DEMOCRACY AND THE ORGANIZATIOI VOLUME 2 • MOISEĬ OSTROGORSKI

CW01669143

Publisher's Note

The book descriptions we ask booksellers to display prominently warn that this is an historic book with numerous typos or missing text; it is not indexed or illustrated.

The book was created using optical character recognition software. The software is 99 percent accurate if the book is in good condition. However, we do understand that even one percent can be an annoying number of typos! And sometimes all or part of a page may be missing from the book. Or the paper may be so discolored from age that it is difficult to read. We apologize and gratefully acknowledge Google's assistance.

After we re-typeset and design a book, the page numbers change so the old index and table of contents no longer work. Therefore, we usually remove them.

Our books sell so few copies that you would have to pay hundreds of dollars to cover the cost of proof reading and fixing the typos, missing text and index. Therefore, whenever possible, we let our customers download a free copy of the original typo-free scanned book. Simply enter the barcode number from the back cover of the paperback in the Free Book form at www.general-books.net. You may also qualify for a free trial membership in our book club to download up to four books for free. Simply enter the barcode number from the back cover onto the membership form on the same page. The book club entitles you to select from more than a million books at no additional charge. Simply enter the title or subject onto the search form to find the books.

If you have any questions, could you please be so kind as to consult our Frequently Asked Questions page at www.general-books.net/faqs.cfm? You are also welcome to contact us there.

General Books LLC™, USA, 2012. ISBN: 9781459076020.

DEMOCRACY aND THE OEGANIZATION OP POLITICAL PAETIES BT

M. OSTROGORSKI

In Two stjmss

Vol. n

TRANSLATED FROM THE FRENCH BT FREDERICK CLARKE, M.A.

FORMERLY TaYLORIaN SCHOLaR IN THE UNIVERSITY OF OXFORD

WITH A PREFACE BT

THE RIGHT HON. JAMES BRYCE, M.P. aUTHOR OF "THE aMKRICaN COMMONWEaLTH" ILontion MACMILLAN AND CO., Limited NEW YORK: THE MACMILLAN COMPANY

1902

 FIRST CHAPTER THE FIRST PARTY ORGANIZATIONS IN THB UNITED STATES

I

The first germs of political extra constitutional organization in the American Republic are to be found in the clubs of the colonial period, which flourished mostly in Boston. These clubs represented groups of men generally bound by professional ties (Merchants' Club, Mechanics' Club) or by ties of friendship, and meeting regularly in taverns or in private houses. Towards the sixties, when the relations between the government of the mother-country and the colonies began to get strained, the clubs naturally became a centre of political discussion, and very soon, reinforced by patriotic societies such as those of the "Sons of Liberty," they supplied the impulse for resistance to the arbitrary acts of the British Parliament. Among these Boston clubs a conspicuous place was taken by the Caucus club, which included the elite of the patriotic party. In the more or less secret meetings that bore this odd name, which had such an extraordinary future before it, and the t point for the learned, public affairs had long been a subject of discussion, whether current business before the colonial Assembly, or, and especially, local elections. The first mention of such gatherings relates to a period preceding the American Revolution by more than half a century. Gordon, the English author of the history of the American Revolution, refers to the Caucus as follows: "The word is not of a novel invention. More than, fifty years ago, Mr. Samuel Adams' father and twenty others, one or two from the north end of the town, where all the ship business is carried on, used to meet, make a caucus, and lay their plans for introducing certain persons into places of trust See above, Vol. I, p. 120. and power. When they had settled it they separated, and used each their particular influence within his own circle. He and his friends would furnish themselves with ballots, including the names of the parties fixed upon, which they distributed on the day of election. By acting in concert, together with a careful and extensive distribution of ballots, they generally carried the elections to their own mind. In like manner it was that Mr. Samuel Adams first became a representative for Boston."

Another description of the Caucus, dating from February, 1763, is given in the journal of John Adams, who was himself about to become one of its most important members: "This day learned that the Caucus club meets at certain times in the garret of Tom Dawes, the Adjutant of the Boston regiment. He has a large house, and he has a movable partition in his garret which he takes down, and the whole club meets in one room. There they smoke tobacco till you cannot see from one end of the garret to the other. There they drink flip, I suppose, and they choose a moderator who puts questions to the vote regularly; and selectmen, assessors, collectors, firewards, and representatives are regularly chosen before they are chosen in the town."

The club now had such a recognized authority with the public that it addressed open appeals to the electorate signed with its title of " The Caucas. " Soon afterwards, probably for more forcible action in different parts of the town, two other Caucuses were formed, the South End Caucus and the Middle District Caucus, which, in concert with the first, the North End Caucus, promoted the cause of the Patriots. It was the North End *The History of the Independence of the United States of America,* Land. 1788, 1, 3(55.

"The Works of John Adams, Boston, 1830, Vol. II, p. 144. The *Boston Evening Post* of the 14th May, 1764, contains the following notice: "To the freeholders, etc. — Modesty preventing a personal application (customary in other places) for your interest to elect particular persons to be your representatives, we therefore request your votes for those gentlemen who have steadily adhered to your interest in times past, especially in the affair of Trade by sending timely instructions requested by our agent, relative to Acts of Trade, late pending in Parliament.

"Your bumble servants,

"The Caucas." (Reproduced in R. Frothingham, *The Rise of the Republic of the United States,* Boston. 1S72, p. 169.) *Life and Times of Joseph Warren,* by R. Frothingham, Bost. 1858, p. 50. Caucus which decided to resist " with their lives and fortunes" the introduction of the tea on which the home government had imposed a duty, and instigated the famous demonstration in Boston harbour when the English cargoes were thrown into the sea. It was also to the initiative of the members of the Caucus, and especially of one of them, Samuel Adams, that was due the creation of the " corresponding committees," of that formidable organization of the patriotic party which paved the way for the Revolution and independence. The corresponding committee of Boston, composed of twenty-one members chosen in public meeting by all the duly qualified electors, took up the agitation openly, at the instigation of the Caucus, which operated secretly. In imitation of the Boston corresponding committee numerous committees were formed throughout the colony of Massachusetts, chosen in each town either in public meetings or by the legal voters. The other colonies, with Virginia at their head, followed this example; their committees were appointed by the colonial assemblies, but before long popular committees arose by the side of them, elected in the towns by the votes of the inhabitants. The corresponding committees kept up regular relations between all the parts of the future republic, convened conferences of delegates of the district, exhorted the population to unity, and implanted in the public mind the resolve to withstand British oppression; acting in broad daylight, they mobilized, so to speak, the opinion of the colonies, to intimidate the government of George III and bring it to its knees. Then when the means of an amicable solution of the conflict were exhausted, the combustible matter accumulated by the corresponding committees caught fire and kindled the great conflagration which destroyed England's rule over her American colonies forever.

History of the Sier/e of Boston, B. 1849, pp. 29, 30, by R. Frothingham, and *Life of Warren,* 238-240, by the same author, who had in his possession the authentic minutes of the North End "Caucas" for the period from 17721774. The book bore the inscription, "Began 17(7 records lost." The minutes of the Caucus which have just been referred to disclose that the Caucus summoned the correspondence committee before it... "appointing a committee of three to wait on the committee of correspondence and dexire their attendance...." *The Rise of the Rep-Mic,* 313, 327.

The secession of the colonies put an end to the task of the corresponding committees. The constitutional liberty for the defence of which they had risen was assured by arms. But it was often menaced by the Americans themselves during the early years of the new republic, which were so full of troubles. The great economic distress which afflicted the whole country after the close of the war, and which often made men seek a remedy in such panaceas as the unlimited issue of paper money or still more extravagant measures, brought out groups of malcontents, who organized representative conventions to remonstrate with the constituted authorities, with the Assemblies, or even to step into their place. This movement gave rise, during the years 1784-1786, to a whole mass of "county conventions" in the States of New England, especially in Massachusetts and Rhode Island. These conventions of delegates, however, in which the petty extempore politicians held forth, had an ephemeral existence; after a noisy session of a few days they dispersed. A few years afterwards, when the Constitution was already firmly established, the contagion of the French Revolution produced in the United States, as in England, political organizations on a permanent basis, in the form of "Democratic Societies," which were an imitation of the Paris Jacobins Club.-They soou spread into all the States, into the towns and the villages, and, by means of corresponding committees, kept up relations with each other. Under the pretence of defending liberty and the rights of man, they indulged in demonstrations which constantly grew noisier and more extravagant. They voted resolutions denouncing tyrants and approving the Paris Jacobins, applauded all the excesses of the Terror, glorified the French Revolutionists at banquets, and furiously attacked all the constituted authorities in the United States The Democratic Societies became an element of disturbance and a menace to public order, so much so that President Washington, in his message to Congress of the 4th of November, 1794, felt obliged to call the attention of the country to these "self-created societies." They tried to defend themselves, but did not find favour with the public. The defeat of the French Terrorists on the 9th i Cf. McMaster, *History of the People of the United States,* I, 300-312, 337. See above, Vol. I, p. 124.

Thermidor, which shortly supervened, completed the discredit of the American political clubs, and after a few years they expired, while continuing up to their last moments to vent their malignant invective and to envenom the election campaigns. II

The election contests, which were too often exceedingly keen in those days, were not so much between parties clearly divided by principles and programmes, as between factions torn by local and personal rivalries. Even on the great stage of the political life of the new republic, in the Congress of the United States, the division into parties produced by divergent interpretations of the Constitution took some time to consolidate itself and acquire an organization. Washington's great authority imposed, during his presidency, a sort of truce, not strictly observed, however, on the animosities of the extreme Democrats, led by Jefferson, and of their "Federalist" opponents, whose most brilliant representative was Hamilton. The local organization of parties was consequently still more slow to grow up; in any event, it had at the outset no need of a rigid structure, for the reason that the number of voters was generally limited by the qualifications for the franchise, that the elective offices were not numerous, and finally because in American society, especially in New England, there was still a ruling class, that is to say, groups of men who, owing to their character,' their wealth, and their social position, commanded the confidence of their fellow-citizens and made them accept their leadership without a murmur. I The candidates were nominated in town meetings or county meetings, but in reality these general gatherings simply ratified selections made beforehand by the small coteries of leaders in their private caucuses, so that it may be said with an excellent historian that the latter "were still the skeleton of the party organization." *j* Thus on the occasion of the presidential election of 1796, John Adams was attacked with extraordinary violence in Pennsylvania by the democratic clubs (cf. McMaster, II, 2il7).

Alexander Johnston's *Nominating Conventions* (Lalor's Cyclopajdia of Political Science).

In Pennsylvania, where the strife of factions was particularly keen, a rough outline of an elective organization of parties appeared sooner than elsewhere, but for a considerable time it proceeded by uncertain and unconnected spurts in which it would be difficult to discover a regular evolution. We do find at a pretty early stage traces of meetings composed of delegates who were supposed, more or less rightly, to have been chosen by their respective townships (as was the case with the ephemeral county conventions of 1786 in Massachusetts), but more often these county meetings, where candidatures were adopted, were mass-meetings open to all, in which the people of the neighbourhood were numerous, while the inhabitants of the more remote localities were barely represented. To nominate candidates for elective offices which went beyond the limits of the county, the views of the inhabitants of various counties were often ascertained by means of a very extensive correspondence; a number of circulars were despatched, and from the replies received a list was drawn up of the candidates who had received the most votes, and it was returned by the same channel for ratification by_t;he counties. These consultations were led by a few public-spirifecPmen with a taste for election work, who made themselves acotresponding _committee for the.occasion. Side by side with this mode of proceeding another was also practised, which consisted of making the nomination of the candidates for the Senate of the State or for the Federal Congress in conferences of representatives of various countieW"conferees," "electors"), appointed for this purpose in county meetings, and of submitting the selections to the ratification of the general county meetings, which, as in the primitive democracies, theoretically retained their full powers. The practice of delegation gained ground, however, and in the first years of this century it seems to have been already fairly common in the counties. There were a few isolated attempts, the first of which even goes back to the year 1788, to bring together delegates from the whole State for nominating candidates for Congress or for the elec Two more instances are perhaps to be found in Pennsylvania, during the twenty-five or thirty years after 1788, to wit, in 1792 and 1812. For the facts relating to these conventions and for the other antecedents of the organization of parties in Pennsylvania, see *Nominating Conventions in l'enn»ylvania,* by J. S. Walton *(The American Historical Review,* January, 18U7).

toral college entrusted with the election of the President and the Vice-President of the United States.

But all these meetings of delegates were composed in an anything but regular way; too often the representation of I different localities was neither complete nor direct. The decisions taken in them, however, were not binding, so to speak, on any one; at one time it was the leaders who, of their own authority, made modifications in the settled lists of candidates, according to the requirements of the electoral situation, at another the local voters recast the "ticket" as they thought proper; the distinction of parties was even not always observed, and mixed lists were made up. The candidates, in their turn, did not consider themselves bound by the nominations made, and often the competitors for elective offices who had not been accepted went on with their candidatures just the same; they offered themselves directly to the electorate. This method of "self-nomination," very common in Pennsylvania down to the first years of this century, was still more so in other States. In Massachusetts, which, although it furnished the earliest political organizations during the revolutionary period, did not develop them for many years to come, the candidates were often proposed by means of letters sent to the newspapers by a friend or an admirer, who' signed with a more or less expressive pseudonym: "An Elector," "Candidus," "The Whole Truth," "Fidelitas," etc. Still in the early years of the nineteenth century we find already in Massachusetts conventions of county or congressional district delegates, which are destined to grow here alongside or above the public meetings where candidates or delegates were directly nominated, and to which in New England the name of "caucus" begins to be given, accompanied sometimes with the epithet "general," as if to distinguish it from the special caucuses of the electoral wire-pullers.2 i F. Wi Dallinger, *Nomination for Elective Office in the United States,* N.Y., 1897, p. 23.

In Massachusetts we come across the same name with a still more sonorous epithet — "grand" — applied even tc free popular representative assemblies. See *Proceedings of the Grand Caucus,* composed of Delegates from the several towus in the county of N. Assembled... February 9, 180!), Pro Bono Publico; and to examine into the present state of the Union whether the people of New England are rie for rebellion, and whether means

While becoming customary with the parties, the conventions of delegates did not at once supply them with a fixed groove in their extra-constitutional existence, for as yet they had no permanent organization themselves. In fact, they were called into being in each particular case by the private initiative of a caucus, of a coterie of politicians who chose to issue summonses, or of a public town meeting which invited its neighbours to send delegates to a common rendezvous. The extra-constitutional organization of the American parties started *by* taking up its abode in a borrowed sphere, belonging to the constitutional structure — in the State Legislatures and then the Congress of the United States.

For the elective offices bestowed in each State by the whole body of its voters, such as the posts of Governor and Lieutenant-Governor or the functions of presidential electors, the necessity of a preliminary understanding as to the candidates was still greater than for the smaller territorial units, and it could only be suitably effected in a single meeting for the whole State. But to organize such general meetings of representatives of all the localities in a regular way was by no means easy in ordinary times, both on account of the means of communication in those days, which made a journey to the capital of the State a formidable and almost hazardous undertaking, and of the difficulty of finding men of leisure willing to leave their homes for the discharge of a temporary duty. However, men enjoying the confidence of the voters of the State were already assembled in the capital in pursuance of their functions of members of the Legislature. Were they are to be used to prevent their resistance to measures of government. Printed Mass. 1809. This pamphlet is also curious from another point of view, as showing the incredible amount of hatred which partisans contrived to excite in the popular mind against the Federalists.

It is needless to recall the main outline of the constitutional fabric of the American republic, the federalized form of which has led to the creation, in each of the States of the Union, of an independent legislative and executive power, of a legislature and a State Governor chosen by the people, while the Union has been provided with a special legislative body, the Congress of the United States, composed of a House of Representatives elected by the citizens of the States, on the basis of population, and of a Senate in which each State, whatever its population, is represented by two members chosen by the legislature of the State. At the head of the executive power of the Union are the President and the Vice-President, elected in the second instance by persons chosen for this purpose, in the present day, in all the States by the people. not in the best position for bringing before their constituents the names of the candidates who could command the most votes in the State? This reflection occurred to the public, and in particular to the members of the State Legislatures themselves, and they laid hands on the nomination of the candidates to the State offices. The members of both Houses belonging to the same party met semi-officially, generally in the legislative building itself, made their selections and communicated them to the voters by means of a proclamation, which they signed individually. Sometimes other signatures of wellknown citizens who happened to be in the capital at that moment were added, to give more weight to the recommendation of the legislators. To make it more sure of prevailing, the latter soon adopted the system of corresponding committees, which devoted their energies throughout the State to the success of the list.

This practice of recommending candidates for the State, which rapidly became general in the whole Union, began very early. The first instance of it is found in the State of Rhode Island in 1790, when the Governor and the LieutenantGovernor were recommended in this way. In the same year the rival parties nominated in a similar manner their candidates to the post of Governor in Pennsylvania, in joint meetings of the members of parties in the Legislature and the constitutional convention, which was convoked at that time to give a new Constitution to the State. In 1793 we find the members of the Legislature making the nomination of the Governor by themselves. In 1795 the State of New York adopts this method to propose John Jay as Governor.' After 1796 it appears as a settled practice in all the States. And in this way is introduced, for the first time, a permanent party J organization, nestling under the wing of the Legislatures and composed of their very elements. It rises above the more or less fortuitous town and county meetings, in which choice is made, either directly or in the second instance, of candidates *The Development of the Nominating Convention in Rhode Island,* by Neil Andrews, Jr., Publications of the Rhode Island Historical Society, Vol. I, Providence, 1893.

J. 8. Walton, *Nominating Conventions in Pennsylvania.* J. G. Hammond, *The History of Political Parties in the State of New York,* Albany, 1842, Vol. I, p. 90. for local elective offices, and in this respect it presents a somewhat striking analogy with the incipient organization of the revolutionary epoch, in which side by side with the corresponding committees of towns formed by the people, on the model of Boston, there were established in the various colonies, on the more aristocratic plan of Virginia, corresponding committees appointed by the colonial assembly. The semi-official control of the selection of candidates for the higher offices assumed by the members of the State Legislatures, was undoubtedly also tainted with "aristocratism," but the electoral body acquiesced in it with a fairly good grace. The Legislature, after all, represented the most important elements of that body; it had a plentiful share of the men of the old "ruling class " who were still regarded as the natural leaders of society, and by the side of them an ever-growing proportion of young politicians thrown up by the democratic leaven which was continuously agitating the country. The action of these men seemed to offer more guarantees for a satisfactory choice and to present more respectability than the mass-meetings, or, as some thought, mob-meetings, in which candidates were selected for the other offices. The private character of the semi-official meetings in question held by the members of Legislatures got them the nickname of Caucus, by analogy with the secret gatherings of the Caucus started at Boston before the Revolui tion. The name of "legislative caucus" became their formal title in all the States. Besides the candidates for the offices of Governor and Lieutenant-Governor, *i.e.* the heads of the executive power of the State, the legislative caucus also nominated the Electors, in cases where they were appointed by the people, the members of the electoral college which chose the heads of the executive power of the Union. But the nomination of candidates for the functions of Electors soon lost its importance, for in the meanwhile there had arisen within the Federal Congress a Caucus which, like the legislative caucuses of the States, took in hand the nomination of - The federal Constitution, in entrusting the election of the President and the Vice-President to a college of Electors chosen in the States in number equal to that of their representatives in Congress, has left the mode of selection of the Electors to be settled by the States. In several of them the Legislatures assumed the right to appoint the Electors in legislative session, while in other States they gave it to the people. candidates for the Presidency and the Vice-Presidency and entered on a course in which the power conferred on the Electors was destined to disappear.

Ill

In the first two presidential elections the choice of the candidates took place of itself, so to speak: Washington was marked out on all sides for the chief magistracy of the new republic; he was elected and re-elected by acclamation to the Presidency, and with him John Adams to the Vice-Presidency. But after Washington's imminent retirement, in 1796, the struggle began. About the anti-Federalist candidate there were no differences of opinion; he was, of course, Thomas Jefferson, while on the Federalist side there was not the same unanimity in favour of John Adams. whose occupancy of the dignity of Vice-President for eight years, by the side of Washington, pointed him out as the latter's successor. In spite of some intrigues against him within the ranks of the Federalists, he was nevertheless elected. But the antipathy with which he inspired several Federalist leaders, and especially Hamilton, broke out with renewed vigour at the approach of the election of 1800. The want of unanimity in the Federalist camp was aggravated by the confusion caused by the death of Washington, whose great prestige alone still shielded the Federalist party, which was daily losing ground in the country although it had a majority in Congress. The imminent danger of the success of Jefferson and of the triumph of radicalism in the government appeared to the Federalists of the Congress to demand their intervention in the presidential election, from which the Constitution had carefully banished them. For some time past the Federalist members of Congress, and the Senators in the first place, had been in the habit of holding semi-official meetings, to which the familiar name of caucus was applied, to settle their line of conduct beforehand on the most important questions coming before Congress. The decisions arrived at by the majority of the members present were considered as in honour The Con.' office-holders from the injl ion prohibits the appointment of members of Congress and e United States as Electors, in order to protect the executive! of the Legislature and generally to ensure its independence. binding the minority; being consequently clothed with a moral sanction, they gave these confabulations an equitable basis and almost a legal authority. In this way there grew up at an early stage, at the very seat of Congress, an extra-constitutional institution which prejudged and anticipated its acts. It was now about to reach out still further and lay hold of a matter which was entirely beyond the competence of Congress. It appears that this was done at the instigation of Hamilton, who, being anxious to push Adams on one side and to prevent the election of Jefferson, wanted to get the electoral manoeuvre which he had hit upon for this purpose sanctioned by a formal decision of the members of the party in Congress. The latter took the decision, nominated in consequence the candidates for the Presidency and the VicePresidency of the Union, and agreed to try and get them accepted by the Electors. This nomination became the precedent, for a practice which completely destroyed the whole scheme of the provisions of the Constitution for the election of the President. The electoral device adopted by the Federalist caucus became known through a private letter from one of its members to his constituents; the Caucus took care not to give it out in its own name, it wrapped all its proceedings in profound secrecy. And when a journalist of the opposition, the famous W. Duane, denounced them in his paper *Aurora,* published at Philadelphia, and attacked the actual practice of the caucuses, the "Jacobinical conclave," he was called before the bar of the Senate for his " false, defamatory, scandalous, and malicious" assertions, and barely managed to escape from the formal proceedings which had been taken According to the mode of voting then in force, the Electors voted for two persons as President and Vice-President, without specifying which of the two they chose for President and which for Vice-President; the one who obtained the greatest number of votes became President. Hamilton's plan consisted in associating a second popular candidate (Pinckney) with Adams and in recommending the Electors, in order not to scatter their votes, to give both candidates an equal number of votes, in the hope that Adams, being one or two votes short, would be beaten by his colleague.

Cf. Hamilton's letter to T. Sedgwick, of May 4, 1800 *(The Works of Alexander Hamilton,* cd. by J. C. Hamilton, N. Y. 1856, Vol. VI, 436). *Memoirs of the Administration of Washington and John Adams,* by Geo. Gibbs, N. Y. 184(i, Vol. II, p.:H7; *The Life and Correspondence of Ilufus King,* N. Y. 180ti, Vol. Ill, pp. 238, 240. against him. In the anti-Federalist press of Boston a violent protest was also made against "the arrogance of a number of Congress to assemble as an electioneering caucus to control the citizens in their constitutional rights." But this did not prevent the Republicans themselves, the anti-Federalist members of Congress, from holding a caucus, also secret, for the nomination of candidates to the two highest executive offices of the Union; they had only to concern themselves with the Vice-Presidency, however, since Jefferson's candidature for the first of these posts was a foregone conclusion. It seems that Madison, the future President of the United States, took the leading part in this caucus.

At the next presidential election, in 1804, the Congressional Caucus reappeared, but on this occasion it no longer observed secrecy. The Republican members of Congress met publicly and settled the candidatures with all the formalities of deliberative assemblies, as if they were acting in pursuance of their mandate. The Federalists, who were almost annihilated as a party since Jefferson's victory, in 1801, gave up holding caucuses altogether. Henceforth there met only a Republican Congressional Caucus, which appeared on the scene every four years at the approach of the presidential election. To strengthen its action in the country it provided itself (in 1813) with a special organ in the form of a corresponding committee/ in which each State was represented by a member,. I and which saw that the decisions of the Caucus were-respected. I Sometimes the State caucuses intervened in the nomination of I candidates for the presidencyIJFlEe Republic; they proposed I names, but in any event the Congressional Caucus always had te last word. Thus in 1808, with two powerful competitors The author of this attack, signed " Old South" (the pseudonym of Benjamin Austin, a well-known Republican writer), gives us on this occasion a good specimen of the style of the times. Addressing a Federalist writer who has given the news of the Federalist caucus, he reproaches him in these terms: "What! Decius! are you daring enough to arrest the votes of Americans by telling them that their servants in Congress have already decided the choice? Are you so abandoned as to stab the Constitution to its vitals by checking the free exercise of the people in their suffrage? If you *are* thus desperate..." etc. (quoted in Niles' *Weekly Register,* Baltimore, XXVI, 178).

Niles, XXVII, 06. Cf. *Annals oj Congress,* sitting of the Senate, 18th March, 1824, speech by Smith of Maryland. for the succession to Jefferson, Madison and Monroe, both put forward in the influential Caucus of Virginia, the Congressional Caucus pronounced for Madison, while taking the formal precaution to declare that the persons present made this recommendation in their "private capacity of citizens." Several members of Congress, who did not want to have Madison, appealed to the country, protesting not only against the regularity of the procedure of the Caucus, but against the institution of the Caucus itself. The Caucus none the less won the day, the whole party in the country accepted its decision, and Madison was elected. The same thing took place in 1812 in spite of an attempted split in the State of New York, the Legislature of which officially brought forward its illustrious statesman, De Witt Clinton, against Madison, who was seeking re-election. In vain did the Legislature of New York, in a manifesto issued for the occasion, try to stir up local jealousies, by protesting against the habitual choice for the presidency of citizens of the State of Virginia, against the perpetuation of the "Virginia dynasty"; in vain did it appeal to democratic susceptibilities by denouncing the usurpation by the coterie of the Congressional Caucus of a right belonging to the people. Madison was re-elected. In 1816, when the Caucus met again to choose a successor to Madison, Henry Clay brought in a motion declaring the nomination of the President in caucus inexpedient, but his pupposal was rejected; a similar resolution introduced by another member shared the same fate. The Caucus adopted the candidature of Monroe, who was Madison's favourite, just as this latter was in a way designated to the Caucus by his predecessor Jefferson. The majority obtained by Monroe was but slighty (65 votes to 54), but as soon as the result was announced Clay at once requested the assembly to make Monroe's nomination unanimous. Such was the weight which the decision of the majority of the Caucus had with every member, it was considered binding in honour on him as well as on every adherent of the party in the country who did not care to incur the reproach of political heresvf'oiNi. postasy. Under cover of these notions there arose in the fcewican electorate the i R. Hildreth, *History of the United States,* VI, 65.

» Niles, III, 18. s *Ibid.,* X, 59.

convention, nay, the dogma, of *regular* candidatures, adopted in party councils, which alone have the right to court the popular suffrage. Complying with this rule, the Electors, who, according to the Constitution, were to be the unfettered commissioners of the people in the choice of the chief magistrate, and to consult only their judgment and their conscience, simply registered the decision taken at Washington by the Congressional Caucus.

The authority of the Congressional Caucus which got its recommendations accepted with this remarkable alacrity and made the "nomination" equivalent to the election, rested on two facts. On the one hand, there was the prestige attaching to the rank of the men who composed the Caucus and to their personal position in the country. They represented in the capital of the Union the same social and political element, and in a still higher degree, which the members of the legislative caucuses represented in the States, that is, the leadership of the natural chiefs, whose authority was still admitted and tacitly acknowledged. The elevation of Jefferson to the Presidency, which it is the fashion to describe as the "political revolution of 1801," was in point of fact only the beginning of a new departure. Far from upsetting the old fabric at once, it installed democratic doctrines in governmental'theories, but not in the manners of the nation; and a quarter of a century will be needed, with the exceptional aid of events of a Cf. the address of the Legislature of New York already mentioned, Niles, in, 17: Mat. Carey, *The Olive Branch,* Philad. 1818, chap. 78, on the Congressional Caucus.

As is well known, the authors of the Constitution were much concerned about the special precautions to be taken for ensuring the choice of the best men for the chief magistracy and for preserving it from intrigue and corruption. They hesitated to entrust the election to the turbulent and unreflecting masses, but they were not less apprehensive about leaving it to an assembly. Between the direct democracy and oligarchy, they thought they had discovered a middle term in a special body of Electors emanating from the people. The idea was that these men, taken from outside official circles (the members of Coogress and office-holders of the United States being made ineligible), scattered throughout the Union and charged with a temporary mission, beginning with the vote and ending with it, would be inaccessible to corruption and would obey only the dictates of their conscience and their intelligence, the high standard of which had marked them out for thc confidence of their fellow-citizens. Cf. *The Federalist* (the celebrated commentary on the Constitution written in 1788, by Hamilton, Madison, and Jay), No. LXVIII, from Hamilton's pen. vol.. n — c non-political character, to draw the practical conclusions from these doctrines and theories and make them part of the political hahits of the people. The lattej still took its orders from the men who impressed it by their superiority and who naturally formed a somewhat exclusive and intimate circle. The members of the Congressional Caucus and the members of the legislative caucuses of the States, or, to use Hamilton's expression, "the leaders of the second class" constituted in fact a sort of political family, and the latter spontaneously became the agents of the Congressional Caucus; they were, in the language of a contemporary, "as prefects" to it,8 set in motion by a simple exchange of private letters. Again, the members of the Caucus represented the *force majeure* of the interests of the Republican party, which enforced discipline, which compelled obedience to the word of command from whatever quarter it proceeded. Rightly or wrongly, the anti-Federalists believed that the Republic and liberty were in mortal danger, that they were menaced by the Federalists, whose political ideal was the English constitutional monarchy, and who, having no confidence in the people, in its intelligence and its virtue, were bent on an autoritarian "consolidated" government. The denunciations of the alleged monarchical plots laid by the Federalists, which their opponents spread abroad in the time of Washington even, look like silly calumnies in these days, but they obtained credence with the simple mindsndoctrinated by the Democrats. The egregious blunders of theTj'eaeransts in power, their measures retwcting the liberty of the press and individual freedom, brought the popular exasperation against them to a climax. The Federalist party soon succumbed, but the recollection of the dangers, real or imaginary, to which liberty and equality were exposed by it, survived it and for many a long day was a sort of bugbear which the leaders of the victorious party had no scruple about using for the consolidation of their power. To prevent the Federalists from returning to the charge, the Josiah Quiney, in the picture which he has left of Washington society in 1826, remarks that "the glittering generalizations of the Declaration were never meant to be taken seriously. Gentlemen were tho natural rulers of America after all" *(Figures of the Past,* Boston, 188.'!, p. 2ti4).

Works, VI, 444 and *passim.* » Niles, XXVII, 38.

Republicans had to carefully guard against divisions, and it was to avoid them, to concentrate all the forces of the party in the great fight for the Presidency, that the Congressional Caucus obligingly offered its services.

This system of intimidation was reinforced by an electoral method which made the minority absolutely powerless and gave the Caucus an exceptional vantage-ground.

IV

The Constitution having left it to the States to settle the mode of appointment of the presidential Electors, the States took the opportunity to adopt a variety of systems; here the State was divided into as many districts as there were Electors to be appointed, and each district appointed its own; there the citizens of the whole State voted for all the Electors 'on a general ticket; finally, in several States the Legislatures took the choice of the Electors into their own hands.-The. first system allowed either shade of political opinion its proper influence, whereas the two last, which soon spread over the greater part of the Union, ruthlessly stifled the voice of minorities, or even enabled a minority to usurp the rights of the majority. Even in States where the district system was in force, the majority laid out the districts in such an arbitrary and irregular way that they included very slight majorities of its adherents, side by side with very large minorities of its opponents; the districts were not always composed of adjoining territories, nor was their representation equal; one elected one representative, while another would elect two, three, or four. It was the eternal craving for domination, which in American political society, the first formally based on right, on the legally expressed will of the majority, adapted itself to This skilful carving out of electoral districts with the object of conjuring away the real majority, soon became popular under the nickname of "gerrymandering." It comes from the State of Massachusetts, where an irregular delimitation of the electoral districts, made, in 1812, in the interests of the Democratic party, gave them an odd-looking outline. A coloured map of them having been published in a newspaper, somebody amused himself with giving a district, which presented a particularly sinuous shape, a few pencil touches, making it exactly like a salamander. "No," said somebody else, "it is not a salamander, it is a gerrymander," alluding to the Governor of the State, Gerry, who belonged to the Democratic party.

the new circumstances: deprived of the use of brute force, it set up, from the very beginning, majorities and minorities seeking to circumvent one another by devices of vote-counting. The divergent views on the Constitution and its interpretation, which broke out from this early date, gave the sanction of principles and convictions, often sincerely held, to these efforts to supplant the other side by expedients of electoral legerdemain; styling itself here "Republican party," there "Federalist party," the majority or the pretended majority everywhere tried to annihilate the minority in the name of the good cause.

To the cause embodied in the "party" was added another preoccupation connected with a political prejudice which was one of the most powerful factors in the organization of the new republic and in its early life. It is notorious that the Union was formed with great difficulty, that it was, to use a celebrated expression, wrested "by grinding necessities from a reluctant people." The old colonies, freed from British rule, varying greatly in territory and population, were extremely jealous about their "sovereignty," and mortally afraid of being absorbed in the federation, or of falling under the swatof the large populous States, with their wealth and power. IF After many stirring incidents, amid which the new, scarcely fern republic seemed on the point of perishing by anarchy, the Union was at last established on the footing of a compromise, which allowed the federal government only expressly stated powers, and conciliated the small States by giving them a representation equal to that of the larger States in the federal Senate But the House of Representatives was composed of members elected in the States on the basis of population, and there, as well as in the college of Electors, which is the numerical counterpart of Congress, large States and small States confronted each other again as such. The States, even the large ones, which followed the district system, which elected their representatives by districts where the majority belonged now to one party and now to the other, could not help returning a mixed set of members, divided against themselves, incapable of reflecting the individuality of the State, while the States that chose their members on a general ticket, which prevented the different opinions in the State from coming out with their due weight, secured a homogeneous and compact representation. This being the state of affairs, the pious solicitude for the autonomy of the State sanctified, in its turn, the party greed which used the general ticket as a weapon for overthrowing competitors; it became a measure of self-preservation necessary for safeguarding the position of the State in the Union. For these reasons some States which originally adopted the district system abandoned it for the general ticket. Virginia set the example from the year 1800, while condemning the general ticket in the preamble of the law which introduced it.

But the advantages offered by the general ticket for ensuring the supremacy of the party and the sovereign individuality of the State could be secured only on condition of the single list being regularly put into shape somewhere on behalf of the people which was to vote it; otherwise the desired concentration could never be carried out over the whole State. This being so, the Congressional Caucus and its local agencies had only to come forward; they undertook to prepare the lists, and the people accepted the duty of voting them. *Vlhe* general ticket called for the Caucus, the Caucus smoothedthe way for the general ticket, and each made over to the other the rights of the people, the full and independent exercise of the electoral franchise. While the general ticket claimed to prevent the "consolidation" of the States, the Caucus consolidated in each State power in the hands of a few. Moreover, a dissentient presidential Elector having no chance of being returned under the general ticket, the "imperative mandate" became logically and almost spontaneously the rule for the Electors, to the advantage of the candidates adopted by the Congressional Caucus. Thus, in the first and in the second instance, voters and Electors both abdicated their independence.

Sometimes, when the electoral contest was particularly keen, and the issue seemed doubtful, the leaders of the caucuses, fearing that the defection of a few supporters might prevent these automaton-Electors from securing all the popular votes necessary for investing them with the office, got the appointment of them transferred to the Legislatures in which they commanded a majority made up of themselves. It was not uncommon for the electoral system to be changed on the very eve of the elections, the general ticket or appointment by the Legislature being substituted, by a sort of legislative *coup d'itat,* for the district system. Disregarding all principle and all rule, the party in power shuffled the electoral arrangements like a pack of cards to suit the convenience of the moment.

These malpractices, as well as the chaos of electoral systems they brought with them, soon caused a revolt in the public conscience, and a movement was set on foot to demand a uniform and really popular mode of election, on the basis of the district system. An amendment to the Constitution of the United States was to enforce it on the whole Union. Proposals in this direction had already been submitted on several occasions to Congress, starting in the year 1800, but after the elections of 1812 they became more common. In the proposals brought forward from 1813 onwards, almost every year, either in the Senate or in the House of Representatives, one of the principal arguments against the general ticket was that it encouraged or necessitated the regrettable practice of the Caucus. It was pointed out with sorrow that the Caucus, combined with the general ticket, had destroyed the whole economy of the plan devised by the authors of the Constitution for the election of the President. To quote one of the many speeches delivered on these occasions and which, by the way, throws light on the whole problem of the permanent party organizations in its relations with the electoral regime: "In the choice of the chief magistrate (by the Electors) the original primary act was to be theirs — spontaneously theirs. The Thus for instance Massachusetts, which voted in the first three presidential elections on the district system, in 18(10 exchanged it for appointment of the Electors by the Legislature, then, in 1804, decreed the general ticket, and in 1808 reverted to appointment by the Legislature. North Carolina practised the district system down to 1804, and in 1808 substituted for it the general ticket, which, in 1812, made way for appointment by the Legislature.
The first proposals were brought before the House of Representatives on the 11Sth of March, 1800, by Nicholas, then by Walker on behalf of the Legislature of New York on the 15th of February, 1802; by Stanley on behalf of the Legislature of North Carolina on the 20th of February, 1802; in the Senate by Bradley on the Kith of April, 1802, etc. *Annate of the Conyress of the United States.* The debates and proceedings in the Congress of the United States, 13th Congress. 1st session, speech of Pickens in the House of Representatives, tlm 3d of January, 1814.
Electors were free to choose whomsoever they pleased.... How hideous the deformity of the practice! The *first* step made in the election is by those whose interference the Constitution prohibits. The members of the two Houses of Congress meet in caucus, or convention, and there ballot for a President or Vice-President of the United States. The result of their election is published through the Union in the name of a recommendation. This modest recommendation then comes before the members of the respective State Legislatures. Where the appointment ultimately rests with them, no trouble whatever is given to the people. The whole business is disposed of without the least inconvenience to them. Where, in *form,* however, the choice of Electors remains with the people, the patriotic members of the State Legislatures, vieing with their patriotic predecessors, back this draft on popular credulity with the weight of their endorsement. Not content with this, they benevolently point out to the people the immediate agents through whom the negotiation can be most safely carried on, make out a ticket of Electors, and thus designate the individuals who, in their behalf, are to honour this demand on their suffrages. Sir, this whole proceeding appears to be monstrous. It must be corrected, or the character of this Government is fundamentally changed. Already, in fact, the Chief Magistrate of the nation owes his office principally to *aristocratic* intrigue, cabal, and management. Preexisting bodies of men, and not the people, make the appointment. Such bodies, from the constitution of nature, are necessarily directed in their movements by a few leaders, whose talents, or boldness, or activity, give them an ascendancy over their associates. On every side these leaders are accessible to the assaults of corruption. I mean not, Sir, that viilgar species of corruption only, which is addressed to the most sordid of human passions, but that which finds its way to the heart, through the avenues which pride, ambition, vanity, personal resentment, family attachment, and a thousand foibles and vices open to the machinations of intrigue. Their comparatively 'permanent existence' and concentrated situation afford the most desirable facilities for the continued operation of the sinister acts. It is not in nature that they should long operate in vain; nor is it in nature that the individual elected by these means should not feel his dependence on those to whom he owes his office, or forego the practices which are essential to ensure its continuance, or its transmission in the desired succession.... I dare not promise that the adoption of this amendment by the States will put an end to cabal, in-

trigue, and corruption in the appointment of a President. No human means can be adequate to that end. But I believe it demonstrable that this amendment will deprive cabals of facility in combination, render intrigue less systematic, and diminish the opportunities of corruption.... Faction cannot but exist, but it will be rendered tolerant."

But the general ticket had its ardent defenders, who dwelt with vehemence on the dangers which the substitution for it of the district system would present from the standpoint of the rights of the States and the balance of power between the small States and the large ones. At the same time some of the most virulent champions of the general ticket admitted the serious abuses which had crept into the presidential election by declaring, like Randolph, that the appointment of Electors had become "a mockery — a shadow of a shade." But they insisted that the district system was no remedy, that the mischief lay, not in the electoral system, but in the practice of the Caucus: "Divide the State into districts, will that destroy the Caucus? Oh, no; the men whose interests it may be to preserve the monster will still protect him. He will laugh at your vain attempts, and again and again trampling down the weak defences of the Constitution, he will, as it shall please him, or rather as it shall please the existing Executive, make and unmake Presidents with the same ease as did the Prstorian cohorts the masters of the Roman world.. .. No, Sir, let the majority of Congress cease to dp evil. Let them scorn to be made the instrument of party, to elevate any man in violation of the Constitution. Let them meet no more in Caucus. Thus, and thus only, Sir, can the object be accom *Annals oj Conyress, ibid.,* speech of Gaston, pp. 842, 843; see also the speeches of Gholson, same sitting; of It. King and of Harper in the Senate, March 20, 1816.

Ibid., 14th Congress, 2d session; speech of Randolph, of the 18th December, 1816; of Grosvenor, of the 20th December, 1816; of Barbour in the Senate, January, 1819. plished." The partisans of the district system, on their side, persisted in asserting that the "so objectionable practice was inseparable from any mode of undivided vote," that it was this which made the Elector a machine set in motion by the caucusticket.

From year to year these arguments were repeated on both sides, but the solution of the question made no progress. The House of Representatives — where the populous States, which derived additional power from the general ticket system or from the appointment of the Electors by the Legislature, easily commanded a majority — systematically rejected all proposals for amending the Constitution. In the Senate, where the small States were represented on the same footing as the large ones, the district system met with a much more favourable reception. Three times the amendment obtained the constitutional majority in the States' chamBer, but it was never able to command two-thirds of the votes in the popular section of Congress. The fortress of the general ticket thus remained intact, and, under its shelter, the Caucus continued its existence. J

V

Yet the external defences with which the general ticket encircled the Caucus could not long protect it, for its own forces were giving way, the two great forces, social and political, of the leadership and of the categorical imperative of the party. They had been slowly but steadily declining almost from the beginning of the century which witnessed the elevation of Jefferson and the triumph of democratic doctrines in the theories of government. The annihilation of the Federalists put an end to the division into parties, and Jefferson's famous remark, "We are all Republicans, we are all Federalists," was destined shortly to represent the real state of things. The survivors of the Federalist party gradually fused with the Republicans, and when Monroe came into power, the old landmarks were definitively obliterated; the Constitution which had aroused so many passions and animosities now inspired every citizen with sentiments of admiration and Speech of Grosvenor, quoted above.

Speech of Pickens, of the 18th December, 1810. adoration; under its-«agis the country was advancing with giant strides, released from all party preoccupation; "the era of good feelings" had dawned in political life. And yet the Congressional Caucus, in putting forward its candidates, repeated the old refrain which exhorted the people to rally round them to confront the enemy, when there was no enemy; it invoked the sovereign cause of the party when the "party" no longer had any particular cause and represented only a memory of the past. But the less the ruling politicians were separated by differences on points of principle, the more readily did their narrow circle become a field for intestine ' and for intrigue. Hardly had Monroe's second administration begun (in 1821), when they were seized with the "fever of president making." Several candidatures arose; all the candidates claimed to represent the firm of the Republican "party"; each candidate had his' friends in Congress, who intrigued and plotted for him, waging a secret and pitiless war on all his rivals. They would have been glad enough to back up their claims with principles, with "great principles," but no distinctive principles could be discovered, not even with a magnifying glass. One of the candidates for the Presidency, Crawford, hit upon another expedient: being Secretary of the Treasury in Monroe's administration, and digpasing_af, a somewhat-eattensiveatrojiage, of places and favours to bestow, he did nOtscrupIe to use them to secure adherents. These bargainings and cabals seemed to justify the complaints of the intervention of members of Congress in the presidential elections, so often made in the course of the periodical debates on the general ticket. The prestige of the leadership could no longer shield the practices which were indulged in at Washington, for this prestige was profoundly impaired; it had been systematically undermined for a quarter of a century by the social and economic revolution which was going on in the American republic. *The* pn-rtQ-snma.l hierarchy which Puritanism had set up in New England, and which was the outcome of an alliauce i "Could we only hit upon a few great principles and unite their support with that of Crawford" (one of the candidates), wrote a Senator ou his side, "we should succeed beyond doubt." *(Martin Van Buren.by* E. M. Shepard. p. 92). between the magistracy, the clergy, property, and culture, was collapsing. The eclipse of the Federalists, who were the living image of government by leaders, robbed it of one of its strongest supports. The influence of the clergy, which had been one of the main props of the Federalists, was being thrust out of lay society. On the other side of the Alleghanies, on the virgin soil of the West, a new world was growing up, free from all traditions, because it had no past; instinct with equality, because its inhabitants, who were all new-comers, parvenus in the elementary sense of the word, resembled each other. And this country of the West was advancing daily in population, in wealth, and in political importance. The old States were also celebrating great triumphs, due to the marvellous rise of their commerce and their industry; but their new prosperity acted rather as a dissolvent of the old order of things, it created a new class of rich men, composed of successful merchants and manufacturers; these *nouveaux riches* supplanted the old ones, without, however, taking their place in the esteem and the reverence of the people. The rapid growth of the cities helped to destroy the old social ties. At the same time the individual was being directly urged by men and things to shake off the old servitudes, or what was represented to him as such. The triumph of Jefferson, in 1801, without effecting a democratic revolution in habits, gave an extraordinary impulse to the propaganda of democratic ideas, *Jl* nade them the object of an almost ritual cult. Politicians R vied with each other in repeating that the voice of the people is the voice of God, that before the majesty of the people everything should bow. Writers popularized and gave point to these ideas. In pamphlets composed for the farmers and the mechanics they preached a crusade against "money power," banks, judges appointed by the government, and against all the other aristocratic institutions, the sale existence of which was an insult to the sovereign people. I

The lesson which the America citizen learnt from things was not less stimulating. Material comfort was increasing Cf. W. Duane, *Politics for American Farmers,* being a series of tracts exhibiting the blessings of free government as it is administered in the United States, compared with the boasted stupendous fabric of British monarchy. Washington. 1807.

with unprecedented rapidity. The series of great inventions which marked the beginning of the century, the steamers which sped to and fro over the vast republic, at that time richer in large rivers than in roads, the natural wealth which sprang from the soil, gave each and all a share in the profits of the economic revolution. Endless vistas of activity opened before every liHiaWtanTo'l' the Union; the soul of the American citizen swelled with pride, with the confidence of the man who is self-sufficing, who knows no superiors. The political sovereignty which was conceded to him with so much deference soon appeared to him as a personal chattel. And then to exercise his proprietary right over the commonwealth, he had no need of another person's intelligence; was it necessary for his success in private life'!" The leading citizens, therefore, who in Congress or in the Legislature of his State, meeting in caucus, dictated to him his line of conduct, the choice of his representatives, became a set of usurpers in his eyes. Jealous of their pretended superiority, he grew impatient of their domination.

The small group of these trained politicians, assembled in the capital of the Union, was now plunged in intrigues aiming at the chief magistracy of the republic, and these intrigues were about to have their *denouement* in the Congressional Caucus, if the established precedent were followed on this occasion again. Would it be followed? Would they dare to do it?—were questions asked in various quarters. And before long the Union became the scene of a violent controversy about the next meeting of the Congressional Caucus; it was discussed in the Press, it occupied the public meetings, the State Legislatures voted resolutions upon it. One of the candidates for the Presidency, 4rew _Jackson, who was not a politician, and who was in more than one respect a *homo novus,* could count but little on the favour of the Congressional Caucus; so his electoral managers came to the conclusion that' to make his success more certain it was indispensable to overthrow the Caucus, and they therefore took an important part in the campaign started against it. Most of the numerous manifestations of public opinion were hostile to the Caucus.

On thi8 point we have the evidence, not to say the avowal, of Jackson's principal election agent, Major Lewis, in the *Narrative* which he supplied to Parton, Jackson's biographer *(Life of A. Jackson,* III, 21).

The popular meetings almost without exception condemned the nominations made by the Caucus as a flagrant usurpation of the rights of the people. The State Legislatures were more divided. In the East the legislative caucuses of New York, Maine, and Virginia pronounced for the old practice of nomination by members of Congress, but in Maryland and in some States of the young West the Caucus was rejected with indignation by formal votes of the Legislatures in official session. At the head of these States of the West was the State of Tennessee, General Jackson's native country. The local legislative caucus hastened, in August, 1822, more than two years in advance of the election, to record a vote recommending him for the chief magistracy. Then the Legislature of the State, acting in its official capacity, passed resolutions energetically condemning the practice of the Congressional Caucus and communicated them to all the Legislatures of the Union. The reception given by these latter to the intervention of their sister of Tennessee was not of the warmest; the great majority of the Legislatures abstained from considering the communication; in others, except in a few cases, it was received rather with disfavour.4 But in the popular meetings, and in most of the newspapers, the attacks on the Caucus continued without intermission.

Among these many meetings should be mentioned a " numerous meeting" of citizens of Coecil County, Maryland, of the 4th September, 1823, and a "numerous and respectable " meeting of citizens of Jefferson County, Ohio, of the 2d December, 1823. Their resolutions with long-winded preambles expressing identical views present a significant contrast in tone and reasoning; those of the old Maryland in the East (see Niles, XXV, 40) bear the stamp of laboured legal argument, while the language of the young State of the West, overflowing with enthusiasm, pays no heed to all the "whereas," and bluntly proclaims: 'The time has now arrived when the machinations of the *few* to dictate to the *many,* however indirectly applied, will be met with becoming firmness, by a people jealous of their rights... the only unexceptional source from which nominations can proceed is the people themselves. To them belongs the right of choosing; and they alone can with propriety take any previous steps" (p. 4 of the report of the meeting, published in pamphlet form). a Hammond, II, 129; Niles, XXIV, 139; XXV, 292, 370.

« Xiles, XXV, 137-139.

See especially the message of Governor Troup of Georgia to the Legislature, and the decision of the Senate of the State of New York (Niles, XXV, 293,323). VI

In Congress the intrigues of the rival factions also continued; the friends of all the candidates, excepting those of Crawford, resolved to take no part in the Caucus, for if they attended it, they would be obliged, in pursuance of the nonwritten law of caucuses, to'bow to its decision, were it voted by a majority of one only, and to give up their favourite candidates at once; in any event, if no candidate obtained a majority in the Caucus, as was becoming probable owing to the multiplicity of candidatures, they would all issue from it with lowered prestige. A preliminary canvass has proved that two-thirds of the Republican members of the Congress refused to meet in caucus; Crawford's partisans none the less persisted in convening it. By way of meeting the reproaches which were levejled at the Caucus of being a "Jacobinical conclave," its organizers decided that it should be held in public. It took place on the 14th of February, 1824, in the hall of Congress. Directly the doors were opened an enormous crowd thronged into the galleries, but on the floor of the brilliantly lighted chamber the seats of the members of the Caucus remained almost empty. At last it was ascertained that of two hundred and sixteen members summoned, sixty-six had responded to the appeal. Crawford obtained an almost unanimous vote, but it was that of a small minority of the party only, and the result simply proved the inability of the Caucus to effect the concentration which was its *raison d'etre.* Nevertheless it issued a long manifesto to demonstrate the necessity of persisting in the old practice and to warn the public of the disastrous effects likely to ensue from its abandonment, which would not be confined to the election of the President and the Vice-President, but would shatter the whole system in force of nominations to elective offices and ruin Republican ascendancy. The signatories of the manifesto insisted that no less a mutter than the "dismemberment or the preservation of the party" was at stake. Salvation therefore lay in the maintenance at all hazards of the traditional organization of the party.

1 Niles. XXV, 391.

The manifesto made no impression on public opinion, and the champions of the Caucus soon had to withstand a great onslaught which was made on them in Congress. The handle for it was given by the everlasting question of the electoral regime, of the general ticket, or the district system. A long discussion arose in the Senate, which was transformed almost immediately into a passionate debate on the Caucus. In the preceding discussions the Caucus had been placed in the dock as the accomplice of the general ticket; now it was its own case which came before the court. Rufus King, one of the last survivors of the generation which had founded the republic, opened fire with a long indictment of the "new, extraordinary, self-created central power, stronger than that of the Constitution, which threatens to overturn the balance of power proceeding from its division and distribution between the States and the United States," to degrade the Legislature, to hand over the government to coteries of men "regulated by a sort of freemasonry, the sign and password of each at once placing the initiated in full confidence and communion with each other in all parts of the Union," etc. In supporting Rufus King's attack, other Senators protested against the assertion that the recommendations of the Caucus were but' a simple expression of opinion of private citizens, and that they committed nobody. It was precisely the influence attaching to their capacity of members of Congress which was the foundation of the Congressional Caucus, according to its opponents. And, in fact, they added, can it be maintained that the meetings which take place in the hall of Congress with their chairman in the Speaker's chair and the officers of the House at the doors, are meetings of private persons? It would be arguing like the priest who, when insulted on his way to church, threw off his gown exclaiming, "Lie there, *divinity,* until I punish that rascal"; and then, "having, in his private capacity, inflicted the chastisement, resumed the character of clergyman and proceeded to preach up charity and forgiveness of injuries, love to God an good-will towards man." The perpetuation of the Congressional Caucus will *Annals of Congress,* 18th Congress, 1st session, sitting of the 18th March, 1824, pp. 355-362.

Ibid., p. 382, speech of Hayne. open the door to the greatest abuses and to corruption. "It is an encroachment on the sovereignty of the people, the more alarming, inasmuch as it is exercised in the corrupt atmosphere of executive patronage and influence. Make me President, and I will make you a Minister, or Secretary, or, at all events, I will provide you with a good berth, suited to your wants if not to your capacity.... The President and Congress were intended by the wise framers of our Constitution to act as checks each upon the other, but by the system at present practised, they lose the benefit of this salutary provision." The defenders of the Caucus, far more numerous in the Senate, took rather a high tone with its opponents. There was nothing, they declared, new-fangled in the caucus system, "it originated with the Revolution itself. It was the venerated S. Adams or his father who first suggested it. Was there any intention to recommend a man who was abhorrent to the people? If the people are united in favour of another man, the recommendation would not weigh a feather. The old adage is that by its fruit the tree shall be known. What has been the result of this practice for the last twenty years? Has your Constitution been violated? Is not our happy situation an object of congratulation? Is not every nation which is striving to break the fetters of slavery, looking to us as the landmark by which they are to be guided? These are the fruits of this system, which has been followed, in relation to the presidential election, from 1800, up to the present day; which has been sustained by the people; and which has some of the greatest names of the country to support it." The attacks on the Caucus were due rather to the rancour of a defeated party or to personal considerations. "It was by the Caucus," said Senator Noble, "that the power then in the hands of Federalists was dislodged, and from my youthful days I said Amen! and so I say now." Developing this idea, the president of the last Caucus, Smith, declared in his turn that it was by the Caucus that the Republican party had been brought into power. "The bridge which has carried me safe over, I call a good bridge.... I act as a party man and *Annals of Congress, ibid.,* pp. 412, 413, speech of Branch. *Ibid.,* 391, 3U2, speech of Barbour of Virginia. *Ibid.,* 374. have no hesitation in saying that I wish to keep my party in power; that I believe the caucus system is the most effectual means; and that when we cease to use it, we shall thereby deprive ourselves of one most powerful instrument.... In a government like ours, where many of our great officers are elected, there must be some mode adopted whereby to concentrate the votes of the people. The caucus system is certainly the best. For the Presidency, for instance, is it not rational to suppose that the members of Congress have better opportunities of knowing the character and talents of the several candidates than those who have never seen them and never acted with them. However, the Caucus mode is denounced, and now let us see what is to be substituted!"

The debate lasted for three days, more than twenty speakers took part in it. At last the Senate, wearied out, adjourned the discussion *sine die.* But it was clear to every one that the verdict had been given, that the Congressional Caucus was doomed. After the fiasco of the last meeting of the Caucus, from which two-thirds of the Republican members of Congress absented themselves, the great debate in the Senate gave it the finishing blow. "King Caucus is dethroned," was said on all sides. And it made no attempt to recover its sovereignty; the animadversion which it aroused in the country was too great.

Now, at this distance of time, and in the light of subsequent events, that hostility appears less justified. The indictment of the Congressional Caucus was undoubtedly, to a certain extent, made up of constructive charges. The exasperation of personal and party strife, as well as the ardour of the democratic spirit with its exuberance of youthful vigour, had inevitably exaggerated, or at least anticipated, certain abuses of the Caucus. In particular the alleged prostitution of patronage, and the bargaining between the Presidents and the members of Congress, which were painted in such sombre colours, do not seem to have presented a grave aspect, however justifiable may have been the apprehensions with regard to the future. Intrigues were not entirely absent from the proceedings of the Caucus, but they do not appear to have given rise to actually corrupt practices. The personages raised to *Annals of Congress, ibid.,* 395-398. VOI-. II.— *V* the Presidency by the Caucus were not so much its creatures as men designated beforehand by public opinion, or by a very considerable section of it, owing to their great services and their character. The Caucus has none the less produced untoward effects, which were destined to weigh heavily on the whole future of the Republic, by establishing disastrous precedents and habits of mind which American political life has never been able to throw off: nullifying the scheme devised by the framers of the Constitution for the presidential election and transforming the Electors into lay figures, the Caucus has made the chief magistracy of the Union an object of wire-pulling; and to get its schemes sanctioned by the people, it has implanted within them a respect for party conventionalism, for its external badge, has drilled them into a blind acceptance of *regular nominations.* VII

As the authors of the manifesto issued on behalf of the last Congressional Caucus had foreseen, its collapse entailed that of the whole system of nomination for elective offices by caucuses. The legislative caucuses in the States had also to retire before the rising democratic tide. Their ranks had already been broken into before the explosion of democratic feeling, which began with the third decade of this century. In the legislative caucuses composed only of members of the party in the Legislature the districts in which their party was in a minority were left unrepresented, and yet decisions were taken in them which bound the party in the whole State; sometimes, even, the caucus represented only the minority of the party in the State. To meet the complaints made on this score, the caucuses decided, towards the latter part of the first decade, to take in delegates elected *ad hoc* by the members of the party in the districts which had no representatives in the Legislature. In this way a popular element was introduced into the oligarchical body of the caucuses and with powers expressly conferred. It mattered little that this innovation was not due, in the first instance, to the feeling that the caucus was usurping the rights of the people, but to the fact that it did not provide the party with a materially complete representation. The gap was made, and it was destined to go on widening until the whole people could enter by it. Rhode Island is perhaps the first to supply an example of a " mixed" caucus, about the year 1807, for the nomination of candidates to the high offices of the State. The following year we see it introduced into Pennsylvania, after a campaign in which the proposal to entrust the nomination of the candidates to special delegates did not find much favour with the population, which held that the sending of delegates would cause "trouble and expense " and divisions in the party into the bargain. It was the Republican caucus which, to silence the rival faction, itself invited the counties represented by non-Republicans to send delegates on-the basis of local representation to the Legislature, to join with the Republican members of the Legislature in nominating candidates for the post of Governor and Lieutenant-Governor. This first mixed caucus met on the 7th of March, 1808, at Lancaster. The violent strife of factions which filled the political life of Pennsylvania produced in about ten years a new variation in the constitution of the bodies which made the nominations of the candidates. The sharp attacks of the faction of the "Old-school Democrats" on the "intrigues of the Executive, and of his servants the Assemblymen," decided their rivals to summon, in 1817, at Harrisburg, a popular convention of delegates from the counties, in which the members of the Legislature were to sit only in the absence of special envoys from their county. The name of convention, which, from the very beginning, was used to designate gatherings of citizens from several places, or "general meetings," became in the meantime the regular appellation of the representative meetings of delegates. The Harrisburg convention was attended by sixty-nine delegates and forty-four members of the State Assembly. The "mixed caucus" thus made room for the "mixed convention," the principle and basis of which were of a popular nature, and to which the members of the Legislature were admitted on a subsidiary footing only. Very often they received a quasi Neil Andrews, *The Develop, of the tfomin. Convert,* in Rhode Island. *Pennsylvania Politics early in this Century,* by W. M. Meigs (Pennsylvania Magazine of History and Biography, Vol. XVII, Philad. 1873).

M Carey, *The Olive Branch,* 1818, p. 4fi2. — Meigs, the article just quoted. mandate to this effect: the populations, who did not care about choosing special delegates, "authorized" their representatives in the Legislature to sit in their stead; or, again, the convention admitted them by a special vote, they were "voted in as members." The mixed convention was destined to be replaced eventually by the pure convention, composed solely of popular delegates elected on each occasion *ad hoc.* This last form of convention gave a definitive and permanent form, in party government, to the principle and the practice of the authority delegated by the people, the haphazard antecedents of which we have seen arise at the dawn of the American Republic, in the conferences of delegates of the townships of the county, or of delegates of several counties, or even in the sporadic conventions of State delegates. The first pure convention was organized in Pennsylvania in opposition to the first mixed convention of Harrisburg, and on the same day, by the rival faction, which declared beforehand that the Harrisburg convention was only a "mongrel Caucus," and convened its own at Carlisle. Yet the "mongrel Caucus " won the day, and it was not till 1823 that both parties adopted the system of pure conventions.

In most of the other States the legislative caucus disappeared more slowly. In the State of New York the democratic society of Tammany demands, as early as 1813, the summoning of a convention of delegates for the nomination of candidates for the posts of Governor and Lieutenant-Governor. But no effect is given to this recommendation; the legislative caucus holds the field. The first mixed caucus appears in New York, as a party move, only in 1817, and in 1824 it is still the caucus which makes the State nominations. But in the course of the same year the conventions of delegates started by the convention of Utica, which was "called to put down the caucus," are permanently established. "The whole caucus system," as was proclaimed at this convention, "had been execrated deep from the hearts of the people. A This procedure was followed in Rhode Island, in 182T. See Neil Andrews, *op. cit.* Meigs, *loc. cit.* ; Walton, *loc. cit.* For the nomination of presidential Electors precedents are found of pure conventions in Pennsylvania, even before 1817. » Hammond, I, 437; II, 156.

tone of indignation and disgust at it had gone forth in the land. It could no longer stand." In Massachusetts it is only in 1823 that special delegates are added to the members of the legislative caucus. In Rhode Island, where the participation of popular delegates

in nominations made by the members of the Legislature was introduced at an early stage, the people shows no readiness to depute its delegates. In 1824 it appears that barely a few towns responded to the appeal to send delegates; that in a convention of more than seventy members there are not more than twelve or sixteen who have been really elected. In several States the pure legislative caucus continued to make the nominations of Governor and Lieutenant-Governor even for some time after 1824.
These facts, which show how great the popular inertia, the force of habit, or the prestige of the leadership, were in face even of the rising tide of democracy, explain in a concrete way how the Congressional Caucus was able, in spite of the attacks made on it, to hold its own for no less than a quarter of a century and wield its oligarchical power, with the aid of a few small groups of men scattered throughout the Union. But if democratic feeling did not at once become an irresistible force, if it did not advance by leaps and bounds, it none the less accumulated in the mind of the nation by a daily, hourly process, while the legislative caucus, giving birth to the mixed caucus and the mixed convention, was itself paving the way for the new *cadres;* only an accident was required to make the pent-up force explode and shatter the old ones. This accident was the fall of the Congressional Caucus of 1824, which sheltered the old leadership, which supplied it with a centre of action. And its collapse was all the more complete that the " party" on wh'ich it leaned had long since lost all vitality, having no longer any distinctive principles or object and aim of its own. Everything therefore tumbled down at *Tibo' speeches* delivered in the New York State Convention, September 1824, with the proceedings of the convention, N. Y. 1824, p. 11. —Cf. the *Avtobiugraphy* of Thurlow Weed, Boston, 1883, p. 117, who says that the convention which met at Utica in August (24 September?), 1824, was the beginning of a new political era. Niles, XXIII, 343. And even this mixed caucus did not make State nominations, but busied itself with the impending nomination for the Presidency of the Union. Neil Andrews, *op. cit.* the same blow: the organization of the party, which was trying to keep it going after life had departed from it, was destroyed, and the leadership which had clung to this corpse fell with it. One era in the political life of the United States came to an end and another began.

SECOND CHAPTER THE ESTABLISHMENT OF THE CONVENTION SYSTEM

I

After the collapse of the Congressional Caucus in 1824 the political situation still presented a somewhat chaotic aspect: the old parties were broken up, the new ones were not yet in existence; the leadership was doomed; the extra-constitutional machinery of the legislative Caucus, which was the base of operations of the parties and the leaders, still worked after a fashion in a good many States; by force of habit people resorted to it automatically, but it had received its death-blow. All these elements were about to be renewed, but the mode of this renovation and the effects attending it will supply the subject of a thrilling drama which is still being enacted, down to the present day, on the political stage of the great American Republic.

The failure of the last Congressional Caucus had almost nullified the nomination of Crawford made by it, and instead of the usual recommendation of a single candidate, public manifestations occurred in various quarters in favour now of one and now of another of the four competitors. They proceeded alike from the State Legislatures, which we have seen formally intervening to recommend Jackson even before the last meeting of the Congressional Caucus,—from semiofficial gatherings of the members of Legislatures meeting in caucus, from mixed caucuses, from State conventions composed solely of delegates, and finally from large meetings of citizens. Everywhere people expressed their opinions, declared their preferences, and they did so with a feverish eagerness, as if they wished to make up for the long abstention enforced upon them by the exclusive power which the Congressional Caucus had wielded. The grand jury and the petty jury proceeded in court, "in their private capacity," to vote for a President; companies of militia did the same as soon as their drill was over; people attending public auctions, passengers on steamers, took advantage of being together to record a vote on the election, which absorbed the whole country more than any previous presidential election. But at the final vote in the College of Electors none of the candidates for the Presidency secured a majority, and, in accordance with the Constitution, the election passed to the House of Representatives. Of the three candidates who had obtained the most votes in the Electoral College, Jackson, John Quincy Adams, and Crawford, it chose the second, a statesman of the highest eminence, of consummate experience, of an austerity of character approaching the virtue of antiquity.

Hardly had the new President entered on his duties when his less fortunate competitors and their followers in Congress began a pitiless war on his administration, a war prompted mainly by the spite and greed of factions leagued against a man whose fault was the possession of power. The arch-contriver of this coalition was the Senator of New York, Martin Van Buren, who has left a name in the history of the United States as one of the protagonists and forerunners of the great managers and crack wire-pullers. During the presidential campaign of 1824 he zealously supported Crawford's candidature in the Congressional Caucus. After Crawford's defeat, Van Buren discerned in his competitor Jackson the coming man, the winner at the next presidential election, joined him, and organized a great campaign on his behalf. Installed in the Senate, he attracted hungry people to his side, amalgamated, amid the ruins left by the old disjointed parties, factions and coteries which had no distinct bond of union in the way of common political aspirations or definite lines of conduct, and several members of which had often taken up diametrically opposite attitudes on the questions of the day. Van Buren began their training by accustoming them to offer a concerted resistance to all proposals of the Government tending to use the federal authority for the economical development of the country. Looking about for a pretext for this mechanical opposition conducted by him, ami fully alive to the binding i Niles, Vol. XXVI, pp. 194, 221, 269, 332, 333.

efficacy of principles so pathetically testified to by his fellowworker in the Congressional Caucus of 1824, Van Buren hit upon the idea of reviving the old cry of violated or threatened State rights, which the public conscience, however, did not believe to be in any way imperilled. The country, which was peacefully enjoying its growing prosperity, was unaware of the usurpatiou of the federal power which was being denounced to it. Besides, did not some of Jackson's followers, and Jackson himself when Senator, have occasion to vote in the direction of "federal usurpation "? It was just the same with the question of customs' duties, which did not furnish the elements of a hard-and-fast division of parties either. Later on circumstances will turn these questions into a war-cry and provide Jackson's party, transformed into the "Democratic" party, with its platform, but in the meanwhile this party was simply a personal coalition, devoid of principles. Even if it were already "inclined to principles," as a recent enthusiastic biographer of Van Buren puts it ingeniously, it none the less presented, in American history, the first example of a national party created not to give shape to ideas, but to form a conquering army, that is to say, on an essentially mechanical basis. It had therefore to look for its main support to a powerful organization in the country. Van Buren set to work to provide for this want with an exceptional competence acquired by a long apprenticeship in his native State, which had early developed the arts of the politician. II

The part played in this connection by the State of New York, and the precedents which it created, were of such importance as to deserve special mention. The motley mass of the cosmopolitan population of the great Atlantic city soon precluded the austere government of a ruling class such as obtained on the Puritan soil of New England, and its political life had long been an uninterrupted series of struggles of rival *condottieri.* These were supplied at one time by great families, the " Could we hit upon a few great principles," etc. See above, p. 26.

1 " Van Buren and his coadjutors, however, led a party as yet of inclination to principles, rather than of principles" *(Martin Van Buren,* by E. M. Shepard, 1888, p. 132).

Livingstons, the Clintons, the Schuylers, with a large plebeian following, like the *optimates* in Rome, at another by successful careers of parvenus, who generally allied themselves with the patricians. More intelligent than the Roman *plebs,* less wretched and above all more alive to their capacity of "men and citizens," the people of New York required to be managed with skill, with science, to be drawn into either of the rival camps. Necessity produced the men and created the scientific modes of action. Among the first of these clever manipulators of the electoral material to which tradition goes back was Aaron Burr, the man who, after having attained the VicePresidency of the Republic, dragged out the long and miserable existence of a Cain, abhorred as the murderer of Hamilton and as a traitor to his country. With no private means, poorly connected, but full of resource and possessing considerable personal charm, Burr was able to gather round him, in the city of New York and in most of the counties of the State, men of a similar stamp, who combined great skill and activity with unbounded devotion to their chief. Over the whole area of the State they formed a sort of net, the meshes of which served for catching the voters. A born organizer of men, Burr had all the less scruple about managing them because his practical philosophy of politics was profoundly imbued with military conceptions. His principal maxim was that the citizens ought to be governed at elections by the same rules of discipline as the soldiers of an army, that a few leaders ought to think for the masses, and that the latter had only to render a blind obedience and march at the word of command. The voters were indeed like pawns on a chess-board, set in motion by an elaborate strategy resting on a thorough knowledge of the various elements of the electorate and on a consummate skill in combination and negotiation, whether in the making up of the lists of the candidates, or in the distribution of rewards after the victory in the form of public offices and dignities. For principles and convictions nobody cared a rap; they "had no need of this hypothesis," as the politicians of New York might have said, applying the celebrated remark on God to their own case. Aaron Burr had a host of imitators. One of his leading dis Cf. Hammond, Vol. I, pp. 136, 172, 203.

Statesman's Manual, Vol. II, p. 1139.

ciples, the most eminent in fact, was Martin Van Buren. He absorbed the current practices with the air around him; he assimilated them at an early stage; he knew by personal experience the ups and downs of *condottiere* politics with its triumphs and its proscriptions. A marvellous cleverness "which amounted to a genius for intrigue, without being identical with it, seconded his talent and his intelligence. A fortunate temperament enabled him and inclined him to play the game in perfect style and with the easy bearing of a gentleman. He never ventured to breast the current; he did not defy events, he preferred to adapt himself to them. Not having been able to prevent the establishment of universal suffrage in the State of New York, on the occasion of the revision of the constitution of 1821, he at once set to work, with all the power of his methodical and organizing mind, to spread the net for the new voters. Election committees, which penetrated into the most remote localities of the State, enrolled the voters and, communicating with the capital, Albany, concentrated all the threads in the hands of Van Buren and a few associates, whom he formed into a junta which received the name of The Regency.

Beneath.these head wire-pullers there grew up a large *personnel* engaged specially in politics, at New York in the first instance, and then in other places, attracted everywhere by a desire for public employment. From the very foundation of the United States, the advantages attaching to the management of public affairs had not only let loose ambitions but also, and in a still greater degree, cravings of a purely material kind. The lucrative posts, on a comparatively modest scale, which the federal service or that of the States could offer, were sought after with an eagerness such as one would have never expected from a democratic people with whom equality of station appeared to exclude a taste for official titles, and in a country absorbed in business where untold profits could be realized. However, so it was. But for a considerable time the office-seekers were stopped by the small number of places as well as by the existence of a ruling class, which had a prior claim on them, in the natural course of things. This competition had a good deal to do with the democratic ferment which set in during the first decades of the century. But in proportion as the old generation which had founded the Republic disappeared, as the development of the country entailed that of the public service, and the political contingents increased both through the extension of the suffrage and the violent rivalries of parties which brought every available force into the field, the scramble for the loaves and fishes became closer and keener. There arose a whole class of men of low degree who applied all their energies in this direction, who sought their means of subsistence in politics, and especially in its troubled waters,—men readw to sacrifice everything to this object, devoid of all scruple. I The social and political state of affairs in New York, referred to above, was particularly favourable to the rise of this type of individual. The neighbouring State of Pennsylvania, also a prey to factions and extremely democratic in tone, had likewise at an early stage let in the small politicians. In the other States they were not so common, but everywhere they presented, by the beginning of the third decade of the century, a distinct element which lowered politics and gave an invidious signification to the very term of " politician," the original, etymological meaning of which denoted simply persons engaged in public affairs. In its altered meaning "this term," as Niles wrote in 1823, "is selected as conveying an idea of persons who have little if any regard for the welfare of the republic unless as immediately connected with or dependent on their own private pursuits, — who, as a great party leader said of himself, are 'men of principle according to their interest,' who have respect for the 'loaves and fishes,' who always bow to a 'rising sun,' and stand prepared to dance round the 'golden calf. ' They are the opposite of statesmen.. .. There are little knots of these politicians everywhere, and at least two out of three of each gang are either office-holders or office-seekers, and each gives or takes the influence that he himself or his fellows may possess, to advance particular views or keep honest and honourable men in the background. Their proceedings are the antipodes of truth and justice. They are the 'fag ends' of the human family. What other men call conscience, they regard as a matter to be bought and sold, as convenience or opportunity offers...."

» *Weekly Register*, Vol. XXIII, p. 370. HI

The arts of management developed in the political atmosphere of New York were now about to be applied by Van Buren on a more extensive scale and on a larger stage. He formed committees throughout the Union to sweep up adherents for Jackson and stir the electorate by speaking and writing, in public meetings and private gatherings, glorifying Jackson, replying to the attacks of his opponents, fiercely assailing Adams' administration by a series of concerted movements. The staff required for the performance of this task, and a picked one, was ready to hand,—the "politicians." They flung themselves headlong into the campaign on behalf of Jackson, who appeared to them as the "rising sun." The committees supplied them with the material, popular sentiment offered them a moral, base of operations. As soon as J. Q. Adams became President, in 1825, Jackson's friends shouted that the will of the people had been violated by the choice made by the House, for the chief magistracy, of J. Q. Adams in preference to the candidate most favoured by the popular vote, Andrew Jackson. The Constitution no doubt left the House complete freedom of choice, but it had used it in a manner contrary to the democratic principle, to the *"demos krateo* principle," as was said by Senator Benton, who had learnt his Greek in the Far West. Adams' election was therefore purely and simply an act of encroachment on the popular sovereignty; by means of the letter of the Constitution the people had been balked of its rights! These charges, which Jackson himself and his friends kept on repeating throughout the country, aroused a. profound indignation, a regular exasperation against the enemies of the people in honest and simple souls. The affront offered to the national will cried for vengeance and could only be wiped out, declared Jackson's followers, by his election to the Presidency for the next term. But it was not only a conflict of abstract principles; Jackson's name was not merely the rallying-cry for the battle of the "democratic principle against the theory of the Constitution," but also for the battle of *Thirty Years' View*, Vol. I, pp. 47, 49.

Ibid., Vol. I., p. 47.
the "people" against the caste of men of intelligence, of culture, of wealth, of social refinement, of historic traditions. These men aroused popular jealousy not only by the monopoly of political power which they enjoyed and which caused the revolt against the Caucus, they irritated the susceptibilities of the masses still more by the social supremacy which they assumed and which made them in fact a sort of caste on the levelled soil of the Old World. General Jackson, on the other hand, without being a demagogue, had no equal in flattering the instincts and the passions of the people; he had his virtues and, in a still higher degree, his defects. The people recognized their own flesh and blood in him; the stern qualities of the "old hero" convinced them that he would be the man to make a clean sweep of the enemies of the people installed in power and to put an end to the "aristocratic corruption" which was rampant in the Government. For this was how the people pictured to itself and others pictured to it the administration presided over by that old stoic J. Q. Adams, the "chief fault of which was that it was too good for the wicked world in which it found itself."

The politicians vigorously exploited the feelings which inclined the masses towards Jackson, conducting their campaign with an unprecedented virulence. He was triumphantly elected. He and his friends regarded their success as the victory of the democratic principle and the affirmation of the right of the people to govern themselves; "it vindicated the *demos* in their right and in their power," as Benton said. So the enthusiasm of the "demos" was immense. Jackson appeared as a new Joshua, who led the chosen people into the promised land wrested from the "enlightened classes," and the people following in Jackson's train flocked to take possession of it. "It seemed," relates a witness, "as if half the nation had rushed at once into the capital. It was like the inundation of the northern barbarians into Rome, save that the tumultuous tide came in from a different point of the compass. The West and the South seemed to have precipitated themselves upon the North and overwhelmed it. On i *Andrew Jackson,* by W. G. Suniiifr. 1S90, p. 118.
Thirty Years' View, Vol. I, pp. 47, lit
that memorable occasion you might tell a 'Jackson man' almost as far as you could see him. Their every motion seemed to cry out victory! Strange faces filled every public place, and every face seemed to bear defiance on its brow." "Persons have come five hundred miles (with no railways!) to see Jackson," wrote Webster, "and they really seem to think that the country is rescued from some dreadful danger." The scenes which followed the ceremony of the taking of the oath by the new President were a sort of symbol of the legal revolution which had just been carried out and of certain effects which it was destined to produce. On his return from the Capitol, from the legislative building, to the White House, the residence of the President, Jackson was preceded, accompanied, and followed by an enormous crowd-which hurried up from all sides. The crowd broke into the White House, filled all the rooms in a twinkling, pell-mell with the high dignitaries of the Republic and the members of the corps diplomatique; in the great reception hall men of the lower orders standing with their muddy boots on the damask-covered chairs were a sort of living image of the taking possession of power by the new master. When refreshments were handed round, the rumour of which had attracted the crowd, a tremendous scramble ensued, crockery, cups, and glasses were smashed to pieces, rough hands intercepted all the ices, so much so that nothing was left for the ladies, as a historian relates with consternation. This fury with which the people flung itself on the refreshments was destined very soon to become highly symbolic.
rv

The vast popular army which marched triumphantly through the streets of Washington dispersed to their homes, but one of its divisions remained, the corps of marauders which followed it. This was composed of the politicians. They wanted their spoils. The victory was due to their efforts, and as the labourer is worthy of his hire, they deserved a reward. By Letter of Arthur J. Stansbury, quoted by Parton, *Andrew Jackson,* Vol. HI, p. 1(K).
Webster's Private Correspondence, Vol. I, p. 473, quoted by Parton, *ibid.,*
way of remuneration for their services they demanded places in the administration. They filled the air of Washington like locusts, they swarmed in the halls and lobbies of the public buildings, in the adjoining streets, they besieged the residences of Jackson and his ministers. Jackson hastened to admit the justice of their claim. His official newspaper had already announced beforehand that he would "reward his friends and punish his enemies." The punishment began at once. Many government servants were dismissed without a hearing and without a word of explanation, and for the sole reason that they were or were suspected of having been hostile to Jackson and that their places were wanted. They were turned adrift without pity; neither long service nor special competence was of any avail. Every official was henceforth at the mercy of informers. A reign of terror set in in the public departments. During the first year of his Presidency Jackson cashiered or got rid of more than two thousand persons, whereas all his predecessors together had dismissed, from the foundation of the Republic, only seventy-four public servants, of whom several for cause. The new men who were put in the place of the old ones were often quite incompetent; their sole merit was that they had "helped Jackson." Several of these appointments were so scandalous that the In the horde of office-seekers which descended on Washington there was one man who was shamefaced enough to say as he walked along the street with Amos Kendall, Jackson's confidential associate: "I am ashamed of myself, for I feel as if every man

knew what I came for." "Don't distress yourself," replied Kendall, " for every man you meet is on the same business" *(Autobiography of Amos Kendall,* 1872. p. 30H). " The gloom of suspicion pervaded the face of society. No man deemed it safe and prudent to trust his neighbour, and the interior of the department presented a fearful scene of guarded silence, secret intrigue, espionage, and tale-bearing. A casual remark dropped in the street would, within an hour, be repeated at headquarters, and many a man received unceremonious dismission who could not, for his life, conceive or conjecture wherein ho had offended " (Parton, Vol. Ill, p. 212).

Barely a week after Jackson's accession to office, Clay wrote from Washington: "Among the official corps here there is the greatest solicitude and apprehension. The members of it feel something like the inhabitants of Cairo when the plague breaks out; no one knows who is next to encounter the stroke of death, or, which with many of them is the same thing, to be dismissed from office. You have no conception of the moral tyranny which prevails here over those in employment" (Carl Schurz, *Life of Henry (. lay.* Vol. I, p. 335).

Senate refused to confirm them, and it would have vetoed at least half of the whole number if it had dared to lace popular clamour. For the people would not stand any discussion of Jackson's acts; to all criticism of the dismissals of officials and of the other arbitrary acts destructive of all sound republican government which marked the Presidency of the "old hero," the "people" had but one invariable reply: "Hurrah for Jackson!"

The "rewarding of friends and the punishment of enemies," carried to such lengths by Jackson, was not a practice altogether unknown in the United States. It had been in vogue, and for a considerable time past, both in the State of New York and in Pennsylvania. As has been incidentally mentioned above, even in Aaron Burr's time, towards the close of the eighteenth century, in the contests of the New York factions, the winning side laid hands on the available public offices. One of the most celebrated faction leaders in New York, De Witt Clinton, developed and perfected the practice by turning out all the men in office who had been appointed by the beaten faction. With each swing of the electoral pendulum the proscriptions began over again. "The public mind," writes Hammond of the year 1811, "has become so accustomed to see men ejected from office on account of their opinions that such changes ceased to be matters of surprise or to produce any excitement." This system, started under the regime of appointment to offices, was continued under that of election to them introduced with universal suffrage, in 1821. Caught at once in the toils of the elaborate organization directed by Van Buren and his associates, universal suffrage bestowed public offices on the politicians selected for this purpose by the wire-pullers. The party victorious at the poll obtained all the places. That appeared to it logical and justifiable. And when, some time afterwards, in the Senate This practice was encouraged in a marked way by the oligarchical mode of appointment to offices, which was in the hands of a small council of a few members of the State Legislature, that is to say, of the party which had, for the moment, a majority in it. For the very instructive if not edifying history of this Council of Appointment, see Hammond's *Political History* 0/-Veto *York,* ami a special article by J. M. Gitterman, "The Council of Appointment in New York," *Political Science Quarterly,* 1802, No. 1.

Vol. I, p. 280. VOL. II E of the United States, Van Buren was accused of having initiated these practices, one of his associates of the Regency, Senator Marcy, protested against the charge as not involving anything reprehensible: "The politicians *preach* what they *practise.* When they are contending for victory they avow their intention of enjoying the fruits of it. If they are defeated, they expect to retire from office. If they are successful, they claim as matter of right the advantages of success. They see nothing wrong in the rule that to the victor belong the spoils of the enemy." This remark about "the spoils to the victor " became famous and passed into every-day language.

The division of the spoils was now transformed from a local practice into a national system. It was one more contribution to American political life from New York, which had started the arts of management for the purpose of manipulating a vast electorate in a motley city devoid of civic spirit and given over to factions, and which had created the type of politician to carry the work out. The "spoils " which served for feeding them, which supplied the *condottiere* leaders with the sinews of war, were the logical completion of the system. The whole Union was destined to fall a victim to this system, because its political situation became similar to that of New York. The old political supremacy wielded by the elite of the nation, and which radiated from Washington, having been shattered with the congressional Caucus, the leadership crumbled into a thousand fragments; it passed to an innumerable crowd of petty Jocal leaders who stood nearer to the masses, but who too often were only needy adventurers. And yet it was their services which had to be resorted to for building up the party without principles which was got together under Jackson's name, and to keep up this mechanical aggregation there was nothing but the artificial cement of "rewards and punishments." To dis-. pense with it on the day after the victory would be to lose the fruit of one's labour, to break up the party. Consequently, even if he had wished to do so, Jackson could not have resisted the demands of the "praetorian band which claimed the reward of the hard-fought contest "; while his Secretary 1 Niles, Vol. XLIII, p. 8.

From the letter of A. J. Stansbury, written after the inauguration of Jackson, and quoted above. of State, who was no other than Martin Van Buren, had only to indulge at Washington in the practices which were so familiar to him in his native State, to present a living link between the spoils system in New York and in the Union.

The hecatombs of office-holders, which were henceforth to be regularly repeated at each change of President, were facilitated to a considerable extent by a law passed iu 1820, which fixed four years as the term of service for several categories of officials: district attorneys, officials in the customs service, paymasters, and some other officers. It appears that the object of the law was to secure greater accuracy and promptitude in the settlement of the accounts of disbursing officers, and to rid the service of dishonest men without further procedure, while those who were blameless could be reappointed for fresh terms. But this law was interpreted to mean that at the end of four years the post became *ipso facto* vacant. It might then be transferred without scandal to another man, so that each new President, without even using or misusing his right of removing public officers, had at his disposal several thousands of appointments, and extremely important ones, for distribution at his discretion, that is to say, for rewarding electoral services. In vain were repeated attempts made to repeal this law. On the contrary, the special use to which it was put was extended more and more, even to posts to which it did not apply at all, on the pretext that in a democratic government public offices were not personal property, and that every citizen had a right to share in the emoluments of the public service. Jackson boldly proclaimed or. embraced On this point we have the evidence of Calhoun and Webster, who, relying on their personal recollections, asserted on several occasions that the authors of the law of 1820 had no political object in view. See the speech of Calhoun of the 9th of February, 1835, on the extent of executive patronage (*Works,* Vol. V, p. 153), and that of Webster in the debate of the 14th of May, 1846, in the Senate, on the dismissal of public servants *(Congressional Globe,* Vol. XV, p. 819). But on the other hand, J. Q. Adams maintained that the law was passed at the instigation of Crawford, who then held the office of Secretary of the Treasury, and wanted places to distribute to pave the way for his presidential candidature (*Works,* Vol. VII, pp. 424-125). See Benton's report to the Senate, of the 4th of May, 1826 (*Thirty Tears' View,* Vol. II, p. 138), the debate iu the Senate of February, 1835, and of February, 1836 *(Congressional Debates,* Vol. XI, part 1, pp. 109,576; Vol. XII, part 1, p. 367). this doctrine in his first presidential message, in which he defended the dismissals carried out by him, explaining that the welfare of the service demanded frequent change of officials, for those who were permanent fixtures inevitably became indifferent to the public interest; that the service lost more by keeping them than it gained by their experience; and to facilitate the rotation which "constituted a first principle in the Republican creed," the President proposed to extend it legally to all offices without exception, by bringing them under the operation of the law of 1820.

Far from being of advantage to the public interest, the application of these "first republican principles" of the rotation and division of the spoils very soon threw the whole of public life into grave disorder. It deteriorated the public service by destroying all stability in it, by setting up intrigue and favour in place of merit, competence, and professional zeal, and leaving the door wide open to adventurers and hungry mercenaries. The organized parties alone benefited by this system, which procured them an army of election agents scattered all over the country and ready to do anything to secure the triumph of the party; for their own fate was at stake, and the election contest became for each of them a life-and-death struggle. Those who wanted to oust them joined the camp of the party in opposition with the same desperate resolve to conquer or to die. The contingents of these two armies were recruited and renewed as it were spontaneously, with a regularity and a fulness which kept pace with the growth of their permanent *cadres.*

V

This organization, as we are already aware, was supplied by the delegates' conventions, which from 1824 onwards developed by a continuous process into a highly finished system. The active campaign conducted on behalf of Jackson, during the years 1825-1828, gave a great stimulus to the movement. Jackson's supporters, as well as those of J. Q. Adams, who was put up for re-election, got the conventions to meet in most *Statesman's Murvtal.* President's messages from 1789, by E. Williams, New York, 1849, Vol. II, p. 702.

of the States, and procured manifestations from them in favour of one or the other candidate. In the state of dissolution of parties which was a feature of the period, the conventions had no standard to raise but the name of the candidate of their choice, and we meet with nothing but "Jackson conventions," "Anti-Jackson conventions," "Administration conventions," or "Friends of the administration conventions." Established at first in a more or less sporadic fashion, the conventions became general and spread throughout the country, falling according to the territorial units and electoral divisions into State, district, county conventions, etc., and ended by covering the whole Union in a regular and exhaustive manner. This process, which began towards the end of Monroe's administration, took no less than a quarter of a century. It was delayed by the same causes which had prolonged the existence of the legislative Caucus and had made it outlive itself after 1824, especially by the *via inertiae* of old habits and the inadequacy of means of communication before the introduction of railways. In the East, where the ground had been so admirably prepared, especially in New York and Pennsylvania, the States of the politicians, the popular representative party organization developed quickly and at once laid hold of the electorate, but it was not quite the same thing in the South and the West. The nomination to elective offices by assemblies of delegates was not yet general under Jackson's first Presidency even in such States as Maryland and Virginia, and still less so in the rudimentary States beyond the Alleghanies. The candidates often offered themselves, as in the old days, either through the medium of the newspapers, or by making a personal canvass of the voters, travelling through the county or the State to have a talk with people and solicit votes. Naturally there A distinguished American publicist, Mr. Talcot Williams, remarks accurately enough, that each advance in the development of American parties has been determined by the extension of means of communication. The convention in New York reached its culminating point after the opening of the Erie Canal; the national convention took its full flight towards the period of the extension of railways, and the direction of the national campaign from a single centre became possible only after the telegraph lines had spread over the whole territory of the Republic. (Party Government in the United States, Lalor, *Cyclopedia of Pol. Science,* III, 114.)

» Nile, Vol. XXX, p. 449; Vol. XXXII, p. 115; Th. Ford, *A History of Illinois* from its commencement as a State in 1818 to 1847, Chicago, 1854, p. 201.

was no discipline among aspirants belonging to the same party, and not unfrequently there were several rival candidatures; to clear the ground of them recourse was sometimes had to an arbitrator, who settled which of the candidates was to retire. In certain parts of the West the new system soon got acclimatized, for instance, in Ohio; in others, as in Illinois, it had more difficulty in obtaining a footing. Introduced, about 1832, by the immigrants from the Atlantic coast, it was received with suspicion by the fierce democrats of the prairies, who detected in it a "Yankee contrivance destined to abridge the liberties of the people, by depriving individuals, on their own mere motion, of the privilege of becoming candidates, and depriving each man of the right to vote for a candidate of his own selection and choice." In the course of the session of the State Legislature of 1835-1836, at Vandalia, there was a great semi-official debate on the system of conventions. In this it met with determined opponents, but it was none the less making its way in every part of the State, being extended to almost all the elective offices. The Jacksonians became ardent promoters of it, to the great exasperation of the Whigs, whose numerical inferiority was further accentuated owing to the discipline which the convention system ensured in the ranks of their antagonists. Having refrained for some years from adopting this system, the Whigs found themselves at last obliged, out of self-defence, to imitate their rivals. The decision arrived at on this point, after a Whig mass meeting, was announced to the people of Illinois in a circular, stating its objects and reasons, drafted by a young member of the Legislature, named Abraham Lincoln, the future President of the United States. But whatever were the suspicions and the personal or local 1 Niles, Vol. XXXV, p. 5. 2 *Ibid.,* Vol. XXIV, p. 242, the letter on the delegate system.

A History of Illinois, p. 203.

« *Ibid.,* p. 204.

6 This circular, dated the 4th of March, 1843, signed by Lincoln and two other persons, but due entirely to bis pen (see *Abraham Lincoln, A History,* by J. Nicolay and J. Hay, I, pp. 218, 21!l), contains word for word the passage from the New Testament which later on became, in the mouth of Lincoln, the famous war-cry against slavery: "A house divided against itself cannot stand." (The text of the circular is reproduced iu A. Liucoln's *Complete Works,* New York, 1891, I, p. 77.) opposition which the convention system encountered, they could not prevail against it nor retard its advance, for it corresponded to too many interests and wants, passions and cravings. The democratic impulse which carried Jackson into power had found expression, in the constitutional sphere, in two important facts: the introduction of universal suffrage into the newly formed States and into several old States where it had not yet been established, and the very considerable extension of the elective principle to public offices. The number of voters increased and the task of each one became vast and highly complicated. And yet. many new members of the sovereign people, especially in the industrial and manufacturing centres which were beginning to arise, had no insight into public affairs, and almost all had no spare time. The haste to get rich was infecting the whole nation with such intensity that in point of fact the effective exercise of its political rights was becoming rather an embarrassment to it than otherwise. It could not leave it to a particular social class such as that which was formerly invested with a certain moral hegemony in the commonwealth: the traditional leadership had ceased to exist. In the absence, therefore, of a quasi-organic social element, some artificial organ was required to discharge the duties which the political indifference of the people left unperformed. And if an organ of this kind managed to come into existence, the nation, which was becoming engrossed in its material interests, would have relinquished its political powei to it without complaint of usurpation. Yet the pride and the consciousness of its strength which filled the new American democracy could not assent to a formal abdication on its part. With the greedy feeling of the miser who, too covetous to spend his wealth, takes his pleasure in the contemplation of it, the American, busy as he was in other directions, felt the need of handling, so to speak, from time to time, and as often as possible, his rights as member of the sovereign people and of thus giving himself the illusion of enjoying them.

The new institution introduced into the political life of the United States — the conventions — met all these requirements, which seemed contradictory at the first blush, admirably. The convention, by nominating the candidates for all the elective offices and settling the programmes, relieved the American of the most difficult task for a citizen of a free country, brought it within the reach of the busiest man or the meanest capacity. And this humble voter appeared none the less to remain absolute master of the situation, since it was from him that the members of the convention held their mandate; they were his envoys, his clerks. Nay, the prerogatives with which the Constitution had invested him were extended by the operation of the conventions: not only could not a member now be created without his intervention, but not even a simple candidate; in a word, the conventions gave the citizen more opportunities for manifesting his will in quasi-constitutional forms than were offered by the Constitution. Again, the conventions satisfied ambitions and appetites, of a more or less legitimate kind, aroused by the advent of new social strata. By formally assigning candidatures for elective appointments, the popular Organization provided a ladder for the "new men" who had not enough influence and, perhaps, merit to climb up of themselves. To others who, eager for a sphere of public activity and influence, could not find room within the limited area of the Constitution, the conventions offered a sort of substitute for it in their organization modelled on the constitutional fabric with their hierarchy, their powers, their dignitaries. Finally, they were of still higher value to the more vulgar and far more numerous ambitions, represented by the new breed of politicians which grew and multiplied under the fostering sway of the great economic outburst of the age. This latter not only kept individual energies engrossed in the pursuit of wealth to the detriment of the proper attention required by public affairs, but it upset society by whirling it all into a sort of vortex, in which some rapidly achieved success, while many others were carried off their feet and in a way flung out of the ranks. The numerous *diclassts* who had failed in private professions turned their attention to public business and swelled the throng of. those who were trying to exploit it on New York methods. Powerless if they remained isolated, they found in the conventions a rallying centre and almost a social position.

All these advantages which the conventions offered, from various points of view, were completed and enhanced by the establishment, towards the end of Jackson's first Presidency, of a central Organization, in the form of *national conventions,* composed of delegates specially chosen by all the States of the Union. Placed on the top of the local conventions, the national convention formed with them a complete extra-constitutional machinery which became the axis of party government now definitively installed in the American Republic, and which confronted the constitutional fabric as its counterpart, providing for each of its grades special assemblies of party Electors, who nominated to the respective public offices. The national conventions were composed of delegates chosen by the State conventions and the district conventions, which, in their turn, were composed of delegates sent by the county conventions, while these latter emanated directly from the primary meetings of the citizens in the cities and the rural districts. The ward in the cities and the township in the counties supplied the base of the electoral Organization. While the local conventions took charge of the elective offices in the States and in Congress, the national conventions undertook the duty performed by the congressional Caucus for a quarter of a century, that of nominating the candidates for the Presidency and the Vice-Presidency of the Union. At the outset the local conventions — the State conventions, for instance — discharged several functions; they made nominations to various offices at the same time, to those of Governor and Lieutenant-Governor, to seats in Congress, etc. But Proposals in the direction of entrusting to similar national delegations the choice of the candidates for the chief magistracies of the Union were put forward even in the time of the congressional Caucus. At first it was desired to widen its base by introducing into it special delegates from the States in which the party, being in a minority, had no representatives in Congress, after the fashion of the mixed caucuses of the State Legislatures (the proposals of the writers, John Binns and Matthew Carey; cf. *Olive Branch,* p. 452). In 1822 a convention of delegates from all the States, with instructions, is expressly proposed, but its recommendation of candidates was to be submitted to the people only as an indication of public feeling, without influencing in any other way the final choice made by the presidential Electors, who were to vote in perfect freedom (Niles, Vol. XXI, p. 403). The following year, in the midst of the ardent controversy aroused by the expected convening of the congressional Caucus, fourteen representatives of Pennsylvania in the Congress published a declaration disapproving of the meeting of the Caucus, and one of them added the opinion that the sole means of restoring harmony in the party would be a national convention (Niles, Vol. XXV, p. 306).
soon the "division of labour" found its way into the nomination business and a special convention met for each office or group of offices to be filled up. Side by side with the conventions, which met from time to time only for the discharge of their special and momentary duty, there grew up a permanent Organization in the form of committees for each territorial unit, for the State, the county, the township, the ward, which summoned the conventions and the primary assemblies, undertook all the preliminary business, and in general managed the election work.

The new democratic structure thus erected, from base to summit, in place of the old shattered party apparatus, was on much broader lines and far more comprehensive; but it nevertheless brought about a concentration of power and a compression of public opinion and of its preoccupations, which increased at each stage of the

Organization. In proportion as the conventions composed of successive delegations stretched out, they got farther from the popular source, leaving behind them a long line of systematically eliminated minorities.-This concentration was followed by a centralization of the objects pursued at the various points of the political circumference. Each set of conventions serving as a support to the higher one, the county convention to that of the State, the State convention to the national convention, each had to pave the way for the next, to subordinate its acts to the preoccupations of its superior. Terminating, by an unbroken series of links, in the national convention, which had to provide for the chief magistracies of the Union, the convention system inevitably made the nominations to every public office, down to those of the township, dependent on the considerations which determined the choice of the President and the Vice-President. To ensure the success of a certain candidature for the Presidency, it was necessary to have a national convention favourable to it; this could only be attained if the State conventions, from which the latter emanated, were composed of members ready to choose their delegates from that point of view, and so on. In this way national politics, that is, relating to the presidential election, became the axis of the whole convention system, making all the elections, even the strictly local, purely municipal ones, contests of political parties waging war for the possession of the White House. No doubt the extreme fierceness of the struggle between the followers and the opponents of Jackson, which made everything subordinate to his success or his defeat, powerfully contributed to infect all the elections without exception with "politics," but the convention system set up the same result as a logical postulate independent of the passions of the moment.

VI

The national convention, which took the place of the congressional Caucus, as regards the selection of candidates for the two chief offices of the Republic, did not succeed to it at once. After the fall of the congressional Caucus there was an interregnum of a few years. When the power of the congressional Caucus came to an end, the State conventions tried to step into its shoes, but concurrently with them State Legislatures and, in some cases, legislative caucuses, also came forward to get possession of the presidential nomination. And it was to the combined action of all these various bodies that was due the nomination, in view of the election of 1828, of Jackson on the one side and of Adams on the other. But soon both State Legislatures and caucuses definitively retired before the conventions, and the choice of candidates for the Presidency was made over for good to the national conventions.

The first national convention was brought about by a casual episode which had agitated the Union for some years, by the anti-masonic movement. A freemason in the State of New York, who wanted to write a book divulging the secrets of the order, having disappeared in a mysterious way, a report was circulated that he had been captured by the freemasons and murdered by them. The indignation aroused by this alleged crime soon extended to the adjoining counties and, outside New York, to one State after another. Anti-masonic associations sprang up, measures were demanded against the freemasons in general, and the members of other secret societies bound by an oath. The anti-masonic contagion spread with extraordinary rapidity, and in a short time the enemies of freemason ry became so numerous that they thought themselves strong enough to contest elections throughout the Union on the question of freemasonry. They started an organization, held conventions to select candidates for the highest elective offices in the States, and finally resolved to try and carry the Presidency in order to get a strong opponent of freemasonry elected and dislodge it from the political power which, according to its antagonists, was its principal object. A general convention of ninety-six anti-masonic delegates, from different parts of the Union, met at Philadelphia, in September, 1830, and having affirmed, in a very lengthy report, the political danger presented by freemasonry, invited all the citizens of the United States who were hostile to secret societies to send delegates, corresponding in numbers to their representatives in Congress, to a convention, with instructions to nominate candidates for the Presidency and the Vice-Presidency. The convention met in the following year at Baltimore; one hundred and fourteen delegates were present, almost all of them from the East; Ohio was the only Western State which sent delegates. It decided that the candidates should be chosen by vote and that the majority required for election should be three-fourths of the members present. The voting took place in a second sitting, and the candidates nominated fought the presidential contest throughout the Union. Defeated at the polls, the anti-masons soon disappeared as an organized party.

But the example of the national convention which they introduced was followed immediately by the opponents of Jackson and then by his supporters. The former had amalgamated, more or less satisfactorily, under the common denomination of *National Republicans.* Their most brilliant champion, Henry Clay, was clearly marked out for contesting the Presidency with Jackson, who stood again in spite of the recommendations which he had made in his messages against the reelection of the President. On the invitation of the Caucus of the National Republicans of the Maryland Legislature a national convention of delegates of this party met at Baltimore in December, 1831. It became the true prototype of *The Proceedings of the United States Anti-masonic Convention,* held at Philadelphia, Sept. 11,1830. Philadelphia, 1830.

The Proceedings of the Second United States Anti-masonic Convention, held at Baltimore, Sept., 1831. Boston,

1832. those great periodical party assizes which from that time to this have played a unique part in the political life of the United States. From this point of view the details connected with the meeting of that convention deserve to be related.

The convention was attended by one hundred and fifty-six delegates, representing eighteen States and the District of Columbia; five States (Georgia, South Carolina, Alabama, Missouri, Mississippi) did not appoint delegates; the sixth, Illinois, elected one, but he did not put in an appearance. The States were very unequally represented; thus Tennessee had only one delegate, Louisiana and Indiana two, while the District of Columbia, adjoining Baltimore, had five. Evidently in the remote States there were not, owing to the difficulties of travelling, enough persons ready to accept the mission; for the same reason, sixty-five delegates did not answer the roll-call, twelve of whom, however, arrived before the close of the convention. After having chosen a temporary organization and instructed the delegations of the States to examine the credentials of their members, the convention appointed a permanent organization, with James Barbour as president, and decided that the nomination of the candidates should be made by calling over the States in their geographical order (Maine, New Hampshire, etc.), each delegate rising in his place to declare the name of the person for whom he gives his vote as the candidate for the office of President of the United States in opposition to Andrew Jackson. The name of Henry Clay having been repeatedly mentioned in this connection, the president, "after making such prefatory remarks as he supposed proper," laid before the convention a letter which he had received from Clay. In this personal letter Jackson's illustrious rival expressed his regret that several delegates had been sent to the convention with instructions to vote for him, Clay; he held that all restrictions on the freedom of deliberation and decision of the convention were inexpedient, that the convention ought to have the power of freely comparing the merits of different candidates. No doubt, Clay was sure of being nominated; but his formal disapproval of the instructions given to the members of the convention is none the less worthy of note. Clay was nominated unanimously, and a committee of eighteen members, one for each State, was ordered to notify to him the decision of the convention. The deputation repaired for this purpose from Baltimore to Washington and brought back his acceptance on the following day. In the third sitting, which, in pursuance of a decision taken the day before, opened with a prayer read by a clergyman, the convention proceeded to nominate a candidate for the Vice-Presidency. _ John Sergeant was proposed and seconded for this office, and each delegate having voted for him *viva voce,* he was proclaimed candidate, after which a committee of five members was directed to notify his nomination to him in person. Before separating, the convention adopted a long address to the citizens of the United States, which was really an indictment of Jackson's administration. It also took care to appoint a central State corresponding committee in each State which had none, and to recommend to the several States to organize subordinate corresponding committees in each county and town in their respective States, and, finally, approved the suggestion of a general convention of "Young Men of the National Bepublican Party." From a feeling of patriotic loyalty the convention proceeded in a body to the residence of Charles Carroll to pay its respects to the "sole survivor of those benefactors of the human race who affixed their names to the Declaration of American Independence."

In conformity with the decision taken by the Baltimore convention, the "convention of young men" met at Washington in May, 1832. It was composed of three hundred and sixteen delegates, who unanimously approved the nomination of Clay and Sergeant. The speeches made on this occasion were "in strains of eloquence but seldom equalled." Clay paid a visit to the convention, which listened to his speech standing. It concluded its labours by voting ten resolutions, which defined the policy of the party and which anticipated the custom since adopted by the conventions of drawing up the "platform" of the party. Following the example of its elder sister, the "convention of young men" repaired in a body to Baltimore *Journal of the National Republican Convention,* which assembled in the city of Baltimore, Dec. 12, 1831, for the nomination of candidates to fill the offices of President and Vice-President. Published by order of the convention, Washington. 2 Niles, Vol. XLII, p. *200.* to greet John Carroll, and then made a pilgrimage to the tomb of George Washington at Mount Vernon.

Lastly Jackson's followers, the Democratic Republicans, met in their turn, in national convention, at Baltimore in May, 1832, not to nominate the candidate for the Presidency, who was of course Jackson himself, but to solemnly proclaim the candidate for the Vice-Presidency. Jackson chose Martin Van Buren for this post, to reward him for his devotion to him, but Van Buren was far from enjoying general consideration in the country; he did not command the support of the party by himself. The convention was to be the means of obtaining it for him; this plan was hit upon, even before the convention of National Republicans, by Jackson's intimates, who formed a sort of occult government around him known as the " kitchen cabinet." Instead of holding councils of his constitutional advisers, Jackson fell into the habit of discussing affairs of state with a few subordinates who were in his confidence, and in whose society he felt more at his ease; he was not obliged to submit to the formality of a regular discussion, but could carry on a general desultory conversation over his pipe. One of the leading members of this kitchen cabinet, Major Lewis, "the great father of the wire-pullers," who had displayed prodigious activity and consummate skill in Jackson's first election, set to work to organize behind the scenes, in favour of Van Buren, a movement which was the first example of great manifestations of opinion, apparently spontaneous, but in reality produced by a machinery with popular forms which screened the doings of the wire-pullers. Lewis conceived the idea of getting the plan of a national convention adopted by the members of a State Legislature, who, having put it forward with the authority belonging to the representatives of the people, would be followed by other Legislatures, with the result that local and consequently rival nominations would be pre 1 Niles, Vol. XLH, p. 236. " Lewis was the great father of the wire-pullers. He first practised in a masterly and scientific way the art of starting movements apparently spontaneous, at a distance, and in a quarter from which they win prestige or popularity, in order that these movements may produce, at the proper time and place, the effects intended by the true agent, who, in the meantime, prepares *to* be acted on by the movement in the direction in which, from the beginning, he desired to go" (Sumner's *Jackson,* p. 77). vented. Another member of the kitchen cabinet, Amos Kendall, put himself in communication with an influential member of the Legislature of New Hampshire, and brought about the meeting of a legislative Caucus, which issued a formal summons for a national convention. The famous "Globe" newspaper, edited by a third member of the kitchen cabinet (F. P. Blair), pronounced the idea an excellent one, explaining that it was the best plan for "obtaining unanimity in the party and ensuring it lasting power." Jackson's satellites in the other States took up the proposal on their part, and finally the scheme was brought to a successful issue. The convention, which met accordingly, acclaimed Jackson and nominated Martin Van Buren for the Vice-Presidency by a considerable majority (208 out of 283 votes). The number of delegates present was 344, from every State except Missouri.

The convention adopted some rules in its procedure which had very pregnant results in the future. It decided first of all that the majority of the delegation of each State should appoint one of themselves to vote on behalf of the State, each State being entitled to a number of votes equal to that which it possesses in the Electoral College. In this way the majority of the delegation not only suppressed the opinion of the dissentient members but appropriated their votes. Besides this the convention resolved that for the choice of candidates, as well as for all decisions connected therewith, a majority of two-thirds of all the votes should be requisite.4 The effect of this rule was that even a majority of half plus one was reduced to the position of a minority, and that to escape therefrom it was obliged to take up with a solution which, perhaps, was not in accord with its real wishes, yielding to the exigencies or the manoeuvres of a fraction which constituted the true minority.

The triumphant re-election of Jackson, in 1832, confirmed his prestige with the masses and his power over the "politicians," who obeyed him implicitly,— so much so that during An outline of this plan was given in a private letter from Lewis to Amos Kendall, published by Parton, Vol. Ill, p. 382.

Summary of the Proceedings of a convention of Republican delegates from the several States in the Union, for the purpose of nominating a candidate for the office of Vice-President of the United States, held at Baltimore, in the State of Maryland, May, 1832. Albany, 1832. the whole of the second term of his Presidency he was able not only to continue and accentuate his autocratic policy, but was even in a position to designate his successor, like a Roman emperor. It was the trusty Martin Van Buren, Vice-President by the grace of Jackson, who was destined to inherit the presidential office. And on this occasion again it was by means of a national convention that he was to be proposed to the suffrages of the Electors as the deliberate choice of the party. The opposition to this plan, which began to show itself at an early stage, was declared by Jackson to be high treason against the people. While in certain States the Legislatures pronounced for the summoning of a national convention, in others they rejected it, having resolved to run another candidate (Hugh White), the nominee of a dissentient fraction of the party, against Van Buren. The convention met on the 20th of May, 1835; it was composed to a great extent of office-holders, that is, of men absolutely under the thumb of the administration. "The whole proceedings of the convention," says a Baltimore newspaper, "has been management, management, management." The New York delegation, with its leader, Silas Wright, Van Buren's ex-colleague in the Albany Regency, beat time, and the convention executed the required movements. Martin Van Buren was chosen candidate for the Presidency. But the followers of White in Tennessee would not disarm; they refused to recognize the nomination, contesting the right of the convention to impose a candidate. It is curious that among the objectors was a representative of Tennessee in Congress, J. K. Polk, the future President of the United States, nominated himself for the Presidency eight years later, by a convention, and who but for this would i " You are at liberty to say on all occasions," wrote Jackson, in a letter of the 23d of February, 1835, intended for publication, " that regarding the people as th true source of political power, I am always ready to bow to their will and to their judgment; that discarding all personal preferences, I consider the true policy of the friends of Republican principles to send delegates fresh from the people to a general convention, for the purpose of selecting candidates for the Presidency and Vice-Presidency, and that to impeach that selection before it is made, as an emanation of executive power, is to assail the virtue of the people, and in effect to oppose their right to govern" (Niles, Vol. XLVIII, p. 81). *Ibid.,* p. 39. » *Ibid.,* Vol. XLVII, p. 378. *The Baltimore Patriot,* quoted by Niles, Vol. XLVIII, p. 248. Vol. ii—*r* never have been able to attain, even in his wildest dreams, to the chief magistracy. Greater weight attached to the resolution voted by the Senate of the Illinois Legislature, which proclaimed that every person eligible to the office of President had an incontestable right to come forward as a candidate for it, without the intervention of caucuses and conventions. "We disapprove," concluded the Senate, "of the system of conventions which Van Buren's party is endeavouring to thrust upon the American people, and we hold that this system is destructive of freedom of voting, contrary to republican institutions and dangerous to popular liberties."

These protests were fruitless; they were not destined to be repeated; the system of national conventions was installed for good and all in American political life, and its power to dispose of party nominations was no longer to be challenged. The system was not yet thoroughly settled, but this was only a matter of time, of a few years. The anti-Jacksonian party, which had for some time past taken the name of Whig, did not hold a national convention for the election of 1836; allied with heterogeneous groups whose sole bond of union was,hostility to Jackson, it could not hope to carry a general convention to a successful issue. The opposition therefore nominated several candidates, Whig and others, at one time in State conventions, at another by Legislatures, at another in public meetings. But this was the last occasion on which this variety of modes of presidential nominations, which we have seen arise after the collapse of the congressional Caucus in 1824, occurred simultaneously. At the presidential election of 1840 Whigs and Democrats both had recourse to national conventions, which from that time became the only central official party organ.

VII

The working of the new Organization revealed almost at once the unhealthy politico-social conditions amid which it 1 Niles, Vol. XLIX, p. 4. s *Ibid.,* p. 384.

Some isolated examples of presidential nominations made outside national conventions may be found later on, but they were rather manifestations in favour of certain candidates than formal nominations. was introduced. In the East as well as in the West it was monopolized by the politicians; the representative meetings of the party, in which the choice of the candidates had to be made, were too often only so in name; the mode in which they were got up and their decisions were marked by fraud and flagrant abuses. The primary meetings out of which sprang all the successive delegations constituting the hierarchy of the conventions were deserted by the great body of citizens, and the politicians, aided by their friends, easily got control of them and bestowed on themselves the nominations to the more or less lucrative posts which they coveted or which they wanted to keep. The Organization in all its grades was full of office-holders; they not only acted behind the scenes, but attended the various conventions in a body as delegates, and very often formed the great majority in these assemblies; 3 in election time they devoted all their energies to the support of the candidates of their party. Attempts were repeatedly made to prohibit the intervention of public officers in politics, but without success. The committee appointed to examine the most important of the many proposals submitted to Congress with this object, the bill introduced into the Senate by Crittenden in 1838, declared in its report that "it was not merely the right but the duty of office-holders to busy themselves in elections, to shape public opinion, and to influence and to direct the people in the choice of their representatives, The historian of Illinois, already quoted, states that " the people did not attend the primary meetings; a few only assembled who were nearest the places of meeting, and those were too often professional politicians, the loafers about the towns, who, having but little business of their own, were ever ready to attend to the affairs of the public.... Conventions themselves were got up and packed by cunning, active, intriguing politicians, to suit the wishes of a few. The mode of getting them up was for some active men to procure a few friends in each precinct of a county to hold primary meetings where delegates were elected to county conventions, who met at the county seats and nominated candidates for the Legislature and for county offices, and appointed other delegates to district and State conventions, to nominate candidates for Congress and for Governor"... (p. 206). " At the late State convention to nominate a Governor, etc., at Herkimer," writes Niles in 1831, "there were present 119 members, of whom there were 69 public officers, and of these 69 no less than 19 were officers of the United States. *It is thus in every State of the Union,* and it is not worth while to use the many particulars that are before us" (Vol. XLIII, p. 100). Many instances of similar facts are given *passim* in the same volume and in the following volumes of the *Register.* and that if they withdrew themselves from this high responsibility they would deserve to be declared infamous and to be stigmatized as idiots and mutes." The assembly adapted the conclusions of this report and ordered ten thousand copies of it to be printed, which were distributed throughout the States. The officials openly neglected their duties for their "work" in the party organizations, because this "work" alone counted and bore fruit. "Politics is the business of the office-holder," observed a newspaper of the day, "as much as agriculture is the business of the farmer. It is his trade, the craft by which he thrives. Hence he is interested to establish some means by which he may control them, and the conventions are the very thing for him. The multitude cannot go to caucuses and conventions; they are necessarily made up of the office-holders and their agents; and when they once agree upon their man, he is put forth as the regular nomination."

These few sarcastic remarks, in fact, put the whole case in a nutshell, showing as they do the *raison d'Mre* of the conventions and the character of the men who manipulated them, as well as the means by which they managed to carry their schemes and impose their will on the electorate. Their decisions commanded respect, because they were taken in the formal conventions of the party, because they appealed to its common creed. The notion of "regularity" which had crept in under the congressional Caucus survived it. Even in the absence, or rather owing to the absence, of distinctive principles forming a natural line of demarcation between the parties, this notion haunted minds seeking for some landmark in the void of ideas, and, conventional as it was, the *regular nomination* appeared to supply them not only with a practical criterion but with an ethical principle which could not be disregarded on pain of moral forfeiture. True, if the voter refused to vote for the candidates chosen by the convention, "no one could be punished for treason in so doing otherwise than by

Cf. the speech delivered at Louisa, Va. , on the 9th of September, 1839, by W. C. Rives, who had been accused of having supported the "gag law," as Crittenden's bill was called, in the Senate (Niles, Vol. LVII, p. 109).

2 *The Newark Daily Advertiser,* July, 1835, quoted by Niles, Vol. XLVIII, p. 304. losing the favour of his party and being denounced as a traitor; which was almost as efficacious in restraining the refractory as the pains and penalties of treason, the hanging and embowelling of former times."

To this moral constraint was added another imposed by the practical necessities of the vote, and which definitively stifled the independence of the voters. The number of the elective offices, and consequently of the elections to be conducted, having become very large, the custom arose, at the instigation of the politicians, of holding them 'all at once, for the offices of the city, of the county, of the State, and of the Union, and on a single list. This list, since known as the "slip ticket," was the material embodiment and the confirmation of the confusion of the politics of the Union with the business of the State and local affairs, introduced by the system of conventions. All the same, it was becoming difficult, and even impossible, for voters left to their own inspirations to make up a voting paper which began with the ward officers, and ended with members of Congress and presidential Electors. The conventions and their committees helped them out of the difficulty by making up the ticket for them, and the voters were forced willy-nilly to accept it and vote it whole, even if several of the candidates entered on the list were obnoxious to them; for if they did not vote it in its entirety, they increased the chances of the opposite side, which would vote its whole list.

Independent candidatures having disappeared, owing to the principle of regular nominations and to the slip ticket, the battle was really fought by the rival party Organizations; the voters simply registered the decisions taken for them and without consulting them. The great body of the citizens were reduced to the position of dummies, or rather they had reduced themselves to that position by withdrawing from public life. Resides, there was not much in it to keep them there. The subordination of local elections to national politics robbed *A History of Illinois,* p. 206. Senator Rives, of Virginia, says in the speech quoted abflve: "Have we not seen that principle of party obedience enforced by the *rack* and the *gibbet,* the denunciations of the Press, the deprivation of office, and the interdiction even of social communion, by affixing to the *doomed* offender the foulest epithets of moral and political disgrace?" local public life of its natural interest, and it became all the less capable of fostering civic spirit. Not only did the commercial classes which formed the great majority of the nation become completely engrossed in their private interests, but political indifference infected even the intellectual leaders of the nation, the men in liberal professions, to the profound astonishment and regret of European investigators.;Disheartened by the advent of mediocrity and of the political mercenaries who excluded men of sterling worth and high principle from public life, and disgusted by the excesses of a shameless Press which sprang into life during Jackson's presidential campaigns, the more cultivated section of the nation soon withdrew into its tent, thus accentuating the political lethargy which crept over the community. "We have lost all sensibility," said Calhoun in the Senate; "we have become hardened under the action of pernicious practices and principles which are characteristic of the age. Things which a few years ago would have shocked and roused the whole community are now hardly noticed." In the midst of this general political apathy, public business fell to the politicians of the conventions like a *res nullius* to the first occupant The separation of society from politics became the leading fact of the situation; the nation had, as it were, split into two absolutely distinct parts: a large majority, which was toiling, developing, and growing rich, and a small, active minority, full of passions and still more of appetites, which was monopolizing political action. The privileged sphere which this minority had invaded, the public administration, was soon filled with an atmosphere of corruption; scandalous abuses speedily came to light in it. The congressional enquiry into the frauds committed in the New York customhouse (which received two-thirds of the payments made into all the customhouses of the Union) revealed a most shameless system of plunder of the treasury and of the public, which had been going on for years, through the connivance of officials whom the spoils system converted from servants of the State into H. Martineau, *Society in America,* 1837, the chapter on Apathy in Citizenship.

2 *Works,* Vol. II, p. 440. Speech of Fe-

bruary, 1835. The celebrated cases of Swsirtwout and Hoyt. tools of their dishonest superiors; as for these latter, they were too faithful adherents of Jackson and Van Buren to be supervised. VIII

These scandals, which laid bare the systematic prostitution of the public service to a party Organization, would not, perhaps, have roused public opinion if the country had been in. a prosperous state. But it was suffering severely from the economic crisis which broke out in 1837, soon after the retirement of Jackson and the accession of Van Buren. The depreciation of the paper currency, brought on by Jackson's financial policy, destroyed public credit, forced the banks to stop payment, caused a general rise in prices, closed factories and workshops, and threw numbers of workmen out of employment; bread riots even occurred. Van Buren had nothing to do with this catastrophe, but as it broke out under his Presidency he and his party were made responsible for the disaster. The remedy seemed to lie in a change of government, and the country resoxmded with the cry: "Away with the spoilers!" The Whigs took advantage of this to form a coalition against Van Buren, in which genuine indignation, roused, as it were, from a lethargic slumber, was a certain factor, but which taken all together had no object but the seizure of power. The Whig party no doubt contained the elite of the community, the men of means and of intelligence, but here as well as in the rival camp the politicians held the outposts and directed the operations.

The Whig national convention, which met, in 1839, at Harrisburg to nominate the candidates for the Presidency, supplied only too eloquent proof of it. The candidate was marked out. beforehand by the whole history of the party which for the last fifteen years had been contending with the Jacksonian democracy; he was the great Whig leader, Henry Clay, an illustrious statesman, a great orator, and gifted with a personal charm which won all hearts. But the politicians did not believe implicitly in his success; they were afraid that at the election he would not be able to rely with certainty on the support of various factions of the ill-assorted coalition formed against Van Buren, and they were not less apprehensive, perhaps, of Clay's commanding personality when installed in the White House. For several reasons they wanted a candidate of a less pronounced individuality and not so compromised in the great struggles which had brought Clay into the front rank. But how to get rid of the idol of the great mass of the party, who were prepared to rally round him once more? The national convention, this new organ of the *voxpopuli,* supplied the politicians with the means of carrying out their design,— to get it said, in the name of the people, who doted on Clay, that they did not want Clay. Instead of voting on the candidates in full convention, it was decided to make the selection behind the scenes by means of successive votes taken by stages: the delegation of each State instructed a committee of three persons to communicate with the committees of the other delegations and to report their views, after which each delegation voted separately on the candidates for the Presidency, and if these votes, added together, gave the majority to any one candidate, the result was submitted to the convention, with which the final decision rested. In case no candidate obtained the majority at the votes of the respective delegations, their committees were to begin their conferences over again and make fresh reports to their principals, and so on until a majority gathered round a name to be laid before the convention, the vote of the majority of each delegation being counted as the vote of the whole State. This complicated procedure, which set in motion five-andtwenty small separate committees working in the dark and meeting only to spy on each other, to take each other's measure, and finally to haggle over the terms of the bargain which would not bear the light of day, was admirably adapted for the choice of candidates by process of elimination, by first of all disposing of the most prominent candidates. Wearied by the interminable conferences of the committees and by the series of successive votes, the delegates were naturally induced to accept the first solution offered, which, of course, had been prearranged by a few wire-pullers. This last task was discharged in the convention by some delegates from New York with a consummate politician, Thurlow Weed, at their head. Under his skilful management Clay, who appeared to have the majority of the delegates on his side, was placed in a minority in the separate votes of the delegations, and finally the convention agreed on the name of a somewhat obscure personage, General Harrison, an honourable man, but whose principal claim consisted of the victories won by him thirty 'years previously in encounters with tribes of Red Indians. And it was in favour of this old man, with no weight or experience as a statesman, without political ideas or a programme, that Clay saw himself rejected by his own party, whom he had so often led to battle amid the cheers even of his opponents. In their justifiable exasperation Clay's friends shouted treason. In reality there was none whatever, from the standpoint occupied by the Organization of the party. It was not its business to give expression to feeling or to affirm principles, but to carry the election; the Presidency was a prize to be won. If Clay, in spite of his glorious past, or on account of that past, did not offer satisfactory guarantees of success, did not the most elementary practical sense enjoin that he should be thrown over and another candidate adopted, were he ever so inferior to him. The rejection of Clay by the national convention was therefore quite in the logic of the system.

The election campaign which now began revealed the methods by which men put forward by this system could be foisted on the country in spite of their mediocrity. Hitherto all the candidates for the Presidency had been statesmen of more or less eminence, with a national reputation; Jackson had no record as a statesman, but he was borne along by the impetuous torrent of triumphant democracy; Van Buren had been thrust on the nation by the immense prestige of Jackson. Harrison possessed none of these qualifications. But the Whig Organization set to work to "raise enthusiasm" in his favour by devices, by systematic efforts which aimed especially at the imagination and the senses of the masses. Monster meetings, processions, parades, spectacular entertainments of every kind, songs, were all so many opportunities for shouting, for howling out Harrison's name without further reference to the virtues and qualities which marked him out for the chief magistracy. A Democratic newspaper in the East having said, by way of ridiculing the mediocrity of the Whig candidate, that if Harrison were given a log cabin and hard cider he would rather stay at home in the West, the Whigs immediately took up the remark as an insult to their candidate, adopted "log cabin and hard cider" as their motto and made it their war-cry. Harrison was the "log cabin" candidate, the man of the people, living its frugal and simple life and cultivating all its virtues, offering hospitality to every passer-by, who found the door open and a glass of cider on the table, whereas Van Buren inhabited a palace and eat with gold spoons and forks. Everywhere log cabins were run up, models of them were paraded in procession through the streets, ornaments for women were made of them, medals were struck with them. Pictures were circulated wholesale throughout the country representing Harrison now as a victorious general, now as a labourer driving a plough on his farm or welcoming old comrades at the door of his cabin. Meetings organized in the open air drew enormous crowds, people brought their wives and children, the number of persons present was reckoned by the acres of ground which they covered. Torrents of oratory flowed at the meetings, but it was devoid of sense; it did not seek to enlighten the mind or to bring home convictions, but to strike the imagination. This effect was obtained mainly by political songs composed for the occasion, which, passing from mouth to mouth, produced a downright frenzy, absurd as they were. Clubs and associations of The most famous of these songs was " Tippecanoe and Tyler too. " Tippecanoe was Harrison's nickname given him in memory of his victory over the Indians at Tippecanoe; Tyler was the name of the candidate for the VicePresidency adopted by the Whig National Convention at the same time as Harrison for the Presidency.

Tune: Little Pig's Tail.

What has caused this great commotion, motion Our country through *1*
It is the ball rolling on
For Tippecanoe and Tyler too —
Tippecanoe and Tyler too —
And with them we'll beat little Van,
Van, Van, Van is a used-up man,
And with them we'll beat little Van
Like the rushing of mighty waters, waters, waters,
On it will go,
And its course will clear the way
For Tippecanoe and Tyler too, etc.

young men were formed throughout the country with the special duty of keeping up the hurly-burly. The Union was turned into a huge fair; for months there was a continuous carnival, with a whole people for actors. A monster procession at Baltimore, in May, 1840, gave the best picture of it. All the States sent delegations, some of which, that of Massachusetts, for instance, numbered not less than fifteen hundred persons; they formed an immense line stretching for miles, and advancing each with a band in front and banners bearing more or less allegorical inscriptions: "Tippecanoe and no reduction of wages," "W. H. Harrison, the poor man's friend," "We will teach the palace slaves to respect the log cabin," "The prairies are on lire," "Mene, mene, tekel, upharsin,— Thou art weighed in the balance and found wanting." The log cabin was not only mentioned or depicted on the banners, several delegations exhibited log cabins of natural size, drawn by horses with riders in fantastic costumes. The log cabins were adorned with all the accessories of these primitive dwellings,— skins of animals, horns, and especially barrels of cider, from which the delegates refreshed themselves liberally as they walked along. In some log cabins the idyll was completed by live raccoons running over the roofs and by the smoke issuing from the chimney of the cabin in which a squirrel was being cooked. One of the greatest successes of the procession was a huge ball ten or twelve feet in diameter, rolled by mountaineers from the Alleghanies clad in the costume of their wild country. In this carnival procession were to be found Clay, Webster, and the other Whig leaders driving in state in a barouche drawn by four grey horses. To serve the good cause they lowered themselves to the buffooneries by which it was sought to carry the multitude. These methods succeeded admirably; the success of "Tippecanoe and Tyler too" at the poll was extraordinary; the majority obtained by Harrison over his rival, Van Buren, surpassed all expectations; the Whig victory was complete.

IX

This victory also marked the definitive triumph of the new order of things in the existence of the parties, which had been Niles, Vol. LVIII, pp. 147-1B6.

taking shape after the fall of the congressional Caucus in 1824. The fifteen years that had elapsed since then were the formative period of this order of tilings, the elements of which have been brought out one by one in the preceding pages. They may be summed up in a few words. The old political parties, which had lost their *locus standi,* had been reconstituted in an artificial way by means of an amalgam of numerous factions, "without one ounce of honest principle to choose between them," as J. Q. Adams remarked. These various contingents were united by the "magnetic" power of leaders like Jackson and Clay, whose commanding personalities constituted in a way the stock-in-trade of the new parties, while the democratic organization of the conventions supplied them with permanent *cadres.* The men who filled these were for the most part bent solely on satisfying their appetites, and the "division of the spoils" became the cohesive force of the party. "A national party became an army of occupation," as a historian puts it, "under a commander-in-chief, intrenched in the offices, and with all the resources of national influence at command, to resist, if need be, majorities and public opinion."

Jackson's autocratic temperament and the personal enthusiasm which he inspired established a military discipline and a blind devotion to the leaders, which transformed men into automatons. But success being the sole object which this conquering horde pursued, and to which it subordinated everything, this devotion was not that of the vassal of by-gone days, loyal in prosperity and in adversity; it was proportioned to self-interest, to the advantage to be gained. A Henry Clay was pitilessly thrown aside directly his chances of victory seemed to decline. The qualities of the leaders, their personal worth, ceased to be of consequence as soon as the party Organization was sufficiently developed through the vigorous impulse given it by the powerful individuals who made it a success. The Jacksons and the Clays having disappeared, or being put on one side, the Organization stepped into their shoes as a joint-stock company takes the place of the private individuals who have founded the firm. The will and good i *Memoirs,* Vol. DC, p. 187.

3 J. Schouler, *History of the United States,* Vol. IV, p. 464. pleasure of Jackson, the imperious charm of Clay, which carried away the multitude, were succeeded by the interest of the "party" represented by any one stamped with the hallmark of its Organization; a figure-head sufficed even for the chief magistracy. The leadership became, so to speak, impersonal and anonymous, up to its highest grade, after having suffered so many losses in its "intermediate ranks" (to revert to Montesquieu's expression) even before the accession of Jackson.

The devotion of the great mass of the voters was henceforth to be bestowed on the abstract entity of the party, being upheld by the superstitious respect for forms which had taken possession of the American political mind. This fetish-worship was developed on one side by the explosion of the democratic feeling which exalted Jackson, and which he, in his turn, exasperated, by constantly appealing in his thundering voice to the "people," by threatening the opponents of his policy with outbreaks of the wrath of the " people," overbearing legislative assemblies with his capacity of elect of the "people "; good sense, equity, political proprieties, logic of the Constitution, — all were obscured by the fumes of the incense which was burnt before the new idol, the "people." Its sacred will was that of the party in majority, and could be known by the outward signs of its Organization coming "fresh from the people," the mere democratic and representative trappings of which commanded respect. To follow these signs became the whole duty of the believer, constituted all the observances of his political religion of loyalty to the party. This twofold democratic formalism, both moral and material, was superadded to the superstitious adoration of the Constitution, of the written instrument, which had taken root in the public mind almost from the beginning. Hardly had a few years elapsed after the violent disputes about the adoption of the Constitution, when it appeared to the Americans as an almost superhuman creation, as a revelation of political truth offered to the whole human race, which had been walking in the darkness. Beyond the reach of rational criticism, it lent itself only to theological exegesis; the rage of controversialists, who Jackson's own words when recommending the national convention which was to nominate Van Buren.

each pull the words of Scripture their own way, no doubt found free scope in the conflicts of the "strict constructionists " and the "loose constructionists," but both bowed down with equal fervour before the letter of the Constitution. Rising on this substratum of constitutional fetish-worship, the formalism introduced into every-day politics, into that of the parties, under the auspices of the new Organization, definitively cut off the American political mind from free enquiry by a sort of iron circle, by making it revolve in the fixed orbit of party regularity.

The industrial evolution and the economic upheaval which took place during the decade of 1830-1840, on their side, if they did not as yet seriously impede the expansion of individualism, were not exactly favourable to it: individual enterprise was beginning to give way to joint-stock companies (corporations), capitalism and monopolies appeared on the scene, the equality of conditions was disappearing.

Engrossed in his material interests, the citizen was not, and did not even wish to be, aware of the part of dummy which he was playing in political life, where the professionals had installed themselves as masters. To give his casting vote to one or the other side, he allowed himself to be roused for a moment from his indifference, or he roused himself under the spur of events; but in both cases the habitual passivity of his political mind yielded only to a strong shock given to his senses; he started only when dragged along with the crowd, worked upon by methods which appealed mainly to popular feeling, and of which the "Tippecanoe and Tyler too" campaign was such a striking picture, not to say a caricature. When the alarm raised by the election contest subsided, citizens and professional politicians could return in peace to their daily preoccupations, the former to attend to their private affairs, the latter to unblushingly exploit the public interest.

Such were, at the moment when the Republic of the United States was entering on the second half-century of its existence, the cardinal points of the political situation, which the development of the party Organization brought out, or helped to Cf. in *Ver/assung und Demokratie der Vereinigten Staaten von Amerika,* by H. von Hoist, Vol. I, Diisseldorf, 187:;, the very acute chapter entitled Die Kanonisirung der Verfassung und ihr wahrer Charakter.

bring out, in a direct or indirect way. These points, of an uncompromising distinctness, which beset the political society of America, constituted so many premises, which were bound to reveal their effects, as its evolution proceeded, with everincreasing fulness. We shall see them unfold themselves with an only too perfect logic, as we follow the course of the party Organization step by step in the electoral struggles for supreme power in the Union, in the solution of great national problems, in local public life, as well as in the play of the machinery of the Constitution, and in the relations of the economic sphere with the State.

THIRD CHAPTER THE EVOLUTION OF THE CONVENTION SYSTEM

I

The change of parties in power, effected by the election of 1840, only made it more evident that the political manners and methods brought into fashion by the Jacksonian Democracy were not a transitory manifestation, due to the character or the traditions of the Democratic party, but that they were taking permanent root in the political society of America. Immediately after the defeat of Van Buren's party it appeared clearly that there would be no solution of continuity. The Whigs had rushed into the fight to the cry of "Away with the spoilers," but hardly was the battle over when they flung themselves on the spoils. The twelve years' waiting in opposition had given a keen edge to the Whig appetites. As on the accession of Jackson, Washington presented the spectacle of a city invaded by office-seekers, but on this occasion they were still more numerous. The new means of locomotion, the railways, which did not exist in 1829, facilitated this invasion of the hungry host in a peculiar degree. Before the new President had entered on office his future ministers were beset by applicants, who were not all small, needy politicians; among them were members of Congress, senators of the United States, who were eager for places. When Harrison John Bell, who was to have a ministerial post in the future administration, was overrun two months even before his installation by place-hunters, to such an extent that he wrote: "I am growing pretty sick already of this thing of office in my own case, and the increasing tide of application from new quarters that daily beats against my ears gives me spasms. In truth, I begin to fear that we are at last, or rather that our leading politicians are, in the several States, chiefly swayed by the thirst for power and plunder. Would you think that Senator Talmadge is willing to descend from the Senate to the New York Custom House? This is yet a secret, but it is true!" (Letter from J. Bell to Governor Letcher of the 13th January, 1841. Coleman's *Lift* took up his abode in the White House, the rush became tremendous; the applicants literally pursued the ministers and the President day and night; they besieged the former in their offices or in their homes, and even in the streets; a good many candidates for office slept in the corridors of the White House, to catch the President the next morning as soon as he got up; there were no fixed times for audiences, the " log cabin " President indulged in a simplicity which allowed every one to have access to him. But his great age could not stand the fatigues and worries caused by the never-ending crowd of applicants, and he died after one month of office.

The Vice-President, Tyler, who, in accordance with the Constitution, succeeded Harrison, was not a genuine Whig. Originally a Democrat, he parted from Jackson without embracing the Whig creed. But the managers of the national convention of Harrisburg, who cared little for principles and were bent only on success, thought it a good move to couple the name of Tyler (" Tyler too ") with that of General Harrison to catch the votes of the malcontent Democrats. Having become President, contrary to all expectation, Tyler dropped the Whig mask with which the wire-pullers had disguised him, and prevented the Whig party from reaping the fruits of their victory in carrying the legislative measures which were dear to their hearts. Disowned by the Whigs as a traitor, the President did not inspire the Democrats whom he had deserted with much confidence either. But as full of infatuation and ambition as he was weak-minded, Tyler fancied that he could create a personal party which would carry him triumphantly into the Presidency for another term, or even for two terms. To recruit adherents, the President laid hands on the public service; he turned out the officials devoted to the Whigs, and replaced them by his own creatures. He gained nothing by this; it was the genuine Democrat candidate who won the victory at the presidential election of 1844. As soon as he came into power, the new President in his turn upset the public service, and still more completely than his predecessors had done; almost all the federal officials were changed to make room for the victors.

of J. J. Crittenden, Vol. I, p. 136, quoted by Hoist, *Verfassungsgeschichte der Vereiniglen Staaten,* Vol. I, p. 358). VOL. ii — o

From that time it became the rule that every change of President involved as a matter of right that of all the public servants appointed by his predecessor of the opposite party. As soon as the new President entered on his office, the "guillotine of the party" was set going for the greater triumph of the so-called democratic principle of "rotation," which was alleged to be essential to the preservation of popular liberties. For the struggle for office kept the political mind of the nation on the alert while participation in public honours was an incentive to the citizen to remain loyal to free institutions. "It is a great American principle," said a speaker from his place in the Senate, "it lies at the foundation of our government." In vain did men of the stamp of

Webster and Calhoun raise their voice against these practices and these theories. "He will be asserting," cried Calhoun, "one of the most untrue and monstrous propositions on the face of God's earth who says that this is a popular doctrine. What! a popular doctrine. This a popular doctrine? It is the very reverse. It is the doctrine to create a king and to annihilate liberty!" The next President, Taylor, had no doubt declared that he would make "honesty, capacity, and fidelity indispensable prerequisites to the bestowal of office," but hardly was he installed (in 1849) when his conscience bade him reward the members of the Organization of the party which had brought him into power.

Speech of Senator Allen, of the 14th of May, 1846 *(Congressional Globe,* Vol. XV, p. 819). Since then, evidence in favour of rotation has been sought for even in the erudition of past centuries. The principle of rotation is alleged to be contemporary with the very discovery of America. Ferdinand and Isabella wrote in their famous " formal lecture," addressed to the new governor of Hispaniola, Ovando: "Also let there be change of authorities, so that many may have a share of profit and honour, aud be made skilful in affairs." "This pregnant sentence contains the whole philosophy of rotation in office," as an American publicist gravely remarks (W. Martin Dickson, " The New Political Machine," *North American Review,* January, 1882, p. 50). Speech in the Senate, of the 14th of May, 1846 (Calhoun's Works, Vol. IV, p. 300). " I did not think it wise or just," he said, " to kick away the ladder by which I ascended to the presidency; colonels, majors, captains, lieutenants, sergeants, and corporals are just as necessary to success in politics as they are to discipline and efficiency in an army." "If the country," he remarked to one of his ministers, " is to be benefited by our services, it seems to me that you and I ought to remember those to whose zeal, activity, and influence we are indebted for our places. There are plenty of Whigs just as capable and The members of the beaten party had only the Press in which to vent their ill-humour and denounce the proscriptions in which the victors indulged. But soon even the recriminations stopped, people learnt to consider the periodical dismissals not only as natural but as justifiable. When the Democratic President who entered the White House in 1853 made a clean sweep of the public service, the opposition Press countenanced this conduct by its silence or even by its formal acquiescence. At last there was no need even of a change of the party in power to carry out the hecatomb of office-holders, the principle of rotation enjoined it even when the party was confirmed in power by the new election; those who had feasted were obliged to make way for their hungry political coreligionists. The Democratic President Buchanan, who succeeded, in 1857, to the Democrat Pierce, yielded with a good grace to the reasons adduced in favour of changing the officials in any event, to reward election services and keep up the Organization of the party. The rotation was carried out so consistently that the author of the famous formula "The spoils to the victors," Marcy, could not help remarking: "They have it that I am the author of the office-seekers' doctrine that 'to the victors belong the spoils,' but I certainly should never recommend the policy of pillaging my own camp." as honest, and quite as deserving of office as the Democrats who have held them at two or three presidential terms. Rotation in office, provided good men are appointed, is sound republican doctrine" (Thurlow Weed's *Autobiography,* Vol. II, pp. 175,176).

" The constant practice and advocacy of the policy by party leaders has so debauched public opinion that a change of officers in the civil service had come to be regarded as a necessary accompaniment of a change of party control. From the year 1853 we must date the cordial recognition by politicians and people of the principle 'To the victors belong the spoils.'" (J. F. Rhodes, *History of the United States from the Compromise of 1850,* N. Y., 1893, Vol. I, p. 400.) " I cannot mistake," wrote Buchanan in a private letter, "the strong current of public opinion in favor of changing public functionaries, both abroad and at home, who have served a reasonable time. They say, and that, too, with considerable force, that if the officers under a preceding Democratic administration shall be continued by a succeeding administration of the same political character, this must necessarily destroy the party" (quoted in Rhodes, Vol. II, p. 248). *Ibid.* II

Presidential "patronage," that is, the power of appointing to public offices, having become the life-blood of the organized parties, their main efforts were brought to bear on the national conventions in which the choice of the candidates for the Presidency was decided. The party staked its fortunes in them for the term of four years at least, and its managers were of opinion that the game could not be played with too much skill. They set to work so well that the history of the national conventions became a long record of tricks, of stratagems, of unscrupulous manoeuvres, or sometimes even of scandalous acts. The Whig convention at Harrisburg gave a foretaste of this in 1839. The Democratic convention of 1844 continued it. The Democrats, put to rout by "Tippecanoe and Tyler too," had quickly recovered their ground in the congressional elections, and appeared to have all the more serious chances of success in the presidential election that the country had derived little benefit from the Whig administration. The general feeling in the Democratic party assigned the Presidency to Van Buren, who, in fact, had not deserved ill of his party and had fallen a victim to a situation created by other people. When the delegates to the Democratic national convention were appointed in the States, it was understood that they should vote for Van Buren. But in the meanwhile an event occurred which inspired the wire-pullers of the party with apprehensions about Van Buren. The question of slavery, which had for some time past been slowly agitating the country, became all of a sudden a burning one, in consequence of the plan formed by the slaveholders for extending the area of slavery by the annexation of the old Mexican province of Texas. The slaveholders of the South furnished the Democratic party with a very considerable number of its contingents. In the defence of their "domestic institution," they took their stand on the sovereign rights of the States, of which the Democrats were the traditional champions. This point of contact soon brought about a close alliance between the two, the former, however, making the support which they gave the Democrats subordinate to their private interest. When the question of the annexation of Texas was distinctly raised, just before the presidential election of 1844, Van Buren pronounced, more or less clearly, against annexation. The Democrat managers considered that by making this declaration he had seriously impaired his chances of success in the South, and to avoid being wrecked with him they decided to throw their great leader overboard.

They accomplished their purpose at the national convention. The mercenary elements, the men who were bent solely on office, and who were ready to vote for any one who could get it for them, adventurers, speculators in land and scrip, who had cast a covetous glance on Texas, were, it would appear, largely represented in the convention. Most of the delegates had instructions to vote for Van Buren; the point was to provide them with a pretext for deserting him. For this recourse was had to a device of procedure, just as the Whigs had done to get rid of Clay. Without giving the delegates time to look round, the Democratic convention was persuaded into adopting the decision that the candidates for the Presidency and the Vice-Presidency must obtain a majority of two-thirds of the votes to be validly nominated. The same procedure had already been followed at the two first Democratic conventions, but as there was no difference of opinion then as to the persons to be nominated, it was not of any consequence. Now a onethird vote was enough to ensure Van Buren's defeat. At the first ballot 151 votes out of 266 were cast for him, but this absolute majority was no longer sufficient. At the second ballot he received still fewer votes, at each fresh ballot he lost some; after the seventh ballot Van Buren's friends withdrew his candidature. The minority then stepped in with a comparatively speaking obscure candidate, James K. Polk. He obtained only 44 votes; but his very mediocrity appeared to a good many delegates as a sort of guarantee of success; According to Benton's account, this convention presented a "motley assemblage, called democratic — many self-appointed, or appointed upon management or solicitation — many alternative substitutes — many members of Congress, in violation of the principle which condemned the Congress presidential caucuses in 1824 — some nullifiers, and an immense outside concourse. Texas land and scrip speculators were largely in it, and more largely on tho outside. A considerable number were in favour of no particular candidate, but in pursuit of office for themselves — inflexible against any one from whom they thought they would not get it, and ready to go for any from whom they thought they could" *(Thirty Years' View,* Vol. II, p. 591).

being little known in the country, he gave umbrage to no one, and he might, after all, they thought, ultimately secure a majority. The next ballot at once disclosed numerous adhesions to Polk, and then a wild stampede set in; delegations which had just cast their vote for other candidates recanted in headlong haste and went over to Polk, and when the balloting closed, it turned out that Polk had been nominated unanimously.

Thus Martin Van Buren, the political legatee of Jackson, the tutelar genius and almost the creator of the Democratic Organization, was thrown over by it for a Polk. The indignation among Jackson's old set was great. They laid the blame on the "two-thirds rule," which had done all the mischief. But it is only fair to add that they did not stop there. And just as several members of the congressional Caucus had declared in 1824 that they would no longer take part in a meeting which usurped the rights of the people, so Van Buren's friends could not find language strong enough to denounce the convention, which, according to them, was "the first instance of a body of men, unknown to the laws and the Constitution, assuming to treat the American Presidency as their private property, to be disposed of at their own will and pleasure; and, it may be added, for their own profit." In reality the convention simply followed the path marked out by the Jacksonians themselves. It was the formal application of the "*demos krateo* principle," which they so confidently set up against the Constitution itself, that invested "men unknown to the Constitution" with the right of disposing of the Presidency, and made their decisions, whatever they might be, binding on the members of the party. The exercise of this right derived from a formal source, entailing no responsibility and productive of material gain, attracted above all the mercenary politicians, and they naturally, judging men and things by the standard of their own interests, of their proprieties of the moment, had no line of conduct to follow but the opportunist one, in the lowest sense of the word. It was no use for Van Buren being, next to Jackson, the sole, the real leader of the Democratic party; the members of the conventions held that the true leader is the one who provides the loaves and

» *Thirty Years' View,* Vol. II, p. 595.

fishes. The best candidate for the Presidency was not the one with the most sterling qualities, but the one who was likely to win, who had the best chance of penetrating into the fortress and opening its gates to his followers. In this policy of results the sole criterion was that of suitableness, of "availability." "He is not available," was henceforth a candidate's death-sentence.

The opportunism of the politicians of the conventions, which tended to keep the best men out of power, was reinforced by the opportunism of the eminent leaders themselves, which dealt the political leadership its death-blow. Here again it was the presidential campaign of 1844 which gave a melancholy exhibition of it, and especially in the Whig camp. The Whigs, repenting in a way the affront offered to their glorious leader, Henry Clay, at the preceding election, nominated him on this occasion for the Presidency by acclamation. The Whig national convention, when adopting his candidature, passed, for the first time, resolutions defining the principles of the party, its " platform" (following the Democratic party, which inaugurated this custom in 1840), but the burning question of Texas, behind which the slaveholders ensconced themselves, was passed over in silence to avoid giving offence to the southerners. Clay was not allowed to observe the same reticence; in the course of the election campaign he had to state his views, and at first he declared himself opposed to the annexation of Texas; but before long he whittled down his declaration more and more, in order not to estrange supporters in the South, and went so far as to say that he would be glad to see the country eventually forjn part of the United States. This rather too clever attitude cost Clay the votes of a good many strong opponents of slavery, who preferred to affirm their creed, without any chance of success, in the person of an independent candidate frankly hostile to the extension of slavery. This desertion caused the defeat of Clay, whose success appeared to be perfectly certain on this occasion. The disappointment was keenly felt throughout the Union by Clay's numerous admirers; men and women shed tears; many despaired of the future of the Republic and of democratic government on seeing a Polk preferred to Henry Clay, the great Clay.

Yet so far as his defeat and not Polk's success was concerned, it was due not so much to the failings of popular government as to those of leaders who, amid their faint-hearted calculations of votes to be won or lost, cannot or will not have the courage of their opinions, who keep back the plain unvarnished truth from the people. No doubt the confused mass of voters under a popular form of government, and the constant uncertainty as to what they think and what they want, demoralize public men who wish to win the multitude, to get as large a following as possible. But still more do the men who, in their efforts to thrust themselves on it, shirk responsibility, who, instead of walking straight before it, twist and turn from side to side, still more do these would-be leaders bewilder the electorate. And if the leadership has declined in democracies, it is because the prominent leaders who happened to be still left standing have preferred to lower themselves to the shifting and wavering caprices of the mob; helping to demolish the leadership, they were themselves buried in its ruins. Clay was a highly pathetic instance of this in the history of American democracy; he fell, never to rise again, and the leadership with him; he was the last great Whig chief, almost the last great party chief in the proper sense of the word. And it is only once, in exceptional circumstances, amid the storm and stress of civil war, that a man will again come forth from the ranks to lead the nation and save it by dint of courage and genius springing from his own uprightness.

The eminent statesmen who were not eliminated by the conventions retired from the field of their own accord. This course was taken by Calhoun, the great rival of the Van Burens and the Clays. On the eve of the election of 1844 his candidature for the Presidency was mooted for a moment. But he would not allow it to be brought before the national convention, and in a published letter he gave his reasons, arraigning the whole system of the conventions with all the power of his sombre logical genius. Finding fault, in the first place, with the constitution of these assemblies, he proves that they are no more a direct expression of the popular voice than they are a true representation of the party: "Instead of being directly or fresh from the people, the delegates to the Baltimore convention will be the delegates of delegates; and of course removed, in all cases, at least three, if not four, degrees from the people. At each successive remove, the voice of the people will become less full and distinct, until at last it will become so faint and imperfect as not to be audible. To drop metaphor, I hold it impossible to form a scheme more calculated to annihilate the control of the people over the presidential election, and vest it in those who make politics a trade and who live or expect to live on the government." Then Calhoun points out that the convention, the representation of which is modelled on that of the States in the Congress, is in no way a faithful reflection of the party in the different States, the States where the party is in a minority, even in a hopeless minority, send-. ing to the convention as complete a number of delegates as the States where the party is in a very large majority, so that a small fraction of the party can thrust its candidate on the majority, upon which the President and his Administration will have to lean. "Objectionable," proceeds Calhoun, "as I think a congressional caucus for nominating a President, it is in my opinion far less so than a convention constituted as is proposed. The former had indeed many things to recommend it. Its members, consisting of senators and representatives, were the immediate organs of the State Legislatures, or the people; were responsible to them, respectively, and were for the most part of higher character, standings, or talents. They voted *per capita,* and, what is very important, they represented fairly the relative strength of the party in their respective States. In all these important particulars it was all that could be desired for a nominating body, and yet could not be borne by the people in the then purer days of the republic. I, acting with General Jackson and most of the leaders of the party at that time, contributed to put it down, because we believed it to be liable to be acted on and influenced by the patronage of the government — an objection far more applicable to a convention constituted as the one proposed than to a congressional caucus. Far, however, was it from my intention in aiding to put that down, to substitute in its place what I regard as a hundred times more objectionable in every point of view." 1 *Works,* Vol. VI, pp. 240-249.

An anonymous pamphlet published about the same time at Washington under the title of "An Appeal to the Democratic Party on the principles of a

The triple eclipse, compulsory or voluntary, of Van Buren, of Clay, aud of Calhoun, witnessed by the "presidential year" of 1844, marked in a definitive way the transfer of the supreme power, under the system of the conventions, to the inferior set of men. Those of the great surviving leaders who attempted to return to the charge only exposed themselves to bitter humiliation. Pursued by his dream of becoming President, Clay stood again in 1848, but the Whig National Convention again rejected him as "unavailable" and once more gave the preference to an obscurt "military hero." The meanness of the devices resorted to at the national convention for keeping out the great Whig leader must have thrown into the shade the odiousness of the first" base betrayal" of 1840. But this conduct was now in no way exceptional, as a friend of Clay pointed out when he wrote to him in his letter of condolence: "The party leaders, the men who make Presidents, will never consent to elevate one greatly their superior; they suffer too much by the contrast, their aspirations are checked, their power is circumscribed, the clay cannot be moulded into an idol suited to their worship." Or as Benton said in less figurative language: "The man they choose must always be a character of no force, that they may rule him; and they rule always to their advantage, constituting a power behind the throne greater than the throne."

When the nomination of Polk at the convention became known, there was a general cry of astonishment throughout the land: "Who is Polk?" But the country was destined to receive at the hand of the conventions even more inferior candidates for the succession to the Washingtons, the Jeffersons, and the Jacksons. Polk was only the first of a long line of "dark horses" who at the last moment won the party race. As an eminent man could not be agreed on at the convention, after a good many intrigues a dark horse was put forward. After a number of fruitless ballots the dark horse appeared all at once on the course, labouring along with a few votes behind national convention for the nomination of President and Vice-President of the United States," and reprinted in the *Charleston Mercury* and then in *Niles' Register,* Vol. LXIII, pp. 258 seq., develops the same considerations in an argument of remarkable logical power which unquestionably betrays Calhoun's authorship.
Private Correspondence of Henni Clay, quoted by Hoist, Vol. I, p. 597. 2 *Thirty Years' View,* Vol. II. p. 595. the cracks; but gradually he outstripped them, and before long was seen to be leading. Thus in 1852 Franklin Pierce was proposed for the first time at the twenty-fifth ballot by fifteen supporters; at the fortyfifth he had not more than twentynine; at the forty-eighth he managed to get fifty-five; at the forty-ninth he obtained two hundred and eighty-two, almost a unanimous vote. Completely unknown the day before, he was placed at the head of the nation. Pierce was succeeded by Buchanan, also a weak man. And it was with helmsmen of this calibre that the ship of the Union was nearing the terrible storm which the slavery question was preparing for it.
The people were helpless. Imprisoned in the convention system and the dogma of "regularity," they could only ratify unconditionally the selections made for them, and Benton was not far from the truth when he said: "The people have no more control over the selection of the man who is to be the President than the subjects of kings have over the birth of the ch ild who is to be their ruler." "And," added this old associate of Jackson and Van Buren, "until this system (the convention system) is abolished, and the people resume their rights, the elective principle of our government is suppressed." The democratic evolution appeared to contradict these apprehensions; in face of the convention system, the elective principle was continually extending in the government, it was applied even to judicial functions. For more than half a century the appointments to judgeships in all the States (excepting Georgia) had been quite beyond the reach of the fluctuations of the popular vote; they rested with the executive or the Legislatures; but the West became impatient of the conservative barrier of an irremovable judiciary, and in 1832 the State of Mississippi inaugurated the system of judges elected for a term of years by the people. This system spread from one State to another in the West and in the East, and even forced itself on the large and old State of New York, which sanctioned it in its new constitution, in 1846. The terms of the elective judgeships even then often appeared too long, and they were shortened in a good many States. All the more was the same course pursued with regard to administrative appointments, the tenure *Thirty Years' View,* Vol. IL p. 596.
Allen's speech in the Senate already quoted. of which became more and more precarious. "The good democratic doctrine of short terms of offices — immediate responsibility to the people " — willed it so. But the more the number of elective offices increased, and the more the short duration of the terms made elections of frequent occurrence, the wider became the sphere of activity of the conventions and the greater their electoral monopoly, as was generally admitted by all thoughtful citizens. Thus the more the theory of radical democracy added to the prerogatives of the people, the more their power diminished in reality, under the

convention system.

III

In the meanwhile the knot fastened round the body of American democracy by this system was being drawn tighter, owing to the increased strength of the old bonds as well as to the new ones which were added to them. The party loyalism embodied in the Organization was becoming more enthusiastic and more intolerant. The party became a sort of church, which admitted no dissent and pitilessly excommunicated any one who deviated a hair's breadth from the established dogma or ritual, were it even from a feeling of deep piety, from a yearning for a more perfect realization of the ideal of holiness set before the believer. The Democratic party was specially conspicuous for the strict discipline which it enforced on its followers, and on the slightest breach individuals or groups were made to feel the weight of its hand. As far back as Jackson's time, towards 1835, a small group arose within the Democratic party desirous of making the practice of its principles more earnest, of reverting to the purity of the Jeffersonian creed, without the smallest idea of starting a schism. But the promoters of this "party of equal rights" did not venture at first to come forward openly, they felt obliged to keep their meetings secret and to continually Senator Sevier's speech at the same sitting (of the 14th of May, 1846).

" It has, therefore," relates a distinguished foreign observer, who visited the United States in 1852, " become a common mode of expression that the 'people ' have in reality very little to do with any of those elections, but that they are ' wire-pulled' by the individuals who make it their business to manage them" (H. Seymour Tremenheere: *The Constitution of the United States Compared with Our Own.* L. 1854, p. 220). change the place, like conspirators; then, when their position became clearly defined, a torrent of abuse and invective was showered on them; they were branded as worse than malefactors, they were "disorganizes." The inquisitorial spirit of the party spread even to relations which were entirely nonpolitical in character. Thus, pn the denunciation of a Democratic convention committee, two officers of the federal army were brought before a court-martial, at Baltimore, on the charge of having made purchases for the commissariat of the army from members of the Whig party. No harm had been done to the Treasury by it; on the contrary, it was proved that the stores had been purchased at a cheaper rate than could have been obtained from supporters of the administration. But, held the convention committee, to buy everything from enemies and not frorn friends was an insult to the Democratic party which deserved punishment.

The opponents of the rival Organization, however, were recognized as belligerents, but the neutrals, the independents, who had not enlisted in either army, were put beyond the pale. The two Organizations united against them in a common outburst of hatred and contempt and in one and the same wish to "exterminate this pestiferous and demoralizing brood." Blind devotion to the party, to the label of the party, became so imperative that even very sensible men came to conceive of the " party" as an entity independent of the principles which it was to promote or oppose. Several anti-slavery Democrats (among whom were men who afterwards attained 1 Quoted by Hoist, Vol. I, p. 307, from a speech of H. Clay, of the 10th of July, 1840.

The semi-official democratic paper, *the Globe,* of July, 1843, having denounced the non-descripts, the no-party men, as "public plunderers and pirates, *kostes humani generis,* who are entitled to no favor or mercy from any honest man," the Whig paper, *The Richmond Whig,* declared: "We shake hands with the *Olobe* on this. We concur with it heartily in desiring the extermination of this pestiferous and demoralizing brood, and will do whatever we can to effect it.... Let the Whigs and Democrats everywhere resolve that the gentry who are too pure to associate with either of them, or to belong to either party, shall not use them to their own individual aggrandizement. Let them act upon the principle that the Whig or Democrat who h:is sense enough to form an opinion and honesty enough to avow it, is to be preferred to the imbecile, or the purist, or the mercenary who cannot come to a decision, or is ashamed of his principles, or from sordid considerations is afraid to declare them" (Niles, Vol. LXIV, p. 331). considerable eminence, such as W. Cullen Bryant and David Dudley Field) strongly disapproved of the declaration of the national convention of 1844 in favour of the annexation of Texas, but none the less decided to vote for Polk, who had accepted this platform, disregarding his pro-slavery sympathies, and seeing in him only the Democrat.

The contingents arrayed under the formal conception of the party kept growing larger and larger. In the first place the tribe of office-seekers multiplied. The deeper the spoils and rotation system took root, the greater became the chances of the aspirants, and in consequence the number of people who competed increased; instead of five candidates for one place there were now ten or twenty. The inevitable disappointment of the nineteen competitors by no means discouraged them; on the contrary, it stimulated them to fresh and more vigorous efforts on behalf of the party Organization, in order to establish a stronger claim on it; everybody expected that his turn must come considering the play of the system and the stability which it had acquired. The growing eagerness of the numerous candidates for public offices made them fall into the hands of those who had the most cleverness and the fewest scruples, so that the mere title of public officer became a moral disqualification. And yet these men were the main prop of the system; they were its corner-stone.

At the same time it received new and abundant material from the foreign element introduced by the continuous immigration, which assumed enormous dimensions from and after 1831, each succeeding year flinging larger and larger masses of emigrants on American soil, mostly from Ireland and from Germany. Owing to the facilities offered by the American naturalization laws, the immigrants began to enjoy the rights " Time was when it was an honor to be an officer, for few but honorable men could get there. Now it is in and of itself rather a disgrace; and it is difficult to avoid the suspicion that a man must have been the mean, cowardly, cringing, servile tool of party, a mere cat's paw, in order to get into office; and unless we know his character from some other source, we can hardly help despising him from the fact that he is in office" (letter from Illinois, of the year 1843, Niles, Vol. LXIV, p. 351).

The number of immigrants, during tire decade of 1831-1840, exceeded half a million; during the following decade of 1841-1850 it reached almost a million and a half. of citizenship after a short period of residence. Ignorant, with no political education, these new members of the commonwealth took service at once in the party organization and blindly followed the word of command. Coming from countries the inhabitants of which were languishing in wretchedness and degradation, as in Ireland, or gasping under the vexatious regime of police-ridden and grandmotherly governments, as in Germany with its *Polizei-Stoat,* the emigrants could not resist the seduction of the word "democrat" and joined the ranks of the Democratic Organization wholesale, bound hand and foot. Small elective offices or distributions of money and spirituous liquors kept them, especially the Irish, loyal to the party. The Whigs, exasperated at seeing the enemy's army receive these accessions every year, laid the blame on the nationality of the Democrat combatants who contributed to their defeat, and exclaimed bitterly: "Ireland has reconquered the country which England had lost!" No doubt the clannish habits peculiar to the Celtic race made the Irish immigrants ready to enlist in battalions, but it was the party Organization created on American soil which turned these habits to account; in their isolation and in their indifference to the political conflicts of the new country, it would have been difficult for the emigrants to influence its destinies without the elaborate convention system which concentrated and flung at a single stroke into the political balance of the United States all the ignorance and all the corruptibility represented by the Irish.

Complaints of the foreign infiltration were soon succeeded by acts, revolts were stirred up, an endeavour was made to form a league against the political influence of the immigrants, but these attempts came to nothing, and, far from weakening the organization of the Democratic party, which absorbed the great majority of the immigrants, only helped to increase its power. Drawing strength from religious passion and inspiration from the old Anglo-Saxon cry of "No Popery," the political animosity aroused by the Catholic Irish took shape in a "Native American Party," with the object of excluding from public office all those who were not born on American soil. This movement, which, after having achieved considerable success at the elections in 1844, died out to come to life again a few years later in the more formidable movement of the "Know Nothings," was in flagrant contradiction with the fundamental principles of American institutions, which rested on equality and on liberty of conscience, as well as utterly opposed to the economic interests of the new continent, which required settlers. The "American Party," therefore, in spite of and owing to Whig sympathy, merely succeeded in throwing the foreign arrivals into the arms of the Organization of the Democratic party. Considering the Democrats as the only friends of the poor people and of the immigrants, the only set of men who were in favour of complete equality for all without distinction of birth and religion, the newcomers were all the more ready to follow the beck and call of the Democratic wirepullers. They blindly adopted the tickets given out at the party conventions and supplied the Organization with what was called "voting cattle."

Finally, besides the growing horde of the professional politicians and the ductile mass of immigrants, the party Organization met with a great accession of strength, after 1840, in the slavery question, which bound to it more closely than ever the upper strata of society, of American stock, possessing a competency and culture. This problem, which had long been flickering in a sort of demi-obscurity, rose on the political horizon of the Union during the decade 1840-1850 in all its grandeur, and threw a crude and trying light on the society of the North. With the exception of a select resolute group impelled towards the question by their strong feelings and generous sympathies, nobody cared to face it; it disturbed the habits of a community engrossed in its affairs, it shocked its notions of propriety, it injured its interests, for it demanded from it self-examination and perhaps action. The best way of escaping from the horrid apparition was to shut one's eyes. But in that case some fixed support was required for moving across the open surface of political life, a sort of railing which could be followed automatically. The party Organization supplied this railing; you walked with your party straight before The adherents of this movement formed a secret order, divided into grades, whose very name, which it appears was "The Sons of Liberty," or the " Order of the Star Spangled Banner," was not known to the members of the lower grades, and to all questions about their organization and its object they were In the habit of replying: "'I don't know," "I know nothing"; this got thorn the popular nickname of " Know Nothings. " you, without heeding anything else, without even allowing your attention to be distracted by the scandals of the spoils system and by the prostitution of politics to the vulgar ambitions and appetites identified with the party Organization. The fear felt by the well-to-do class of losing its footing and knocking up against the slavery question, if it left the beaten track of the party Organization, was all the more paramount in men's minds because the abuses of the convention system came before them mainly in their local aspect, whereas they could not help conceiving the danger of a conflict on the subject of slavery in its general aspect as a conflagration setting the whole Union in a blaze. Hypnotized by the slavery problem, the political society of America, which, in the state of intoxication produced by Jacksonism, had got entangled in the toils of the party Organization, abandoned all attempts at extricating itself. And by way of self-deception, it hardened itself in a fanatical party loyalism, scarcely spontaneous or sincere, but sanctified by the supreme necessity of *quieta non movere. TV*

This maxim, however, which contains all the philosophy of decayed political or social systems, could not prevail against the voice of conscience and the logic of events which so often comes to its aid. The traditional parties were the less able to maintain the *status quo* that they no longer had any real basis themselves; all that was left them was the name and style under which they traded. The differences of opinion on financial and economic questions which set the Jacksonians and their opponents by the ears and consolidated them into two rival parties of Democrats and Whigs, had long since been settled; the national bank ceased to preoccupy the Whigs themselves, who at Clay's instigation and under his leadership had fought so many desperate and fruitless battles in that field; nothing was heard either of the problem of internal improvements; finally, even the tariff question, the protectionism which the Whigs had championed with ardour, no longer drew a line of demarcation between the parties; in the votes on the subject of customs duties many Democrats and Whigs were VOL. II—H found on the same side. With the obliteration of these questions, therefore, which evidently did not contain the elements of permanent divisions, the parties inevitably lost their distinct individuality. It could not be restored to them by the only real question which was agitating the country, the slavery problem, for the divergencies to which it gave rise no more coincided with the division into Whigs and Democrats than did the worn-out problems of their old creed. Inside each of these parties there were opponents as well as upholders of slavery; the southerners, whether they belonged to the Whig or to the Democratic party, were generally favourable to this "domestic institution " of their section of the country, whereas the Democrats and the Whigs of the North, and especially the Democrats, were divided on the question, the majority, however, being opposed to the extension of slavery. In a word, slavery and anti-slavery men corresponded rather to the division into South and North, and in no way to that into Whigs and Democrats, and the rearrangement of the parties on a genuine basis could not have been accomplished without the break-up of the old organizations. But the latter clung desperately to life and refused to stand aside, on the specious pretext that the line of geographical separation drawn by a division into opponents and upholders of slavery would split up the Union materially. Fearing the effects, they could devise no better remedy than to make away with the cause, or at all events to ignore it. They organized a conspiracy of ambiguity and silence around the great national problem which cried for solution, and for a long series of years the used-up parties tried to hold their ground against the logic of events by means of endless stratagems, falsehoods, and recantations, which only made the political atmosphere heavier and the storm more inevitable. The Whig Organization was specially conspicuous for this attitude; it made it its vital principle. By subordinating everything to the supreme preoccupation of keeping up its *cadres,* of remaining a *national* organization, it embraced the policy of the bat which showed the birds its wings and hobnobbed with the rats.

The question was raised in a distinct and by no means revolutionary manner by the celebrated Wilmot Proviso. When President Polk, the slaveholders' man, after entangling the country in a campaign on their behalf against Mexico, in order to rob it, in defiance of the law of nations, of Texas, submitted, in 1846, a demand for a credit of two millions to be used as an indemnity for the vast territory of which the neighbouring republic was being despoiled, a Democrat from the North, Wilmot, moved the addition of a clause to the bill, providing that slavery (which in pursuance of the "compromise of Missouri " of 1821 was prohibited only in the northern Territories above 36 30' north latitude) could not be introduced into the annexed territory. Supported by the Whigs of the North and by a minority of the Democrats of the North, the Proviso was carried in the House of Representatives but lost in the Senate. Two years later, in 1848, it was reintroduced in the form of an independent motion, but no longer found the same favour either with the Democratic faction of the North or with the Whigs, who had, however, secured a majority in the House. They were thinking only of the impending presidential election, and of how to win it without compromising themselves. If they decided either way, they were lost, in the one case estranging the free opinion of the North, in the other forfeiting the support of the southerners.

The solution of this singular and apparently hopeless problem of political fence-riding with which the Whigs were confronted found a surreptitious aid in the state of the public mind, which was weary of politicians' intrigues and of artificial party divisions. People sighed for a President under no obligations to the mercenary politicians, commending himself to the public by his personal qualities; in a word, an honest man and nothing more. General Taylor, a brave soldier, who distinguished himself in the Mexican War, seemed to many persons to combine these conditions, and in various parts of the Union manifestations occurred in favour of his presidential candidature; he was acclaimed in "meetings of the people," in gatherings of "Native Americans" and elsewhere, with a clear indication of the independent character attributed to him and of the hope that he would become the President of the whole country and not of a party, that he " And whereas he is particularly agreeable to us as the people's candidate for the presidency, from the fortunate circumstance that he has been entirely aloof from the party conflicts of the country, has formed no ' entangling aliiwould bring about a new state of things by breaking up the old party organizations. But these manifestations against the thraldom of party were destined only to be the last gleam of a light that had long been feebly flickering and was now well-nigh extinct in men's minds. Taylor agreed to be the people's candidate and his prospects of success appeared to increase daily, but they were intercepted by one of the very organizations which he was meant to destroy. The Whig Organization, seeing a formidable rival in Taylor, hastened to take him up on its own account. The candidate outside parties longed for by the people became in its eyes the candidate outside political principles and convictions, who alone could be adopted by it without risk. The worthy general, who always Btood aloof from politics and never voted, was the very ideal of the Whig Organization; he himself admitted, in letters written with much artlessness, that he had only " crude impressions on matters of policy," and he allowed himself to be persuaded that he was a Whig, "although," he added honestly, "not an ultra one." Fearing that their candidate's excess of naive sincerity might compromise the adoption of his candidature, the wire-pullers assigned him a small committee of supervision,8 which drafted all his political letters for him, with the shades of meaning and mental reservations that the game appeared to demand.

The ground was sufficiently prepared when the Whig national convention met; Thurlow Weed exerted his wire-pulling talents ances' with intruding politicians or wire-workers; and if elected, would have no debts to pay with the offices and money of the people for partisan electioneering services; and whereas, as president, he would be unfettered, and could give full play to the honesty of his nature as the president of the whole country and not of a party" (Niles, Vol. LXXIII, p. 7'J).

" He was nominated for the express purpose of breaking up the old organizations... and if elected would do all in his power to break down the old parties. Ho was nominated to bring about a new state of things" (quoted by Hoist, Vol. II, p. 290). The "committee of safety," which became a permanent feature, had, however, its precedent, having been already created for the first " military hero," proposed by the Whigs for the presidency in 1840. Harrison was also placed under a committee intended to check any excess of language on his part. The Democrats even maintained — it was the chairman of the Democratic national convention who asserted it from his seat — that General Harrison's guardians never let him out of their sight, and accompanied him to the post-office when he went to fetch his letters, to prevent him from making unsuitable replies (Niles, Vol. LVDX p. 148). in it as at the famous convention of Harrisburg in 1839, and Taylor's candidature was carried without any difficulty, although his attitude on the burning question of the day remained an enigma to everybody. There were, however, some delegates who, in their devotion to the anti-slavery cause, wanted to be reassured. After Taylor had been nominated for the Presidency, one of them tabled a resolution binding the nominee to the fundamental principles of the Whig party, which were opposed to the extension of slavery, to the acquisition of territories by means of conquest, etc. The chairman of the convention refused to put the motion to the vote. After the nomination of the candidate for the Vice-Presidency (Fillmore) a delegate brought forward a resolution declaring that the two candidates adopted had been so as Whig candidates. Another delegate wanted to pass a resolution denying the right of Congress to authorize slavery in the Territories. The chairman declined to put these proposals to the vote as well, and the convention broke up without having made a political declaration. Afraid of proclaiming a principle, a conviction, the Whig party had an "available" candidate as its sole bond of union. During the election campaign the Whig Organization continued to carefully keep up the ambiguity of Taylor's position, representing him in the North as a genuine Whig and in favour of the Wilmot Proviso, while his capacity of planter and slaveowner was calculated to dispel' all suspicion and hesitation on the part of the voters in the South. Thanks to this combination and to the divisions in the Democratic party Taylor was elected, to the greater triumph of the Whig firm, and its Organization at once proceeded to distribute dividends on the orthodox method of distribution of the spoils, and we are already aware how Taylor lent himself to it.

But hardly had the victors taken their seats at the banquet when the spectre of slavery appeared, in a menacing, terrifying attitude. The slaveholders were becoming more and more aggressive in their wish to extend the territorial area of slavery; they even talked of breaking up the Union. At the same time in the northern States the revolt of men's consciences against slavery and the pretensions of its sup Greeley and Cleveland, *A Political Text-book for ISlio,* p. 15.

porters was growing more formidable and causing a deeper and deeper split in the Whig ranks; but the "party" chose to ignore it, and, without formally giving way to the slaveholders, made itself powerless to withstand their encroachments. This contradictory situation, over winch the party Organization threw its aegis, showed itself most conspicuously in the very

State of the North which was the greatest hotbed of the anti-slavery agitation, in Massachusetts, and here too was the best field for observing how complex were the factors which lay at the root of this situation, and how and by whom they were combined to produce the effect described. Some clung to the *status quo* out of devotion to the Union; a resolute attitude appeared to them bound to bring about an explosion and hasten the split; forgetting the adage of *propter vitam vivendi perdere causas,* they thought they could not sacrifice too much to their patriotism. Others were restrained by the feeling, inherent in the race, of superstitious respect for the existing social order. The high standard of culture on which Boston prided itself contributed its quota to this ultra-conservative frame of mind by filling the atmosphere with the timorousness of intellectual refinement and its aristocratic indifference to anything capable of stirring the vulgar herd that crawls at its feet. The churches, generally timid, if not servile, in face of the powers that be, exerted the same deadening influence. The trading class, a very numerous one, which was absorbed in money-making and had considerable interests at stake in the South, regarded all these individuals with convictions who meddled with what did not concern them as tiresome busybodies, and, engrossed in its selfish pursuits, demanded peace at any price. Others, alive to the situation created by the slavery problem and sincerely devoted to the cause of freedom, thought that they could best' fight the good fight by remaining in the ranks of the old party. Others, bound by old associations or by feelings of personal attachment to Whig leaders, thought they would be wanting in self-respect, be guilty of inconsistency, if they did not continue to walk obediently behind the "party," little as was the life left in it. Finally, the ambition of those engaged in a political career and the appetites of the mercenary politicians looked on it as a means of keeping what they had got. The party Organization bound all these scruples, prejudices, timidities, weaknesses, ambitions, and cravings together by dragging them after the politicians; it became their broker, with no idea but that of earning its brokerage, of obtaining all the places for its own men without sharing with others, as would have been necessary if the party were reconstructed on a new base with fresh elements. Offering a shelter, a permanent refuge, to all the timorous minds and selfish interests, the Organization of the party saved them from the necessity or the temptation of looking things in the face, and, false to its own radical and democratic origin, became a tool of the most abject conservatism. To get rid of the divergencies which in spite of its efforts were constantly arising between the adherents of the party, who were nicknamed the "conscience Whigs," and the others, the "commercial Whigs," the Organization hit on the ingenious plan of "agreeing to disagree," and of continuing to fly the Whig colours. If indifference could follow this advice, how would conscience reconcile itself to it; by what devices would it stifle the voice that cried within it? Such was the question that was continually recurring in the course of events which, far from solving it, only envenomed it. The demand of California to be admitted into the Union as a State, with exclusion of slavery, the debates on the " Compromise of 1850" which was proposed as a settlement of the controversy, the disputes on the finality of this instrument, and the mental distress caused by the duty it enjoined of restoring fugitive slaves to their masters, were so many opportunities for demonstrating over and over again the irremediable division between the southern Whigs and the anti-slavery Whigs. The national convention of 1852 tried to bring about an apparent agreement between them by a supreme quibble, selecting a colourless candidate, a "military hero," to please the North, and adopting a programme to suit the South, almost the same as that which the Democratic convention had approved a fortnight previously. This was the last straw; the southern Whigs thought it safer to vote for the Democratic candidate who was of the same timber as the platform; the opponents of the extension of slavery mustered behind an independent candidate, and there remained only a Whig minority which consented to "support the candidate while spitting upon the platform on which he stood." This candidate was beaten, and the "Whig party" was left on the field. The Organization did not despair of bringing it to life again. A more frightful decomposition only set in. In Congress several leading southern Whigs became supporters of the Democratic Administration, and when the slaveholders and their victorious northern allies cut away the last legal barrier against slavery by repealing the "Compromise of Missouri" of 1821, all the Whig members from the South (with one exception) voted with the Democratic majority. The northern Whigs were left alone. The Whig *national* Organization was dead beyond a shadow of a doubt; it could no longer block the path, as it had done for so many years, of the champions of liberty, that is, of the non-extension of slavery, the road was clear; only its corpse still lay across it for a time.

V

A number of Whigs who had a sincere hatred of slavery, who preferred human liberty to the integrity of the party, had not waited for this crisis to leave the Whig Organization and take their stand on a plain, straightforward anti-slavery platform. But for many a long year they had to fight not only to defend and to propagate their opinions, but even for their right to organize themselves on this particular footing. The conception of parties as kinds of churches taking charge of all the manifold moral interests of the faithful, of their whole soul considered for this purpose as one and indivisible, and exercising over them a universal, catholic jurisdiction, had sunk so deep into the public mind that the mere fact of forming a party to champion a particular cause, and nothing but that cause, seemed in itself wicked, immoral in the highest degree; people do not join a church to affirm their belief in a single dogma. To avoid shocking public opinion, therefore, the first anti-slavery organization, which was formed under the name of the " Liberty party," felt bound to place on record a formal abjuration of this heresy, by solemnly declaring, in its platform of 1843, that the Liberty party was not "organized merely for the overthrow of slavery," that it did not originate in a "desire to accomplish a single object, but in a comprehensive regard to the great interests of the whole country." This asseveration in no way saved the Liberty party from attacks at the hands of men who piqued themselves on orthodoxy and political good sense.

When the movement launched by the Liberty party took a fresh start, just before the presidential election of 1848, in the form of the "Free Soil party," which frankly declared its hostility to the extension of slavery to regions which were free from it, its adherents, who came mostly from the Whig side, were branded as "renegades and apostates," while even sincere opponents of the extension of slavery, such as Benton, who was turned out of the Senate by the slavery men after a long and most distinguished career, thought the notion of an independent party of this kind simply absurd, and even took steps to get the Free Soil Organization dissolved. "It was an organization entirely to be regretted," declared Benton, "its aspect was sectional, its foundation a single idea, and its tendency to merge political principles in a slavery contention.... It went... to narrow down the basis of party organization to a single idea; and that idea not known to our ancestors as an element in political organizations." But, on the other hand, the Whig party, which resorted to endless prevarications and lies to avoid facing the grave question of the day, and which was not even his party, received a testimonial from Benton because it kept within the generalities which befit a party worthy of the name: "The, Whig party, so far as slavery was concerned, acted most nationally; they ignored the subject, and made their nomination on the platform of the Constitution, the country, and the character of their candidate."" It is remarkable that the same reproach of narrowness of base was addressed to the Free Soil party by the man who, twelve yeaTS later, was to be borne into supreme power by an Organizati on, on the strength of the one idea which called it into life — by Abraham Lincoln. The future President, before he belonged to the nation and to humanity, during the obscure period of his political career, when lost in the crowd of politicians, followed the narrow path of the Whig party, with E. Stanwood, *A History of Presidential Elections,* Boston, 1896, p. 151. » G. W. Julian, *Political Recollections,* Chicago, 1884, p. 64. *Thirty Years' View,* Vol. II, p. 722.

which he was connected. When supporting the regular candidature of Taylor in 1848, Lincoln, who from his youth up had conceived a hatred of slavery, pointed out with emphasis that the "Free Soilers" (who had run a candidate against Taylor) "were a party of one idea or principle, good enough in itself, but not broad enough to found a party on."

The Whig party was rapidly decomposing when those of its members who were sincerely opposed to slavery were still waiting for the opponents of slavery, the Free Soilers or others, to come over to them for the purpose of fighting the good fight under their banner, of becoming partners in their old firm. Eventually the disgust inspired by the behaviour of the Whig party drove most of its supporters out of it; but, enfeebled by the mental servitude in which they had so long been kept, they did not venture to openly throw off the yoke, and they fled into the darkness of the "Know Nothings," of the secret association which to the charm of mystery added the sincerity and honesty of its aspirations, whatever may have been the verdict of good sense on it. But in spite of the numerous adhesions brought to it by the deserters from the old parties rent by the terrible controversy, the party of the "Know Nothings" could not hold together long, both on account of the fancifulness of its object and because the slavery question with its divisions followed the "Know Nothings" into their subterranean retreat, like the terrible eye symbolizing conscience, in the song of the *Legende des Slicles,* which "was always there." They were obliged to break up and come out into the light of day to take sides for or against slavery and facilitate a rational and honest rearrangement of parties. A few Whig fragments were still left here and there, in New York, Massachusetts, Ohio, which refused to dissolve, like reptiles which have been crushed and whose severed joints still give signs of life. But soon they mingled with the dust, the road was clear, and all the opponents of the extension of slavery, the number of which increased with marked rapidity Cf. *Memoirs and Letters of Charles Sumner,* by E. L. Pierce, Boston, 1893, Vol. m, p. 170.

" Thousands eager to bolt from the old parties, but fearful of being shot down on the way as deserters, gladly availed themselves of this newly devised 'underground railroad ' in escaping from the service of their old master" (Julian, p. 141). towards 1854, under the provocations of the slaveholders, were able to meet freely and form an organic whole, however different their origin and however divergent their opinions on other subjects. This body soon received the name of the "Eepublican " party. Born in the States of the West (Michigan, Wisconsin), where party organization was less developed than in the East, and where consequently more facilities existed for spontaneous popular movements, it attracted Whigs from the East loosely connected with the organization of the party, Free Soilers, Know Nothings who had seen the error of their ways, Democrats who managed to throw off the party yoke, and spread, about the year 1856, over the whole North. In place of the stereotyped party organizations which stubbornly and selfishly impeded the solution of the vital question of the Republic, there now arose, on the one side, a living organization, inspired only by frankness and disinterestedness, which was bound to make the forces massed on the other side take a decided line. VI While just as deeply divided on the question of the extension of slavery as the Whig party, the Democratic party preserved an appearance of unity and cohesion, thanks to the discipline which was its distinguishing characteristic and to the concessions which it was continually making to the slaveholders, under the influence of its Organization. It was the latter which delivered the party into their hands and which always prevented it from regaining its freedom, from breaking its bonds. In the contingents of the Democratic party formed under Jackson the slavocrats of the South were in a minority; the majority of the party, contributed mainly by the North and the North-West, was not favourable to the extension of slavery, but from 1844 onwards the minority took the helm, in consequence of the change of front of the Democratic National Convention, which threw over Van Buren and adopted a candidate favourable to the annexation of Texas, to avoid risking the fruits of the victory, the "spoils." By a selfish scheme of the Organization, the Democratic party found itself all at once committed, whether it liked it or not, to a new policy, which was to change its own destiny and that of the country and land it in a catastrophe. Having at the instance of its Organization lent its name to the Texas intrigue, which was the starting-point of all the further encroachments of the slave power, the Democratic party became, if not its champion in ordinary, at all events its surety, and in each new phase of the operation undertaken by the slaveholders it had to renew its endorsement, on pain of breaking the connection, by subscribing to the "Compromise of 1850" at their request, by pledging itself afterwards to the irrevocable finality of this instrument, by abolishing the prohibition of slavery in the northern Territories (the compromise of Missouri). But these successive concessions, being of little use to the slaveholders, who were overrun by the development of free labour in the new Territories and unnerved by the growing opposition of public opinion in the free States, the flexibility of which, great as it was, had its limits, the alliance between the slaveholders and the northern Democrats could not last. The party Organization resorted to all manner of manoeuvres and expedients to maintain it. The Democratic national conventions played in this conjuncture a game much resembling that of the Whig conventions, at one time rejecting motions (as for instance that of Yancey, in 1848) which contained straightforward proposals on the subject of the extension of slavery; at another allowing (as in 1848 and in 1856) two sets of delegations from the same State to take their seat, the one in favour of and the other opposed to slavery, each of which claimed to represent the State; now introducing into their platform articles formally condemning all anti-slavery agitation and then disavowing them during the election campaign (of 1852) as "rotten planks"; or again selecting colourless candidates, like Pierce in 1852 and Buchanan in 1856; or adopting platforms of a. machiavellian duplicity, like that of 1856, which perfidiously invoked the doctrine of " popular sovereignty," by proclaiming that the Congress had no right to allow or forbid slavery in the Territories, and that the Territories were free to admit or prohibit it in their constitution. But as the Territories adopt a constitution only at the moment when they are admissible as States, the convention threw no light on the question as to what regime should be observed in regard to slavery during the, perhaps exceedingly lengthy, interval between the formation of the Territory and its elevation to the rank of State. To prevent the doubt being cleared up by the person of the candidate, the national convention selected a northerner, Buchanan, who had not taken up any line in the events of the last few years, because he had spent them abroad in diplomatic employ, and was able, as a newspaper observed, to "prove an *alibi* in the question of the day."

But all these machinations were only half-sucecessful. The measure of ambiguity was well-nigh full. Buchanan was elected, but the defection of Democrats who went over to the Bepublican party in the North was so considerable that the slaveholders, ill at ease, resolved to play their last card. Having lost faith in the meaningless formulas and pettifogging devices offered by the northern politicians, and being accustomed to drag these politicians at their heels by the mere threat of seceding from the party and the Union, they demanded from the federal authority a formal acknowledgment of the right to own slaves in all the Territories, with or without the consent of their inhabitants, just like any other property. The northern politicians, who had taken their stand on the theory of "popular sovereignty" in making the earlier bargains with the slaveholders, could not stultify themselves by complying with this new demand without losing most of their supporters in the North, while the slaveholders in their passionate advocacy of their cause put it before the integrity of the party, and would not recede. The artificial union of the party's ill-assorted fragments could no longer be maintained.

The split that was brewing during the whole of Buchanan's Presidency, which was filled with struggles between the administration devoted to irreconcilable slaveholders and the northern Democrats, came to a head at the national convention of the party, which met in 18G0, at Charlestown. It was in vain that the delegates from the North brought forward a wiredrawn programme of the kind which national conventions knew so well how to concoct, for this supreme effort to stave off the catastrophe was only a supreme quibble. The platform reproduced that of 1856 with its puzzling resolutions on "popular sovereignty," by declaring that "Democratic principles are unchangeable in their nature," and added a paragraph pledging the party to abide, as regards the question of slavery in the Territories, by the decisions of the Supreme Court on questions of constitutional law. As soon as the majority of the convention had voted this platform the southern delegates withdrew, and there being no longer a quorum for nominating the candidates by the two-thirds majority prescribed by the rules, the convention had to adjourn without having accomplished its task. The dissentients met in a separate convention and adopted an out-and-out slavery programme, allowing every citizen to settle in the Territory with his property, slaves included, which the Federal Government was bound to protect in case of need. For the choice of candidates, however, three or even four new conventions were held by the various Democratic fractions, which resulted in several rival lists. The semblance of union in the party disappeared; the long struggle between the ambiguous situation kept up by the Organization and the naked truth of the slaveholders' aspirations was at an end; the Organization was shattered, without even being able to take credit for its exertions in trying to get the vexed question out of the way. For however reprehensible the cause of slavery may have been from a political, economical, and humanitarian point of view, ft rested on sincere convictions, on clear and straightforward ideas; and if it deserved to succumb, it was entitled to fight just as much as it was bound to submit to opposition. And political wisdom even which condemned the principle of slavocracy, as well as morality which abhorred it, required that it should not be withdrawn from the contest, that this contest should be a frank and open one, held in the light of day.

The break-up of the old organizations now made this contest possible; freed from the trammels with which these organizations had enveloped them, the principle of liberty on the one side and that of slavocracy on the other could stand up, meet face to face, and fight it out. But the conflict could no longer be settled in a peaceful way; it was too late for that; the South had gone too far in its pretensions to allow itself to be nonsuited by a simple electoral verdict; it was systematically forced against the wall of *sint ut sunt aut non sint* by the temperament of its race and the dangers which appeared to threaten it no less than by the attitude of the party organizations. A feudal stock, born and bred for domination and command, proud and fearless, with a profound sense of its individuality, it could not humble itself before the Yankees without committing a moral suicide. Finding itself more and more driven into a corner by the world of freedom rising out of the " great desert of the West," and feeling the ground slipping from beneath its feet, in spite of the verbal arrangements devised by the party organization, slavocracy was obliged to be always seeking new fulcrums, to be continually raising its terms. And it daily became all the more aggressive and intractable, because the resistance opposed to it was invariably made up of concessions, and it was confronted solely by parties ready to do anything to prolong their existence and following the lead of organizations which, with love of the Union always on their lips, were only venal go-betweens. When the election of Lincoln to the Presidency announced the victory of the party of principles, slavocracy thought the death-knell of its sway in the Union had sounded, and it denounced the federal compact; the North flew to arms to defend the integrity of the Union; and the slavery conflict was left to the arbitrament of blood and iron.

FOURTH CHAPTER THE EVOLUTION OF THE CONVENTION SYSTEM *(continued)*

I

In the crisis brought on by the slavery question the old parties foundered, but the system of organization by which they made head against wind and tide survived them, during the tempest of the Civil War as well as after the re-establishment of the Union; it even took a fresh start under cover of the distress and the perils of the fratricidal struggle, and of the political, social, and economic transformation which the Union underwent on issuing from the war.

The "Republicans," who represented the fresh current in the life of the parties, adopted the machinery of the organization in vogue, the convention and committee system, in all its fulness; it was in such common use thawfc commanded acceptance almost like a natural phenomenon, anil indeed a party whose origins were so laborious, and which lAd to contend against such powerful opponents, could not but gain by adopting an organization, ready to hand, of the type sanctioned by popular habits. But in proportion as the power of the new party increased, it attracted to itself the professionals and the political parasites who try to feed on the vital substance of parties; the machinery of conventions, which they had learnt to manipulate with such skill, gave them every facility for getting in. The moral principles which lay at the root of the "Republican" party, and the lofty enthusiasm which inspired its adherents, precluded the self-seeking politicians from becoming the masters of it, but they none the less formed a considerable element in the party. While the first Republican national convention, of 185(;, presented a sort of extemporized gathering, most of the members of which had no formal credentials, but who were all animated by the purest and noblest sentiments, the second national convention, of 1860, was already composed of regular delegations from the several States, but with a very large contingent of politicians and wirepullers. Throughout the proceedings of this convention, including its principal achievement, the nomination of Lincoln, wire-pulling was at least as great a factor as spontaneousness and devotion to principles. Indeed, the selection of Lincoln was determined by considerations of "availability," in accordance with the tradition of national conventions; he was preferred to the candidate who was the history of the party personified, its brain and its heart, to William Seward. The nomination of Lincoln brought tears to the eyes of many opponents of slavery, who saw in it a fresh triumph of the opportunism habitual to party organizations ("rather success than Seward "), but for once in a way the wire-pullers of the convention were mistaken; Lincoln turned out to be a man of courage, of force of will, and of moral grandeur such as is seldom met with in history.

But if these eminent qualities helped him to overcome the formidable rebellion of the South, he could make but little use of them against the political traditions bequeathed by the old party organizations,— against rotation and the spoils' system. It appears that at his accession Lincoln had decided to appoint Republicans and Democrats indiscriminately to offices, but this intention was never put into practice. The secession flung most of the Democrats on the side of the enemies of the Union; the Republican party remained its chief, if not sole, prop, and the very safety of the 'tTnion seemed to demand that the Republican party should be supported at all hazards, and that public posts should be entrusted exclusively to its adherents. Sb the horde *at* officeseekers, whose principal claim was their "Republicanism," soon won the day. To make room for them one of the most appalling hecatombs of officials known in the history of the American public service was carried out. Thus the best representatives of the Republican party were led into continuing the old courses which they condemned, and not only to ensure the immediate future of the party, but to meet personal obli i W. H. Lam on, *The Life of Abraham Lincoln,* Boston, 1872, p. 458.

VOL. II — I -y gations, to pay for past electoral services as well. Lincoln himself happened to be in this predicament, and he was the first to do as he was bid. At the Republican national convention of Chicago the wire-pullers who supported Lincoln concluded, without his knowledge, a bargain with two important delegations, those of Pennsylvania and Indiana, by the terms of which the latter promised to vote for Lincoln, who in return was to give their favourites, Caleb Smith of Indiana and Simon Cameron of Pennsylvania, posts in the cabinet. As typical "politicians," both of them had little to recommend them in point of moral qualities for the highest positions in the Republic. The appointment of Cameron in particular gave rise to strong protests from respectable citizens of his own State. But the managers of the convention, who had carried the vote in favour of Lincoln, insisted on his redeeming the promise made by them for his benefit. Lincoln's position was a most embarrassing one. He is supposed to have said: "All that I am in the world,—the Presidency and all else,— I owe to that opinion of me which the people express when they call me 'honest old Abe.' Now, what will they think of their *honest* Abe, when he appoints Simon Cameron to be his familiar adviser? " He made the appointment. The result was what might have been expected. The war department entrusted to Cameron, which had just at that time to cope with exceptional difficulties of organization, became a hotbed of corruption. The numerous bargains and contracts entered into for the requirements of the war by Cameron's administration were tainted with fraud, to the greater advantage of the Secretary's relations and friends. At last Lincoln was forced by public opinion to intervene; he relieved Cameron of his post and appointed him to an important embassy in Europe. Probably the same considerations of "honour and safety" which, according to Lincoln's biographer, had prevented him from repudiating the compact made by the wire-pullers, precluded him from simply dismissing the man of the Chicago convention. In very many cases of less importance Lincoln showed the same deference to the demands of the influential personages of the party Organization; he let them have places for their i Lamon, *The Life of Lincoln,* p. 460. Cf. A. K. McClure, *Abraham Lincoln and Men of War Times,* Philad., 1892, 3d ed., pp. 138-147. *protiyis,* even for unworthy ones. Besides making more than once appointments inspired solely by the interests of the party, the President had no scruple about intervening, if necessary, iu election contests to support the "regular" candidates with all the weight of his authority. II

Throughout the whole of the Civil War the situation was too critical to dispense with the services of the system of party organization which, in the terrible struggle that the Government of the North had to maintain, placed its rear in safety. After the victory the Organization had to receive its share in the results, and while the opponents of slavery tried with feverish ardour to gather up and preserve the moral fruits of the victory, the Republican Organization showed no less eagerness to grasp its material advantages. It flung itself at a bound on the reconquered States of the South, and carried out to the letter the famous maxim of "the spoils to the victor." The territory which the Organization invaded had hitherto almost escaped from the system introduced by the Jacksonian Democracy after the eclipse of the leadership embodied in the legislative Caucus. The social and economic conditions which favoured the establishment and the development of the popular party Organization in the North and in the West did not exist in the South. The South and the rest of the Union formed practically two nations, two different races, each with a distinct civilization.

G.W. Julian records a typical case, in which, having warned the President against a bad appointment which he was about to make, he received the following reply: "There is much force in what you say; but in the balancing of matters, I guess I shall have to appoint him" *(Political Recollections,* p. 183). Julian also relates a case of this official pressure exerted in his own favour: In 1864 the local convention in Indiana nominated Julian as candidate for Congress; but the editor of a local newspaper set to work to patronize Julian's opponent, who had been rejected by the convention, and was standing as an independent candidate. And as the editor of the newspaper was at the same time a federal office-bolder, Julian appealed to Lincoln. "You can rest assured," replied the President, "that Mr. llolloway this was the name of the editor-official shall support you openly and unconditionally, or lose his head. " As a matter of fact, Holloway, on a threat of dismissal, had to give way *(ibid.,* p. 244).

With the steam era in full swing, the slave-holding South remained an essentially agricultural country, of scattered populations, and relatively few and unimportant urban agglomerations, in which manufacturing industry was barely represented, and the arts and crafts had attained a very moderate degree of development. Slave labour excluded all free effort, and kept the South apart from the economic movement which carried away the North and the West in a sort of whirlwind. It prevented the rise of a powerful middle class, composed of small farmers, like those who constituted the moral force of New England, of captains of industry, of manufacturers, of leading traders, of superior artisans, who drew from their material independence and from the success achieved by their dogged and untrammelled will the consciousness of their dignity as men and citizens. Immediately beneath a somewhat limited number of planters, in addition to the coloured slaves, came a wretched mass of men of white race, "mean whites," sunk in ignorance and poverty, physically free, but kept by their wretchedness in a close economical and political dependence on the planters. The latter, as the sole possessors of wealth, formed a ruling class in the State which was the flat negation of democracy; in the South the republican form required by the Constitution of the Union covered an oligarchical power wielded by a few thousand rich planters. They formed an elite which in more than one respect presented a striking resemblance to the old gentry of England, and combined with the chivalrous qualities of a feudal race a fair intellectual culture, which they derived not so much from authors as from orators, like the Greeks in the agora, and a great breadth of mind, except in what concerned the institution of slavery, which warped their judgment and impaired their moral sense. Drawing into their orbit the less wealthy planters and the men of liberal professions in the cities, this elite wielded an even vaster and stronger social and political leadership than that which obtained in England in the old days, for the reason that the structure of the society of the South and of its political life was more *igalitaire,* more levelled; that there was no hereditary aristocratic class, separated, if not by the law, at all events by social conventions, from the rest of the population; and that all the members of the white race, down to the wretchedest, were united, owing to slavery, in the same feelings and prejudices and in the same interests; in a word, because the moral cohesion of society in the South was perfect, and made it a sort of vast family or clan, in which the younger members followed their elders spontaneously and naturally. Respect for authority in all its forms was absolute.

This state of things created a political atmosphere which was anything but favourable to the birth and development of the two primordial elements of political life in the Northern States, that is to say, of the democratic formalism which took possession of the public mind, and of the race of mercenary politicians who, under cover of this formalism, laid hands on the political machinery. The great mass of voters had no need of the abstract notion of "regularity" and of cut-and-dried resolutions of the would-be representative conventions for shaping their policy; they followed implicitly the men to whom they were bound as if by feudal ties; every great family had its political following, with a crowd of dependents, great and small, who rushed up at the first summons. Again, even apart from the restrictiops on the suffrage which prevailed in the old States of the South, politics and the principal public functions were practically a monopoly of the ruling class. Politics were for this class not so much a career as a vocation; young members of good families were initiated into it at an early age, and tempered their southern ardour in the controversies of the day on constitutional law in which the women themselves took an interest. It was almost always from this class, and from among the men who gravitated towards it, that the members of the legislative assemblies, and of Congress in particular, were recruited. As a rule, they were kept in their posts for years together, the great Democratic principle of rotation being by no means in favour. The executive offices were also unaffected by it, and attracted men of distinction all the more naturally that the latter were seldom able to find a situation in commerce or industry, which were in a very backward state. The elective functions were few in number; most of the offices were filled up by the executive or by the Legislature. In one of the most important States,— in South Carolina, — down to 1861, the presidential Electors themselves were not chosen by the people, but appointed by the Legislature, as was the practice in some States of the North in the days of the congressional Caucus.

The need, therefore, of a party election machinery did not make itself felt here to the same extent as in the North and in the West, and the convention system did not acquire the same importance in the South. There was little of the same formal regularity in it; the lower grades of local conventions, those of counties and of districts, hardly existed at all in practice; besides, the communal elections were generally uninfluenced by party considerations; the State conventions were more gatherings of leading men, who were brilliant speakers as well, than the product of successive delegations formed according to rule. This was the case especially in the old States,—Virginia, the two Carolinas, and Georgia,— where the social leadership was particularly strong and the drift of public opinion was all in one direction. In the newer States of Tennessee and Kentucky, in which society was more democratic and parties were evenly balanced, the party Organization was more highly developed. But, taken as a whole, it was far behind that of the North, leaving the electorate a very considerable amount of independence in the South. Very often the candidates came forward of their own accord, without having received the investiture of any convention, a thing which had become wellnigh a physical impossibility in the North. Nor was there the same need, in the South, of the committees which canvassed the voters in concert with the candidates. The candidates as a rule did not meddle with electioneering; their special field of activity was the stump, in which they broke a lance with their opponents, and in debates with the rival candidates they treated the public and themselves to tournaments of eloquence which flattered their chivalrous tastes. The victor in the debate was afterwards the victor at the polls. The necessary amount of wire-pulling, more of a patriarchal kind, was done, not by professionals, but by natural go-betweens, the most important of whom were the overseers of slaves on the large plantations. These individuals, who played a considerable part in the economy of Southern society, served as a connecting link

"The best man in debate won the votes at the polls" *(The Life and Times of W. L.Yanasy,* by J. V. Du Bose, Birmingham, Ala., lS!tt, p. 13D).

between the planters and the "mean whites," and in this capacity exercised considerable influence over the latter, which made them the great electors of the locality, and even enabled them often to mould the policy of their masters. Monopolizing politics, the members of the ruling class no doubt used them for the narrowest and most selfish of interests, to defend the accursed institution; but however sordid the motives by which they were guided, their object was rather the interest of their class, of the " section," than that of individuals. Public functions were never a source of personal gain to them; they looked on them aa a means of gratifying their dignity, their pride. The small places, which did not hold out these inducements, were left to people who were akin to the type of the "politicians" in the North, but for this very reason the type in the South was a poor and stunted one; the professionals of politics played an altogether subordinate part there. AH this was changed after the Civil War, when the victors gave the suffrage to the whole ignorant and degraded mass of freed negroes and cut off the old leadership by depriving the men who had pronounced for secession of political rights. The old political society was dissolved; the new one presented only incoherent elements. The Republican party undertook to bring them together, as much with a view to consolidate the results of the victory, and in particular the emancipation of the negroes, as to keep itself permanently in power. For this purpose it made use of the party Organization in vogue in the North. The negroes adapted themselves to it with extraordinary rapidity; without understanding anything of the issues of politics, they grasped its externals admirably,— the devices and stratagems of organization, the dodges and tricks of procedure at the meetings,— and in a short time they manoeuvred in the conventions and the committees like veterans. They were controlled by whites, some of whom had hurried down from the northern States, and who got the nickname of "carpet-baggers," since become famous, from their exasperated opponents. Many of them were very re Introduced on this occasion for the first time into political language, and since then transported to the other side of the Atlantic, into England, where, however, it obtained a very moderate and almost inoffensive application,

Cf. Vol. I, p. 448.

spectable men, who were really bent on working for the triumph of the principles of liberty and the moral regeneration of the South, but the majority was composed of adventurers, who had come to make their way in the conquered country. They found associates on the spot in the "mean whites," released from their old social ties by the fall of the slave power, in ex-overseers of slaves, accustomed to electioneering work under the slavery regime, etc. In concert with those southerners who joined the Eepublican party (the "Scalawags," as they were called in the South), and with the help of the negroes enrolled in its organization, the carpet-baggers got into possession of the electoral machine. When installed in power, the negroes and their white mentors indulged in an unprecedented robbery of the public purse. They made the Legislatures issue bonds on the State to provide for public works, which were never taken in hand, and shared the proceeds among themselves, leaving the tax-payers to submit to fresh taxation; they openly passed fraudulent disbursements or swelled the expenses incurred for furnishing offices, etc., in the wildest fashion, fitting them up, for instance, with clocks at $480 apiece, with chandeliers at $650. the nickname of "carpet-bagger" originated in the American North-west, at a time when in this still virgin country there were founded *soi-disant* banks of issue which, for the better concealment of their shady speculations, led a wandering existence, like wild-cats (" wild-cat money "). The notes issued by them were secured by the mortgage of land; but to escape from legal proceedings in case their notes were protested, the speculative bankers neglected to provide for a place of business, which the law omitted to enjoin on them. Having no permanent office, they circulated their paper by means of itinerant agents, who carried them in carpet bags, and were dubbed "carpet-baggers." A journalist of the South, an old carpet-bagger, having exhausted his stock of opprobrious epithets on the Yankee intruders, at last flung in their face his own nickname, which was at once adopted by the whole Press. I take this explanation from the novel by Albion W.

Tourgee, *A FooVs Errand, by One of Themselves,* N. Y., 1880, p. 106. Whatever may be its value as a work of fiction, this tale is a historical document of undeniable importance for understanding the South during the period of *Reconstruction* which followed the close of the war. Thus in less than four months the legislature of North Carolina voted more than 25 millions in bonds, mostly intended for railroads, of which 14 millions were issued and sold at from 9 to 45 per cent, of their nominal value. In South Carolina the debt of the State rose in the space of four years from 51 millions to 181 millions, without any public work of importance having been executed or begun. The four years of Republican domination cost Louisiana 10b' millions of dollars.

The public offices were distributed among illiterates; in one State there were more than two hundred negro magistrates unable to read or write; justice was openly bought and sold. For years it was a regular Saturnalia, exhibiting a caricature of popular government, and supplying, as it were, a demonstration *ab absurdo* of the effects of a rough and uneducated universal suffrage worked by the perfected machine of a scientific organization flying the party flag. On the specious pretext of defending the cause of which the Republican party was the champion, its Organization offered these gangs of thieves a base of operations, when it did not openly place itself at their head. Several public posts were simply a branch of the Organization; its officers, chairmen of committees, etc., unblushiugly combined their duties with federal or State functions.

While the local leaders of the Organization, most of them vulgar spoilsmen, were absorbed in plunder, the great chiefs pulled the strings from Washington, settled the candidatures for the most important posts in the southern States, and made the leaders of these States manoeuvre to suit the requirements of their policy, not knowing exactly, or not wishing to know, what was going on under tho rule of the carpet-baggers. The Republican Organization had to be supported in the South at all costs. The federal government itself, the administration of President Grant, on more than one occasion placed the military at the disposal of the Organization in its election straggles. The most typical case of this kind occurred in Louisiana. The Republican Organization of the State not having succeeded in carrying its candidates at the election of 1872, the defeated candidate for the governorship, Kellog, disputed the validity of the election. A judge who was a friend of his signed an order for the occupation of the legislative building by federal troops, to prevent the members elect of the Legislature from taking their seats. An illegal returning board, a tool of the Republican Organization, proclaimed Kellog Governor, and gave out the names of another set of men as elected to the Legislature; these sham members were the defeated candidates of the Republican convention. The intruders were admitted into the legislative building, and they organized themselves officially. At the same time the two contending parties made most earnest representations to the federal government. The managers of the convention who supported Kellog and his friends telegraphed to the President, stating that if the judge's order were confirmed, it would " save the Republican majority and give Louisiana a Republican Legislature and State government." The attorney-general replied from Washington that the government of the Union recognized Kellog's Legislature and government. The real government of the State telegraphed on its side to Grant, begging him to defer his decision until a committee of citizens arrived in Washington to explain the case. The attorneygeneral replied on the President's behalf that the visit of the delegates would be useless, that the President had made up his mind, and that he would not change it. At the same time Grant sent an order to the officer in command of the troops at New Orleans, bidding him "use all necessary force to preserve the peace and recognize the authority of the Republican governor."

The misdeeds of the Republican Organization exploiting the negro vote soon flung almost all the respectable white population into opposition; the humiliation of being governed by the slaves of yesterday, and of being ruthlessly plundered by their leaders, the carpet-baggers and scalawags, made the whites forget all their political differences, and they united under the flag of the Democratic party, without giving a thought to its principles, but simply because it was the opposite of the Republican party, of the party of the blacks. Without stopping to consider the questions of the day on their merits, they voted invariably for the measures and the candidates of the Democratic party, good or bad. The whole South solidified into this attitude, which got it the nickname of " Solid South," and became a mere appendage of an electoral machine. Political formalism invaded its whole existence. The comparative freedom from party spirit which existed before the war in local elections, and to some extent even in others, disappeared altogether. Party organization, so loose in the South before the war, was made supreme there, together with its system of "regular" nominations. The frame of mind developed in the southerners under the slavery regime naturally inclined them to such a renunciation of private judgment. The institution of slavery, raised to the level of a dogma by its champions, proclaimed a Divine ordinance, held absolute sway over men's minds; every one who ventured to attack it, or even to discuss it, was put beyond the pale, and the terrible consequences of social ostracism stifled the desire for and the habit of free speech. Fostered by the concrete fact of slavery, the subjection of the public mind passed as a legacy to the abstract notion of party which succeeded the slavocracy, and, steeped in the feelings which had created the Solid South, it gave fresh strength and wider scope to the power of "regularity." The whites, intrenched behind the Organization of the Democratic party, had soon succeeded in dislodging the Republicans in the South. They achieved it both by their superior strength of a homogeneous and self-reliant society and by means of electoral frauds or acts of intimidation aimed at the new coloured citizens, and justified in equity by the necessity of preventing "negro domination" to "save civilization." But when the negroes had been reduced *per fas et nefas* to impotence, the Solid South, which arrested the free current of political life in the South, still continued to exist; guard was mounted around it, the politicians watched over it, in order not to lose their situation. Their tribe had grown and multiplied in the South since the close of the Civil War. We have seen them appear on the scene in the form of carpet-baggers, of scalawags, and of subaltern negro politicians all hoisting the Hepublican standard. Soon they installed themselves in the opposite Democratic camp as well. The old leaders of the South, whom the victorious Republicans thought they had dethroned by depriving them of their political rights (which, however, were restored to them in 1872), speedily regained their influence, because they represented at their fullest the passions and the grudges of the conquered, and still possessed the economic supremacy which made even the emancipated negroes in search of a livelihood gravitate towards them. But they could not exert their political influence in the old way after the suffrage was extended and the party Organization system, bringing in a large staff of workers, was developed throughout the country. The old leaders had all the more need of new intermediaries between themselves and the mass of the voters that most of the whites of good position, ruined by the war,!?ave up politics and devoted themselves entirely to retrieving their fortunes. The vacant place was at once taken in the Democratic camp by mercenaries, the number of whom naturally increased after the Democrats got the upper hand again; a good many scalawags who controlled the negroes in the Republican organizations went over to the enemy to "save civilization" threatened by the negroes, that is to say, to make more sure of the spoils. The general pacification and the marvellous economic transformation undergone by the South «lter the war only improved the chances of the professional politicians, by concentrating the vital forces of the country in industry and commerce, and by making its politico-social situation like that of the North. In order not to be disturbed in the enjoyment of the spoils which the Democratic politicians derived from State and municipal offices, and which the Republican politicians found in the federal offices (the federal executive had remained in the hands of the Republicans for twenty years without a break after the war), the politicians made the populations, in spite of the profound changes that had ensued, keep their respective positions, taken up during the troublous times which followed the war. They went on, the one side sounding the alarm against "negro domination," and the other "waving the bloody shirt" of the war waged against the "rebels," to get the faithful followers of the parties to vote at their behest with a *sancta simplicitas.* Having thus helped to create and maintain the "Solid South," the party Organization identified with it the whole Union: it forced people to take up the feud at every point of the territory where there were "Republicans" and "Democrats." The Organization derived additional strength from this situation, as well as from several other effects of the war, which went far beyond the new state of things created in the South.

Ill

The war introduced profound changes into the whole national existence; it imparted a new character to its political, economical, and moral relations, by stamping them all with a common trait, which might be described by the term "inflation," applied specially to one of the effects of the war,—the inordinate extension of paper money. In fact, everything became "inflated,"— the political authority of the Union over the States, trade, manufactures, currency, patriotism, style of living, enthusiasm for the public weal, and exploitation of the public weal. While revealing itself in these manifold aspects, inflation, by a rebound, gave an extraordinary impulse to party organization.

The political life of the Union was marked by an excessive development of centralization. In the first place, the issue of the war, which in itself was a struggle between State rights, — between the right of the States to have such institutions as they liked,— and the sovereignty of the Union, was the triumph of the principle of centralization. The "imperial spirit" which the federal government continued to display after the war was over, and in particular the measures of "reconstruction" of the South under the military regime set up by the victors in the subdued States, converted the principle into a fact. The amendments of the Constitution, which enlarged the jurisdiction of Congress over the States, and the laws passed in pursuance of these amendments (as well as the decisions of the Supreme Court of the United States), added the sanction of law to the reality of the fact. The development of the public services of the Union, caused by the new financial requirements and by the extension of the federal jurisdiction, gave the Washington government a number of new officials; distributed over the States, they linked them to the centre. Economic life exhibited a still greater concentration and fusion. The extension given to railroads and telegraphs made distances of no account, and did away with the comparative isolation in which the populations of the States had hitherto lived. The great industrial undertakings created by a colossal combination of small capital, and reaching from one end of the Union to the other, united the inhabitants of the different States in common interests. Thus, in public life and in the economic sphere, the citizen, began to feel himself more and more a small part of a great whole;

his personality was gradually dwindling. The military discipline enforced during the four years of a war which had been waged, not with a foreign enemy, but with an adverse political party, inflicted a no less serious blow on the individualism of the citizen. It accustomed one set to passive obedience, the other to command, and, as it were, lent sanction in civil life to the ideas of Aaron Burr, the great protagonist of electoral organization, who held that voters should be drilled like soldiers in an army.

Side by side with the authoritative spirit and the centralization which penetrated into political life, and the concentration which pervaded the economic sphere, there took place in the latter an unprecedented expansion of forces and activities, which, in its turn, contributed to the moral decline of the citizen. Manufactures and commerce advanced by leaps and bounds on the establishment, for the requirements of the war, of high customs duties, which stimulated home production, and owing to abundant issues of paper currency, which caused an apparent plethora of money. Restored, after the close of hostilities, to peaceful avocations, the population plunged, with an ardour all the greater that it had long been restrained and impeded by the anxieties of the war, into the pursuit of wealth, of money-making. Taking advantage of the fluctuations in the value of paper money, speculation invaded everything; soon there was no limit to it. Money was made with surprising facility, and was spent still more easily. Tastes and appetites were freely indulged in. Everybody contracted expensive habits of living; people thought they could afford anything; the idea of the value of money was lost to a certain extent. And along with the common measure of material things, the notion of moral worth grew dim as well. Success, or the craving for success, seemed to justify everything. Besides, people had. no time to waste in scrutinizing acts and men from an ethical point of view; they were too much engrossed in the frantic race for wealth.

To this coarse materialism was added the unbounded enthusiasm aroused by the war. Enormous sacrifices had been made to save the Union, millions of slaves had been given their liberty, blood had been "shed like water" without hesitation; people were conscious of this, they prided themselves on it; they got drunk v.ith patriotism all the more readily and sincerely because it better concealed the decline of the national character. And to turn this patriotism to account, the feelings which it inspired were invested, so to speak, in the party of the Union,— the Republican party, — like a capital to be kept intact and left to fructify; all the moral enthusiasm accumulated in the struggle was deposited with the party, and party feeling increased in volume. Powerful enough before the war, it was already almost a superstition; now it became a passion. Engendered by conventionality and selfish rivalries, it cast off its impurities in the crucible of civil war and appeared in a sort of ideal glow. It burned with a flame which was unceasingly rekindled on both sides by the blast of the Solid South. The Republican party became holy in the eyes of its adherents, like a living image of the country; all who were not traitors to the Union and to humanity were bound to be with it. The Democratic party became all the more endeared to its followers. This *inflation* of party feeling, far from making up for the civic shrinkage produced by the manifold currents of centralization and by industrial expansion, which had created a pernicious moral atmosphere and absorbed individual energies, only delivered the citizen more effectually, bound hand and foot, into the power of the party embodied in its Organization. The latter could exploit the civic indolence, as well as trade on party fanaticism, in a way it had never been able to do before.

While the moral sources of its influence got extended, the Organization secured improvements in its machinery in the direction of centralization, which increased its material hold on the mass of voters. About the year 1866 a central committee was created at Washington, to control throughout the Union the elections to the House of Representatives, which had hitherto been left to the local organizations. It was composed of members of Congress appointed by their colleagues of the same party (in the proportion of one member to each State), and in this way it revived to a certain extent the old congressional Caucus, which, however, only looked after the presidential elections. The new central organ, called the Congressional Campaign Committee, in watching the electoral situation in the congressional districts, penetrated more deeply and more continuously into local political life than could be done by the permanent committee of the national convention, which made its appearance on the eve of, and solely in view of, the presidential election. Again, in the States the local permanent Organization, represented by standing committees appointed by the conventions, evolved small executive committees, which absorbed all the election work to such an extent that the role of the large committees became a purely nominal one. Finally? in the very large cities, like New York and Philadelphia, the ties which bound the followers of the party were drawn closer by means of permanent associations. Before this the Organization of the party called the voters together for the special occasion only, for the election of delegates to the convention, but when this duty was accomplished, the members of the primaries melted away into the mass of citizens, like their delegates to the conventions, which in fact were only temporary gatherings of the adherents of the party. The growth of the population in the large centres, stimulated by the industrial expansion, and the eminently fluctuating character of this population, made it more and more difficult to keep up party ties there. By regularly enrolling their adherents in associations, in great political clubs, the Organization got the elements of the primaries and the conventions ready to hand, as well as the voters who were to vote on election day for the candidates adopted at those conventions. Elsewhere the first grade of the Organization was also put on a more solid footing, owing to the very centralization which, favoured by the exceptional extension of railroads and the telegraph, knit all the parts of the Organization more strongly together. While becoming more than ever the groundwork of the system, the primary meetings remained, none the less, more than ever devoid of spontaneous and genuine life. The absolute power of the small cliques of managers, who settled everything behind the scenes, was such a common thing with them, that the old appellation of Caucus, in the sense of secret meeting, of cabal, was revived and applied in everyday language to the primaries, either term being used indifferently, and finally extended to the whole system of the representative party organization, of which the primaries were the basis, under the name of "caucus system." The professional politicians, who filled the Organization at all its stages, executed their movements, under the direction of the managers and the wirepullers, with such uniformity and with such indifference or insensibility to right and wrong, and operated with such unerring certainty on the electorate, that they evoked the idea of a piece of mechanism working automatically and blindly, — of a machine. The effect appeared so precisely identical that the term "Machine" was bestowed on the Organization as a nickname, which it bears down to the present day, even in preference to that of "Caucus." IV . The new powers, both of a moral and material kind, which the Organization derived from the situation created by the Civil War, enabled it to take the whole electorate in tow. Having thus come into possession of the electoral monopoly, the Organization could all the more easily thrust itself on the government, and especially on the executive, which disposed of the places in the Federal service required by the Organization for feeding its machine. Since the introduction of the spoils' system, the Organization had always pressed heavily on the exercise of the presidential patronage. Now it was about to strip the executive completely of this prerogative, and the latter was in too weak a state to resist. This weakness was due to a multiplicity of causes, some of them developed by the Caucus and the party system, the others lurking in the economy of the constitutional fabric set up by the founders of the Republic. The first source of the President's inferiority lay in his own origin, in the mode of his election: he owed it to the Organization of the party; it was a convention of its delegates which had nominated him, having taken him, perhaps, out of obscurity; the innumerable committees of this Organization had worked up the electorate to vote for him; in short, he was its creature. Could he forget this in power? had he not contracted obligations to its leaders, even without having entered into any explicit engagement? How, indeed, could he turn his back on the men who had fought hard for the White House on his behalf, who had made personal and pecuniary sacrifices to ensure his triumph? We have already seen Lincoln, when grappling with this fatal situation, give in on more than one occasion, at a time when he enjoyed the highest power ever wielded by a chief magistrate in a republic with free institu VOL. II—K tions. It is therefore not surprising that the successors of the great President should not have exhibited more firmness. The anxiety about re-election, which haunts almost every President in his first term, could not but increase their conciliatoriness towards the local leaders of the Organization. But personal obligations were not the only ones which the President contracted towards them. The party system, which had made its way into the government behind the back of the Constitution, and which was developed and intensified by the Caucus, made the President a party chief, or a trustee, who, on entering the White House, received the fortunes of the party as a deposit. As the party's success at the elections depended on the efficiency of the Organization, the President had to take good care not to weaken the latter, not to damp the zeal and ardour of the numerous workers who led the electoral troops. Consequently when, after the battle, a local leader requested the President to give his lieutenants places available under the rotation system, and for which he had already pledged himself to them, the President had no alternative but to comply; for if he refused, he ruined the political credit of the local leaders, as well as the chances of the party in the district.

But even if he wished to rise above personal calculations and party preoccupations, and take refuge in the letter and the spirit of the Constitution, this was of no avail, for it was there, within the four corners of the Constitution, that the managers of the Organization were on the watch for him; they guarded all the approaches to it. The scheme of the Constitution, which, for the better protection of liberty, had organized the great branches of government,— the legislative, the executive, and the judiciary,— as co-ordinate powers counterbalancing each other, was warped in practice. The separation Lincoln himself admitted his powerlessness as regards the party. The following is a still more characteristic remark of his than that related by Julian, and quoted above: During his first presidency a member of Congress, one Jones, had got a certain Smith appointed postmaster in the chief town of his district. Subsequently, having a personal ground of complaint against him, he asked Lincoln to turn him out. "And I must turn him out," said the President to one of his friends. "I don't want to, but I must, — there is no help for it. " To which his friend replied, " Are you President, or is Jones President?" "Jones is President," answered Lincoln promptly. (*Nation* of New York, 1872, Vol. XV, p. 69.) of powers, which was to ensure the object aimed at, was the primary cause of its failure. On the strength of a mistaken interpretation of the English Constitution by Montesquieu, the principle of the separation of powers was introduced into America and was enforced there in the direction of absolute separation. Although they had laid the foundation for it, the authors of the Constitution, some of whom, and those the most eminent, had seen through the mistake of the *Esprit des Lois,* had refrained from pushing to extreme lengths the separation of the public powers in regard to their mutual relations. But under the influence of the prejudice created by the false doctrine, that separation was soon accentuated and completed by the abolition of direct relations between the executive and the legislative; in pursuance of a custom which obtained the force of law, the President and his ministers communicated with Congress in writing only. However, the more the Union developed, the more complex its political life grew, the less possible did it become for the legislative and the executive to act separately or at a distance from each other, the sphere over which their operations extended, that of the interests of the country, being one and indivisible. Whether it was about legislation or for the annual appropriations of the budget, the executive had to confer and treat with the legislative, and the partition set up by the Constitution fell down under the irresistible pressure of realities. But as they were not able to meet in public, the representatives of the two powers were obliged to negotiate and bargain privately, in corners, and in these encounters the legislative, armed from head to foot through its power of adopting or rejecting bills, was always at an advantage. The controlling supervision of public opinion, which was unrepresented at these meetings, bore upon the legislative all the less that the latter's organization had undergone a practical revolution, in pursuance of which the activity of Congress became concentrated in a number of secret committees, which prepared all the business of the public sittings to such an extent as to make them a mere form. In fact, in certain specified cases the Constitution had deviated from the principle of the separation of powers by making the ratification 1 *Ct. The Federalist,* No. XLVII. of treaties and of appointments to the more important offices subject to the approval of the Senate. But the effect described of the separation of powers was only further accentuated by this enforced co-operation, which gave the legislative a formal hold over the executive, and all the more irresistible because the sittings, even the plenary ones, of the Senate devoted to the cousideration of the presidential proposals relating to treaties and appointments (executive sessions) were (and still are) secret.

Closely pressed on various sides by the legislative, the executive was obliged to yield, and, in order to live, was reduced to purchasing the support of the members of Congress with the favours at its disposal. Towards the middle of this century this practice became a regular one, and Pierce and Buchanan bought legislation like an article of commerce with the places which they distributed to the *protigis* of the Senators and the Representatives. To the organic weakness of the position was added that of the men who filled it; the convention system made it impossible, apart from chance, for men of strong character to attain to the chief magistracy; for in the words of Benton, quoted above, "The man they choose must always be a character of no force, that they may rule him. " After the war, the prestige and the independence of the President suffered a fresh eclipse. The conflict of Congress with President Johnson, which culminated in the impeachment of the President, was a long series of mortifications and humiliations for him. Before this supreme ordeal Congress took from him, by the law of Tenure of Office of 1867 (repealed twenty years later), the right of dismissing officials whose appointment was subject to the approval of the Senate. The President could only suspend officials in and for the duration of the parliamentary recess. The officials whom he wished to turn out remained in thoir offices until the persons whom he selected to replace them were confirmed by the Senate. Johnson's successor, General Grant, borne into the White House by his military glory, personally enjoyed an immense popularity which might have emancipated him from the politicians, but his utter inexperience in civil business and his want of discernment in the choice of men placed him at the mercy of the leaders of Congress, who were only too ready to trade upon his weakness. Thus, by a combination of divers causes and circumstances, the executive gradually declined and the legislative obtained the ascendency.

But at the same time the latter in its turn lost its proper character, and became the stronghold of the leaders of the party Organization. The seats in Congress being the highest electoral prize that could be won, with the assistance of the Organization, its local managers naturally coveted them for themselves, and when the Machine acquired the strength which enabled it to operate with certainty, it systematically placed them in these important elective positions. Or — to put the same thing in another way, considering the situation created by the development of the Caucus in a somewhat different aspect — access to elective offices being possible only with the assistance of the Machine, the men who attained to the highest of them, such as seats in Congress, were almost always those who wielded the greatest influence in the local organizations. They were, therefore, the persons to reap the benefit of the superiority gained by the legislative over the executive. Deriving strength from the latter's weakness, the managers of the Organization, disguised as members of Congress, forced the executive to make over the whole federal patronage to them. Besides, the impossibility of the federal administration, with no local organs of its own, deciding by itself on the appointments necessitated by the periodical rotation of an ever increasing number of offices, had at an early stage paved the way for this encroachment on the part of Congress. Often perplexed by the host of applications from the office-seekers, the administration, even before the Civil War, used to consult the respective members of Congress, who were supposed to be better informed as to the merits of the local competitors. Lincoln, engrossed by the cares of the war, systematically referred to them for all appointments to local offices; he did little more than countersign the selections made by the Representatives or the Senators.

After the war the eclipse of the executive was complete and definitive, and the members of Congress entered so thoroughly into the part of dispensers of patronage, which they had assumed, that they considered it as a right, as a prerogative, of their position. Foremost among those who enjoyed this privilege came the Senators, to whom their constitutional power, as well as the special prestige attaching to their capacity of representatives of sovereign States, gave more influence. They regularly took in hand the distribution of offices in their States. If the district was represented in the popular branch of Congress by a member of the party in power, it was he who disposed of the offices to be given away in that district; if not, they reverted to the Senators (or the single Senator of the party in power, if the second Senator belonged to the opposition); the higher offices of the State fell in any event to its Senators, whose decision was final. The Senate, which, under the terms of the Constitution, was entrusted with the duty of confirming by a majority the important presidential appointments, had admitted, by the unwritten law of the "courtesy of the Senate," the exclusive right of the Senators of each State to approve or reject the proposals of the President relating to their State; consequently all the other Senators concurred with their colleague without looking into the case. This procedure being a settled thing, the President made himself ridiculous if he ignored the recommendations of the Senators; it was better to accept them with a good grace, that is to say, send to the Senate only lists submitted beforehand by the Senators interested. In practice this state of affairs admitted of a good many exceptions, but, generally speaking, it amounted to the President having the signature and the Senator the choice. When this result was achieved, the Machine and the spoils' system entered on a new phase; from more or less disguised plunder, the division of the spoils became a sort of public service, in which the Senator, as leader or representative of the local Machine, was made, as it were, receiver and paymaster general for the State, with district receivers in the persons of his lieutenants. Thus all the threads of the extraconstitutional party organizations converged in the Senate of the United States; this citadel of the Constitution became their nervous centre.

V

Such was the situation when Grant took up his abode in the White House. His immense prestige, and the unbounded con tidence of the Republican masses who had carried him into power, could do nothing against it. After a few half-hearted attempts at resistance, he became its accomplice. Public opinion being drugged, as it were, the executive reduced to impotence, and the legislative captured by the Organization, the latter came out all the more boldly; it allowed freer scope than ever to the mercenary contingents which filled its ranks, and started on a new era of scandals and corruption in public life, which recalled and surpassed the worst days of Jackson. The practices of rotation and division of the spoils were never before carried to such a pitch. The heads of the departments, with a few highly honourable exceptions, handed them over to the Organization of the party. To provide places for its creatures, a clean sweep of officials was carried out, amid a hurricane of intrigue and delation. The degradation of the public service, which was very considerable before Grant, reached its height. Filled with men who were often disreputable and incompetent, it became a veritable hotbed of corruption. The shameless nepotism in which the President himself, honest as he was, indulged, and the pernicious influence of those about him, to which he was amenable, contributed not a little to this result, but the greater part of it was due to the Organization, whose sole anxiety was to put its own men in office and screen them to the utmost of its power. It was under the aegis of the Organization, when not with the connivance or the complicity of its representatives, that the traffic in public functions, the waste of public money, the frauds in the collection of the government revenue, which marked Grant's Presidency, were committed, especially during his second term. Never did the government show its intimacy with the wirepullers more openly. Generally they had kept behind the scenes, formed "kitchen The terms in which contemporaries refer to this are almost identical with the language quoted above, describing the reign of terror in the departments at Washington after the advent to power of Jackson. "Every clerk," said a writer six months after Grant's accession, "distrusted his neighbor, and the air of the Treasury, which in ordinary times is not altogether pure, now seemed heavy with the whisper of delators. The new administration began its career by creating or encouraging in its service the same system of spies and secret denunciation which is usually charged as the crowning disgrace of an absolute despotism " *(North American Review,* October, 1869, p. 455, " Civil Service Reform ").

cabinets." Now the foremost dignitary of the Caucus, the Chairman of the National Committee, Mr. Chandler, publicly combined this post with that of Secretary of the Interior, and it was not to this latter that he gave the best of his time and energy. As we have seen, the administration even placed the military at the disposal of the Organization, in the South, to "strengthen the party." The government shielded the Organization, and the latter did the same for the government. At the expiration of Grant's first term all the State conventions rose for him as one man, and in the national convention he was renominated unanimously.

"And public opinion, in the main, did not protest; it made no sign, hypnotized by the imaginary dangers which threatened the Union from the "rebel" South. "Men went on fearing the dead lions of secession and slavery more than the living dogs of political corruption." With Grant in power, people were at all events sure that the order of things established by his victories would not be impugned; and then, business was not bad, money was easily made. This attitude of public opinion, half anxious and half indifferent, allowed the influence of the Machine in the party to take the form of a regular despotism, although it was becoming less and less representative of the party. The official party shed from head to foot the eminent or merely disinterested citizens, who, after having been brought into the held by the great slavery crisis, returned peaceably to their homes, or, which was the case with a small elite, openly broke with the official party, sickened by the scandals which it exhibited. The most high-minded and illustrious of the Republican leaders, the Charles Sumners, the Schurzs, the Trumbulls, the Cabinet ministers who were honest and opposed to the Machine, the Coxes, the Hoars, the Bristows, withdrew or were thrust on one side by the clique which surrounded Grant. The official party divested itself of everything that resembled principles, ideas, or ideals, and left the Organization only the mercenary element. Towards the close of Grant's second Presidency the separation of this element represented by the Machine from the great mass of 1Geo. S. Merriam, *The Life and Times of Samuel Bowles,* N.Y., 1885, Vol. II, p. 87.
the adherents of the party who met only on the day of the elections to cast a common vote, appeared complete.

Grant's successor, Hayes, who got in at the national convention as a dark horse, proved a thoroughly honest man. Accepting the presidential nomination, he declared himself an opponent of the spoils' system: "It ought to be abolished. The reform should be thorough, radical, and complete." Promising to "use all the constitutional powers conferred on the executive to pass this reform," and holding that it might be "best accomplished by an executive who is under no temptation to use the patronage of his office to promote his own re-election," he announced beforehand that he would not be a candidate for a second term. Hayes was elected (in 1876), and set to work resolutely to carry out his promises. But thereupon most of the leaders of the party which brought him into power, the managers of the Organization, rose up against him. During the election campaign they had fought for him withoiit formally endorsing his programme; they made no comment on his protests and promises, considering them perhaps as a good bait for catching the votes of the credulous. But when they saw that the President was in earnest, their state of mind was one of stupefaction and revolt. Hayes tried to strike at the corrupt officials, imposed and supported by the Caucus, and to bring about a formal separation of the officeholders from the Organization, which was full of them. To put an end to the scandalous promiscuity existing between the two, he passed an order forbidding federal office-holders to take part in the management of political organizations, caucuses, conventions, or election campaigns. The Machine took up this order as a challenge, and its trusty friends, three leading officials in New York, seriously compromised in the corrupt practices of which this city was a hotbed, and reduced thereby to the alternative of resignation or dismissal, had the audacity to openly defy the President. They got themselves elected delegates to the State convention, and one of them, Mr. Cornell, even procured his appointment to the most militant post in the Organization, that of Chairman of the State Committee. Hayes was forbearing enough to offer these rebellious officials compensation if they would give up the offices in which they had compromised themselves. After waiting in vain for their resignations, he dismissed them. But for the appointment of their successors the President was obliged, under the Constitution, to obtain the consent of the Senate, and it was there that the men of the Machine were on the lookout for him. At the instigation of the head of the Organization of New York and Senator of this State, Roscoe Conkling, who had stirred up the revolt against the presidential order there, the Senate, of which he was one of the most influential leaders, rejected the presidential nominations. The dismissed officials remained in office, under the law passed by Congress at the time of its conflict with Johnson, which had deprived the President of the absolute right of dismissal of officials appointed with the confirmation of the Senate. In the next session of Congress Hayes sent up his candidates again, to meet with a fresh rejection, and it was not till the third session, after more than a year of private negotiation with Senators, and humble entreaties, that the administration succeeded, and even then thanks to the help of Democratic Senators, in definitively getting rid of the three unfaithful New York officials. Hayes lost heart and began to give way. Making use of his constitutional right of veto he still struggled with the Senate, in which, moreover, his party was no longer in a majority, but he did not succeed in purifying the public service and in freeing the executive from the power of the Machine; he submitted to it, though with somewhat less docility. For one good appointment he made two bad ones, under the pressure exercised by it. During his administration there were far fewer scandals than under Grant; the behaviour of the Organization became more decent. The most sympathetic judges claimed that "the oil of the Machine was of a better quality and had no offensive odor," but they could not gainsay the stubborn fact that the Machine was still in full swing. And then, it must in fairness be added that Hayes himself brought fuel to it by rewarding the services rendered to him at the presidential election, which had been so hotly contested, although he had not bargained with the agents of See the letters of the Secretary of the Treasury, John Sherman, to the Senators Allison and,J. Morill, quoted in *The Last Quarter Century in the United States,* by E. B. Andrews, Lond., 1897, Vol. I, p. 246.

» *Nation,* Vol. XXVI, p. 164.

the Organization. It was all very well to forego re-election and dispense with their help for the future, but he could not escape from the debt which he owed them for the past.

Edified by Hayes' experience, his successor, Garfield, showed no intention of taking the bestowal of offices out of the hands of members of Congress. But while lending himself to the spoils' system, he provoked, from his very accession, the violent animosity of the famous Roscoe Conkling by the way in which he interpreted the division of the spoils. The conflict which broke out between the President and the Senator, and which offered the public the rich treat of a big political scandal, was chiefly remarkable for the evidence it supplied of the lengths to which the insolent pretensions of the powerful Machine leaders could go. The new President, desirous of ingratiating himself with all the factions of the party in the State of New York, made a few appointments without reference to, or even against the wish of, Roscoe Conkling, who, however, was not forgotten. But Conkling considered the fact of not having taken his advice and obtained his consent for the appointments in question as a breach of faith on the part of the President, and he called on him to mend his ways. On Garfield's refusing, Conkling wanted to play the old game of 1877 by asking the Senate to reject the candidates submitted by the President, but the assembly would not follow him on this occasion. Conkling looked on this as a flagrant violation, at his expense, of the rule of the "courtesy of the Senate," and he appealed from the President and the Senate to his electors. He and his trusty colleague of the State of New York sent in their resignations; they were not re-elected. But in the meanwhile the appetites aroused by the spoils brought about a far more serious collision; among the horde of office-seekers who invaded Washington, expecting more, it would appear, from Garfield than from his predecessor, one, being disappointed or having lost patience, assassinated the President. This tragic death surrounded him with the halo of a martyr for the cause of the emancipation of the public service from the politicians, which he had not had the time or the strength of will to embrace, and won over public opinion to it better than years of political propaganda could have done. The shock given to opinion helped to make Congress pass a law which withdrew from the favouritism of the administration, or, what came to the same tiling, from the exigencies of members of Congress, a certain number of offices by having them filled by competitive examinations. This reform, carried in 1883, was the starting-point of an important movement in the political life of the United States, as will be seen in a subsequent chapter, where the subject will be fully dealt with, but it could not restore the free use of the presidential prerogative in regard to appointments and cancel the encroachments of the Congressmen. Meanwhile, it is enough to point out that the appointments for which the President has to obtain the confirmation of the Senate have not been affected by the new law, the intervention of the Senate in these cases being prescribed by the Constitution.

For the moment the actual effect produced by the awakening of public opinion was to detach enough supporters from the Republican Organization to ptit an end to the monopoly of power which it had enjoyed for nearly a quarter of a century, and bring into the Presidency, under the Democratic flag, a man of undaunted courage and incorruptible honesty, Mr. Grover Cleveland. But the career of this President even, which shed such a lustre on the independent exercise of the executive power, gave the best possible proof of how difficult, not to say impossible, it was for the President, in the state of things described above, to curb the Organization of the party. In spite of the purity of his intentions, upheld by an indomitable will, Cleveland was not able, especially during his first Presidency, to free himself either from personal obligations to the Organization, or from the anxiety of maintaining the strength of the party of which the Organization made itself the caretaker, or from the necessities imposed by the constitutional relations between the President and Congress, and exploited by the Organization in its own interest. Cleveland was by no means a mere tool of the spoils' system and rotation; he made several excellent appointments without a thought of party, but he none the less changed the greater part of the federal office-holders, of course putting Democrats into the place of dismissed Republicans. In doing this he showed himself far more scrupulous than his predecessors, but among the appointments made by him there were some scandalous ones in the literal sense of the word. He made them with reluctance, but still he made them. For instance, in the State of Maryland he appointed to important posts, at the bidding of the Machine, persons taken from among its creatures, some of whom were real criminals, and of the worst kind. The reason was that the head of the Democratic Machine in Maryland, one of the most questionable politicians in the whole Union, was the chairman of the national committee which conducted the presidential campaign on behalf of Cleveland, and he was besides Senator of the State in the Congress of the United States. In this triple capacity he was too strong even for a Cleveland, so much so that the President, replying to the indignant protests of the respectable citizens of Baltimore, told them that he could not help it, for if he refused the candidates of Mr. Gorman, the Senator in question, the latter would revenge himself by getting the Senate to reject his appointments; or, again, he urged them to summon a mass-meeting to protest against the appointments which he had made at the request of the said Senator. By a strongly worded circular (of the 14th of July, 1886), Mr. Cleveland revived President Hayes' order forbidding federal office-holders to engage in active party politics, to take part in the management of caucuses and conventions, etc. But this circular remained a dead letter, at least as regards the Democratic office-holders; it simply served as a pretext for turning out a number of officials of Republican origin whom the administration had found in office. Public opinion, more keenly opposed under Cleveland than under his predecessors to the spoils' system, was not sufficiently so to intimidate the Machines and their representatives in Congress. In regard to great economic problems, such as the currency and customs-duties, which directly affected the material well-being of the masses and kept their susceptibilities on the alert, the President made a brave fight of it with the factious Senate, especially during his second term (1893-1897). When it was a question of appointments to offices, this bellicose ardour cooled down, was tempered by mutual concessions. Made on both sides with a bad grace, and, perhaps, laboriously negotiated, they Cf. L. B. Swift, "Civil Service Reform: A Review of Two Administrations." *Forum,* Vol. XIV, p. 205.

vindicated neither the prerogatives of the President nor the interests of the public service.

The Republican President who filled the Democratic interregnum between Mr. Cleveland's first and seQond Presidency,"' Mr. Benjamin Harrison, had no occasion even to try his strength with the Machine. If he ventured to defy anything, it was public opinion, indignant at seeing the President, in violation of his promises as candidate, revert to the worst traditions of the spoils' system. In the space of one year, thirty thousand employees of the postal department were changed, for no other reason than that given by the postmaster of a town to the postmen whom he discharged: "You have done your work well. You are gentlemen, but you know, boys, you are Democrats." The prostitution of public offices to the party and its myrmidons reached its highest pitch by spreading to the cabinet itself, which was put up to auction, as it were; the proprietor of a large dry-goods store in Philadelphia was rewarded with a post in the cabinet for having supplied the committee that conducted the presidential campaign with a considerable sum of money, a great part of which was notoriously employed in purchasing votes. A precedent was created, and similar things occurred under each of the subsequent administrations. Mr. Cleveland's second administration appointed to an embassy in Europe an individual whose sole claim was the payment of $50,000 to the election fund. In face of the outcry caused by this appointment, the extemporized diplomatist sent in his resignation. Four years afterwards, when Mr. McKinley's Cabinet was being formed, the choice which he made for the post of Secretary of War was attributed to a heavy money contribution towards the presidential campaign, which unfortunately could not make up for the flagrant incompetence exhibited by this minister during the war with Spain, and then with the Filipinos, in which the Republic soon got itself entangled.

The general attitude of Mr. McKinley towards the spoils' system was anything but revolutionary. Taught by the experience of his predecessor, Mr. Cleveland, he wished above all things to live in peace with the Senate and his party, and from the very beginning he resigned his power of appointing to offices in favour of the members of Congress as meekly and as completely as if the practice were formally prescribed by the Constitution. He made it a rule to simply countersign the appointments recommended by the Senators who represented the party, making good ones if the Senators acting for the Machine proposed them, and bad or detestable ones if the selections made by the Senators were bad or detestable. Thanks' to this conduct, the President now in office established a unique record; of the three thousand appointments submitted by him to the Senate during the first twenty months of his Presidency, not one was rejected. Thus, in the thirty years which elapsed after the Civil War, the state of things which made members of Congress representing the party Organization the dispensers of federal patronage has become rather confirmed than otherwise.

VI

The federal officers, who in reality held their places from the members of Congress, were of course at their mercy, and in the election campaigns they placed all their influence at their disposal, made themselves their most zealous agents. But soon the Caucus was not satisfied with these personal exertions, with these *corvies;* it completed the formula of the *Ancien Rigime* in their case and at their expense by turning them into *des taillables et corviahles d, merci.* All the officials were made liable to a direct and proportional tax for the benefit of the Organization. The practice originated before the Civil War. It crept in at first, under Democratic administrations, during the decade 1840-1850, timidly and slowly. The operations attending the levy of this singular tribute were wrapped in secrecy, and the Press of the party thought it its duty to deny them. In the course of the next decade they increased to a great extent, and under Buchanan they were already thoroughly established. But it was left to the Republican Machine, after the war, to bring the contribution, or rather extortion, system to perfection. The Machine did *Conservative Exsays, Legal and Political,* by S. S. Nicholas, Philad., 1863, pp. 601,502. "Politii-al Assessments," by Dorm an B. Eaton *(North American Review,* September, 1882, p. 201!).

so with perfect calmness and unconcern. Considering that the officials appointed by the administration or elected by the people held their places from itself, the Organization was of opinion that they *owed* it the interest of the capital thus placed at their disposal. The Congressional Campaign Committee, founded about 1866, inaugurated the new era by putting the practice in force with the regularity of a government budget. It demanded from the federal office-holders throughout the Union a percentage on their salaries as a contribution euphemistically described as "voluntary." The local Organizations adopted the same system, and before long there were as many as five categories of "assessments" inflicted on the hapless employees, — federal, State, municipal, ward, and district,— and often they were taxed by more than one committee.

The ostensible object of these assessments was to defray the expenses of the election campaign, such as outlay for printing, postage, and other lawful disbursements. Part of the money collected was really used for this purpose, but most of it fouud another destination, where no check could be applied; it went to corrupt voters and to local managers of the Machine and their "workers." The reason alleged for making the assessed pay up was the necessity of preventing the accession to power of the opposite party, which would turn them out and give their places to its adherents. But the fear of being removed by their own party or of spoiling their chances of promotion, if they refused to contribute, acted with more force on the office-holders, and they submitted to the exaction, which was often rather considerable and extremely heavy for the small employees. The fear was not an idle one; there were, in fact, under Grant's first Presidency, many cases of dismissal of refractory individuals, especially in the State of New York, which, as usual when a means of corruption was to the fore, adopted the system of assessments in all its fulness. Restrained by the disapprobation of public opinion, the Machine men after a while no longer ventured to get people turned " Removals for neglect to pay were remorseless. In the sixteen months from 1869, Grinuel, as Collector of New York, removed 510 out of his 892 subordinates: and Murphy, his successor, in about the same length of time removed 338" (the article by D. B. Eaton quoted above).

out, but they none the less attained their object through the fear which their influence on the appointments inspired. The assessments were demanded in the federal service with exemplary persistency, enhanced by the cruel irony of the wording of the circulars sent by the committees to their victims "You will esteem it both a privilege and a pleasure to make a contribution." The percentage exacted from the officials was sometimes calculated on the basis of a figure several times higher than their real emoluments, the committee supposing that the holder of the office made far more out of it by illicit means, and that he owed the party a proportional royalty. Neither pecuniary position, nor age, nor sex, found mercy with the collectors of the committees. Every one who figured on the pay-roll of a public department was put under contribution, — office-boys, dock-labourers, washerwomen, not to mention schoolmasters and schoolmistresses. The collecting agents of the Organization pursued the employees even into their offices, prowled about the lobbies of the government departments, receipt-book in hand, and lay in wait for the wretched tribute-payers, especially on pay-day. As a rule the Organization of the Republican party in power could count on the indifference or even the connivance of the government. Grant and his successor, Hayes, had, it is true, issued orders prohibiting the payment of assessments, but they remained a dead letter. The Presidents were perfectly sincere, but their ministers were not so. No less a personage than John Sherman, Secretary of the Treasury under Hayes, declared that he "had no objection to the government A curious correspondence took place on this subject between the treasurer of the Republican Organization and General Barlow, from whom he demanded a thousand dollars of " voluntary contribution," although the general's salary made him liable only to a payment of 8120. Barlow sent a cheque for jSl'20, declaring that, as an honest man, he got only the §(,000 assigned to his office. The treasurer sent him back the cheque *(Nation,* 17th November, 1870). In New York, during the presidential campaign of 1SH0, even the policemen were fleeced, a thing which appeared all the more difficult that they held their appointments from a municipal board composed of members of the two parties, and that consequently they could defy the threats of dismissal coming from either side. The Organization got over the difficulty: the committees of the two parties combined and addressed a collective demand for assessments to the policemen. The latter could only pay up. The money levied was shared between the two rival Machiues. Vol. ii — *L* employees making contributions to the fund." The Congressional Committee was therefore quite within the mark in saying, in a circular sent out on the eve of the presidential election of 1880, that "the Committee was authorized to state that such voluntary contributions from persons employed in the service of the United States would not be objected to in any official quarter." And better still, State committees of the Organization asked the chiefs of employees in arrears to help them in collecting the assessments, sent them lists of these persons, whom they described as "delinquents," with the amounts "due" by them.

Under the pressure of public opinion, which as time went on became less tolerant of these abuses, the law of 1883, already referred to, providing for admission to the federal service by competitive examination, tried to cure the evil of political assessments by prohibiting them under penalties. It forbade Senators, Representatives, and office-holders to ask for and receive "contributions," and every one generally to apply for or collect them in the offices, buildings, or precincts where the employees are on duty. The same penalties of fine and imprisonment were enacted against officials dismissing, degrading, or promoting subordinates, or threatening them with or promising the same, for refusal or consent to pay assessments. This law checked the evil, but was very far from putting an end to it. It gave a good many inferior officials courage to resist, and made a good many superior ones disinclined to ask for assessments on behalf of the party Organization. But very often the letter and the spirit of the law were openly and grossly violated, both in the departments at Washington and in the country. The habit had become too inveterate a one, and was kept alive by the spoils' system, which was still in force. Besides, the law, even if strictly observed, did not prevent agents of the Organization who were not members of Congress or federal office-holders from demanding assessments; they could no longer carry on their operations in the very *Nation,* October, 1879, p. 249.

See in the eleventh *Report of the United States Civil Service Commission,* Washington, 1895, Part III: "Investigations of alleged violations of the Civil Service law from 1889 to 1895," that is to say after a lapse of time which allowed the law of 1883 to be tested. offices of the public departments, but they could perfectly well, and they did, pursue their victims into their homes, or even get at them in their offices by correspondence, for a circular of the Attorney-General of the Union (of 1894) has admitted that the law forbids only personal applications in the offices.

The assessments levied on the office-holders found a counterpart in the contributions demanded from candidates for election. The prejudice, or the principle, it that expression is preferred, of "regularity" having made it impossible for any aspirant to an elective office to come before the electors without the introduction of a party Organization, which confers the stamp of regular candidate, the Machines found themselves able to apply the practice of assessments to candidates with even greater success and certainty than to office-holders. The candidates paid the respective Organization a sum fixed by its committee, in return for which the latter put them on its list, that is to say, gave them the nomination of the party, and, of course, pledged itself to do its utmost to ensure their return on election day. The pretext of election expenses, on which assessments were demanded from office-holders, was a more plausible one in the case of candidates, and they had always contributed more or less to the party funds; but before the war these contributions were fairly moderate, sometimes even extremely small. In the South where, in the absence of the Machine, the individual commanded the support of the voters by his social position and his personal merit, especially his eloquence, election expenses hardly existed at all. With the development of the Machine the pecuniary contributions of the candidates were made strictly compulsory, and raised to exorbitant figures, which often exceeded the total of what the office aspired to could bring in, at least by fair means. In the large cities, with New York at their head, practice established a sort of tariff for each set of offices, according to the length of the term and the importance of the place. Thus a judge *i Ibid.,* p. 116.

Cf. the figures given by W. P. Fishback, *A Plea for Honest Electiont,* Indianapolis, 1886. In 1860, Yancey, speaking at New Orleans, remarked that he had been twice elected to Congress, and had not spent five dollars in his two election campaigns *(Life of Yancey,* p. 531). ship, that is to say, the nomination to it, amounted to $15,000; a seat in Congress was rated at $4000; for membership of a State Legislature $1500 was demanded; a like amount for the position of alderman in a city council, etc. The impossibility of getting into the public service by any other channel resulted in a good many perfectly respectable and competent men consenting to pay the assessments, just as people bought offices and commissions in Europe in the old days, to be able to serve the State or satisfy legitimate ambitions; once elected on the list of the Machine to which they had paid the money, they discharged their duties honourably. It was impossible, however, that this should be the rule. Even men who were not dishonest, but who had no private means and borrowed money to pay for their nomination, were naturally inclined to get all they could out of their place during the short elective term, silencing their scruples, if they had any. But many others had none whatever, and under cover of the assessment system they gained admission in increasing numbers, as did a good many notoriously incompetent persons. The higher ranks of the judiciary itself were not spared, and there were judges (happily the case was not very common) whose sole claim was the contribution paid to the Machine. Thus the public service, which was so deeply degraded by the practices of rotation and division of the spoils, received another deadly blow at the hands of the Caucus, by the assessment system; it was no longer only political favouritism, party passion and intrigue, electoral services rendered, that determined admission to public functions but, over and above these, money in its most direct and most ignominious form of use. Public functions were virtually put up to auction. In bringing about this state of things, the Organization assumed the full aspect of which the outline had long been rising into view: from a political combination in the service of a party, it had come down to an industrial concern for making money out of places; it bought votes, worked up this raw material into elective commissions, and resold them with its trade-mark to the highest bidder.

FIFTH CHAPTER THE EVOLUTION OF THE CONVENTION SYSTEM *(conclusion)*

I

The electoral monopoly which the party Organization acquired and consolidated after the war, delivered the public service into its hands and led it to exploit that service commercially. The same monopoly was about to give it access to other and still larger spheres for an identical object. The traffic in places was only the first stage of the industrialism with which the Caucus was to imbue American public life; the Caucus was about to encourage fresh developments, or to conspire with other factors in producing them, or to take the lead itself in it. The first consequence, a fatal and immediate one, of the mode of bestowing public functions which it had established was the growing number of unfaithful officeholders. A certain number of those who obtained their places or their seats in assemblies from the hands of the Caucus, by a more or less heavy payment, hastened, as I have shown, to make money out of them, not only by the emoluments attaching thereto, but still more through the influence and power over the public funds which they involved. Owing their appointments solely or mainly to the favour of a political party, these persons entered on their duties with a very hazy sense of responsibility, and once they found themselves placed by their official position near a source of gain, they were readily tempted to dip into it for their own advantage. In return for a commission they procured government orders, contracts for public works, etc. These practices occurred before the war on a comparatively slender scale, and in a sporadic fashion, so to speak. After the war,— and it is always to this fateful epoch that one reverts in tracing the decline of public morality under various aspects,— after the war the corrupt officials fostered by the Caucus regime began to proceed with method: being brought together by their common tendencies, they combined into a syndicate, which, installed in a public department or in an elective assembly, directed its raids from thence on the public purse, under the aegis of their political party. For greater security the syndicate accepted members of the opposite party. These combinations of plundering politicians soon became tolerably common under the name of "rings." The economic expansion and the unbounded speculation which set in after the war, gave a powerful impulse to the Rings: they let loose appetites and strained men's minds to the utmost in the pursuit of new sources of wealth, while the marvellous development of the whole country, and of the cities in particular, with the manifold branches of their government and their works of every kind, daily increasing in number and importance, multiplied opportunities and pretexts for coveting and laying hands on public money. The public authorities whose duty it was to watch over it, being quite under the thumb of the party Organization, the jobbers and speculators hit on the plan of getting into the Organization and of reaching through it, so to speak, to the objects of their desires.

The Rings found a particularly favourable field for their operations in the municipal administration. The municipal sphere was within easy reach of the petty jobbers, who had only low aspirations; it contained an extensive domain which could be drawn on directly, and offered with more facilities for downright plunder greater chances of impunity; for the members of the city councils, being invariably elected on the ticket of a political party, were screened by the party. Municipal administration, therefore, became in most of the large American cities the scene of flagrant abuses, committed by men who were creatures of the Machine or who had succeeded in capturing it with the object of using it to exploit the public resources. These municipal scandals, often stimulated by other causes which will be pointed out later on, kept pace with the growth of the cities and the development of the Machine which followed closely on it. They appeared in the first instance, and with the greatest force, in the city of New York, which was the first to develop the Machine, and has produced the most finished specimen of it in the form of Tammany Hall. The part which this Organization has played there is so thoroughly representative of the action of the Machine in municipal government that it is necessary to become acquainted with Tammany Hall, and even to linger for a moment on its history, which gives it an exceptional place in the annals of party organization, as well as in those of American political life in general.

The origins of the Tammany organization are very curious; they are a mixture of fable and history. It got its name from a legendary chief of an Indian tribe. A great warrior, a high-minded ruler, an illustrious sage, the father of his people, Tammany, or Tammanend, was a brilliant representative of the indigenous civilization contrasted with that which was imported into the American continent by the men of the old world When the colonists shook off the English yoke, their imagination travelled back to this hero sprung from the very land which they wished to wrest from the despot beyond the seas, and they placed themselves under the patronage of Tammanend's memory. His exploits, to be sure, made him the equal of St. George, the slayer of the dragon, under whose banner the English fought, and who had only the one superiority of being a saint of the Church. To deprive him of it, Tammanend or Tammany was canonized there and then, and there grew up in the revolutionary army the cult of St. Tammany, with a saint's day which was held on the 12th of May, the supposed day of his birth. From the army this cult passed into civil society, in which patriots, and foremost among them the ''Sons of Liberty," founded St. Tammany associations, for cultivating the love of country and of the Republic under the invocation of the legendary hero. The local myth, which appealed to the imagination, was inwoven with the hazy idea of man in the state of nature and of freedom, which haunted people's minds during the whole of the second half of the eighteenth century. The return to nature, to primitive life, extolled by philosophers and poets on the other side of the ocean, found expression here in aboriginal costumes worn on St. Tammany's Day, when men, women, and children, dressed up in feathers and bucks' tails, danced around a pole crowned with a cap of liberty and hung from top to bottom with tomahawks and other Indian paraphernalia. In imitation of the first Tammany society, founded at Philadelphia in 1772, several others were created, at New York, at Baltimore, and elsewhere, but that of New York alone survived.

This society was founded in 1789 by a humble citizen of Irish extraction, an upholsterer of the name of Mooney, to vindicate democratic ideas as against the aristocratic exclusiveness derived from England, which had not entirely disappeared, as, for instance, the institution of the order of Cincinnati, on a hereditary basis, by the ex-officers of the Revolution, apparently indicated. Unlike this society of aristocratic tendencies, the Tammany society declared that its object was "to connect, in indissoluble bonds of friendship, brethren of known attachment to the political rights of human nature and the liberties of the country." To the name of Tammany it added that of the discoverer of America, and took the title of "The Tammany Society or Columbian Order." Created as a secret society, the members of which were admitted and initiated with certain rites, Tammany adopted a singular organization with an Indian nomenclature intended to give prominence to its eminently American character; it was divided into thirteen tribes, corresponding in number to the States which formed the Union, each named after an animal,— tiger, fox, wolf, eagle, etc. The managing committee of the society was composed of thirteen "sachems" (chiefs), one of whom was a "grand sachem" or "great father "; a "sagamore " officiated as master of the ceremonies, and a "wiskinskie" discharged the more modest duties of door-keeper. The members were called "braves "; the place where they met bore the name of "wigwam." The year was divided into seasons of flowers, fruits, hunting, and snows, and each season split up into moons.

During the early years of its existence the society maintained the character of a purely patriotic and philanthropic association which it had assumed, its activity being confined to friendly gatherings and more or less pompous speeches, delivered on the anniversary of Tammany, to sing the praises In 1805 Tammany obtained the privilege of incorporation from the Stat© legislature as a society whose object was " affording relief t« the indigent and distressed members of the said association, their widows and orphans, and others who may be found proper objects of their charity." of liberty and preach republican virtue. Among.its members were Federalists as well as anti-Federalists. "But before long politics crept into it. The frankly democratic tendencies of the society drew it towards the Jeffersonian party and induced it to join in the great electoral contest of 1800, under the influence, it would appear, of Aaron Burr. Inspired by him, the Tammany society set to work to canvass for the Republican-Democratic candidates, to bring forward the voters on their behalf, to procure the electoral franchise for those who did not possess it by means of stratagems, by transferring, for instance, to a single person the title-deeds of several persons up to the amount of the qualification required by the law. From and after this date Tammany became a regular political party organization and took an ever increasing share in the It is to one of these speeches that we owe the authenticated, if not authentic, history of Tammany, the famous Indian chief. This speech was made, in 1795, by S. L. Mitchill, a curious person, who played a certain part in the history of New York, an encyclopaedical *savant,* a Leibnitz on a small scale, and at the same time an ardent anti-Federalist Republican, out of respect for Jefferson the philosopher. (See Hammond, Vol. I, pp. 216,283, and H. Adams, *History of the United States,* N. Y., 1880, Vol. I, p. 111.) The worthy doctor relates, with profound conviction, all the exploits of Tammanend, which exhibit an extraordinary medley of adventures of mythological and biblical personages. "The Grecian Hercules does not appear to have achieved greater exploits." For many a long year he maintained a terrible struggle with the Evil Spirit, who took a malicious delight in tormenting the great Indian chief and his people. At one time he would make poisonous plants and stinging nettles spring up, which emitted noxious exhalations, the fumes of which killed people; at another time he would send rattlesnakes, which infected the country, etc., etc. Tammany's courage and sagacity had invariably got the better of the machinations of the Evil Spirit; and having finally defeated him, he devoted himself to the arts of peace by governing his people wisely and happily, on principles which, by a sort of retroactive effect, turn out to be none other than those of the Declaration of Independence: "There was no force, no violence, in his measures, but general consent and concurrence of sentiment conferred on him all the authority he possessed. He disdained usurpation of power, and would sooner have been bound, loaded with weights, and cast headlong into the lake, than attempt any invasion of the people's rights. If he obtained influence, that influence was conferred on him by the citizens; and they trusted him with power because they were confident he would not abuse it" *(Life, Exploits, and Precepts of Tammany, the Famous Indian Chief,* being the anniversary oration pronounced before the Tammany Society, or Columbian Order, in the old Presbyterian church, in the city of New York, on Tuesday, the 12th May, 1795, by Samuel Latham Mitchill, M.D., F.R.S.E., Professor of Chemistry, Natural History, ami Agriculture in the College of New York, N. Y. Printed by J. Buel, Mdccxcv, 36 pp.).

contests which filled the public life of New York. It was the centre of the humbler voters, attracted by its popular tendencies tand kept together by the social cement of its gatherings and brotherly feasts. The suffrage in New York being subject to a property qualification (down to 1821), these voters belonged not so much to the populace as to the lower middle class and to the category of artisans, and it was from men of the middle class that they received their impulse. For a long time, therefore, the Tammany society preserved a decided stamp of respectability; it included among its members a good many property-holders and tradesmen of good repute, and its dignities of sachems, etc., were much sought after in these circles, the dull existence of which they brightened up a little. The austere tone of people in modest circumstiinces, earning an honest living by hard work, and with the fear of God before their eyes, — which forms the groundwork of the Puritanism that took its rise on Anglo-Saxon soil, — found an echo naturally enough in the grave personages of the Tammany society, and more than once its spokesmen uttered warnings, on the solemn occasions of its anniversary, against the bad habits and the vices which were invading the country, such as billiards, stage-plays, extravagant dress, the wild race for wealth. Bidding their hearers beware of what they considered as the pernicious propensities of the man, they appealed also to the citizen, adjuring him to cultivate independence of mind, to make it the criterion in the choice of representatives, and to constantly exercise an unfettered judgment.

But in proportion as the society got entangled in party politics and in the strife of factions, which was so bitter in New " If political independence is the boast of our country, *individual independence* should be the characteristic of merit. We should value it in a man as the apple of the eye. It is a pledge of honesty, it is the cradle of virtue.... Theenora of such a man aresacred.... Inselectingyourdepositoriesof public trust in every department of the State, the Society cannot too earnestly press upon your minds the propriety, nay, *necessity,* of selecting men of *independent minds"*... (Address of the Society of Tammany, or Columbian Order, to its advent members, and the members of its several branches throughout the United States. New York, 1819, 40 pp.). This very curious address, which breathes a generous and genuine spirit of liberty and republican virtue throughout, apart from a few bombastic passages and some nonsense about the effect of protection and the remedies for economic depression, is full of wise and noble thoughts.

York, there gathered round it an ever increasing number of people who, without having been admitted as members of the secret society, followed it in the election contests and formed a sort of purely political appendage to it which soon developed into a gangrenous excrescence. They constituted alongside the society the "general meeting," transformed later on, when the plenary meetings became a material impossibility, into a representative " general committee." Two great facts radically chauged the character and tendencies of Tammany. In the democratic struggle the aristocratic element, represented in New York by the Clintons, the Livingstons, disappeared, and the plebeian and somewhat venal following on which these power-loving patricians leaned, turned towards Tammany. At the same time the introduction of universal suffrage, effected in 1821, enlarged this following and created a new atmosphere, in which democratic aspirations, being now gratified, lost their mystic fragrance, and in which the Puritan spirit of the toiling lower middle class evaporated. Tammany was invaded by the mob element. Again, the voting strength which the Tammany organization contributed to the Republican-Democratic party soon made its services appreciated and gained them rewards in the form of places handed over to its members. As early as under Madison's Presidency Tammany had a share in federal patronage, the extent of which did but increase with its electoral influence. Tothefederal patronage was added that of the State, and especially of the city, not to mention the elective offices for which Tammany fell into the habit of recommending candidates, on behalf of the Democratic party, even before the introduction of the convention system. These *latifundia* ruined Tammany morally, while developing and confirming its power. Its enormous patronage placed a whole army of officials at its beck and call and turned them into election agents; but at the same time it attracted to and permanently established in Tammany the mercenary elements which had lost no time in over Niles remarks with reference to this, on the eve of the municipal election of 1834: "The 'Tammanies' have the benefit of an old organization, the respect for 'regular nominations,' an army of officers of the United States and of the State and city of New York of about five hundred men, who have many dependents, whose persons and purse are at the command of the party, and the 'spoils' amount to a million a year. All these will be 'on duty'" (*Weekly Register,* Vol. XLVI, p. 82).

running the Organization down to its inner circle of initiated members, although the post of "great father" and several "sachems" continued to be bestowed, for a time at least, on men of acknowledged respectability. Towards the year 1835 Tammany's entrance on this path was an accomplished fact. However, the prestige attaching to its democratic and, as it were, mythological origin, and to its long career of more than half a century, parallel with that of the Union, remained an asset of Tammany, as well as its character of the official, "regular" organization of the Democratic party.

The establishment of the popular system of conventions, together with the extension of the elective method to public functions, ended by placing the Democratic party, which Tammany claimed to represent, irrevocably in its power: the followers of Tammany flocked into the primaries and the conventions, and, by virtue of the people's right, distributed, in the name of the

Democratic party, the nominations which every orthodox Democrat ratified on election day by his ballot because they were made by the Organization of his party. And as the majority of the population of the city of New York was connected by tradition with the Democratic party, Tammany became the master of the city and of its municipal administration. During the following decade, from 1840-1850, Tammany gained considerable reinforcements from the European immigration. The tide of immigration, which, entering through New York, spread over the whole Union, left in that city, as a sort of residuum, the wretchedest, the feeblest, portion of the human cargo dumped down on the shores of America. This class of immigrants, composed for the most part of Irishmen, was marked out as the prey of the leaders of Tammany in search of heedless or corrupt votes; they let themselves be enrolled by it like so many sheep, and by their ever increasing number formed a sort of rock, which served henceforth as a foundation for the power of Tammany. Still their contribution to the demoralization of Tammany and of the political life of New York was probably not so large as some American writers represent it, for the corruption began under the property qualification regime and was developed under universal suffrage and took firm root in the soil of New York, through the action of Tammany, even before the era of naturalizations *en* masse set in. What is true is that the naturalized aliens supplied Tammany with a large contingent, which enabled it to renew, so to speak, its stock of American origin and to continue and extend its mischievous operations.

When the mob elements attracted to Tammany's standard became numerous enough, they were grouped into permanent associations, organized in the form of "clubs" or "gangs," or incorporated into existing organizations such as the firemen's companies. Later on these organizations were reduced to a uniform type of electoral district associations for each of the political subdivisions of the city. The associations culminated in a central committee, which possessed discretionary powers over the whole Organization. The members of the associations were admitted only after a strict selection and had to promise absolute obedience to the Tammany leaders. They filled the primaries and the conventions in which candidates were nominated, and carried the vote by violence if necessary; then on election day they arrived in compact battalions to deposit the Tammany ticket in the ballot-boxes, and often, to secure it a majority, they perpetrated frauds, the most common of which consisted in a person voting several times under different names. Tammany thus constituted an army of democratic mamelukes, who bolstered up, under republican forms, a real system of despotism, wielded by a handful of men. To support this army Tammany had the disposal not only of a great number of places in the municipal administration, but of a large war fund provided by the contributions of the office-holders, by the assessments which it began to levy at an early date. It was Tammany, one may say, which inaugurated the system since naturalized throughout the Union. It pitilessly squeezed all those who obtained or expected a nomination through its good offices.

The respectable citizens, too engrossed by their avocations, did not interfere, not realizing what was going on, or they deliberately winked at the wrong-doings of Tammany out of At the time of the first election of the mayor of New York under popular suffrage, in 1834, the assessments system was already working regularly. On this occasion Tammany fixed the contribution of all the employees of the city at the exorbitant rate of 10 per cent of the annual salaries (Niles, Vol. XLVI, p. 34).

love for the party of which it had constituted itself the regular Organization, and which it led to victory; it supplied the party with compact majorities at the State and presidential elections, and the Democratic leaders, even the most eminent of them, endured it when they were not cajoling it. Having thus inveigled the party, Tammany wielded over it a tyrannical power, which it turned to account in the sordid interests of its managers and of their creatures. By the prescriptive right which it acquired over the machinery of the party, it got such a tight hold of it that if the party tried to unfasten its bonds, it divested itself of its Democratic status. It was enough for Tammany simply to close its doors, in the material sense of the words, against the rebels and recalcitrants, to put them outside the party. The Tammany society, after having for years held its meetings in taverns, according to the custom of the day, built a house for itself, which was commonly known by the name of "Tammany Hall," and which became not only the seat of the society, but also the head-quarters of the political party Organization that had sprung from it. By extension the name of "Tammany Hall" was soon applied to the whole Organization, so as to become synonymous with it. This confusion of meaning, which set up an association of ideas between the building and the party which it harboured, obtained a political recognition in the admission that whoever was excluded from the building was excluded from the party, from its regular organization. The Hall being the property of the secret society, its sachems posed as judges of the party orthodoxy by allowing some and refusing others the use of the Hall. A faction of the party, which had been denied admittance in this way, contested the right of the society to meddle with the affairs of the party, for the reason that by its As early as 1835 a New York paper pointed this out in terms in which there has been next to nothing to change since: "The Society influences the committees, directs the office-holders, and rules the destinies of the party. It presses on the Democracy like an oppressive incubus, crushing and restraining the free and glorious c irculation of independent sentiment and democratic principles. The corrupt adherents will not, and the timid portion of the party dare not, murmur against that political organization. Many men of broken fortunes have joined this society and obtained office. Most of the officeholders in the city and State belong to this political machine which rules the party" *(The New Yvrk Evening Post,* of November, 1835, quoted by Niles, Vol. XLIX, p. 217). statutes it was only a charitable society. The sachems affirmed this right in a formal decision delivered in the "Grand Wigwam," in which they declared that "no doubt charity was one of the objects contemplated in the organization of our society, but that virtue is not diminished by adding thereto the more extended beneficence which looks to ttie good of the whole country, and the political rights of every class of its citizens." Acting on this decision, the sachems of Tammany, in concert with the leaders of the party Organization, often resorted to this summary expedient to stop the revolts which broke out in the ranks of the party. Thus the formalist principle of party regularity, which enslaves political consciences, was materialized even more than is the loyalty of subjects through monarchical hereditary right; the loyalty of the followers of the Democratic party was addressed not only to its name and style, but to the walls of the house in which it had its central office.

The members of the Democratic party who were in revolt against Tammany, or who were simply dissentients, had no resource but schism or alliance with the opposite party. They tried both. In the course of the last sixty years there occurred, in fact, more than one rebellion against Tammany in the Democratic ranks, from the formation, towards 1835, of the "party of equal rights," mentioned in a preceding chapter, down to the more recent secessions of the rival Halls, such as Mozart Hall, Apollo Hall, Irving Hall, County Democracy, and several others. For the most part these revolts and secessions came from family quarrels. The spoils being of course not enough to go round, those who considered themselves hardly used discovered that Tammany was a corrupt organization, and appealed to the indignation of good citizens. Sometimes the Republicans thought it a good opportunity for joining the malcontents and inflicting a defeat on Tammany Hall, but the Republican Organization was intent only on the spoils and was quite ready to sell itself to Tammany for a mess of pottage. In any event, the attempts at revolt against Tammany could not be successful, or permanently successful, for it had over Address of the Grand Council of the Tammany Society, or Columbian Order, upon the subject of their recent decision relative to the political use of Tammany Hall, February 4th, 1853. N. Y., 1853.

its rivals the enormous superiority of the monopoly of "regularity" which it had secured; of a long unbroken existence; of a consummate experience in the art of wire-pulling acquired in the course of that existence; of a vast army of "workers" provided by the office-holders and the militant members of the Hall; and of a plentiful supply of places and money, with which it bought the leaders of the dissentient factions, or even its antagonists of the opposite party. These resources enabled Tammany to return quickly to power, even when it happened to be defeated by a coalition of dissentient Democrats with the Republicans or with independent citizens.

The use which Tammany made of its power, especially during the period after the war, had nothing in common with the interests, of the party under the banner of which it operated; considerations of political principles or proprieties were henceforth utterly foreign to it; it did not care either, or but slightly, for the gratifications of ambition procured by the enjoyment of power; its sole aim was to secure and exploit the vast material resources of the city. In this the Tammany men displayed an unexampled rapacity and effrontery; they applied themselves to the plunder of the city property with a regularity and a coolness which imparted a singularly piquant flavour to the ceremony of initiation of new members of the Tammany society, at which the following lines were sung: —

"Sacred's the ground where Freedom's found,
And virtue stamps her name."

Under the wing of the party, Tammany installed municipal corruption permanently in New York and made it the worstgoverned city of the American continent, in which the most elementary wants of the citizens were unattended to, and which constituted a living and abiding reproach to modern civilization.

Of the 41 mayors of New York elected by the popular vote from 1834 down to 1897, 32 were Democrats, of whom 24 belonged to Tammany, and in eight cases were re-elected once or twice, whereas the dissentients were successful only eight times, and mostly thanks to the support of Republicans and Independents. n

The systematic robbery of the public purse, carried on in the city of New York under the auspices of Tammany began, it would appear, about 1850, when, in consequence of the extension of the city, the need for better means of transport than the omnibuses ushered in the era of concessions to railway companies. From that time the rings got a firm footing, but it was in the following decade, from 1860-1870, that they reached their apogee. Towards the middle of this decade the municipal administration was already entirely in the hands of a clique of a few persons who pulled the strings of the Organization of the Democratic party. Settling the ticket for regular candidatures among themselves, they filled the municipal bodies, and even the State Legislature, with their tools, and got them to vote expenditure which committed the finances of the city to millions of dollars, in the form of sinecures, public works, taking up land for public purposes, "opening of new streets," subsidies and more or less fraudulent gifts to various associations, etc. Most of the newspapers were paid to hold their tongue; their owners were squared by the municipal advertisements given to them; the reporters all received an annual douceur of two hundred dollars. Among these engineers of municipal corruption a certain Tweed arose, who gave his name to the ring which has remained the most famous of them all. This man, who with unheard-of audacity looted the capital of the new world, was in reality a vulgar rogue, whose name under ordinary circumstances would not have got beyond the reports of the police court. A chair-maker by trade, lazy and unskilful, he soon gave up his business and all regular work and launched into speculation and caucus politics. A jovial fellow, with a fund of vulgar *bonhomie* and an exuberant nature, he managed to make many friends among the lower orders of the city and to win supporters in the party Organization, which enabled him to obtain several elective posts, one more important than the other. In these offices he found opportunities for jobbery and for acquiring influence over a "The Government of the City of New York," *North American Review,* October, 1866.

VOL. II—M number of voters. But Tweed's ambitions, or rather appetites, were of no ordinary kind. Having come into contact, in the municipal life of New York, with a few individuals almost as obscure and just as greedy as himself, they spontaneously combined for the same object of laying hands on the city. But how were they to get a hold on it? They had no need to look for the lever of Archimedes; it was there, concealed in the party Organizations which distributed power. The strongest Organization was Tammany Hall, and the conspirators directed their steps towards it. By a series of skilful movements they made their way into its General Committee, got Tweed appointed chairman, then obtained admittance into the Tammany society, which, renovated by an infusion of fresh elements, elected Tweed to the dignity of "Grand Sachem." Tweed and his associates were now absolute masters of Tammany Hall, and from that moment the city of New York was virtually at their feet.

The principal members of this clique were, in addition to Tweed, an obscure attorney, another and more cultivated lawyer, with literary and artistic pretensions, but who was only a notoriety-hunter, and an ex-auctioneer, who had gradually risen in the political world from the post of secretary of a ward caucus. These four constituted the managing "Ring." Disposing through Tammany of nominations to offices, they filled the whole municipal administration with their creatures, raised to the bench worthless individuals who sold justice " like grocers," but who faithfully served the Ring by screening its offending *protigis* from the rigour of the law, or by granting it other favours. The members of the Ring took the most important and influential posts in the municipal administration for themselves; thus Tweed got himself appointed street commissioner, an official who had under his orders a very large staff of employees and of labourers. A number of sinecures created for the purpose increased the total of people on whose votes the Ring could depend. Extensive public works served as a pretext for giving, at the cost of the rate-payers, real or fictitious occupation to a mass of people, who in return carried out the political orders of the Ring. This enormous patronage which it dispensed to the lower orders, with the assistance of Tammany Hall, was the rock on which it founded its power. With it the Ring captured first of all the citadel of the party, — the primaries,— which were frequented only by humble citizens, and then it made these men vote for its candidates at the elections. To complete their number, that is to say, to create voters at its beck and call, the Ring procured naturalizations *en masse* of aliens in violation or in contempt of the law. The judicial procedure established by the law for this purpose was turned into a pure farce by the judges devoted to the Ring; they considered and decided more than fourteen hundred applications a day; in the course of the year 1868 they thus admitted more than forty-one thousand aliens. Moreover, the Ring organized on an equally extensive scale a fraudulent registration of voters, by getting fictitious names put on the register, which were used afterwards for voting. At the poll the election inspectors appointed by the Ring made a false return, so that at the election of Governor in 1868, the number of votes given, or rather counted, in the city of New York turned out to be eight per cent in excess of the entire voting population. The Governor elected was the candidate of the Ring, and he could exercise in its favour the right of vetoing such decisions of the Legislature as were likely to paralyse the intrigues of the new masters of the municipality. The Legislature, however, itself fell in with the plans of the Ring. The latter was directly represented in it by Tweed, who got himself elected senator and succeeded even in obtaining the chairmanship of the most important senatorial committee. By dint of lavish bribes to the members of the assembly, he procured from the Legislature a law which modified the charter of the city so as to extend the jurisdiction of the mayor, and transfer several powers in regard to the assessment and apportionment of taxes, and some other important decisions, to a committee composed of the mayor and of three other high municipal officials. But the holders of these four positions were no other than the four members of the Ring.

Screened on all sides, Tweed and his associates quietly robbed the city exchequer. For instance, they got friends to buy plots "An Episode in Municipal Government," by C. F. Wingate *(North American Review,* 1874, 1875, 1876). of land which the city afterwards acquired for public purposes at extravagant prices; or sent in fictitious claims, which the city paid without asking a question; or again, and very often, forced the contractors and tradesmen to swell the totals of the accounts and to hand them the difference between the real price and the invoice price. These last were of a fabulous extravagance, of which the building and furnishing of the law courts constitutes an imperishable monument; according to the estimate, it was to cost $250,000, but it swallowed up from eight to thirteen millions, without being finished; each chair cost $407, and the rest in proportion. Among the various items in the accounts there were also safes down for more than $400,000. The Ring carried on its operations for several years quite unchecked, the bribed Press keeping silence, and the electorate being dragged at the heels of Tammany, which it followed out of party loyalty or personal interest. The money embezzled by the leaders of the Ring flowed in a golden stream, as we are already aware, among a vast number of voters, in various forms, so that the latter only profited by the regime of plunder. Taxes they had none to pay; the rich paid them, and if *they* were fleeced, where was the harm? The number of voters interested in one way or another in the prosperity of Tammany and its Ring was not less than half of the electorate of New York. Intrenched behind Tammany Hall, which provided it with the popular vote, the Ring might have continued its exploits for a long time, and it was a mere chance that stopped them in 1871. One of the fellow-workers of the Ring, who thought he had not been sufficiently rewarded, and who had in vain prosecuted a claim on the municipal funds, got cognizance of certain fraudulent accounts, through a small municipal employee, and took them to a newspaper. The scandal became public; good citizens shook off their torpor, organized themselves, and forced the courts to intervene. The members of the Ring, by betraying one another to save their skin, facilitated the enquiry opened into their misdeeds, but considerable efforts were required to dislodge them. Unmasked and publicly convicted, Tweed snapped his fingers at public opinion and the law by asking: "What are you going to do about it?" and what was more characteristic, he was not left in the lurch, not only by the troop of his lieutenants and sub-lieutenants, but by the voters of his district, who triumphantly re-elected him to the Senate of the State. Eventually the Ring was defeated at the municipal election, and its principal members and acolytes were prosecuted or forced to abscond or retire. The operations of the Ring cost the rate-payers $160,000,000 at the lowest computation; the consolidated debt of the city increased by more than $100,000,000, and the annual expenditure was doubled.

But the lesson was of little service to the city of New York; after a short time, when the champions of honest government got slack, Tammany recovered itself, and in 1874 it was once more in possession of the mayoralty. The Republican Organization, the rival of Tammany Hall, contributed to this result itself, by a manoeuvre which will be repeated over and over again in the municipal history of New York; the independent citizens having opposed a candidate to that of Tammany Hall, the Republican Machine brought into the field another candidate of its own, on the pretext of not jeopardizing the prestige and cohesion of the Republican party, which would be needed in the coming State and national political battles. These tactics, which divided the forces arrayed against Tammany, had the natural result of letting its candidate get in. The Republican Organization was not so very sorry for this; a secret understanding with its rival of Tammany Hall secured it a share in the spoils. The upshot of the revolt of 1871 against Tweed's Ring was to bring about a partial weeding of the bench and of the upper administrative staff, and to stop the flagrant waste of public money. Tweed's Ring disappeared, but its place was taken by a small coterie of politicians of low degree, who were just as dishonest, and who ruled the party Organization just as autocratically. For a time Tammany was more careful in the choice of its candidates, but simply in order to lull the vigilance of the voters by making them believe that it had turned over a new leaf. Besides, it pursued these tactics only with the most conspicuous offices which headed the list. The rest of the ticket was filled up as These figures are taken fmni Lalor's *Cyclopedia of Political Science,* the article, " Tammany Hall," by Talcot Williams.
before with corrupt or vulgar men, not excepting the members of the town council.

Continually perfecting its Machine, Tammany Hall drew more and more closely within its organization the lowest strata of the population, and in particular the "dangerous classes," the men who are on the borders of the criminal class when they do not form part of it. The publicans and the keepers of all kinds of low resorts, enrolled by fair means or foul in the Organization of Tammany Hall, served it as recruiting sergeants among the large proletariate and the gaol-birds who swar'med in New York. The managing staff of Tammany itself, too, came up to a level which was not much higher. However, at the head of the municipality Tammany Hall still tolerated more or less respectable persons, who served as figure-heads. A temporary eclipse of Tammany having brought Democratic mayors, elected in spite of it, into the Town Hall for a few years, Tammany thought it a good move, in order to ingratiate itself with respectable voters, to raise the standard of respectability of its candidates still further, and it procured the election of a very distinguished mayor (A. S. Hewitt) itself. But in the end Tammany grew tired of these tactics when it saw that these mayors wanted to govern the city in the interests of the city. Appealing, with the surreptitious assistance of the Republican Organization, to the time-honoured political divisions which split the rate-payers into two hostile camps in spite of the identity of their interests in municipal government, Tammany Hall, from 1888 onwards, installed in the mayoralty, for one term after another, individuals who were akin rather to the section of the electorate which haunted saloons and gambling-hells. The Tammany men were now a family party, and shameless corruption recommenced on a gigantic scale.

Taught by Tweed's experience, however, his successors The enquiry conducted in 1889 by an independent New York paper proved that the executive committee of Tammany Hall comprised 28 professioual politicians, 1 person convicted of murder, 1 man indicted for murder but acquitted, 1 person prosecuted for bribery, 4 professional gamblers, 5 exkeepers of gaming-houses, 4 saloon-keepers, 5 ex-saloon-keepers, 3 ex-pugilists, 0 members of the Tweed gang, IS ex-car-conductors, 1 lawyer, 2 *soi-ilixant* lawyers, etc. *(Nation,* 1894, Vol. LIX, p. 4).
changed their *modus operandi;* they took care not to swell the taxes; they even gave the rate-payers the illusion of economy and reduced taxation (the appearance of which was obtained by the fact that part of the current expenditure was defrayed by loans, by the increasing revenues of the city, and by the fall in the rate of interest on the municipal debt, while the higher valuation of the ratable property brought down the relative rate of taxation. To make up for this the Tammany men developed a complete system of blackmailing. The principal instrument of this plunder was the police; they levied a regular toll, prescribed by a fixed tariff, on all the saloons, houses of ill-fame, and gambling-hells; extorted money, on false pretences or on no pretence at all, from small traders whom they had the power of molesting. Other perfectly lawful businesses were subjected to a tribute: steamboat companies, insurance societies, banks, etc., paid blackmail in return for the "protection" accorded to them. The police captains and even the policemen had to buy their places from their superiors by payment of large sums, according as the district was more or less "rich," that is to say, contained more loot. Part of the money thus extorted went to the head men of Tammany; it appears that they fixed beforehand for each ward and district the amount of the blackmail which was to be paid to them, and left the police all that it succeeded in getting over and above this. Tammany even took care that sources of extortion should not be wanting; it used all its influence to obtain laws restrictive of the traffic in spirituous liquors, prohibiting the sale of them on Sunday or at nighttime, or increasing the amount of the license, etc., and then sold the protection of the police to the offenders. Every interest, lawful as well as unlawful, which was dependent on the municipal administration, was blackmailed by Tammany. "The government of the city in fact became a huge market, in which the officers might as well have sat at little tables and sold their wares openly." Tammany financiering, *ibid.,* p. 318. See *The Independent* of the 13th September, 1894, the article by Frank Moss, one of the counsel who prosecuted the enquiry into the administration of the police before a committee of the Senate, which became famous under the name of the Lexow Committee.
« *Nation,* Vol. LVIII, p. 460.

The revelation of these scandals, due to the courageous initiative of private individuals, produced, in 1894, a revolt like that formerly directed against Tweed and his gang; it took place under the same conditions and had the same effects; the independent citizens and those Democrats who were indignant at or jealous of Tammany, having made common cause with the Republicans, the coalition defeated Tammany Hall and carried out a cleansing process in the administration, in the ordinary as well as the metaphorical sense of the words; it reformed the police and had the streets swept, which under the Tammany regime had been left in a dirty state from motives of economy. But at the next election, when a vigorous attempt was made to enforce, in an unmistakable way, the supremacy of municipal interests in the administration of the city, by choosing a mayor and other municipal candidates solely for their competence and their character, irrespective of all party considerations, the two rival Organizations once more made friends, and, as usual, their parties followed them, with the result that Tammany Hall came back into power. Rather than see the mayoralty slip from the party Machines, the Republican Organization preferred to hand over the city to Tammany, its rival. It did so by running a third candidate and thrusting him, because he was a Republican, on the Republican voters, although it knew perfectly well that he could not get in. The occurrence, which was not a very novel one in the history of New York, on this occasion derived exceptional gravity from the fact that this election (of 1897) inaugurated a new era in the municipal life of the American metropolis, which, owing to an amalgamation of New York with Brooklyn and other neighbouring agglomerations, became the second largest city of the world, and offered an enormous stake to those who were contending for its administration.

III

This very summary sketch of the history of Tammany Hall and of the municipal administration of New York, which is indissolubly connected with it, certainly presents a unique career, but by no means an exceptional one; the same features will be found in that of most of the large cities of the Union; Tammany has only exhibited them in a singularly exaggerated form. Moreover, some of these cities were not better off than New York, and had a history somewhat resembling and parallel with that of Tammany Hall. Thus almost at the very moment when Tweed's Ring was being overthrown at New York, amid shouts of general indignation, in the second municipality of the Republic, in Philadelphia, a Ring was being installed which was to be master of the city for years to come. This was the Gas Ring, the most famous, next to Tammany's, in the annals of American municipal life. Of the factors which made the Tammany Ring possible and ensured its success, several were absent in Philadelphia; it did not possess a living tradition of party loyalty as old and as materialized as that embodied in Tammany Hall; in its population the alien element introduced by the constant flow of immigration was not very considerable; the Quaker city, too, had no populace like that of New York, but, on the contrary, contained a very large medium class composed of small tradesfolk and well-to-do artisans, occupying their own houses, and in their capacity of ratepayers directly interested in good municipal government. But all these advantages were more than counterbalanced for evil by the unusual perfection of the party Machine, with the help of which the Gas Ring captured and bled the city. From this point of view the history of the Gas Ring is particularly characteristic.

The anxieties of the Civil War having kept the good citizens more than ever away from the primaries, the latter fell completely into the hands of the least exalted social elements. With their assistance a few needy and ambitious individuals succeeded in getting places in the gas department, which was a dependency of the municipality. Having under their orders a very large number of employees and workmen (as many as two thousand), these personages conceived the idea of turning them into political agents by making them take up the business and assume the power of the party Organization. Methodically distributed among all the wards of the city, the Gas Department people filled the primaries and, thanks to their number and their discipline, secured majorities for the delegates whom their employers pointed out to them beforehand. The commaud of such a compact mass of "workers" had made the leaders installed in the gas department an important electoral factor, and soon procured them valuable alliances in the other municipal departments. These contributed to the Gas Ring their quota of employees, who were reinforced by the employees of the contractors and tradespeople doing business with the municipality, of the saloon-keepers, as well as of the numerous servants of the street-car companies, in which the head men of the Ring became shareholders. All these troops formed a single army, marching at the order of the Ring, with the police on its flanks. A friendly mayor filled the whole force with politicians of low degree, who voted in the primaries as citizens, induced the humbler voters to attend them, and got rid of the independent ones by their power as' police officers; they prevented them from getting into the primaries; at the elections they screened the electoral frauds which it was their duty to prevent, and made things unpleasant for those who protested. Intrigue and corruption by means of sinecures in the gas department or elsewhere definitively silenced opposition and gave the Ring complete control of the primaries and the conventions, that is to say, the monopoly of the regular candidatures. No candidate hostile to the Ring could obtain a nomination. No one who had not given pledges to the Ring could be elected, not only to municipal assemblies, but even to the State Legislature or Congress. For the Ring, following the example of its prototype of New York, took care to ally itself with the dominant political party; at New York the Democrats were in a majority, and the Ring there became Democrat; at Philadelphia the Republicans were in power, and the Ring hoisted the standard of the Republican party, and out of party loyalty almost all its followers voted the ticket privately settled by the Gas Ring. The compact battalions which the latter brought to the Republican party were such a valuable reinforcement to it that the independent Republicans, imitating the attitude of the leaders of the Democratic party in the State of New York towards Tweed and his successors, or of the Republican leaders towards the carpet-baggers in the South, did not care to look too closely into the means by which these contingents were supplied to them; in the situation created by the war their great object was the success of the Republican party, which seemed to them bound up with the safety of the Union. Then when the problems raised by the war passed out of the acute stage, another preoccupation, of an anything but sentimental kind, made the interest of the Eepublican party paramount; it became the champion of protection, from which Pennsylvania, a pre-eminently manufacturing State, benefited most. To maintain the high customs duties, the manufacturers of Philadelphia and of the State silenced all scruples and made over to the Organization their votes and those of their numerous workmen, whose interest was, or was represented to them as, identical with that of their employers. The upshot was that the Ring managed to fill the whole municipal administration and most of the town councils with its creatures, and to plant its garrison in the State Legislature.

Once in power, the Gas Ring exploited the city exchequer just as methodically as, but with more prudence and decency than, the Tammany Ring; the controllers of the Gas Ring took care to entrust the high municipal offices to more or less respectable personages, whom they used as figureheads, while they themselves kept behind the scenes; nor did they rob with the same effrontery as Tweed and Co. But the city of Philadelphia was no better off; the price of gas was exorbitant, and the enormous income which it brought in to the municipality disappeared by means of a mysterious system of accounts; the city debt increased at the rate of three millions a year, without any important improvement being introduced into the municipal plant; to meet the interest on the ever growing debt the rates were made heavier and heavier; "inefficiency, waste, badly paved and filthy streets, unwholesome and offensive water, and slovenly and costly management have been the rule for years past throughout the city government." Petition presented in 1883 to the State Legislature by several leading citizens of Philadelphia, who describe the condition of the city in these terms: "Philadelphia is now recognized as the worst-paved and worst-cleaned city in the civilized world. The water supply is so bad that during many weeks of the last winter it was not only distasteful and unwholesome for drinking, but offensive for bathing purposes. The effort to clean the streets was abandoned for months, and no attempt was made to that end until some public-spirited citizens, at their own expense, cleaned a number of the principal thoroughfares. The system of sewerage and the physical condition of the sewers are Exploiting all the resources of the city, the Ring did not spare even the charitable institutions and the prisons,— it imperturbably took its tribute of them. It made electoral coin out of schoolmasterships, and filled the schools with incompetent teachers. It sowed the seeds of corruption everywhere; it set up a hotbed of it in the municipal assemblies; it contaminated even the courts of law. Like the Tammany Ring, it stopped the mouth of the press by regular subsidies, so that not a single paper could be found to plead the cause of honest government. It manufactured majorities at the polls by means of frauds in voting and in the counting of the ballots; it bought votes wholesale and retail, forcing all those who received salaries from the city to provide the wherewithal for corruption. The policemen entrusted with the dirty work already described were also taxed at twenty dollars a head and more, and their captains at a much higher figure. The air reeked with corruption.

The power of the Machine, which shielded the Ring that was responsible for this state of things, was reinforced by certain peculiarities of municipal organization in America to which I have already alluded, by saying that they stimulated municipal abuses. This organization, which was by no means uniform, presented in several cities, and those the largest ones, a tangled heap of administrative bodies placed pell-mell by the side or on the top of one another, of small committees and commissions with independent powers and separate accounts, which, added to the complication of the system, made it impossible to control those bodies. At Philadelphia " thirty-two departments or executive arms, all independent of each other, and of any head save councils, divided the management of affairs, and reduced responsibility to a minimum." The confusion and irresponsibility which resulted therefrom were further accentuated by the frequent changes which the State Legislature made in the notoriously bad,— so mnch so as to be dangerous to the health and most offensive to the comfort of our people. Public work has been done so badly that structures have had to be renewed almost as soon as finished. Others have been in part constmcted at enormous expense, and then permitted to fall to decay without completion." *City Government in Philadelphia,* by E. P. Allinson and B. Penrose, Baltimore, 1887, p. 61 ("Johns Hopkins University Studies in Historical and Political Science").
organization of the city. In most of the States there was no organic municipal law securing the government of the cities a certain measure of stahility; each city received from the Legislature its charter, which prescribed its administration somewhat minutely, and which might be changed at any moment in its smallest details. Practically deprived of self-government, the cities were at the mercy of the Legislatures, or rather of the small groups of their members who used their powers to experiment on the municipal charters for reasons which were often of an interested nature. If sinecures were wanted, recourse was had to the Legislature, which created new offices in the city departments with nominal duties; if the object was to turn out political opponents, or, on the other hand, to save friends from the risks of an impending election, the Legislature obligingly voted a law which abolished the offices of the firstnamed or prolonged the terms of the second; was it desired to grant a financial company privileges not contemplated or prohibited by the law, the Legislature was called in and forthwith voted a bill accordingly. The municipality, even if it was honest, was not master in its own house.

There was thus a permanent conspiracy between the faulty legal organization, which destroyed the responsibility of the municipal authorities to their constituents, and the party Machine, which did away with the responsibility of the municipal voters to themselves and the interests of their city. The more the ramifications of the Machine extended in the city and beyond it, the more grave and mischievous did this conspiracy become, and it reached its highest point when the majority in the municipality and in the Legislature belonged to the same party and the same Machine. In New York, where the State Legislature generally had a Republican majority, Tammany Hall, which was supposed to represent the Democratic party in the city, could not expect any favours from the Legislature in Albany, and might even be seriously embarrassed in its operations by the intervention of the Legislature. But at Philadelphia the majority in the municipality belonged to the same party that was predominant in the State Legislature; and as the latter's majority was made up with the vast vote of the city of Philadelphia, the Ring which ruled the city was sure of support in the Legislature. In vain, therefore, did independent citizens appeal to the Legislature, whose somewhat excessive powers in the matter of municipal regulation might have been used as a check on municipal abuses. Nor could these citizens count on the support of the Democratic opposition, for the men who ran the Republican Machine, that is to say, the Ring, came to a secret understanding with the managers of the Democratic Organization, and in the wards where the independents were too numerous, got in Democratic candidates who promised to do as they were told, just as Tweed proceeded when he bought Republican caucuses in New York. Left to their own resources, the independents had great difficulty in contesting even a single one of the many elective offices to be filled up; for, apart from the monopoly of regular candidatures, the Machines secured that of the ballots, thanks to the slip ticket system. In fact, if the electors were asked to vote for a single independent candidate while acquiescing in the return of the "regular" candidates to the other offices, it was necessary to provide them with ballot-papers containing, together with the name of the independent candidate, those of the candidates for all the other posts, and with alterations for the different electoral districts of Philadelphia besides; and if the Republicans as well as the Democrats were appealed to on behalf of this independent candidate, all these tickets had to be supplied in duplicate. Thus the Machine drew a sort of iron circle around municipal life; from whatever side good citizens approached, they were confronted and driven back by the Machine. Many attempts were made to dislodge the Ring; they failed time after time, but in the end the assailants managed to effect a breach in the fortress, and, gaining ground step by step, amid a series of incidents which I shall have another opportunity of relating, succeeded at the expiration of ten years in overthrowing the Ring. But, as in New York, the triumph of the good citizens was uot of long duration. The municipal administration once more fell under the yoke of the Machine, whose managers exploited it on more or less commercial lines. Abuses were not so flagrant, but extravagance none the less continued to characterize the municipal government of Philadelphia. This extravagance is attested by t wo sets of figures, which speak volumes: During the twelve years which followed the defeat of the Gas King (lKtcs-lNW

Among the other large cities, several, especially Washington, New Orleans, San Francisco, Cincinnati, Chicago, were hardly better off than Philadelphia or New York in the matter of Rings. Elsewhere municipal disorders occurred on a smaller scale, but under almost similar conditions; that is to say, that wherever municipal resources whetted people's appetites, and a large population devoid of natural cohesion and public spirit, but abounding in floating and corrupt elements, and wedded to the notion of " regularity," could be easily taken in tow by the party Machine, the latter allowed the municipal property to become the prey of the boldest spirits. Almost all the cities whose population exceeded 100,000, or even a lesser figure, had their Rings. At one time a Ring was deliberately formed to plunder the city by a few persons who were trying to capture the Organization of the predominant political party for that purpose. At another the Ring developed almost automatically through the play of the party system. The plan of fighting municipal elections on political lines, without reference to the special fitness or even to the integrity of the candidates, brought into municipal life many individuals of questionable public spirit, who soon discovered that the government of the city offered opportunities for extravagance and jobbery, and they took advantage of it with more or less audacity or more or less moderation. Sometimes it was a formal Ring with a regular organization the current expenditures of the city rose from 13J millions of dollars (in round numbers) to more than *3'2* millions (137 per cent), whereas the value of the rateable property increased from 554 to 770 millions only (37 per cent).

1 Three years of Ring government (1871-1874) saddled the city of Washington with a debt twice as large (in proportion to the population) as that contracted by the whole Union during the four years of civil war; and what the city got in return in the form of the public works, which had served as a pretext for this extravagant expenditure, was valueless; thus the wood pavement cost four millions of dollars, but it was so badly done that it had to be renewed at a fresh cost of 91,420,000 (see *Nation,* Vol. XLII, p. 28; Vol. XLV, p. 47). An eminent citizen of this city sums up the career of the municipality under the government of political parties as follows: "It has made the city hall of Chicago an asylum of party retainers, who live on the public revenues, control party management, and stand between the people and their government. It culminated in Chicago in 18115, in a common council which was literally a den of thieves. Some three fourths of the members banded themselves together to plunder the public and to blackmail corporations" *(The Mnnii-5pnl Outlook,* by Edwin B. Smith, Chicago Municipal Voters' league, ISM), p. 7). which carried on the exploitation of the city, after having gained a footing in a municipal department, which served it as a citadel whence it directed its operations; such was the celebrated Ring of San Francisco, which was installed in the fire department. At another time the Rings were more in the nature of temporary and intermittent combinations. For the better concealment of their designs, they often fastened on a single municipal department which offered them something to exploit or the means of making money. This department was frequently that of the police, as in New York under the late rule of Tammany.

When the scandals reached their highest pitch, or the burden of taxation became intolerable, revolts broke out against the corrupt Rings and the Machines, as in New York and Philadelphia. That is to say, the good citizens shook off their indifference, rose, organized themselves, beat to arms, and marched against the enemies of the public weal intrenched behind the Machine of the predominant party. The independents combined with the rival party for this purpose, detached honest citizens from the party in power, and often succeeded in overthrowing the Ring. Many of these revolts introduced new tendencies, new currents, into American political life caught in the toils of party organization, and for this reason the most important and the most characteristic of these attempts at emancipation will be considered in their proper place. For the moment, so far as the history of the growing influence of the Caucus in municipal life and the direction taken by the latter under its impulse is concerned, it need only be pointed out that the revolts in question, even the most successful, the most victorious ones, were but incidents, which merely made a break in the prescription of the power of the Machine. Hardly freed from its yoke, the American cities for the most part soon fell under it again, for this simple reason, that the principal factors of the situation remained the same. When the anger provoked by the sudden revelation of the scandals calmed down, and when the vigilance of the good citizens began to tire, which was always pretty soon, the permanent forces on which the Machine rested, after having been in abeyance for a moment, asserted themselves once more. They afflicted the great majority of voters with a dimness of sight, and even those who had some clearness of vision were content to ask, like the member of Congress, who, having come into the House while the claims of two rival candidates to a contested seat were being investigated, and having been told by a colleague that "they are both rascals," enquired: "Which is our rascal?" In one form or another, therefore, in a greater or lesser degree, the municipal abuses upheld or encouraged by the Caucus continued to be common occurrences in most of the large cities. In all parts of the country they stamped municipal administration, not to mention the moral effects, with two leading traits which constitute the material result of its career since the Civil War: an excessive increase in the debt of the city, and the utter inadequacy of its municipal plant. Of the colossal sums expended, a certain portion went into the pockets of the plunderers, and the greater portion, which was devoted to legitimate objects, was misapplied by untrustworthy or incompetent agents, leaving the cities with no thoroughly developed or well executed public works.

IV

The direct exploitation of municipal interests, on the brutal methods popularized by Tweed, was at an early stage supplemented, and afterwards more and more replaced, by indirect exploitation. This last method was peculiarly favoured by a special phenomenon of the economic expansion, the stimulating property of which in the corruption of municipal government I have already, pointed out. The special economic factor referred to was the rise of joint-stock industrial concerns, of corporations. While imparting to corruption a fresh development, often of a more subtle but of an exceedingly penetrating kind, it enabled the party Organization at the same time to take a more direct, more personal share in the prostitution of the powers of government to private interests. The extraordinary outburst of manufactures and of specidation, after the war, brought about a concentration of capital unprecedented in history, which made a comparatively limited VOL. II — N 178 number of capitalist combinations masters of most of the economic functions of the country. Daily spreading further and further, the companies overran the American continent all the more easily that the notions and the habits of individual freedom and non-intervention of the State, which had passed into dogmas, secured industrial liberty, and that the legislator trained in these notions and habits was taken unawares by the unexpected evolution of industrial relations. While rendering great services to the community and developing its economic life with increasing force and rapidity, the corporations exhibited insatiable greed and, as it were, an innate tendency to push their way by trampling on individual interests, or on the weaker interests which crossed their path. They tried to create monopolies by crushing competition *per fas et nefas*. Will the State remain a passive spectator of this power, or will it use its authority to arrest this coalition of selfish interests, which in their career of encroachment may constitute a danger for the general interest, or in any event will it be watchful enough to stop direct usurpation on their part? These were the questions raised from the very beginning. The answer given by the course of events was not satisfactory; the organs of government showed themselves at the outset indifferent or even too obliging to the corporations. With culpable complaisance they made over to the companies large portions of the public property entrusted to their care, and by their tolerance facilitated the abuses in which the latter indulged. The corporations, which had command of money, used it lavishly to buy the support and the connivance of which they stood in need.

Their operations were directed in the first place against municipal administration, with a view to obtaining from it concessions which consisted of the right to run undertakings of public interest, to utilize the public thoroughfares or the land of the city for streetcars, railways, railroads in transit, gas works, electrical supply, water works, etc These concessions or "franchises," out of which the companies made a profit, consequently represented for the cities which had the disposal of them an asset for which it was only right to obtain a return. But the companies more often than not managed to get the franchises gratis, or by payment of an absurdly small due; they bought the members of the city councils, which were generally filled, thanks to the Caucus, with politicians of a low stamp. The steady growth of the cities and the technical improvements in the means of transport and communication increased the number of the franchises and their value, and along with them the opportunities for corruption. The traffic in franchises became very common in the large cities; it created a particular species of town councillors, which acquired a melancholy popularity under the name of "boodle aldermen,'' from whom the corporations bought the ordinance of the council, or who even of their own accord organized a syndicate to hold out a public right until a purchaser could be found. The municipal freebooters, organized in "rings" or "combines," thus found a means of making money without taking it directly out of the pockets of the ratepayers, but the loss was none the less enormous to the latter; for if the companies had paid the cities for the franchises, or paid what they were worth, there would have been no need, as has been calculated in the case of New York, for instance, of municipal taxes to defray the city expenditure. The corporations obtained numberless other favours which consolidated their monopoly, to the detriment of the citizens, or even of future generations, bound by the culpable complaisance or negligence of the municipalities. With their complicity the corporations even evaded payment of their proper quota of rates, and paid only a very small portion of them, leaving the burden to be borne by the poorer ratepayers. While buying boodle aldermen directly whenever they could, the companies, which had considerable interests at stake, hit The word "boodle," used in vulgar parlance, and especially in thieves' slang, to denote money or booty, has become synonymous with money used for bribery, especially for bribing aldermen. Cf. C. L. Norton, *Political Americanismn,* N. Y., 1890, and E. Brown and A. Strauss, *A Dictionary of American Politicn,* N. Y., 1892.

A. R. Conkling, *City Government in the United States,* N. Y., 1895, p. 176.

'The triennial report, of 1898, of the Bureau of Labour Statistics of the State of Illinois, points out that the tax on dogs brings in more to Chicago than that on the street-car companies. "In 18X6 the dogs paid.'J7,918 for the few privileges they enjoy, while the street-car companies paid jS.'SO.MO; but soon afterwards the dog. having less influence in legislative halls than certain financiers, bad to bear the larger burden." In 1896 the dog-tax yielded t?84,48'J while all the street-car lines together brought in only $58,828. upon the plan of supplementing this resource by trying to pack the councils in their own way and for their own convenience, to get in men who would be at their disposal from the beginning. With this object the corporations laid hands on the machinery of the party Organization; they intervened with their money and their creatures in the primaries and the conventions to secure the nomination of accommodating candidates, or even constructed the party Machine from top to bottom for their own use on the method adopted, for instance, by the Gas Ring in Philadelphia, and did as they liked with the political Organization which distributed elective offices; or again subsidized the existing Machine, which, in return, gave them the benefit of its influence with its nominees, on the principle of *do ut des* applied to all concerned.

The relations of this kind between the party Organizations and the corporations grew up not so much in municipal life as in the larger spheres of the States and of the Union, in which the big companies took their full flight. With interests extending over the economic surface of the country, and with an unquenchable thirst for gain, they needed still more the complaisance of Congress and of the State Legislatures. But to buy their members singly, as plain aldermen were bought, was not such an easy matter, owing alike to the great number of the legislators, which would have rendered the operation an expensive one, and to their higher character and rank, which made attempts to corrupt them more hazardous. The party Organizations very often provided a way of getting round them more cheaply and more effectively: the representatives elected with the all-powerful aid of the Organizations, or even with their money, contracted obligations towards them which had no need to be expressly stated; they flowed from the nature of human relations. Entering into alliance with the Organizations, by means of heavy contributions to their funds, or even by paying them the whole bill of the election campaign, the corporations obtained a hold over the representatives. "I wanted," declared Jay Gould, the celebrated speculator, to a legislative committee of enquiry before which he was summoned as a witness, "I wanted the Legislatures of four States, and to obtain control of them I made the Legislatures with my own money; I found this plan a cheaper one." Direct legislative bribery was not on that account unknown; not often met with in Congress, it was far more common in the State Legislatures; but even in these assemblies a large proportion or most of the members were not to be bought, and if they showed themselves too obliging to the corporations, it was more often because their dependent position with regard to the party Organizations and their powerful backers forced them to be so. A member of the Legislature of New York has pathetically explained this by saying to a journalist: "I want to be honest, and I am honest; but I am the slave of the Organization, and if I kick out I am politically ruined." Often the companies made use of the machinery of the party Organizations to introduce their own agents into the State Legislatures and Congress, so that they were directly represented in these assemblies, like constituencies, by several members, who formed a ring there devoted to their special interests. In the years immediately following the war Congress was ruled by a set of industrial rings of this kind which made common cause on log-rolling principles.

Under one aspect or another the party Organizations appeared as the base of operations for all the great private interests in their efforts to bend the power of the State to their own selfish ends, efforts which have filled the greater part of the history of the United States since the Civil War. The railroad companies took the lead in the attack delivered by monopoly on the power of the State as representing the public interest. The construction of the immense network of railroads, their financial management, and their working were marked by flagrant abuses, committed for the benefit of small rings of financiers and speculators, with the help or the tolerance of the State. Almost all the railroad lines were built at an excessive cost, with subsidies in money, and especially in grants of land made by Congress out of the national property. Too often these concessions, by which in the fourteen

years from 1861 to 1875 a territory of more than 163,000,000 of *Money in City Elections,* an address before the Commonwealth Club in New York, March 21, 1887, by Joseph E. Bishop.
The North American Review referred to this subject in 1869 in the following terms: "A net-work of rings controls Congress, and forms a hedge which marks the limit within which argument and reason may prevail" *(The Session,* April, 1869, p. 617). acres had passed into the hands of the companies, were granted to shady speculators, who commended themselves to members of Congress by their lavish contributions to the funds of the party Organizations in their States, and to whom many a Senator owed his seat. The vast tracts of land obtained from the government made the companies a quasi-feudal power in the respective localities, and supplied them with ample material for banking and stock-exchange speculations. To obtain the capital required for building the lines, the concession-holders issued stock, with which they indulged in reckless and fraudulent gambling, of which the public, who invested their savings in these securities, was the victim; and it was almost impossible, owing to the inadequacy of the law, to call the company directors to account; sometimes, even, at their instigation, special laws passed by the Legislatures screened their predatory operations. But the most crying abuses came to light in the working of the lines, in the arbitrary application of freight tariffs, "abuses so glaring in their proportions as to savour of fiction rather than actual history" the directors allowed different terms to different customers, which enabled the one to crush all competition, thanks to reduced rates, and ruined the others.

A few years after the war it became clear that in the case of railroads free competition did not supply the required regulator of economic relations, that it was absolutely necessary to have them supervised and regulated by the State. Thereupon the companies began a desperate struggle to escape from the State, and for a considerable time they held it in check, because they had succeeded in introducing their owu contingents into the forces of the State arrayed against them, by means of the direct corruption of the lobby, as well as through the medium of the party Organization. Their money and their Report of the committee of enquiry on railroads appointed by the Legislature of New York in 1879, and generally known by the name of the Hepburn Committee, from its chairman, Mr. A. B. Hepburn *(Report of the Special Committee on Railroads,* Albany, 1871), p. 7).
" Lobby " is the word applied to legislative brokers, a very common class in American legislative assemblies, in which they exercise their persuasive arts on the members, either with money or other inducements, to obtain their votes for or against the bills in which the employers of the brokers are interested. large staff (the railroads had as many as 900,000 employees in the Union) enabled them to manipulate the machinery of the Organization in more than one State, by drawing to their side the low ward politicians, who were only too ready to sell themselves. They concluded alliances with the most corrupt Machines and Rings, of which the agreement between the Erie Company and Tammany Ring may be quoted as an instance. Often the high officials of the companies sat on the important party committees and pulled the strings from them. They equipped and kept up political Organizations for their own use, and ran them as they pleased, like their trains. If a Senator had lifted up his voice against them at Washington, the "railroad kings" ordered the Organization in his State to fall upon him and prevent his re-election. These "kings" intervened in all the presidential elections; they tried to settle to their liking the elections of governors, of the principal officials, of judges, of members of legislatures, and even the composition of committees in the assemblies. Certain States became completely dependent on the railroads, were "owned" by them. Thus the New York Central controlled the State of New York, the Pennsylvania Railroad ruled Pennsylvania and extended its sway over Ohio, the Central Pacific was master of California. All theorgans of government in these States were at their beck and call. In Congress even the railroads wielded a decisive influence; a good many of their magnates had seats in the Senate, forming almost a quarter of the assembly; other members of it were their agents.. At one time the railroad companies appeared to be a real menace to the republic and to liberty. Their omnipotence recalled the part which slavery had played in the political and economic destinies of the United States before 1860. "The old slave power," remarked the former anti-slavery champions, "acted as a unit and had a combined capital in human flesh estimated atff!200,000,000. It ruled the nation forty years. It was exceedingly difficult for a northern man to stand up in Congress and look that power in the face, but we believe it has been quite as difficult for a member of Congress, North and South, to withstand the purposes of the railway power. The danger is different but not less." The analogy, whether G. W. Julian, "Pending Ordeals *ol* Democracy" *(International Review,* complete or not, at any rate applied to, and could be accounted for to a great extent by the role which the party Organization played in both cases: it espoused the interests of the companies just as it had served as a bulwark to slavery.

When the populations of the North-West and of the Pacific slope, in their exasperation at the abuses of the railroads, revolted (Grangers' Movement, Farmers' Alliance), too readily ascribing to them all their economic embarrassments, they had to sever their connection with the regular party Organizations and wage open war on them; for their enemy, the railroads, was always entrenched behind them. Over and over again they succeeded in defeating the coalitions of the railroads with the party Organizations and in getting laws passed which curtailed the power of the companies, but these coalitions continued all the same, and frequently had their revenge. Most of the laws enacted, which were often extravagant and unpractical, were repealed, or their application was paralyzed by the connections which the railroads possessed in the Legislatures, the government departments, and even in the law courts. In the meantime the economic abuses thrown in the teeth of the companies became to a certain extent less pronounced, under the influence of the popular agitation as well as in the natural course of things, yet the companies still remained open to attack, and the support of the Organizations was always valuable to them for warding it off. The legitimate attacks provoked by the monopolist power and the corrupt influence of the companies were followed by others which were not so; the unpopularity of the companies with the public made them a target for venal legislators, who brought in bills directed against this or that company with the sole object of being paid to withdraw their proposals. The companies fought these blackmailers (called "strikers ") with the same devices which they employed to buy the laws of which they stood in need,—lobbying and influence of the party Organizations, to which they made regular contributions, in the nature of insurance premia, "for protection." Treating their relations with the parties from a commercial point of view, the companies paid no attention to their principles or programmes, combining with one party in one State and with its rival, if in a majority, in another, according to the rule laid down by the "railway king" referred to above, Jay Gould, the master of the Erie line, who declared before another and more recent committee of enquiry: "In a Republican district I was a Republican; in a Democratic district I was a Democrat; in a doubtful district I was doubtful; but I was always Erie." When the companies had grasped the notion of an insurance premium, they fell into the habit of subscribing to the funds of the Organization of both parties in the same State or the same city, with the knowledge of both, just as insurances of the same property against fire or other accidents are effected in several companies simultaneously.

Precisely similar relations grew up between the party Organizations and the various monopolized industries which came after that of the railroads in the economic evolution of America, during the decades from 1870 to 1890, and the most important of which obtained a far-reaching notoriety under the name of "Trusts." The most powerful trust, moreover, that of petroleum, represented by the Standard Oil Company, was created with the privity of the railroads, which allowed it special rates for freight, and by the very community of interests which arose between them was drawn into the same methods of action on the government. The other trusts, however, acted in the same fashion, for they all owed their existence and their unchecked growth more or less to the negligence or the improper intervention of the authorities, which it was their interest to perpetuate. In any event they had an interest in not being interfered with gratuitously, and they were glad to pay for their "protection." The directors of the Sugar Trust, the most important after the Petroleum Trust, had admitted this before the committee of enquiry of the Senate of the United States, representing it as perfectly natural, and even as right and proper. The dialogue which took place on this occasion between the Senators conducting the enquiry and the directors of the Trust was highly edifying. The committee was appointed to clear up the suspected connivance of certain Senators with the Trust in the vote for high duties on sugar. The Trust benefited by the ultraprotectionist tariff, which closed the American market to foreign refiners, until, in 1894, on the revision of this tariff, Report of the committee of 1879, quoted above, p. 51.

undertaken with a view to lower the duties, the House decided to admit sugar duty-free. But the Trust secured, the support of a few Senators, headed by a famous Machine leader, who nullified this decision and got the old tariff on refined sugar raised still higher, so as to make the Trust, whose industrial organization had already killed all rivalry at home, safe against competition from abroad. The representatives of the Trust summoned before the committee of enquiry denied that they had contributed to the funds of the national Organization of the party, while admitting, with more or less reticence, that they had done so in the case of the party Organizations in the States, the dealings with which were beyond the jurisdiction of the federal committee and might be admitted without putting the witnesses under the obligation of giving full details. "Contributions to local political organizations," declared the president of the Trust, "have always been made by corporations, before the Trust and by the Trust and the American Sugar Refining Company, and no doubt will continue to be. It is a very suitable and proper thing to do."... "We have a good deal of local protection for our contribution."... "Wherever there is a dominant party, wherever the majority is very large, that is the party that gets the contribution, because that is the party that controls the local matters." "Then," asked a Senator on the committee, "the Sugar Trust is a Democrat in a Democratic State and a Republican in a Republican State?" "As far," was the reply, "as local matters are concerned, I think that is about it." "You think," asked the Senator of another representative of the Trust, "it is perfectly laudable for the American Sugar Refining Company (the official name of the Trust) to contribute large sums of money, by the thousands of dollars, for the purpose of influencing elections in the country, do you?" "I have," replied the other, "always understood, or for many years, that it is the custom of both parties to solicit from corporations and individuals contributions for the carrying on of their political campaigns, and that it is the custom of corporations and individuals to respond to such invitations." Senate's Reports, second session, 53d Congress, Vol. X (Report of the Committee, August 2, 1891, N006), p. 350. "Do you think it is perfectly proper?"... ." I think as parties are now managed it is perfectly proper." While certain industrial interests, of a more or less local scope, only asked not to be disturbed in their practices by the government, other undertakings sought the intervention of the State to get an artificial value authoritatively imparted to their products throughout the country. The first bought "protection" retail, now from one and now from the other party, according as whichever of the two had the local majority, or from both at the same time. The second, whose interests and appetites could obtain satisfaction only through the complaisance of the legislators at Washington, allied themselves with one of the two national parties which were contending for supreme power. In this respect the Sugar Trust, which depended to a certain extent on the customs tariff, formed a transition between the monopolies of both kinds and their respective *modus operandi.* Foremost among the private interests of the second category came the manufacturing industries, which can be placed in a privileged position by protective customs duties. The somewhat mild protectionist tendencies, which struggled with varying success for more than half a century before the Civil War, received an extraordinary impulse during the war, which imperatively demanded additional sources of revenue, and which brought into force with this object, in 1861, a higher general tariff, supplemented in succeeding years by new and partial enhancements of the customs duties. It was understood that all these enhancements, caused by exceptional circumstances, should be of a provisional character only. But these fiscal measures, adopted while the Republican party was in power, exactly suited the manufacturers, and being desirous of perpetuating them, they attached themselves to that party and made it their tool and the obedient servant of their interests. They supplied the Republican Organization with "fat," with money for its election campaigns, and in return they obtained protective duties for their products which enabled them to make enormous fortunes. It was no use for the budget to show a large surplus of receipts every year; the duties were kept up just the same, subject only to frequent readjustments, some being raised and some lowered.

i *Ibid.*, p. 393.

The accession of a Democrat to the Presidency, in the person of Mr. Cleveland, and the extremely firm attitude taken up by him against excessive protection, only had the effect of bringing the Republican Organization and the manufacturers closer together, and of spurring them to exceptional efforts. The Republican Organization having made up its mind to "fry all the fat out of the manufacturers," declared to them in a confidential circular: "We want money, and want it at once." The manufacturers, and especially those of Pennsylvania, appealed to by Mr. Wanamaker, got together very heavy sums for the next presidential campaign, of 1888, a large portion of which was employed in buying votes, and by dint of corruption they brought the Republicans back into power. The latter hastened to repay the advances with some coin of their own making: Mr. Wanamaker received a post in the Cabinet as his brokerage, and the manufacturers were presented with a new tariff still more prohibitive than the preceding ones, that which became famous under the name of the " McKinley tariff." The economic difficulties created by the exaggerations of this tariff helped to reinstal Mr. Cleveland in the White House, but the manufacturers set to work again, and by means of an underground agitation conducted throughout the country brought the Republican Organization to adopt Mr. McKinley himself as presidential candidate for the next term. He had the good luck to see the opposite side take up with the mad programme of free coinage of silver, which made the depreciated white metal the monetary standard on the basis of its old ratio to gold. A good many Democrats, preferring their country to their party, separated from the latter, and to stop the silverites with their plan, which threatened to bring about a financial catastrophe, they did not hesitate to vote for the Republican candidate, Mr. McKinley. It was clearly understood that the election was to be fought, not on the tariff, but on "sound money." Thanks to the help of the dissentient Democrats, the "gold Democrats," Mr. McKinley was elected. But once in the White House he remembered only the support of the manufacturers, and hurriedly summoned an extraordinary session of Congress to "get the tariff revised by its friends." The Republican majority elected on the currency question hastened to offer the manufacturers a new ultra-protectionist tariff (the " Dingley tariff "), leaving the settlement of the monetary standard, which the financial stability of the country demanded, in abeyance.

The campaign of the silverites, conducted under the name and style of the "regular" Democratic Organization, was, in its turn, to a great extent a speculation of wealthy industrial interests trying to exploit the power of the State for their own advantage. They consisted of the owners of silver mines in the West, who demanded measures for ensuring their product an artificial market and then an artificial price, higher than the market value, just like the manufacturers. The increasing production of silver, owing to the discovery of new mines in the Far West, while steadily lowering the price of this metal, made it less and less fit for serving as a measure of value. But guided by the interests of the Republican Organization, which wanted the votes of the mining States to round off its national influence, and in particular to discharge the obligations of the party to the manufacturers, the Republicans in power passed on two successive occasions laws which obliged the Treasury to effect regular purchases of silver at the market rate, and to mint it in the legal ratio to gold of 16 to 1, although the silver dollar, while legal tender, had practically gone out of circulation, and the commercial ratio in which the two metals stood to each other had fallen as low as 31 to 1. The producers of silver, not content with having a forced buyer in the person of the Treasury, wanted to deprive it of its seigniorage as well, in order to pocket the difference between the legal ratio and the commercial one themselves, and they demanded free coinage of the metal, coupled of course with the *imprimatur* of the State, which would give their commodity a forced currency. But in the meanwhile the accumulation in "the Treasury of silver paid for by notes redeemable in gold put the latter at a premium, and the law for the compulsory purchase of silver had to be repealed. Thereupon the silver men recommenced their agitation. Having resolved to make a fight for power, they took as their weapon the Organization of the Democratic party, which party appeared to be specially infected with the popular prejudice that credits the State with the power of indefinitely increasing the "volume of money." The sinews of war contributed by the wealthy owners of-the mines, trading on this prejudice, got the better of the Democratic Organization, and the latter made over to the champions of the white metal the votes of the bulk of the "regular" adherents of the party. The coalition, which took its stand on the platform of "free silver," attracted a good many radical and revolutionary elements, who imagined that they were combating plutocracy in combating gold; but if the Democratic Organization had won, its victory would have mostly benefited the big silver producers, who would have been able to sell their commodity at double the price.

Following the example of the large industrial or speculative undertakings which I have just described, all the other private interests which had something to hope or fear from the State, which could be affected by legislation, paid tribute to the party Organizations, bought their support and patronage with ready money; and when they were slow about asking for it, the Organization thrust it on them to get the price of it. It was not only undertakings with legitimate objects if not methods, which tried to mix up their interests with those of the party Organizations in this way; enterprises which could not bear the light, conceived and carried on in contravention of the law, to defraud the Treasury, also skulked behind the party Organizations, which were only too ready to admit that one person's money is as good as another's. In short, it was the extension of the methods of Tammany Hall in all their fulness to a larger sphere.

Developing step by step, the material exploitation of the electoral monopoly acquired by the party Organization reached its climax; from a broker in offices it rose to be a trafficker in political influence; along with elective posts it sold the power residing in them, beginning with the adjudication of contracts, government orders, and public works, and ending with a wholesale and retail trade in legislation and "protection."

V

Thus in the political as well as in the industrial sphere with its relations to the State the party Organization became the great go-between for greedy private interests in their dealings with the authorities. This singular function, which it (lischarged with a quasi-constitutional regularity, soon made it develop a special and improved organ. The systematic exploitation of public offices, with "what there is in it," by the manipulation of the election business, became a more and more complicated undertaking in proportion as the number of voters increased and their social, ethnic, and economic differences grew more marked, as was the case especially in the large cities after the war. To be successfully carried out, this undertaking required efforts brought to bear on numerous and diverse groups, and yet directed by a single mind. The punctual execution of the word of command along the whole line could be ensured only by the individual responsibility of those who transmitted it. The discipline of the troops rested on the unquestioned authority of the immediate chief. That authority was equally important during the battle and after it, when the time arrived for dividing the booty; it alone could allot to each his share by silencing individual jealousies and preventing rebellions. The more principles retired into the background in the existence of the party organizations, leaving the spoils their sole object, the greater was their need, in order to live and act, of a strong personal government. It appeared, by a natural evolution, after the war, in the person of the autocratic Machine leaders, who wielded power like the "tyrants" of the Greek cities. In America they received the name of " boss," which has become as popular as that of Caucus and Machine. The name dates from the Dutch period in the history of New York, and comes from the Dutch word "baas," which means master, employer, and had long been common in every-day language as a respectful appellation addressed by an inferior to a superior. But after the Civil War it became a political term applied sarcastically to politicians, who, in spite of democratic appearances, ruled despotically and wielded a usurped power. This invidious acceptation of the word "boss" has not obliterated its original meaning, and in familiar language it continued to be employed in a nonpolitical as well as a political sense instead of "chief," "leader," to denote respectable politicians, and even those in the highest position. Still in the news of the day and in politi In a political conversation which I had with a Democratic Senator at Washington he repeatedly used the expression "our boss," without further cal controversy the term "boss" was always used of party dictators, controllers of corrupt Machines, brought into power and keeping themselves there by their instrumentality.

The large cities were the first to develop this species of rulers on the American continent, thanks to the heterogeneous character of their inhabitants, of their numerous populace with its caesarean instincts, which always incline the masses to embody their political feelings in a man. Imbued with these propensities, which the wretchedness and ignorance of the masses made it so easy to trade on, the populations of the big cities lent the politicians their large stock of personal loyalty, which, passing from hand to hand, like a bill of exchange with successive endorsements, was ultimately invested in a supreme chief. This man, who took the lead because he showed the most energy and skill in managing those who knew how to manage the masses, had only to transform the loyalty dammed up in the party channel into votes and public offices to make it the foundation of his power. His sole obligation was to assign their quota of the profits which he made to all the intermediaries who collected the electoral raw material and passed it on to him. The liability was not a very heavy one, if the offices and other sources of gain were abundant. All these conditions happened to be first combined in the home of Tammany, in New York, and it was there that the first bosses made their appearance. Tweed, whose figure is familiar to us, was exactly a "boss" who, while leaving the forms of popular government intact, practically monopolized its powers and ruled the city despotically. It was to him, it appears, that the term "boss" was first applied, but he had his precursor before the war in the person of Fernando Wood, who organized the mob and with its support became the dictator of Tammany Hall. Several times mayor of New York, he sold public offices by auction, getting cash payments of $10,000, $20,000, and even $50,000 for them. His star paled, however, before that of Tweed, and he accepted from the latter a seat in the Congress of the United States for his old age. The brilliant career of Tweed was prematurely cut short by his imprisonment, but the position of boss did not long description of the person intended. He was speaking of Mr. Grover Cleveland, at that time (18%) President of the United States.

remain vacant. After a short interregnum it was held by John Kelly, who for many years autocratically ruled Tammany Hall and the city, *urbem et orbem,* disposing of the resources of the city, fixing its budget, deciding who was to get the various municipal offices, who should represent the city in the State Legislature, who should be returned for Congress, who elected judge. Mayor, town council, executive committees, party conventions nominating candidates, simply registered his wishes, his orders. After Kelly's death his dignity passed without disturbance, quite smoothly, as in a monarchy where the succession is well established, to his lieutenant, who is down to the present day the reigning boss of New York. In the other large cities boss rule also asserted itself, without presenting the same continuity and the same fulness of power as in New York and Philadelphia. Sometimes the boss was overthrown, either by a sort of palace revolution planned by jealous rivals, or by a coalition of the good citizens, exasperated by the municipal abuses for which the boss was generally more or less responsible. But often it was only an interregnum. The victorious party itself evolved a boss, who took up the business of the dethroned "tyrant."

The boss also made his appearance in the political sphere of the States. He was called into existence there by the same necessities as in the cities: the Organization scattered over the vast area of the State required a head, especially in view of its relations with the federal executive, who, in pursuance of the system of spoils, apportioned them as rewards for electoral services among the "workers" in the States. To make these distributions the President stood no less in need of responsible intermediaries. As we are already aware, this dutywas assumed by the Senators; they were generally the State bosses. Having attained their position by a process of natural selection, like their prototypes of the cities, they wielded, thanks to their influence over the State Machine, a similar power, which in certain States, headed by New York, Pennsylvania, and Maryland, bordered on pure absolutism. They distributed the nominations, that is to say, decided who should be candidates for the Legislature and for the other high offices of the State; they collected the assessments; the State Legis VOL. II — O lature, which they had made with their Machine, was at their orders; they settled who should be appointed Speaker of the House, what laws it should pass and what reject, who should be elected Senator of the United States. Upholding their authority by the bestowal of federal offices, which the President conceded to them in consideration of that very authority, the State bosses felt the need of a firm footing at Washington, and for this object the seats in the Senate, which shared with the President his prerogative of appointing to the high offices, were specially valuable. The State bosses, therefore, emerging from the retired position in which the city bosses often remained, generally got themselves appointed Senators, and in the double capacity of State boss and Senator they could take a high tone with the President and impose their will on him. We have already met with this type of boss in the person of Conkling of New York and Gorman of Maryland. Pennsylvania, Illinois, Ohio, Indiana, California, and several other States also gave the Senate a line of bosses who had shot up on their soil. A good many State bosses were not able to get into the Senate because the Legislature of their State was in the hands of the opposite party, but that did not prevent them from wielding their power in their State with the full support of the President, if he belonged to their party. For instance, Conkling's pupil and successor in the dignity of Republican boss of the State of New York lorded it absolutely over that State for many years without having a seat in the Senate or any public position whatever. Sometimes the bosses abstained from taking this seat for themselves, and put into it devoted followers who served as their mouthpieces. Far more often this part of underling to the boss was played in

Congress by the members of the House of Representatives, who owed their seats to his good pleasure. Most of the State bosses, when they had attained to power, managed to keep it a very long time, sometimes for their whole life; in Pennsylvania it had even become hereditary; after a long reign a boss transmitted the dignity, with his seat in the Senate, to his son. In the States where the Machine had not developed to any great extent, bossism naturally found the ground less favourable, but the tendency towards this regime was exhibited almost everywhere, appearing in one place with well marked traits, in another assuming a vaguer or fainter outline, according to the local circumstances and the somewhat changeable conditions of the moment in the local life of parties.

The role of Senatorial boss, considerable as it was, remained, however, confined to the affairs of their States, especially to matters of patronage; it did not extend to government in general, to national policy. Bossism made a tentative movement in that direction, but it led to nothing. During Grant's Presidency a sort of syndicate of powerful bosses was formed in the Senate, including Conkling, Cameron, Chandler, Morton, and others, called the " Senatorial Group," which, with the President's connivance, dictated the policy of the national government. But after Grant's departure the bosses' syndicate disappeared. Hayes gave them the cold shoulder. They might, perhaps, have recovered their power if their audacious endeavour to thrust Grant's presidency on the country for a third term had succeeded. But respect for the venerable tradition bequeathed by George Washington, which did not admit of a person holding the chief magistracy for more than two terms, proved stronger than the intrigues of the bosses. Since then the attempt to play at mayors of the palace in a federal republic has not been renewed, and the bosses have fallen back upon local affairs in the States and the cities.

Moreover, almost from the very outset of their career, they had been strongly tempted by interests other than those of politics in the original, in the European sense of the word. The system of "regular" nominations and assessments, which brought in money, opened out to the boss commercial prospects along with the gratifications derived from the enjoyment of power. Those prospects were widened in a marked degree by the expansion of speculation and industry, which made capital inclined to secure the connivance of the authorities by means of corruption. Instead of being practised individually on the members of the Legislatures and councils, the corruption was soon brought to bear, for the sake of greater economy and efficiency, on the party Organizations, which made and unmade those bodies wholesale. But to come to an understanding with them for this purpose, and to keep up the delicate and continuous relations which the plan required, the capitalists, the corporations, stood in need of intermediaries who could be relied upon for the discretion demanded of a go-between and who possessed unquestioned influence. The political boss, the autocrat of the Machine, who had just broken through the shell of the spoils' system, happened to be at hand to discharge this duty, and the capitalists entered into a coalition with him. Their subscriptions to the party chest were henceforth paid to the boss, and with these extensive resources at his disposal he increased his power in the Organization tenfold; he no longer depended solely on the assessments for conducting the election campaign, and on the patronage, on the places which he could distribute, for keeping his men loyal; he had a fund of his own with which he could provide for everything and make his will law for all the politicians who were dependent on the Organization, or who gravitated towards it. These increased means of influence which the corporations and other capitalists supplied to the boss, even gave the impression that it was capitalism which had created the boss; that the phenomenon of bossism was due, not so much to the evolution of the government of the country, as to its commercial development. There is some exaggeration in this view; capitalism does not create commodities, it only turns them to account; it buys what is for sale, men as well as materials. Capitalism has only raised the stature of the boss; it has enhanced his powers and his means of action, having found in him a highly perfected instrument. As the boss held in the hollow of his hand the members of the city councils or of the Legislatures, whose election he had procured by his resources and his absolute authority over the Machine, he was able to supply the corporations with " protection " on easier terms; obeying his word of command, those legislators voted the laws which the corporations needed or threw out those which interfered with them. The boss centralized political influence in his own hands, and made himself a broker or wholesale dealer in it. In proportion as the boss asserted himself in this direction, he drove the "lobby" into the background, just as in commerce and industry the small shop-keepers or manufacturers retired This view has been recently presented with much spirit in an interesting little volume by Mr. J. J. Chapman, *Causes and Consequences,* N. Y., 1898 (published in Englaud under the title, *Government, Democracy, and other Essays).* before the large stores and the factory. Thus at the centre of the political market, in the State of New York, the "lobby" in the State Legislature, which was flourishing up to a recent period, has been supplanted in the last ten or twelve years by the Tammany Hall boss or the Republican State boss, according to the shifting fortunes of parties. It was with them that the corporations now had to deal, whether they liked it or not, by purchasing their support or by submitting to blackmail. Living to a great extent on the corporations, bossism burst into full bloom in the States where big capitalist interests were concentrated, where companies were most numerous, such as New York, New Jersey, Pennsylvania. But in almost all other places where the

Machine created the boss, he used his political position as a business man; he appeared as a Janus with a double face, as a political dictator and as a broker in legislation and administration, or at all events a dealer in nominations. Following the general tendency of his time and of his environment, which preferred hard cash to public honours, the boss, when it was not necessary for his trade, as it was in the case of the State boss, and even, then, was ready to forego the ostensible exercise of public functions and content himself with occult power and the chances of making money. He reduced politics to a business in the ordinary sense of the word.

VI

The advent of the commercial boss marked the furthest point in the evolution of the party Organization. It indicated the complete elimination of political principles and ideas from its existence. Clearly they were no longer what kept the organized parties together, and the latter were living an artificial life. In fact, the quarter of a century which has elapsed since the constitutional settlement of the problem of the South, in 1870, has been simply one long demonstration of this fact. The Democratic party was only a party of resistance opposed to the Republican party, and this latter, called into being by a particular national problem, by the struggle against the extension of slavery, had accomplished its task. The South having been conquered and pacified after a fashion, the Republican party had henceforth all the less reason for existence that it had been formed out of dissimilar elements united on the sole question of slavery. But the Republican party did not see this; it was bent only on keeping itself in power, by substituting for its vanished principles an unreasoning discipline which saddened its early champions, by trying to rekindle the dying flame of the conflict with the South, by combining with the privileged interests of the manufacturers, and by shirking a straightforward attitude on other questions. But these questions thrust themselves on the parties against their will, and bursting in upon them sowed discord in their ranks, especially the financial problem, which threatened to upset the whole economic life of the country. Soon there was no question at all on which the respective parties were agreed among themselves. The Republicans of the manufacturing East were interested in the protectionist tariff; those of the agricultural West did not care about it; while a good many Democrats in the East were drawn by their interests towards protection, and even in the South, which was becoming a manufacturing country, the anti-protectionist ardour of the Democrats was cooling down. The desire to obtain " cheap money " by means of an unlimited paper currency, which seized on large sections of the population throughout the Union, brought dissension into the Democratic party (the "greenbackers" movement); then, when this desire took shape in the demand for free silver, it made fresh havoc in the Democratic party, while it divided the Republican party, sweeping before it like a tornado the Republican States of the West, inhabited by farmers involved in debt and on the look-out for panaceas which would enable them to repay their creditors. One of the founders of the Republican party, G. W. Julian, expressed his sentiments on this point in the following terms: "The work which had brought it together had been accomplished, but its discipline was not to be relaxed for a moment. On the contrary, the leaders were not only in favor of perpetuating the Organization, but they treated it as an institution. It was an enduring establishment, corresponding to the old-fashioned idea of a church, outside of which no good thing can exist, and inside of which all good things must originate. It was a master to be served, if not a deity to be worshipped. Its continued existence was indispensable, not only to the welfare but the life of the Republic, against which the 'rebels' were still plotting; and whoever denied this was to be counted as an enemy of his country" (" The DeathStruggle of the Republican Party," *North American Review*, 1878, p. lo2).

the capitalists of the East, with as little coin as possible. The time-honoured war-cry against the "rebel" South was powerless to restore the old unity of the Republican party, and even among the Republican whites in the South the attempt of their coreligionists in New England to bestow on them a new force bill (in 1890), to protect the vote of the negroes with federal troops, found no echo.

In reality it was another antagonism that was coming to light, no longer between the North and the South, but between the manufacturing East and the agricultural West, an economic antagonism complicated by social divergences which in many parts of the country were breeding revolt against the existing order of things, which savoured of plutocracy. But the parties had not the skill or the power to adapt themselves to the new state of affairs; they shirked looking the new problems in the face; they did not hear the mutterings of the social storm; for they were engrossed by the Organizations, which had but one idea: *Beati possidentes!* They did not trouble themselves about divisions within their own ranks; they had no objection to their members taking up opposite attitudes in different States or districts, according to the interests or the prejudices which predominated there, provided that the firm, in the name of which power was obtained and exploited, continued to exist. As in the days of the slavery conflict, "they agreed to disagree," in order not to shatter the party Organizations. In fact, it was exactly the same game in every respect, with the one exception that at that time it was less complicated, because there was only a single question which parties tried to make away with, whereas now the troublesome questions and the motives inspired by them intersected each other.

Every Congress, beginning with the Forty-third (of the years 1873-1875), threw into stronger relief the moral decomposition of the parties; very often there was cross voting on each side, a good many members called Republicans voting with members called Democrats, while other Democrats made common cause with Republicans in opposition to the firstnamed. Between the parties *qua* parties there was no longer any fixed line of demarcation, and to recognize them it was necessary, as has been remarked, to put labels on their members. Parties and members shifted their position with regard to the questions of the day according to the changing currents of the popular moods in different parts of the country, and the greater or less chances of inveigling the popular suffrage with this or that attitude. The grave problems of legislation were for the parties only something to play at heads and tails with. There was so little to choose between the platforms of the two parties that they might have been exchanged without ruffling the susceptibilities of their adherents. The platforms competed only in the vagueness and ambiguity of their declarations designed to catch votes. Nor did the distinctive criterion which was absent from their political principles appear in the moral character of either party; they were equally corrupt, and the corruption of each supplied the other with its reason for existence. "Turn out the rascals" was the cry to which the Republicans were dislodged from the Presidency, in 1884, after a quarter of a century's rule, — the same cry which served as a rallying word at New York against the Democratic Organization of Tammany Hall, and against so many other Democratic Machines.

Mr. Cleveland, whom this victory brought into the Presidency as nominee of the Democratic party, courageously tried to restore to it its individuality by making it take up on its own account the reform, which was imperatively demanded, of the improper taxation introduced by the protectionist tariff. The wire-pullers viewed this attempt with disfavour, being afraid of losing the protectionist element lodged within the party. But Mr. Cleveland, declaring war against protection, on the eve of the general election, by his famous message of 1887, forced the parties to fight on this question. The Democratic party lost the battle, but it seemed to have recovered its moral unity. It did not keep it for long, no more than its rival. Indeed, in a short time the situation was once more complicated by the preoccupations arising out of the silver agitation which was invading both parties. The Republicans returned to power, and being in a hurry to pay their debt to their allies, the manufacturers, by voting them a new and higher tariff, encountered the ill-will of the members of Congress from the Western States, who cared more for the 1 *Nation,* 5 August, 1886, p. 10.

free coinage of silver than for the increase of the customs duties. Not daring to oppose the Silverites directly, nor to consent to their demand, the majority of the Republican party granted them an instalment, to obtain their support for the tariff, in the form of a new law obliging the treasury to make regular purchases of the white metal (the Sherman Act of 1890). The path towards the financial disaster, which the wholesale introduction of a depreciated standard was bound to bring about, lay open, but the Republican Organization was safe, for a moment. When, two years later, the question of the unlimited coinage of silver was distinctly raised in Congress,— without success, however,— the Republican party in the Senate and in the House of Representatives split in two. It was the same with the Democrats, who had all voted as one man against the Sherman Act almost the day before. As the silver movement was gathering strength among the Democrats in the West, the national Organization of the party, which hitherto had prudently ignored the silver question, adopted, at the national convention of 1892, a platform which expressed its views on this burning question in terms that were a masterpiece of ambiguity and were intended to throw a veil over the divisions to which it gave rise, and to conciliate, or rather to inveigle, the opponents as well as the adherents of the silver standard. When, in the following year, the financial panic made the repeal of the Sherman Act of 1890 an imperative necessity, the parties in Congress showed themselves once more divided.

The silver agitation, which continued to make greater and greater havoc in the country, culminated at last in the crisis of 189G, which clearly showed how artificial, inconsistent, and dangerous was the existence of parties which, having outlived themselves, still cumbered the political stage. The decisive struggle was approaching, and the leaders of the parties were still shilly-shallying. The Republican candidate for the Presidency, put forward at an early stage by the manufacturers,— Mr. McKinley,— very communicative on the tariff question, evaded a straightforward declaration on the attitude which he was about to take up in the great controversy of the day; the curiosity evinced by the public on this point was resented by the wire-pullers of the party as premature and almost improper. They were waiting for clearer indications as to which way the cat would jump. At last, when it became evident that the Democrats were going over *en masse* into the silver camp, and that the big commercial interests in the West, on which the Republican party generally leaned, were on the side of gold, the national convention of the Republican party, of that party which had done so much to encourage the silverite demands and exasperate the crisis by its shuffling and its haggling, declared for gold, with a verbal proviso in favour of bimetallism. Three weeks later the national Democratic convention made a violent pronouncement in favour of free silver, and thereupon the last vestige of hesitation disappeared in the opposite camp: Mr. McKinley, who had supported the silver men in Congress, came out as the uncompromising champion of "sound money." The Democratic party, overrun by the silverites, was left shorn of its traditional principles, but it none the less kept its old name and style, the saving grace of which decided a very large proportion of its adherents to vote for silver irrespective of their convictions. Thus, even when the logic of events, getting the upper hand, had brought about an honest stand-up fight on the financial question, which for years past had been hanging like a Damocles' sword over the country, the situation was still a warped one. No real, natural regrouping of parties took place on this question. The attitude of the Republicans after their victory showed this only too clearly: instead of devoting themselves to a definitive solution of the question at issue, to prevent a relapse, they returned forthwith to the tariff, to satisfy the financial supporters of their Organization. The defeated Democrats, while still clinging to the free silver plank, were unconsciously relaxing their hold; when they parted from it they completely lost their footing in the situation created by the victorious war with Spain carried on under the auspices of their rivals of the Republican party. Nor was the new and grave problem of "imperialism," propounded by this war, and which deeply divided the public mind, able to bring the parties into line again; for the want of agreement showed itself in each of them. The effete parties were still walking in confusion and chaos. A short interview published not *long* ago presents a picture of this condition of the parties, the spontaneous vividness of which duties the brush

Under somewhat different aspects the spectacle presented by the last quarter of a century, which we have just been reviewing, was thus always the same: the parties in a state of disintegration, of moral decomposition, and unable to unite in accordance with natural affinities. It was in vain that, almost from the commencement of the new era which marked their disintegration, expectations were indulged in of their transformation on a genuine, living hasis. New life could not be infused into their effete frames; the existing Organizations prevented the necessary metamorphosis. Rebirth for the parties meant death to them. In preventing the regeneration of the parties the Organizations became all the more indispensable to them, for in the void of ideas and of principles in which the parties were living they needed an artificial prop. By supplying them with this the Organization weakened them still more; they were bound to acquiesce in and connive at the corruption on which the Organization subsisted; for if they had tried to interfere with it, they would have cut away the hand which supported them. And the more the Machine was perfected, the more valuable did it become to them and the more it degraded them by enabling them to dispense with principles in thought and conduct. The progress of the of the historian: On the eve of the elections to Congress, of November, 1898, a journalist was asking the representative of the Democratic Congressional Committee to what questions he was directing his campaign of "political literature," and in what light he was presenting them to the electorate. He inquired, for instance, if the silver question constituted now the main issue as in 1896. "Not exactly that," was the reply, "but the silver question is in the foreground."... "Are you sending that literature into New York, Connecticut, and the Eastern States?"... "We are not sending them much of any kind. They prefer to conduct their campaigns on State issues."... "Is your campaign literature taking any stand upon territorial expansion, imperialism, and questions of that sort?"... "No, those are not party questions. The Democratic Congressional Committee cannot afford to take sides upon a matter in which there is so much disagreement among members of the party in and out of Congress."..." What are you doing with the war, — are you criticizing its conduct?"... "No, we are simply sending out criticisms of other people, mostly Republicans."... "Are you attacking the Dingley tariff?"..." On two grounds: We are showing that it is a disappointment as a revenue producer in time of peace, and that its schedules bear unevenly upon the poor."... "But you do not attack the principle of protection in itself?"... "No, we prefer to confine our attack upon the tariff to the lines I have indicated, as being safely within the limits of our present party policy" (despatch of the 20th October, 1898, from Washington to the *Evening Post* of New York).

Machine, with the boss at its head, was therefore not only an indicator of the moral decomposition of the parties, but one of its efficient causes.

The Organization contributing to the moral disintegration of the parties, impeding their transformation and at the same time keeping them artificially alive, marked the furthest limit of the action of the Caucus which imbued the whole political existence of the country. We have seen the strength of this complex power gradually accumulate, in the course of the evolution which we have followed step by step, as the historical phenomena one after another revealed it to us. To fill up the unavoidable gaps attending this method of observation, to gauge the power of the party Organization in its daily action, together with its limitations, or rather the power of the political and social forces of which it is the resultant, we shall now proceed to consider its working from the statical point of view.

FIFTH PART FIRST CHAPTER THE LOCAL ORGANIZATION

I

The body of the Organization of American parties contains the following three essential organs: the primary assembly of the members of the party from which all the powers of the Organization emanate; the committee of the party which is the controlling power within it; and the conventions of the delegates who choose the candidates for elective offices on behalf of the party. We have had many an opportunity of observing the movements of these organs without having been able to inspect them in detail. We shall now proceed to make this inspection, which will disclose to us, if it is permissible to go on using biological terms, their anatomical form and their physiological functions, as well as their nervous system.

The primary assemblies of the members of the party bear the name of "caucuses" in New England and in certain States of the West, and that of "primaries" or "primary elections" in the rest of the Union. They meet in each city ward or rural district, at tolerably frequent intervals, to make direct choice of the candidates of the party for the local offices assigned to the ward, but especially to appoint delegates to the various party conventions, who select candidates for public functions on all the other steps of the hierarchical ladder. In almost every case the primaries simply serve as a cell for the numerous conventions of the party. The details of their organization vary a great deal, not only from State to State, but in different parts of the same State. This organization is determined sometimes by rules, sometimes, and more often, by custom and precedents. In principle, the primaries are composed of all the adherents of the party, but those who lay claim to the title must have it confirmed by the party Organization. In a few large cities a preliminary selection is already made; there the followers of the party are grouped into associations, or permanent clubs, and all those who are members of them are allowed to sit in the primaries. The discretionary right of admission or exclusion possessed by these associations, or clubs, has too often made them close bodies, and has enabled a small fraction of the party to assume the power of speaking and of taking decisions on its behalf. In New York especially the political monopoly of the associations has been one of the factors of the power which the " Machine " has acquired there. In the very great majority of cases, where the permanent nucleus does not exist in the regular form of associations or clubs, the organization of the party is started in the primaries, to which are admitted the electors who declare that they have voted for the candidate of the party at the last election, or who, in general, profess the creed of the party. They are bound to make good these declarations in case they are challenged by any member of the party. The meeting, or more often the committee, has to decide the point in dispute.

But whether the admission to the primaries of the adherents of the party is beset with more or less extensive restrictions, in practice the great majority of the voters keep away from these assemblies. The proportion of voters who take part in At certain periods the Republican associations of New York contained hardly a tenth or an eighth of the whole of the Republican voters of the city. In a letter addressed, in November, 1879, to the future President of the Uuited States, Chester A. Arthur, Col. G. Bliss, ex U. S. District Attorney, estimated the number of persons allowed to vote in the Republican primaries of New York at six thousand. "The rolls," he said, " are deceptive; in one district half the names of those on the rolls are not known in the district. These bogus names afford a convenient means for fraudulent voting."... "The rolls of many of the districts are full of names of men not Republicans, and are used by the managers to perpetuate their control of the associations. On the other hand, desirable members, good Republicans, who have an absolute right to become members, are excluded. Sometimes this is done by a direct rejection, but of toner by a refusal to vote upon the names presented."... "At elections (primaries) they are or are not members, according as they are or are not prepared to vote a ticket satisfactory to the controlling powers." When it suited the Organization, on the other hand, it entered an altogether exaggerated number on the lists of the associations. The Republican Machine adopted this course in 1805 to obtain a larger representation at the State convention, which was about to select delegates to the national convention of 1896.
the primaries varies from 1 to 10 per cent. The principal cause of this abstention is the indifference of the citizens, who are too much engrossed in their business or their domestic, affairs or their pleasures. This is especially true of the cities; in the country districts the meeting of the primary is a small pastime, which attracts people for want of anything better. A good many abstentionists are greatly encouraged in their attitude, if not justified, by the fact that the primary is almost invariably in the hands of a coterie of politicians, who make it their business. The citizens who are outside the clique are reduced to impotence in the primary. While the politicians who manipulate them form a compact group, the former find themselves helpless and isolated. The conditions of existence in the large cities, which have done away with neighbourliness, make the respectable citizens strangers to one another. They would have, in order to cope with the politicians, who had come to an understanding beforehand, to lay their heads together as well; but too often they have no point of social contact for this, and even no material opportunities. The diurnal and nocturnal existence of a citizen is divided, not only between two districts situated at two extremities of the town, but perhaps even between two large cities, like Brooklyn and New York, the first of which is in a way the sleeping-place of the second. The cohesion which is wanting to the respectable citizens when they get to the primary can scarcely be achieved at the meeting itself; for discussion, exchange of views, which bring men nearer each other, do not take place in the primaries. They have lost their original consultative character, prescribed by the classic type of the "town meeting" of New England, which was the great civic school of the Kepublicans of the Xew World. The primary, which was intended to be a town meeting for the members of the party, has ceased to be so almost everywhere in the cities, and has become a formal gathering where the sole business is to vote; just as at an election, with this difference, that the members of only one party vote, and that they vote only on representatives of the party. The lists of the candidates voted on are settled beforehand, and

very often each elector as he comes into the room receives several ready printed. True, every citizen is entitled to propose candidates of his own, but he will get no support in the VOL. II — P meeting; and then the delegates to be chosen are often so numerous that a previous understanding is absolutely neces-sary. The lists presented at the primary are generally prepared behind the scenes, where the politicians "make up the slate," as is said in their slang. Probably on one occasion a schoolboy's slate had been used for noting the names of the candidates to be proposed, and the word has acquired a generic significance, a verb even being formed out of it, "to slate," to be "slated," which means to be chosen as a candidate by the local politicians. Provided with the slate, the presiding officers of the primary make the meeting adopt it by a series of movements regulated with the precision of a military parade. These movements are executed with such rapidity and such *ensemble* that the good citizen does not know what to make of it. If he ventures to intervene, he is easily silenced by means of the niceties of the procedure, with which he is very seldom familiar. The presiding officers always have the last word, even if they do not apply the standing orders in an arbitrary fashion In one way or another the programme is carried, point by point, in the form in which it was settled beforehand behind the scenes. The good citizen is reduced to playing the part of an involuntary dummy amid involuntary dummies of the " ring," which manages the local Organization. In the course of a conversation which I had with a member of the general committee of Tammany Hall, and in which he showed the utmost frankness on the subject of the methods of Tammany, he said to me: "Next week we shall have some primaries. I will take you there and you will see everything." — " How am I to see, since you have just admitted yourself that the whole system is only a 'tomfoolery of popular government'?" "Oh," he replied with a smile, "you will see everything that any American citizen can see."

Soon afterwards I had an opportunity of attending a Tammany primary in one of the most popular wards of New York. It took place close to the drinking saloon kept by the district leader of Tammany Hall and Senator of the State in the legislature of New York. His portrait in oils adorned the platform on which the dignitaries of the Organization took their seats. They opened the sitting and put a certain number of motions to the vote. Reading them out in an automatic way, they despatched the business with precision and rapidity. The public, which was fairly numerous, evidently belonged to the dregs of the population. There was no disorder; on the contrary, the electors displayed complete apathy towards all that was being done on the platform. When the chairman repeated the usual formula: let those who are in favour of this motion say "aye," and those who are of a contrary opinion say " no," they did not even muster up energy to bring out the "aye." Once only a n

The stronghold of this "ring" is the local committee of the party. Each political subdivision, the rural town or the city ward, or even the ward precinct, has its committee, appointed annually at the primary of the party. Above this committee of first instance there are, in the local Organization, one or two more committees: the ward committee in the cities, which is generally composed of the members of the precinct committees; and the county committee, which is the central committee for the county with its towns and villages, or the city committee in the large cities which have a central independent Organization. The members of the county committee are appointed by the committees of the wards and of the towns or by the respective delegates of these territorial units to the county convention; the city committee is formed in a similar way. That is to say, the direct influence of the electors on the composition of the committees of the party expires on the threshold of the committee of first instance. In certain States (in Indiana, for example) the electors do not even choose the members of the committees of first instance; these members are appointed by the chairmen of the superior committees. Thus the local committees, not to mention the higher ones, the State and national committees, are cast in a centralizing mould.

The local committee, which is the permanent representative of the party Organization, of the primaries and of the local conventions, is supposed to be their executive organ, with the duty of exerting itself, especially during election time, to ensure the success of the candidates of the party within its jurisdiction. In reality it manages, it manipulates the whole Organization, and in particular during the stage which precedes the election, that of the nomination of candidates. Generally, it is the committee which makes up the slate, and member, seated astride a chair and with his hack to the platform, bellowed out " No!" but nobody seemed to take him to task for this discordant cry. They knew that he was at heart an excellent citizen, who had uttered it simply to break the monotony of the proceedings. But in a short space of time all was over: the ceremony had lasted barely ten minutes. The room emptied in a twinkling, and everybody rushed off to the drinking saloon.

it forces it on the primary because it wields a predominant power there. It is the committee which convenes the primary, which selects the date and place of the meeting to suit its own convenience, which settles its procedure, which presides over the assembly until the officers are elected. Very often it is the committee, again, which appoints the "inspectors of election," who have to receive and count the votes; and if it selects inspectors who are hostile to a particular candidate and are unscrupulous, that candidate is a lost man. Being entrusted with the duty of keeping the roll of membership, the committee decides beforehand who is entitled to take part in the primaries, or, at all events, directs the meeting how to decide in case the dispute is brought before it. In a word, all the business of the primaries is "cut and dried" by the committee. Once in power the coterie easily keeps there; possessing a sort of mortgage over each future primary, the committee gets itself reappointed from year to year.

The influence of the county committee, to which the ward committees and village committees of the district lead up, is still more excessive. It rules over the local Organizations with powers which are sometimes despotic. Generally, it frames its own rules and by-laws, and makes, at its good will and pleasure, those of the Organizations over which it presides. Among other things, it fixes the qualifications for voting at the primaries, and it can make them difficult enough to reduce the number of the adherents of the party entitled to vote. The county committee decides, without appeal, on all the contests which arise in the Organization. It wields disciplinary powers in it: it can suspend, or even turn out, the officers of the associations or of the local committees. Nay more, it can dissolve a whole local Organization, when it encounters opposition in it, or refuse to recognize it as the "regular " Organization. The central committee of Tammany Hall reserves to itself even the right to revise the nominations of candidates made by the conventions or the committees, and to fill up the places of the adopted candidates by others " wherever the honor, preservation and integrity of this organization (of Tammany Hall) shall require such action. " In California the usurpation of the committees has gone farther still: they have assumed the right of appointing the delegates to the conventions themselves without convening the primaries at all. The county committees generally contain a very large number of members, especially in the big cities; the central committee of Tammany numbers more than fourteen hundred persons; elsewhere the total is much smaller, but still pretty considerable, and naturally it is incapable of attending to the delicate duties which devolve on it. In practice, therefore, one of its many sub-committees concentrates all the powers in its hands. In Tammany Hall the reins of government are held by the "committee on organization"; it is this body which is invested with the power of revising and substituting all the nominations made. In other places it is also a small committee that pulls all the strings. Often the other committees exist only on paper; they are not convened, and serve solely for conferring titles on the "workers" of the party.
in

In order that the programme settled behind the scenes by the committee and its henchmen may be faithfully executed in the primaries and successfully carried out, the politicians have devised an elaborate system of tactics and strategy, with the object of preventing discordant voices arising in them or of nullifying their effect if they should command a hearing. In the first place, everything is done to keep the citizens who do not belong to the dominant clique away from the primaries. The meeting is fixed for a date when it would be impossible for them to come, — for instance, during the very hot months' when most of the well-to-do citizens go away for a holiday. The hour and the place of meeting are generally selected with the same object. It is held in an out-of-the-way place or in an unpleasant, if not dangerous, neighbourhood, where a respectable man would not care to set foot. Very often, and Here are some specimens of their names. The county committee of the Republican party of New York possesses the following sub-committees: on organization, on election officers, on appeals, on finance, on abuses and grievances, on naturalization, on public meetings, on printing. The county committee of the Democratic party at Chicago has treated itself to fourteen sub-committees: executive, finance, judiciary, primaries, contests and appeals, printing, on halls, on speakers, naturalization, registration, on education, auditing, on discipline, on city organization, on town organization.

perhaps most often, the primary is held in a public-house, or a few doors off one, or in a livery stable, or in a back shop. The people who crowd round the door, and those who occupy the front places inside, belong to the category of tap-room frequenters, with a strong contingent, in the large cities, of the representatives of the criminal or semi-criminal class; and they deliberately, by their filthy language and objectionable conduct, disgust the respectable citizens who venture into these meetings. To make good one's right to take part in the primary, it is even necessary, sometimes, to use one's fists, — a form of exercise which has little attraction for welldressed men, unless they happen to be blessed with a combative temperament which is not afraid of a boxing-match.

When the moral and physical violence to which the Ring of the politicians resorts to keep away opposition is not sufficient, or is not expedient, they have recourse to frauds which, from long practice, have been reduced to a system, not to say a science, the time-honoured methods of which have their special terminology. The proper notice convening the primaries is published too late or is not published at all; so that the initiated alone are informed in time. To attain the same effect, the primaries are appointed quite unexpectedly, before the usual date. This is a "snap" primary. The meeting is not forestalled; it is advertised early enough, but the place where it is to be held is selected at the farther end of a large ward; most of the electors will not have the material possibility of getting there in time, and however expeditious they may be, they will find that the meeting is over, that there is no longer a primary; this is called a "stolen" primary. The citizens whom the Ring mistrusts may arrive in good time, but they will meet their match: the Ring has taken care to pack the meeting, to fill it with people devoted to them or in their pay, picked up in the public-houses or at the street crossings, who will swamp all opposition by their numbers. This is a "packed" primary. Generally it is made up of persons who A courageous and extremely combative politician, who at the present moment holds the post of Governor of one of the largest States of the Union, expressed his regret to me, in connection with this, that the good citizens were too " effeminate." "I am not afraid," he said, "of the primary people; I am quite ready to have a bout of fisticuffs with them." are strangers to the ward or who belong to the opposite party. In the large cities there are strolling companies of such voters, who travel to order from one ward to another. Often the boss of the opposite party politely lends his meu for the evening. These are small services which the rival bosses are very glad to render each other, out of professional free-masonry as well as from interest, —for to maintain discipline in the ranks of one's troops the enemy must not be disorganized.

If, after all, the opposition is still too numerous, it is reduced by frauds in voting and in counting the votes, although ostensibly special precautions are taken to avoid mistakes. The local Organization of the party, the Association, or the first annual meeting of the primary, or the committee, appoints every year special commissioners to superintend the operations of voting and of counting the votes in the primaries, —" inspectors" or "election judges." But in practice the inspectors, who generally owe their appointment to the Ring and are in collusion with it, are there only to screen frauds and to perpetrate them. The lists of the members of the party are full of names of persons who are not electors in the locality, who are dead, or who have never existed. A good number of names on these "padded rolls " are distributed to the imported hirelings who vote, and even several times over under different names ("repeaters"). The election inspectors imperturbably accept all the voting-papers, down to the "pudding ballots" containing several votes on very thin paper, wrapped up together, and then, when the counting begins, they unroll them, and enter them, one by one; often they put a certain number of voting papers, with the names of their favourite candidates, into the ballot-box beforehand (" ballot-box stuffing"), or, while the votes are being counted, they dexterously conjure away papers bearing the names of their opponents, or drop papers containing the names of friends out of their sleeve, or even make an untrue return of the figures obtained by the different candidates. In cases where the vote is open, and where heads are counted, the inspectors declare that the adherents of the Ring have a majority, even if they were in the proportion of 1 to 2. It is therefore an axiom that the candidate who has the election inspectors on his side is sure of success. It is true that there is a remedy against these frauds and, in general, against the irregularities committed at the primaries: an appeal lies to the county or city committee, but that committee hardly ever decides against the manipulators of the primaries, for it is composed of their political friends and allies, of their "own cousins," as a boss put it who was explaining to me why it is a waste of time to complain to the committee. It is not uncommon for the dissatisfied parties to take the law into their own hands during the primary, by engaging in a regular fight, which sometimes ends in bloodshed. The intervention of the police, which endeavours, with more or less impartiality, to preserve order and stop brawls, is pretty frequent. On the other hand, a good many primaries pass off quite calmly, to wit, when there is no opposition to the dominant Ring in the district. In that case, the handful of persons who manipulate the local Organization, perhaps not more than four or five, come together, and, after having played a game of cards or indulged in some other recreation, go away; the primary is considered as having been held, on the strength of which the certificates of the delegates supposed to have been elected are signed.

Opposition, if it does occur, rarely proceeds from the good citizens concerned about the honour of the party, about political honesty; they keep away because they are under the impression that the people whom they are likely to find at the meeting are all rogues. Generally, the attack is led by a rival faction of the politicians, which covets the places to which the primaries are a stepping-stone. Of the two factions the one which wins the victory in the primary, by getting its lists of delegates to the conventions voted, will have every prospect of being recognized as the "regular" one entitled to the rewards. A contested primary is therefore an affair between the office-holders and office-seekers, the "ins" and the "outs," which does not concern, so to speak, the great mass of the citizens. The latter are dragged into the contest in a passive way, by the members of both rings of politicians, who move heaven and earth to get as many people as possible to vote in their favour. They make use of every kind of argument: they appeal to the friendship of some, to the compassion of others, by representing to them that their livelihood, the subsistence of their families, is at stake; they promise favours and places, or even resort to direct corruption in its different forms, — from the distribution of drinks and cigars down to the payment of money. This last argument sometimes leads to considerable expense, which is defrayed by contributions from those immediately interested, from the office-holders and the candidates, from the central Organization, or perhaps from third persons who will need the favour of the nominees of the primaries and conventions, such as the financial or industrial companies. However, patronage in its different grades constitutes of itself a considerable fund for bribery. In order to add to the number of their respective adherents, the rival factions resort to the above-mentioned stratagems and frauds in the primaries, and then the sole question is, which of the two will out-general the other, each of them being quite prepared to take the rough with the smooth.

The reader, however, will be better able to grasp the situation by a small picture drawn from life by Mr. Theodore Roosevelt, the distinguished statesman and writer, who, having been sent in 1891 to Baltimore to make an enquiry into the breaches of the law of 1883 relating to political assessments, followed the operations of the primaries there in person: —

The primaries, he wrote in his official report, held on March 30, were marked by a very bitter contest between two factions of the Republican party.... In its essence it was, without doubt, mainly a fight between the office-holders on one side and the disappointed office-seekers on the other, the " Johnson-Airey " men representing the former and the " Henderson-Stone " the latter.... As far as I could find out from the witnesses there seemed to be no question of principle at stake at all, but one of offices merely.... Seemingly, many of them regarded victory in the primaries as of more importance than victory at the polls, because the former gave the control of the party machinery, and would therefore, in their own language, entitle them to " recognition " in the distribution of patronage.

As a whole the contest was marked by great fraud and no little violence. Many of the witnesses of each faction testified that the leaders of the opposite faction in their ward had voted repeaters, Democrats, and men living outside of the ward in great numbers, and I am inclined to believe that in this respect there is much reason to regard the testimony of each side as correct in its outline of the conduct of the other. Accusations of ballot-box stuffing were freely made, with much appearance of justification. A number of fights took place. In many wards there were several arrests; in one or two cases so many men were arrested that the police patrol wagons could not accommodate them. In several cases the judges of the election were themselves among those arrested. The judges, three in number, in each ward, sat within a house at a window opening on the street, and the voters at the primary were marshalled in a line outside, surrounded by a great crowd of onlookers. Each party or faction had its ticket holders, who presented its ballots to the voters, and its challengers, who challenged those of the opposite party. Much complaint was made in certain wards of one side or the other being " in " with the police, who would accordingly arrest and drag out of the line voters of the opposition faction, and would decline to do so in the case of voters of the protected faction. In many of the wards furniture wagons were hired to bring voters up to the polls. The ward workers stood about shouting, challenging, occasionally fighting, seeing that the ticket holders peddled their tickets actively, keeping the furniture wagons sharply on the move, taking doubting or wavering voters into the saloons and treating them to beer; and in short, the whole aspect of the primaries, save only in those wards where there was no contest, bore no distant resemblance to the parliamentary elections described in Charles Lever's novels.

One of the incidents of the day was an effort on the part of Marshal Airey to drag a judge, whom he accused of misconduct, out of the window, a fierce scuffle being the result. In another ward a Johnson clerk detected, as he thought, signs of cheating, and broke open the ballot-box, taking out two huge handfuls of so-called "pudding " ballots; whereupon the two Henderson judges threw him out of the window, and all three were arrested.

In some wards the use of the so-called "pudding" tickets seem to have been quite common.... There was considerable complaint of bribery; in some cases votes were said to have been bought for money; in others, the charge was that outsiders, not Republicans, possibly not residents of the ward, had been offered drinks to participate in the primary. Most of the witnesses spoke of the cheating in a matter of-course way, as being too universal and too common in primaries generally to lie worthy of notice, and a great number of them did not seem to bear any special malice against their opponents for having cheated successfully, — if anything, rather admiring them for their shrewdness, — and frankly testified that it was only lack of opportunity that had hindered them from doing as much themselves. Two of the witnesses, both Henderson adherents, employes of the customhouse, testified with refreshing and cheerful frankness to this effect. One of them remarked, anent fixing up "pudding " tickets: "I would have done the same. thing myself; I believe in doing anything to win."... The testimony of the other ran as follows: "I don't say I wouldn't cheat in the primaries. Whoever gets two judges, wins." *Q.* "Each side cheats as much as it can?" — *A.* "Certainly, that's the way; I do it just the same as they do. They had two judges." *Q.* "How do you do your cheating?" — *A.* "Well, we do our cheating honourably. If they catch us at it it's all right; it's fair. I even carried the box home with me on one occasion. I have broken up more than one election."...

All of the office-seeking or office-holding ward workers who came before me evidently believed that the business of managing primaries, and, in fact, the business of conducting politics generally, belonged of right to the office-holding caste....

The money for defraying the expenses of the Johnson-Airey faction at the primaries in this, the eighth ward, was raised almost solely from among the office-holders.... Some fifty dollars was thus raised. Ten ticket holders, or ticket peddlers, were paid two dollars apiece to work up the vote; $2.50 was paid for one half the rent of the window; seven dollars was paid for tickets; the balance went to give a new suit of clothes to a young man who was a clerk of the Johnson-Airey faction, and who discovered, as he claimed, apparently with much reason, that the Henderson people were cheating. He then burst open the ballot-box, and was thrown out of the window by the Henderson judges. All were arrested in consequence.... In the sixth ward over one hundred dollars were raised, all the expenses of this ward being paid by the office-holders. Ten or twelve dollars went in printing and room rent, ninety-four dollars were expended in paying fortyseven ticket holders two dollars apiece to work up the vote, — an expenditure so excessive for the purpose as to suggest that it was really a form of bribery. Deputy Marshal B marshalled the vote at the primary, getting two hundred voters together in a body; but the primary was broken up with violence before the vote could be polled.

However great the scandals which enable one of the two factions to carry the primary, it is generally left in undisputed possession, and the opposition has but one resource: to split, to "bolt." It separates from the "regular" faction, threatening to fight it at the polls. Sometimes it goes farther, and convenes a primary composed of its own adherents, and selects a rival set of delegates, claiming for itself and for them the party orthodoxy and denouncing the rival faction as an usurper. But all these manifestations are almost always devoid of effect, and often even of sincerity. The delegates chosen in the dissentient primary may come to the convention, but they will not be allowed to sit; the "regular" delegates will always be admitted, even if they have been elected by the minority of the party. The dissentients will be obliged to submit, they will not go so far as a real "bolt," for that is equivalent to burning one's ships, to cutting oneself off wantonly from communion with the party and its earthly rewards. Something like a cosmic catastrophe must occur to make a member of the Organization "bolt" for good and all. The uncompromising attitude of the dissentients is often only a manoeuvre, "they talk big things" with a view to "recognition," to induce the victorious faction to promise them a share of the booty. That is what generally happens, unless the quarrel of the factions is envenomed by long-standing grudges and tierce animosities; these latter, however, seldom create an impassable gulf; the politician is too great a realist to be influenced by sentimental trifles.

It does happen that the primaries are conducted fairly, without frauds or stratagems; but this is rather the exception. In certain cities there have not been honest primaries within living memory. In the East, the cities of New York, Philadelphia, and Baltimore hold the record for fraudulent primaries; Boston is purer, but by no means irreproachable. The West is not much better off than the East; even the rudimentary States of the Pacific slope, such as Oregon and Washington, where there are hardly any large cities, are afflicted with the same complaint. In Oregon, for instance, the largest city in the State has a population of less than fifty thousand inhabitants (according to the census of 1890), and yet the primaries are marked by all the abuses which party organization has made familiar in the East. In the rural districts the state of things is far better. The primaries are better and more numerously attended, and are, consequently, more representative of the parties. It is more difficult, if not impossible, to commit most of the frauds which characterize these meetings in the cities, such as voting repeaters or by persons who are strangers to the locality and to the party: the people know each other well. Nevertheless, the rival factions do not scruple to resort to tricks of a bucolic ingenuity to monopolize the primaries. Thus the country folk have enriched the vocabulary of stratagems with the term "jumping" a primary: one of the two factions unexpectedly brings up reinforcements, which have been hastily collected by means of a waggonette driven through the locality and stopping at the doors of friends, who are told to "jump in." In order to hold the primary without opposition, the chairman, having put his watch on, hurriedly opens the sitting and despatches the list of business with lightning speed, and then, when the other people arrive at the real time, the primary is over; they protest, the chairman pulls out his watch, the protesters do the same, the watches are compared, but the vote cannot be upset. The public, when they learn what has taken place in the primary, treat it only as a joke; they consider it "smart," and, at most, the chairman will perhaps be asked the next day when he is met in the street, "And how is your watch to-day?" However, in the rural districts themselves, less innocent frauds are resorted to; sometimes the practices indulged in by the manipulators of the primaries in the cities are followed more closely. IV

The selections of delegates made in the primaries are not always so bad as might be expected from the practices which are in vogue in them. Among the elected are to be found respectable persons, who hold aloof from the primaries, and are not aware of the means by which they have been returned. In choosing these persons, the politicians of the primaries are influenced by various motives. Sometimes they place them at the top of their lists to get the other less recommendable candidates through more easily. The ingenuous elector, finding in one of these lists, handed to him at the door, the name of one or two citizens of good repute, makes up his mind to put it in the ballot-box, after having conscientiously, but "I have known a gang of ward workers and repeaters to leave St. Louis and spend an afternoon voting at the primary election of an adjoining county. Candidates for State offices and their friends are making the county primaries worse hy introducing the frauds of the city Into them" (Communication from St. Louis, Missouri, to the *National Conference on Practical Reform of Primary Elections,* held in New York City, January, 18!)8; Chicago, p. 148).

fruitlessly, scanned it. Sometimes these good delegates do not accept the mission, but their name will all the same have served as a flag to cover the merchandise of the politicians. Occasionally the latter abstain from selecting men of their own making in order not to raise respectable opinion, if it is very strong in the district, against them on the day of election; the better element in the electorate thus acts as a check on the politicians of the primaries, but — and this point cannot be too strongly insisted on — in an altogether relative degree, and more often hardly at all. As a general rule, the delegates chosen in the primaries are not up to the moral and intellectual standard of the average of the party; they are below it, and a long way below it.

The powers conferred on the delegates are unlimited in theory; the latter are supposed to be guided solely by their own judgment in the discharge of their duties. But this is not-the case in practice; often they receive imperative instructions to vote at the convention for certain candidates, whose names have been voted for with this object in the primaries. The lists of the persons proposed as delegates often contain the words "pledged" to so and so; that is to say, if they are elected they will vote at the convention for a particular candidate, so that the voter in the primary is warned of the use which will be made of his vote. Generally he is not much the wiser for this as regards the selections to be made. In the majority of cases the delegates are really, if not formally, pledged; the boss, or the aspirant to a public function, has put them forward and got them elected, through his intrigues or his money, on the well-understood condition that they will vote for him, or as he directs them. Occasionally the lists of the candidates for the delegacy, which are handed to the citizen attending the primary, contain the definite statement "unpledged "; but this may be only a trap to catch the unwary. The delegate who is formally "pledged" carries out his bargain; sometimes he lets himself be persuaded by pecuniary or other arguments to transfer his vote to rival candidates; but this is rare.

In any event the delegate is simply a transmitting agent. In certain localities, therefore, the primary, whose real choice is the candidate for the elective office, has left it to him to appoint the delegates to support him at the convention on behalf of the district. In certain States the primaries have assumed in a formal way the direct and definitive selection of the candidates (of course apart from candidates to local elective functions, who are always chosen by the respective primary); that is to say, they do not send any delegates to a convention, which, in that case, does not take place. This system, which is known by the name of "Crawford County system," because it was first started in Crawford County in Pennsylvania, is also in use elsewhere, — in Ohio, in a few other States of the West, but especially in the South. It is not, as a rule, applied to a territory of larger area than a county, and it consists of the following: Each primary votes for the candidates who are standing for the county offices, the result of the vote is communicated to the county-town, where the figures obtained by each competitor are added up, and the candidate who heads the list is declared nominated. The Crawford County system is applied most extensively in South Carolina, where the primaries have the direct choice of the candidates for Congress, and even for the whole State.

The power which the primaries thus wield, either directly or indirectly, over the selection of candidates, runs through the whole line. They determine the character and the acts of all the conventions which succeed one another, from the county or city convention up to the national convention, for all these conventions emanate from the primary as from a source. They determine the nominations to all the public functions, from the most humble ones up to that of President of the Republic. And these nominations again decide the election, by the intrinsic force of party loyalty: confronted with the alternative of going over to the enemy or of voting for the candidate recommended by the Organization of his party, the elector submits to the ticket which it has settled. In places where the party is in a majority, the nomination is equivalent to election, so much so that often most of the voters do not think it necessary to turn out and go to the poll, the result of the vote being a foregone conclusion for their party and its duly nominated candidate.

1 have found this mode of appointing delegates of the primaries in force in certain parts of the State of Illinois.

Consequently all those who aspire to public offices, or who deal in them, or who want to exploit the influence which they carry with them in executive or legislative spheres, have their eyes turned towards the primaries: the politicians start by ensconcing and fortifying themselves in the primary; it is their base of operations and their citadel. The power of the boss over the Machine consists, above all, in the power of managing the primaries; if he is master of them he holds the conventions in the hollow of his hand, and if he can make his will prevail in the conventions he will drag the majority of the party after him. The candidate who wants to be adopted by a convention, however high it may be, must, to succeed, first make sure of the delegates chosen in the primaries; it is therefore the primaries that he "works" by intrigue and corruption if the Machine does not do it for him. It is also in the primaries and by the same means that operations are begun by the business men and the jobbers who are on the look-out for contracts and public works; by the industrial companies, the banks, the railways, which need the favour of the representatives of government; the delegates will deliver over to them the candidates and the office-holders, whom they have called into being, and make them the humble servants of those capitalists; the work of the " lobby" is carried on, or begun, in the primaries. In short, the whole representative government on which the political life of America reposes, within the parties and in the State, is shaped by the primaries, and it is on them that are consequently brought to bear all the attempts which seek to make the public interest subservient to private ends. But these attempts are met only by the indifference of the good citizens and the perversity of the bad ones, which, combined, make the primaries a fraud and a farce, a "tomfoolery of popular government," to use the language of the member of Tammany Hall.

This state of things did not fail to attract public attention at an early stage, and there was no lack of discussion, of imprecation, and exhortation. The good citizens who abandoned the primaries to the politicians were adjured to attend these meetings regularly; but the appeal proved ineffective, and by dint of continual solemn repetition the injunction "attend the primaries" became a joke. Various more or less ingenious schemes were mooted for reforming the primaries. At last the legislator even was called in to defeat the craft and guile of the politicians. But all the remedies proposed, and especially the legislative ones, which will be considered in detail in one of the concluding chapters, met with scanty success. The primaries are still what they were.

In any event the role of the party member, whether more or less unreal and delusive, ends in the primaries: as soon as he has, or is supposed to have, recorded his vote for the delegates he disappears from the political stage; he no longer has any power as a party member. Political activity is now transferred to the larger stage of the conventions, with a new set of actors.

SECOND CHAPTER THE CONVENTIONS

I

The convention system is extremely complicated, and, at first sight, even somewhat confused. Composed of representatives of the people assembled in party meetings, the conventions are invested with the mission of pointing out to the general body of the party the candidates for whom they may vote. But as the elective offices are exceedingly numerous, and the areas of their territorial jurisdiction are by no means identical, and as the party Organization entrusted with the choice of candidates is formed on a strictly representative basis, those charged with this duty cannot be the same for all the offices within the limits of the State, or even of a part of the State. The first complication comes from the federative system of the American Government, with its double set of parallel functions in the State and in the Union. A State sends to Congress ten or twenty representatives, and a hundred or a couple of hundred members to the legislative assembly of the State, and, consequently it is divided, with a view to the federal elections, into ten or twenty districts, and into one hundred or two hundred for the legislative elections of the State. The delegates of the party in one of these last districts cannot, therefore, choose the candidate for a congressional district, or *vice versa,* without infringing the representative principle. Hence the necessity of holding two conventions of delegates: the one composed of delegates from all the primaries of the congressional district which will elect the candidate for Congress; and the other containing delegates from the primaries of the much smaller district which has to return a member to the local legislative assembly. However, the legislative offices are not the only ones which are filled up by election: the judiciary and the principal executive offices are so as well, not to mention those connected with local self-government, the municipal offices and others. But their jurisdictions do not tally with any of the districts carved out for the various legislative elections, and they cannot possess an identical party representation. Consequently, each public office to which a particular territorial subdivision is assigned requires a special convention of delegates to settle the candidature on behalf of the respective party. If many offices in the same electoral unit have to be filled up, for instance those of the State, — Governor, Lieutenant-Governor, State Secretary, State Treasurer, Attorney-General, judges of the Supreme Court, etc.,— the selections of the candidates are made in a single convention, called the "State convention." It is the same with county or city offices, which, very often but not always, are dealt with in a single "county convention" or "city convention." But in any event, the string of conventions is a very long one. Sometimes it begins with the county convention; at others, in certain cities, with the ward convention, which nominates the local candidate for the town council in a "councilmanic" or "aldermanic convention "; above which comes, for municipal government, the city convention, which settles the candidatures for the dignity of mayor and other municipal offices. The small cities dispense with city conventions; their municipal candidates are chosen in the primaries. The principal conventions, apart from those of the county and city, are as follows: the legislative assembly district conventions, for selecting the candidate for the State legislative assembly; the senatorial district, for choosing the candidate for the Senate of the State; the congressional district, for selecting the candidate for the House of Representatives at Washington; the judicial conventions; and, finally, the State conventions, not to mention the national conventions, which nominate the candidates for the Presidency and the Vice-Presidency of the Republic. Among the conventions, some proceed from the primaries by direct elections, others by elections at two or even three degrees, to wit, the State conventions, whose members are generally elected by the conventions of legislative districts; and the national conventions, which issue, in part at least, as we shall see, from the State conventions. As the national conventions will be dealt with in a special chapter, I leave them out for the moment, so that the description given in the following pages will refer solely to the lower conventions.

The number of the delegates sent to each convention is not a fixed one; it is determined by the respective county, city, or State committee, according to the number of votes polled in each locality by the candidates of the party at the last general election. Usually, the figures of the presidential election, and still more often of that for the State Governor, are taken as a basis of calculation. Thus, for instance, to each electoral division are allotted one or two delegates, plus a delegate for every hundred votes polled in it by the candidate of the paTty for the post of Governor. The totals of membership of the conventions vary indefinitely with the conventions and the States; some are composed of a few dozen members, while others have several hundred or more than a thousand, and occasionally even as many as two thousand members. Each delegate is given a deputy (" alternate "), to take his place if he is prevented from attending. If both are absent, the other delegates of the respective locality, or, in practice, the chairman whom each local delegation to the convention selects as its mouthpiece, appoints, of his own authority, an outsider to take the place of the delegate. Often this power is used to introduce into the convention a personage whose oratorical gifts or talent for intrigue make him specially valuable; the delegate is withdrawn, and taken in again when this extraordinary auxiliary has performed his task.

The composition of the conventions from the standpoint of the moral, intellectual, and social character of their members, is a somewhat motley one, for although they are managed by professional politicians, they are not recruited exclusively in their circles. No doubt, a considerable proportion of each convention consists of office-seekers or office-holders, and, in general, of mercenary politicians. The convention is for them The orders of Presidents Hayes and Cleveland quoted in a previous chapter, forbidding otlice-holders to belong to the conventions, could affect the Federal officials only. In the case of State and municipal employees, it is only in one or two places that such a prohibition exists, imposed either by the regulations of the parties or by the public authority.
a sort of stock exchange, where they sell and buy political influence, payable in places or money, or, at all events, get to know each other, put in their claims, and form connections which they will turn to account later on. Their rank and their ambitions vary with the grade of the conventions, from the small fry of the ward or district conventions up to the bigwigs of the State conventions. The politicians are not oblivious of the maxim that you must cut your coat according to your cloth, but one and all, in their respective spheres, are there, according to the expressive slang of the Machine, "not for their health, but on business. " In the same category of delegates are often found persons who are simply agents for big private concerns, for railroad companies, and other societies which want to introduce their garrisons into the political fortresses. Other delegates, without being professionals, derive gratifications of *amour-propre* from the ephemeral position of delegate, were it only, perhaps, the extremely modest one of seeing their names appear in the local paper; or, if they are of a vigorous temperament, opportunities for more or less violent emotions. Along with these delegates, small folk full of petty vanity, are found personages of higher rank in the social scale, well-to-do, and perfectly respectable, who are not above the homage paid to notoriety, and who accept and court it all the more readily that they think they are performing a duty in so doing. Their disinterestedness, however, is not always complete, even in the matter of places and other " good things "; if they do not try to get them for themselves, they come to obtain them for friends. Finally, there is a category of obscure, humble delegates, free from the cant of these respectable personages, and sincerely desirous of discharging their mission for the public good.

The distribution of these different categories among the conventions is a very unequal one; in any event, the first category, that of office-seekers and mercenary politicians, is found in all of them and is particularly numerous and influential in the States where the Machine has reached a high point of development. In a general way it may be said that the least reputable, not to say often the lowest, conventions are the city conventions, as well as the county conventions which include a large city, for instance Cook County, Illinois, in which the city of Chicago is situated; they often exhibit a collection of political bandits, of rogues, and of actual criminals. In the country districts where there are no large cities, the county conventions keep up to a very fair moral and social standard. The best are the State conventions, in which are often to be found many very respectable citizens; among them a certain number are purely decorative personages, who have no real influence, and whose usefulness consists in unwittingly screening the manoeuvres of the smart members. The State conventions, however, are deteriorating; they are falling more and more into the hands of the professional politicians, and the least respectable and least well-meaning elements are gaining ground in them. All these observations apply to both of the two great parties indiscriminately. It is true that shades of difference can be discerned in their respective conventions, but these distinctions do not go much beyond appearances. Thus the Republican conventions have a good many negroes, especially in the South, where the coloured people form the great majority of the Republican party. Elsewhere, and especially in the large cities of the East, and to a certain extent of the West, the Republicans are, on the contrary, supposed to belong to the higher class, while the Democrats attract the dregs of the population. But it is impossible to generalize. I have attended a district convention of Tammauy Hall in New York, where one felt oneself among " gentlemen"; the district in question is inhabited by a superior class. I carried away altogether different impressions from a Republican State convention in the central West, which was not conspicuous for decorum or even for cleanliness; the floor covered with spittle, and the atmosphere reeking with tobacco, reminded one more of a pot-house, in spite of the very large dimensions of the hall; the demeanour of the public which thronged the staircases confirmed this impression.

Among the 723 delegates of a convention of Cook County, held at Chicago in 18%, there were 17 persons who had been tried for homicide, 7 who had been convicted of this crime and who had served their sentence, ttt5 who had served terms in the penitentiary for burglary, 2 for picking porkets, 7 gambling-house keepers, 2 keepers of houses of ill-fame, 24i5 saloon-keepers, 14 lawyers, IS doctors, 148 political employees, 15 ex-policemen, t5 farmers,;i justices of the peace, 71 without occupation, etc. *(American Review of Rpripws,* Sept., 18!I7, the article by R. M. Eusley, entitled "The *sine qua* fie/i of Caucus reform.")

Is the *personnel* of the conventions, with which we have just become acquainted, representative of opinion, does it reflect it? A distinction must be drawn between political opinion in general and the opinion of the parties, for the two are by no means equivalents; the divergence between them increases from day to day; a number of people who help to form and mould public opinion, and especially the enlightened section of it, are outside the regular parties, or are only connected with them in a nominal way. Consequently, when opinion in general. is concerned, an unhesitating reply in the negative must be given to the question. The representative pretensions of the conventions with regard to the opinion of the parties would be more justified, but can only be admitted with qualifications, for even among the trusty adherents of the parties a certain number never come in contact with the Organizations; and, again, the latter gather round them electoral elements which do not belong to the class of professional politicians. The final upshot is that the conventions represent more than the Machine and less than the party.

II

This inherent defect of the conventions is in no way made up for by the manner in which they discharge their mandate, by the procedure, the practices, and the habits which obtain in them. The conventions are summoned by the respective committees, which, as a rule, have been appointed at the preceding convention, from the county committee appointed by the county convention up to the State committee chosen by the State convention. The chairman of the committee, or a person specially designated by him, opens the convention and conducts the preliminary proceedings until the Permanent Organization is chosen. The powers of this "temporary chairman" are immense; it is he who really decides or prejudges the cases of contested credentials, for he selects the committee which is invested with this duty, and which can with impunity unseat delegates duly elected, but hostile to the candidates of the Organization. This constantly happens in cases where the party is in the hands of a Machine, and the latter has not succeeded in carrying all the primaries. It is no use for the delegates of the opposition having been elected by an enormous majority, and it is in vain that they form a majority at the convention; both are of no avail. The adherents of the Machine who have been defeated in the primary start a sham contest, claiming to have been duly elected; or they go so far as to " bolt," to hold a new primary and choose their delegates, with the result that two rival delegations appear at the convention The standing committee which gets up the preliminary work of the convention draws up the roll of the delegates whom it considers as duly elected, and transmits it to the temporary chairman; the latter allows them all to take their seat, leaving their rivals, the real delegates, to bring their case before the committee of credentials; this committee, after a sham investigation, at which the contestants are heard in support of their claims, submits to the convention a report deciding against them; the convention in which the pretended delegates, admitted provisionally as *prima facie* ones, have a majority, forthwith ratifies the proposals of the committee, and the Machine and its candidates remain masters of the position. It is therefore an axiom that "the temporary chairman is the convention." While the committee of credentials is deliberating, the permanent officers are chosen, and after the report on the contested seats and other reports, if need be, have been adopted, the convention proceeds to its proper work, which is the choice of the candidates for election. As soon as the voting is over and the "ticket" is settled, the convention adjourns *sine die,* having taken care to reappoint the committee, whose powers will continue until the next convention.

This procedure is expanded and becomes more complicated, according to the rank of the convention and the political situation. In the higher conventions, especially in the State conventions, the programme is far more elaborate and more decorative. The sitting is opened with prayers read by a clergyman. The temporary chairman appoints, on motions brought in by different members, in addition to the committee on credentials, a committee on permanent organization, which will propose the permanent officers, and a committee on resolutions, which will draw up the programme of the party with declarations on the questions of the day. The resolutions are generally adopted without amendment or discussion. Often some other proposals and motions are submitted or even speeches are delivered, but they are all in the nature of interludes. It rarely happens that these manifestations of opinion offer any real importance. When the country is agitated by some problem or other, the agitation sometimes finds an echo in the conventions, even outside the all-important period of the presidential election, especially in the States of New England, where the habit of public discussion is more deeply rooted. The speeches made and the resolutions voted on these occasions should undoubtedly be noted like all important indications capable of throwing light on the perpetual riddle in democracies: what is the real opinion, what does the people think? But the insufficiently representative character of the conventions, in most cases, prevent them from serving as a good barometer of opinion, even in stormy times. The speeches and the resolutions indulged in at the conventions have almost always only a theatrical value.

In the meanwhile the permanent officers are appointed, the selection of whom is always made with care. The president is generally an influential personage in the party; he is followed by a long array of honorary vice-presidents and honorary secretaries, whose titles are a means of recognizing faithful party service. In taking the chair, the president produces a long speech, prepared beforehand, which, in more or less high-flown language, glorifies the party, recalls its achievements in the past, its "immortal principles," and vigorously attacks and anathematizes the rival party. The candidates are proposed by delegates of note in eulogistic, and more or less lengthy, speeches, which however will have very little to do with the success of the aspirants to the nominations. The choice of the latter as a matter of fact has more often than not been already settled in the primaries, where the decisive battle is fought by the rival candidates, with the result that the man who has " got the delegates " will carry the vote of the convention. The vote is taken under the supervision of a special committee appointed for this purpose. After the proclamation of the result, the friends of the defeated candidate move to make the nomination of the winner unanimous — a proposal which is carried amid deafening applause. To the candidates adopted for the higher posts, and who are generally close at hand, a special delegation is deputed to notify them of the choice and to conduct them ceremoniously into the hall where the convention is sitting. The president introduces the nominees to the assembly in a complimentary address, and they respond briefly. Each of these incidents supplies a fresh pretext for applause and cheers.

Thus, apart from the business transacted behind the scenes, the conventions appear as essentially show assemblies, entirely devoid of the deliberative character which should be their distinctive mark and their *raison d'etre.* The absence of genuine activity and of initiative is accentuated by the way in which the proceedings are all settled beforehand. These arrangements are undeniably useful: they simplify the work of the conventions, and very often enable them to despatch their somewhat heavy programme in a few hours. But the order which prevails is too perfect: everything that is said and done is rigidly prescribed, nothing is left to chance; it is the cut-and-dried system in all its beauty. The temporary chairman, the permanent officers, the members of the different committees, the delegates who will propose the various motions, who will introduce the candidates, all down to the last man, are agreed on beforehand; the "slate" has been made up. The whole thing goes like clock-work, and the convention presents the spectacle, which rejoices the heart of the party managers, of a "harmonious" convention. This "harmony" may be depended on in places where the Machine is absolute master of the situation and the result has been prearranged in the primaries. But it is not the rule; there are plenty of States, or parts of a State, where the Machine has not asserted itself with that degree of power which we have seen it display in New York or in Pennsylvania. In a good many places the party Organization is far less rigid; in others the authority of the Machine is in a state of unstable equilibrium, or, even if it rests on a firm basis, it now and then has to cope with revolts, which break out, in the first place,in the primaries, where opponents manage to elect hostile delegates. In that case "harmony" is spoilt in the convention, and the proceedings in the latter are made as lively as in the primaries by the rival factions; there is sometimes a "fight," not only in the figurative sense in which this word is used by the politicians to describe their contests, the police are called in, delegates are ejected. The Machine can, as we have seen, turn out delegates disturbing the "harmony" without using physical force: by getting a sufficient number of delegates unseated it may give itself a majority. The Machine does resort to this expedient, but it is not always at its disposal; the situation does not always assume this simple aspect. The convention often happens to be split up into several groups, each of them perhaps having its favourite candidate, and none of them strong enough to compel the others to follow 'it. In addition to this, a good many delegates come to the convention unpledged, without having committed themselves to any one whatever, and meaning, either honestly or from corrupt motives, not to make up their minds, not to dispose of their votes, until the last moment. To secure all these delegates the persons interested, that is to say, the party Organization or the candidates and their friends, have to use diplomacy. This term is extremely comprehensive in this connection; it extends from simple entreaties, preferred with more or less skill, down to manoeuvres of every kind, and bargains, including direct bribery.

These operations, which make up the work of "getting the delegates" inaugurated at the primaries, begin several weeks before the convention; the delegates are pestered on all sides, they are approached with flattery, with civility, with promises of places, or,of money, or of favours of various kinds; every argument is brought to bear. The last, and often the main assault, is delivered at the convention itself. The managers of the different candidates open their "head-quarters" in the hotels of the city in which the convention is being held, whence they direct the attack and where they entertain the delegates and persons capable of influencing them. On the eve of the convention a party is given them, at which there is no stint of refreshments of every kind; often the candidate presides at it. The delegates are not insensible to these marks of attention; but the wary ones require something more positive. The favourite plan consists of "deals," bargains between the representatives of the various groups of delegates, who divide the candidatures between them by throwing over some of their candidates and entering into a reciprocal engagement for the rest: "You vote for our candidate, and we will vote for yours "; the withdrawal of the candidates and of their adherents is bought by definite promises of public offices guaranteed by the Organization of the party. A more or less considerable number of delegates remain outside these bargains,—they are the respectable delegates of various grades and categories; generally their honesty of itself delivers them into the hands of the professional politicians. The psychological sketch which I have given of this class of delegates has enabled the reader to divine that when confronted with professionals skilled in all the arts of their trade they would fall an easy prey to them. This is especially the case with the rural delegates. Lost in the crowd of delegates, they are swept along by a sort of wave, without having a clear idea of what is going on. Apart from the delegates of their locality they know nobody, and they shrink timidly into a corner; thereupon some of the strangers accost them with a mixture of unceremoniousness and cordiality,, and, introducing themselves, manage to interlard their conversation with a lot of flattery and humbug; they charitably warn the delegates against the intrigues of the concocters of candidatures, and, out of pure friendship, give them "tips " of good candidatures for which they can safely vote. A few minutes more, and a fresh set of brokers comes to hunt them up. The worthy delegates listen and meditate. The sitting is opened, the "patriotic" speech of the chairman makes a favourable impression on them. Then come the various motions, the nominations, and the voting; the elaborate tactics which govern all these evolutions are quite lost on our delegates, and, eventually, they follow the lead of their obliging mentors. The methods by which well-meaning delegates are inveigled are more or less coarse or refined according to the persons who are operated on; but with the variations which the consummate tact and skill of the professionals suggest, they succeed only too often, even with people who are accustomed to deal with their fellow-creatures, and who in their own sphere of activity exhibit good sense and perspicacity; these faculties are evidently quite special in their application. Consequently, however considerable the contingent supplied by the honest delegates often may be, the part they play is, in the majority of cases, a passive one. They help to make the convention a "harmonious " as well as a discordant one. In the latter case, an understanding is often extremely difficult to arrive at, each rival group sticking to its candidates. Thereupon one ballot succeeds another without result; no candidate has a majority. No one will give way. It is a deadlock. Sometimes this lasts for days, and the number of ballots which have been taken reaches unheard-of figures, especially in the small conventions, where, at first sight, it would appear easier to come to terms. Thus, not long ago (in 1897), at a senatorial district convention in the State of Iowa, the candidate was nominated after the 6021st ballot.

in

What is the character of the candidates turned out by the conventions which we have just seen at work? It differs a great deal, according to the several kinds of conventions. The lower grade conventions, that is to say, those which provide for the less important elective offices, as a rule produce candidates who are decidedly bad, from the standpoint of morality and intelligence. The nominations go to the "workers" of the Organization, and, in general, to the politicians of low degree, in return for their services, or in recognition of the position which they have won in the caucuses and the committees. This applies, in the first place, to the candidates for the local offices in the cities, and pretty often in the counties. The legislative candidatures are, considering their importance for the political life of the country, the worst of all. The candidates for the House of Representatives at Washington are, for the most part, inferior men. As for those who get the nominations for the State legislatures, their principal failing is a very inadequate stock of morality. The conventions of rural legislative districts, being made up of a better class of men, are more strict in their choice; they are very often likely to lay their hand on decent, if not intelligent men; but in the large cities the selections are deplorable in the great majority of cases, although, again, the best representatives also come from the cities. It is otherwise with the candidates for conspicuous offices, the holders of which are always under the public eye, such as the Mayor, the State Governor, the Treasurer, and other high State officials, the judges of the superior courts. The candidatures of these latter are, happily, often, though by no means always, unaffected by party considerations; sometimes the judicial nominations made by the convention of one party are "endorsed " by the convention of the opposite party. As a rule, which is subject to very considerable exceptions, the conventions do not introduce disreputable or incompetent men into the higher judiciary, but, in any case, the party origin of the judges heavily handicaps their independence, as will be pointed out in greater detail further on. With regard to municipal offices, a movement is beginning to take shape (to which I shall also have another opportunity of referring), which tends to make the personal merit of the candidates the criterion of choice. The high executive offices are invariably filled by party candidates, but the conventions which nominate them, in particular the State conventions, take care to select decent candidates, so as not to run counter to public opinion and expose the Organization of the party to a revolt, and perhaps to a defeat. It may, therefore, be said in a general way that the nominations to the higher offices are of a satisfactory character, and sometimes even hit upon persons out of the common run.

But most of the "good" candidates are afflicted with an inherent defect, *i.e.* their weakness of character, their lack of energy and will. In this respect they are a reflection of the category of "good" delegates whom the politicians take into the conventions, and who often impart a tone of respectability to the State conventions. This weakness of character easily makes them the tools of the astute politicians, who may become "a power behind the throne greater than the throne," and this is what often induces a party Machine or a boss to select them in preference to men of a higher stamp, who would not submit to play the part of a dummy. But even in places where the party Organization is not strong enough, nor corrupt or ambitious enough, to dictate to the officials who owe their nomination to it, superior men have little prospect or desire of being adopted by the conventions. We have noted in our historical investigation of the system of the democratic Caucus, that in proportion as it developed, eminent, or simply distinguished, individuals withdrew from or were thrust out of political life or public functions. Now we can lay our finger on the fact and its cause, that we know the meaning of the three words "getting the delegates," which are inscribed on the door of American political life like the three well-known words over the entrance of Dante's Inferno. What man of real merit would care to seek admittance at this portal? If he did, he would always run the risk of being knocked down and trampled on in the crush which frequently takes place there. And even if the door were opened to him, if he did win the prize, would it be of a nature to make him forget the purgatory which he has had to pass through? By no means. Most of the public offices, from the standpoint of their rank, of their powers, of the pecuniary advantages attaching to them, hold out a very poor bait to ambition or the love of gain. In the whole hierarchy of the service of the State there are not ten really important posts. The emoluments are wretched, compared with those of employees in private concerns. The position is a most precarious one, for the elective terms are short, not exceeding two years on the average, and rarely extending to four (except for certain judgeships, the term of which is fourteen or even twenty-one years). The chances of re-election are almost *nil.* On the other hand, the liberal professions and industrial and commercial pursuits offer, amid the steady growth of the country, an endless field of activity, in which the most gifted minds and the strongest energies can find worthy scope and win triumphs which flatter self-love, excite the imagination, and satisfy the.craving for wealth. Political functions, that is to say, those which are considered as such in Europe, seats in legislative assemblies and ministerial posts, cannot have much attraction either for Americans, far less than in the Old World. The American political arena is too small, split up as it is by the federative organization of the Union into a great number of little compartments; the contests which are i Cf. James Bryce, *The American Commonwealth,* Vol. II, ch. LVIII: "Why the best men do not enter politics." fought in it, even on the large federal stage, almost entirely turning on business questions, have no dramatic interest capable of attracting doughty combatants and a numerous public whose shouts and applause stimulate and reward them. Nor does the position of legislator confer a patent of social nobility, as it used to do in the dawn of American political life, and as it still does in the present day in England; there is no such thing as a social nobility in the United States, and the members of the legislative assemblies would be the last persons to come in for it: the discredit into which they have fallen is too great. "Low as a congressman" is a saying one often hears, and the members of the State legislatures are in still greater disrepute; their seats are anything but sought after by men of real worth, "they go begging." Consequently, when the Organization of the party steps out of its own surroundings to look for candidates, and it does so, it cannot go very far. It has not much choice, even if it is inclined to forego the monopoly which it has created in favour of the class of professional politicians.

Restricted by so many more or less organic conditions, some of them due to the compressive power of the Caucus, others to the general conditions, political, social, and economic of the American Republic, the circle of those eligible by the conventions is still further narrowed, owing to two prejudices which have obtained the force of political customs or laws. One has made a dogma of the principle of local representation in its strictest sense, according to which elective offices can be filled only by persons residing iu the political subdivision in question, so that to stand, for instance, for Congress, it is not enough to be an American citizen, nor even a citizen of the State, but you must also be domiciled in the congressional district which has to elect its representative in the House. A man of the highest eminence, with a national and, perhaps, universal reputation, if he is not a prophet in his own little country, cannot enter political life, nor re-enter it if he has lost the favour of his constituents or of the ruling clique. For instance, Mr. Gladstone, who, in the course of his stirring career, had to change his constituency several times, would have been excluded from the American Congress from the outset. In consequence, the choice of a convention which nomi241 nates the candidates is reduced, even for the highest offices, to the local residents, whatever their moral and intellectual worth. But this restriction is accompanied by another which aggravates it in a marked degree, and which is connected with another American prejudice, that of rotation in public offices. I have explained, in the proper place, that in England the M.P. is ipso *facto* candidate for re-election, that the Association of the party, unless there has been a regular quarrel, readopts him without discussion, for the sole reason that he is the sitting member. In the United States this is a reason why the representative should give up his place to somebody else who has not yet held it. Custom has fixed a maximum of occupation for each "office: one term, two or three, and once this limit is reached, the holder, whatever his merit and the services which he might have been able to render in the future, owing to the experience acquired, must retire; "he has had enough," "he should step aside to give somebody else a chance. " In the South, the old practice of the slave-holding days has not yet been quite given up; the conventions frequently nominate representatives for one term after another. In New England, also, people like to keep good old servants, and the maximum of tenure is longer there than in the other States of the North; but there, too, and in the most enlightened States, like Massachusetts, for instance, unreasoning rotation triumphs owing to the prejudice of local representation. A legislative district is composed of several localities, of six or seven towns, which elect a member together. Accordingly, to distribute the honours fairly, to "pass the honours around," on each occasion a representative of another town is elected in turn.

Thus everything conspires to ensure the adoption at the conventions of candidates stamped with the common hallmark of mediocrity. But far from being a blemish, this quality generally becomes the first condition of their success at elections. We are already familiar with the expression "available candidate," *i.e.* the one who is likely to poll the most votes, and we are aware, from the history of the presidential candidatures, that his principal characteristic consists in having no character; not possessing a strongly marked individuality and not having compromised himself in the con VOL. II — B troversies of the day or in the struggles of factions, he is the most apt not to displease the electors and to slip in under the party flag. These qualifications and claims of an "available candidate" apply just as much to offices below that of the President; in each case the most suitable candidate will be the one who has not made himself conspicuous in a good or a bad sense, who has had no opportunity of making enemies, who has not been mixed up with militant politics. In fact, the virtues which the candidate must possess are all of a negative order; in the way of positive qualities the standard to which the candidate must come up is not a very lofty one. In the first place, the candidate must be a clean man; that is to say, there must be nothing against him, he must not have the reputation of a dishonest man. In places where the Machine is very powerful, the moral shortcomings of its candidate would not be, strictly speaking, an insurmountable obstacle, but, as a Tammany leader has explained to me, with the high authority which belongs to his Organization on this particular subject, far greater efforts and much more money would be required to get in a candidate of that kind. In the absence of proof to the contrary the habitual obscurity of the candidate is very often sufficient to raise the presumption of honesty in his favour. It is by no means necessary that he should be above the average in his respectability nor, generally speaking, in his personal eminence. Intellectual ability will always be useful to the candidate; it is just as well that he should be a good speaker, but it is not indispensable. Nor is the prestige of wealth an important factor in the United States for winning popular suffrages. The local influence wielded by the candidate is no doubt a source of superiority to him, but personal influence is a commodity of eminently uncertain, unstable value in the market of American life; amid the general fluctuation to which existence in the New World is liable personal positions change with a kaleidoscopic rapidity, a man is up one day and down the next.

When we bear in mind, therefore, the qualifications of the "good candidate " in England, we see how much fainter the individuality of the candidate is in the democracy of America. The complexity of the American elective system would be alone sufficient to account for the difference. In England the elector votes for a candidate, in America for a ticket on which all the numerous candidates are jumbled together. The English candidate must, to a considerable degree (which, it is true, is being diminished by the Caucus), depend on himself; he has to face the crowd alone, all eyes are upon him, he has more need than his American congener to be a good speaker, to impress the intelligence or the imagination by his personal ability. The American candidate is only an ingredient of the more or less scientific compound represented by the ticket. Apart from the elementary consistency which every ingredient ought to possess, its particular and distinctive nature is of value only to the extent in which it can accelerate cohesion. Appealing to an electoral body composed of various groups, the ticket will be all the more successful with it because its composition presents a reflection of these groups, because it establishes an affinity between them in the person of its candidates; that is to say, gives a special representation to the various groups. There is no question whatever here of a representation of interests, as the European reader, familiar with this notion, might be inclined to suppose; for most of the "interests," either social, so far as they exist in the United States, or professional, hold aloof from political life and furnish it with no basis of classification. The diversity of the elements of the electorate, which the politicians deem it advisable to take into account, reposes on distinctions which divide it by vertical, and not horizontal lines, such as affinities created by ethnical origin, in a lesser degree by religion, and by various other more or less spontaneous or voluntary associations, down to those which are founded on a community of tastes and pleasures, such as that of cyclists, for instance. The individuals who make up the slate take care to put on it, according to the composition of the electoral population, an Irishman, a German, a Scandinavian, a Czech, or, in other orders of ideas, a farmer, a cyclist of note. It is a race between the two rival tickets which shall form the fuller and more perfect collection of these species. Thus the criterion of an available candidate is completed: when his qualifications are not confined to negative virtues, when he possesses personal claims, they are more often than not of a purely external description.

THIRD CHAPTER THE NATIONAL CONVENTION

I

The choice of candidates for the highest executive offices of the Union, for the Presidency and the Vice-Presidency of the Republic, while following, in its main outline, the procedure and the preoccupations which govern the selection of candidates for the State offices, is always invested with exceptional importance. The stake is enormous; it includes the highest prize to which the ambition of an American citizen can aspire; it confers for the space of four years executive powers extending over a whole continent, and among others that of patronage, which has in its hands the life and death, so to speak, of 150,000 office-holders scattered over the face of the Union; it settles the destinies of the rival parties for many a year to come, perhaps. As the popular vote is confined to candidates selected in the national conventions, the attention of the whole country, excited to the highest pitch by the great periodical duel, centres on these assemblies so as to make them a unique institution, and their working under the eyes of the whole fever-stricken nation a unique spectacle. The citizen who pays no heed to the affairs of his State and of his city, which, however, concern him so nearly, fires up on the approach of the national conventions; but, by a singular piece of inconsistency, he does not on that account trouble himself more about the operations which pave the way for them, which determine their character; he does not take more interest than usual, that is to say, he takes hardly any interest, in the primaries and in the local conventions from which the national convention will issue like a cast from a mould. This great gathering appeals rather to the American elector's naturally excitable temperament than to his public spirit. The formation of the national conventions is, therefore, left to the professional politicians. The latter are proportionally far more numerous in them than in the State conventions, which include local notabilities, respectable personages, who, as a rule, stand aloof from politics. These personages are not so eager to accept the gratuitous mission of national delegate, which entails a long journey and an absence of a good many days, involving considerable loss and expense. Out of loyalty to their State they will go so far as to make some sacrifice to attend the State convention, but they are less ready to make it for the Union, which does not hold exactly the same place in their affections. This is especially true of the Southern States, but, in a lesser degree, it applies also to the North and to the West; with all his devotion to the big country, the American has a great and often an extreme attachment for the small one. Personal *amour-propre* has, also, something to do with the abstention of the local bigwigs, who naturally play the first fiddle in the State conventions; whereas in the national conventions they would be lost in the crowd. Moreover, the politicians are very anxious to obtain the position of delegate to the national convention for themselves, for every vote which helps to make the future President there has a high commercial value; it gives its owner claims on the gratitude of the future administration, which takes the form of places from an embassy in Europe down to a postmastership in the Far West. There are, no doubt, a certain number of delegates whose sole aspiration is to lend a hand in the great work of the party, out of devotion to its cause, or from mere vanity which courts opportunities for coming forward. But the great majority, and they may be estimated at nine-tenths, are occupied exclusively with their own interests at the convention. In the crowd of politicians who flock to the conventions all ranks are represented: Senators of the United States, State Governors, and so on down to aspirants to modest places; and each of them has an "axe to grind."

The representation at the national conventions is established on a fixed basis: each State sends to them, whatever the importance of the party in that State, twice as many delegates as it has Representatives and Senators in Congress; for instance, the State of New York, which has, in virtue of its population, Repeated attempts have been made to establish the representation at the national conventions on a basis proportioned to the numerical strength of the thirty-four members of the House of Representatives, plus two senators allotted to each State indiscriminately, deputes seventy-two delegates; the State of Delaware or of Montana, which has but one Representative in Congress and its two Senators, sends six delegates to the convention. Besides this, the Territories, represented in Congress by delegates only without a voice, and the District of Columbia, not represented at all, are empowered to take part in the conventions. Their populations are not allowed to vote for the President; but in order to develop party life in the Territories, the organizations of the parties concede to them, and to the District of Columbia by courtesy, a representation at the conventions, which at first consisted of two delegates and has been recently raised to six. The House of Representatives, having at the present moment 357 members, and the Senate 90 for the forty-five States, the double number of the delegates to the national conventions gives a total of 894 plus 42 delegates for the Territories of Alaska, Arizona, New Mexico, Oklahoma, Indian Territory, Hawaiian Islands, and the District of Columbia. In addition an alternate is appointed for each delegate to take his place in party in the respective States, as shown by the votes given to its candidates at the last election. But the States in which the party was in a minority, and this was notably the case with the

Republican party in the South, always opposed this reform which would have lessened their representation, and especially the share of their politicians in the " spoils." The inhabitants of the District of Columbia, which contains the federal capital, the city of Washington, built on neutralized ground not forming part of any State, and placed under the jurisdiction of Congress, are permanently excluded from voting (except those who have a legal domicile elsewhere). As for the Territories, which are the new parts of the Union, generally reclaimed from the great wilderness of the Far West and not yet formed into States owing to their imperfect economic and political development, which are as yet only embryo States, they do not acquire the right of voting for presidential Electors until they are admitted into the Union as States.

Of late years there have arisen, alongside the regular parties and in opposition to them, new parties, such as the Prohibitionists, whose principal object is to obtain laws prohibiting the sale of spirituous liquors, and especially the Populists, who promote agrarian and semi-socialist-collectivist schemes. These parties have adopted the same organization as the regular parties; they put forward candidates of their own, chosen in State and national conventions. The basis of representation in their conventions is not modelled on Congress or the Electoral College, but is fixed in proportion to the number of the adherents of the party in the different States, as shown by the vote at the last elections. The last national convention of the Populist party was composed of more than *I'M)* members, that of the Prohibitionist party had almost as many. case he is prevented from attending. The four delegates who represent the Senators of the State multiplied by two are chosen by the State conventions, and are called "delegates at large "; the other delegates who correspond to the members of the House of Representatives are chosen, to the number of two for each congressional district, by the district conventions. That is the invariable mode of election followed by the Republican party; whereas the Democrats elect in certain States, such as New York, for instance, all the delegates in the State convention; the State being considered, in this particular connection, as alone possessing a political individuality. This conception of the representation of the State, of a highly centralizing character, has received, in the Democratic party, a still more serious application in the form of the "unit rule," which restricts the right of the individual delegates to vote according to their preferences; the State convention, whether it elect only the four delegates at large or all the delegates, can order them to vote in a lump at the national convention, in accordance with the decision of the majority. For instance, if in the State delegation of seventy-two members instructed to vote as a "unit," thirty-seven delegates are in favour of a certain candidate, the votes of the other thirty-five delegates are passed to his credit, although they are hostile to him. Republican State conventions have repeatedly tried to introduce the unit rule; but the national conventions, beginning with that of 1860, on each occasion admitted the right of the delegates to vote as they pleased. On the other hand, the State conventions of all the parties, without distinction, often give the delegates peremptory instructions to vote for a particular presidential candidate. However, these instructions leave the delegates a certain latitude; for if the candidate who has been prescribed to them does not succeed in obtaining a majority, they will have to choose one from among the other competitors, and at their own discretion, so that in reality the delegates come to the national convention with full powers.

The convention meets in the summer of the "presidential year," that is to say, of that in which the people will have to choose, on the first Tuesday in November in leap year, the presidential electors who, according to the letter of the Constitution, elect the President and the Vice-President. The business preliminary to the convention is entrusted to the national committee of the party, which is appointed every four years, in the national convention, by the respective delegations of all the States and Territories, each of them choosing one member. In the beginning of the year, the national committee calls on the State committees to proceed to the election of the delegates, and, at the same time, fixes the date and the place of meeting of the convention. Before the Civil War. the national conventions almost always met in a city of the East, by preference at Baltimore; but since the extraordinary development of the West, which has shifted the geographical and economic centre of the Union, the parties have been in the habit of holding their grand council in a city of the central West, at Chicago, for instance. The enormous influx of visitors caused by the sitting of the convention, and perhaps, also, local *amour-propre,* makes several cities compete for the honour of having it. They plead their cause before the national committee through numerous deputations, composed of hotel proprietors, representatives of the chambers of commerce, judges, politicians. These extemporized advocates, while apologizing for not possessing the "wisdom of Solomon and the eloquence of Demosthenes in order that they might know just what to say," often deliver lengthy, eloquent, and argumentative addresses, in a public sitting, sometimes enforcing them by poetical quotations. The applicants promise to provide, in addition to a large sum of money to defray the cost of the convention and the travelling and hotel expenses of the members of the national committee and their wives, all the elements of comfort required by visitors, including fine weather. In other cities the heat is unbearable in summer, but in their city never; and for a very good reason: "we do not keep that kind of weather," as the spokesman of a certain city stated before the Democratic national committee in its session of 1896. II

A few days before the opening of the convention, the city in which it is to be held assumes a special aspect, "a conven *Report of the Democratic Xational Committee Meeting* held at Washington, D.C., January Hi, 18!i(i, p. 30.

tion aspect"; the streets, adorned with a profusion of flags and bunting flying over the crossings, the hotels inhabited by the delegations, and other political "head-quarters," are thronged by a huge crowd, "a convention crowd "; favoured by "a convention weather," it makes a continuous hubbub, "a convention stir," from morning till evening, and even later. The whole town is swamped with "enthusiasm," "convention enthusiasm," or, if the expression is preferred, "pre-convention enthusiasm." The arrival of the delegations provokes the first outbursts of it. Each State delegation arrives in a body, accompanied by a more or less considerable number of fellow-citizens of their native State, who escort their delegates. Very often the delegation comes with a band and in a special train containing sleeping-cars, a saloon-car, and a refreshment-car, the stock of liquors in which, being sometimes on too large a scale, provokes the exasperation of the Prohibitionists. At the station a solemn reception awaits the delegation. Zealous political co-religionists formed into clubs for the duration of the presidential campaign, or delegations which have already arrived, go to meet the new delegation and welcome it with harangues and applause re-echoed by the shouts of the assembled crowd. Then the whole company walks in a procession to the hotel in which the delegation has engaged rooms. To the sound of drums and fifes, in the midst of a frenzied crowd, the new arrivals march past, adorned with badges, medals, and ribbons bearing the name of their State, all wearing, perhaps, a special costume, which consists, for instance, of white hats, "liners" trimmed with silver lace, and carrying yellow walking-sticks. The delegation is preceded by its banner, and perhaps it displays yet another emblem, such as a gilt alligator, or even a live eagle which has come all the way from the Rocky Mountains.

Each State delegation has its official abode or, as the expression is, its "head-quarters" in a hotel, known from afar by a large sign and flags. It occupies, according to the rank of the State and the more or less active or retiring part played by it in the presidential campaign, a single room in which a hapless delegate in his shirt sleeves sits on duty, or a whole suite of apartments which are always full of crack politicians and wire-pullers. The head-quarters is the meeting-place not only of the members of the delegation, but of all the citizens of the State who attend the convention, either to help the different candidates in the campaign or as spectators. If all of them do not receive a plentiful supply of drinks and cigars at the head-quarters of their State, they are all sure to obtain badges with the name of the State there; endless batches of men and women come to fetch them, and it is not until they have pinned them on their breast that they consider themselves in proper trim and, as it were, entitled to swell the crush and the uproar prevailing in the city. The number of visitors who have come simply as sight-seers is enormous. It is a huge fair which attracts people from all quarters, and they cannot always get rooms, in spite of the number of hotels and their vast accommodation. The "head-quarters " of the States are the principal point of attraction for the crowd; the streets adjoining them are blocked to such an extent that it is sometimes necessary to stop all wheeled traffic. Inside the hotels matters are still worse. In the evening especially, when the visitors are joined by the inhabitants of the city after their day's work, it is no mean achievement to get into and out of the hotels occupied by the principal head-quarters; you do not walk, you are borne along by the crowd; the huge building is invaded, as it were, by a conquering army. These invaders, however, are very peacefully inclined; they are in quest of emotions only, and. they procure them at a very cheap rate by figuring in the show which they provide themselves. A small section is also under the impression that it is taking part, by its presence, in the selection of the future President of the United States; and it is not altogether wrong. The presidential candidatures are concocted under the auspices of the. crowd.

The candidatures are almost always numerous. They are spoken of a very long time before the meeting of the convention. It may be said that people begin to talk about the candidates for the next election, and discuss the claims of personages considered as "presidential possibilities," almost the day after the inauguration of the new President. Aspirants to the chief magistracy start an "underground canvass" at an early stage, to prepare their candidature. If they are very rich or, what comes to the same thing, if they have attached themselves to important special interests, such as manufacturers enriched by a protectionist tariff, or powerful companies or "trusts," they conduct this underground canvass with much method, —they systematically work the primaries from which will issue, step by step, the national convention. In any event, during the year which precedes the meeting of the convention, in a good many States the general feeling, or rather the feeling of the politicians, settles down in favour of one of its more or less eminent citizens as candidate for the Presidency of the Union. This feeling stamps him as the "favourite son" of his native State and makes him a competitor. Every national convention is confronted with halfa-dozen or more "favourite sons" of somewhat unequal merit and reputation. Some have had a fairly long political experience either in Congress or as member of the Cabinet or State Governor; others, and this is not so common, have hardly had an opportunity of winning their spurs in public life, but have achieved a local position, especially through the arts of the politician. Some are not known at all outside their own State, the popularity of others extends beyond its limits, and a few have a national reputation. Side by side with these candidatures brought forward with perfect good faith, there are others which are a mere speculation — almost a form of blackmail. A powerful boss who is absolute master of the delegation of his State, since it was chosen by *his* machine, who, consequently, controls several votes at the convention,! runs a candidate with the sole object of selling his withdrawal at a high figure. The candidate thus marked out for the part of pawn is, perhaps, the only person unaware of the fact; as State Governor or ex-ambassador he thinks that the honour offered to him is perfectly natural. Sometimes the boss gets himself nominated as presidential candidate by the State convention, and he will remain so up to the very last moment; as soon as he has made his deal with the probable winner, has bargained for the amount of presidential patronage to which he considers himself entitled, he will go over to his side with I the whole delegation of the State. Among the genuine candidatures, a good many are put forward only as a matter of form, without any chance of success, simply by way of tribute to the distinguished citizen who represents the dignity of the

State for the occasion. Perhaps the good fortune of being a "dark horse," who will be chosen at the eleventh hour in preference to more distinguished aspirants, is in store for some of these "favourite sons," and they will be looked on as "dark horse possibilities"; but the "dark horse" is just as likely to be an outsider and to appear for the first time at the last moment only. The dark horse is not necessarily an obscure personage; on the contrary, he may be very well known in the country and perhaps be extremely popular (as, for instance, General Sherman, the hero of the Civil War, who ranked among the dark horses at the Republican convention of 1884); but he does not appear to command acceptance as a presidential candidate. On the other hand, some of the candidates, one or two, are brought out of the ruck from the very first (this was the case, at the same convention, with J. G. Blaine and Chester A. Arthur, at that time President of the United States). Their great national reputation, their high rank in the party, or the part played or special position occupied by them in the political conjunctures of the moment, or their character, which exercises a fascination over the masses, give them an exceptional force of attraction. They are not only "favourite sons " of their respective States, but general "favourites "; and the personality of this or that "favourite" appears to be so commanding that he becomes the " logical candidate" of the situation. But that is no proof whatever that he will be adopted by the convention; the "favourite," as we shall see, is more likely than not to be beaten.

To whatever category the aspirant belongs, even if he is a hot "favourite" and the "logical candidate," the progress of his candidature must depend on the herculean efforts put forth during the few days which precede the convention, and in the course of the session itself. Each aspirant has at his disposal for this purpose not only the delegation of his State, which plunges wildly into the fray, but numerous special workers, all controlled by a head manager, an expert in this particular line, and who generally belongs to the delegation of the State and is sometimes a well-known personage. Their efforts are directed not only to the delegates, whose votes are asked for, but also to the outside multitude, with a view to creating a moral atmosphere favourable to the aspirant and pressing on the delegates with the weight of public opinion. This twofold propaganda, which constitutes what is called "the boom" or "booming," in political slang, is full of dramatic and spectacular incidents. The part of the programme intended for the outside public is addressed almost exclusively to the senses. True, speeches are made to the public, mass meetings are got up in front of the hotels, and speakers discuss the situation and the merits of the candidate from the balconies. But the favourite plan is to make the candidate popular by demonstrative methods, — by exhibiting and shouting out his name, by spreading abroad the reproduction of his physiognomy. The head-quarters of each candidate is provided with large bales of his portraits, with leaflets relating his glorious life, and, especially, with badges bearing his name and his likeness, which it distributes to all comers. Every citizen who puts on this ribbon or button publicly confesses thereby his belief in the candidate, and is qualified for making proselytes, who, perhaps, are converted solely by the artistic execution of the badges. On the building occupied by the head-quarters, above the banner with a picture of the candidate, is displayed his name, in huge letters, and in the evening it reappears in the form of luminous globes, the varied colours of which attract the gaze of the crowd.

But the most important part of the boom of the candidate in the streets consists of concerts, serenades, parades, and processions, by day and by night. The persons figuring in these processions, who are often obliging auxiliaries impelled by disinterested "enthusiasm," are imported by hundreds and thousands from the candidate's own State and from elsewhere. They are formed into companies, generally wearing a special dress, and, headed by a band, they walk through the streets to show how many admirers the candidate possesses. And the smarter their bearing and the more picturesque their uniform, the more they impress the crowd in favour of the candidate. Along with these sights for the eye, the boom includes a very important vocal element, in addition to the band, and which consists in bellowing out the candidate's name; the aforesaid companies, in the course of their processions, or special bands, numbering perhaps hundreds of persons, scour the streets uttering more or less articulate cries in which the candidate's name can be distinguished. They overrun the hotels, and, jostling each other in the passages, execute their repertoire, consisting of a single refrain, "Jones for President!" or, at the most, some lines like the following: —

Ho, ha, he!
Who are we?
We are the Bland Club from K. C. (Kansas City).
We're hot stuff!
That's no bluff,
Vote for silver and you'll have stuff 1
or again: —
He's a runner; he's a winner;
Wahoo waugh! Wahoo waugh I
Billy McKinley I Billy McKinley!
Wahoo waugh! Wahoo waugh I

These gymnastic and vocal propagandists form one of the three factors of the situation, along with the delegates and the spectators. While acting on the latter, they are meant to impress the former in the long run; and, to a certain extent, they perhaps succeed in doing so.

But, in any event, the conversions effected by the boom in the street cannot be of importance. Not so with the boom which goes on inside the various "head-quarters," and which aims directly at the delegates. This kind of boom also tries to puff the presidential aspirant, but by more refined methods. After having discreetly reconnoitred the hostile and rival positions, the managers of each aspirant direct their attacks toward the weaker points, in order to capture as many delegations as possible. They endeavour to spread abroad the impression that their client is most likely to obtain a majority; that it is, consequently, good policy to join him instead of persisting in the support of an aspirant doomed to defeat. They quote, with some stretch of their imagination, the delegations which have "mentioned" or even "endorsed" their aspirant; they have on their office table ready-made lists, copies of which they eagerly distribute, and which show, State by State, the exact total of the votes which he will poll at the first ballot, —a total which is always exaggerated. A few members of the delegation are detached as "missionaries," and visit the head-quarters to make proselytes; they ask to be heard by the delegations, and, in more or less closely reasoned speeches, they plead the cause of their candidate before one delegation after another, and perhaps prove the weakness of his competitors. They are received courteously and listened to attentively; but a straightforward answer is seldom given them. Everybody is on his guard; the ground on which one treads is full of pitfalls. Everything depends on the combinations which are being formed elsewhere, and you never know exactly what to believe; sinister rumours are continually circulating; at one time you are told that the adherents of the presidential aspirant A and those of B have combined, and that creates a new situation, the surface of the electoral chessboard is radically changed thereby; at another time comes the grave news that a "break" has taken place in the delegations of this or that State: they can no longer be depended on. Each moment brings a fresh element of anxiety; you live in a state of perpetual apprehension. A certain number of delegates, ranked among the "doubtful" ones, that is to say, who are not definitively committed to a particular candidature, are not proof against all these tactical movements, and let themselves be easily frightened into joiuing this or that aspirant who seems to be coming to the front and who must, consequently, be propitiated. In reality, it is all a matter of bargaining: they calculate, they appraise, they buy, they sell, but the bargain is rarely stated in definite terms; there is a tacit understanding that the delegate who gives his vote will have a claim on the lucky winner. Only a small number of delegates are bought straight out with cash. This is especially the case with the negro delegates of the Southern States, in which the local organization of the party, and notably of the Republican party, having but few followers, often keep up a nominal existence simply in order to have the right of sending delegates to the national convention. This class of delegates sells itself to the highest bidder; but, mindful of his dignity, the coloured gentleman plays a deep game and at first refuses to treat, and then, when the price has been agreed on with him, perhaps he has to be watched, and, to prevent him from coming in contact with the representative of a rival aspirant, who might entice him away, he is "shadowed" by a sort of detective, who never lets him out of his sight. Mines and countermines are laid the whole time. Laborious negotiations proceed all along the line; it is a continuous series of conferences, of councils of war, of confabulations, in which the leaders expend and exhaust their energies. A conspicuous politician at the convention rises almost with the dawn and retires long after midnight to snatch a few hours of sleep, frequently interrupted by the bands, which have not found the daytime and the evening long enough for making a noise in. The small fry of delegates also stay up very late, being detained at the bars, where they stimulate their enthusiasm or relieve their feelings in songs, some of which "are not in the hymn-book." On the Sunday preceding the opening of the convention the agitation reaches its height, in spite of the Anglo-Saxon Sabbath; it is the day of the crisis on which the process of "crystallization" takes place, on which the combinations are definitively settled, on which the principal actors have come to an understanding about the candidates and the programme. But this does not make the final result any more of a certainty; the convention almost always has great surprises in store.

in

The sittings of the national convention are public, and generally attract from 10,000 to 15,000 spectators. The members of the convention alone number nearly 2000 persons, consisting of 930 delegates and as many alternates. The convention, therefore, always sits in a building of vast size, and generally erected for the purpose. The opening of the doors is awaited by an enormous crowd, a portion of which will be excluded for want of tickets. This gathering is taken advantage of to start a propaganda, *in extremis,* in favour of this or that presidential aspirant: the vocal performers use what voice they have left; here and there a few impromptu orators perhaps deliver They are admitted by tickets which are partly sold to cover the expenses of the convention and partly distributed to the delegates, who can give them to their friends. A considerable number of these latter tickets too are dealt in, and often become the object of wild speculation.

speeches ou the political situation; other propagandists, without saying anything, carry about emblematic demonstrations of the superiority of this or that candidate. A crowd of hawkers offer emblems of less profound meaning in the form of walking-sticks, pins, buttons with the likeness of the presidential aspirant, small national flags, paper fans which the heat makes acceptable, prospectuses of restaurants started for the occasion, etc. The attitude of the crowd is excellent; it exhibits the good humour and undefinable air of intelligence which are the unfailing characteristics of American crowds. It knows various political personages who will be talked of at the convention, or who will be among the principal actors there, but of the convention itself, of the way in which it is formed, it does not know much; not only has it no inkling of all the manoeuvres to which the convention has given rise, but it does not know whence the members of the convention come, from whom they derive their power; it is no use questioning these people one after another, their answers are confused and involved or sometimes absurd, —and yet they are all electors.

At last the doors are thrown open, the crowd rushes in and occupies all the seats in a twinkling, without any disorder. You find yourself in a vast amphitheatre (I am referring especially to the Chicago Coliseum, in which I witnessed the famous Democratic national convention of 1896), and the scene which meets your gaze just at first is unquestionably a very imposing one: the eye can scarcely take in the amphitheatre, the benches and galleries are black with people, the bright July sun plays upon the human sea through the innumerable panes of glass which form the roof of the building. All the galleries are hung with flags and bunting encircling the portraits of the great ancestors of the Republic; their line is not very long as yet, but it is a glorious one: they are the Washingtons, the Jeffersons, the Jacksons. A muffled hum of For instance, at the Republican convention of 1896 three men stood outside, the one tall, gaunt, unshaven, clad in rags like a beggar, with an umbrella in tatters and carrying a banner on which was written, "Look out for hard times and cold days if McK. is beaten." Two other sandwich-men confronted him, the one fashionably dressed and with the inscription, "The workman under the McKinley Bill," the other in rags, lean and with a halfstarved look, representing "the workman under the Wilson Bill" (which lowered the protectionist customs duties).

VOL. II—S voices fills the vast enclosure like the mutterings of the ocean gathering its waves before it lets loose the storm, while from above issue other sounds of a clearer and more melodious kind: on a gallery over the presidential platform an orchestra, completely hidden by the hangings, plays popular airs and wafts down upon the crowd the sweet and tender strains of "America ":

My country, 'tis of thee,
Sweet land of liberty,
Of thee I sing.
Land where my fathers died,
Land of the pilgrims' pride,
From every mountain side
Let freedom ring.

In the meanwhile the chairman of the national committee ascends the platform, knocks on the desk with the gavel, and calls the convention to order, after which a clergyman offers up a prayer to invoke the blessing of Heaven upon the labours of the assembly. The clergyman is chosen without distinction of cult or sect, but always with reference to tactical considerations. The Republican convention of 1896 was opened by a rabbi; the object was to avoid giving offence to the bigoted Catholics and Protestants by selecting a minister of the opposite persuasion; but on the following days recourse was had to the services of Christian clergymen. The prayer recited by the minister is of his own composition; sometimes this prayer steps out of ecclesiastical commonplace, assuming a mild tone A hammer resembling that used by auctioneers, which corresponds to the president's bell on the Continent in Europe. The gavel used at each convention generally has its history, it is made out of a piece of wood from a historic house or tree, or one claiming to be such. It often has a symbolic aspect, being composed of several pieces equal in number to that of the States of the Union, each State being represented by a piece coming from its soil; or again, as at the conventions of 18!V, when the great battle was fought on the question of the silver standard, the gavel presented to the Republican convention was fitted with pieces of gold at both ends, while the gavel offered to the Democratic convention was made of sixteen bits of silver and one bit of gold to represent the legal ratio of 16 to 1, which the Democrats wanted to maintain in spite of the depreciation of silver. There are always amateurs ready to present the convention with a gavel; "the Man with the gavel," who has become a sort of institution, appears before the convention, often at a very Inopportune moment, and handing over his gift, delivers a little address which is meant to be impressive.

of theological freedom, or even sounding a note of protest against the existing social and political order of things. After the prayer the chairman of the national committee, on behalf of the latter, submits to the convention the names of the temporary organization of the convention, which are, as a rule, adopted by the assembly without debate. The temporary chairman receives the gavel from the chairman of the national committee and delivers a speech, which is hailed with applause and shouts. This is the first explosion of the enthusiasm of the crowd, which is destined to reappear only too often in the course of the session.

The convention begins by selecting its four great committees, viz. the committee on credentials, on permanent organization, on rules and order of business, and on platform or on resolutions. The roll of all the States is called, the chairman of each delegation announces the names of the members, one for each committee, whom it appoints to act on them. Thereupon the convention adjourns, and the committees set to work at once in order to submit their reports on the following morning. If the reports are not ready, the convention does its best to kill the time by listening to addresses delivered by speakers who step into the breach, by taking cognizance of resolutions and memorials presented to the convention on matters of public interest, or considered as such by Here are one or two extracts: " We praise Thee, O Lord. We acknowledge Thee to be the Lord. All the earth doth worship Thee, Father everlasting... may liberty ever drive away oppression; may virtue ever dominate darksome vice, and may Thy kingdom come and Thy will be done on earth, and so may the great true democracy, good of all people, the sublime philosophy of the Commoner of Nazareth, everywhere prevail."

Or again: "Almighty God, Father of Men and Ruler of the universe... guide then the choice of this convention so that its nominees in character and conviction shall represent the spirit of modern Democracy, a progressive Democracy, of a Democracy that is arrayed on the side of the masses as against the classes, and that strives to lift from the shoulders of the people the burdens borne for the benefit of the favoured few. May the nominees of this convention be in touch with the multitude of toilers that bear the heat and burden of the day, and lead them to victory, not for the sake of mere spoil of office, or of power, but for the sake of inherent principles." The Democratic national convention of 1806 departed from this rule, and after a violent discussion rejected the candidate of the committee for the temporary chairmanship who represented the gold faction, the majority of the convention having been won over beforehand to the cause of the white metal. their authors, and which include proposals of a most preposter» ous kind. The most important reports of the committees are those of the committee on credentials and of the committee on resolutions. The former decides all the cases of contested seats. These last are always numerous; sometimes individual delegates contend for the position, at others two complete delegations appear for the State, each claiming to be the duly elected one. These rivalries hardly ever represent different currents of opinion; they proceed exclusively from the desire for "recognition," — the delegation which is admitted will he able to aspire to favours at the hand of the Government which the convention will bring into existence. The cases have already undergone a preliminary investigation by the national committee on the eve of the meeting of the convention, and a lengthy one, for the contending parties are generally very tenacious and fond of quibbling. On the strength of this investigation, the national committee (appointed four years before by the preceding convention) draws up the temporary roll of the members of the convention; the committee on credentials of the sitting convention settles it definitively. As in the State convention, it generally admits those who are supported by the local regular organization of the party, and if there are two complete delegations of a State they are often reconciled by the admission of both, with a half vote for each delegate, unless the hostility between the two delegations is irremediable and a majority in the convention cannot be formed without the full vote of one of the two rivals; in that case a sufficient number of delegates are invalidated to break down opposition on the pretext, whether true or not, that they have not been properly elected. Sometimes the decisions of the committee on credentials are not ratified by the convention; but this seldom happens. After the report of the committee on credentials, the convention considers the report of the committee on permanent organization, which submits to it the names of the permanent officers of the convention. This list, which, by the way, is settled beforehand by the national committee, is accepted without opposition. The permanent chairman delivers a long speech on the political situation, repeatedly and frantically interrupted by cries of approval, which are a sort of instalment offered by the crowd of the shouts with which it will shortly receive the platform to be submitted by the committee on resolutions.

The platform, which is supposed to be the party's profession of faith and its programme of action, would appear to be the main business of the convention; in reality, it is only a farce, — the biggest farce of all the acts of this great parliament of the party. The platform presents a long list of statements, almost on *omni re scibili et quibusdam aliis,* relating to politics, in which everybody can find something to suit him, but in which nothing is considered as of any consequence by the authors of the document, as well as by the whole convention. It is a catalogue revised and enlarged from one convention to another. If a new problem is beginning to stir the country, if any question not only of a political but of a social or humanitarian nature is interesting public opinion for the moment, the platform hastens to re-echo it, in order to show in words the party's solicitude for the particular cause. It is not even necessary that American interests should be involved; it is enough if the question affects the elector's sensibility as a man, if it strikes some chord or other within him. It is therefore considered good taste to insert in the platform of the party an expression of sympathy with, for instance, the persecuted Armenians in Turkey, and good policy to declare for Irish Home Rule, and to protest against the harsh treatment of the Jews in the dominions of the Tsar, the Irish and the Jews having many coreligionists and congeners among the electors of the United States. All the more are the authors of the platform on the look-out for the special preoccupations of American citizens, which stir the public mind or disturb private interests. For instance, the scandals of the spoils system having exasperated opinion and made "civil service reform " a question of the day, the platforms of both parties hasten to add a strongly worded paragraph in favour of the reform, which all the delegates in quest of spoils of course hate like poison; and every future platform reaffirms the pious declaration. If there is an urgent problem which demands a straightforward solution, the concoctors of the platform endeavour to word it in language which can bear different constructions, to compose a "straddling" one. This is a game which they enjoy as thorough proficients; and the reader will remember that it is in the traditions of the national conventions, and he is aware of the part which tins conjuring away of the problems of the day has played in political contests. Exceptionally, at times of grave crises which distracted the party, when there was no loophole, the platform has met the question of the day with a straightforward answer which, on two occasions, was the signal for a formal split in the party; to wit, at the Democratic convention of Charleston, in 1860, on the subject of slavery, and at the Democratic convention of Chicago, in 1896, about the free coinage of silver.

But, apart from cases of this kind, the sole object of the platform is, in the present day, as formerly, to catch votes by trading on the credulity of the electors. The declamatory form and the ambiguous statements of this document of the party both tend in this direction. As an indication, therefore, of the policy of the future administration elected on this platform, the latter is of no value. In this respect, the letter of acceptance of the candidate adopted by the convention, in which he states his aims and his views on the great questions of the day, is far more important. Whether the President will keep the promises of the candidate or not, in any event, you hear not the manufactured voice of a machine, but the living accents of a man whose personality marks him out for and lays him open to responsibility. The platform has just as little significance and authority for Congress. Its members consider themselves in no way bound by the programme laid down in the convention, for they know perfectly well under what circumstances and with what men Here is the first paragraph of the platform adopted at the Republican convention in 1896: "The Republicans of the United States, assembled by their representatives in National Convention, appealing for the popular and historical justification of their claims to the matchless achievements of thirty years of Republican rule, earnestly and confidently address themselves to the awakened intelligence, experience, and conscience of their countrymen in the following declaration of facts and principles:

"For the first time since the Civil War the American people have witnessed the calamitous consequences of full and unrestricted Democratic control of the government. It has been a record of unparalleled incapacity, dishonour, and disaster."...

The letters of acceptance of the rival presidential candidates correspond to the addresses to their constituencies issued by the leaders of the English parties, sitting in the House of Commons, immediately after the dissolution of Parliament which marks the beginning of election time. tal reservations it has been promulgated. The promises of the platform which the party that has come into or remained in power has not redeemed, will only provide matter for violent denunciations in the next platform of the opposite party, which will arouse the indignant enthusiasm of the assembled crowd, expressed in applause and shouts loud enough to shake the walls of the building. One must be sparing, however, in the use of terms describing the uproar in which the convention, delegates as well as spectators, indulges, for it is about to assume proportions setting all figures of speech and metaphors at defiance; one must, therefore, not exhaust too soon those which ordinary language has at its command. This tumult will continually interrupt the last two and the most important acts of the convention, after the adoption of the platform, viz. the introduction of the aspirants and the ballots. IV

All the States are invited, in alphabetical order, to introduce their aspirants. Those who have any respond to the invitation by putting up speakers to support the claims of their "favourite sons," or, in general, of the men whom they prefer. These champions are carefully selected beforehand from among those delegates who are most conspicuous for their eloquence, as well as for their influence. The principal spokesman of each aspirant makes the nominating speech in his favour, then another delegate, or several delegates, second the nomination in less elaborate speeches; and so on until the list of the States and of the aspirants is exhausted. It is only when all these torrents of eloquence have ceased to flow that the voting begins. The nominating speeches are looked on as the aesthetic treat and the *piice de resistance* of the entertainment. The eulogium of the aspirant is generally pompous and bombastic; it tries to be at once persuasive and affecting. It dwells on the aspirant's special chances of being elected if he is adopted as a candidate; it tells the story of his life, beginning with the days of his childhood and his youth. If they have been full of toil and hardship, so much the better: that will melt the hearts of the audience; if he has had to go barefoot for want of shoeleather, that is a real godsend; the people, "the plain people," will recognize in him "one of themselves," and the others will share this feeling out of democratic snobbery. For there is nothing so becoming in American society as the humble beginnings of a successful man, as the poverty and misery which have faded into a reminiscence in his life. Whatever the real position and the notoriety of the aspirant, if he be only an obscure favourite son incapable, perhaps, of attaining the dignity of a dark horse, the speaker who eulogizes him never considers himself under any restriction in the choice of terms for glorifying him; tho speech teems with the most extravagant epithets and with metaphors of extraordinary boldness. The orator lays under contribution the poets, mythology, modern history, ancient history, and that of Rome in particular. Daniel Webster, who had to touch up President Harrison's inaugural speech, said afterwards: "It was a very stiff job. I killed no less than fourteen Roman consuls." It appears that these consuls have left issue. At the Democratic convention of 1896 a candidate was introduced in these terms: "We give you another Cicero — Cicero to meet another Catiline." Another candidate, a farmer from the West, was put forward as "that illustrious statesman and patriot, that Tiberius Gracchus;" and the speaker adjured the convention to vote for the American Gracchus "by the ashes of your ancestors; by the memories of your great and venerated dead; by the love which you bear to.your children; by the duty which you owe to posterity; in the name of all that men hold sacred." In the majority of cases, the authors of these impassioned appeals know perfectly well that their clients have not the faintest chance of obtaining a majority in the convention, and all the delegates and the public are aware of it too; but the grand specimen of eloquence is none the less delivered and listened to with conviction, for, as in the theatre, if the actors and the audience did not look as if they believed that it has all really happened, there could be no play at all.

It is remarkable, as illustrating the psychology of the American elector, that for more than sixty years, from the date at which one finds the prototype of the nominating speech, the national convention style of eloquence has not changed, amid the incessant progress of American society. I subjoin, as a matter of record, the text of that speech, delivered at the Democratic convention of 1835, in favour of the candidature of R. M. Johnson to the Vice-Presidency (the candidate for the Presidency, Martin Van Buren, was marked out by the all-powerful will of Jackson, and it was useless to recommend him by harangues of the delegates):

Who is he? If, Mr. President, you could transport yourself to the

"Far West," you would find upon one of her green and sunny fields, surrounded by the implements of husbandry, a personage whose plain and simple garb, whose frank and cordial and unostentatious bearing, would tell you that he had sprung from the people — that he was still one of them, and that his heart, in all its recollectious, its hopes and its sympathies, was blended with the fortunes of the toiling millions. But, sir, his seared and shattered frame and limping gait would tell you, too, that the story of his life was not confined to a mere recital of household hospitalities or neighbourhood charities. That story is no legend of obscure or doubtful authenticity; it lingers not alone in the kindly bosoms of friends, but every tongue in the Republic can give it utterance, and the brightest pages of your country's history have caught lustre from its glowing record. When this nation was agonizing and bleeding at every pore, when war had desolated with fire and sword your northern frontier, and the best blood in the land had been vainly spilt upon its plains, he left the warm halls of Congress for the bleak winds of the Canadas; and, waiting for no summons of the recruiting officer, he rallied about him the chivalry of his State, and dashed with his gallant volunteers to the scene of hostilities, resolved to perish or to retrieve the national honour. With daring impetuosity he pursued and overtook the enemy — threw himself like a thunderbolt of war into the thickest of the fight — fought hand to hand and eye to eye with the Briton and his savage myrmidons — poured out his blood like water — triumphed and returned home with the richest trophies of the campaign. Sir, his deeds rely not for recollection or blazonry upon musty records, nor yet upon caucus or convention addresses; they have been spoken in the thunders of victorious battles, they have been written upon the hacked and broken armour of his country's invaders. His life has been one of unfaltering, unswerving devotion to freedom and to the people. The people "love him because he first loved them." His popularity rests upon no calculation of political chances. It is not seated in the arithmetics, but in the deep and ardent affections of his country....

... His fame, like that of our venerated chief magistrate, spreads everywhere — alike in the wilderness and with "city full," penetrating into the far valleys, climbing to the hill tops, and reaching in its kindling, animating influences every log cabin beyond the mountains.... There is a voice from the great valleys of the West; from all her cities and cottages. There is a voice from the East, from the North, and the South; there is a voice from the fields of the husbandman, from the workshops of the mechanic, from the primary assemblies of the people, from the conventions of neighbourhoods and States, calling aloud for the elevation of the war-worn soldier, this tried and uncorruptible patriot, this advocate of the destitute and downtrodden, this friend to freedom and to man. Such, sir, is Richard M. Johnson.

Let us now turn to a nominating speech made at a recent convention. I take the conventions of 1884 at random. Here is an address delivered at the Republican convention in favour of a candidate who obtained 13 votes out of 813. After having sketched the history of the Republican party and of its glories, the speaker narrates the life of the aspirant:

X. was born in North Carolina. He draws from southern blood and southern soil and southern skies the generous chivalry of a nature that abhors cant and hypocrisy and falsehood, and feels the stain like a wound. Thirty-four years ago he came, a poor, barefooted, penniless boy, to the rugged soil of Connecticut, where breathing its free air, listening to its free speech, and taught in its free school, he laid the foundation of a manly character and life in principles which are as enduring as Connecticut's everlasting hills....

The fierce light that beats against a presidential candidate will explore his record iu vain, and he will come out brighter from the blaze. His life is gentle, and the elements are so mixed in him that nature might stand up and say to all the world "This is a man."... If he is nominated, all elements can support him, for he is a radical conservative and a conservative radical; a friend of Garfield and a friend of Grant. Sir, if he should be nominated, it would ensure you Connecticut by a 10,000 majority. It would weld together with fervent heat the dissensions in New York. It would blaze through the State of Garfield, that daughter of Connecticut, more beautiful than her mother.

It would carry the Southern States, for he is the only candidate that this party would have named who was born on southern soil. It would please all parties and all professions, for he is a lawyer, editor, soldier, statesman, orator. It would take the people, for he is what the people all love — God Almighty's noblest work, an honest man. Such a nomination would sweep from the storm-beaten coast of the Atlantic to the Golden Gate of the peaceful sea. With him elected in i Niles, XLVIII, 217.
vigour of his life and plenitude of his powers, beloved at home and respected abroad, with our free institutions and our imperial domain, we should need no Bartholdi statue standing at the gate-way of commerce with uplifted torch to typify the genius of liberty enlightening the world, but our history under a Republican President, administered upon a Republican policy, would of itself bear witness to all times, and to all people, that America is the greatest, freest, most prosperous country upon which the sun in his course has ever looked down.

Here is another short extract from a speech made at the rival convention, at that of the Democratic party, in favour of an eminent aspirant, who was triumphantly adopted at the second ballot — Mr. Grover Cleveland:

Grim and grey, personally fighting the battles of the Democratic party, I stand to-day to voice the sentiment of the young men of my State when I speak for Grover Cleveland, of New York. His name is upon their lips, his name is in their hearts, and he is the choice not only of that band of young men, but he is the choice of all those who desire for the first time, as young men, to cast their votes in November for the candidate nominated by this convention. They love him, gentlemen, and respect him, not only for himself, for his character, for his integrity and judgment and iron will, but they love him most for the enemies he has made.... Every breeze brings to us what would seem to be indications of victory, but we cannot accomplish victory without recruits. Those recruits are at our bidding: young, middle-aged, and old; you see them in platoons and regiments, brigades and divisions. Every one of them bears upon its banner first "Cleveland of New York." Let the countersign of the great Democratic camp in November be "Cleveland," and then men can make their way to it, and recruited as we shall be, our Ides of November will not be a Waterloo, but will be a glorious sun of Austerlitz and Wisconsin.

The eloquence of the speakers, however great it is or appears to be, only produces its full effect when accompanied by the more or less noisy manifestations with which the audience greets the speeches and the names of the presidential aspirants who form the subject of them. Every speech is interrupted and brought to a close by more or less frantic shouts; being looked on as a criterion of the aspirant's popularity, these outcries impress the delegates, make the weak hesitate, and sometimes decide the wavering. The campaign managers The speaker was a delegate of the State of Wisconsin.
of each aspirant, therefore, considering these manifestations as a card in their game, procure them by means of a paid *claque,* judiciously distributed over the enormous hall. This is the last and the most impressive act of the "boom" organized on behalf of the aspirant; inside the convention building the boom becomes an apotheosis. As soon as the aspirant's name is uttered, the delegates who support him and the paid applauders jump up on their seats and break into cheers or other less articulate cries, which are immediately taken up by a more or less considerable section of the crowd. The latter are only too ready to make a row, they have almost a physiological need of this relief; it is enough for the *claque* to give the signal for them to go into convulsions. If the aspirant is a favourite, a very popular man, whom the forecasts place in the first flight for the presidential race, the delirium reaches an indescribable pitch of intensity. Hardly has the speaker pronounced his name when his portrait, which has been held in reserve, is hoisted aloft and carried about the hall, every one is on his legs, shouting, screaming, tossing hats and handkerchiefs into the air, waving small flags and open umbrellas. It is a sort of pandemonium or Bedlam. If one could imagine a crowd of fifteen thousand persons all attacked at once with St Vitus' dance, one would obtain a faint idea of the scene presented by the convention. The chairman with his hammer is quite helpless, it is in vain that he tells the band to play in order to tranquillize the assembly; a duel begins between the orchestra, which energetically strikes up the "Star-Spangled Banner," and the yelling crowd; now and then a few sounds from the instruments are audible, but they are instantaneously drowned by the shouting. The orchestra tries to play " Dixie," or "The Girl I Left Behind Me"; it is of no avail, the crowd refuses to listen. The paroxysm is at its height. Here a delegate takes off his coat, hoists it on a walking-stick, and, waving it with both hands, begins to dance, probably in imi A well-known American journalist and ex-diplomatist has hit on another simile to give an

idea of the uproar which he witnessed on a similar occasion at a convention: "Imagine all the hogs ever slaughtered in Cincinnati giving their death squeals together." (Murat Halstead, *Caucufee of 1860.* A history of the natioual conventions, Columbus, ISliO, p. 145.) This city, which has the nickname of "IVrcopolls," possesses the largest slaughterhouse for hogs. 209 tation of King David dancing before the Ark. Another enthusiast, at the further end of the hall, creates a precedent himself by taking off his boots and waving them one on an umbrella and the other on a stick. The crowd does not stop until compelled by fatigue, by exhaustion. Spectators who know what is coming have taken out their watches from the very beginning, like certain travellers at the entrance of a long tunnel. The duration of the uproar, carefully noted down, is not only of importance for the effect of the moment; it is formally placed on record, and later on people will point out that the uproar for McKinley did not last more than twenty-two minutes, that is to say two minutes less than that with which Blaine was honoured.

The series of panegyrics of the aspirants continues, each has his more or less well-sustained boom; but all at once a slight incident renews the uproar of a short time back. The speech on behalf of a much-talked-of aspirant is at an end, but his boom, which has been started in the regulation way, flags, and his adherents are pained to see that it is about to die out when it has hardly begun. At this point, however, a young woman in one of the galleries, dressed entirely in white, stands up, shouts out the name of the aspirant at the top of her voice, seizes two small flags, and whirls them round like windmills with her bare arms. Her cries and her gestures attract the attention of the adjoining groups, then of others, and, finally, of the whole meeting; and the fifteen thousand persons, adherents as well as opponents of the aspirant in question, greet his youthful admirer with unearthly shrieks, which last for several minutes. The delegates of the aspirant's State go to fetch the intrepid damsel, and, under their escort,, with a heavy banner, adorned with the aspirant's likeness, in her hand, she marches in triumph across the hall in the midst of the raving crowd; she is hoisted over the partition which separates the seats of the delegates from those of the public, and is invited to take her place among the delegates. The whole meeting, delegates as well as the public, yells its loudest, — they are all glad to be able to enjoy another fit of hysterics. The most astonished person of all is the heroine of the incident, which she has brought about quite unwittingly; she only obeyed a voice from within, like Joan of Arc; perhaps 270 she had a vague recollection of the woman with the white umbrella who roused the enthusiasm of a preceding convention.

At last the long string of panegyrics is at an end; wearied with oratory and overcome by the tremendous physical exertion, every one takes breath to prepare for the new and supreme emotions to be afforded by the ballots.

V

The voting for the candidates is attended with the same publicity as all the proceedings which have gone before it: as the name of each State is called out, in alphabetical order, the chairman of the delegation announces to whom it gives its votes. In the Democratic conventions, where the "unit rule" is in force, the votes are all credited to a single candidate, that of the majority of the delegates, and the chairman of the New York delegation, for instance, declares, "seventytwo votes for so-and-so," although thirty-five delegates are against him. In the Republican conventions, where each delegate is entitled to vote as he pleases, the chairman of the delegation announces several candidates, if there is occasion for it, mentioning at the same time the number of votes given to each. However, even in the Democratic conventions each delegate has the right to challenge the declaration of his chairman; in that case, the clerk of the convention calls the roll of all the delegates, who each state the name of their candidate. This does not alter the result, all the votes are given to the candidate chosen by the majority; but the minority gets an opportunity of making a public demonstration in favour of its candidate. Sometimes the chairman of the State delegation mentions him spontaneously and with a good grace, saying "so-and-so among the delegates wish to record their votes for that splendid type of New England Democracy X, but under the operation of the unit rule I cast the twenty-two votes of the State for Y." The majority which an aspirant must obtain to be proclaimed candidate is a bare majority with the Republicans, and a two-thirds one with the Democrats. The reader is aware that the "two-thirds rule" is of very old standing, and will recollect the way in which it was used in certain Democratic conventions to disqualify popular aspirants, such as Martin Van BureD. Repeated attempts have been made to abolish the "two-thirds rule," but without success; it has become part of the Democratic patrimony. It is still just as far from answering the purpose which its authors had in view and which, moreover, has never been accurately ascertained. According to one version, the rule was adopted in the interest of the Southern States, which wanted to prevent the free States of the North and of the West from thrusting a President on them against their will. Another explanation is that the majority was fixed at two-thirds to ensure complete harmony between the President and the federal Senate, a portion of whose members is renewed in two-thirds of the States almost at the same time as the occupant of the chief magistracy of the Union. As has always been the case, the two-thirds rule somewhat facilitates intrigue, but it does not delay the gathering of a majority round some name or other more than on the Republican side, owing to the unit rule, which, by automatically assimilating the minorities, quickens the coagulation of the various elements of the convention.

The manoeuvres and the intrigues

relating to the person of the future President, which have been carried on by managers and powerful State bosses, may be paralyzed by the force of public opinion, which sometimes imposes its candidate on the convention with inflexible persistency. The politicians, at least the big ones who are working for themselves, are in that case defeated before the battle begins. Thus, for instance, in 1892 the head politicians of the Democratic party, along with Tammany Hall, were hostile to Cleveland's candidature; but in the country at large it aroused the greatest enthusiasm; and the politicians had to yield and give him a majority at the first ballot. His Republican rival, Harrison, who then filled the Presidency and was seeking renomination, was opposed by several State bosses, who combined to ensure his defeat; but the bulk of the delegates did not follow them, believing in Harrison's success with the electorate, and brought him in also at the first ballot. However, such a direct pressure of opinion is of extremely rare occurrence. Generally, when the balloting begins, the situation is still very uncertain, for it depends entirely on intrigues and manoeuvres which, although they have been prosecuted unremittingly, have not yet led to a result. The first ballot, therefore, is hardly ever decisive; it barely gives approximate indications of the strength of the rival forces, which are simply mustered. To make an impression on the convention, the managers of the principal aspirants try to bring up all their following and to show "presidential strength," except when a smart manager holds back a few votes for the second ballot with the object of proving that his aspirant is gaining votes, and of making this example contagious. Most of the delegates, who are running obscure "favourite sons," are free from all these preoccupations. They have voted for these aspirants and will vote for them again in one or two ballots, for conscience' sake, either to carry out their instructions or from "State pride"; but they are really waiting, and waiting very impatiently, for the moment when they can decently throw them over and join the winners. But who is to win; who will be the man? This is the question which consumes all the human beings packed in the huge building, and growing more and more overwrought and unstrung; each fresh ballot is expected to furnish the answer. The chiefs of the staff of the various aspirants, alone keeping a cool head amid the general excitement, combine the movements on the board. All the dispositions suggested by the last ballot must be made immediately, for the ballots follow each other without a break. Hurriedly, the heads of different delegations exchange a few words, give a word of command; or a delegation of a large State withdraws for awhile to come to an agreement; these conferences are sometimes particularly passionate and uproarious. During the first ballots the great object of the aspirants and their champions is to wear out their rivals, especially the favourites, to disable the eminent aspirants, in order to clear the ground. For this pur There have been a few cases in which the candidate obtained a majority at the first ballot, besides those of Cleveland and Harrison in 1892, which I have just mentioned. Quite recently, in 18!Hi, Mr. McKinley was nominated at once, and before this, Grant in 1808 and 1872, Lincoln in 1864, Henry Clay in 1844, and Martin Van Buren in 1835. The last-named was adopted at the convention of 1840 without a ballot. The same honour fell to Mr. Cleveland's lot in 1888. On the other hand, in several cases the number of the ballots has lieen very large: Garfield was adopted, in 1880, at the 38th ballot; Pierce, in 1852, at the 49th, and Scott, in 1852, at the 53rd ballot.

pose, a coalition is easily formed between all the mediocrities whom the others of course stand in the way of. At the same time the forces of the big aspirants are hindered from combining. To prevent an alliance between A and B, who are leading, a considerable number of votes are given to B. The adherents of A, concluding that B is a most dangerous rival, instantly break with him. At the next ballot the number of votes obtained by B falls off, and then he is beaten irredeemably; he will get no more recruits, and desertions will even take place in his own ranks. To keep the totals of the eminent aspirants stationary, after several successive ballots, is also an important result; it is hoped to wear them out, to tire their adherents, and with a view to this the followers of aspirants who are doomed to failure will go on voting for them ballot after ballot. For a certain number of ballots, therefore, it is only a sparring match; votes are given to aspirants and withdrawn from them; are borrowed for one ballot and scrupulously returned at the next.

On their side, the favourites, as well as the aspirants of the second class, try to gain the votes of the humble aspirants, to "get their strength." The question is, which of the powerful aspirants will succeed in detaching the most votes of this description. All the negotiations and the manoeuvres which preceded and have been carried on during the convention have tended in this direction; and it is now, under the running fire of the votes announced for the various competitors, that the supreme decision must be taken by those delegates who command a more or less considerable amount of "presidential strength." When they have satisfied themselves, after a few ballots, that their own candidates have no prospect of success, they go over, with a quiet conscience, into the camp of a more fortunate aspirant. In so doing, they no doubt consult their own interests, that is to say, sell themselves as dear as possible and, perhaps, also let themselves be carried away by personal sympathies and antipathies; but these interests and these feelings even are guided by considerations of a general kind. Having given up his pet aspirant, if he had one, each delegate tries to join the ranks of a " winner," of an aspirant likely to carry the day in the country, and to procure for VOL. II — T the party power with all its consequences. In a word, he looks out for the "available candidate" among the aspirants. The general conditions of "availability " are already familiar to us, and it need only be added that the aspirant to the Presidency must combine them in the highest degree in all that concerns the negative qualifications for the position. As for the others, if the aspirant has a certain amount of popularity, if he is personally "magnetic," so much the better, that will be a good card in the game. His physique is not immaterial either. His political position, perhaps a very poor one, is capable of being advantageously made up for by that of his State. If this latter is a doubtful State, in which the parties are evenly balanced, it may not be able to resist the temptation of having one of its sons in the Presidency, and may, on this occasion, give his party a majority, which majority will, perhaps, be decisive for the victory of that party in the whole Union, if the State is a large one like New York, for instance, disposing of thirty-six votes in the Electoral College. A State of this kind is, consequently, looked on as a "pivotal" State, and the aspirant who belongs to it is ipso *facto* an available candidate. New York, which has long played the part of pivotal State, has, therefore, imposed many presidential candidates on the national conventions. A State in which one of the two parties has a permanent majority, and which cannot turn the scale in favour of that party in the presidential contests, or a very small State, like Maine, for instance, is not on that account deprived of the chance of supplying a presidential candidate, but, then, the latter must be a man who holds a very leading position; this was the case with J. G. Blaine, a citizen of Maine.

It may well and more often than not it does happen that after several ballots none of the favourites succeeds in detaching enough votes from his rivals to obtain a majority. This is the moment for the "dark horses" to appear on the course. They must not forestall this moment; if they come forward at the first ballots to try conclusions with the favourites, they run the risk of being hopelessly beaten at oucn. Their merit resides precisely in the character of *makeshift* which they possess; and they can only turn it to account when a feeling of weariness comes over the assembly. The dark horses sometimes try to force the hand of the convention by combining their small groups, "bunching their votes"; but it is not easy for them to come to an understanding, for the coalition can only be made for the benefit of one of them. They have to trust rather to chance to bring the right man out of the ruck. Perhaps a favourite, despairing of his own success, will, to prevent the triumph of the rival favourite, himself transfer all his "strength," at a single blow, to a dark horse; perhaps the latter, by laboriously increasing his total at each successive ballot, will command success in the end.

Each ballot is followed with the utmost anxiety by the whole assembly, and it invariably gives rise to noisy manifestations. During the roll-call of the States the adherents of the various aspirants applaud and utter shouts of delight as soon as a delegation announces that it votes for their man. When the result of the ballot is proclaimed, an explosion of enthusiasm, often ending in a grand uproar, greets a rise in the total of votes obtained by an aspirant. If the rise is accentuated at the following ballots, the crowd of delegates and spectators becomes delirious. More or less unearthly shrieks, cries of animals, hats thrown into the air, red umbrellas opened, flags and banners frantically waved, start the pandemonium afresh. The standard of the State to which the aspirant in question belongs, planted in front of the seats of its delegates, is pulled up, and in a twinkling it is surrounded by the standards of several other States, which salute it, and all form a procession, which marches several times round the.hall along its unencumbered passages. The sitting is practically interrupted; it is impossible to proceed to a new ballot; in vain does the chairman cry out to the secretary in a stentorian voice: "Call the roll"; the delegations do not answer, it is not worth while. At the next ballot, the hero of this manifestation has perhaps lost some votes, and the star of another aspirant has suddenly risen; with the fickleness that belongs to crowds, the convention, forgetting the man whom it cheered barely half an hour back, rushes madly after the new momentary favourite of fortune. The uncertainty as to the final result continues down to the ballot in which an aspirant who already holds a good position is reinforced by an important group of delegates, who give up their aspirant or aspirants. This change of front, which soon grows like an avalanche, constitutes the "crisis" or "break," and raises the excitement of the audience to its highest pitch. With nerves strained to the utmost, the public awaits the dramatic moment from the second ballot onward, and says to itself on each occasion: "It will come this time." This moment sends a thrill of anticipation through the politicians of the convention and causes them a violent emotion, in which they indulge with a fueling of delight. As soon as the "break" takes place, the whole assembly has an epileptic fit, stamping on the floor, yelling, carrying round standards in a procession, etc., in the way with which we are familiar. The politician whose influence has brought about the break will, of course, be in good odour with the candidate when the latter has become President; he can count upon an embassy or some other "good thing."

Sometimes the ballot in which the "crisis" has taken place is the last, sometimes one or two more ballots are required to gather a majority round the name of the lucky winner; but his success grows more marked with each moment, and a little sooner or later he will "be landed." When his triumph appears tolerably certain, a sort of panic seizes on the delegates who had hitherto voted for other aspirants, and they rush to join the winner in a wild race, which is called the " stampede." One after another, they are in a hurry to retract their vote before the ballot is closed. Here is an old man who jumps on a chair as nimbly as his bulk will allow him, and cries out in a choking voice: "Mr. Chairman, Mr. Chairman!" and when, at the expiration of a moment, which has evidently seemed to him like an eternity, he catches the chairman's eye, he announces that his State changes its mind, and gives its fifteen or twenty votes to so-and-so. Several other heads of delegations make a declaration to the same effect. The reader will remember that Polk carried the nomination under similar circumstances. This was the first instance of a stampede. To prevent the stampede and the break-up of their troops, the champions of the rival aspirants, who see the hurricane coming, have but one resource, which is to obtain the adjournment of the convention; but the latter is generally too excited to consent. Repeated attempts have been made to prevent stampedes by formal rules of procedure of the conventions. At the Republican convention uf 1870, the Many changes in the votes are no longer of use to the winner, who already has his majority; but delegates who want to "get in his band wagon" make them all the same, in the hope of establishing a claim on the future President; true, they cannot aspire to the title of "original McKinley men" or "original Bryan men," but they have joined before the formal proclamation of the successful candidate. As soon as the result of the last ballot is announced, the champion of one of the defeated aspirants proposes to the convention to make the nomination of their fortunate rival unanimous. The motion is carried, a grand uproar of the regulation kind, with the war-dance of the standards, greets the happy event, the band strikes up "Hail to the Chief," and the assembly goes mad for half an hour or so.

But there remains the selection of a candidate for the VicePresidency. This task does not detain the convention long; not that the aspirants to the second dignity are less numerous, but because the assembly is already exhausted, and because it is not in the habit of attaching much importance to the post of Vice-President, whose influence in the government of the Union and the distribution of offices is *nil.* The reader is aware that this view of the Vice-Presidency as an office that can be held by anybody has, on occasions, cost the Republic dear, when, owing to the death of the President, the VicePresident has become chief of the State. The struggles of Congress with Tyler (1841-1845) and afterwards with Andrew Johnson (1865-1869), who were raised unexpectedly to the Presidency, have left behind them painful memories on which not a thought is bestowed when the candidate for the VicePresidency is chosen. The conventions make use of this candidature to gratify personal or local vanity, which it is advisable to soothe or turn to account. They bestow the honour as a consolation stakes on one of the defeated aspirants to the Presidency, or on a citizen of a different part of the country to that to which the candidate adopted for the chief magistracy belongs. If the latter comes from a State in chairman refused to accept a change of vote announced in the course of the ballot. The Democratic conventions of 1884 and 1888 inserted a provision to the same effect in the mles which each convention adopts for the transaction of its business, but it has not been renewed.
the West, the Vice-Presidency is given to an Eastern man to silence the jealousy of the populations of the East. It is desirable that this person should also be very rich, "a man with a barrel," so that he can contribute a large sum to the expenses of the election campaign; and often the place is one for a millionnaire. The procedure for the selection of the candidate for the Vice-Presidency is just the same as for the Presidency: roll-call, introduction of the aspirants in highfaluting speeches in which they appear surrounded with a halo of virtue and glory; several consecutive ballots, and the shouts of the crowd; but these latter already betray a certain weakness and lassitude, the arms move mechanically, all the voices are hoarse.

At last, after a session of several days, the end is reached; the convention adjourns *sine die.* All is over. As you step out of the building you inhale with relief the gentle breeze which tempers the scorching heat of July; you come to yourself; you recover your sensibility, which has been blunted by the incessant uproar, and your faculty of judgment, which has been held in abeyance amid the pandemonium in which day after day has been passed. You collect your impressions, and you realize what a colossal travesty of popular institutions you have just been witnessing. A greedy crowd of office-holders, or of office-seekers, disguised as delegates of the people, on the pretence of holding the grand council of the party, indulged in, or were the victims of, intrigues and manoeuvres, the object of which was the chief magistracy of the greatest Republic of the two hemispheres, — the succession to the Washingtons and the Jeffersons. With an elaborate respect for forms extending to the smallest details of procedure, they pretended to deliberate, and then passed resolutions settled by a handful of wire-pullers in the obscurity of committees and private caucuses; they proclaimed as the creed of the party appealing to its piety, a collection of hollow, vague phrases, strung together by a few experts in the art of using meaningless language, and adopted still more precipitately without examination and without conviction; with their hand upon their heart, they adjured the assembly to support aspirants in whose success they had not the faintest belief; they voted in public for candidates whom they were scheming to defeat. Cut off from their conscience by selfish calculations and from their judgment by the tumultuous crowd of spectators, which alone made all attempt at deliberation an impossibility, they submitted without resistance to the pressure of the galleries masquerading as popular opinion, and made up of a *clcujue* and of a raving mob which, under ordinary circumstances, could only be formed by the inmates of all the lunatic asylums of the country who had made their escape at the same time. Here this mob discharges a great political function; it supplies the "enthusiasm" which is the primary element of the convention, which does duty for discussion and controls all its movements. Produced to order of the astute managers, "enthusiasm" is served out to the delegates as a strong drink, to gain completer mastery over their will. But in the fit of intoxication they yield to the most sudden impulses, dart in the most unexpected directions, and it is blind chance which has the last word. The name of the candidate for the Presidency of the Republic issues from the votes of the convention like a number from a lottery. And all the followers of the party, from the Atlantic to the Pacific, are bound, on pain of apostasy, to vote for the product of that lottery. Yet, when you carry your thoughts back from the scene which you have just witnessed and review the line of Presidents, you find that if they have not all been great men — far from it — they were all honourable men; and you cannot help repeating the American saying: "God takes care of drunkards, of little children, and of the United States!"

FOURTH CHAPTER THE ELECTION CAMPAIGN

I

When the curtain falls on the conventions, the first act of the formation of the American representative government is at an end; the nominations made by the rival parties are submitted to the sovereign people, and it is for the latter now to give its decision. Up to this point not much has been seen of the people, although it has been talked of a good deal; everybody quoted its authority, acted in its name, took pledges on its behalf, but this everybody was almost entirely made up of the class of professional politicians only. All that we have seen take place has taken place between them; they made plans, set on foot intrigues, conducted manoeuvres against one another, negotiated, bargained, fought battles. The stake was the public weal, but the people appeared to have nothing to do but patiently await the decisions of the politicians, and then simply countersign them. However, the hour for signing is at hand, and the politicians, a prey to anxiety, alternating between hope and fear, are obliged to face the people restored *ipso facto* to the full exercise of its powers. Hitherto the contact between the party Organization and the electorate has been very slight; they were much less in touch with one another than we have seen to be the case with the party representatives and the bulk of the electors in England. The more or less methodical action exerted over the electoral masses by the English Caucus in the interval between the elections has no counterpart in the United States; here that action is compressed into the efforts made during tl»e brief space of election time, and it is hardly a figure of speech to say that the American party Organization snatches the verdict from the electorate at a single stroke, that it carries the position by a sort of furious assault. The result is not the less brilliant, on the contrary even; for the besieging army supplied by the American Organization is infinitely superior to the troops of the English Caucus in point of generalship, recruiting, dash, and discipline.

This is the proper time for reviewing that besieging army. We will begin with the staff. It is represented in the first place by the "national committees" of each party appointed every four years at the national conventions. Consisting of one representative from each State and each Territory, the national committee numbers about fifty members. Its principal duty consists of conducting the presidential campaign throughout the Union. After the close of the campaign the national committee subsists, but it falls into a state of suspended animation to revive at the expiration of three years on the approach of the next national convention, which it will convene and of which it will take charge until the latter is definitively organized. As it has not the character of a permanent representation of the party, the national committee of the party in power does not exercise any influence over the Administration or its policy. The chairman of the national committee of the victorious party is, perhaps, the only member who possesses a certain authority with the President. Among the other members of the committee some are consulted, when appointments to offices are concerned: if the party in a State has no Senator in the Congress of the United States, the member of the national committee from that State is the person who enjoys the influence belonging to the Senators in matters of patronage with the President. The chairman is chosen nominally by the committee, but in reality he is always selected by the presidential candidate, who has the greatest interest in the good management of the campaign. Once he has chosen his man, the candidate places his fortune unreservedly in his hands. The chairman wields the power of a commander-in-chief in regard to everybody. The members of the committee are his lieutenants, each in charge of his own State and working on the spot. The head-quarters, which had been always established at New York, has lately been transferred to Chicago. There the chairman presides over a small executive committee of a few members; the whole national committee is seldom convened. If need be, the chairman dispenses even with the assistance of the executive committee; formal considerations are the last to trouble him; he summons to his counsels persons who have no title in the hierarchy of the organization, he sends for them from all quarters. Through the medium of the respective members of the national committee he is in constant communication with all the State committees, but he does not fail to address these latter directly, he corresponds with their members personally to swell their importance and spur them to action. Although he is supreme chief, his authority does not rest solely on the power of command entrusted to him, for his troops are supposed to consist of free men. Tact and other diplomatic virtues are the qualities which the chairman must possess in a high degree, which make his power a reality and extend his influence beyond the point where these powers come to an end. Not having the right to command, he can make himself accepted as umpire. The strife of factions which rends the parties in so many places, the rivalries of the big local politicians all fraught with dangers to the happy issue of the campaign, can be appeased by the skill and the tact of the national chairman intervening as mediator.

The most delicate of the duties devolving on the chairman is to procure the sinews of war, and to spend the money collected in the most judicious manner. He appeals for fuuds to the trusty followers of the party who believe that its success is bound up with the greatness of the country, to the clients of the party, if the latter has any special ones, such as, for instance, the manufacturers who benefit by the protectionist policy of the Republican party; the intimate friends of the candidates for the Presidency and the Vice-Presidency who are well off are not applied to the least. A clever, ingenious, and energetic chairman always manages to fill the chest. But the important thing is to make a good use of the contents; for, besides the current expenses, there are others which demand much discrimination, especially the purchase of votes and of venal assistance. A little money well employed may be more useful than ten times the amount spent in other ways. Like a general who chooses the strategic points for the disposition of his troops, the national chairman distributes and skilfully brings to bear his pecuniary resources at the different points of the immense'electoral battlefield formed by the Union. The members of the national committee communicate, for this purpose, to the chairman calculations made in concert with the local Organization, but it is the chairman's insight which decides. The powers of the chairman in all matters of finance are discretionary; he is accountable to no one. Besides, the expenditure incurred is wrapped in secrecy, for a good deal of it could not bear the light of day; and after the close of the campaign the national committee is in the habit of destroying all its papers; it makes "a bonfire of forgetfulness" of them. The legitimate duties of the national committee, which also require very large sums, consist mainly in organizing the oratorical and literary campaign on behalf of the "ticket" of the party over the whole area of the Republic. The methods of this propaganda will be examined further on in detail. I will only point out here that it is directed in each State by the respective member of the national committee, who conducts, like a commander of the corps, all the operations of the campaign in his State, under the orders of the executive committee at head-quarters.

Alongside the national committee, each of the two great parties possesses another central committee, at Washington, — the congressional committee. This committee is in some sort a reminiscence of the old congressional caucus, and is composed of members of Congress chosen by their colleagues and political co-religionists of the House of Representatives and the Senate. The members of the Republican committee are appointed, to the number of one for each State, by the Republican Senators and Representatives of each State meeting in private caucus; the selections for the Democratic committee are made separately by the Representatives of each State choosing one from among their number, and by the Democratic Senators electing nine delegates in a general meeting. If the State has no Democratic Representatives or Senators, the congressional committee takes to itself an outside representative of the same State. The existence of the congressional committee is as temporary as that of the legislature from which it emanates, and it disappears with the expiration of the powers of the particular Congress. Considerations of general policy are even more foreign to the congressional committee than to the national committee; it pays no heed to platforms or programmes, and simply endeavours to ensure the success at the congressional elections of the candidates who bear the party label, whatever their political complexion. It divides all the congressional districts into three categories: the good, the hopeless, and the doubtful; almost neglecting the first two groups, it directs all its efforts toward the districts of the last group. Its means of action consist of overt propaganda, by speaking and by "political literature," aud of methods of a more secret kind, in which the distribution of money fills, it would appear, a not inconsiderable place. The sinews of war are supplied to the congressional committee by wealthy members of the party, but these donations are much smaller than those made to the national committee; the disinterested or calculated generosity of the donors is reserved for the presidential campaign in which the great stake is played for. The congressional committee intervenes actively in the election campaigns in the "off years," that is to say, those years in which the congressional elections, which take place every second year, do not coincide with the presidential election, for instance, in 1894, 1898. At the request of the candidates interested, it sends them speakers and "political literature" for distribution, and, perhaps, money as well. But the committee does not remain inactive in the interval between the elections; it follows the fortunes of the party in the districts attentively; it analyzes the vote at each succeeding election by counties; and if it notes a fall in the number of votes polled by the candidate of the party, it makes an enquiry into the causes. Perhaps the fault lies with the factions which are devouring each other, or the candidate is not a popular one, or the policy of the party is creating discontent, or the rival party is employing too energetic and too persuasive methods of propaganda. The congressional committee interposes to smooth down these difficulties. It is in constant relations with all the county committees in the Union; the latter point out to it the special steps necessary to retrieve the fortunes of the party in their congressional district, and in general make the congressional committee the confidant of their troubles. On the opening of the presidential campaign the congressional committee places all its resources at the disposal of the national committee and becomes its close ally, foregoing its own initiative even in what concerns the congressional elections, for in the "presidential year" all the elections follow the fortunes of the contest for the Presidency.

The powers which the national committee wields for the whole Union are exercised in a subordinate capacity in the States by the State committee, and in each county by the county committee. These three committees multiplied by the number of the counties, which amounts to about 2200, form so many rays running from the centre to the electoral circumference. The *personnel* of these committees contains only the officers of the army of the party Organization, from the generals down to the subalterns. Below them extend the vast battalions of the privates and non-commissioned officers enrolled in the local committees of the city wards, of the villages, and, perhaps, also of the "school districts," which are subdivisions of rural neighbourhoods. In every village or "school district" of any importance there is a local committee of the party, composed of three to five militants, who watch over its interests, report what they see, and execute the orders sent to them. The ward committees in the cities have a much larger number of members. The total of these troops, of all the parties combined, may be estimated, of course quite approximately, at from 800,000 to 900,000 men, exclusive of the corps of officers supplied by the higher committees, which contain not less than 50,000 persons. While in England the militants of the party Associations are almost all amateurs, inspired solely by sentimental considerations, and submitting to discipline only so far as it appears to them compatible with the needs of the cause and with their personal dignity, in the United States almost all those who compose the immense army of the party Organization are experts, trained in their business, and spurred by the incentive of personal interest which bends the will and silences all conflicting sentiments. In fact they are, for the most part, themselves candidates for, or aspirants to, places, or they are trying to get them for relations or friends. Realizing, to some extent, the philosophic conception of the Utilitarians, they are obliged, in order to compass their ends, to work for the other candidates of the party, all along the line, with the same zeal which they would display in their own behalf; for each candidature is only an atom, a line of the ticket of the party which the average elector accepts or rejects in a lump. In voting for Mr. McKinley as President, he will vote at the same time for the Republican candidates for the other functions, those of State Governor, congressman, etc., to the end of the list. Between all the committees, therefore, from the national committee down to that of a school district in a remote corner of the Far West, there arises a co-operation founded on the closest community of interest; the ardour and the energy of each is placed at the service of all, and the moral forces of the Organization are increased tenfold, just as its material forces have been increased owing to the system of committees radiating from the centre.

This army constitutes the regular and permanent machinery of the Organization. It is increased, for the term of the campaign, by numerous auxiliaries, who may be divided into three categories: one is made up of humble servants engaged by the committees and paid by the job; the second is also due to the co-operation of individuals, but they come forward out of devotion to the party or enthusiasm for the cause; and, lastly, the third category contains auxiliaries formed into companies, troops organized for the occasion. The most common type of these corps of free-lances is afforded by the clubs.

II

The American political clubs are very different from the English clubs, as the temporary character borne by the former is enough to show. Permanent political clubs are not entirely wanting in the United States, but the part they play in political life is almost *nil.* They are not in the least a regular organ of the party, as in England, a focus of political action and influence the rays from which dart continuously over the surface of the community. In the first place, in America there are no central party clubs, like the Carlton or the National Liberal Club in London; the federative organization of the United States and the absence of a capital evidently stand in the way of this. In New York, in Philadelphia, and in. several other important centres, there are, of course, large clubs, as, for instance, the Union League clubs, the clubs founded since the Civil War by the Republicans, and which are sure to be found in all the large cities of the East. While exceedingly noteworthy in the. matter of their appointments, these clubs are on a smaller scale than the London clubs, and not only from a material point of view: they are recruited in a closer, more exclusive way, reflecting in this respect the general character of the big American clubs which try to be more aristocratic than the English clubs. The absence of a nobility, of an upper class created by the law and recognized by the national manners, is made up for in certain American cities by coteries, which form into magic circles, to which admittance can be gained only by showing one's credentials, or what they are pleased to consider as such. Being founded on this principle, the smart clubs admit only a very small number of members with extravagant entrance fees and subscriptions. The select political clubs have not escaped this tendency to social exclusiveness, and besides that, they are much less homogeneous than the English clubs as regards the political views of their members, because social considerations fill too large a place in the choice of the members, and especially because the latter are getting to change their party more and more frequently. Republicans who have voted for Mr. Cleveland none, the less remain members of Republican clubs; Democrats who have openly given their votes to Mr. McKinley continue to belong to Democratic clubs; so that a good many clubs are Republican or Democratic simply because they were founded by members of one or the other party. In England, a Tory who has gone over to the Liberal side could not remain a member of the Carlton for an hour; social relations, which are not governed exclusively by snobbery, would not permit of it. In the United States the social divisions, while sometimes painfully narrow, are superficial, and, amid the kaleidoscopic existence of the Americans, lack the stability which would give them the property of a political cement. The big American clubs are, therefore, unable to serve as a connecting link between society and political life, to bring the two into touch with one another.

Alongside these political clubs, which are little distinguishable from non-political ones, there are others, in several large cities, of a much less exalted kind, whose members are almost all politicians. The necessities of "politics" often bring together, as in a disreputable resort, men of very different social position, culture, and manners. For the most part, however, these clubs are filled with politicians of low degree; apart from the mercenaries of politics, the "workers," they are frequented only by the men who buy their influence, such as contractors for public works and government purveyors. The clubs serve all these people as a place of meeting, not to say a haunt, where they discuss their business and also indulge in the pleasures of social intercourse. The most distinguished of these clubs, if it is permissible to use the epithet, is the Democratic club of Tammany Hall in New York. The big boss of Tammany holds his receptions there daily, receives the homage of his lieges and of office-seekers, and dispenses justice to them, like Saint Louis under the oak at Vincennes. The subscription to the clubs is purely nominal; the expenses are almost always borne by a head politician, a "leader," who makes the club the citadel from which he directs the political operations necessary for getting hold of an elective post for himself or for his favourite candidate. Often the club is named after this politician, "Jones' Club," or "O'Brien's Association," as if its members wanted to proclaim that they were only a band devoted to a chief. Sometimes the clubs are, as in England, under the patronage of the local congressman, whom they "bleed" by extorting subsidies from him or by making him pay their debts. They are not of much use to the head politicians, for if there are several of them in the electoral division, they are likely rather to afford opportunities for the jealousies of the small politicians wrangling over the spoils, and to keep alive the spirit of faction. The clubs of the politicians also try, like the English party associations, to combine politics and pleasure, by organizing balls in winter, excursions in summer, outings, "chowder parties," or "clambakes "; but even in these cases, the politicians keep to themselves and their own set without attracting the bulk of the electorate. In England, political fetes are organized for the electors, it is on their "social tendencies " that people try to work for the benefit of the parties under whose auspices the fetes take place; here it is a family affair of the "workers" formed into clubs. The latter thus only throw into clearer relief, by the quality of their members and their social intercourse, the separation between the world of politicians and the rest of the population, just as the select political clubs had shown us the social elements collected in them as devoid of influence on political life.

Moreover, the number of the permanent clubs is small in comparison with the area of the Union and its electorate. Of late years attempts have been made to extend the system and to widen the sphere of recruitment. In 1888 the Republicans formed clubs all over the territory, and combined them into a national federation under the name of Republican National League. This organization claims to possess more than two million and a half of adherents and about twenty thousand clubs. But in reality most of the clubs have only a nominal existence, — hardly one club in a hundred has premises of its own; generally they hire a room for the occasion, and their meetings are few and far between. The Democrats have followed the example set by their rivals and have also founded a number of clubs, federated into a National Association of Democratic Clubs which number nearly four thousand affiliated clubs. Both federations hold conventions every year or every two years, in which they amuse themselves by passing resolutions defining the policy of the party, and which are not exactly remarkable for their wisdom. The members of these clubs are, to a great extent, office-seekers who have been glad to find a new base of operations for their designs on the public purse, and young men not belonging to the world of professional politicians, but attracted by the titles of president, vice-president, and other dignities which the clubs provide for their youthful vanity. The managers of the parties try to turn this vanity to account for their requirements and to transform the young clubmen into election agents.

There are, however, permanent clubs, and in very large numbers, which, without bearing this name, and without having any ostensible connection with politics, wield very great electoral influence. These are the drinking-saloons, especially in the large cities, where they play a leading part in the government, and which will be referred to again. The VOL. II U lower orders spend their leisure time in the bars and form their opinions on things in general there, under the auspices of the saloon-keeper, who is their guide, the director of their conscience. The party organizations and the candidates therefore find that their most valuable helpers for manipulating the electorate are the saloon-keepers, and the latter must be rightly ranked among their regular auxiliaries. In the case of a good many drinking-saloons, this is even their sole reason for existence; they would not be able to subsist without the remuneration which they receive, in one form or another, for the services which they render to the candidates.

Of course, the drinking-saloons take in only the dregs of the population. To lay hand on the higher strata of the electors, the election organizers make up for the limited development of the permanent political clubs by temporary clubs formed for the duration of the campaign. The "campaign clubs" are associations of citizens who have their regular avocations, and, in ordinary times, pay little or no heed to politics. The great date of the presidential election reminds them of their civic duty. They respond piously to this sacred appeal. United by a community of political views, that is to say, by the predilection for one party over another which they imagine they profess, these citizens enrol themselves in a club flying the colours of their party or of its candidate for the Presidency of the Republic, to strengthen themselves mutually in their creed, for the two or three months that the campaign will last. They meet, perhaps, every evening for this purpose of edification; they listen to speeches which glorify their candidate, they sing political songs, absorb enthusiasm for the party ticket, and diffuse this enthusiasm around them, in the club and outside it. This action and reaction comes all the easier to them that, in the majority of cases, or at all events very often, they do not present fortuitous aggregations, the atoms of which are brought together in a haphazard way, but groups formed in accordance with more or less natural affinities, due to a common occupation, race, or religion. Thus each presidential campaign is the signal for an outburst of clubs, Republican and Democratic, of commercial travellers, of clerks of dry-goods stores, of lawyers, of merchants, of railroad employees; of workmen's clubs formed, not by wards, but by workshops, the workmen in a large factory dividing, perhaps, into two clubs, the one Republican, the other Democratic; clubs of coloured men; Irish, German, Jewish, Polish, Swedish clubs; and even Republican or Democratic ''cyclists' brigades." If they cannot or do not care to *sentire idem de republica,* the members of these clubs develop enough *esprit de corps* to unite on the ticket. Some will confine themselves to fortifying their party faith, others will strive to make proselytes by delivering speeches, distributing leaflets, or, again, by manifestations in the streets in favour of their candidate. For this last purpose special clubs are started, called "marching clubs," with the particular duty of walking about in procession and making a noise in the streets and squares, in honour of the party and its candidates. We have already come across clubs of this kind in the city where the national convention was held, and where they carried on a gymnastic and vocal propaganda in favour of the presidential aspirants. They were an anticipation of the marching clubs. Generally, these clubs are formed in each locality after the work of the national conventions is finished, and they display their activity in the months of September and October, when the election campaign is in full swing. Their usefulness to the parties is of a twofold kind: they help greatly to keep up " enthusiasm," and they gather to their standard young electors attracted by the quasi-military organization of these clubs; their members wear a special uniform and hold varied grades, such as captain and colonel. By 'a conventional courtesy these titles are henceforth always conceded to these electoral warriors in social intercourse, by virtue of the saying: "Once a captain, always a captain."

Of late years the craze for campaign clubs has spread to the schools, the colleges. Political clubs were not unknown among American students; they were a means, like any other, of enlivening their existence; but since the presidential campaign of 1892 the students have definitively descended into the lists to help the parties, by speaking or by other forms of propaganda. In any event, the college club, which for a few months plunges the young men into a political party atmosphere, serves the purpose of keeping them warm for the next presidential campaign. In almost every college or university there are formed, for the duration of the campaign, clubs of students of both parties. The Republican clubs federated themselves, in 1892, into an American Republican College League; the Democratic student clubs adopted, in 1896, a similar national organization.

The number of the electors enrolled in the campaign clubs is undoubtedly very considerable, and can hardly be below 1,500,000 or 2,000,000. If to these volunteer forces are added the paid combatants, they will all together, with the regular army of the party Organizations, make up the enormous total of 3,500,000 to 4,000,000 out of an electoral population of 15,000,000, or 16,000,000. That is to say, there is one militant, entering heart and soul into the fray, to every four or five electors. This applies to the Organizations, both regular and irregular, which openly fly party colours. But there are also non-political Organizations, economic or others, which can, however, be of some assistance to one or the other party, according as the latter serves the particular interest which they have in view or embodies their sentimental preoccupations, by its general tendencies or its past. For instance, the Wool Growers' Association, which is interested in a protectionist tariff, will naturally contribute its influence to the Republican party. In the same way the unionist association of veterans of the Civil War, "The Grand Army of the Republic," being in sympathy with the Republican party, which headed the war for the integrity of the Union, will work for it at the elections, without intervening officially *qua* Organization. On the other hand, the Confederate Veterans' Union, the association of veterans of the slave-holders' army, will, in a similar manner, 'turn towards the Democratic party in the Southern States.

Ill

And women? Has the great role of helpers of the regular party Organizations which we have seen held by women in England nothing to correspond to it in the United States? Being aware of the exceptionally independent position enjoyed by women on the other side of the Atlantic, the reader would expect that they would have plunged into militant politics even far more extensively and ardently. In reality, nothing of the kind takes place. After half a century of victorious progress in the social sphere, American women have remained outside political life, both because they had not shown a strong enough wish to get into it themselves, and owing to the resistance offered by the men. The agitation in favour of the "rights of women" had no doubt begun earlier in the United States than in England, towards the close of the first half of this century, but it encountered only indifference and hostility. The part allotted to women was always based on the old feminine ideal expressed by the words *domo sedit lanam fecit.* The conservative spirit of the East, where the social conceptions of the old mother-country had held their ground with great tenacity, threw all its weight into the scale to repress any attempt at emancipation on the part of women. That a woman should speak in public seemed a monstrous thing. Soon the passions of the day stepped in. A good many women entered the lists to take part, and a very honourable part, in the abolitionist agitation, on behalf of the negro slaves. The hostility which greeted the abolitionists, those unwelcome intruders, did not spare women, who often had to face the violence of crowds, attacks from the pulpit and in the press, and social ostracism. When, after the liberation of the negroes, the slaves of yesterday were invested *en masse* with the political suffrage, the agitation for obtaining the same privilege or the same "inalienable right" for women recommenced with renewed force, but with little success. The attempts to insert an amendment for this purpose into the federal constitution, like that which conceded political equality to the negroes by a general measure applying to the whole Union, failed, as did also nearly all the partial attempts made on the legislatures of particular States with the same object. It is only in a few rudimentary States of the Far West (Wyoming, Utah, Colorado, Idaho), of little economic importance and culture, that women have obtained

'A woman who was one of the pioneers of "feminism" in the United States, Miss Susan Anthony, having read a paper to a convention of school teachers of the State of New York, a personage of note said to her: "In matter and manner I could not criticise your essay; but, my dear young woman, I would rather have followed my wife and daughter to the grave than to have had either of them stand here before this audience and read that address." political rights, and in a fourth State of the West (Kansas) the rights of municipal electors, whereas in England women are entitled to vote in all local elections throughout the country. The question of woman suffrage continues to be raised by.its champions with tenacity, from year to year, in the different State legislatures; but it is invariably negatived, either by one or the other House of the legislature, or, when its advocates have succeeded in carrying their vote and obtaining the assent of the executive, by the people which has to ratify constitutional changes.

Public opinion and the legislator have shown themselves much more ready to allow women, in the government of the commonwealth, a small place outside the political sphere, to wit, in school administration: in more than half of the States of the Union women are entitled to vote at the elections for school officers, and to be elected to those posts. Some States which refuse women the school vote concede them the eligibility, therein representing the tendency which during the last quarter of the century has become general in American social life, and which consists in letting the individual merit of women assert itself as freely as that of men in the achievement of personal positions. The benefits of the free expansion of the individual, of that principle which dominates American life and which is its mainspring, were extended to women; the national manners and the law gradually admitted their right to embrace such avocations and professions as they please, up to that of the bar, and even of the ministry in certain churches. The West, the vast expanse and immense resources of which opened up boundless horizons to individual energies, took, as it were, for its motto, "Live and let live, and every man to his liking." Free from the narrow views, from the conventions and the prejudices of the old societies, which serve as a bulwark for vested rights and selfish interests, the West gave the impulse to the social emancipation of women, and that movement soon made its way into the old States of the East. The traditional inequalities sanctioned by the common law in the civil status of women, and especially of married women, were abolished in one State after another; the wife became the equal of the husband, of the man, as regards the disposal of her property and the care of the children.

In social relations she was already almost his superior, being treated by the men with an exceptional deference which has a faint savour of the chivalry of the Middle Ages. Carefully sparing the woman, in the well-to-do or even barely well-to-do classes, so much as the knowledge of his anxieties about the struggle for existence; taking upon himself alone all care and all responsibility; making himself, as some say, foolishly a beast of burden for the pleasure of the woman, — the man ensures her leisure which the woman often knows how to make a good use of by devoting herself to mental culture. The pursuit of this culture, even when of a superficial kind, does not only enhance the distinction of the American woman that makes her one of the most interesting phenomena of the New World. It leads women to fall back upon themselves rather than turn upon society, while making them often step out of their home life to satisfy their intellectual curiosity more fully. In fact, they form numerous organizations for this purpose, associations for reading and discussion, in the form of women's clubs, which are very common not only in the highly cultivated States, like Massachusetts, but even in those of the West and of the Pacific slope. When the women study social problems, among other things, they do it rather as dilettantes than as militant reformers, because they have no personal grievances to urge against society. Those among them who are prone to action find a noble employment for their faculties in the moral and philanthropic movements to which American women have rendered, and continue to render, conspicuous service. "Practical politics" is the last thing to tempt their ambitions; it has been made too contemptible by the "machines" and the "bosses." The pursuit of notoriety, it is true, is not less prevalent in the United States than elsewhere; on the contrary even, it is carefully stimulated by a sensational press which breaks down, without encountering much resistance, "the wall of private life," and is always keeping before the world the women (as well as the men) whose social position exposes them to the curiosity of the public, and who, in their turn, are not sorry to minister to it with their sayings and doings. But the comparatively limited section of society which has a craving for the gratifications attending this publicity, prides itself too much on its elevated tastes to look for these gratifications in i politics, which, in their eyes, is infected especially with the taint of "vulgarity." The American women therefore who court the applause of the crowd, try to deserve it rather by their fashionable exploits or by their distinction in sports, by aspiring, for instance, to the title of " champion " of something.

The upshot of all these circumstances combined is that American women, taken as a whole, care far less for political action than their English sisters. This indifference, due as it is to divers causes, supplies us with a fresh proof of the separation which exists between society and politics in the United States. Content with having made the most of the great social fact of the expansion of the individual, for the development of their own individuality from the economic, intellectual and social standpoint, American women pay no heed to the postulates of the abstract doctrine of human equality which constitutes the principal basis of the political claims of women. There are a number of societies whose object is to obtain the political suffrage for women, and which prosecute their undertaking with much enthusiasm; but alongside these societies are women's organizations carrying on an opposite propaganda. In places where women are already entitled to the political or the school vote, they have not shown much eagerness to exercise their right; pretty considerable at the start, the number of women who vote grows smaller and smaller. Women have managed in several localities to get themselves elected to various positions, to municipal office in Kansas, and elsewhere; but in the very States which had made them eligible, to a greater or lesser extent, they still have to contend with the prejudice which considers their sex as a fatal obstacle to holding office. Recent elections in the feminist State *par excellence,* in that of Utah, have shown that when women are competing with men for elective posts, they cannot count even on the general support of the electors of their own sex. All the more deep-rooted is the old prejudice entertained by the men on the subject of women taking part in public life. A good many of them, among the least hostile, consent or resign themselves to it for the reason given by an elector, who, when asked to vote for two female candidates for the school board, yielded after some hesitation with the remark: "Two ladies cannot do much harm anyway."

The reader will now understand why the services of women had not been applied for by the political parties nor offered to them, as in England. The Prohibitionist party, which is more a philanthropic organization, was the only one to countenance the co-operation of women; in the conventions of this party it is not uncommon to see women among the delegates. In the old parties there are only one or two instances of women sent to the State conventions. The Democratic national convention of 1896 was the first to contain a delegate and four alternates of the weaker sex, who came from the State of Utah. In the election campaigns women were rarely met with canvassing as party emissaries; a few stepped into the breach for their husbands, turning to account all the seduction of their persuasive eloquence, and sometimes with signal success. Nor did they make their appearance on the stump, except in the West, where the spectacle of a woman on the platform did not shock the simple folk of the new districts; and the greater the distance from the East, the more the case became less uncommon. The presidential campaign of 1896 was marked by rather important changes in all these respects. Both in the East and in the West a good many women "took the stump" with ardour, to speak on behalf, some of Mr. McKinley, others of his Democratic competitor, Mr. Bryan. In several places the women, like the men, organized themselves in campaign clubs, with different names such as " auxiliary clubs," " Women McKinley clubs," "Women's Silver Leagues," etc. It would appear even that "marching clubs" were formed, composed of women,and which manoeuvred in the streets in military fashion with the precision of old stagers, executing the words of command of the lady captain, "Right by file," "Column right," "Open order," etc. After all, the assistance rendered by women to the party Organizations, in this celebrated presidential campaign, was not very great, and it should be referred to only as a symptom of the changes which are creeping into electoral manners.

More interesting and, perhaps, more pregnant with consequences for the party Organizations, is the rSle which women are beginning to play in the contests of public life, in opposition to the regular parties. The profound corruption which these parties have introduced into that life is more and more giving rise to attempts at ousting them from the municipal administration, which they have contaminated most and with which party politics has the least legitimate connection. Independent municipal candidates are run against the candidates of the party machines, as I have already mentioned incidentally and as I shall explain at length farther on. Guided by the same feelings which inclined women to social action in the philanthropic sphere and in the solution of moral problems, where they displayed such admirable devotion and intelligence, a number of women descend into the arena to fight for the purification of municipal life. They attach themselves to independent municipal leagues or form even, for this purpose, special organizations confined to their own sex; they take an active part in election campaigns, by canvassing, by distributing "political literature," or even by making speeches. Sometimes it happens that they conduct this electoral propaganda on behalf of persons of their own sex, when it is a case, for instance, of elections to school office, and when they think the women candidates are in a position to serve the good cause. IV

So much for the contingents of the party Organization and its auxiliary troops. The contingents of the electors which the first named have to encounter, are formed under the law which lays down the conditions for the exercise of political rights. Nevertheless, their real composition is, to a certain extent, subject to the influence of the party Organization, which can modify it more or less, to suit its convenience, by intervening in the preliminary procedure necessary for establishing each individual elector's right to vote. This procedure consists of a periodical registration of all the electors, as in Eng An Interesting campaign carried on under these circumstances is related in a little book published in the Annals of the American Academy of Political and Social Science, of July, 1895, *The Story of a Woman's Municipal Campaign,* edited by Mrs. Talcott Williams. This publication is a collection of reports and notes relating to the campaign conducted, on behalf of two women candidates for the school board of Philadelphia, by the Civic Club, which is a women's organization, founded "to promote by education and co-operation a higher public spirit and a better social order." The interest of this volume goes beyond the campaign in question, and makes it worthy of the attention of all those who study the elective regime in the United States. land. But in the United States it is much less complicated and beset with fewer precautions. This is not due only to the fact that the electoral qualifications in force in England are many and various, of dissimilar origin and nature, while in the United States it is manhood suffrage, pure and unadulterated, which predominates. In several States of the Union more conditions are attached to the right to vote than in many a country of universal suffrage in Europe. Apart from the general conditions of age and residence, some States, such as Massachusetts, Pennsylvania, Florida, require the payment of a polltax, or of municipal taxes (South Carolina); Rhode Island gives the municipal vote only to persons rated in respect of property of a minimum value of $134; the constitution of Connecticut imposes a moral and intellectual qualification: "a good moral character and the ability to read an article of the constitution or of the codes"; Massachusetts, Maine, Delaware, and Wyoming also insist on the elector being able to read the constitution; California requires the same, since 1893, from the new voters; most of the Southern States have recently inserted in their revised constitutions similar provisions requiring that the electors shall be able to read or even explain the text of the constitution, and framed with the sole object of keeping the negroes away from the poll. Although complicated with these limitations on the right to vote, the electoral registration of America mounts guard over it far less jealously than the English registration system. Both of them thus express the different conceptions of the right to vote produced by the development of American democracy on the one hand, and of the old mother-country on the other. The English legislation on the subject gives voice to the conception which looks on the vote as a privilege; in the American laws it appears rather as a right of man. English statute law and the tenor of English judicial decisions hamper registration with so many restrictions and formalities that the elector is rather prevented from making use of his right; in the United States, the law is anxious to give the electors every facility for exercising their rights, at the risk of admitting even non-qualified persons.

For a considerable time preliminary registration was unknown in the United States; every citizen who claimed to be qualified was allowed to give his vote without further ado, unless his right was contested there and then, in which case the point was decided forthwith. This regime, which existed in England before 1832, when the number of electors was extremely limited, survived in the United States the introduction of universal suffrage and the increase iu the number of elections due to the extension of the elective method in appointments to offices. But it soon gave rise to grave abuses, which became worse with the development of the large cities, especially in New York, where it was no longer possible to know who was who in the ever-growing multitude of electors. The steady influx of European immigrants in its turn increased the opportunities for fraud. The electoral contests were decided by persons who were not qualified to vote or who were not even naturalized Americans. The introduction of a preliminary system for ascertaining the real electors had evidently become a vital necessity, and yet it was opposed as an anti-democratic and anti-republican measure. A bill introducing registration into the city of New York having been laid before the legislature of the State, in 1840, by the Whigs, who had suffered from the spurious Democratic electors at the last elections, the Governor of the State, himself a Whig, and who was the illustrious William Seward, gave his opinion against the bill. For, as we read in Seward's autobiography, "his views had always inclined toward free, uncontrolled, and universal suffrage." He drafted a message of veto in which he apprehended that the bill would subject voters to unnecessary difficulties and would reduce the number of votes polled in the city, not so much by preventing illegal voting as by hindering lawful voters." Looking at things from the standpoint of his party, Seward held that the measure in question "tended to alienate the undistinguished poor, especially those of foreign birth, from our side, by teaching them to regard the Whigs as hostile to their rights." The Governor only consented to forego his veto at the earnest entreaties of his political friends. The law thus passed was repealed in the i Cf. Niles, Vol. XX, p. 100.

W. Seward, *An Autobiography,* with a memoir of his life, by Fr. W. Seward, N. Y., 1891, Vol. I, p. 475. Horace Greeley, *Recollections of a Busy Life,* N. Y.. 1ST;!, p. 313. Thurlow Weed assured H. Greeley on this subject that Seward " would have preferred to lose his right hand " rather than sign the bill. *(Ibid.)* following year; and it was not till 1859 that the registration of electors was reintroduced, in the teeth of a somewhat strong opposition, which was continued for a long time. In his messages to the legislature, of 1870 and 1872, the Governor of the State of New York expressed himself in unfavourable terms on the utility of laws relating to the registration of electors, for the frauds went on just the same. In the other States compulsory registration did not meet with a better reception. At the present moment there are still eight States which have abstained from passing laws on this subject; in three States (West Virginia, Texas, Arkansas) registration is even prohibited by the constitution; lastly, the State of Indiana, which had a law, no longer has one; the representatives of the parties in that State assured me that they were none the worse off, that the reciprocal surveillance which the parties exercised over the voters was enough to prevent abuses. In several States, among the very ones which have adopted the system of registration, it is not applied in a general way: sometimes previous inscription is obligatory only in the very large cities, optional in the others, and not allowed in agglomerations of less importance (Missouri); sometimes a particular group of electors is exempted from registration, as, for instance, in Rhode Island owners of real estate of a minimum value of $134, leaseholders of an estate at an annual rent of at least seven dollars, and all those who have previously been upon the voting-list and who pay a property tax of one dollar a year and upwards; or again, persons who have not been entered on the register are allowed to vote if they make an affidavit, attested by sworn witnesses, that they really possess the electoral qualifications (Illinois).

According to the laws in force in the various States, and which present a very considerable variety, a periodical census of all the electors is held on the eve of the presidential elections; that is to say, every four years, or before the general elections in the States, every two years, or every year (in New Orleans, for instance), or, on the contrary, at much longer intervals, every ten years (as in Boston). The electors desirous of securing their right to the vote have to appear in person before the registration officers and state their qualifications. When they have been questioned as to these qualifications and examined in the reading of the constitution, in places where the law requires this attainment, they may be required to confirm their declarations by an oath, which is administered to them there and then. If the declarations made by the electors before the registration officers are not contested by anybody, the persons making them are duly inscribed on the register. Every elector can appeal to the courts of law against a refusal to make an entry or against a wrong entry. Besides this, to facilitate the detection of mistakes, the complete lists, or, at all events, the lists of the contested electors, are published and posted up. In the interval between one registration and the next, the new electors are entered in a supplementary list, upon their application, while the names of the electors who have died, changed their residence, or lost their right to vote for some other reason, are struck off by the officers in charge of the register. In a few States only the lists are drawn up otherwise than on the strength of the personal declarations of the electors; in some of these (Pennsylvania, Massachusetts, excepting the city of Boston) the government officials, especially the assessors of taxes, themselves undertake the duty of collecting and verifying the necessary information, by analyzing the lists of taxpayers or by making house to house visits. In certain other States (Illinois) the register is a revised transcript of the poll list of the last election; in addition to the names which appear on that list the registration board enter those of all other persons who are known to them to be electors, and omit the names of persons who have died or removed from the district. At the time of the registration, the electoral qualifications determined by certain periods, such as age or residence, are referred not to the moment of inscription on the register, but to the date of the coming election, so that a minor who will have attained his majority on the day of the election is already entered on the list. It is the same with terms of residence required for obtaining the vote. Moreover, these terms are generally very short: an elector must have resided in the State one year, in the county or the city from two to four months, and in the electoral district thirty, or even twenty, days before the election.

The persons in charge of electoral registration always bear an official character, but in the majority of cases they are representatives of the parties, chosen by the public authority in equal numbers from each of the two great parties, or even appointed directly by the committees of the parties; the "election inspectors," whom we have seen at work in the primaries, often form the registration board. In some States of New England (Connecticut, Delaware, Rhode Island) the business of registration is included among the municipal duties, and is entrusted to municipal councils or to special registrars elected in town-meeting. In the Southern States, it is generally the Governor of the State who appoints for each county a registrar, or supervisor of registration, "acompetent, discreet, and fair-minded person," as the law of Florida has it. However, almost everywhere the direct or indirect connection of the registration officers with the political parties and their committees, is too strong to allow of the perfect independence of these officials. That independence is constantly put to the test in the discharge of their duties, in which the party Organizations intervene very actively.

The committees of the parties devote their special attention to making their adherents register and to getting them registered. On the eve of the registration, they send them reminders, which mention the date and place of registration; they look up defaulters and bring them in person before the registrars; they pay the poll-tax on behalf of electors in places where it is required for obtaining the vote; they instruct a lawyer to conduct the appeals of their followers in the courts; and, lastly, in a good many cases, they help to bring on the register creatures of their own who have no right to be there. Frauds of this kind are tolerably common. Indeed, the extraordinary facilities for registration, as shown by the very summary sketch of the system in force in the United States which I have just given, put a sort of premium on these frauds: to wit the personal declaration of the elector which lies at the root of the system, and which is accepted until disproved, the shortness of the terms of residence, and the share which the parties too often have in the appointment of the registration officers. One of the favourite expedients resorted to for obtaining fraudulent registration is "colonization" of electors: vagabonds and tramps are imported into the city and housed in lodgings for a few days to manufacture a sham legal domicile entitling them to be put on the register. Often this formality even is dispensed with: fictitious names and addresses are given in. Or, again, the same persons present themselves for registration in several election districts, or even several times in the same district under different names. These frauds are not always easy to prevent, even with all the good will and honesty of the registration officials, for it is a difficult matter to prove the identity of people, in the case of negroes, for instance, who all resemble each other. In several States the register contains a more or less detailed description of each elector, his age, colour, his height measured in inches, and even his weight into the bargain (Boston), or other particulars which may establish his identity. In certain States registration frauds have been reduced to a system, and employed with singular audacity, as an *instrumentum regni,* by the Machine. For instance, the famous Democratic Machine, which for many years, after the Civil War, ruled over the State of Maryland, kept itself in power by means, among other things, of the registration frauds which it organized. In England, as we have seen, the registration system also gives rise to abuses, but not altogether of the same kind: there it is the practice of improper objections and exclusions which is the curse of the system; here, on the contrary, it is the inflation of the register. In both countries abuse and fraud have only developed in a highly reprehensible manner, have emphasized, the rigorous principles which govern the right to a vote in each of them, the principle of privilege and the principle of individual right; it looks as if these abuses were in a way the penalty for the niggardliness with which the electoral right was doled out, on the one hand, and the heedless liberality with which it was distributed on the other.

Along with registration, the party Organizations devote themselves, in much the same way, to the naturalization of aliens likely to increase their electoral contingents. In the cities each large party committee has a permanent sub-committee in charge of the naturalization of immigrants. But it is especially on the eve of the elections that the Organizations start off in pursuit of all the aliens who can be naturalized. The Organizations make them go through all the necessary 305 formalities, pay the naturalization fees for them, and keep them warm, so to speak, for the coming election. Not unfrequently the committees or the candidates interested procure naturalization for aliens who have not complied with the requirements of the law, that is to say, obtain fraudulent naturalizations. The reader will remember how Tweed's Ring manufactured naturalized electors *en masse* in New York. These frauds are much facilitated by the extreme liberality of the American naturalization laws, and by the careless way in which the public authorities, especially the courts of law, verify the qualifications of the applicants. In certain States, the party committees get aliens admitted just before the elections in regular batches, a hundred or more per day, of people who barely understand English. The federal law requires a previous residence of five years for obtaining the status of an American citizen, but in a good many States (in fifteen) the immigrants are allowed to vote on a simple declaration of their intention to get naturalized and after a term of residence in the State varying from three to eighteen months.

Besides this, even in States where definitive naturalization is required, it is sufficient to obtain it on the eve of the election to have the right to take part therein. Thanks to the shortness of this interval, the Organizations keep an easier hold on the new citizens whom they have just introduced into the electoral body, and reap the fruit of their labour swiftly and surely. In the State of New York it was enough, down to 1895, to have obtained naturalization ten days before the election to have the legal right to vote. The law of 1895 (chap. 927) has extended this term of ten days to ninety, and at the same time forbids party committees and candidates, on penalty of a fine, to pay naturalization fees or to incur any expense with the object of procuring the naturalization of aliens.

V

The registration of electors and the naturalization of aliens having settled the legal composition of the electorate, the party Organization proceed to attack the latter directly. They These fees, however, are very low, much lower than in France, and even than in England; they seldom exceed half a dollar. VOL. II — x begin by reconnoitring the ground and making an estimate of the forces available on each side. All over the Union, in each locality, polling lists are drawn up showing which party each elector is going to vote for; if he has not made up his mind or has not given an indication of his choice, he is ranked among the doubtful. Special agents, paid by the party committees, scour the country to assist in this task and to make a more exhaustive political enquiry about each particular elector; they take down a quantity of details relating to his person, his race, his religion, his business, his circle of acquaintance, his pecuniary position, to whom he owes money or is under any obligation. In short, a sort of political and social survey is made for each locality. The data supplied by it are grouped and transmitted from one committee to another, along the whole line, up to the national committee. Each committee will derive from it useful information for determining its policy in its respective territorial area: the national committee will pass over all the States in which the preliminary poll has disclosed a very large majority favourable or hostile to the party and to its candidate for the Presidency; it has no need to convert the majority in the first case and it will never succeed in converting the majority in the second; it will, therefore, concentrate all its efforts on the States in which the majority is inconsiderable or uncertain, where the parties are so well matched in point of numbers that a small group of electors may turn the scale in favour of either side; winning this small group will mean winning the whole State. The same calculation holds good for the divisions and the subdivisions of the States and for all the local elective posts which have to be filled up. Although their interests are absolutely identical, the various committees, from that of the county up to the national committee, may, however, by reason of this very calculation, divide their efforts: the national committee, having no chance of getting its candidate for the Presidency a majority in a certain State, will leave the party to its fate there, but in several districts of that State in which the party is able to return congressmen, members of the local legislature, and other office-holders, the respective committees of that party will plunge into the fray with all their might. Thus the poll taken in each locality is of general import for the whole Union, as well as of special significance for each political subdivision in the States.

Generally there are two polls: the first goes on in the beginning of election time, in the mouth of September, and serves as a basis for the whole campaign; while the last is completed at least a fortnight before the election (which takes place on the first Tuesday of November) and furnishes hints for the dispositions to be made at the eleventh hour. In the States where the issue of the contest is always uncertain, which have the reputation of "close" or "doubtful" States, such as Indiana, each elector is asked what his views are on three separate occasions, ninety, sixty, and thirty days before the election; it is the second poll which gives a really faithful picture of the situation. Owing to the exceptional care which was always bestowed on the taking of the poll, its results used to be considered very trustworthy. But for some years past they have become more and more tainted with uncertainty, owing to the abrupt oscillations in the political sympathies of the electors, who have grown more capricious and more independent. The enquiry is supposed to be made on the eve of each election, but in the immense majority of cases it is held only for the great elections of the presidential year, unless the off election is of exceptional importance, such as certain elections for State Governor or even municipal elections. On no occasion, probably, is the mind of the electors probed with such care and method as for the municipal elections of New York, in which the wonderful Machine of Tammany Hall works to perfection, and the "braves " of the "Great Wigwam" fight *pro axis et focis.* The poll enables the party organizers to settle on the distribution and the best use of their means of action over the electorate. These means of action, established by long practice, are sometimes of a general scope, sometimes they present the character of arguments *ad hominem.* The former are aimed, as in England, at the intelligence and the senses of the voters, but are so under different conditions and often, also, in different forms. Those intended to act on the brains consist of speech and print.

VI

Eloquence is lavished on the electors in a continuous series of meetings of every kind, of every shade of importance, and in every place; from mass-meetings which attract thousands of people, the meetings go down to small gatherings in outof-the-way country spots, attended by a handful of farmers. Sometimes they are held in immense enclosures built expressly for the occasion, sometimes they take place on large lawns or at street-crossings. Sometimes the assemblage is a promiscuous one, sometimes it is composed of special groups, professional or others, commercial travellers, clerks in dry-goods stores, etc. Wherever there is, and whenever it is possible to collect, a gathering of human beings, floods of oratory are poured forth on behalf of the parties, day after day, during the whole of the campaign. Appealing even to the lowest strata of the electorate, who can hardly be reached by print, the meetings, in fact, do succeed in attracting electors of every degree. According to an estimate made on excellent authority, the proportion of electors who do not attend meetings hardly exceeds ten per cent. However, it is only in the "presidential years " that this great flocking together of electors occurs. In the "off years" the stump is more or less idle, and special circumstances are necessary to make the election campaign become "a speaking campaign" in these years. During the presidential campaign there has been so much speaking, and in such a high key, that the words of the innumerable orators have not yet died away and still resound in the ears of the electors at the ensuing local elections; so in the "off years" the programme is confined to small ward meetings and others, and then at the next presidential campaign the high pressure operation is repeated.

The meetings are got up by the committees; this is one of the most important, if not the most important, of their duties. The national committee supplies the eminent orators, who have a national reputation and who travel, by its direction, from one State to another, to make the great hits; the State committees procure the less important speakers. There is no lack of performers. All the committees, from the national committee and the congressional committee downwards, receive hundreds of offers, all more or less interested. The best speakers are engaged, like tenors, at so much a night for a certain number of evenings, or by the week, and are more or less highly paid. Those who come next in order of merit only get their travelling expenses and perhaps a small allowance for their time. Lastly, all the rest, and they form the very great majority, give their services gratuitously in the hope of obtaining a share of the booty, after the victory, in the form of some place or other; although generally disappointed in this expectation, they do not lose heart, being persuaded that their turn is sure to come next time, and the committees do not contradict them. Yet the number of paid speakers is on the increase, people grow less and less inclined to serve the party for nothing: "there is less patriotism and more selfishness," as the representative of a national committee has mournfully remarked on this subject. The speakers are taken principally from among politicians and members of the bar; they also include journalists and men who are in business and can talk; one meets, too, with clergymen who are sometimes more successful on the stump than in the pulpit. The candidates, on behalf of whom the election campaign is conducted, of course have their place marked on the list of orators, which, however, is not the most important one; they are lost in the crowd of speakers who have to fight for the ticket, especially at the general elections of the presidential year, when all the notabilities of the party descend into the arena, Senators of the United States, State Governors, or even ex-Presidents of the Republic.

All the speakers are, during the campaign, under the orders of the State committee. The latter draws up the list of the places, with the dates, at which each of them will have to speak. Along with his marching orders the speaker pretty often receives from the committee ammunition, in the form of arguments, of facts, of statistics. It not infrequently happens that the committee asks a speaker sent on an important campaign to submit to it beforehand his speech, which it will touch up, perhaps, pointing out what should be said and what left unsaid. When the battle is fought on an important practical problem, the committees, in the most contested States, take still greater precautions: before despatching their speakers to the four quarters of the State, they call them together and have them coached up by experts, who impress upon them the different aspects of the problem, point out to them the possible objections, and the' replies to be made thereto. The pupils of these extemporized schools of political eloquence are far from being novices in the art of the stump, members of Congress even and other politicians of a certain rank are to be found amongst them. The committees take care to suit the speakers to the audiences, according to affinities determined by ethnical origin, which differs so widely in the United States, and the intellectual character of the population. To meetings mainly composed of Irishmen speakers of the same race are told off; the vast agglomerations of Germans and Scandinavians, which are found in so many States, are harangued in German or in Swedish or Norwegian. The committees do not forget either that speakers who would be successful before country audiences may cut a very poor figure in the cities, and *vice versa.* Similarly, the committees make special provision for districts whose inhabitants, of more sober temperament or more highly developed intelligence, are not easily carried away by fluent talkers with pathetic intonations and gestures. These "hard-headed" districts must be dealt with by speakers who can appeal to reason, who can present good logical arguments; in other places it will be enough to excite passions and prejudices and to tickle the innate sense of humour of the Americans.

It is eloquence of this last kind which is the predominant type in the party meetings, and which has given the terms of "stump" and "stump oratory," already so familiar to us, their peculiar meaning. This style is the most appreciated because it best suits the national temperament. The fact is that beneath a frigid exterior, under a reserved and taciturn appearance, the

American is a highly sensitive, emotional, and excitable being. His delicate and rapid perception, which makes him vibrate in response to the whole gamut of human feeling, also makes hira run along it with an impetuosity which prevents him from concentrating his thoughts, from analyzing them at length, and from weighing the thoughts of others. Feeding his sensibility with.strong emotions, he finds in that sensibility itself a faculty which enables him to seize with equal subtlety and swiftness the ridiculous side of things; this is the sense of humour which acts as a kind of relief to this excitable being and preserves his equilibrium. A telling hit fires the American, another sends him on the opposite tack, with results perhaps affecting the gravest interests of the Republic. Rhetorical language, sonorous and grandiloquent phrases, take him at once; the verbiage of generalities imposes on him all the more easily that they flatter his imagination, developed amid the vast expanse of a continent with inexhaustible resources, which open up boundless horizons to all comers. By calling up before him the most comprehensive and elevated general idea, that of his native land, of the great American people, one is always sure to move him or make him think that he is moved. The most closely reasoned argument may be demolished by an amusing reply or by a telling retort which strikes the imagination.

While kept at this level by the temper of the multitude, stump oratory has on the other hand no fountain-head from which to draw loftier inspirations, to take models of an eloquence nobler in tone and form and richer in thought. Public Daring the presidential campaign of 1884 the three words, "Rum, Romanism, Rebellion," brought about the defeat of the Republican candidate and gave the victory to his Democratic rival. A member of a deputation which went to greet Blaine, the Republican candidate, expressed in his harangue the hope that he was against "Rum, Romanism, Rebellion." This epigram enraged a large number of electors, who were Catholics and saloon-keepers, to 8uc.h an extent that a good many of them, in the State of New York, transferred their votes to the Democratic candidate, Mr. Cleveland, or abstained from voting. It was thought that these votes, which gave Cleveland the majority in this State, had decided his election.

Hence the advice which a comic paper puts in the mouth of an old politician giving hints to his son who is about to make his first appearance on the stump: "Stick to the American eagle and to our own dear native land as much as possible." In a Western State, at a "joint" meeting, the Republican speaker, a very eminent advocate, delivered a most remarkable speech on behalf of his party. His Democratic opponent rose and confined his reply to the following words: "My friends, whenever there is a great criminal to be defended, my friend (the Republican speaker), who is the greatest criminal lawyer in the State, is always retained to conduct that defence. To-night the Republican party is on trial for its life; how desperate is the case is clearly shown by the fact that our greatest criminal lawyer has been called in to work the old wonder with his eloquent tongue." Then he sat down, and that district went against the Republicans at the next election. (Fr. H. Hardy, " The Making of a President," *Fortnightly Review,* August, 1896.) life in America was not always unprovided with such a source, but that source has dried up. Political eloquence, of the true kind, which once shone with such lustre in the United States, has steadily declined for the last forty or fifty years. The Clays, the Websters, the Calhouns have left no successors; their traditions are only a reminiscence of the past. The great political eloquence departed with the old leadership towards the close of the epoch which preceded the Civil War. It was one of the attributes of that leadership which, springing from social ascendency, found in this precious gift, at the end of its career, its highest and noblest expression. It was not only the giants whose names have just been mentioned who wielded over their fellow-citizens the sublime supremacy of speech. They shared it with numbers of less important men who all, aiming at the same effect, felt the same responsibility. The "great speech" which they delivered from time to time was the fruit of long preparation; it was the event heralded by the news-writers and expected by the public, on every important occasion, as a duty which the speaker had to discharge to his fellow-citizens by pointing out to them their duty, by enlightening their conscience. This speech, reported in full by the newspapers, was read and pondered over, and it powerfully helped to form public opinion. In the South political eloquence was quite a social function: it brought the members of the community closer to each other in every-day life, it united them in the same ideas and the same feelings; and while sometimes arousing passions, it provided food for the mind. Addressing audiences enamoured of oratory and possessing a certain Culture, the speakers in the South had to go back in their debates to the very principles of government, to its historic evolution, to examine the questions of the day in their manifold aspects. "These discussions were therefore, in fact, a sort of political school wherein lectures were delivered for the education of the masses," as a political veteran reminds us.

The social and political conditions which had undermined the leadership have also deteriorated representative govern Reuben Davis, *Recollections oj Mississippi and Mississippians,* Boston, 1889, p. l04.

ment, the strength and dignity of which ennoble public speaking and which in declining inevitably drags down with it political eloquence. With the development of the system of secret committees and party caucuses, in Congress as well as in the State legislatures, and with the advent of the Machine, which filled the assemblies with inferior men, these bodies had ceased to be deliberative assemblies; it was no use making a display of eloquence when the vote was decided beforehand by the resolution of the party caucus or of the committee; the most cogent reasoning, the most solid debate, was of no avail against the word of command of an influential boss. Being unable to change the votes, the speeches made in the assemblies could only be addressed to the country at large, and in the very great majority of cases simply to the electors of the member of Congress who was on his legs, and who was unknown in the other constituencies and had but little interest for them. Owing to this the speeches escaped the criticism of an assembly composed of men of the same intellectual calibre, or of a higher, one, than that of the speaker; the latter could say what he liked, he was talking only "for Buncombe." And before long the House thought it could and should dispense with these speeches, by authorizing its members to insert in the official reports, the *Congressional Record,* the harangues which they had not delivered, but had only announced in a few words; they were supposed to "develop their remarks" in the printed text. Nor had the members of the legislative assemblies any need to be good speakers to be returned by the electors; "getting the delegates" became far more important; and it was to the cultivation of that art, and not of the art of oratory, that embryo politicians henceforth devoted themselves. The wonderful rise of the press, with a power of expansion unparalleled in any other country, has helped in its turn to diminish political eloquence. Having undertaken to deliver ideas regularly and i During the celebrated debate on the "Missouri Compromise," in 1821, which settled the question of slavery in the Territories, a representative of a North Carolina district which included the county of Buncombe, insisted on speaking, in spite of the advice of his friends. "It is for Buncombe," he said to them, "that I want to speak." From that time, " to speak for Buncombe" passed into a proverb, denoting speeches with an objective other than the convictions of the audience. at the customer's door, so to speak, the press has driven the old purveyors of political thought into the background; and the latter naturally try rather to adapt themselves to the new state of things, to serve the public expeditiously and cheaply, that is to say, with little expenditure of intellect on the part of the producers as well as the consumers. Lastly, the very nature of the questions which interest public opinion at the present day is not very favourable to a lofty and aspiring style of eloquence. During the forty years which had preceded the Civil War, the controversies bore upon the very foundations of public order, on guarantees for liberty won amid tears and blood, on the rights of the people, on the dignity of man outraged in the slave. These questions, which thrilled the public mind, had given place, after the war, to economic problems, concerned with tariffs, currency, etc., and which appeal to preoccupations if not of a sordid at all events of a very prosaic kind. If in bygone days the great political orator who informed, not only the political conscience, but the moral conscience, of the citizens, appeared as a sort of *vates,* he could hardly reveal himself as such in discussing customs-duties on pig iron or wool.

Yet the tone of political oratory, which has necessarily had to alter with its subject-matter, has not grown business-like. On the contrary, it has become, especially outside legislative precincts, rather frivolous than otherwise. The extraordinary development of after-dinner speeches has brought about a great change in this direction. Banquets and dinners have, for the last quarter of a century, given public men more and more opportunities of stating their views, of initiating the public into the problems of the day. Coming as a sort of gastronomic complement, the speeches made on these occasions have aimed especially at being digestive and agreeable to the palate, have sought to keep the guests in a good humour, to make them laugh. It became the fashion for the gravest individuals even, meeting for some object of public interest, when once at table, to vie with one another in facetiousness, to see who could tell the most amusing stories, the most side-splitting anecdotes. To be able to make such a speech at a public dinner now almost forms part of a "gentleman's" education, to use the oldfashioned expression. Those who excel in it are the object of an enthusiastic admiration on the part of the public, which would never be bestowed on an eminent statesman; in the eyes of men who pride themselves on refined tastes, they rival the celebrated actors and actresses who send the multitude into raptures. The great artist of the after-dinner speech, who is a genius in his line, enjoys a national reputation; and his art may carry him a long way, as far as the Senate of the United States, especially if he possesses a large fortune into the bargain, and, of course, the friendship or the neutrality of the boss of the State. Owing to this, post-prandial eloquence has become, to some extent, a classic model for stump speakers; but the latter, who address less refined audiences, naturally often season their oratorical viands with coarser condiments.

It is only fair to add that stump eloquence, while preserving the characteristics which have just been described, has also of late years come under the salutary influence of the serious discussion of economic facts and ideas, started by President Cleveland's famous message, in 1887, on protectionism. This message brought the problem before public opinion and forced all those who canvass that opinion to take it up. Again, the stump has benefited, without any merit on its part, by the decline of parliamentary eloquence: eminent or distinguished speakers, for whom there is no longer room in Congress, take their eloquence to the stump, in important conjunctures. This fact has become of real significance in the course of the last decade. A good many speeches of a most remarkable kind, and which promoted political education in the true sense of the word, have been made on the stump and by orators not belonging, or no longer belonging, to the political set. These speeches lead me to make another general reservation in regard to the character of political eloquence in America. There are in the United States orators of real distinction, of lofty intellect and great talent; but one must hasten to add that they are extremely rare, and some of them do not always combine with these gifts that nobility of political character without which the most remarkable orator is only a gladiator. It is not possible to resist this impression in listening to a speaker who, with transcendent art, seems to strike the noblest chords in the human breast, when one reflects that the day before this same speaker belonged to Tammany Hall or was, or still is, connected with another Machine. All the more vividly is the image of gladiators evoked by the minor speakers who are engaged by the party committees to perform feats of oratory before the assembled multitude. The very euphemisms with which the language of the day describes stump orators, by calling them "spellbinders," and saying, "let loose the spellbinders," recall the combatants of the arena. The elaborate organization which directs the exploits of the "campaign orators," while admirably adapted to the purpose in view, accentuates and amplifies the metaphor. It is the same arena as in the amphitheatre of antiquity, but the material progress of contemporary civilization enables it to be transported at will; steam-power carries the spellbinders from city to city, from one station to another, and at each stopping-place, before the assembled crowd, they go through their performance on the railway platform. If they are spellbinders of the first water, a special train is put on for them, which follows the route and the timetable fixed by the committee to suit the convenience of its campaign, and which sometimes goes the round of several States.

Below the spellbinders there are in the service of the committees other oratorical gladiators, of a very modest kind, hardly deserving the title, but who are none the less useful. To this category belong workshop and factory talkers, workmen who have the gift of gab and who are paid by the committees to harangue their comrades. Other speakers, equally humble, are told off to speak at street-crossings to crowds which they gather round them. They often meet with opponents, who are only accomplices, and the two sides carry on a sham debate, which of course always ends in the discomfiture of the party opposed to that for which the accomplices are working.

Genuine debates between two opponents are becoming more and more rare. Formerly these "joint debates" were tolerably common; they were almost a public institution in the South; at political meetings the representatives of the various i This appellation is derived from the stereotyped phrase used by the newspapers, which, in reporting a speech, say of the speaker, " he kept his audience spellbound," etc. opinions "divided the time" between them. But they were also known in the North and West. The most celebrated of these debates, which took place in 1858, between Lincoln and Douglas, then rival candidates in Illinois for the post of Senator, was followed with rapt attention by the whole Union; they were discussing before the country the burning question of slavery. After the Civil War, the face-to-face debate, which enabled the citizens to grasp then and there the arguments pro and con presented by public men, disappeared almost entirely. "For the last twenty years," as the political veteran already quoted wrote in 1888, "this practical union between politicians and people has not existed. Only one party is allowed to speak, and the leaders of that party no longer debate, they simply declaim and denounce. Upon this crude and windy diet the once robust and sturdy political convictions of our people have dwindled into leanness and decay.... The evil of mischievous assertions is greatly lessened when free discussion is allowed, and error exposed and combated by the unsparing vigor of an opposing party." In the South, however, beginning as soon as the border-state of Maryland, the joint debate still reappears sometimes. Thus in the election campaign of 1896, in this or that State one might have seen the three rival candidates for the post of Governor, Republican, Democratic, and Populist, going their rounds together through the State, or the Republican and Democratic candidates for a seat in Congress engaging in an oratorical duel on the occasion of a fair which attracted the crowd. It was the development of the press again which, to a great extent, was the cause of the joint debate going out of fashion, or at all events which supplied a pretext for dropping it; it was alleged that speeches made on the other side were brought within the reach of every citizen by the newspapers, which now penetrate everywhere. For the value of this argument, I need only refer to the observations which I have made on it when speaking of political meetings in England.

The speakers represent one party only and address similar audiences. These meetings are attended almost exclusively by the faithful followers of the party; not only the adherents of the opposite party but even the "doubtful" electors keep *Recollections of Mis»issippi,* p. 195.

away from them. If the election campaign is a particularly fierce one, the opponents go to the meeting to create obstruction, which reaches a high pitch of turbulence, but is not marked by personal violence or abuse. In ordinary times the electors of each party are almost a family group in their meetings. The somewhat faint attempts at frequenting meetings of political opponents are rather discouraged by the party Organizations. The latter no doubt show each other the civility of sharing the hall, in places where it is difficult to get one; they hire, or even build a hall, at joint expense, but each party uses it on different evenings. Their tolerance does not go beyond this, being hardly equal to that of

American religious communities in which the same place of worship often not only serves for several cults at different hours, but in which sometimes heterodox congregations exchange their preachers for one or two Sundays. The object and effect of American political meetings is, therefore, not so much to instruct and convert as to edify the audience, to strengthen them in the party creed. The great expedient of the American stump is to "raise enthusiasm," just as at English meetings, but in a much greater degree, which is accounted for by the idiosyncrasies of the American temperament referred to above, and by the moral and intellectual calibre of the speakers on the other side of the Atlantic. Yet the value for propagandist purposes which the meetings possess in this respect, in the eyes of the parties, is declining, for the intellectual standard of the American electors is getting higher, — they are not so easily caught by the artifices of the stump. On the other hand, it must be pointed out that the action of the meetings is not absolutely confined to the production of "enthusiasm." In the course of a presidential campaign so many speeches are made, the question of the day is turned inside and out to such an extent, that it is impossible for the electors not to learn something. The great mass only carries away, it is true, extremely hazy notions, but a small section ends by getting more or less insight into the problems under discussion. VII

While the meetings are intended to take the bulk of the electors by storm, down to the least cultivated, the more intelligent electors are canvassed by means of the Press, newspapers, pamphlets, leaflets, etc. In the eyes of the Organizations, the newspapers do the most execution, and the former put forth very considerable efforts to make them serve their ends. The very great majority of the newspapers are already in sympathy with the "regular" parties; a good many of them keep up more or less close relations with the Organizations, and, as we are already aware, are even sometimes one of the strongest buttresses of the Machines and the bosses. The role of the Press as a party instrument dates from the rise of the political wire-pullers in the States of New York and Pennsylvania, and it asserted itself definitively under Jackson. The press was methodically attached to the Organization of the party; it submitted to the latter's unreasoning discipline, with the sacrifice, not only of its independence, but also of moderation and good faith. The famous "Kitchen Cabinet" developed the "manufacture of opinion" by means of the Press, with such consummate skill that it apparently took in Jackson himself. By way of reward, the Press was allowed from the outset a share in the profits of the spoils system." The relations thus established between the Press and the organized parties continued from that time forth on the same basis. After the civil war, when the importance of the Press increased The virtuous indignation of Niles found particularly violent epithets to describe the degradation of the press enslaved by the parties: "The *organized* party press is as reckless of justice as are the bands of robbers and murderers who infest the Apennines. It has no discretion, and instead of being the 'tyrauts' foe, the people's friend' (which is the motto on the grand banner of the profession), it becomes the tyrants' slave, the people's foe... Individual printers and editors, as other persons, *will* do wrong, but when *bodies* of them are marshalled and ' ear-marked ' and 'collared ' to cry out, ' God is God and Mahomet is his prophet,' and kiss the black stone in gangs — they are no better than..." etc. (*Weekly Register, 1833,* Vol. 46, p. 307, the article, "The Organized Press.") Article by Noah, editor of the *New York Evening Star,* quoted in Niles, *ibid.,* p. 391.

The total of this " reward " distributed under Jackson to the press in the form of offices and other sources of gain, is estimated by Niles at $200,000 a year *(ibid.,* p. 307). with the general development of the country, the co-operation of the newspapers became still more valuable, and it rose in price; editors or proprietors of big newspapers were appointed offhand to diplomatic posts of the first class, to Paris, Berlin, St. Petersburg. In the case of the big newspapers the *do ut des* is tacitly understood, with the others the party committees often negotiate formally. The papers place at their disposal, for the advocacy of the candidates and the policy of the party, not only the pens of their editors, but also their columns by inserting this or that communication or article which the committees supply them with. For this purpose there are, at the head-quarters of the parties, and often also attached to the State committees, press bureaus which prepare copy for the newspapers in the form of telegraphic despatches, editorials, correspondence, etc. Often the committees have the article inserted by paying for the space taken up by it, according to the tariff for advertisements.

The number of papers is, however, so great that it would be impossible for the committees, even apart from the expense, to keep up relations with all of them, to wit, with the small local papers; the party Organizations achieve this through the system of publicity known by the name of "patent inside," which has introduced manufacturing methods into the editing of periodicals. central agencies regularly supply several thousands of periodicals with the greater part of their copy, — literary, political, and scientific articles,—with which the publishers fill up the "inside" of the paper, adding the local news and the advertisements on the first and fourth pages. Often the publishers have no need even to get this copy set up, they receive stereotyped plates of it all ready for the press. This system, which gives extraordinary facilities for equipping and publishing a newspaper with little outlay, puts the small papers in the power of their purveyors, the " press syndicates." The national party committees come to an understanding with these agencies and get them to accept political copy or plates, which the agencies will pass on to their customers of the respective political persuasion. The six most important press agencies are able to get a communication reproduced in sixteen thousand papers. The political matter thus inserted in the local journal does not take up much space, barely two columns perhaps, but it none the less serves its purpose, for this paper is very often the sole instrument of civilization in the district, — nothing else is read there.

In estimating the political effect of the press, inspired by the parties, one may say in a general way that it is in the inverse ratio to the intelligence of the reader. The newspapers do not wield much influence over intelligent readers; that influence is on the decline with them, as in England; they no longer read the editorials, and for the same reason, owing to the want of good faith which characterizes the political articles. It is not quite the same thing with one important category of newspapers, viz. those published in the German language, which are somewhat numerous and widely circulated in several States. Edited with less lightness of touch and less passion than the newspapers written in English, the German newspapers are more substantial and more sedate; they command the full confidence of their readers, who peruse them scrupulously and absorb the leading article. Besides, the American newspaper written in English has less pretensions to direct the political conscience of its readers, to lecture them; it considers itself in the first place as a purveyor of facts, true, if such can be obtained, or otherwise. The comment on the facts, the criticism, is thrust into the background. The rush for news which engrosses the American newspapers, from the leviathans of the press down to the smallest fry, might have served as an outlet for the violence of political controversy, if it had not in too many cases been itself a source of demoralization to the reader whose morbid curiosity the newspaper simply stimulates by constantly dishing up scandals, crimes, or, at all events, gossip. The breaking up of the matter of the paper into a number of short paragraphs, which I have referred to in my remarks on the cheap English press, is carried to extreme lengths in the American journals, and assuredly is not more likely, in the United States, to fix the reader's attention and discipline his mind. The political matter is presented in the same fashion, that is to say, it is not of a kind to instruct and enlighten the reader. Recent years have witnessed the rise of an independent press whose growing influence is an excellent omen, as I shall have an opportunity of explaining farther on; but that press has as yet conquered but a VOL. II — T small part of the field, and the other press still holds its ground.

This state of things is all the more grave, from the standpoint of the political education of the electoral masses, that the press is their only source of political instruction outside election time. In the interval between the elections the party Organizations take but little pains to disseminate political facts and ideas among the electors, as is done by the party Associations in England, to an utterly inadequate extent, it is true, as I have taken care to point out. Nor do the American electors possess the resources offered by the periodical meetings of English M.P.'s with their constituents. To keep in the good graces of their electors, the English members of Parliament are obliged to "come down" as often as possible and make speeches; defending the policy of the party with which they are connected, they have to discuss the legislative measures which that party brings forward or opposes. The members of Congress, and still more those of the State legislatures, are relieved from this obligation by the fact that they owe their seats in the first place to the Machine or to their skill in "getting the delegates "; besides, the shortness of their elective term makes it almost useless for them to present themselves to their electors before the next election, at which they will more often than not be prevented from standing again, owing to the rule of rotation in office. In the days when the Senate of the United States was composed of distinguished men, of the political elite of the nation, there was in most of the States at least one Senator who discharged the function of political educator by his speeches and his communications on the questions of the day; he helped to form public opinion and to store the public mind. This type of Senator has disappeared now that, under the regime of the Machine, money opens the doors of the Senate to any one who is willing to spend plenty of it. Public men, as a rule, rather avoid facing public opinion, they shirk stating their views on the questions which interest it; for fear of compromising themselves they remain "non-committal": rightly or wrongly they hold that under a democratic government it is not permissible for those who wish to be honoured with the confidence of the people to have views of their own, or, at all events, to put them for ward; that it is better, with their ear always bent towards the ground, to steer their course by the shifting views of the multitude. The prominent lawyers, the notabilities of the bar who contributed their quota to public discussion, let themselves, after the war, like the rest of their fellow-citizens, be engrossed by business, by their professional avocations, putting their talent at the disposal of the big financial and industrial companies, and deliberately depriving themselves of the leisure which might have been spent in disinterested study and have been of service to the commonwealth.

There was, before the war, yet another public educator who diffused enlightenment with very appreciable effects, — the lecturer of the "lyceum." The lyceum was a sort of free university for the mental culture of grown-up persons, provided in an intermittent way by men of letters, amateurs or professional lecturers, who generally came from outside and made tours through the country. At a time when communications were not so easy as they are nowadays, the arrival of the lyceum lecturer was a great local event which was eagerly looked forward to by the public. The lectures afforded instruction and edification, while they relieved the monotony of existence, especially in the winter time. The lecturer treated literary, scientific, ethical, and political subjects, often with talent and almost always with honesty. Members of Congress were not above ascending the platform of the lyceum, during the parliamentary vacation. The illustrious abolitionist champions also spoke in it. Daniel Webster, Channing, Emerson, Theodore Parker, Charles Sumner, Wendell Phillips, H. Ward Beecher, and G. W. Curtis might have been heard in the lyceum. During the decade of 1850 to 1860 the lyceum reached the highest point of its development and usefulness, but after the war it underwent a complete eclipse. It was killed by the press and also by the passion for notoriety which infected the lecturing staff and the public: the lectures were too often offered by speakers of both sexes who were dying to appear on the boards, without having any serious claim on the attention of the public; the latter, in its turn, smitten with the fever and the frivolity which invaded society after the war, went to the lyceum to enjoy a show, an exhibition, and demanded lecturers whose notoriety ranked them with theatrical stars, and worth seeing on that account.

Left without guidance by those who could or should have supplied them with a clue to the labyrinth of political affairs, American citizens have no means either of acquiring the rudiments of political knowledge before beginning life, that is to say, at school. Political and historical studies have been and, to a great extent, still are much neglected in American instruction. These studies have made marked progress, during the last few years, in the sphere of higher education, but they are still poor in quality or nonexistent in secondary and elementary schools. Even in the high schools (secondary schools) the teaching of history occupies a rather subordinate place, while in the elementary schools it hardly exists; towards the end of the curriculum national history is introduced into it and then brought to a close with Washington's Presidency. Political studies are still less favoured; a pupil has but little chance of learning how his country is governed, who makes the laws, by whom and how the city which he inhabits is administered, unless he goes through the high school, the programme of which generally includes a course of lessons on the political organization of the country. But the number of children who attend the high schools is very small; everybody is in too great a hurry, in the United States, to rush into practical life and get on, while the wonderful precocity of the young Americans encourages this tendency. A child leaves the elementary As recently as the year 1890, the President of Columbia College said: "Our higher institutions have neglected almost wholly to instruct the young men whom they undertake to train in the principles of the government under which they are to live and of which they are to be a part, and in the duties which are to devolve upon them as citizens. Every other branch of their culture has been sedulously cared for. They are taught a great deal about the properties of matter, but very little about the passions of men; much about the perturbations of the planets, but very little about the interactions of parties; much about the constitution of the solar system, but very little about the constitution of the United States.... Indeed, so far is the teaching of our colleges at present from being suited to prepare young men for the proper discharge of what, under our constitution, is really the most important duty before them in life, that it almost seems to have been purposely planned to evade that object." (F. Barnard, "The Degradation of our Politics," *Forum*, April, 1890.) Out of the total of school attendance in every grade of public instruction, in 1896-1897, which amounted to 16,265,097, there were only 584,904 children in the high schools and other similar establishments, and 217,763 receiving higher education. *(Report of the Commissioners of Education* for the year 1896-1897, Washington, 1898, Vol. I, p. 1.) school with nothing in the way of civic instruction but the Declaration of Independence learnt by rote, like a saying lesson, and the notions of "patriotism" inculcated by the ceremonial displays of the flag of the Union.

No doubt, special instruction in this or that subject, even if it bears directly upon politics, is not enough to make the citizen; it is the cultivation of the intelligence in general that improves the judgment of the future elector; it is the sum total of what is taught in the school that develops it. Are not the American schools, then, very good? They inspire the great mass of American citizens with a boundless confidence, and the latter say, with a pride which at the same time has something touching about it: "We have the best schools in the world." In truth, nowhere else in the world is instruction lavished so generously and with such a feeling of democratic fraternity; the school is the base of the political edifice in America, it is the kernel of the State by very reason of the latter's legal organization, which makes the "school district" the elementary administrative unit, which groups the citizens in the first place around the school whence all the rays of public life are projected as from a luminous centre. But the manner and the methods with which instruction is given in these schools provoke strong criticism on the part of the elite of American society; its best representatives are of opinion that the teaching in the public schools is almost exclusively concerned with cramming, with exercising the memory at the expense of the faculties of observation, of analysis, aud of reasoning; that this teaching is of an eminently formal and mechanical kind, as if its business were to make automata and not men. The difficulty of raising the standard of the masters who impart this instruction, and who are very often incapable of giving any other, is all the greater that the choice of the teaching staff and of the school authorities who have to submit to popular election is frequently subordinated to party i One of the highest American authorities on education said to me on this subject: "Have you ever been in the East, have yon ever seen an Arab school with the children all repeating their lessons together? well, it is just the same with us." Cf. C. W. Eliot, "Wherein Popular Education has Failed." *Forum,* December, 1892; J. M. Rice, *The Public School System oj the United Statei,* 1893.

politics; school offices form part of the "spoils." The spirit of the education given at school to young Americans, *qua* Americans, is not less strongly animadverted on by men of sound judgment on the other side of the Atlantic: according to them, that education strives to develop in the young the " patriotic" sentiment in its narrow aspect, which takes no account of the rest of humanity and is apt to look on other countries and other nations, if not with contempt, at all events with an indulgent pity. The national self-sufficiency or conceit thus drilled into the youthful mind, in its turn, does not much help to form the political judgment. No doubt the great exertions and sacrifices to which the Americans submit for the spread of education have not been in vain, the intelligence of the masses has made and continues to make notable progress; their horizon is broadening, they are getting a better notion of the issues of politics, but without exercising the critical and discerning spirit necessary to save them from the thousand and one pitfalls which beset the elector whose vote is wanted.

The utter inadequacy of political culture among the electoral masses has attracted the attention of sensible men, and has given rise, in the last few years, to several attempts at making good the deficiency by political instruction given in the public schools, as well as to adults, by means of lectures, classes, etc. In some States, the public authorities have joined in this movement and have procured the insertion in the programmes of a course on "civics" (a word coined as a substitute for "politics " degraded by the "politicians "), devoted to the constitutional organization of the State and the Union. But it is mostly private initiative which carries on the work, by starting societies for the study of the questions of the day, debating clubs, lectures, either independently, or, to a certain extent, under the auspices of the organizations created for the general education of adults, such as the "University extension," the "Chautauqua," and others. All these attempts, which are highly creditable and cannot fail to bear fruit in the long run, are, however, in the nature of isolated and scattered effort; the action of private initiative, which has its great merits, also sometimes has its defects, which deprive it of the advantages of a general direction and extensive propelling power. The vast area of the Union, split up into so many States, also presents an obstacle to propaganda; the endeavours to spread political education made in one State are not known in several others, so much so that even people who are in the business, so to speak, have no accurate information on the subject. Lastly, it must be pointed out that the small amounts of political instruction offered to adults by private initiative hardly reach the lowest strata of universal suffrage; with but few exceptions, this instruction does not go below what would be called in England the middle class.

When all is said and done, one finds that the American is left to himself for the discharge of his duties as a citizen. The intellectual curiosity which is such a good trait in his character remains in abeyance, is not satisfied in a systematic way. With a real wish to grasp the political problems of the day, he is reduced to fugitive and superficial impressions. His extremely quick and resourceful mind readily inclines him to content himself with them, to persuade himself that he understands everything, that he has got to the bottom of everything. An imperfectly ecjuipped critic of things and ideas, he is not, it would seem, a better judge of the men who present them; perhaps the excessive confidence which characterizes social intercourse in a new society — where one is ignorant of, and, out of good nature, does not inquire into people's past history — and in a business community — where the spirit of unbridled speculation procures unlimited credit for the first comer — encourages this want of criticism; in any event, the absence of political culture is not calculated to diminish it when political problems have to be faced. So when the average man descends into the arena of public life, at election time, he is — he who is so intelligent and so clever in practical life — like a Samson shorn of his strength; and the Philistines of the party Organization have an easy task when they undertake to provide his "political education" offhand, in view of the vote which they want to snatch from him. To the elector, whose food during the years which intervene between the elections has been confined to the opium of the party newspapers, they administer a stronger dose of it, adding, by way of an extra, the apparently more solid nutriment of "political literature " or "campaign documents."

The "literature" consists of pamphlets, leaflets, posters, handbills, etc. , bearing on the questions and persons at stake, and, of course, composed in the interest of the party. At each headquarters there is a "literary bureau" with a staff of writers who draw up the "campaign documents." The most important of these "documents," published in the form of pamphlets, are mostly presented as speeches delivered in Congress. In a certain number of cases this is only an expedient used, not so much to impress the imagination of the readers as to secure the exemption from postage accorded to official documents, to every speech made in Congress and sent by one of its members to the electors, however great the number of copies. As custom allows the insertion, in the *Congressional Record,* with the assent of the House, of speeches not really delivered, and even after the close of the session, pamphlets are published in it, in view of the election campaign, with

the addition of a phrase which gives the appearance of a speech: "Mr. Speaker, I have here a speech delivered by..." or " an article written by... and I propose, with the consent of the House, to insert it in my remarks. The matter referred to is as follows "; and then comes the pamphlet in its entirety, or even a chapter of a book. It was in this way that were circulated, under the Congressional stamp, writings by Henry George, the author of "Progress and Poverty." As a rule, the value of these pamphletspeeches varies; some are more or lass instructive, but the great majority consist only of declamation and denunciation of the opposite party. They are not much read, however; most electors put them on one side, while somewhat impressed by their arrival; the elector who receives a pamphlet in the big yellow Washington envelope with the official heading is greatly pleased to find that his name is known to the national committee. The pamphlets, as is also the case in England, are mainly of service for supplying facts and arguments to minor speakers and to the local debaters who retail and amplify them. The great committees even publish, for use in 1 In this way the committees of the parties forward several millions of copies of a single speech without expense; that is to say, at the expense of the taxpayers. In the presidential campaign of 18% the official envelopes alone placed at the disposal of members of Congress for the despatch of documents cost the Treasury more than $140,000.
this way, special repertories, well got up, under the title of "campaigu books" or "campaign text-books," which contain, along with many statistics, short monographs on the political questions before the public, official documents, declarations of the party, indictments of the policy of the opposite party, defences of their own, etc. There is one category of pamphlets which, being not such dry reading, is more acceptable to the recipients, viz. the biographies of the candidates for the Presidency, and sometimes also for posts of less importance. These biographies are composed in prospectus style for the requirements of the election campaign and are known, in consequence, by the name of "campaign lives "; they form a historical type of their own which has no resemblance whatever to Plutarch. Sometimes, however, the campaign lives of the presidential candidates are penned by real, and even illustrious men of letters, while their heroes are obscure mediocrities; thus the biography of Pierce was written by Hawthorne, the author of "The Scarlet Letter."

The type of "campaign literature" which is the most read, and which produces the most effect, is represented by leaflets, or even little bits of cardboard, with a few dogmatic assertions unaccompanied by argument. The controversy on the currency system, for instance, is settled on them by a few figures stating peremptorily that under the gold standard debts have increased by so and so many millions. That is enough for the elector, he is convinced: "I know it's true, it comes from the national committee." Similarly the superiority of protectionism is demonstrated by a series of small leaflets intended for the farmers, the front page of each leaflet exhibiting a picture of an agricultural product, — apples, butter, honey, poultry, sheep, cows, — with an explanatory note showing at what rate the article in question paid duty under the McKinley tariff, to what amount the customs-duties were lowered by the Wilson Bill of the Democrats, and how much the American farmer loses on each head of cattle, each pound of butter, each dozen of eggs, etc. On the back of the leaflet are given the three respective figures for a number of other agricultural products, with the conclusion, "Stand by Eepublican Principles, Protection and Sound Money." The greatest success is obtained by "pictorial literature," that is to say, by illustrated leaflets and handbills with symbolic pictures, caricatures, etc., representing, for instance, monometallism in the form of a man with only one eye and one leg, and thus furnishing self-evident proof of the absurdity of opposition to bimetallism. As a large proportion of the electors who have more or less recently come into the country do not understand English sufficiently, the "campaign documents" which are considered the most important, big speeches, small cards or leaflets, are brought within their reach by translations into their mother tongue, — in German, in French, in Italian, in Swedish, in Polish, in Czech, in Hebrew, in fact, in almost all the languages of Europe. Throughout the campaign all the polyglot "literature" is distributed unremittingly and with much method, especially in the "doubtful" States. Provided with copies of the electoral register in every part of the country, the committees despatch their "literature" to all the electors; but it is the "doubtful electors," as disclosed by the canvass, who are the special object of their attentions; they overwhelm them with communications, they leave them no peace, and send them at short intervals now a pamphlet, now a newspaper, now illustrated leaflets. As in the case of the other methods of electoral propaganda, the distribution of "documents" occurs only during the presidential campaign; and it is only by way of exception that it takes place on the occasion of other election campaigns.

In particularly grave conjunctures, the party Organization does not monopolize the action intended to influence the public mind. The appeals addressed to public opinion in these circumstances come from independent sources as well. A mobilization of all the living forces of the nation takes place along the whole line. As a matter of course the independent press, that which is not an agent of the parties or which is bound to them by very loose ties only, intervenes with much energy. The Church itself, whose absolute independence of the State makes it indifferent to party strife, the churches of every denomination put themselves in motion when the great problems of the day, or even the person of the candidate, appear to raise moral questions ruled by the Decalogue. The question of the double standard and of the free coinage of silver is an economic one, but the preacher submits to his flock whether it is honest to pay one's debts in a depreciated metal and to despoil one's creditor with the hypocritical aid of the law. In a similar spirit, ministers of religion stand up in their churches against a corrupt State boss, the cup of whose iniquities is running over, or against the plunderers and receivers, or the accomplices of the gang of Tammany Hall. Taking up the narrower standpoint of church morality, clergymen publish letters in the newspapers to recommend a candidate, for instance, the candidate for the Presidency of the Republic, as a pious, God-fearing man. Individual citizens, more or less eminent representatives of social groups, of professions, come forward in like manner to throw the weight of their opinion or of their prestige into the scale, by means of a public declaration solicited by an interviewer of the press or spontaneously addressed to a newspaper. Often the paper takes little plebiscites among these persons by publishing the views of a group of college presidents, of a group of bankers, of a group of lawyers, of a group of workmen in some trade, etc. Although got up for reporting purposes, to procure copy, these consultations add to the mass of ideas and opinions put into general circulation on the occasion of the election campaign.

FIFTH CHAPTER THE ELECTION CAMPAIGN *(conclusion)*

I

The means of propaganda which have just been reviewed and which aim, or are supposed to aim, at the intelligence of the electors, are very largely supplemented by others intended to act on the imagination. The latter appeal in the first place to the senses, and are meant to "raise enthusiasm." This mode of action is already familiar to us from our English experience; but in America it is applied with an amplitude and a wealth of resources by the side of which the efforts of the English party Associations cut a very poor figure and mark the infancy of the art. The reader need only recall the famous presidential campaign of "Tippecanoe and Tyler too," in 1840, to be aware that the art of stirring up the electors by making a noise was at a very early stage brought to a rare pitch in the United States. The noise is produced by a set of regular'devices, to which the American organizers themselves give the collective title of "the Chinese business." Foremost among the usual methods come the mass-meetings, whose principal attraction for the crowd that cares little for political eloquence consists of musical interludes executed by orchestras and choruses. The signal is given, as soon as election time begins, by the "ratification meetings," summoned on the pretext of ratifying the selections of candidates made in the conventions. Another ceremony which affords repeated opportunities for stirring up the crowd is the "banner" or "flag raising " — the inauguration of the flag or of the banner of the party, generally adorned with the portraits of the candidates for the Presidency and the Vice-Presidency. Amid the din of speeches and bands, the huge banner is planted in front of the head-quarters of the committee, and in other parts of the city hung across the street. As the campaign progresses, one mass-maeting is held after another, with no particular pretext. They are organized in large covered buildings or in the open air, and announced by puffs in the newspapers and by handbills in which the speakers and the music are eulogized beforehand. Singing does not fill as important a place in the programme as music, and it by no means consists entirely of political songs.

Far more picturesque are the processions and the big processions called parades, of which we have already had a foretaste at the national convention. Every city and every rural district treats itself to these during the campaign, and they would think themselves almost disgraced if they were deprived of them. We are already familiar with the special organization of "marching clubs," which file through the streets for the glory of their party. Fireworks, torch-light processions, cavalcades on horseback or on bicycles, ridden by hundreds or even thousands of men and women wearing a special uniform, bicycle orchestras, aquatic parades with hundreds of boats in a row, parades in the streets attended by large contingents of the followers of the party, are so many means of testifying to the enthusiasm which animates its members. Some of these demonstrations attain really gigantic proportions, such as the great parades in New York, for instance, when more than a hundred thousand men march past a few leading members of the party, sometimes with the presidential candidate himself at their head, accompanied by bands, flags, and banners, in the midst of a million spectators. It is a general review of the forces of the party held like a military review. The troops are under the orders of a grand-marshal and a number of assistant marshals, adjutants, and captains. The various companies are generally formed by professions or trades: store clerks, merchants, barristers, etc. All classes of the population are represented, from the princes of finance down to the common people; heads of business firms and members of the bar fall in, shouting themselves hoarse, in honour of the candidates of the party, just like ordinary labourers. The ridiculous side of the spectacle they present does not occur to them nor to the spectators of the show, — it is lost in the feeling of duty towards the party, in the pious wish to conciliate the God of electoral battles by rites of some kind or other. For they consider that the party is served by making its numerical strength conspicuous, by conveying an impression of the combative ardour which animates its adherents, even if this is achieved by methods savouring of the travelling circus. In reality, all this rumpus of parades and processions wins but few votes for the party, but it keeps up "enthusiasm" in the camp and awakens the apathetic, rouses them out of their indifference, forces them to fix their eyes on the cause of the party embodied in the performers. It is a method of attracting the attention of the crowd which has taken such deep root in American life, that even the reform movements which appeal to the intelligence and the moral sense of the citizens do not feel at liberty to dispense with these practices. The regular parties have all the less scruple in persisting in them despite the heavy pecuniary sacrifices which the organization of these manifestations demands. The electioneering effect of the parades and the marches-past is beginning to decline, thanks to the spread of enlightenment; yet these manifestations do not become fewer in number; they even assume new forms, such as, during the campaign of 1896, the pilgrimages to the residence of the presidential candidate, each made up of hundreds or thousands of persons from all parts of the Union, of every calling, sex, and colour.

In the'rural districts, the "Chinese business" produces perhaps more effect, but of course does not attain the same proportions as in the cities, it is combined with the forms of intellectual action. The whole neighbourhood is invited to a "rally," — this is the name given to political meetings attended by the inhabitants of several localities; the farmers generally come in large numbers, on horseback, in breaks, or on foot, often with their families. Political speakers sent down by the committees hold forth in a covered enclosure to audiences which, especially in the West, are composed of men and women. Outside, in the square, there are other talkers, the The cost, for instance, of a " torch-light procession " and of the uniforms worn by the members of the "marching clubs," in a large city, amounts to $25,000 or even $40,000 (£5,000-£8,000).

"fakirs," the pedlers, also attracted by the rally; in language which, if not more truthful, is often more amusing than that of the political speechmakers, they puff their varied wares, including everything from objects and accessories of the toilet, playthings, confectionery, down to Webster's dictionary, which is commended in touching terms. In the daytime a "procession" takes place: the faithful followers of the party, adorned with emblems, scour the country, headed by a band; the negro village barber, wearing a costume trimmed with gold, beats time with indescribable dignity. In the evening all the houses are illuminated and a torch-light procession concludes the "Chinese business." The fete, however, still goes on; the speakers reappear, and, in the open air, on the green, by the flickering glare of the torches, they harangue the assembled crowd. Bareheaded, exposed to an autumn wind, the "spellbinder" discourses, and, in a voice showing signs of fatigue, but which he tries to make as stentorian as possible, repeats, for the twentieth time perhaps in the day, the asseveration: "When the American people will rise in their might and majesty-y-y "; but the attention of the wearied public is distracted, there are only a few groups listening here and there, the rest are talking, the young people are flirting in the dim light. Besides, the reporter has already sent off his long telegram to the big newspaper of the district, in which he has somewhat anticipated all the details, like a man who knows what goes on at "enthusiastic manifestations."

In addition to the large meetings and demonstrations intended to call forth "enthusiasm," the electioneering propaganda of the parties that aims at the senses also resorts to practices which procure the senses gratifications of a more personal kind, such as picnics, dances, and dramatic entertainments, etc. As in the English "social meetings," organized under the auspices of the parties, political harangues are here introduced into the programme as interludes. However, this particular kind of "mixture of politics and pleasure" is not very common in the United States. In the old days, before the Civil War, political picnics were in vogue, especially in the South, and were known by the name of "barbecues," be The word "barbecue," which means ox, pig, etc. , roasted whole, is very probably derived from the French *(burbe* a *queue),* although a native origin cause animals roasted whole, at a fire lighted in the open air for the occasion, were often consumed at them. The barbecues were the great social and political rendez-vous; the planters came to them with their wives and daughters and accompanied by a number of servants; the best political speakers of the district used them as a practising ground. Their eloquence was lavished as generously as the provisions on the assembled crowd. Often the debates were "joint" ones; political opponents feasted together and in the intervals indulged in oratorical tourneys. Sometimes this lasted for several days, and invitations were sent out beforehand for a "protracted" barbecue. In the South and in the West the barbecues still take place; occasionally the programme includes, besides the political speeches and the meals, athletic contests, dances, sports, horse races. In the East the barbecues are less common and not so picturesque; it is more a sort of fair for which the railroad companies consider it a good opportunity to organize excursion trains.

Lastly, another external device, and a very common one, which is used for manifestations in favour of the party and its candidates, is the display of political emblems which recall, symbolically or directly, the persons and the names of the candidates and the cause of the party. We find this practice already resorted to in the first presidential campaign which was conducted in a noisy fashion, amid violent competition, — the campaign of 1824; but the industry of the Old World had to be drawn on for obtaining the article, in the form of silk "presidential vests" made in France, stamped with the likenesses of the presidential candidates: Adams, Clay, and Jackson, to suit all tastes. In the present day American industry more than suffices to meet the demand, and sometimes exhibits great ingenuity and mechanical skill in the invention of party emblems. The most common ones are the badges, and especially the "buttons," small, round tin plates bearing the portraits of the candidates in enamel, with or without a motto.

is also assigned to it, from which is supposed to come the Spanish word *barbacda,* borrowed from the Aborigines by the first explorers of the New World. See a delightful description of the barbecues in Davis, *Recollections of Mississippi,* pp. 108, 2iH. Cf. also *Life of Yancey,* p. 330.

» Niles, Vol. XXVI, 69.

As soon as the election campaign opens everybody, old and young, men "worth millions of dollars" and ragamuffins who sell newspapers or black boots at street-crossings, adorn their buttonhole with a party "button," on which may be seen the picture of the great man who is candidate for the post of President or Governor, with the inscription: "lam for McKinley; are you?" or, "Silver is good enough," "16 to 1," "McKinley and protection." The political button, however, is only a variety of a decoration which has been in favour for some time in the United States and is adorned with maxims of every kind. Even in Congress grave legislators may be seen sporting a button with a motto containing, for instance, the following terse formula which sums up the whole morality of "politics ": "Don't kick." The " button" has become a craze which has invaded even the elementary schools, in which boys and girls cover themselves with a lot of buttons bearing inscriptions, some of which are anything but suited to the age and the sex of the children. In a good many places the school authorities were obliged to intervene and refuse admission to scholars decorated with "motto buttons." An exception, however, was made in favour of "political buttons," because they, as was said by the chairman of a school board which had taken prohibitory measures, "would tend to make the boys patriotic."

All these practices, which are meant to act on the imagination through the medium of the senses, do not quite exhaust the "Chinese business "; another set of practices may be included in it which try to impress the imagination through the intellect. These are the charges, the claims, the bets, and the straw votes. The " charges " are libellous accusations brought against the candidates of the opposite party. They occur so regularly in the course of each election campaign that nobody believes them: it is only "campaign lies. " Yet they are brought all the same; they resemble a firework which leaves nothing behind it, but for the moment it has made a noise. The "claims" are forecasts backed by figures which predict success for the party; they "claim " for it in advance so many votes, those or these counties, or such and such a State. A very carefully conducted canvass can no doubt furnish a trustworthy basis for estimating the coming vote; but these estimates or claims are always exaggerated with the object of VOL. II—*l* stimulating the ardour of the " workers " and the generosity of the subscribers to the party funds. There are certain highly skilful and extremely shrewd politicians who are looked on by many people as prophets able to lift at will the veil which conceals the electoral future. The estimate published on the eve of the election is often vouched for by the signature of one of these famous experts, and it is settled after a long conference of the executive committee of the party. The national committee itself is not above drawing up and publishing bulletins of claims in view of the presidential vote.

To confirm the belief in the success of the candidates of the party and to decide the waverers, bets laid on the candidates as on race-horses are largely resorted to. It is an old national habit, in the United States, to back one's opinion, even on the most trivial subjects, by laying a bet; formerly there was even a general formula: "I bet you a beaver hat." Now the phrase is simply "a hat." The custom of betting soon spread to elections, and in particular during the keenly contested presidential campaign of 1824, with heavy money stakes. At the outset bets in money were made mostly by the politicians, nay, even by statesmen of the first rank, such as Martin van Buren, for instance. His correspondence contains letters on this subject which might have been written by a bookmaker. Among the rest of the population the election bet came into fashion first of all in the form of harmless wagers in which the stake was the classic hat, a box of cigars, a bottle of wine, or certain grotesque performances which are much in vogue down to the present day, and which consist, for instance, in walking down the main street with one's coat turned inside out, in wheeling the winner in a barrow, or in rolling a pea along the pavement with a toothpick. In the last presidential campaign an enthusiastic admirer of Mr. McKinley pledged himself, it would Occasionally, however, something else was substituted for the beaver hat. The illustrious statesman, Hamilton, who was also a great advocate, was arguing one day before the court of the State of Vermont. One of his arguments did not commend itself to the judge, and the latter interrupted him with the remark: "You are wrong, Mr. Hamilton, I bet you a bowl of punch on it." "May it please your Honour," replied Hamilton, "/ never drink punch." The judge had a reputation of a contrary description. *(Travels through the northern part of the United States, in the year 1807 and 1808,* by E. A. Kendall, N. Y., Vol. 1809, III, p. 208.) Nilee, Vol. XXXVI, p. 332.

appear, to have all his teeth pulled out if Mr. McKinley was not elected. But alongside these playful proceedings the election bet also became a pretext for gambling in all classes of the population and among persons of all ages. This form of gambling is much stimulated by the party committees, who have made it a regular means of influencing the electors, by laying bets themselves, or through others, on their candidates; the more these candidates are backed and the longer the odds given, the more their success must appear certain to the electors who have not made up their minds. The committees therefore, to encourage the gambling, themselves provide the layers of the odds with money, and spend large sums on this account, which are afterward entered under "sundry election expenses" or some other vague heading. The law has intervened to prohibit election bets, which are often also used as a means of bribery. As early as 1839 a law was passed in this sense by the legislature of Maryland, making all bets or wagers about an election punishable by fine. At the present moment similar laws exist in a great number of States (New York, California, Ohio, Indiana, Michigan, Missouri, Wisconsin, New Jersey, Delaware, Connecticut, etc.), making persons who bet, or who shall become interested in the bet, liable to fine, imprisonment, to the loss of the right to vote or to be elected; but all these laws are a dead letter, they are never put in force.

The "straw votes " are a general rehearsal of the impending election, conducted in certain sections of the population or in certain localities for the purpose of eliciting the views of the electors. These polls are held on the stock exchange, in large factories, or other establishments containing a great number of electors; the vote is secret. Or a canvass is made, by a return of votes collected from house to house or by means of post cards addressed to a large body of electors. The result of these anticipating votes furnish "evidence " of the strength of the candidate and of the "hopeless " weakness of his rival. Being often taken in a genuine way, by a newspaper, for instance, for the purpose of gauging public opinion, these ballots are always apt to influence those electors who like to be on the winning side.

n

The extraordinary development of these electioneering methods which, by appealing now to the intelligence and now to the imagination, operate collectively on large masses of electors and appear to whirl away all classes of the population, with far greater force than in England, by no means excludes the direct action of man on man, so powerful in the old society of the mother-country. The arguments *ad hominem* which are addressed to the electors individually find plenty of scope in the United States, first of all in the classic form of the canvass, of the personal solicitation of votes. The importance of the canvass is somewhat diminished in America by the decisive role of the nomination, which discounts the result of the election and which makes the candidates bring their efforts to bear, not upon the electors, but upon the delegates to the convention. For instance, in the South where, owing to the traditional supremacy of the Democratic party, the nomination of the candidate is equivalent to election, personal canvassing is not much practised. But wherever parties are evenly matched, in all the "doubtful" States, it is carried on energetically. The *modus operandi* varies a good deal. The lower strata of the electorate are canvassed by paid "workers" (the law does not prohibit this as it does in England), who visit them in the evening to "devil out the voters," according to one expression. The workers strive not so much to argue with the electors as to make themselves pleasant; they shake hands with negroes, they invite the bystanders to have a drink; the offer is only too readily accepted: half-a-dozen are asked, and fifty present themselves; people hurry up from all sides as soon as the report spreads that a politician has come down and is standing treat. The canvasser is generally of a social status somewhat higher than that of the canvassed, but he is obliged to adapt himself to them, to descend to thenlevel. As the decisive moment approaches, redoubled efforts are made to win the "doubtful " electors, one by one; emissaries are sent to them who have a special influence over them, to whom they are under an obligation, or whom they wish or are obliged to stand well with for some reason or another. The minute reconnoissance of the positions made at the beginning of the campaign, in the form of a poll, has indicated who is to be taken in hand and in what way. In the rural districts, where everybody is known, with all their ins and outs, the emissary is clearly marked out; he takes charge of his man to put him in the right way, "he is horseshading him," as is said in the West. The canvassers of this sort are zealous auxiliaries who look for no reward but the success of the party and the satisfaction of having contributed to it. The Organization has the moral right to requisition, on the eve of the election, every faithful follower of the party for the work of conversion; and all respond to the pious appeal.

The candidate himself does not always take a personal part in the election; each candidate has his own method. Generally he pays a visit to the most important electors; but if he is an inferior man, from a social and moral standpoint, as is often the case with municipal or legislative candidates, it is better for him not to meet the respectable electors. Instead of this, he will go from one drinking-saloon to another to ingratiate himself with the frequenters of the bars. A candidate who is careful of his dignity shrinks from doing this, and acts on the electors through the stump. In the cities, however, it is not so necessary, nor is it easy for the candidate to bestow many marks of personal attention on the electors; he has no points of contact with the heterogeneous and floating populations of the large cities; he would not know how to address them, what to say to them. Personal action will be more effectively exercised over them through the men of the Organization, of the Machine, who are rubbing up against them every day, who always have their net spread to catch them. In the rural districts, on the other hand, the candidate must show himself. He is exempt from the baby-kissing business, which does not exist in America, but he is not at liberty to shirk that of hand-shaking; he is obliged to stop at the streetcrossings, to chat with people, to show that he has no pride about him. A good many candidates proceed with method in The expression "to horseshade," "to be horse-shaded," which means to talk politics, is derived from the habit which country folk had, when they came to church on Sunday, of putting their horse in a shady corner and sitting down there themselves to discuss political affairs with a friend, whom they met at this great rural rendez-vous.

their country rounds: provided with a carriage and a stock of cigars, they visit all the electors, and if they are not known in the district, they get a member of the local committee to accompany them. The visitors come in, the candidate is introduced, a cigar is offered, and a brief conversation is started, the remembrance of which will perhaps be fondly treasured up by the inmates. Later on, the good woman of the house will say to a guest: "Two or three months ago, the very chair in which you are now sitting was occupied by Congressman So and So." There is, however, a category of candidates debarred by custom from intervening personally in the election campaigns, viz., the candidates for the Presidency; their greatness is supposed to prevent them taking the field; their adherents may move heaven and earth, but they themselves must remain in the background and calmly await the popular verdict. Yet this rule or custom has been more than once departed from; several presidential candidates have descended into the lists, by hurrying from one State to another, by making speeches, and giving innumerable hand-shakes to the thousands of men who had flocked together to listen to them or to see them.

The civilities of the candidate and the endless variety of arguments employed by the canvassers and their volunteer assistants to induce the elector to vote their way, act, or are supposed to act, by free persuasion. But sometimes these arguments are supplemented or replaced by the force of the authority wielded over the elector by the person who asks for his vote. This form of pressure is mostly exerted by employers of labour. It would appear to be not so uncommon in the East, which is the great stronghold of capitalism; in the West the independent spirit of the workmen makes them less inclined to submit to it. The foreman or the masters give the workman to understand that the rate of their wages, or their engagement itself in the factory or workshop, will depend on the defeat or the success of the candidate; if personal exhortations are not ventured on, they are conveyed to the workmen in a quasi During the presidential campaign of 1896 the "silver" candidate, Mr. Bryan, led the attack in person and " beat the record " of all his predecessors by the number of miles which he travelled, of the speeches which he delivered, and of the hand-shakes which he distributed.

anonymous manner by handing to them on pay-day, in an envelope containing the money, a little puff of the candidate or of the party favoured by the employers; or bills are posted up in the workshop stating that if a particular candidate is elected the wages will fall, or the factory will be closed or have to restrict its out-put. In a good many States (of the West as well as of the East) the legislator has felt bound to intervene and prohibit the use by the employers of "pay envelopes " containing the names of candidates or political mottoes or arguments, and the exhibiting in their establishments of placards or notices intended to influence the vote of the workman. m

Lastly, the most direct argument addressed to the personal interest of the elector consists, as in other countries, of the purchase of votes for cash. Less common than is generally supposed in Europe, bribery plays a considerable part in the political life of America, and an increasing one. The reader will remember how inexpensive elections were before the Civil War. It was only in three or four large cities, with New York at their head, which already contained a wretched population exposed to the temptations of ignorance and vice, that money was had recourse to for getting votes at elections. But after the war, the exasperation of party spirit and the extraordinary development of the spoils system, which made booty the sole object of election contests, led to bribery being used as a regular weapon. The rapid growth of the cities, inevitably accompanied by the rise of a poverty-stricken and semi-criminal class, the arrival of wretched emigrants from Europe, and the extension of the suffrage to the besotted negroes, had, in their turn, swelled the venal contingents. The appearance on the political stage of the rich "corporations" and, in general, of the big industrial and financial concerns trying to pack the legislative assemblies, the executive, and the judiciary, greatly helped to supply the funds required for buying votes. The economy of the American electoral system, which makes the result of the presidential election depend on a few "pivotal" States, whatever the distribution of the whole popular vote in the Union, has facilitated the concentration of bribery operations, and thereby put a premium on them. These States, ranked among the "doubtful" ones, four or five in number, are "drenched with money" during the presidential campaign for buying the "floaters," the "wavering" electors who sell themselves to the highest bidder. Elsewhere bribery is also practised, but in a very unequal fashion. In some parts of the Union electoral manners are tolerably pure, but in others bribery is a permanent institution. And what is remarkable and somewhat unexpected is that the cities are not the sole or even the principal seat of it. Even in the contaminated cities, bribery is not always individual: the "workers," the small "leaders," rather are bought, who wield an influence over a certain number of poor electors, and make them vote as they tell them to without paying them expressly for their vote. The parties often secure, in much the same way, the votes of the members of the workmen's trade-unions: the leaders "sell them out" to the parties, without the workmen having a suspicion of it. The electors who deliberately sell themselves belong, in the cities, mostly to the dregs of the population. In some cases, when the bargain has been struck before the polling-day, the vendors are put under lock and key up to the moment when they deliver the goods; they are collected a day or two beforehand in one place and kept there to be brought to the poll afterwards under proper escort, as was done formerly in England in the rotten boroughs. This is especially the case with the negroes in the Southern cities. The coloured electors are bought wholesale and retail. Yet, thanks to the progress which the negroes have already The reader is aware that the President and the Vice-President are chosen by the College of Electors, in which each State has as many votes as it has Senators and Representatives in Congress, and that these votes are really given by the Electors of the party which has obtained a majority in the respective State, at the popular vote. As the populous States are the most strongly represented in this College, a very small majority obtained by one party in these States can give it a majority in the Electoral College, although it may not have secured, as indeed has happened on more than one occasion, a majority of the popular suffrages in the whole Union.

This practice was known in England by the name of "cooping" or "bottling. " Cf the *Report on the Municipal Vorimrations in England and Wales*, of 1835, Vol. IV, pp. 2.;10 and 2488, and the report of the *Select Committee on Parliamentary and Municipal Electionn*, 18f9 *(Blue Books*, 1868-6i, Vol. VIII, p. 83). The term " cooping " is also used in the United States. made in a moral and intellectual point of view, and which promises well for the future of this sorely tried race, the number of venal coloured electors is growing less; there are negroes impressed with their dignity as citizens who cannot be bought for any consideration.

The most shameless venality is often met with in the country districts, particularly in the States of the Atlantic seaboard, nay, even in New England, inhabited by the descendants of the Puritans. Votes are sold there openly like an article of commerce; there is a regular market quotation for them. And it is not only needy people who make a traffic of their votes, but well-to-do farmers, of American stock, pious folk who always go to church on Sunday. If the farmer's son is an elector and dwells under the paternal roof, the father receives the price of his vote and of that of their "help," who is under a sort of moral obligation to vote for the same candidate as his master. A good many would not take a bribe from the party which they regard as hostile; they keep faith with their own party, but they none the less demand money for their vote, in the form of an indemnity for their trouble, for loss of time, and travelling expenses. In some country districts a quarter or a third of the electors make money out of their votes. The proportion of venal electors in the whole Union, town and country, has been estimated at more than eleven per cent, from special enquiries carried on in different localities.

Bribery was up till lately carried on with all the more facility that the vote was not absolutely secret; the buyer could follow his man to the ballot-box and see if the latter had really put his voting-paper in it. In the same way the foremen in factories kept an eye on their workmen. Electors were even exposed to intimidation and personal violence at the Sometimes the proportion is still higher. I have seen the reports of the local organizations addressed to a State Committee, of a rather "doubtful" State, one month before the presidential election of 1806. These reports referred in more or less explicit terms to districts where it was necessary to buy votes: some said in diplomatic language that it would be advisable to keep the money in hand for the end of the campaign; the others gave straight out the exact number of the electors who would sell their votes; in one country district, out of 17.3 electors, there were 101 to be bought.

Cf. " The alarming proportion of Venal Voters," by J. J. McCook, *Forum*, Vol. 15; "The Sale of Votes," by J. B. Harrison, *Century*, Vol. 47; "Money in Practical Politics," by J. W. Jenks, *ibid.*, October, 1892. hands of desperate election agents, who prevented them from voting as they liked or forced another "ticket" on them. The scandals which attended the taking of the vote under these circumstances, and the wholesale bribery which marked the presidential election of 1888, were at last too much for public opinion, and contributed to the adoption in almost every State, in the course of a few years, of the great electoral reform known by the name of the "Australian Ballot." The new method of voting, thus called because it is in force in the English colonies of Australia (as also, by the way, in the mothercountry), ensures absolute secrecy for the vote by the plan of official voting-papers, distributed exclusively by official agency and deposited by each voter in such a way as to prevent the contents being seen. The names of the candidates of all the parties are declared, in the manner and within the period prescribed, to the public authority, which classifies them all on a single voting-paper printed under its directions. Each elector who comes up to vote receives from the election officers a copy of the voting-paper, withdraws into an isolated compartment to mark on the list the candidates of his choice, and gives up the paper folded in such a way as to avoid any particular signs. All persons other than those recording their vote are kept at a distance; the public is forbidden to approach within fifty to a hundred yards of the railed enclosure behind which the voting is going on. The "Australian" system has, in fact, put an end to the open intimidation and to the coercion which were practised on the electors; the elections are now, with few exceptions, conducted in an orderly manner; the public market for votes which was held, in New York and in other large cities, outside the pollingplaces, has also been put down. But bribery goes on just the same and has not diminished: means have been discovered of "beating" the law; devices have been invented which enable the bribers to assure themselves that the bribe-taker has really performed his part of the bargain. In other cases the elector's vote is not bought, but his abstention from voting, which is easy to find out; electors of this kind form a rather Formerly the elections were often disturbed by sanguinary brawls, in which firearms were even sometimes used, especially in the South. Similar eases still occur, but rarely. numerous class humorously called "fishermen," they are prevented from voting because they have gone out fishing. Or what is still safer and simpler, the elector is paid not to apply for registration; he will not be able to vote even if the other side succeeds in making a convert of him.

While adopting the Australian Ballot, a good many States have added to the penal provisions directed against electoral bribery. The law of Indiana has even given the elector who has taken a bribe to vote or to abstain from voting, the right of suing the briber for three hundred dollars. Following the example of the English Corrupt Practices Act, of 1883, which is fondly imagined in the United States to have banished bribery in England to an almost antediluvian past, the legislatures of several States have dealt with the expenses of the candidates. The law of New York compels the candidates to submit to the proper authority, after the election, a detailed account supported by affidavit of all the moneys contributed or expended by them, or through others, directly or indirectly, to secure their election. As the law imposes this obligation on the candidates themselves only, the latter hide behind the committees, stating that they have made over nearly all their money to them, and the committees are not obliged to render an account of the way in which it has been spent. The legislatures, guided by the politicians, have thus doomed the law to failure. Its only effect is to disclose the total of the sums spent by the candidates and to prove, what has long been well known, that the candidate's expenditure often exceeds the amount of the emoluments attache to the office. The laws of the States of Massachusetts, Michigan, Kansas, and Colorado have gone farther: they require the committees as well as the candidates to render an account; but they also content themselves with the purely moral sanction of public opinion, leaving the candidates and the committees to spend what they think fit, as before. In a third group of States, a positive sanction has been added in the form of provisions prescribing a maximum of election expenditure which cannot be exceeded on pain of fine and invalidation of the election. In certain States (Ohio, Missouri, Minnesota) the maximum is based on the number of the electors; in other States (California, Nevada) it consists of a percentage on the salary of the post aspired to by the candidate, and on a scale which rises with the duration of the elective term. In the State of Montana the maximum is a fixed amount. A good many of these laws are exceedingly minute in their provisions, and would leave no loophole for the candidates and the committees if they were enforced. But this is not done. It may be said that they never are enforced. Some candidates swear to false statements of their expenditure, while others often look.on their obligation to render a detailed account as a joke, and make it up in a humorous way. Besides, the strict application of the law would be impeded by the fact that, as a rule, there are several candidates on one ticket, and that the committee incurs on behalf of the whole ticket many items of expenditure which cannot be divided; it would, consequently, be difficult to apportion the exact share of each candidate for the purpose of ascertaining whether the legal maximum has really been exceeded or not.

The bribery of the electors has its corollary and complement in the bribery of the election officers which conduct the ballot. Up till lately this form of corruption was even more far-reaching, at least in its effects, than the purchase of individual votes. Dishonest "election inspectors," suborned on behalf of a candidate, altered the result of the ballot for his benefit, assigning him a majority of the voting-papers although he had received a minority of the votes. The methods by which this result is attained are the same as those which we have seen practised in the primaries: fraudulent votes (recorded by electors who are disqualified, or who vote under an assumed name, or several times over) are deliberately admitted; votingpapers bearing the name of the favoured candidate are slipped into the ballot-box; or during the counting of the vote he is credited with more, and his rival, who has really won the election, with fewer votes than they have received, the one is "counted in" and the other "counted out" by the favour of the election board. In some large cities the election was falsified not so much by the purchase of votes as by these frauds which completed the registration frauds and constituted a more Thus in a city of the State of New York a candidate for the post of alderman submitted the following account: "for newspapers $10, janitor service $15, hacks and carryalls 520, refreshments and cigars $200, for renewing old acquaintances and forming new ones $900; total $1136." expeditious and less expensive mode of procedure. In the South these practices were introduced, after the Civil War, to "save civilization" from the new coloured electors; but gradually people got into the habit of committing the voting frauds at the expense of white political opponents. The Australian Ballot has remedied this abuse not only by supplying official voting-papers, but by providing that the ballot-boxes shall be placed in the voting-room so as to be under the eyes of the public; that they shall be examined before the polling begins, and that the parties or the rival candidates shall be at liberty to station watchers and challengers within the polling rooms; and, lastly, that the counting of the vote shall take place in public and forthwith. These measures have stopped the frauds to a very considerable extent, but they have not been sufficient to put an end to them altogether. To make them quite impossible, in spite of the dishonesty of "election inspectors" and the want of vigilance of the public, voting machines have been invented in which the elector has only to touch a knob or knobs to record his vote for one or more candidates, and in which an automatic counter registers the number of votes obtained by each candidate. It appears that there are still technical difficulties to be overcome to make the machines thoroughly answer their purpose, while safeguarding the secrecy of the vote; yet voting machines have already been used in a certain number of elections, and not without success.

No doubt the most effective invention would be one that would touch the public conscience, for if the voting frauds and the bribery of electors occur so frequently, and if they are inadequately repressed by the law which, however, has no lack of prohibitory clauses, if the candidate ventures to make a joke of the enactment which requires from him an account of his election expenditure — if all this is possible, the fault must lie in the tolerance shown by public opinion. Not that public opinion approves these practices; on the contrary, they are most strongly reprobated, and not only by the public in general; the better set of politicians, with certain exceptions, also look on them with disgust. But this is more in theory, Except in the South, where most of the States have not adopted the Australian Ballot.
in principle. When it comes to fighting the opposite party, people shut their eyes; they acquiesce in buying "floaters" as in one of those melancholy necessities with which "politics," as well as war, is fraught, but which must be faced if the battle is to be won. And it must be won, for if you are a "man," an American, you cannot let yourself be beaten; even if you leave yourself out of account, there is the sacred cause of the party whose triumph must be assured at all hazards, for the salvation of the country. The opposite party resorts to bribery; then why should not your own party, which is the good, the just one, also benefit by it? If the other side would leave off bribing, one would be only too pleased to follow its example; but no one will be the first to disarm. And so it comes about that men who are perfectly honourable in private life stoop to organize electoral bribery, to superintend the details of it, or, at all events, to knowingly supply the material for it; they subscribe to the "campaign fund," with more than a suspicion that part of their money will be spent in buying votes. The elector who sells himself, including the well-to-do and pious farmer of New Hampshire, has still fewer scruples: he has been brought up by the Caucus and Machine system in the notion that "politics" is a " business" in which, as in any other business, some people buy commodities and others sell them; and why should he let people who will make money out of his vote have it for nothing? IV
The money spent in bribery adds very perceptibly to the election expenditure considered as legitimate and which by itself is very heavy, in spite of the Australian Ballot, which has curtailed it by introducing official voting-papers prepared by and at the cost of the State, of the city, etc. The legitimate heads of expenditure are as follows: the hire of halls; the payments made to speakers, to canvassers, to "workers" of every kind; the making up and distribution of "political literature"; advertising, postage, and telegrams; the distribution of campaign emblems and "buttons," uniforms, banners, and torches used in processions and parades; the conveyance of electors on the polling-day, etc. In addition to the expenses actually incurred, large sums remain in the hands of the go-betweens, of the agents, but they none the less help to swell the total. Election expenses are, in consequence, extremely high in the United States. Where does the money come from? It is supplied by the candidates, by the office-holders, and by private donors. The candidates, who have, as a rule, already paid the party organization a certain sum for their nomination, contribute their quota toward the election expenses; sometimes the contribution, which is often pretty high and perhaps exceeds the whole salary of the office, is voluntary; sometimes it is levied under the "assessments" system. In some States (for instance, Massachusetts, Montana) the legislator has taken the trouble to forbid the committees to demand "contributions" from the candidates and the latter to comply with the demand — a platonic prohibition, as the candidate has a direct interest in coming to an understanding with the committee. On the other hand, the legislator of New York, acting perhaps on the saying "we preach what we practise," which was the preface to the famous formula of "the spoils to the victor," and on the more recent utterance of the present boss of Tammany Hall, who declared that "they the Tammany men were not hypocrites,"— the legislator of New York provides that "the authorized representatives of the political party, of the organization, or of the association, to which the candidate belongs," shall have the right of demanding money contributions from the latter. The presidential candidates themselves subscribe to the "campaign fund "; if they are not rich, they must, and this applies to all candidates, have rich friends ready to step into the breach and to loosen their purse-strings. Often the candidate, to forward his election campaign, launches into personal expenditure independently of that which will be incurred with his money by the committee.

The office-holders, who are liable to the tribute of "assessments" for the benefit of the party, have been a little less squeezed since the law of 1883 has taken the federal employees These last categories, as well as the payment of canvassers, are, as the reader will remember, declared illegal by the English law, and would *ipso facto* unseat the M. P. on whose behalf they had been iucurred.
appointed by competitive examinations out of the clutches of the parties, and has forbidden the officials of the Union to demand and to collect "political contributions " in the federal de-

partments. The law is sometimes infringed and often evaded; to avoid coming within its scope, the party committees who ask for subscriptions are composed of persons who are not federal office-holders, and they do not solicit the contributions in the offices themselves. Yet, as I have already had occasion to remark, the law, as a whole, has checked the abuse of the assessments in the comparatively limited sphere to which it applied; the mischief is no longer epidemic, it occurs in a sporadic fashion only in the federal service. But in the service of the States and the municipal service, the *personnel* of which is much more numerous, there is no legal obstacle to the levy of the assessments, and no means of refusing them with impunity; and they are still demanded and paid. It is a remarkable fact that often they are not paid solely by the office-holders, federal and others, belonging to the party in power, but also by the employees belonging to the party in opposition; for they "feel that the desk, not the man at it, owes just so much to the party in power." Such is the hold which the custom of assessments has obtained over the public mind that it has become, in the eyes of many people, almost a part of the natural order of things.

The gifts of private individuals who are not candidates nor office-holders make up a very large proportion of the "campaign fund." It is on the committees, each in its own sphere, from the national committee downward, that the duty devolves of procuring these offerings to the sacred cause of the party. In the very great majority of cases they are due to anything but disinterested considerations; they are a pure speculation, an investment of money which later on should yield a good return in favours that the men elected with the money of the donors have at their disposal. First and foremost come the representatives of the big industrial or financial concerns, "corporations," or individual capitalists, which by a heavy contribution to the "campaign funds" obtain a sort of mortgage over the future administration or legislature; we are already aware that for the sake of greater security many a *Eleventh Report of the U. 8. Civil Service Commission*, p. 227.

corporation subscribes to the funds of both parties at the same time. Wealthy private individuals give money with the same object, — to establish a claim on the gratitude of the future administration which will repay them with honours for themselves, extending to a seat in the Cabinet or an embassy, or with places for their friends and their proteges. Lastly, there is a category of donors who expect and desire nothing but the success of the party; some subscribe out of pure "patriotism," pure devotion to the "cause," while others are actuated by sporting motives which make them enjoy a good fight for its own sake; they "plunge" for their party as they would for a race-horse. More often than not both kinds of motives, of "patriotism" and of sporting excitement, are blended in the minds of the donors and make them submit cheerfully to pecuniary sacrifices, which sometimes reach a high figure.

V

But still greater and more profitable than these funds subscribed by zealous partisans, is the capital which consists of the feeling of loyalty to the party, diffused throughout the great mass of the electorate. Not to mention numerous employees of all classes who owe their position to the party, and aspirants to offices, several times as numerous, who hope to obtain places through it, — most of the electors are bound to one or the other of the two great parties by various ties, the strongest of which are personal associations, the company which a man keeps, tradition, habit, the prejudice created by these factors or engendered by considerations of private and public interest of a more or less rational or irrational kind. After all, the name of the party is its own justification, in the eyes of millions of electors. They say, with a well-known politician, an ex-Senator of New York, "I am a Democrat" (or "I am a Republican," as the case may be), just as a believer says, to explain and justify his faith, "I am a Christian!" The reader knows how, and through what political circumstances, party devotion, which is rather an unreasoning sentiment all the world over, has been intensified in the United States and raised to the level of a dogma, — VOL. II —2 A the dogma of "regularity," which makes the party creed consist in voting the "straight party ticket," whatever it may be. The sins against the religion of the party are sins against the ticket. They fall under two heads, "scratching " and " bolting." A member of the party who withholds his vote from one or some of the candidates entered on the party ticket, while voting for the rest, is guilty of "scratching": he "scratches," he strikes out the names of the candidates to whom he objects. The elector who altogether rejects the ticket adopted by the Organization of his party commits the graver offence of "bolting"; his perversity makes him a "bolter," an apostate. Nevertheless, the theologians of the religion of the party discuss the point whether there can be cases in which bolting may not be considered as a deadly sin. As for setting limits to the obligation of blindly voting the ticket, the doctrine has never gone beyond platonic declarations like that of the following resolution, voted in 1880 by the Republican State convention of Massachusetts: " The duty of all Republicans loyally to support the candidates of the party, and the duty of nominating conventions to present candidates who are acceptable to all Republicans, are reciprocal duties, of equal force and obligation."

The exceptions are scarcely admitted in theory, while the rule is strictly upheld. Directly the candidates are proclaimed by the convention, their rivals and their opponents are bound to submit, to rally to them, and even to fight by their side and for them. This is called "falling into line." And the higher the political position of a member of the party, the more imperative is his duty to fall into line: he has perhaps violently opposed the candidate before his formal nomination, accusing him of every possible crime; but as soon as that candidate has received the investiture of the party Organization, he "takes the stump" on his behalf, and is at a loss for terras in which to extol his virtues and his talents. The humble party follower never has an opportunity of hearing the candidates on the ticket criticised by any one but open enemies belonging to the opposite party, who are of course the fathers of lies. He turns a deaf ear to their perfidious remarks, he preserves his party immaculateness, without a single lapse, which enables him to say proudly: "I am a thorough Republican," "I am a lifelong Democrat." He declares: "I have never in my life scratched a ticket," even when the candidates on it were as bad as they could be; he makes the assertion with the pride of the grandee of Spain who, when refusing to deliver up Hernani, says to the king: "Voici mon noble aieul. Il vecut soixante ans, gardant la foi juree meme aux Juifs." The intensity of these feelings of party loyalty varies somewhat with the period and the social environment. In the "presidential years," when the chief magistracy of the Republic has to be won, party loyalty will stop at no sacrifices and will swallow all scruples to attain the end. It pays less heed now than ever to the merit of the candidates on the ticket at whose head is the presidential candidate. In order not to jeopardize the success of the ticket, which represents an indivisible whole, the faithful follower of the party will vote blindly for any one who comes after that candidate; he will vote even for a "yellow dog." Hence, this exceptional year is often called, from that point of view, "the yellow dog year." As regards the intensity of party loyalty according to the social environment, it is greater in the East and, in general, in the country districts. In the East, tradition, hereditary habits, are more powerful; social relations are more crystallized, so to speak; in short, the East is more conservative. Besides, the party Organization, which keeps party loyalty alive like a fire, is more developed in the East than in the West. The mode of life in the country districts encourages mental stagnation in political matters as well as in other respects. The sources of information are indifferent; only one newspaper is read, when it is read, —the official newspaper of the party. New ideas have difficulty in making their way. In the absence of distractions politics are a good deal talked in the villages, contrary to what takes place in the cities; but people only get more confirmed in their traditional views, they edify each other in the old creed of the party. Social pressure, which is much heavier in the country than in the cities, and respect for the world's opinion mount guard around that creed; often it is only at the risk of losing the esteem and the confidence of your neighbours that you can break with your political party. This state of the public mind, which, as it were, congeals the electoral masses, leads " This is my noble ancestor. He lived to the age of sixty, keeping his plighted word eyen with Jews." to the formation of "Republican States," and of "Democratic States," according as the traditional preponderance belongs to one or the other party, and gives these parties "normal majorities."

If this was the case everywhere and always, throughout the Union, the party Organizations would, of course, have nothing to do. But the solid layer of electors permanently attached to the parties is not only enveloped with a floating mass of other electors, it is also liable to be broken into itself. Party loyalty, without being affected by bribery, yields sometimes to personal influences, at others, and more often, to considerations of a general kind, or which have the appearance of such. The first case is when the person of the candidate prevails over the habits of the elector as a party-man; if he dislikes the candidate of his own party, he " scratches " his name on the list — a practice which, without being common, is becoming less and less rare. Or he is attracted by the candidate of the opposite party, perhaps by a single candidate on a long list, and he votes for him. In this way it happens that the whole ticket of a party is beaten, except one candidate, who gets in at the end of the rival list; or, again, one of the candidates on the winning ticket obtains a far greater number of votes than his fellow-combatants, he "runs ahead of his ticket," owing, no doubt, to the greater popularity which he enjoys with the electors of his own party, but often also to the votes given him by members of the opposite party. Perhaps it is the popularity or the local reputation of the candidate, his personal "magnetism," or perhaps even that of his champion on the stump, a "great campaigner," which makes the elector change his mind. In the local elections personal considerations carry very great weight, whereas in the other elections the American elector is not so liable as his English congener to be carried away by them. For, as the reader is already aware, the individuality of the American candidate is, as a rule, much fainter; it is not so much his personal and concrete qualifications that appeal to the elector, as the abstract entity which goes by the name of the "ticket." Often personal preferences themselves, when they are uppermost in the elector's mind, assume a somewhat abstract form; he votes for a candidate whom he does not know and whose political views he does not usually share, solely because the candidate in question belongs to his State or county, he votes for him out of "State pride" or "county pride"; it is the small parochial prejudice which expands into an abstract conception in his mind. In the choice of candidates for the Presidency this mental tendency is often traded on; a candidate belonging to a "doubtful" State is selected in the hope that a good many electors who generally vote for the opposite party will give their votes to this presidential candidate out of "State pride," and increase his chance of success.

Party loyalty is far more seriously impaired by the trend of events, by the new political or simply economic conjunctures which disturb the elector's peace of mind. He feels that he is threatened, or believes that the country is threatened, by what has already happened or is likely to happen, and in his fright he darts out of the beaten party track wherein he is wont to walk. Economic perturbations are those which put party loyalty to the severest test; the ordeal is too trying in the case of many electors. An industrial or commercial depression, a bad harvest, carries disaffection into the elector's mind. The mirage of a universal prosperity to be brought about by some infallible specific, such as the unlimited issue of paper money or the free coinage of silver, is rushed madly after by masses of electors. It is, in fact, a sort of contagious madness; hence the term "craze" is applied to these electoral convulsions. When a "craze" sets in, it sweeps through the ranks of the parties like a hurricane through a forest, uprooting giant trees in its blind fury. Apart from the more or less unusual cases of a "craze," of late years there have occurred almost periodical reactions against the party in power, caused mostly by economic troubles. The reaction breaks out with extraordinary rapidity and intensity. There is no need to wait for the next presidential election; in less than two years, at the first congressional election after the advent of the new President, universal suffrage administers an exemplary correction to the party which it has installed in power, or even gives a majority to the opposite party. Thus, at the presidential election of 1892 the Democrats won with more than 5,500,000 votes; at the congressional elections of 1894 they lost nearly 1,200,000 of them, — a fall which placed them in a minority of 104 in the House against 245 Republican Representatives and 7 Populists. These revulsions are prompted partly by a feeling akin to that of the Buddhist, who beats his idol when it has not granted his prayers, and partly by the more or less vague hope that a change of the party in power and of politics will bring about an improvement in business, etc. In England we have also come across a category of electors who are governed by these considerations, and who vote sometimes for one party, sometimes for another. But in the United States these electors are far more numerous, because the economic situation is much less stable than in the old country. Under the pressure of circumstances of one kind or another, with or without good reason, the current of opinion turns towards a certain party, creates or develops for its benefit a "feeling" which mounts like a tidal wave, submerging everything that it meets. The analogy of the action has led to the transfer of the expression "tidal wave " to the result itself, and to the application of this term to the election which has given the winning side an overwhelming majority. Sometimes the tidal wave falls as rapidly as it has risen, sometimes it lasts for a time; having begun to flow, for instance, at the congressional elections, it reaches a still higher level at the next presidential election, and then subsides altogether. Capricious and undefinable as the tidal wave is, its course is, to some extent, regulated by the communities through which it passes; at one time it is impetuous, at another it moves more slowly. The West is the region where it displays the most force; the equality of social conditions which prevails in this vast tract of country allows the " feeling" to spread without hindrance from one person to another, like a prairie fire, whereas in the East it is interrupted, is stopped, by the barriers arising out of social divisions.

As the federal, State, and local elections are practically mixed up, and all the candidates of the party are brought together on a single ticket, the elector is generally inclined to vote for them in a lump, to put a "straight ticket" in the ballot-box. This confusion, which is due both to the material and to the moral connection established by the party between the different elections, forms, as we are already aware, one of the strongest guarantees for loyalty to the party, along the whole line. Special combinations of circumstances may, however, sever this connection in the mind of the elector and prompt him to divide his vote, by voting for the local candidates of one party and for the candidates for the Presidency and the Vice-Presidency of the Union nominated by the opposite party, and who, owing to this, will perhaps be elected with a "tidal wave" majority. Thus, for instance, at the presidential election of 1896 a number of New York Democrats, frightened at the probable consequences of the silverite programme adopted by the candidate of their party, Mr. Bryan, decided, in order to save the country from a financial catastrophe, to vote for his rival, Mr. McKinley; but at the same time they voted, in accordance with their old habit, the Tammany Hall ticket for the local candidatures. An elector who is thus guilty of a partial infidelity to his party is said to vote a "split ticket." Splitting the ticket is becoming more and more common in local elections, to the detriment of the party; the elector looks, more than formerly, to the personal merit of the municipal candidates, and not to their party label.

Lastly, if breaches are made in party loyalty through certain conjunctures, it is also sometimes undermined by the absence of all special conjunctures: when there are no points of disagreement between the parties, when the latter being void of principles and ideas live only for themselves, when there is nothing to distinguish them one from the other apart from the names which they assume. Party fetishism in that case flourishes inside the parties as strongly as ever, but the state of demoralization to which they are reduced puts a premium on desertion as well as on the formation of new political sects, of "third parties," which are a refuge to honest and often absurd convictions thirsting for the truth, to vague discontent in search of a fulcrum or a lever for action. This, again, is all so much injury inflicted on party loyalty.

The lapses of the feeling of party loyalty are far from being the only form assumed by the electoral fluctuations which I have just described. I have considered them in this aspect because it is more easy to observe the ebb and flow on the shore than in the void of space. In reality the floating mass of electors is only partly derived from the solid mass of party Like the " Know-Nothings," for instance, who arose amid the demoralization of the old parties before the war. The Populist party, recently founded in analogous circumstances, may also serve as an example.

followers; irrespective of the independent and critically minded electors, who are daily growing more numerous within the parties, there is a very considerable number of electors who are in a continuous state of oscillation, so to speak, drifting hither and thither with events. They embody, in political life, the leading trait of the American character, which is instability, — mobility of temperament side by side with a conservative mind. This contradiction, from which no human society is exempt, and which is elicited with special force in democracies by the very form of their government, is brought to a pitch in the United States by the national temperament, the most full of contrasts. And it is this contradiction that the party Organiza' tion has to contend with and which it again exploits. All its efforts, during the electoral period which we have just been reviewing, are directed to this twofold end. The campaign of meetings, of "documents," of processions, and of parades, of acts of pressure of every kind, is meant to turn to account, for the benefit of the respective party, the fund both of immobility and instability which lies in a tangled heap in the electors' minds: the campaign work draws out the feeling of loyalty which is there, though in a latent state; it combats the apathy which envelops this feeling like an outer husk; it revives old prejudices and adapts them to new sets of circumstances; it raises barriers against invasions from outside and restores the balance of minds seized with a "craze," or fascinated by a programme or a man; it sets in motion the floating elements to draw them to its side; it decides the waverers; it lays hold of the weak; it upsets the "normal majorities," and starts or helps on a "tidal wave." In the eminently unstable state of equilibrium presented by the American political temperament, the party which puts forth, in the direction referred to, the most efforts and in a more methodical way, will have the best chance of getting the most votes for itself out of the more or less inert or more or less floating electoral mass, independently of the intrinsic merit of the cause or of the principles which this party represents, or of the force of time-honoured prejudices which protects it. The party which relies on this merit or on this force alone will inevitably be worsted by that which devotes itself to "getting out" the vote, as the saying goes. From this point of view the fate of party contests, however deep the convictions or however ardent the passions to which they give rise, depends on organization. VI

The success of the efforts made to "get out the vote" will, however, be incomplete if care is not taken, at the eleventh hour, to "get out" the voters. Apathy and want of public spirit are so great with many electors that they would abstain from voting if they were left to themselves on the polling-day. The chairmen of the committees write them reminders on the eve of it; on the day itself special messengers, "runners," are despatched to visit them in their homes and, perhaps, to put gentle constraint on them to induce them to move; in the country districts messengers on horseback ride from one farm to another, etc. It is the same as in England. Yet the American elector shows more eagerness to vote. The notion of the duty of voting is more common in the United States, perhaps not so much from the fact that the civic conscience is more enlightened there, as owing to the civic " cant" which, to a certain extent, prevails in the American democracy. The excessive use of the elective system, which necessitates constant appeals to the electors, which demands unremitting exertions to win their good graces, has developed in American political life, to a greater degree than elsewhere, the verbiage about the greatness of the people, about the august majesty of the citizen, about his sacred rights and duties, etc. With these grand words constantly dinned into his head and with a genuine appreciation of them, but wholly wrapped up in his affairs, the American elector readily cherishes a platonic cult for his civic duties. He considers that he owes it to himself to profess this cult, although he has not the time nor the inclination to be a minister of it; and he thinks he puts himself right with his conscience when he goes to deposit his voting-paper on the day of the poll, —the voting-paper prepared for him and without him, — as one goes to church on the day of a great festival. It is a testimonial of piety as well, of civic piety, which he delivers to himself; and, as he can get it cheap, he is quite ready to join in the ritual performance of the vote, which is the sum and substance of his civic religion. Again, nowhere is the elector so canvassed as he is by the party Organization in the United States. This twofold pressure put on the elector reaches its height in the presidential years. The stake involved in the presidential election always appears to the citizen too great for him to hold aloof, especially when with this election is bound up some grave problem of national politics which affect the primordial interests, material or moral, of the country. The party Organization, in its turn, moves heaven and earth at this election.

The result is that the vote in the presidential years yields very high proportions — as much as 95 per cent of the total electorate. The maximum is reached in the " doubtful" States, where the parties fight tooth and nail over the slender majority which may issue from the contest; for instance, in Indiana the parties manage to bring from 90 per cent to 95 per cent of the electors to the poll. It should be noted, however, that the total of 100 per cent represents only electors on the register, that is to say, under the American system, those only who have got on it of their own accord. A good many, in fact, abstain from registering out of political indifference or for other reasons; for instance, in New York it is notorious that a considerable number of citizens avoid it in order to escape from service on juries and from the tax-collector, as the electoral register serves as a basis for settling the lists of jurymen and tax-payers. The consequent divergence between the electoral population and the registered electors somewhat impairs the value of the high proportions of voters. Again, the small number of voters does not always bear the moral and political significance usually attributed to the practice of abstaining from voting. Thus, in certain Southern States, for instance in Mississippi, the proportion of 35 per cent to 40 per cent for the number of voters is considered a good maximum: there is no need of a better, the Democratic party in this State possesses such an overwhelming majority that it is safe from all surprises; it is not worth while, therefore, for the electors to take the trouble to go to the poll, the election was virtually over when the candidates were nominated at the party conventions.

However, in other States, where the greater or less number of votes has a real significance, there are also many abstentions, and the "stay-at-home vote" or the "dumb vote" is pretty large, even at the presidential elections. Most of the abstentionists are so from pure indifference; they do not care about exercising their right, it has not sufficient attraction for them. Some find a better employment for their time; they take advantage of the presidential polling-day, which is a holiday, to go out of town the previous evening for a country excursion or for a little trip to relations or friends. Others do not vote from principle, so to speak; this is especially the case with many persons belonging to the well-to-do classes and who do not deign to put themselves out. A certain number of abstentionists pride themselves on it, like the electors who replied to the canvassers: "I am proud to say I have not voted for twenty years, and I have made a vow never to vote again." — "I never vote; it is hopeless to obtain good government. Free government and universal suffrage are humbugs." With some these diatribes against elective government are only cynical remarks; but with many others the dislike and weariness of politics are perfectly sincere, and are the true cause of their abstention. Lastly, along with the incorrigible abstentionists, there are electors, well-meaning citizens, who take temporary refuge in abstention to express their dissatisfaction with the conduct of their party; they cannot make up their minds to vote against it, but they want to give its leaders a warning and to bring them to reason. This mode of protesting against abuses by silence is not uncommon, and sometimes is a serious blow to those against whom it is directed.

Abstention from voting occurs with special frequency at elections other than those of the "presidential year"; the electors do not attach the same importance to them and are not urged to vote with the same ardour by the party Organizations, whose zeal slackens in the interval, unless the State or municipal election is of exceptional gravity. In this latter case the parties manage to put into the field almost as many voters as at the presidential election. But this is the exception; as a rule the abstentions at local elections are considerable and sometimes even enormous. 3 The cause of good government *The Story of a Woman's Municipal Campaifln,* pp. (K), 61. In most of the large cities the number of voters, at the municipal elections, seldom exceeds 60 %; very often it is below 50 %, and sometimes it barely suffers much therefrom, for the result is that the mercenary elements of the Machines are the most regular in voting. In this connection the question of a compulsory vote has been raised. Before the foundation of the Republic, under English rule, there were in several colonies old laws which imposed fines on electors who abstained from voting, — in the colony of Plymouth and those of Delaware, Virginia, and Maryland. In these two last colonies the fine consisted of a hundred pounds of tobacco; Virginia has even, by a new law, doubled this quantity of tobacco. Quite recently (in 1889) a city of the State of Missouri, Kansas City, went so far as to insert in its charter a fine of two dollars and a half on persons who abstained from voting at a general election; but the Supreme Court of the State has annulled the provision as unconstitutional. The readiness to vote is nowadays in no way inferior to that in the colonial period, of which some persons wish to revive the legislation; on the contrary, it has increased during this century; from the presidential campaigns of Jackson and of "Tippecanoe and Tyler too" onward the proportion of voters has risen almost continuously. But the fact none the less remains true that this progression has not kept pace with the political development of the country and with the growth of the abuses of the elective regime which the vigilance of the electors should guard against, and that the abstention of the good citizens from voting is at the present day one of the causes of the deterioration of the American government.

The vote at the polls which closes the election campaign, in the beginning of November, puts an end, for a time, to the labours of the party Organization, even as regards the presidential election which, under the terms of the law, does not take place till some months later (on the second Monday of the following January). As the reader is aware, the letter of the Constitution provides that the citizens shall confine themselves to voting for the members of the Electoral College who are to reaches 30%. Cf. the statistics of municipal voting in twenty-one large cities of the Union, in the *Publications of the American Statistical Association,* Vol. IV (1894-1896), p. 283.
Cf. Cortland F. Bishop, *History oj Elections in the American Colonies,* New York, 1893, pp. 190-192. elect,

in perfect independence, the President and the VicePresident of the Kepublic. But in reality the presidential Electors are chosen, just like the other candidates, on the recommendation of the party Organization, only to put into the ballot-box the name of the presidential candidate adopted by the national convention of the party. By bestowing its votes on the Electors selected for this purpose, the people ratines the choice of the respective national convention and gives them an implied but imperative mandate to raise the nominee of the convention officially to power. The presidential Electors accept the terms of these instructions beforehand, and proud, or finding it worth their while, to become the mechanical executors of the will of the party, they often contribute large sums to its funds to be invested with their nominal and ephemeral dignity. Although the law leaves them full liberty of action, there is no instance of the presidential Electors having voted contrary to the instructions of their party. Hence, on the evening of the election in November it is known exactly how many votes each candidate will receive in each State at the secret ballot of the Electoral College, in the month of January. It is the supreme triumph of "regularity" and of the party Organization which keeps it up.

The vote once recorded, the role of the people is completed as well. The great assizes which the American people have just held in "their might and their majesty" are at an end. Lord and sovereign judge, they have appeared on the scene at the last moment only, having come from afar, as it were from a foreign land or from the opposite bank. A pontoon bridge is hurriedly constructed to bring together the general public and the community of "politicians," severed from one another in ordinary times. No sooner have they met than the politicians surround and turn the mass of electors by a series of concerted movements, and strive to conquer their minds and lead their wills captive. The efforts expended are formidable and the apparent results are admirable, but it is the triumph of organization applying factory methods to action The names of the candidates of the parties for the Presidency and the Vice-Presidency are often printed at the head of the voting-paper, hut officially no notice is taken of them.

on the public mind. Everything is engines, engineers, fuel, and materials; man plays a more or less subordinate part, as has been shown, for instance, by the position of the candidate. The latter hands over to the committee his money and his person, that is to say, his gift of the gab, — if he has any; the committee shovels them into the furnace along with the money and the gift of the gab of the other candidates on the "ticket" and of the "workers" of every degree, so as to produce the highest possible pressure on the electoral material. In the endeavour to mould this material with the minimum of friction and resistance, all efforts are concentrated on its most malleable points; the living mass is hammered in its most impressionable spot — the senses. The emotions of the multitude are appealed to; it is excited and worked up into a state of hysteria by a set of elaborate methods complacently called an "education campaign," down to the "Chinese business," which, according to a chairman of a State committee, "is politely styled 'political education.'" The extreme nervous tension produced in the electors by the fnrious attacks on their minds, — attacks which are all the more violent because they are crowded into a short space of time, — is inevitably followed by a reaction. The artificial passion for the public weal at once gives way to civic weariness. Exhausted, the great mass of the electorate falls or relapses into a state of prostration. The " politicians " alone are left standing and masters of the field. SIXTH CHAPTER THE POLITICIANS AND THE MACHINE

I

On the great stage of electoral life which we have just quitted, we have repeatedly caught glimpses of a special category of actors, the professional politicians. Still more often have we been confronted with the results of the schemes which they were hatching behind the scenes with a view to bring about the general action on the stage. To grasp this action with its causes and its effects, we must therefore go behind the scenes, catch the professionals of politics in their own haunts, and make them, as it were, sit to us for their portraits.

The American politician, while constituting a separate class in American society, has not a distinct origin. He is recruited from all ranks of the community, as circumstances and personal tastes happen to dictate, by a process of *natural selection.* The germ which produces the politician is the desire to obtain some public office or other. The aspirant may be a low-class attorney just as well as a small employee, an artisan, a cab-driver, a car-conductor, or even a *dielassi,* a social failure. To realize his ambition, he begins to " study politics." It is not the " Politics" of Aristotle, nor even that of Columbia College, but it is none the less a science which demands great application and certain natural aptitudes. It consists of a technical part, which includes a knowledge of the machinery of the party organization, with all its wheels within wheels, — the primaries, the committees, the various sets of conventions, — and of the legal procedure in force for making up the register and taking the vote. While learning the ostensible working of the party and of the election machinery, the future politician fathoms their inner working, the manoeuvres, the dodges, and the frauds by means of which a minority, perhaps an insignificant minority, is transformed into a majority, and a semblance of popular sanction is given to the schemes of a gang of political sharpers. But all these highly useful acquirements constitute, so to speak, only the mechanical side of the politicians' art, which by itself will not carry its man very far. The principal subjectmatter of his "studies " is a sort of empirical psychology. He studies the men about him and their weak points, and by trading on the latter he tries to get as large a following as possible. He begins with his immediate neighbours, who live on the same landing; he extends his advances to the inmates of the whole house, and before long to the next or the next two houses as well. When he has got acquainted with a dozen, or even half a dozen, electors, who are ready, often out of mere friendship, to join him at the elections, he is the possessor of a small political capital, which he will forthwith turn over, and which will become, perhaps, the foundation of his success, of a brilliant success, at a more or less early date. It is like the future millionaire's first ten-pound note. "Owning" half a dozen or a dozen votes, he is received with open arms by the local organization of the party; they make much of him, ask his advice, put him on the committee of the local branch, and even show their gratitude for the voting strength which he brings them in a less platonic fashion. His career of "ward politician" has begun.

In the popular wards of the large cities the small politician has no need to create the political following which he forms around him; he finds it ready to hand in social life, in which neighbourly ties, and above all common tastes and mutual sympathies, give rise to small sets, groups of people who meet regularly to enjoy the pleasures of sociability and of friendship. The street corner serves them as a rendezvous as long as they are in the youthful stage. Then, when they grow older and have a few cents to spend, they meet in a drinking-saloon or in a room hired for the purpose with their modest contributions. Several " gangs " unite to found a sort of club, in which they give small parties, balls, or simply smoke, drink, and amuse themselves. This merry crew is a latent political force; when the elections come round it may furnish a compact band of voters. The small politician therefore has but to lay his hand on it. Often he has himself grown up in the gang and with it; the stirring life of the gang, with its escapades, its quarrels, and its brawls with the members of the rival gangs, frequently gave him an opportunity of displaying his superior faculties of command and of organization; his companions got into the habit of following him in everything. These qualities which he possesses and this confidence which he inspires he can turn to account as soon as he feels his vocation, as soon as he becomes a " practical politician." The agglomerations of the European immigrants offer a no less favourable soil for the growth of the political manipulator of men. Germans, Italians, or Slavs arrive without knowing the language, the manners and customs, and the institutions of the country. But thereupon they find a fellow-countryman already naturalized and at home in the New World, who puts himself fraternally at their disposal; he guides their early steps, he helps them to look out for work, he appears on their behalf before the representatives of the public authority in the ward with whom they have to deal; later on, when the legal term has expired, or even earlier, he procures their naturalization. Day by day the ties which grow up between him and them are drawn closer, he becomes for them not only a friend, an adviser, but an oracle; and full of gratitude for his friendly services, and of admiration for his intelligence, they make over to him with perfect good faith the votes which have just been given them, and which as a rule they do not know what to do with. Here again is an "owner" of votes, who will find a good investment for his modest pile in the electoral market.

When the influence of the budding politician, obtained in one way or another, asserts itself in the precinct, the Organization of the party formally invests him with the position of local leader. He becomes its official representative in the precinct (often known by the name of "captain"), and acquires an indefeasible right to a share of the profits realized by the Organization, that is, to some office suited rather to his merits as a wire-puller. than to his special fitness for it. Often within the ranks of the party the budding politician meets with rivals An interesting description of the social r6le of these "gangs," and of their importance in local political life, will be found in the Rev. R. A. Wood's book, *The City Wilderness,* Boston, 1899. Vol. u — 2 R and competitors; each has his knot of followers, and each seeks to extend his influence. The one who is most skilful in managing his fellow-creatures, in winning them by small services or promises, who best appraises each man's price, who is clever in bringing about understandings and alliances, will come out first and will transform his rivals into his trusty lieutenants. The immediate object and, to a certain extent, the arena of this "struggle for existence" is the local primary; each strives to assert himself in the primary, that is to say, to procure the election of delegates devoted to him. The competitor who succeeds in this will be "recognized" by the higher Organization of the party impassively contemplating the struggle. At the head of his gang, each of them wrangles over every inch of ground, bringing into play all his resources, from the seductiveness of his personal magnetism, of his skill as a negotiator, down to the methods of what I have called the technical portion of the art and which consists in making away with voting-papers, in voting several times under different names, preventing opponents from voting by stratagem or by violence, etc. If the competitors are numerous and pretty evenly matched, there always turns out to be one who, occupying a somewhat more advantageous position, eventually thrusts himself on the others; instead of fighting each other, they all "compromise on him," admit his authority, and follow his lead, in order to secure a more modest but safer share of the booty. Our small politician now has his lieutenants each of whom has his henchmen, and he is supreme in the primary in which delegates are elected to the local convention. His political capital has thus increased.

In the larger arena of the ward or of

the district, he meets with other politicians of the same rank, and there exactly the same process of natural selection takes place, one of them achieves the position of "leader," gains an ascendency over all the "ward politicians," who place their contingents at his disposal and help him to assert his authority over the party organization in the ward, or perhaps even in more than one ward. A few of the cleverest leaders unite and form a "ring" or a "combine," to work up the electoral raw material and exploit " what there is in it. " The organization of the politicians reaches the final stage of its development when the "leaders" find their master in one of their own number who commands obedience by his strength of will, his cleverness, his audacity, and his luck, and who asserts himself *per fan et nefas* in the central conventions of the party, just as his prototype, the "ward politician," asserts himself in the primary. By a common agreement which has no need to be bargained about or expressed, every one wheels into line behind this man, recognizes him as the supreme chief. He is crowned city boss or state boss, as the case may be. At the head of his adherents, he forms with them what is called the "Machine," that is to say an aggregation of individuals stretching out hierarchically from top to bottom, bound to one another by personal devotion, but mercenary, and bent solely on satisfying their appetites by exploiting the resources of a political party. The men of the "Machine" do not accept this nickname, and style themselves "the Organization," usurping the name after having usurped the thing, after having "captured" the party Organization by a series of successful operations in the primaries and the conventions. This distinction between the Machine and the Organization does not exist only in logic, but it often does in fact as well; the power of the mercenary politicians in the party Organization is not universal, there are many places which escape it more or less. Although a constant phenomenon, the Machine is not a general phenomenon. While intending to point out later on the limitations to which its extension is subject, I pass them by for the moment, and, for the clearness of the narrative, I shall refer in the meanwhile to the Machine as if it covered the whole political area of the United States.

Sometimes an ambitious and specially gifted politician quickens or anticipates the process of natural evolution, he "builds a machine" from top to bottom; he finds out men capable of serving him as lieutenants, comes to an understanding with them, and by his manoeuvres spreads his net over the whole city or the whole State. But if he succeeds in this, it is because the social and political elements of the Machine were there ready to hand. However predominant therefore the personal character of the Machine may be, it is unfair to say that its importance is no more than that of a fortuitous and temporary association. True, there are purely personal Machines to be met with which break to pieces on the disappearance of their creator, but as a rule their elements represent a permanent stock forming part of the political circulation of the country. Only one must know how to bring these elements together and keep them together. The strongest attraction and source of cohesion for the politicians are the places in the public service, from the humblest up to the highest, which bring in a little or a good deal of money. Yet most of the Machine men are paid not so much in ready money as in drafts on the future; they are a singularly confiding race, and the hopes which are held out to them suffice to keep their zeal alive for a very long time. The material profits which the politicians receive or expect for their services are seasoned with the social pleasures which they enjoy in the gatherings of their particular circle. The "head-quarters" of the party in the locality, whether established in the premises of a drinking-saloon or elsewhere, is not only an official place of meeting, but a club where one goes to spend the evening, where one is always sure of pleasant company because those who frequent it are united by the same interests and the same aspirations. There the politicians receive their personal friends who are not in politics, and invite them to join in their pleasures. From time to time the head politicians get up special entertainments for their men, cheap excursions, "chowder-parties" or "clambakes," which I have already mentioned when speaking of the politician's clubs. All these gatherings, ordinary or extraordinary, which impart a social relish to political relations, are a powerful means of keeping up the loyalty of the small politicians and of developing to a high pitch the *esprit de corps* which makes them really a machine.

Each Machine being in reality composed of a number of smaller and smaller Machines which form so many microcosms within it, the respective powers as well as the rank of the chief engineers and of their fellow-workmen represent a sort of expanding ladder. This is the case in the first instance with the hierarchy of the Machine's staff: the title and the role of boss do not belong exclusively to the man who controls the Machine in the city or in the State; the leader is the local boss in his own district; the person in charge of the precinct is himself a little boss. However, all the men of the Machine may be divided into three categories representing three distinct grades: the "boys," the "henchmen," and the "bosses." The boys are the simple workers who do the rough work, very often the dirty work of politics. They are the chief performers in the primaries, they are always there in force, to support the leaders with their lungs, and if need be with their fists; they rise like one man against the good citizens who venture into these meetings or against the rival factions; they make themselves the docile instrument of the frauds and manoeuvres conceived by the ingenious brain of the managing ring; they supply the *claque* at the meetings; they do duty in the processions and at the parades; they go the round of the drinking-saloons to pick up the voters; they fetch them at their residences; and generally they are always at the heels of the leaders, which has got them the nickname of "heelers. " Before the recent reform known as the Australian Ballot which introduced official voting papers, the heelers, thronging the approaches of the polling-place, distributed the tickets of their candidates and often resorted to intimidation or violence to thrust them on the electors or to prevent those provided with other tickets from voting. Ignorant, brutal, averse to regular work, the heelers are mostly recruited in the "dangerous" classes, criminal or semi-criminal, from among frequenters of drinking-saloons, from failures and loafers of every description.

The henchmen are the lieutenants and the helps of the bosses; they vary in social position and rank with the position of their masters, from the associate of the small local leader up to the confidential man of the great boss who sits in the Senate of the United States. The henchman is in his territory, if he has one assigned to him, a sort of prefect or vicar who "works" for the boss, who manages the subordinate politicians and the electorate on his behalf. He is personally responsible to the boss for the success of his operations: if he misleads his chief as to the local political situation, if he does not succeed in carrying the primary, if in his district the Machine is beaten at the elections, and if his want of zeal or skill appears to be the cause, he is summarily dismissed from his place in the Machine. Past services and personal position count for nothing; as soon as a man is considered not sufficiently useful to the Machine he is thrown over without pity. Apart from political service the henchman owes the boss personal homage just as his historical prototype the vassal owed it to the lord. He cherishes for the boss a devotion into which affection scarcely enters, but which is a mixture of the obedience of a subordinate whose advancement depends on his superior and of sincere admiration for the doughty chief, the commander of victorious legions on the battlefields of "politics." He sees in him the living embodiment of the virtues and of the ideal of the "politician," which invest the latter with just as bright a halo in the eyes of men who have risen in the primaries as that which encircled the medieval knight. Many a boss keeps his henchmen at a distance, it is only with feelings and gestures of deference that they approach him; others indulge in more familiarity with their lieutenants, but the subordination always subsists and often goes as far as servility, of a kind which a hired domestic would object to.

The boss in his turn owes help and protection to his henchmen, he must defend them with his person, must forward their political ambitions, if they have any, ensure them a livelihood if they are not well off, as is the case with most of his lieutenants, procure them places in the public service, keep them there, however great their incompetence or their neglect of their duties. He will move heaven and earth to place his men, he will risk his influence to achieve it. This is the first reward which he claims, regardless of himself, from the boss above him, or from the head of the executive power who makes appointments. He will besiege the new President, and like the office-seekers under the first Harrison, will be ready to sleep in the corridors of the White House to be the first to catch the President when 1 happened to be with a ward boss of one of the largest cities of the United States. He wanted to give me the hand-book of the party Organization, containing the lists of the members of the committees, etc., but could not lay his hand on it. At this point one of the precinct leaders appeared. Without a word of preface the boss ordered him to fetch a copy of the book from the "head-quarters" of the Organization. The "leader," a white-haired man, accepted the commission obsequiously and ran off like a small boy. When he had gone the boss told me his history, which explains many things in a few words. For the services which he rendered to the Machine in his post of leader, it procured him a place of $900 in the municipal administration. A rival faction of politicians which was fighting the Machine and which had friends in the town-hall proposed to the leader employee to go over to their side. The leader reported the proposal to his Machine and was told to refuse. He obeyed and was dismissed from his office; but the Machine did not leave him in the lnrch. "We take care of him," said the boss to me; the Machine makes up to him his lost salary, pending its reinstallation when it will become absolute mistress of the town-hall, and will be able to capture all the municipal offices.

he wakes: he must have a place for his henchman. If the boss is a member of the Senate he will not hesitate, in order to put pressure on the administration, to obstruct an important measure demanded by the country: he must have a place for his henchman. It is by no means out of chivalry that the boss thus devotes himself to his lieutenants, but to safeguard his own position: if he did not exert himself actively on their behalf, no one would care to "work " for such a chief; or, if with all his good will he were to become unable to get places for his men, he would undergo the same fate; he could no longer appeal to their selfish interest, nor to their imagination; the charm is broken, the prestige vanishes into thin air, and the boss ceases to be a boss. But as long as the ties which unite them to one another subsist, their mutual relations are ruled by an iron discipline, stronger, to use the expression of my American interlocutors, than that of the Roman Catholic Church. A subordinate politician must put his personal feelings completely on one side; his likes and dislikes are to order; he must be ready to exchange them one for the other without a moment's hesitation. Here, for instance, is a political opponent who has been fighting the Machine for years and who has inspired its adherents with feelings of inextinguishable resentment and untold bitterness. For reasons unknown to the public he lays down his arms and comes to terms with the boss; the latter orders his adoption as candidate for an important post; and forthwith in the primaries and in the convention all without a single exception vote for him enthusiastically: the ways of the chiefs of the Machine are unfathomable and the subalterns have only to follow them. This is the case at all grades of the Machine. The principal lieutenants themselves only wait for the word of command; even when the boss consults them, they are under no illusion as to their authority: he is free to listen to their advice or not, as soon as he has given his decision not a word is spoken. The committees of the party Organization, the ward, city, State committees, simply register the will of the boss or of the respective leader, and their members are in reality only figure-heads. All along the line the real power is always in the hands of a single man, the leader. The leader often does 11 put the question to a ward boss, "Does the city boss consult you leaders?" "We call it receiving orders," was the only reply. not think fit even to sit on the committee, he sends to it in his place a friend who votes according to his instructions. The great boss, the city or State boss, generally presides over the central committee, but sometimes he too puts in a lay-figure as his substitute. While devoid of real influence, the committees can depose the bosses, by electing another chairman of the committee in place of the boss or of his lay-figure. This is the formal proclamation of the deposition of the reigning boss to whom his vassals renounce allegiance. n

The Machine is now built, the politicians are sorted and in their proper places for action. Our next step is to see them at work. For this purpose we will begin by following a politician of average importance whose intermediary position places him at the centre of action, such as a sub-boss in a large city, a "district leader" or a "ward leader" in New York, Philadelphia, or Baltimore. This "leader" presents himself to us in the first instance as the engineer-in-chief of the Machine for getting hold of the base of operations of organized parties — the nominations for elective posts. Forestalling the role of the primaries and the conventions, the Machine, as we know already, makes up the slate of delegates and of candidates and gets it simply registered by these party assemblies. For local elective positions, especially for municipal offices and for the delegateships of the primaries, the "leader" makes up the slate of his own authority, and on his own responsibility, that is to say, he has to choose men who are ready, after they are duly elected, to do what the Machine tells them. The slate of the higher elective posts is made up or approved by the boss himself, but it is the business of the "leader" to ensure the success of the slate at the convention, by getting docile delegates elected. Having selected his candidates, who will be presented to the people as the deliberate choice of the convention, the boss instructs the "leader" to "deliver a solid delegation" for these candidates, and the leader is bound to "deliver the goods." If the leader is unable to do so, he signs his deposition as leader. On the other hand, if the lieutenants of a boss, small or great, refuse to "deliver the goods" to him, the boss will not have the wherewithal for carrying on his trade in elective offices. The internal operations of the Machine along the whole line consist, therefore, of these deliveries: each respective leader is supposed to "deliver the delegates" to his superior, from the delegates to the county or district convention up to the delegates to the National Convention. The district leader is the first deliverer. How does he get the "goods" himself? After the delivery of the delegates, the electors must be made to vote for the candidates adopted by those delegates. The district leader again is the chief agent of this operation. How does he succeed in it?

In both cases he gains his ends by corruption and by seduction. The sinews of corruption are supplied him by the Machine; the means of seduction he derives from his own resources. He is amiable with everybody, with the lowest of the low, he is all things to all men. To offend no one, to please every one, that is his motto. He is in constant touch with all the electors of his district, he knows their ins and outs, the strong and the weak points of each man, and how to exploit them. He "understands " all his people perfectly, because he is one of them himself; he is eminently "representative" of the community on which he acts; he is on a moral and intellectual level which is neither higher nor lower than that of the average of the inhabitants of the district: if the district is one which swarms with the dregs of the population, with frequenters of drinking-saloons, the local leader of the Machine is not much superior; on the other hand, in a wellinhabited district the leader always has a respectable appearance, his get-up and his address are gentlemanly, he speaks English correctly, he is pleasing, genial, but without being vulgar. With these apparent virtues he combines certain moral virtues, a very small stock it is true, but which ensure him esteem and general confidence: he is a man of courage, of strength of will, and above all a man of his word. No matter if he is a low wire puller, who sticks at no fraud, or if he has committed breaches of trust in public offices,—he keeps his promises, he is a man of honour. This merit is appreciated in him to the exclusion of all the others because everybody or nearly everybody has something to ask of him; and if he is not asked for anything, he volunteers his services. All aspirants to public office who inhabit "his" district apply to him, from members of the bar who want a judgeship down to crossing-sweepers. In that district he is the sole dispenser of all the public posts at the disposal of the party Organization. The boss or the managing ring of the Machine distributes these offices among the leaders, leaving it entirely to their discretion to make the best use of them for the common cause. This " patronage" intrusted to the leader is the most important part of his ammunition, and makes him undisputed master in his territory; it draws into his orbit the whole tribe of office-seekers who realize that there is no salvation save in him. These are not only the aspirants to elective posts who cannot be elected if they are not on the slate, the slate which is in the hands of the Machine; the non-elective posts in the public departments, down to those of office messengers, are invariably given by favour; to obtain one, you must have what is called a "pull," or "pulls," occult influences which pull the official to make him do something contrary to his duty. Under the spoils system, the public servant who owes his place, not to his merit, but to the choice or to the approval of the party organization, contracts obligations toward it: the representative of the Organization, the leader of the Machine, has a "pull" on him. If the innumerable places in the public service, a good many of which are pure sinecures for the use of the politicians and their creatures, are not sufficient, the leader is in a position to find his people private employment, to get them small places in railroads, in street-cars, and other large private concerns: the companies, as we are aware, have need of "protection," and being anxious to stand well with the all-powerful party organization, they always give a good reception to the applications or recommendations of the leader of the Machine: he has a "pull" on these great employers of labour.

In addition to the places, there are a thousand and one other favours which the representative of the Machine can grant by means of hie influence, favours which imply the weal or woe of the whole existence of many humble folk: permits issued by the police or by other authorities for plying some small trade or business on the public thoroughfare, such as that of costermonger, of vendor of roasted chestnuts, of seller of cooling drinks, of boot-black, etc.; a word from the leader of the Machine is enough to get the poor fellow permission to set up his improvised shop at a street-corner. It is through the leader again that one can obtain a license to open a drinkingsaloon or get it refused to a competitor. The power of his pulls extends even to defying the law itself; it ensures impunity to misdemeanours, nay even to criminal offences, if the culprits are trusty followers of the Machine. Sometimes it is a case only of breaking the law with no guilty intention, such as an infringement of building regulations, but far more often the leader of the Machine uses his power to protect gaol-birds. If the offenders are notoriously supporters of the Machine, the policemen will often think twice about arresting them. When they are arrested, the leader intervenes and applies for their release on bail. Sometimes he may have to spend the whole morning at the police court interceding for one after another of his clients, arrested for being drunk and disorderly, for assaults committed in a brawl, or for other offences. The leader provides the sum fixed by the judge as bail, and then, before the hearing comes on, tries to get the judge to dismiss the case, or at all events to obtain a considerable reduction or a commutation of the penalty. It is not an uncommon thing for the judge himself to be the local leader of the Machine outside the court; in that case the law is squared in a still more summary fashion. If the matter is a more serious one and comes within the province of the prosecuting officers, the Machine exerts its influence with them to get the prosecution dropped. The right which these officers have, in several States, to dismiss a case without giving any reasons, enables them to fall in with the wishes of the Machine, which has a " pull" on them as it has on all the elective officials. If the prosecution cannot be stopped, it can be spun out and the decision postponed. Whatever the gravity of the case therefore, as soon as there is any "trouble," everybody rushes off to the leader of the Machine. He is an inverted tribune of the people, he defends the obscure and the humble against justice, he interposes between them and the arm of the law.

Many other citizens who have nothing to ask or fear from the public authorities, but who are in needy circumstances, also get help and succour from the representative of the Machine: to this one he lends a dollar; for another he obtains a railroad ticket without payment; he has coal distributed in the depth of winter; he makes other gifts in kind; he sometimes sends poultry at Christmas time; he buys medicine for a sick person; he helps to bury the dead by procuring a coffin on credit or half price. He has a kind heart in virtue of his position, and his position gives him the means of satisfying his need for kindness: the money which he distributes comes from the chest of the Machine; the latter has obtained it by the most reprehensible methods, those which we have seen practised by Tammany Hall, but no matter. With this money he can also dispense an ample hospitality in the drinking-saloons. As soon as he comes in, friends known and unknown gather round him, and he treats everybody, he orders one drink after another for the company; he is the only one who does not drink, he is on duty. To the more influential electors a less intermittent hospitality is offered in the clubs of the politicians; admitted by the latter as friends, joining in their amusements, they are socially swept into the sphere of influence of the Machine. The electors who are below the favours or the civilities of the representatives of the Machine are bought right out at the market price. Each man is taken by his weak side. It is like a huge spider's web spread by the Machine over the district. Every new elector is drawn into it at once. As soon as he moves into the locality an enquiry is made about him of the representatives of the Machine in whose jurisdiction his old residence was situated, a visit is paid him, an attempt is made to win him. An answer is found in his case to the invariable question which haunts the Machine: what does he want, what would he like to have? The man who does not wish for anything, who does not ask for anything, is the most painful puzzle to the Machine; it considers him almost as a hateable being.

The favours of every kind granted to those who go with the Machine, the "rewards," find a corollary in the " punishments" inflicted on those who cross its path. It deprives them of their livelihood, it persecutes and molests them with all the resources of its influence. If the man who has incurred its animosity is an employee, it gets him dismissed from his situation; if he is engaged in manufactures or trade, the leader sets the police at him who make a point of worrying him on the most futile or imaginary pretexts; at one time the sanitary conditions of his establishment are defective, at another the carriages or vans which stand outside his door impede the traffic. The tax collector makes a minute investigation into the taxes and licenses paid by the trader who is in the bad books of the Machine, and discovers that he has not been paying the proper sum. The saloon-keeper who remained open after the statutory hour at night and on Sundays, with the countenance of the police, is prosecuted and fined heavily as soon as he has lost the favour of the Machine. The wretched peddler at the street-corner does not escape the vengeance of the Machine any more than the millionnaires; his permit is withdrawn. To vindicate its slighted authority, the Machine makes use of everything, even of corpses, as in the case of Tammany, which, in order to give a too independent undertaker a lesson, ordered the municipal employees at its beck and call to put him on short commons, to send him only one dead body a month.

It would be better, however, to listen to the testimony on this subject of an unexceptionable witness who, after having belonged to the famous Eepublican Machine of Pennsylvania, has recently severed his connection with it in an emphatic way, Mr. John Wanamaker, the owner of a dry goods store, who was made Postmaster-General in circumstances which will be within the reader's recollection. This is the tenor of his evidence:

No sooner does a man show independence, and refuse to indorse the misdeeds of the political Machine than he is taken in hand to be disciplined. If he is the employee of a corporation, he is threatened with discharge; if he is a merchant, he is boycotted; if he is a clerk, the head of the firm is notified that he must be suppressed; if he is interested in a corporation, the company's interests are threatened; if he is a director or stockholder in a bank, large customers are found to threaten the withdrawal of their business; if he is a physician, good patrons object; if he is a lawyer, his clients are given orders and threaten to leave him; if he is a preacher, members of his congregation protest; if a man daring to be independent of political dictation is in debt, he is threatened by those who hold his obligations. This is not the result of accident, but of method. It is the result of a carefully planned and manipulated system that extends into every county in the State, and reaches all classes of business. It is every-day and every-year working machinery; manned by a host of political retainers, who report to the central office the first symptoms of Machine insubordination, and who are expected to advise ways and means of applying the silencing and crushing pressure. But there is a class of men beyond these influences which the Machine must reach. They are men who have to their credit long years of honourable professional and business records; men who are leaders in their respective communities; men whose very names are synonyms for integrity and character; men whom ordinary considerations will not move. These men are a constant menace to the existence of the Machine, and methods must be found to keep them from taking an active interest in politics. To influence these men is set in motion the character torpedo, the reputation-smirching and the good-name-destroying Machine. It is worked by the hands of a gang of place-holders and place-seekers, who risk nothing by trying to rob honest men of their characters. It is a warning of what all who protest must encounter. The blackmailer begins to operate. That most contemptible of human beings — the anonymous letter-writer — starts his miserable work. The scandal-peddler, a moral outcast, labors systematically to poisou society with innuendo, insinuations, and base lies. Detective agencies, composed of low tools and thugs, are hired at great expense to dog the footsteps of those who dare work against the Machine. They are paid to fabricate stories, invent false accusations, and furnish false evidence against any one whom the Machine may wish to destroy. Any man who causes trouble is sure to feel their vengeance. Those connected in any way with the persons of their special hatred are not safe. The youth or the aged are not spared. They do not care for the gray-haired mother or innocent children, and this is why men do not dare to fight. Any man who enters the arena of Pennsylvania politics to-day against the Machine will not escape it

In truth, this system of rewards and punishments cannot lay claim to originality; it is that of the Sicilian *mafia* and the Italian *camorra,* minus the stiletto and the gun, and plus the scientific method.

"While bringing their efforts to bear on individual electors, the leaders of the Machine also make great exertions to cultivate the friendship of men who through their position or their business can procure them adhesions in a lump, who can serve as recruiting sergeants. For this purpose they make friends in the workmen's trade unions, in the factories and the workshops, and even descend to the lowest step in the social ladder to get useful help; they get hold of the keepers of lodging-houses, of gambling-houses, and of every kind of den frequented by the criminal or semi-criminal class, of the saloon-keepers, by ensuring them protection against the police *The Speeches of Hon. John Wanamaker* on " Quayism and Boss Domination in Pennsylvania Politics." Philadelphia (1898) pp. 123-124.

and the law, or by paying them directly. The co-operation of the saloon-keepers is particularly appreciated, and very often the Machine takes them into partnership, and confers on them the post of " captain " of the precinct in which their saloon is situated. The drinking-saloon is, in fact, the great laboratory of the Machine. It is there that a great deal of the electioneering work is done; the saloon-keepers who attend to this business do not always confine themselves to the role of humble auxiliaries of the Machine; their influence develops their ambitions and their appetites, and gives them access to municipal councils, and even to State legislatures, where they look after the interests of their trade, and prostitute their official position to every form of corruption.

To be up to the mark, a leader should also be an expert in the art of fraudulently procuring electoral registration and the naturalization of non-qualified persons. He must be not less familiar with the devices resorted to during the counting of the voting-papers, so as to swell in a miraculous way the number of votes obtained by the candidates of the Machine, and in any event it is his business to rescue from the clutches of the law any of his henchmen who have been caught in the act of tampering with voting-papers.

All this work of inveigling the electors is done both by the district leader and by the small leaders of the precincts or divisions. The latter serve as informers and finger-posts to the Machine; they are continually spying on the inhabitants of their little domain on its behalf. At the same time they operate themselves: the Machine gives them as their share some money and a few subordinate places to distribute. The relative influence attaching to their position of representative of the Machine enables them also to grant small favours and to render services of less importance. If the resources in influence and money at the disposal of the precinct leader are inadequate, he refers to the leader of the district, who almost always finds the ways and means; in cases where that is beyond the tatter's powers, where an exceptionally strong "pull" or an authoritative act is required, the leader applies to the boss.

This is the proper moment for us also to transport ourselves into the higher sphere of the Machine, in which the boss reigns supreme.

III

The operations of the "leaders," which bear rather on the lower strata of the population, enable the Machine to "fix the primaries," to form the conventions of delegates to its liking, and to bring the big battalions up to the poll. But the respectable portion of the electorate would often be capable of rejecting the candidates of the Machine, for these latter are not the most deserving individuals. The Machine cannot afford the luxury of high-class candidates: they would not be able to render it the services on which it subsists; a man of independent mind and anxious to do his duty could not provide it with the pulls with which it obtains the votes of the electors. Besides, some Machines, such as Tammany for instance, are obliged to let in notorious bandits as a measure of precaution: the latter have, either as accomplices or spectators, become acquainted with certain wrongful deeds of the Machine, and they might make dangerous revelations. In any event, the necessities of its existence always impel the Machine to prefer as candidates men who are rather at the lower end of their respective social sphere, whether it is a case of a city councilman or of a member of Congress, or even of a State Governor. To thrust them on the bulk of the party, including its respectable and independent section, there is often required a higher strategy and a special sort of tactics which test the perverse sagacity of the heads of the Machine themselves, of the boss, or of the managing ring.

The A B C of the strategy of the Machine is to shuffle the electoral pack, to mix up its own cause with that of the party whose flag it hoists or with the great political preoccupations of the day, and to create a confusion between the different elections themselves. At the municipal election the issue is never the good government of the city, the state of the pavements or the drainage, but the protectionist tariff, or Cuba, or the Philippines. Why, the particular city election will predetermine the result of the impending State election's, or even of the presidential election — is this the time to look closely into the merit of this or that local candidate? The issue is the general fate of the party in the State and in the Union, and if some electors are prepared to jeopardize it because the candidate for the city council in their ward is not the ideal of all the virtues, they will do this on their own responsibility. The Machine includes men whose political morality provokes strong animadversion; it may be so; it has governed the city or the State like a satrapy; there is, perhaps, an element of truth in this charge; but is it fair to make the party pay for the individual faults of a few of its servants? The enemy is at the gates, and it is the "life of the party," of that grand, of that noble party, which must be saved; who will lift a parricidal hand against it? Sometimes the stake is still higher; the party which the Machine claims to serve is identified with a problem which closely concerns the daily existence of the great majority of the citizens, such as the protection of the national industries or the currency; the defeat of the party means financial ruin followed by the advent of anarchy and socialism; under such circumstances what do men signify? it is the flag which must be followed. And each time the conjuncture is an exceptional one; each time it is a case of *force majeure* which makes it imperative to vote the party ticket as it stands, to vote even for a "yellow dog. " The American's excitability of temperament, which inclines him to exaggeration, and his imagination, which magnifies everything, make this game of the Machine a fairly easy one.

This card-shuffling game is very often complicated by the fact that the Machine slips spurious cards into the pack, it puts forward ornamental candidates or fictitious candidates intended to impress the electors. It selects perfectly respectable men whose reputation and social position appear to preclude the idea that they would make themselves liegemen of the Machine; but owing to their weakness of character and want of perspicacity they become, without being aware of it, tools in the hands of the astute leaders of the Machine; they do what the Machine wants, and shield it with their respectability. This category of candidates is known by the name of " figureheads." A "prominent citizen," who has succeeded by honourable means, pious, known for the interest which he takes in charities, in social movements, full of good intentions, but stung by political ambition or accessible to vanity, the figurehead is highly pleased at being courted by the big politicians who rule the roast at the political board; he lends them a willing Vol. n — 2 c ear and is speedily circumvented. The skill of the heads of the Machine consists in finding out men likely to fall in with this role, and in managing them with the required lightness of hand by discerning the point of resistance beyond which the pressure to be put upon them must not go. The figure-head is almost a classic character, he is to be found at every stage of the political life directed by the party Organization. We have already met with good specimens of the figure-head in the conventions, especially in the State conventions, in the capacity of delegates. Making up the conventions as it pleases, the Machine measures out with consummate art the amount of figure-head stuff, increasing it according to the importance of the convention, and taking care to vary the actors. The respectable personages thus distributed among the conventions give the illusion of free and deliberate choices, and of really representative assemblies, not to mention the heavy subscription to the party funds which they make in return for the honorary position conferred on them. To reward their co-operation, the Machine procures them other functions as well, of a less ephemeral but equally honorary nature. Their role of figure-head, however, is chiefly connected with important elective posts. Placed at the head of the ticket, they cover all the rest of the list with their respectability. The conspicuous office most frequently bestowed on this particular species of "prominent citizens" is that of mayor. The figure-head is to be found also, but not so often, in the post of State Governor, and much more rarely in Congress.

Another species of candidates with which the Machine hoodwinks the electors are the "dummies," the imaginary candidates. Thus the Machine, fearing that its real candidate whom it has in its mind may be rejected by the electors on account of his disreputableness, puts forward another candidate ten times more disreputable. This odious candidature provokes a revolt of the public conscience. Bowing to public opinion, the Machine humbly gives way and withdraws its man, substituting for him the other whom it had selected *in petto*. The public thereupon accepts this latter as the lesser of the two evils with a veritable sense of relief, and congratulates itself on the fresh proof which it has just given of the omnipotence of free opinion in a democracy, the sole manifestation of which is sufficient to make the political bandits hide their heads. The superlatively odious candidate who has vpluntarily retired is a dummy. Sometimes the Machine inverts the procedure; it begins by putting forward an honourable man, then at the last moment it drops him and replaces him by a candidate of its own making. This time it is the respectable candidate who has served as dummy. As a rule, the dummy is a conscious accomplice of the Machine, whereas the figurehead always acts in good faith.

It is not uncommon for the part of dummy, as confederate of the Machine, to be played by the Machine of the opposite party. If this latter is not strong enough to get possession of the spoils, if it has no chance of carrying its ticket against the opposite ticket, it prefers to come to terms with its rival, to help it to elect its candidates, in order to get a share of the spoils as its reward. With this object it makes weak nominations, it chooses for the party which it represents candidates likely rather to repel than attract the electors; it dooms them to failure beforehand, in order to ensure the success of the pretended hostile Machine. For instance, in the State of Pennsylvania, ruled by the Republican Machine, independent citizens, or even Republicans, disgusted with the corrupt regime of their boss, would be inclined to vote, at the election for Governor, for an honest man even if he were a Democrat. The Democratic Machine ought, one would think, to jump at this opportunity of selecting an acceptable candidate. It does exactly the contrary; it chooses a candidate who is personally honourable, but a violent silverite. A good many of the electors who have revolted against the Republican boss cannot bring themselves to turn against the principles of their party and the primordial interests of their country; they abstain from voting, or vote for the Republican candidate, and the latter is elected for the greater triumph of the Machine of which he is the servile instrument. At a municipal election, in which questions of national politics may be of little or no avail to confuse the issues, the confederate Machine selects candidates In every-day language the dummy and the figure-head are often confused, the first term being used for the second, but wrongly so; the figurehead really takes part in the game, although he is prompted,-whereas the dummy, as in whist, is always passive.
whose personality, if not their programme, is enough to repel the honest electors.

These Machiavellian combinations are, however, only some of the forms assumed by the co-operation of hostile Machines which, instead of fighting each other, often find it more profitable to come to terms secretly, and to make "deals." They "trade" the votes of the electors; the Democratic Machine gives its votes to the Republican candidate for the presidency, in return for which the Republican Machine helps to get the head of the Democratic Machine elected to the post of Governor, or helps to carry the Democratic ticket at the city elections. Sometimes the Machines do not even take the trouble to observe secrecy; they settle a " mixed ticket," which the electors are obliged to vote whether they like it or not. Occasionally an influential politician simply "sells out" the votes which he "controls " to the rival Machine. It is quite common, as I have already mentioned in the proper place, for the Machines to help each other to carry the primaries of the party, by the loan of their "boys "; at the elections these little courtesies are borne in mind. When a formidable movement of independent electors, of "reformers," breaks out, an understanding between the two Machines often seems to them the obvious course — the Machine in opposition assists the threatened Machine, not so much in order to save it as to save the Machine regime, the spoils system which supports the politicians.

When the Machine in opposition does not think it advisable to take up this attitude, the Machine attacked by the independents of its own party resorts to the "harmony" dodge: it makes fervent appeals to them in favour of concord, invites them to "harmony conferences " to induce them to disarm. It is lavish of promises of good government, subscribes to everything proposed in the way of declarations of principles, of programmes, even if they contain denunciations of the bosses and of the practices of the Machine, provided that it is allowed to have the candidates. At a pinch, it allows the recalcitrants a portion of the ticket; it is prepared to make sacrifices, for there is but one thing which it cares for — to "maintain a united party "; like Shy lock, it may say: "Sufferance is the badge of all our tribe." It varies the extent of the sacrifices according to the situation; it flings the Cerberus of public opinion a few elective posts bestowed on highly respectable persons; if possible, it selects them from the class of figureheads, otherwise it acquiesces in the complete abandonment of these offices. If the brute is savage and has sharp teeth, the Machine throws it a few more sops. Sometimes the Machine is in such danger that it consents, always "for the sake of harmony," to keep the second and third rate places only for its men. If public opinion declares with special force in favour of a certain candidature, the Machine hastens to adopt it. The flexibility with which the Machine tries to adapt itself to circumstances has no limits; it is capable, in order to mislead public opinion, of changing its skin, of becoming quite "respectable," and of appearing exclusively taken up with the public weal, of even hoisting the standard of "reform," of starting on a crusade against the corruption of the politicians, especially when that corruption is embodied in the Machine of the opposite party. All this lasts just as long as is required for the storm to blow over; when the popular effervescence has subsided, the Machine will revert to its old ways. The promised reforms are made away with; the bills are brought in only as a matter of form, or, if they are passed, they are stripped of their vitality in committee to such an extent as to make them still-born. The homage to honesty and the acts of penitence which the Machine finds itself obliged to do are temporary ordeals for it, interludes only which interrupt its peaceable possession of power. Except in the periods of crises, it cares little for what honest folk think of its deeds or misdeeds; it reckons on the indifference and the apathy of the great mass of the electors; it is convinced that the party will "wheel into line," whatever the men whom it puts in power. Experience but rarely contradicts it; in quiet times it can manipulate the candidatures as it likes, and that is enough to make it master of the position.

Trifling with public opinion, fencing with it or simply ignoring it when it can afford to do so, the Machine, however, always makes it believe that after all it is obliged to do what the "people" want, that it has, in reality, no power. And the "people" accepts this view with much complacency, it knows that the politicians are full of craft and guile, but it has confidence in its own strength, an ingenuous confidence which inspires it, not so much with indignation, as with indulgent contempt for the politicians whom it deems at its mercy. The whole business of hoodwinking public opinion, to which the Machine devotes itself, is powerfully seconded by the party press. The newspapers know what's what perfectly well, but they represent in the first place an industrial concern which depends, in the United States, not so much on readers, on subscribers, as on the persons who supply the advertisements. The Machine, owing to its pulls, is able to procure the newspapers large advertising orders. Besides this, it subsidizes individual editors or bribes them with places given to them or to their relations. In return these newspapers present the facts in a light which is favourable to the Machine, and keep out matter which is compromising for it. Often the boss prefers to secure the good offices of the reporters who regularly insert paragraphs of a few lines, insignificant in appearance, but always worded to suit the Machine, while in the same newspaper the leading articles, which hardly any one reads, are inveighing against the Machine. Certain State bosses practise the system of "patent inside" for their requirements, and fill the local newspaper with articles and news which they get written at headquarters. Generally the small local journal is one of the powerful instruments which the Machine uses to keep public opinion in a state of coma.

IV

Being aware of the fact that the Machine holds the keys of the electoral situation, everybody whose interests are affected thereby acknowledges its power, whether they like it or not. The candidates of the party are the first to realize that they are not at liberty to attain their object independently of the Machine and still less in opposition to it. The Machine is too strong even for candidates who occupy such an exceptional position that they might, it would seem, shake it off; a man of independent character, enjoying great personal popularity, and a "military hero" to boot, whose laurels, freshly plucked in a recent war, throw the multitude into raptures, on becoming a candidate deems it nevertheless necessary to at least perform the rite of going to "see" the boss, just as in Grand Tartary, according to the narrative of Piano Carpini, the Christians, the legates of the Pope themselves, who appeared before the Great Khan, were obliged to conform to the pagan rite of passing between two fires, to show that they were not cherishing any evil designs against the master and were not concealing poison or noxious herbs wherewith to injure him. With the great majority of candidates, the enormous election expenses and the technical complexity of the election business are quite enough to prevent them from courting the popular suffrages with their own resources; if an aspirant is not approved by the Machine of the party to which he claims to belong, he must construct a Machine for himself — like a traveller who would build a railroad for his own use, or an ordinary citizen who would start a factory to procure himself a piece of cloth. Aided by the conditions with which we are familiar, the Machine has succeeded in transforming the elections into an industry, exploited like other industrial concerns, on the method of concentration of capital and labour applied to the raw material. Being able to deliver its product on the most favourable terms, it takes orders, it contracts for elections: does any one wish to become municipal councillor or member of the legislature, he has but to come to terms with the Machine, to "see" the boss and settle the price; the Machine undertakes the rest. As it enjoys a monopoly in its line of business, the Machine can refuse offers without giving any reason, that is to say, forbid an aspirant to become candidate. The boss bluntly informs an aspirant to an elective post that he cannot grant or renew his "nomination," and the applicant must bow to the decision, for the convention which makes the nominations makes them at the bidding of the boss, recruited as it is by his henchmen in the primaries, which are full of their underlings. Again, the tradition of local candidatures which excludes candidates not residing in the constituency, prevents the aspirant shown out by the boss from trying his political luck in another constituency. The boss has thus absolute power over the candidates, he can admit them into or shut them out of political life at will. It also happens that the boss compels a man to stand: in following out his ideas of election tactics, he has settled that the most suitable candidate in the particular conjuncture is So-and-so; it matters little if this individual has no wish to come forward, or if he has an appointment already, he must obey, if he does not mean to give up public life for good. Thus in the course of the last few years the boss of Tammany Hall ordered one of his lieges, a member of Congress, to resign in order to become a candidate for the post of treasurer of the city of New York, and the member of Congress exchanged his title of legislator for that of municipal employee. Quite recently the same boss selected a judge of the supreme court of the State for the more precarious and less remunerative post of State Governor; the judge was about to be re-elected for a term of fourteen years to his dignified and peaceful position, while the success of his party at the election for Governor was doubtful; he none the less obeyed, he resigned his judgeship, was defeated, but he did his duty to the boss and to the party Machine.

So far as it is a question of money to be paid for the candidatures, the Machine may be haggled with, but up to a certain limit; for the large sum which it demands from the candidates is not only intended to enrich the bosses, the latter must also recoup themselves for the heavy expenditure which they have to incur, and for them as well as for ordinary manufacturers there is a cost price below which they cannot go. To obtain a considerable reduction, or even to be exempted from all payment, the candidate must himself represent a certain capital which may be placed to the credit of the Machine just as if it was in cash. To this category belong the aspirants who have many friends and followers, and who are strongly backed by the press, the figure-heads whom the Machine puts up itself in order to adorn its ticket with their names, and lastly men of small means and no influence, but who will serve the Machine with docility in their elective posts, in return for which it undertakes to pay their election expenses; in point of fact they sell themselves just as people sold their soul to the devil, except that there is no formal compact, the bargain is tacitly understood.

The other candidates, however, who have contributed more or less handsomely to the funds of the Machine, also owe it service after their election; every public official must put all his influence at its disposal, that which his office procures him as well as his own. Mr. Wanamaker remarks on this subject: "Down to the borough place, up to the largest post-office appointment, every man who gets a place must make obeisance to the boss.... Each office-holder becomes a servant of the Machine. If he owns a newspaper it must support the Machine.... The straits which a man in the service is driven to to control his relations, and his bank, and his connections of every kind for the boss is ludicrous as well as sad." In this way the power of the Machine extends over all the branches of the government, none escape it, each serves to satisfy its wants and its appetites. The Executive, and in general the officials who are at the head of a department, are the first prey of the Machine, for they dispose of what the Machine wants above all things, — the subordinate offices in the public administrations with which it pays its henchmen and its workers. The departmental chiefs make over to it the patronage which is intrusted to them by the law. The municipal Machine claims it from the mayor; the State Machine gets the State offices from the Governor; the State boss extorts the nominations to the Federal places of his State from the President of the United States. And each of them yields to the exigencies and the entreaties of the respective Machine, for the same reasons which the case of the President has already disclosed to us in the historical sketch of the system of party organization. These reasons apply with still greater force to the lower officials who have to deal, not with several Senators who neutralize each other, but with a single boss, and who have behind them a less brilliant record and before them a long public career to run, with prizes to be gained. Here, for instance, is a local official of as high a rank as State Governor; he is not in needy circumstances, he is sometimes very rich, a millionnaire; but his political future depends entirely on the Machine, it is the Machine which has taken him out of obscurity, and if it drops him he will fall back into it; yet he has further ambitions, he would like to become Senator of the United States, or he even dreams of the White House. The men of the Machine are always at him, and weak character as he generally is, he soon yields, though a man of good intentions. His successor and the successor of his successor will present the same spectacle.4 At the best, oscillating 1 *The Speeches,* p. 109.

A recent number of the *Gazette* of Emporia, in the State of Kansas, conbetween fear of public opinion and fear of the Machine, he will wear himself out in concessions, now to one and now to the other. Patronage is the main, but by no means the only, object of these concessions, and of this game of see-saw in which the Governor indulges toward the Machine; he also exercises in the latter's favour, under its pressure, the other prerogatives attached to his functions. Wherever the boss "owns" the Governor, as the saying goes, he makes him veto the decisions of the legislature which thwart the Machine, makes him pardon the electoral tricksters or the unfaithful officials belonging to the Machine, and who perchance have been convicted, etc.

The legislative power is not less prone to fall into the clutches of the Machines, especially the State legislatures. Congress as a whole escapes this influence in the absence of a national Machine or a national boss. It is only the individual members of Congress, elected with the help of their local Machine, who are under the thumb of the latter like the other local public representatives, and are obliged to render it the services which it demands from them, such as asking the federal Executive for places for the men of the Machine, obediently taking the stump in the local campaigns against the champions of good government, and, in rarer cases, voting in the House as the Machine directs, when it is interested in the particular bill for reasons which are generally of a financial nature. Far more serious is the interference of the Machine with the legislative work in the municipal assemblies and in the State legislatures. In each legislative assembly the Machine "owns" a certain number of members whose election tained, on this subject, a very characteristic exhortation addressed to the new Governor, selected outside the political set after the long and melancholy experience supplied by his predecessors who were ruled by the politicians: "There will come into his council-room unworthy men seeking preferment. They will plead party fealty and party service to justify their claims. X. must be firm. He must throw these men overboard. There will come into his council-room crafty men with schemes for the Governor to further. They will point to their campaign contributions to justify their requests. X. must throw them down. There will come flatterers to steal away the Governor's honour. There will come sugar-coated plans to loot the Treasury; the devil will come to X. and take him into a high mountain and show him the United States Senate — how it lies — and in the next six months he will havo proved himself false to the people or worthy of their confidence. " expenses it has paid; these tools of the Machine form a nucleus which is quickly developed by intimidation and corruption brought to bear on the independent members. The latter are swept into the net first of all by the institution of the legislative caucus, of those semi-official meetings of the members of the party in which they decide, by a majority of votes, what line shall be taken up in the full sitting of the House on each important question; on pain of apostasy, every member of the party is obliged to vote in the way agreed on. Forming a compact group which manoeuvres as one man, the representatives of the Machine easily become masters of the caucus, and always thrust their decisions on it. Besides this, the members, even the most independent ones, are reduced to submission through fear of seeing all the legislative measures in which their constituencies are interested shelved. The speaker of the assembly, chosen in caucus, is a creature of the Machine, and it is he who appoints all the legislative committees, taking care to keep out the members who have shown themselves uncompromising toward the Machine. As soon as a bill brought in by one of these members is referred to the committee, it is smothered there, the committee never reports on it. The more honourable members therefore make up their minds, in despair, to vote for the most scandalous proposals, dictated by the Machine, in order to prevent the interests of their constituents from being neglected. If the Governor of the State is a creature of the Machine, the latter can put pressure through him on the legislators who had rather not "antagonize" the head of the Executive, and all the more easily that he has the right of legislative veto aud other prerogatives. Lastly, a good many members are made tools of the Machine by dint of corruption; some sell themselves; others, and they are more numerous, honest men, generally from the country districts, succumb to the schemes of the agents of corruption who set traps for them, entice them into bad courses, lead them into gambling, etc. The legislation which the Machine demands or extorts from the State assemblies is very varied: sometimes it is the creation of new offices to be distributed among the politicians; the abolition of offices held by the opponents of the Machine ("to legislate out of office "); the reorganization of the public departments enabling the Machine to exploit them more easily; fiscal favours and others to the companies which are its financial backers; the reduction of their taxes; the creation of monopolies in favour of private individuals; and generally all sorts of laws which on one pretext or another give rise to expenditure benefiting certain persons favoured by the Machine.

The Machine interferes in a similar way with municipal government, which is even the principal sphere of its activity and of its evil doings, as we are already aware from the historical sketch of the caucus system. It is more easy to "build a Machine" in a city than in a State: the territorial area is limited; the elements of the population on which the Machine leans are concentrated there and are more homogeneous; the spoil awaits, so to speak, the bosses and the plundering rings — contracts to be adjudged, public works to be given out, "franchises" to be granted, and sinecures to be created in the municipal departments, or rather on the pay-r61 ls.

The administration of justice itself does not escape the influence of the Machine, for the judges, being elective officials, are, like the others, in need of being put on the slate. The subordinate magistrates, the police justices, taken very often from among the "henchmen" of the Machine, are generally its humble servants. It is they who, together with the police, help the Machine to control the lower strata of the electors. Their duties make them the nearest and the most influential public authority, next to the police, with the masses. It is in them that the people should see embodied the majesty of the law, and they prostitute it to the Machine. Of the higher magistrates the Machine wields the most pernicious influence over the prosecuting officers, by making them, as has already been mentioned, dismiss or suspend prosecutions against its proteges. The higher judiciary, chosen with more regard for the importance of their office, discharge their duties fairly honourably so long as " politics" are not involved; but whenever the interests of the party and of its Machine are at stake they are sometimes liable to be influenced by party considerations. The magic effect of the " pull" is not unknown in courts of justice, especially on the occasion of the exercise of the patronage intrusted to the judges, who not only appoint the clerks, but select barristers for many lucrative berths, such as receiverships in bankruptcy, refereeships, etc. The best claim in the eyes of the judge to these appointments is not the legal knowledge and the professional dignity of the lawyer, but his relations with the boss and the Machine; it is the son or the nephew of a conspicuous politician, or a politician himself, a member of the Machine, who gets the preference. The most upright judge, whose position, under the regime of an elected judiciary, is rendered so precarious by the heedlessness and the caprice of the popular vote, which often make him suffer for his honesty, — this judge is, besides, dependent on the good pleasure of the boss. If he has incurred his displeasure, he is a lost man, he will be "turned down "; a frown from the boss is enough to put an end to the most brilliant and most dignified judicial career; he sits in judgment on the judges, and condemns them for the heinous offence of insubordination to the Machine; having got the judge elected the Machine considers it has "the right," as the Tammany boss put it recently, "to expect proper consideration at his hands."

Thus there is no sphere of public, political, and economic activity into which the Machine does not penetrate, in which it does not wield an influence used solely for its own interests. A detailed analysis of the resources supplied by each of these spheres to the operations and the schemes of a Machine, in a large city or in a State, would present a really formidable whole, transcending in importance all that a legitimate government, however vast its powers, can aspire to. Mr. Wanamaker, Cf. the article in the *American Law Review*, 1899, entitled "The Struggle in New York for the Independence of the Judiciary from the Control of the Party 'Boss.'" This opinion was expressed on the following occasion: the Tammany boss asked a Democratic judge, that is to say, a judge elected on the ticket of the Democratic party, to appoint a man of his, a low-class politician, clerk of the court. The judge, who did not see why he should turn out the occupant of the post to make way for the creature of the boss, refused. At the next election of judges, which took place soon afterward, the boss gave orders that this judge, who had discharged his duties with the greatest distinction for a period of twenty-eight years, should be replaced on the list of party candidates by a newcomer whose claims to the bench were *nil.* The convention which nominates the candidates, as usual, simply carried out the order. The excommunicated judge stood as independent candidate with the support of the Republican party, but was defeated at the election.
quoted above, has made out such a list for the Republican Machine of the State of Pennsylvania. Here it is:

Parts Of The Quay Machine *Part A.* — A Republican State Committee, which in every part is subjugated to serve the personal interests of Senator Quay first and the party next, without respect to the will of the people.
Part B. — Great prestige and patronage, controlled by Quay as a United States Senator, with two votes, his own and the other. *Part C.*—Thirty Congressmen, with their secretaries, sixty persons, whose salaries aggregate §180,000 annually, and who are re-

sponsible to the machine for their respective districts. *Part D.*—The 419 officers and employees of the State government, who receive in salaries 81,034,500 annually, and who are selected only because they are supposed to be able to deliver the votes of their districts to any one the Quay machine dictates. These men are all assessed by the bosses. *Part E.* — The State Senate, with every officer, from president *pro tem* down to page-boys, selected to do the machine's bidding. The expenses of the Senate last year were $169,604. *Part F.* — The State House of Representatives, with members, officers, and employees, 267 in number, who drew 3468,302 last year. All committees are selected by the machine, and are chairmened by men who know no will but that of Senator Quay. Thus his machine absolutely controls all revenue and tax legislation. *Part G.* — 8122 post-offices, with salaries amounting to $3,705,446. Most postmasters are made the personal agents of the machine in their respective towns. *Part H.*—4149 county offices, a majority of whom are controlled by Senator Quay's machine, whose salaries amount to $6,000,000. *Part I.* —The Philadelphia Mint, with 438 employees, who receive in yearly salaries $326,665. *Part J.* — The offices of Collector of Port, with 400 employees, who receive in salaries $454,000. *Part K.*—The internal revenue offices, with 281 employees, who receive in salaries $356,400. *Part L.* — The United States Circuit and District Courts, with fortyone employees, who receive in salaries §95,000. *Part M.* — League Island Navy Yard and Senate arsenals, with 585 employees, who receive in salaries $725,000, making a total of 14,705 officers and employees, who receive from the State and National Governments $7,609,911 annually. *Part N.* —The thousands of trustees, other officials and employees of hospitals, State and private; State prisons, reformatories, State asylums, charitable homes, State colleges, normal schools, soldiers' orphans' schools, scientific institutes and museums who are expected to support the machine, or the appropriations of their institutions will be endangered. *Part O.*—The combined capital of the brewers of the State, their thousands of employees and dependent patrons whom they control. It is alleged to have been the money of the brewers that paid the large sums during Superintendent of Mint Boyer's administration as State Treasurer necessary to make good shortages which saved the machine when his cashier, Mr. Livesey, became a fugitive from justice. *Part P.* — Besides the amounts paid for salaries of State officers which have already been accounted for, the Appropriation Committee, who are of Quay's personal selection, disburse $10,000,000 annually to schools, hospitals, penal institutions, etc. The bold manipulation of these funds for the benefit of the machine has educated people to regard moneys received for these purposes as personal contributions from Senator Quay, in return for which they must render help to his machine. *Part Q.* — The State Liquor League, whose members are in every city, town, hamlet, and crossroads throughout the State, and who maintain a permanent State organization, having headquarters and representatives at Harrisburg during the sessions of the Legislature, are always for Senator Quay's machine, and form an important part of the machine's operations. *Part Jt.* — A large number of the Common Fleas Judges throughout the State, who use their license-granting power for the benefit of the machine by rewarding those faithful to the cause of Quay, and punishing those opposed to the machine.

Part *S.* — The millions of withheld school and personal tax moneys that are used to further the interests of the machine. At three per cent interest, the rate that Smedley Darlington testified last week, under oath, his trust company paid, the machine has taken $2,500,000 of your money since Senator Quay began his reign.

Part *T.* — The hundreds of subservient newspapers who are recipients of machine favours, with their army of newsgatherers and correspondents, who are forced to chloroform public sentiment, and hide the iniquities of the machine.

The principal allies and partners of the machine are the corporations. The 15,000 national and State office-holders, and the thousands of other officials connected with State institutions, form a small part of the whole number of obedient machine men who are constantly at the command of Senator Quay, the admitted boss of the machine. The corporation employees of the State who are controlled for Quay's use increase the number to the proportions of a vast army.

The steam railroads of the State employ 85,117 men, and pay them annually in wages $49,400,000. Of this number, the Pennsylvania and Reading Railroads furnish 37,911 and 10,08.3 men, respectively. The Vanderbilt system furnishes 12,432 men; the Baltimore and Ohio, 3616; the New Jersey Central, 2864; the Lehigh Valley, 12,062; and the Delaware, Lackawanna, and Western, 2150. The great street railways of the State, who have received valuable legislative concessions for nothing, give the machine loyal support with 12,079 employees, who are paid in salaries 86,920,692 every year.

That monopoly of monopolies, the Standard Oil Company, pays annually. $2,600,000 to its 3000 employees, who are taught fidelity to Senator Quay's machine. The Bethlehem Iron Works, whose armour plates are sold to the Government for nearly double the contract price offered to foreign countries, influence their employees to such an extent that in the city of Bethlehem it has been found difficult to get men to stand as antiQuay delegates.

The thousands of working-men of the Carnegie Iron Works, it is said, are marched to the polls under the supervision of superintendents and foremen, and voted for Quay candidates under penalty of losing their jobs.

The great express companies who furnish franks to machine followers, one of whom is bossed by Senator Piatt, with their thousands of men, can be counted on for great service to the machine.

The telegraph companies, whose State officials can, it is said, be found at the inner Quay councils, with the thousands of employees distributed at every important point throughout the State, and before whom a large share of all important news must pass, is one of the most dangerous parts of the Quay machine. 1 *The Speeches,* pp. 231-231.

SEVENTH CHAPTER THE POLITICIANS AND THE MACHINE *(conclusion)*

I

The extraordinary powers, unparalleled under the regime of free institutions, which the Machine exercises, centre eventually in a single man — the boss. What sort of man, then, is this, who is able to wield such an authority? Let us look more closely at this personage who is the embodiment of the politicians and their works.

Two principal species may be pointed out in the genus boss: the city boss and the State boss. The type is exactly the same, only the features differ: coarser in the one, they are often more refined in the other. The origin of the boss is always very humble, especially that of the city boss. This latter is a "self-made" man in the strict sense of the word. In the majority of cases, of foreign, Irish, extraction, the child of parents who have recently immigrated, or having himself landed on American soil at a very early age, he has begun his public career in the streets of a large city as newspaper vendor, streetcar conductor, actor in a travelling circus, or, better still, waiter to a saloon-keeper, Irish like himself. There he was initiated into the mysteries of "paltics" by the conversations of the heelers and the ward politicians; he learnt to fathom the recesses of the human heart, with the insight vouchsafed into them by the generous properties of drink; and, having felt his vocation, he enlisted in the army of heelers, with the baton of boss in his knapsack. From a "repeater" (a man who votes several times over under feigned names) he quickly became head of a gang of repeaters, and then precinct leader. In the meanwhile he has, perhaps, mounted still higher on the politico-social ladder by becoming himself a saloon-keeper. Or, less fortunate, he has found his means of subsistence and his social position in a sinecure which the Machine has procured for him in the municipal administraVol. Ii—2d 401 tion. Extending his influence from day to day, he constructed a small local machine; with its aid he became a member of the city council, that promised land flowing with milk and honey in the form of contracts for public works or even of "franchises," of the monopolies coveted by wealthy corporations, which have the excellent habit of paying. As district leader, he swallowed up the other less able district leaders and was left without a rival. A vulgar demagogue, he got the mob on his side, and, by dealing in its votes, he became the Caesar of the Machine and of the city. This stirring and so laborious career has sometimes been within an ace of being stopped by still more dramatic incidents, such as a criminal prosecution for homicide or less serious encounters with the law. However, he will perhaps have lost nothing by waiting; as it were by chance, justice may suddenly wake up, and, like his illustrious ancestor, Tweed, he may some day forget the cares of power in the peaceful retirement of a prison.

The State boss is generally of American origin. His beginnings were also very humble. He has had a more respectable career, although in certain cases his past would not bear closely looking into: one has embezzled public money and has escaped imprisonment through the intervention of the senatorial boss whom he was serving, and who made good the defalcation; another has on his conscience the death of a man killed in a brawl; another was in his youth a confirmed drinker and gambler. Having entered "politics" young, the future State boss has built up his fortune slowly, by the same methods as the lower boss. Working as underling for a big boss, doing his jobs in every part of the State, he has made friends with the local politicians, he has found out their strong and their weak points, and has discerned the use which he can make of each man. With the most powerful of them he has concluded offensive and defensive alliances. Strengthened by these friendships and these supports, extending over the whole State, some purely interested, others not unmixed with personal affection, he has got himself accepted as dispenser of the federal patronage, and, after a series of lucky operations with this capital, has ended by sweeping the whole State into the sphere of his influence.

This brilliant career of a man who from such a humble start has risen to be master of the government of a large city or of a State, — without, as a rule, filling any official position, — is, from one end to the other, the triumph of one supreme quality: skill in the management of men. The organizing genius and the *coup d'ozil* of the strategist and of the tactician, which takes in vast horizons and foresees eventualities, are in the boss only the complement and the amplification of this first quality. With an inevitably limited stock of good things to be provided for an unlimited number of appetites, he performs the miracle of the loaves and fishes, discerning exactly the right slice and cutting off just the proper quantity to be given to each man. To some he offers the solid food of places, of money, and of pulls; to others the unsubstantial diet of promises. He plays with wants and appetites, with credulity and vanity, as with so many counters. He is admirably equipped for this game by his mind, which is profoundly calculating, cool, incapable of yielding to the impulse of the moment, but very capable of taking sudden and bold resolutions to meet the situation. With this uniform type of mind, which is the distinctive mark of the species, the particular temperaments vary: there is the brutal, coarse, overbearing boss; the amiable and even seductive, or "magnetic" boss; or, while devoid of personal "magnetism," mild, smooth-mannered, an "easy boss," nay, even unctuous, like a clergyman, so much so that any one who did not know him would not the least perceive the hoax if he were introduced to him as the Reverend X. Y. Z. But the affability never goes so far as expansiveness: the boss is naturally reserved, coiled up — he has no confidant; this is wiser, at least he is sure not to be betrayed. He hardly utters his plans and his schemes to himself; he turns them over in his head and marks them by means of mental notes, which he will develop under the pressure of circumstances.

This Moltke of the Machine has all the less difficulty in being taciturn that he does not know the six languages in which the great German chief of the staff was silent; the boss often does not even know his own, he cannot speak or write English correctly. It is said of a certain boss, who is at the head of his profession, or is at least one of its most famous representatives, that his whole vocabulary does not exceed three hundred words. In fact, the education which the boss has received is generally of the poorest; he has hardly attended the primary school. Yet owing to the resourceful intelligence and the dogged energy which distinguish the American, many a boss, and especially those who have risen to the position of State boss, ends by acquiring a certain polish which shows itself not only in his dress and his manners, but appears to fill the gaps of his early very defective education. He can turn this semblance of culture which he has acquired to account with the same coolness with which he exploits the varied resources of the Machine; he is capable, on the occasion of the inauguration of a political club, which brings together the pick of the Machine, of quoting the "constitution of the Athenian democracy," or of expatiating on the dangers of the American democracy like a Tocqueville on a small scale. There are bosses who have real intellectual interests. But it is a curious fact that these great manipulators of men do not turn their attention to anything living, among the things of the mind. A famous State boss, one of the most terrible realists of Machine politics, seeks mental relaxation in Assyrian antiquities. The reigning boss of the neighbouring State indulges in the study of theology in the leisure moments left him by "politics." These studies are one of the few things which the bosses do disinterestedly, they could not well boast of them to their followers, on the contrary even. When the rival press, launching out into every kind of attack on the boss, accuses him of having embezzled public money, he gets the statement contradicted by the newspapers devoted to him, or threatens an action for slander, because the Eighth Commandment, "Thou shalt not steal," compels the respect of the great majority. But when the boss is called an ignorant and illiterate man, he takes no notice, and his newspapers are care 1 have had the advantage of hearing a dissertation of this kind from the mouth of a prominent boss, who summed up the position of the American democracy for my benefit, and dwelt on the important part played by demagogues and on the danger that there was of the American people despairing of democracy and preferring a monarch, a " strong man. " After having listened to the boss for more than half an hour, I interrupted him by asking artlessly whether he did not think that one of the dangers to which he referred was the special development of the party Organization. "N-n-no," he replied, "I don't think so. You see, you can't prevent me having influence. I ask my friends to do this or that, and they do it. The newspaper of the rival party, no doubt, will be sure to say the next day,' Boss X. has decreed this.'" ful not to protest and represent him as a scholar, for that might injure him with the masses, with the "plain people."

Cultivated or without culture, the hoss is, in any event, a man of superior intelligence, but of an altogether special kind of superiority, which shows itself in a very delicate appreciation of particular situations. He is incapable of grasping principles; his ideas in politics are hard to discover: he has none, and does not need them. This is not the compass he uses, it is the wind of circumstances and of personal conjunctures which steers the course of the boss. He is incapable of stating his views on the problems of the day. He is neither a writer, nor a speaker, nor even a good talker; on the stump he would cut a poor figure. The stock of eloquence necessary for defending, by speech and by the pen, the name and style of the party under which the boss operates is supplied by others. He confines himself to turning their talents to account, just as he does those of the district leaders and other henchmen; he himself is invariably nothing more than a clever contractor. The few orators who have been discernible among the higher bosses, the senatorial bosses, even the most brilliant of these orators, were simply rhetoricians and polemists, who looked at the great questions of the day in their personal aspect, with reference to the persons who were involved in the various controversies; they never connected their name with a legislative measure or left any other lasting trace of their activity. The opportunism of which the boss is the living embodiment does not allow him to risk taking the initiative; he prefers to walk in the shadow of public opinion. Incapable of contributing to the movement of ideas, he finds it difficult to understand them, he grasps public opinion only in its crystallized state, so to speak; its aspirations and its impulses escape him, and its revolts take him by surprise. Observing and appraising mankind in detail, by their pettinesses, the boss is not qualified to appreciate the moral forces of human nature; a profound judge of men, he does not understand man. He never credits the citizen in general with virtue and intelligence, he is not aware that these qualities exist; his skill lies in seizing on the weaknesses of men. The few moral virtues of the politician which he possesses are narrowed in their exercise in the same way; he is devoted, up to the point of self-sacrifice, to his friends; a man of his word, he is so as long as particular persons are concerned; if he has promised places or favours he looks on his promises as sacred; but if he has promised reforms on the eve of the elections he snaps his fingers at them the day after. The courage and the confidence in himself which distinguish him in his acts fail him in the domain of ideas; growing timorous all of a sudden, he stealthily watches public opinion to see if he can venture to go ahead without suffering for it. The general aspect of men and of things always escapes him; he is a judge only of the concrete, of the reality converted into small coin. In other words, his mind lacks the all-important qualities which make the real leader of men. He has only the intelligence of a great wire-puller.

The methods of the boss are exactly adapted to his mind: he does not like discussion, the clash of ideas; he is a man of underhand action. He shuns the light of day; his element is intrigue, and he revels in it. The resources of his sagacity are expended in combinations of mines and counter-mines. He arranges everything secretly and keeps silence and makes his lieutenants keep silence until the moment comes for facing the public. But, while working in the dark, the boss does not hide himself, he wields his power quite openly. He does not deny this, unless it be from a remnant of modesty or by a refinement of irony, like the boss that said to a deputation of citizens, who had come to advocate a measure of public interest before him, "I quite agree with you, but," he added, timidly, "what can I, a mere citizen, do?" Certain State bosses have their "kitchen cabinets " which are summoned regularly and are followed by reporters, who wait in the passages to find out what has been going on. The publicity attaching to the person of the boss, to his sayings and doings, to his supposed plans, is by no means distasteful to him: he is treated as if he were a great statesman. It must be added that the public also takes pleasure, a melodramatic pleasure, in following the sayings and doings of the boss. He appears to them, according to the description of newspapers which are not in the habit of laying on the colours too thinly, as a sort of Mephistopheles and Cagliostro rolled into one, who has endless tricks up his sleeve. What is he going to bring out of it now, what is he going to do, what has he just done — are so many questions and hypotheses which help to break the monotony of American life. It should be admitted that this curiosity is not the only feeling which gains the boss his undeniable popularity. This man who, sprung from nothing, has reached the very top of the tree, strikes the imagination of the Americans and flatters it. They recognize in him a master spirit. He excites admiration like those *conquistadores* who conquered and plundered empires. Even cultivated men of high integrity cannot always resist this feeling of admiration for the favourites of fortune, honest folk or rascals, which pervades the air of the New World. One would almost think that they are proud of the bosses.

In the eyes of the great mass of the "respectable" members of the party, who do not take an active part in politics and who only hear from afar the din of the clash of arms, the boss, whose name is in every mouth, appears as a sort of paladin who is always in the breach and fighting for the good cause. The hostile cries and the objurgations which accompany the name of the boss die away as they descend further and further into the lower strata of the community, and the name alone reaches these strata encircled with a halo of notoriety. In the remote districts the *sancta simplicitas* of the people procures for the boss an attachment which sometimes is expressed in a touching and disconcerting form when one thinks of the archcorrupter and poisoner of the springs of public life who is the object of these sentiments.3 Yet, as a general rule, the boss A very eminent judge expressed his regret to me that I could not see the Tammany Hall boss, who was not in America. "What a pity," exclaimed the judge, who belonged to a different State and a different party from the boss, "you would have seen a man, a mastermind!" I asked an editor of a large independent newspaper to tell me what was the foundation of the power of the State boss, who was ruling a free republic like an Oriental satrapy. "The pride in him as a leader," replied my interlocutor, drawing himself up. I put the same question, about an odious boss of a large city, to a leading barrister. "Why, he is a leader of men," he replied, with emphasis.

A powerful senatorial boss, a State boss, learnt that a plot had been formed in the greatest secrecy to depose him from power, and that several delegates to the convention had already joined the conspirators. The boss at once decided to appeal to the people, and hurriedly sent out thousands of circulars to all the four corners of the State, couched in the following terms: "I find myself unexpectedly precipitated into a struggle for my political life. I am a candidate for State chairman. Can I have your support?" The first reply does not much care to put his popularity to the test of a popular vote; he does not often stand for elective office himself. Sometimes it is the flagrant inadequacy of his education which prevents him from filling a leading position; but more often he would run the risk of a defeat owing to his reputation of wire-puller and election jobber, whereas, if he keeps behind the scenes, he can quietly pull the strings and secure the return of the men who suit him. The State boss likes to run for the Senate of the United States, for the very reason that he can obtain this position more easily by intrigue and corruption, the Senators being elected, not by universal suffrage, but by the State Legislatures, where the boss is often supreme. In any event, it is not in the public position which the boss sometimes fills that his power resides. That power is by its nature occult and irresponsible.

The boss none the less derives from it

considerable personal profit, both of a material and moral kind. The first is the most important; he makes money, and often he makes a large fortune. For the city boss this is the main, the sole object, as the Tammany boss has of late cynically admitted in public. Cases are quoted, it is true, of bosses who have died poor; but there are many bosses alive and well who are very rich, who are "worth" at least $500,000, while having no avowable source of income. This one has perhaps §5000 salary as Senator, but he lives at the rate of $50,000 a year; he has a house in town, at the seaside, and in the South, amid groves of orange trees. Another has not perhaps even these $5000 salary, and spends ten or twelve times as much, buys land and houses, keeps race-horses, etc. Where does the money come from? In the first place, the boss has absolute control of the which arrived, written in a little girl's hand, ran: "Dear Senator X. Your letter to father received. Father is dead, but mother and I and the boys are here, and we will see that you get the vote for this precinct." *Why is the party "boss"?* — an article written, almost at the dictation of a well-known boss, for a " press syndicate," which supplies articles for reproduction in numerous periodicals. This article, which probably appeared, has been obligingly communicated to me in proof-sheets by the editors of the " syndicate ") When summoned before the committee of enquiry of the New York legislature (Mazet Committee of 1899), controlled by the rival boss,—the Republican State boss, — the Tammany leader, who is the boss of New York City, was led to speak of his profits. "You are working for your own pocket?" he was asked by way of conclusion. "All the time; and you too," replied the boss. party funds. Again, he receives commissions given by the great contractors for public works, by the companies which buy municipal franchises or other favours, commissions paid in cash, or in stock of the company, or by allowing him "to get in on the ground-floor " when the company is floated, which enables the initiated to indulge in stock exchange speculations. In connivance with the State treasurer, his creature, the boss speculates with the treasury balances, or deposits them without interest in private banks, which show their gratitude by a heavy contribution to the party chest, that is, to the boss. Lastly, the boss makes money out of the pulls which he has on the representatives of authority, by ensuring, in return for a share in the profits, a lucrative connexion to business men, to lawyers: a tradesman who has the boss or his son for nominal partner obtains the preference with the municipal administration and his goods are accepted without serious investigation; it is the same with a law firm in partnership with the son of a boss, who is in a better position than any one else for dealing with disputed claims on the public purse or for appearing before legislative committees which examine bills interesting financial companies. It is only fair to add that if the income of the bosses is considerable, their general expenses are so as well; the boss has to spend a great deal to maintain his political position, to keep up the Machine. Sometimes the boss devotes his whole income to this, he does not grow rich by "politics "; but this disinterestedness does not prevent him from getting good things for the members of his family, by means of the pulls described in the instances quoted.

The "disinterested" boss takes to "politics" from inclination; "politics" is his passion, that is to say, not the problems of politics in the ordinary sense of the word, but the intrigues, the combinations, and the gossip of personal politics. It is this kind of politics that he indulges in. When he has company at his table he talks "politics"; when he takes a month's holiday and goes to some island or other he still talks "politics" with the crowd of visitors whom he receives; "he eats, he drinks, he sleeps politics," — as a well-known political personage has said of a famous State boss. The love of power, the satisfaction felt by the autocrat who exalts and humbles men at his good pleasure, is a still more common motive with the boss. He enjoys this power behind the scenes and on the stage. The tribe of politicians worship him as a king. He holds his court even in his country residences; crowds of office-seekers hang upon his nod there. At the city convention or the State convention, often a quarter of an hour before the opening of the sitting, the great mass of delegates know nothing of the slate which they will shortly vote; they try to guess it, and await, as if it were the decree of destiny, the communication of the names which "the old man" — as they affectionately call the boss — has been pleased, in his inscrutable wisdom, to adopt. When the boss condescends to come to the convention and take his seat in a spectators' box — in case he does not care to be a delegate — the whole audience rises and bursts into applause, the band plays "Hail to the chief." The principal lieutenants of the boss are on intimate terms with him, but in their relations there is always the more or less perceptible tone which characterizes those between sovereign and vassal; he is master of them all, he has the last word. He decides without appeal and without circumlocution, he generally speaks with an *imperatoria brevitas.* Yet, among these vassals there are powerful ones, with whom the master A boss who is not unknown to fame, having put me in communication with one of his lieutenants, the latter, by a singular inadvertence, made an appointment with me at a meeting of their committee. The members of the committee arrived one after the other, and the boss himself. For each man he had a civil, for some a kindly word, but always so laconic as to be almost disconcerting. Seated in a corner I watched them; and realizing that the presence of a stranger would only embarrass them, I went up to the boss, and said, " I suppose that your meeting of to-day will not be of great interest tome." "Purely administrative," replied the boss. "But I should be very glad to have a talk with one of these gentlemen." "— 'l right." He cast a glance at the meeting, and said, " Senator!" and turning to me, added: "He has been Senator in the State Legislature." I looked at the whilom *pater conscriptus* of the great commonwealth, and I saw an elderly man with an expressionless face and a lame, misshapen body. "Senator, this gentleman wants to talk politics; you will be hero to-morrow evening at eight o'clock, eh?" A slight wink from the expressionless face showed that he had understood. I went to the appointment half-heartedly, not expecting to get much out of the promised interview. But, to my astonishment, the expressionless face lighted up, and I had a conversation, of several hours' duration, with the Senator, in which he gave me some very interesting information about "politics," while correcting himself occasionally, with the prudence of the Norman peasant who says: "Pour une annee qu'il y a des pommes, il n'y a pas de pommes; pour uue anne'e qu'il n'y a pas de pommes, il y a des pommes." has to reckon, as the King of France had to reckon with the Duke of Burgundy, the Duke of Normandy, the Count of Flanders. From this obligation not even a boss as absolute as the Tammany chief escapes; among his district leaders are men who do not depend on the boss either for their livelihood or for their position, who engage in "politics" from taste and ambition, and who wield an indisputable personal ascendency in their districts, — they have a crowd of vassals and lieges of their own. A State boss, were he as powerful as the Republican boss of Pennsylvania, is exposed to the schemes of some of his lieutenants, haunted by the wish to "set up for themselves." Perhaps it is the Philadelphia boss who is plotting to supplant the master, or it is the boss of the second large city of the State, of Pittsburg, who wants to play at being independent. Sometimes there are open fights; the big boss has a bout with his unruly vassals, like Louis XI. with Charles the Bold, but in the end he comes to terms with them. When he can, he quells revolts by the exercise of authority or by sheer corruption; he deposes the district leader who is guilty or suspected of disloyalty; or he ruins him in his fief, he drenches the primaries with money to prevent the rebel from "getting the delegates," without whom the latter is powerless. To meet extraordinary expenditure, the boss blackmails the corporations, the financial companies, exactly like — and this again is a point of resemblance with feudal manners — the mediaeval king, who extorted money from the burgesses, the traders of his good cities, to get the wherewithal for making war on a rebellious vassal.

Such is the boss in his public capacity. In his private sphere he is often perfectly honourable; his family life is irreproachable, he can be depended on, he is exact in the observances of religion, he has his seat in church. This holds good, also, of the subordinate politicians. The politician, great or small, simply puts in practice, without being aware of it perhaps, the doctrine of two moralities, the one for private, the other for public life. With certain bosses the divergence between the two moralities is not so wide in practice as with certain others, but one and all wield their power for their own interest and not in that of the commonwealth. The boss who uses his influence solely for the good of the party, or even for the good of the people, the virtuous boss, must be relegated to the realm of romance.

The use which the boss makes of his extensive and penetrating power by no means, however, affects the whole of political life: this use is confined to his requirements as an electioneering contractor, as an exploiter of the industry of elections. He does not try, like the tyrants of the Greek cities or of the Italian republics, to assert his power over the *polis* in general, to control all the manifestations of political life. All his designs on the commonwealth amount, in fact, to running the elections as he likes, putting his followers in all the places, keeping out his opponents, protecting the first, making the second harmless, and realizing the material profits attaching to these places and to the influence which they procure. The line of public policy to be adopted, in itself, is a matter of indifference to the boss. The persons even of the actors on the political stage are only of moment to him in so far as they are for or against him at the elections. If he "punishes his enemies," if he brings about proscriptions, it is solely in self-defence; he never meddles with citizens who do not go out of their way to oppose him. If he is often a despot, he is so rather from necessity, as a matter of business, than from inclination. His wish is, on the contrary, to make as many friends as possible, to please everybody; for whatever the source of his power, the material substance of it is composed of the votes of the multitude given to the candidates of the boss. A really intelligent boss is never gratuitously arrogant and despotic; he wields his power of tyrant with moderation and kindliness, and he might repeat the saying of Lord Clive: "When I think of my opportunities, I am astonished at my own moderation " Those who would like to make the acquaintance of such a hoss should read the novel by Paul Leicester Ford, *The Honourable Peter Stirling, and What People Thought of Him*, 9th ed., New York, 1896, — a clever book, written with a thorough knowledge of American " politics." N. This saying of Clive, recalled by Mr. Bryce with reference n» certain city bosses who abstain from robbing (*American Commonwealth*, II, 111), was repeated by one of the most brilliant of American orators, in a recent cele

It might, however, be explained to him that it is no great merit on his part to exhibit so much moderation. That moderation is enforced on him not only by the fact which I have just brought out, namely, that his appetites and his desires are specialized by the very nature of his means of action. Even if he tried to go farther he would fall foul of the rights of the citizen, reserved by the Constitution, those rights against which all the designs of the public authorities, like the waves that beat upon the cliff, are directed in vain. It is no use for the boss being master of the executive and the legislative, they are not omnipotent. The American Constitu brated speech, aimed at the Tammany Hall boss: "This boss need not announce any penalty against an enemy to gratify his vengeance. Let him but express dislike for a person, and ten thousand able men will be raking their wits to invent plans for the annoyance of the luckless individual who has provoked his displeasure. He need never mention the name of the corporation which he has doomed to disaster. He has but to frown upon it, and every city department would forthwith discover reasons for assailing it, while the public, quick to discover conditions affecting credit, would hasten to throw its securities upon the market, as if its certificates of stock contaminated the fingers that touched them. If he determined to establish an engine-house in the back-yard of a recalcitrant citizen, it would bo unnecessary to formulate his desire in words, but all the same the building would soon be in course of construction....

"Indeed, as we survey the extent of his powers and the manner in which they have been exercised, I believe he would be justified in saying with Lord Clive: 'Considering my opportunities, I am amazed at uiy own moderation. ' Consider for a moment his situation, and then tell me if he be not entitled to praise for moderation rather than blame for excess. He can make no public appearance without a hundred hands being ready to carry his bag or his overcoat. To walk with him is distinction among politicians. To be noticed by him is to broaden the horizon of a statesman's prospects. If flattery can affect him, ten thousand tongues are ready to persuade him that never in the history of the world has a statesman so wise, so learned, so eloquent, shed upon a happy country the priceless blessings of his political leadership. If avarice can move him, wealth, beyond its wildest dreams, is within his reach if he will allow it to flow to his feet. Where, in all the experience of man, civilized or uncivilized, can we find a parallel for power like this? No Roman proconsul ever sent to administer a distant province, no Spanish captain-general, ruling a transmarine colony, enjoyed equal power to aggrandize himself or to benefit his favorites. Clive, walking through the treasury of Moorshedabad, where sacks of gold and silver, rubies and diamonds — the accumulated fruits of a tyrannical and unrestrained taxation — were piled on every side, free to take what he chose, no power to question him, no limitation upon his greed, except such as wag imposed upon him by his conscience, — Clive, with the riches of Bengal at his feet, enjoyed no such opportunities as the boss of a great American city." (Speech of Mr. Bourke Cockrau, of the 31st of October, 1898, at New York.) tion has made the fundamental rights of the man and of the citizen safe from oppression by placing them under the sovereign protection of the courts, which can annul as unconstitutional not only administrative acts, but laws themselves; and the judiciary, taken as a whole, is not yet under the thumb of the bosses. No doubt, the barrier thus erected by the pact of the Constitution, for the protection of individual rights, in marking the extreme limit beyond which it is not allowable to pass, still leaves a certain margin for possible encroachment on these rights. Being able to exploit only this margin, this border, the boss makes it wholly and solely subservient to the interests of his electioneering business, in order to get as large a return as possible. The influence of the boss, therefore, being always brought back to these exclusive preoccupations, has only a partial effect on general political life, and the mischief which it does there is, in a way, of a local and sporadic kind. This mischief corresponds more or less closely to the moral and material needs of the boss and of the Machine trying to make their living, in their own way.

The point which is most exposed to the designs of the Machine is, in consequence, the municipal administration, owing to its ample resources offering abundance of loot and being, so to speak, within arm's reach. The finances of a city ruled by the Machine are always heavily burdened with useless and bloated expenditure. The departments are invariably encumbered with a very considerable number of sinecures, the sole object of which is to enable the " workers " of the Machine to draw their salaries; useful public works are knocked down at extravagant rates; the exploitation of the monopolies in the gift of the city is granted for nothing, or for an absurdly small consideration. In a word, the results of "ring" government, which we have witnessed in the municipal history of New York, of Philadelphia, and of some other cities, are a regular feature of American cities ruled by bosses, although in a more attenuated form. The ratepayers certainly suffer from it, they have more rates to pay; but the masses who have no rates to pay have no reason to complaiu of this regime; they gain by it, for the public works of little or no utility which the Machine is always pressing for, in order to have opportunity for plunder, give employment to poor people, arid wellpaid employment, stinginess being by no means the defect of the governments carried on by the bosses. The peculation caused by the Machine is considerable, but, looking to the piratical methods which the latter practises in municipal administration, it ought logically to be even greater. After all, it often turns out that the resources of the cities which are not afflicted with a Machine are not administered much more economically. The depredations committed by the bosses are made up for, to a certain extent, by a better, more responsible administration of the municipal departments, which is due to the members of the councils of these cities and their employees being more disciplined. The Machine which selects all the candidates for public office at its good pleasure, while making them docile instruments, takes care to choose them as well as possible; and once they are installed in their posts, it sees that they do not compromise it. Instead of being responsible to the public, they are so to the Machine; the responsibility is deflected, but it is genuine, and all the more that the power of the Machine is more centralized, more personal, and more immediate. If the Machine is convinced of the necessity of a certain standard of administration, it can enforce it on the persons in office more easily than the electors themselves could do. Besides this, the great mass of small employees are not dishonest; they accept their places from the Machine to earn a humble livelihood. And when they have discharged the first duty of their office, which is to serve the Machine, when this tribute on their time, their exertions, and their conscience has been taken, they honestly give the rest to the public. The municipal administration run by the most corrupt Machine — I mean Tammany Hall — affords striking proof of this state of things.

Of all the public departments in the large cities the most contaminated by the Machine is that of the police, whose co-operation is particularly valuable to it. The police in these The Tammany Hall boss in his evidence, quoted above, admitted that he was in the habit of telling the municipal councillors who were slack in their attendance at the sittings of the Council to be more regular; he " regarded it as one of his functions, as a member of the executive committee of Tammany Hall, to force such attendance." cities is "full of politics "; and so long as it is a question of "politics," that is to say, of the operations in which the Machine is interested, the public cannot count on the protection of the police. It shields from the public the frauds committed, at the primaries and at the elections, by the followers of the Machine; it molests the Machine's opponents when they want to exercise their electoral rights; it winks at the law-breaking drinking-saloons, at the gambling-hells and houses of ill fame, which pay blackmail to the Machine. But in other respects the police really does its duty, and does it, on the whole, fairly well. The other municipal departments are also infected with "politics," but in a lesser degree, and to an extent which varies with the audacity of the Machine and the indifference of the public. The Machine treats them as a preserve for " spoils " — places, contracts, etc. It exploits, with this view, at one time the fire brigade, at another the hospitals, sometimes even the school boards, by putting on them, as a reward, political "workers" for whom nothing better can be found. But, however satisfactory the administration of the cities governed by a Machine may be as a whole, and however properly aud conscientiously the employees may discharge the routine of their duties, the spirit which presides over the administration is always an unenlightened one, with no breadth or life, save in the matter of expenditure. This inferiority makes itself felt especially in educational policy; the schools are better in the cities which are not under the regime of the Machine.

Nor is legislation wholly contaminated by the Machine. The State legislatures, which vote laws, at the bidding of the boss, to swell the resources of patronage or to bestow privileges or monopolies on companies allied with the boss, also vote good laws — laws of public utility. 'It is even easier to obtain swh a law with the help of the boss. Instead of agitating and bringing the pressure of enlightened opinion to bear on the members of the legislature, it is better to apply to the boss; the latter will give the order and the law will go through, like a letter in the post.' The boss will consent to give this order if the measure, whether good or not, appears to him "popular"; in that case the passing of the law will benefit the Machine at the next election. The members of the legislative assembly, in their turn, will pass it with a readiness in which servility blends with confidence in the sagacity of the boss. The great preoccupation of the legislators who, in ordinary times, act only under pressure from outside, is to know, when others than the boss demand a measure, "who is behind them. " Are they supported by numerous and influential electors? The boss's word of command reassures them. It is sometimes more useful to appeal to the boss, not only over the heads of the legislators, but even over the heads of the sovereign people. Well-meaning citizens, who are prosecuting a reform or pursuing a certain course of action, in municipal administration as well as in the government of the State, are able to convert the bosses to their views more quickly than the great mass of the electors, and with a practical effect which is at least just as certain. In these cases boss rule offers the advantages of an "enlightened despotism." The boss exerts the same power to stop obnoxious attempts at legislation coming from individual members of the legislature, who want to blackmail wealthy companies by bringing in bills directed against them. If these companies enjoy the protection, duly paid for, of the boss, he holds up his hand, and the "striker" vanishes like a schoolboy caught in the act. The boss is equally successful in blocking a good measure brought in by an independent member, that is to say, a recalcitrant one in the eyes of the boss. Thus, the boss acts as a disciplining force; he exerts it on the whole political community for good as well as for evil; he keeps a hold and a check on the multitude by the favours and the protection which he procures for them against the law itself, just as he keeps a hold and a check on the executive officers and the legislators.

C But the boss himself is exempt from all disciplining authority; the power which he wields is not only usurped, but it is also irresponsible. He is, therefore, always liable to step out of the moderation which his character of usurper enjoins and which his means of action, as well as the barriers of the constitution, impose on him. As with every autocrat, absolute power makes him lose his head sooner or later; he becomes wilful, arrogant, and tyrannical; he exceeds all bounds in the effrontery with which he and his men use the public resources for their own benefit. At last the public's cup of patience runs over, a revolt breaks out, and the Machine is " smashed." This is the fate of every Machine, as it is of every brigand to end on the scaffold. It is only a question of time. A boss who has more self-control, more perspicacity, remains longer in power; a short-sighted and greedy boss enjoys the present hour without restraint, and precipitates his fall. But just as the death on the gibbet of the bandit of Calabria or the Abruzzi does not prevent him from having a successor in the wilds which were the scene of his exploits, so the Machine which has been "smashed" is soon put together again by the same boss or by another, to meet the same fate in the end as their predecessors. It is a regime which recalls, to some extent, that which was defined by the words "a despotism tempered by assassination." Here the assassination is only symbolical; free institutions enable the revolution to be carried out in an absolutelypacific manner, by the simple action of votingpapers. /The American people have only, according to the stereotyped phrase of the stump orator, to "rise in their might and in their majesty," and everything will come right. In reality, it is not so much in their " majesty " that the people rise as in their fury. For a long time impassive and apathetic, they start up all of a sudden in a paroxysm of wrath and try to vent it on somebody or other; "they want to punish some one." The sovereign people strike without pity and without discernment, guilty and innocent will all do to make up the hecatomb which they must have. Terror runs through the ranks of the politicians; the most powerful of them, the head bosses, on whose smile State Governors and legislators were hanging only the day before, bite the dust. The power of public opinion, which is supposed to weigh heavily, in the United States, on everybody and everything, like the *moira* of the ancients, reaches the politicians in the end, but it reaches them in a more or less/accidental way, which excludes all regular responsibility/ The authority which public opinion wields over the Machine is the authority of Judge Lynch.

The deference and submissiveness with which the Machine is obliged to treat public opinion are, consequently, limited solely to the risk which it runs of awaking the Lynch which slumbers in the breast of the public. The Machine, it is true, pays great attention to public opinion. Every district or ward leader carefully watches the state of public feeling and keeps the boss informed about it. Sometimes a semi-official canvass is taken to ascertain what reception would be given to this or that candidature prepared by the Machine. It is said of certain bosses that they endeavour, like Haroun-al-Raschid, to get at the opinion of people in the streets, in places of public resort, by talking to car conductors, to passers-by, about candidatures or other questions of the day. In cases where it is possible to satisfy public opinion without any great sacrifice on the part of the Machine, the latter does so with alacrity. But this is not often within its power, for if it always consulted the interests of the public, it would ruin its own prospects. If it appointed honest people only to public office, they would not consent to serve it; if it gave up selling "franchises," laws, and "protection" to corporations, where would it get the money which it wants for its up-keep and for the enormous general expenditure which the Machine of a large city or of a State has to meet? The bosses therefore are driven by the force of things to disregard the opinion of honest and enlightened people. The generally apathetic and inert state of public opinion enables them to defy it with impunity, in nine cases out of ten: the difficulty for them is to get over the tenth case; and it is for this purpose that they sound public opinion, to ascertain the approach of the fatal point. As long as they do not think themselves near it, they indulge unreservedly in their practices, and sometimes even take a fierce delight in openly defying public opinion; the more or less imminent danger which they run makes them look on their audacity almost as heroism. They yield only when they cannot help it. When the political situation is narrowed down to one question, submitted distinctly to public opinion, and producing a movement of the public mind in a particular direction, the Machine lies low. When it can descry nothing but the alternative of defeat or submission to the behests of public opinion, the Machine gives way. But often it tries its hand, in spite of this, and it is only after having been beaten that it mends its ways. Then it brings forward excellent candidates at the elections, adopts a humble, cringing attitude, practises virtue, until such time as public opinion goes to sleep again. On the whole, the authority of public opinion in general is only a feeble and yielding obstacle to the designs of the Machine; it imposes only partial restrictions on the latter's power.

There is a special category of respectable members of the party which exercise a certain control over the Machine: these are the wealthy persons who, out of party loyalty, give the Machine large subscriptions to the election campaign funds; they have the ear of the bosses when important candidatures are involved. Far more effective is the check imposed on the Machine by the Machine of the opposite party: whenever the two parties are evenly matched, a small number of good citizens can turn the scale in favour of one or the other party; the two rival Machines are in that case obliged to vie with each other in cultivating the good graces of these independent electors, by making up their tickets with names of men as respectable as the business of the Machine will allow. This intervention of the independent electors as masters of the situation supplies a corrective to the Machine, which is daily growing more important and more efficacious. On the other hand, it is true that the existence of two rival Machines, of more or less equal strength, helps each to hold its own and ensures it the absolute adhesion of the members of the party, who vote for it, in spite of its corruption, in order not to endanger the prospects of the party. Whereas, in places where the feebleness of the Opposition makes the dominant party safe, the Machine is not followed so blindly, and even falls to pieces pretty quickly. There are, however, very remarkable exceptions: in Pennsylvania, for instance, the egregious weakness of the Democratic Opposition does not prevent the Republicans from upholding, in the teeth of all resistance, the most corrupt State Machine that has ever existed in the United States.

The most extensive limitations to which the power of the Machine and of the politicians is subject are to be found in the social and economic character of the particular community. In places where the population is more homogeneous, and forms smaller sots, in which opinion has consequently more consistency and asserts itself with more force, the Machine cannot take the liberties which it does in large cities where public spirit is smothered under the huge agglomerations of heterogeneous elements brought together promiscuously. Its proceedings do not escape the attention of the public so easily, and the Machine is from necessity more circumspect and more moderate in its desires. In places where there are no large public works to be tendered for, or important contracts to be awarded, where there are no powerful corporations with extensive interests depending on administration or legislation, in a word, where the material for plunder is not considerable, the Machine is necessarily frugal and cannot provide a sufficient livelihood for those who have no other means of subsistence. Hence the parts of the Union least contaminated by the Machine and the politicians are the country districts. There• everybody knows each other. Opinion, which is more slow in forming among the rural population and that of small cities, is more solid, more durable, less spasmodic than in the large centres. The electors have both more leisure and more sense of their own value, a narrow and exacting sense, which procures them more consideration, at least in appearance. The Machine, however, does exist among these populations, but it is more respectable, more attentive to the general opinion. It does not assume the repulsive aspect of bossism, it simply appears as a trade-union of all those who live on the party or expect something from it, office-holders, aspirants to places with their relations and their friends. Comparatively speaking, this trade-union is as powerful as the Machine of the large city, and, it may be added, just as corrupt. With their eyes always fixed on the local loaves and fishes and the modest diet provided thereby, the politicians of the small rural Machine make politics subservient to these interests. It is not uncommon in the country districts and the small cities for members of the same family to be distributed in the rival Machines. The South, which is still largely agricultural and where, according to the census of 1890, there were only two cities with a population exceeding 100,000, and only five cities with more than 50,000 inhabitants, does not present a very favourable field for the development of the Machine. Apart from these two large cities, New Orleans and Louisville, the odious type of the boss is hardly met with in the South. Continuing, as it were, the old tradition of the South before the Civil War, the Southern boss, if the chief election wire-pullers may be thus designated, is fonder of the sentimental gratifications procured by power than of gain. This is less true of the Republican party, which occupies, as against the "Solid South," an inferior political and social position. In the West the Machine prospers more, while exhibiting infinite variations in the extent of its power and its misdeeds. The great hotbed of the Machine and of the bosses is still the Eastern States, which are rich and populous, and where social differentiation has made the most progress.

If on the map of the United States all the parts of the country where the Machine has developed were coloured red, the eye would at once be attracted to the right by a large blotch formed by the States of New York and Pennsylvania with a strip of the State of New Jersey on the east, with the State of Maryland on the south, and the State of Ohio on the west. This spot casts a faint shadow to the north-east over New England, while on the other side, to the west, the red will appear in more or less deep tints on the State of Illinois and will stain the neighbouring States, marking with scarlet points most of the large cities, such as St. Louis in Missouri and others of less importance, like Louisville in Kentucky or Minneapolis in Minnesota, and other still smaller ones among the large ones; then, after making a brief pause in the States of the Far West and leaving some patches there, it will flow toward the Pacific slope and deposit a thick layer of carmine on San Francisco; and, finally, jumping right over to the Gulf of Mexico, it will cover New Orleans with a similar layer. A very considerable space will be left hardly coloured at all or will even exhibit the shot colour to be seen in certain fabrics: these are regions or cities where the Machine has no stable and regular existence; rings of mercenary politicians form in them, disappear after a short time, and re-form under favourable circumstances. A good many points again on the map will appear almost white, presenting the touching spectacle of "good Machines. " But this in truth is an abuse of language, an honest Machine is not in the course of nature; it would be more correct to say that there are many local party Organizations which have not degenerated, which have not fallen into the category of Machines. Every Machine represents a party Organization, but every party Organization is not necessarily a Machine. However fair this distinction may be, it must nevertheless be admitted that, in the conditions which govern the life of American political parties, every Organization carries within it the germ of a Machine which is capable of a singularly rapid growth. A population may, so to speak, go to bed with an Organization and wake up with a Machine. Heuce, the "Mushroom Machines" which are a tolerably common phenomenon. In any event, it must not be forgotten that the part of the map coloured red, while only a portion of the whole country, contains almost a third of the population of the United States and represents at least three-fifths of its economic interests. This domain of the Machine is daily growing larger. The Machine is gaining ground, especially in the West, where it is invading districts which appeared to be free from it. It is the steady development of economic interests which paves the way for it; that development produces the wherewithal for exploitation by the Machine, and, on the other hand, it more and more absorbs individual energies and diverts the attention of the citizens from political preoccupations, while leaving still greater liberty of action to the professionals of politics. The new chances thus offered to the Machine are improved in some cases by its somewhat more prudent conduct; in proportion as it consolidates its power, it takes more care not to provoke the opposition of the good citizens. The explosion is bound to come, but it is slower in coming; thanks to the precautions of moral hygiene which a good many Machines adopt, their average life has become longer, they are "smashed" at less frequent intervals.

in

But why should this periodical necessity of "smashing " the Machines exist at all? Why is the power of the Machine, even when mitigated by the limitations and the restrictions which we have just been considering, tolerated in the full blaze of democracy? The varied materials for an answer to this question have already been disclosed to us in the course of our investigation. It now remains for us to recapitulate them in a more methodical way. The first and general condi tion of the Machine's existence and success is, of course, the extraordinary development of the elective regime and of the party system fostered and stimulated one by another. They have created the necessity for a highly elaborate and intricate election machinery, which can be worked only by experts. At the same time they have made the task of the ordinary citizen so difficult as to leave him bewildered and helpless, and ready to submit blindly to any guidance offered. But why should these experts be men of the stamp of "bosses," and how does it come about that they are able to keep a hold on the political machinery and exploit it so easily? What are their particular means and resources? The most common explanation given is that the Machine disposes of a large patronage, or, again, that it lives on rich corporations, and that if it had not one or the other of these resources, or both of them, it would die of inanition. This explanation is only partly true, it only deals with the material resources. Foremost among these, in fact, comes the patronage, the places iu the public service of the Union, of the States, and of the municipalities; these places, supplemented by the hope of getting them, furnish the pay for maintaining the army of politicians who serve the Machine. The more places the boss has to distribute, the more firmly established will be his power. A city boss dreams of becoming State boss, because this last position will make him the dispenser of the State patronage and of the federal patronage. The height of the State boss's ambition is to rise to be a "president-maker," by no means in order to become mayor of the palace to the President and influence the policy of the Union, but in order to secure a preponderating voice in the distribution of the places, including those of the Cabinet. The boss lives as much on the substance of the patronage as on the prestige which the possession of it gives him; and to enjoy both, he must be the sole dispenser of patronage toward whom all eyes are turned. If it were possible to obtain a place irrespective of him, or in spite of him, he would lose caste, the discipline which he wields over his men would be relaxed, and the whole Organization would be "demoralized." The number of the places at the disposal of the Machine is constantly increased by the constituted authorities, under pressure from it. Besides the patronage improperly exploited by the party Organizations there is the patronage conceded to the parties by the law, in the form of seats on election boards. To ensure the impartiality of the proceedings of these boards, they are composed of representatives of the two principal parties, appointed by their respective Organizations and paid out of public money. In a large city like New York or Philadelphia, which has more than a thousand polling-places or thereabouts, each Organization is in a position to distribute a large sum every year on this account.

Next come the principal direct receipts of the Machine — the assessments, the contributions paid by the candidates and by the office-holders. The percentage paid by these last yields of itself considerable sums. To give an idea of them, the case may be quoted of the assessments of the municipal employees in the city of Philadelphia: levied at the rate of two per cent, they provide, out of the $4,500,000 which the city spends in salaries, $90,000 for the benefit of the Machine. The contributions of the candidates are much higher, and no elective post escapes this tribute. Even candidates for the highest judicial office are obliged to pay a large sum which, in New York, for instance, generally run3 into thousands of dollars. The contributions given to the funds of the Machine by private individuals, by wealthy zealots of the party, important as they are, sink into insignificance beside those of the financial or industrial corporations, especially in the States of New York and Pennsylvania. There the corporations pay a regular tribute to the boss, as "price of the peace," that is to say, to be left in peace, to ensure themselves against the hostile designs of the legislators or of the higher executive officers. Besides this, the corporations are liable to extraordinary calls on the eve of a particularly hot election campaign, in which the Machine will have to spend a great deal. It is difficult to form an accurate idea of the amount of the contributions made by the corporations; yet some useful information on this subject may be gleaned from the following data relating to New York: this city is the seat of more than 2100 corporations subject to regulation by the law and, consequently, standing in need of "protection "; their combined capital approaches the total of $2,000,000,000; most of these companies discharge the "price of the peace," and some of them pay $50,000 a year, apart from extraordinary contributions amounting to as much as $100,000.' One may also mention the income which the Machine derives from the fStes and the entertainments which it gets up for its workers: it distributes tickets of admission at somewhat high prices, $5 or $10 each, to the officials and to other persons who are under an obligation to it, such as saloon-keepers, contractors, etc. It is a form of extortion which all these persons are obliged to submit to for the greater advantage of the Machine's exchequer.

The enormous material resources of which the Machine thus disposes are not the only foundation of its success; it possesses also a moral stock which in fact is converted into capital like a security into cash. This moral capital consists of the deliberate or unconscious adhesion of the various elements of the community. The Machine exists and works with their consent, and by no means in spite of them. The first of these social elements on which the Machine leans is made up of its own servants and of its nearest adherents, of the social category which is consequently known by the name of "the Machine element." These people work for the Machine as they would have worked for a manufacturer, a merchant, for any one who might have employed them. They get their living in "practical politics," and they must do so, for does not the wisdom of nations say: "a man cannot live on wind," "people do not go into politics for fun. " The work the men of the Machine do for it is undeniable; the duties of a leader, of a small precinct leader and of his lieutenants, who have to oil all the wheels of the Machine from day to day, are by no means a sinecure; they are extremely absorbing and keep the mind in a constant state of tension. The work is rather dirty; this may be, but there are so many trades which involve handling unpleasant things; every trade has its processes, and "practical politics" has its own; the use of these processes is not so much a matter of ethics as of technique. "It is perfectly idle to ask oneself if it is for good or for evil," said a member of Tammany Hall to Cf. the article by Mr. Joseph Bishop, "The Price of the Peace" *The Century,* 1894, Vol. 48).
me, who gave me a sketch of the methods of the Great Wigwam, "it is neither bad nor good, it is politics." The character of the pay, which consists of "spoils," is not objectionable either, it is almost part of the natural order of things. When the Creator, after making the two great lights of the day and of the night, made the two great political organizations, he ordained that they should divide the public offices between them. It is therefore only fair that these offices should be given to the men who have "worked" for the party, and to them alone. It is a disregard of this truth which would be scandalous and would constitute a danger for the public morality, nay, even for the public order of the American democracy. A small boss once spoke to me with bitterness of the head bosses, who sometimes bestow places on persons who do not belong to the Organization, to the detriment of those who "do the work"; "if this goes on and becomes the general practice, we shall have a monarchy."

It is by following this train of reasoning that the men of the Machine come to consider the independent members of the party who oppose the Machines as hateable and contemptible; these citizens not only prevent them from earning their living, but even try, while posing as champions of honesty, to get hold of the offices, without having "done the work" for the party; they are therefore hypocrites, full of "humbug and cant." At the best, they are only "doctrinaires," "college professors," "star-gazers," for the government without parties which they dream of is an idea as absurd as it is flagitious. The immorality is all on the side of the "reformers," who sacrifice the interests of the party to their vanity and their ambition, who do not scruple to sow discord, whereas they, the men of the Machine, sacrifice everything to "harmony." They feel proud of being "harmonious," being quite ready to waive the other virtues. "Harmony " is for them the sum and substance of morality; it generalizes in regard to public life the sentiments of fraternity which unite the politicians in their private relations, and which assume the aspect at one time of professional solidarity, at another of personal attachment. These sentiments, therefore, do not stop even at the frontiers of the parties. While fighting one another according to the rules of the game, the politicians of the rival Machines are often ready, not only to make common cause against the outsiders, but to help one another, to the detriment of their own parties. For instance, a small Republican boss, to oblige his Democratic colleague and friend, who wants to get a friend of his own, a Democratic candidate, elected to a small post, orders his men to vote for that candidate, although he is a Democrat. The considerations by which the politicians are guided in thus acting have been put into words by one of them, who said to Mr. Theodore Roosevelt, "There are no politics in politics." This enigmatic utterance meant that in the world of politicians no heed is paid to the political conventions of society. Far from being utterly depraved men, the politicians profess rather a clan morality, which is often in opposition with the morality of society at large. The Machine, however, is but strengthened thereby: the perverted clan morality justifies the conduct and stimulates the enthusiasm of the numerous category of those who give their mercenary support to it.

In addition to this category, the Machine has on its side, in the first place, the mass of the people. The criminal and semicriminal elements, the *diclassls* of every kind, who swarm in the large cities, are devoted to the Machine, because it buys them with cash or protects them against the law. In all communities, even the best regulated ones, there is at the lowest depth a social residuum composed of "Catilinarianexistences," — to use the celebrated phrase of Bismarck,— who are hostile to public order, not only from their vicious nature, but also from an inherited feeling of revolt against the State, which has dammed the torrent of individual will and passion. The Machine of the American parties has realized the unique combination which consists of protecting the low "Catilinarian existences" against the public authority by the influence which it wields over this same authority, and, while ensuring them impunity, keeping them in check by this very means.

The popular stratum which is superior in point of morality, but wretched, having only precarious means of existence, and which swells the army of the unemployed, also gets assistance from the representatives of the Machine; the boss regime, with *Machine Politics in New York City,* reprinted in *American Ideate and other Essays,* New York, 18!7, p. 122.

its costly administration of the cities, does but benefit a number of humble folk. The interested philanthropy and the other attentions lavished by the politicians win them the hearts of the people. It is no use denouncing the bosses as public malefactors, laying bare the corruption of Machine rule. The people answer, "It is good enough for us." In fact, they do not see the harm done by the politicians, but they know their urbanity and their generosity. Between a couple of drinks taken at the bar, how many stories are not told of how the local leader of the Machine has got this man out of a difficulty, has given coal to another, has distributed flour among a number of neighbours, has sent wreaths to the humble obsequies of the destitute? Can it be said of such a man that he is a worthless individual? The boss Tweed, when publicly convicted of monstrous depredations and sent to prison, lost none of the esteem and admiration in which he had been held by the lower orders of New York; they were convinced that Tweed had fallen a victim to the nefarious designs of the rich, he who was so kind to the poor. It is of no consequence that the Machine prostitutes itself to the rich, to the "corporations "; its local representatives, who are close to the people, and who are themselves of the people, only get more credit from being so with the masses owing to the feeling of class antagonism which lurks in the popular mind and which is stirred by the sight of those rich; while the money received from them enables the Machine to establish itself the more firmly in the favour of the poor. Besides, the Machine does not relieve their material wretchedness only, it also relieves their moral wretchedness. The leaders of the Machine have a kindly word for the humblest inhabitants of their district; they share in their joys and in their sorrows; they find a sympathetic smile even for the halt and the maimed; they shed a ray of human brotherhood on the most miserable of creatures. They do it automatically, in the way of business, to everybody without distinction; but they none the less appear as ministers of the cult of fraternity in a higher degree than the priests of the churches and the professional philanthropists: they are nearer to the people, they come in friendly contact with them every day, and the people have confidence in them. They offer it a counterfeit of charity and fraternity, but if the people accept it so readily, the reason is that the real article is very rare, or inadequate, or badly distributed in society as it at present exists. The men of higher rank who come down as it were from the moon to exhort the people to vote for honest candidates opposed to the Machine, are strangers to them, and the people have no confidence in them because they belong to another social sphere. The habits of mind and the manners of these latter, even of the most well-meaning of them, often only offer fresh food for popular prejudices; they have too great a regard for themselves; they are too gentlemanly; they are " kid-gloved." Few of them are able or willing to stoop to the methods of the politicians, with which it is easier to get the ear of the people. These last the people does know, they are "the nicest men," and it prefers to vote with them for dishonest candidates, who often are also "the nicest men."

Not that the lower-class elector prefers the corrupt man; he desires what is right at least as ardently as the "kid-gloved" gentleman, his instincts impel him no less strongly toward what is honest and what is just, but he appraises honesty and justice in his own fashion. In his eyes the man who does his neighbour no harm, and who even does him good, cannot do harm to society and to the community. The lower-class elector still judges everything by the standard of private morality; he is as yet incapable of rising to the height of social morality. The primitive morality of the masses delivers them into the hands of the Machine as inevitably as clan morality attaches the tribe of politicians to it. The intelligence of the masses does not preserve them any better from the attraction exercised by the Machine. The effort required to disengage the political questions at stake, to consider them in themselves, and to understand them, is too great. The popular mind is perfectly accessible to reasoning; sound arguments find an echo in it, but the question must be well defined and distinctly presented. Once the problem is grasped, the lower-class elector is just as capable of exhibiting public spirit as any one else. But the difficulty is to get at him and to make him open his mind confidently to arguments coming from outside; here, again, the social differentiation which is at work in the United States, in their turn, as in the countries of the Old World, erects a barrier between the people and the cultivated set, and accentuates the class antagonism which prevents common action.

Among the humble electors there is a large category which, in the opinion of many people, embodies in a special degree this venality, this narrow morality, and this ignorance, and, for that reason, supplies the Machine with most of its supporters. The electoral category thus indicted is formed by the "foreign element," that is to say, by the immigrants. Coming from countries with less advanced political institutions, where they had lived in degradation and in misery, and incapable of promptly assimilating the spirit and the manners of the American democracy, these foreigners, naturalized as American citizens, whose number is counted by millions, cannot but become an instrument of political demoralization and lower the political level of the Republic. It would, therefore, be only too natural that they should supply the Machine, especially in the big cities, with its largest following. I, for my part, was somewhat inclined to share this opinion when I arrived in the United States. But a careful enquiry conducted on the spot has made me, if not abandon it entirely, at all events qualify it very considerably. Almost all the men of sound judgment whom I have been able to consult, in the East as well as in the West, of American stock themselves and some of them of very old stock, protested against the theory according to which the "ignorant foreigners" are the great culprits in the political disorders which afflict the democracy of America. My personal observations have only confirmed me in their view. No doubt, the newly naturalized citizens are, for the most part, ignorant, but the proportion of ignorant electors of American origin is not less great. The wretched immigrants are easily bought, but the poor natives of the country are exposed to the same temptation, and not only the poor ones. I have already had occasion to point out that bribery is rife even in the rural districts of New England among the well-to-do farmers, descendants of the Puritans. Again, in the contests with the rings and the bosses, initiated by good citizens, the latter often obtain as active and disinterested support from the naturalized citizens as from the others. By way of explanation of the phenomenon of bossism, I was sometimes told that "the Irish need a leader. " True, the Irish are easily brigaded and they do not contribute much to the purity of the municipal administration in places where they are in great number, but this great number never constitutes a majority of the electorate; besides, they are by no means inaccessible to good influences. Several other foreign elements supply, taken altogether, excellent civic material, such as the Scandinavians, the Germans, who are always found, the great majority of them, on the right side in all important political conjunctures. Even the Jews who have escaped from the ghettos of eastern Europe promise to develop civic qualities on American soil.

The upshot of the matter is that the immigrants make the task of democratic government rather more complicated; but the difficulty is only relative and temporary. The rising generation is assimilated with remarkable rapidity, and with an abandonment of its early associations that is often too complete for the taste of the older generation. The children, anxious to be the same as their American companions, refuse to speak the mother tongue even at home, and the parents witness with a sore heart the inevitable disappearance of the last fragment of a past which is not less dear to them because it has been spent in tears. The influences to which the young immigrants are subjected and which they in their turn introduce into daily life are those of the American environment. The movement started in the last few years against immigration in a country which had always welcomed with open arms the oppressed and the unsuccessful of the whole world, is not so much founded on facts as due to the calculations of the politicians who, in order to get a little popularity, trade on the spirit of vulgar nationalism and on the professional envy and jealousy which foreign competition excites in certain sections of the working community. The bill against foreign immigration, which had been passed by Congress, was killed by President Cleveland's veto just as he was laying down power. An American who bears a glorious name has summed up the whole question in the following words: "Our danger is not from the contamination of foreigners, but from the surrender of ideals upon which self-governments rest or die." Letter from William Lloyd Garrison, of the 20th of December, 1896, to the editor of the *Evening Post* of New York.

IV

The custody of these ideals is naturally entrusted to the social class which is superior to the masses by its knowledge and its wealth; but this class, which is called in the United States "the better element" because it is better off, does not fulfil its mission; it leaves the public interest to its fate, and, far from opposing obstacles to the Machine, only makes things easier for it. The abdication of the better element is due to manifold considerations which, however, may all be referred to the eminently materialistic spirit that animates the prosperous and wealthy classes. These classes, which present different grades of well-being, meet in one and the same exclusive preoccupation, that of " making money "; they embody in the highest degree the mercantile spirit of the bourgeoisje in the Old World, while exhibiting more nobility than the latter in the use made of their wealth; they measure all things by the sole criterion, "Does it pay/" Now they find that politics "do not pay," that it is not worth while neglecting one's own business to attend to public affairs; that it pays better to submit to the depredations of a Machine than to lose one's time in fighting the bosses, at least as long as they keep within the limits of comparative moderation. The race for wealth which absorbs the Americans takes up all their time, the rich allow themselves as little leisure as those who have to earn their living. The only social class which enjoys leisure is, according to a sally of Mr. Theodore Roosevelt, that of the "bar-tenders" (barmen in public-houses). The few American millionnaires who are not in business take to sport and to other amusements, which fill up their idle time; but it never enters their head even to descend into the political arena. Many members of the better element think themselves "too good" for politics; it is beneath them, it is too "vulgar." They think they have performed their civic duty when they have voted the party ticket on the day of the election; and some even do not go so far as this, they do not vote at all, they are not always aware even that there is an election going on, they would not be able to say where their polling-place is, who is their representative in the legislature. All the more do they neglect the primaries. They never read political VOL. II. —2 f newspapers, or only read the headlines. The most "patriotic" among the members of the better element subscribe to the funds of the party, but refuse to make any personal exertion, to devote their time and their energies. And this seems perfectly natural to them. "Only an English landlord or a 'crank' can go into politics for nothing," as was said to me by a barrister,—an excellent citizen himself, by the way, — who did but interpret the general view of his fellow-countrymen.

This deliberate or unconscious reasoning, — " It does not pay," — which lies at the root of the whole passive attitude of the better element, is complicated by other considerations, some of which, resting on prejudices or sophisms, beguile the citizen who is forgetful of his duties, and appear to justify his conduct,, while others promise a personal reward in return for his abstention. The chief prejudice which sways men's minds, to the greater advantage of the Machine, is party fetishism. This feeling makes many very "respectable" electors shut their eyes to the misdeeds of the Machine; they really believe that it is the other party which is a hotbed of corruption, that theirs is honest by virtue of its name. Others, more clearsighted, groan inwardly, but take care not to kick against the Machine at elections, letting themselves be persuaded that the "life of the party is in danger," and that this is not the time to pick holes in the doings of certain representatives of the Organization; that it is not an act of civic abdication, but only a temporary sacrifice to the paramount cause of the party which is demanded of them. This temporary sacrifice is repeated every time, and every time the " good" citizens, overcoming their repugnance, "vote like men," that is to say, like so many sheep. The timorous conservatism which characterizes most of the members of the better element makes them apprehend unspeakable catastrophes if they should leave the beaten track of the party. They have an inkling that the methods of the Machine are not always clean, but they concentrate their thoughts on the great party work which the Machine performs by "getting out the vote" and descending to the lowest depths of the political community in search of it. The whole economy of the representative system of government appears to them to be realized by this pious and mysterious operation of "getting out the vote," and it is seldom that any one of their number is found to give the reply which was made by the person from whom the representatives of the Machine demanded a subscription for the purpose of " getting out the vote ": "No, sir, I don't believe in getting out the vote; I'll give you some money to keep it in." Electors of a philosophic turn of mind take their stand on the proposition that the American government is a party government, that parties cannot exist without an organization, and that, this being so, the organization must be paid for. They refuse to see in the boss aught but the organizer of victory for their party, and do not see in him the corrupter of the Republic. Other electors, wiser in their generation, but deterred by respect for the world's opinion, are afraid of incurring the reproach which disqualifies a man more than anything else in American life, that of being "impractical," of appearing on a level with a "college professor," capable of imagining that action can be taken in politics irrespective of one's party. Certain electors carry their independence so far as to speak with cynical unconcern of the parties, but, when the election comes, habit reasserts itself, and they cannot even make up their minds to "scratch" the party ticket. In voting for the party, a good many electors vote, not so much for it as against the opposite party, which seems to them the most corrupt of the two; others are hardly under this illusion, but they none the less continue to vote for the party solely to make use of their vote: to give a vote to an independent candidate, who has no chance of being elected, appears to their materialistic mind, accustomed to see every effort crowned with a tangible result, as a sterile act; it is "throwing away" one's vote, as if a man were to throw away money with which he could buy something, whether useful or not is of little consequence; the moral effect of a vote which serves solely to assert a principle, to fling in the face of the world a protest of the conscience, is lost on these electors, because it is only moral. Lastly, certain electors — and their name is legion — have not even to ask themselves if they ought to vote the party ticket or not; they are in blissful ignorance of everything that goes on within their party, of all Jthe political scandals and the misdeeds of the politicians. They do not read the newspapers, or pay no attention to the denunciations, even the most well-meant ones, launched by the press against the Machines and the bosses; the press has, through its own fault, lost credit with the public. The most precise charges brought home to the bosses are treated with incredulity by a great part of the public, and elicit but one reply: "It is only campaign lies." Each of them reasoning in his own way, or not reasoning at all, these electors of the better element all end by voting for the "yellow dog" run by the Machine.

What the party devotion, or the party cant professed by the better element, or ignorance and apathy do to deaden the political conscience of the great majority of this social group, is done, as regards an important section of it, by personal interest. It is no longer the unconscious or half-conscious complicity of humble electors anxious about their daily bread; it is the cool calculation of men who want things which the Machine is able to give. With the help of the Machine they can succeed better in business, as well as in the professions, and obtain honours,—honours which in the levelled society of the United States offer an irresistible attraction to a number of men. One has no idea how many there are who would like "to be something," to get a public office, even for a short time only, sometimes for itself, sometimes to make a stepping-stone of it. Members of the bar cultivate the friendship of the bosses, do not scruple to join Tammany Hall, with a view to some position or other, —corporation counsel, prosecuting attorney, judge,—a position which will make the holder of it known to the public and extend his connection in case he is obliged to return to his profession. Men who are perfectly respectable and intelligent, but who have cast a longing glance on a public situation, look at the Machine with friendly eyes: they are thinking of the "nomination." Those even who have had an opportunity of displaying their independence and their civic indignation discover that "harmony" in the party demands sacrifices as soon as the prospect of an important post is in sight. The representatives of the corporations docilely pay their tribute as "price of the peace," holding that their first duty is to think of the interests of their share-holders.

Those who are not restrained by what they consider as their duty or their interest acquiesce without a struggle or a protest from simple habit or from apathy. The regime of the Machine has so blunted public sensibility that it appears as part of the natural order of things. Shutting their eyes to the fact that it is on the absence of public spirit that the Machine lives and prospers, people regard it as invincible ("you cannot beat them "), accept it with a sort of fatalism. They console themselves by saying that there is no help for it, "you see, it is a plant; it must grow." Even the authority of Mr. Herbert Spencer is appealed to by persons who have caught up his name and that of his doctrine; they put the Machine and the bosses down to "evolution," which there is no resisting. Moreover, this passive attitude is, it would appear, in conformity with good democratic doctrine. "It is," said an ex-Governor of a large State recently, "it is good democratic doctrine to let things alone, trusting to time and to the natural operation of events to mend all the tears." The imperturbable optimism, which is one of the essential traits of the American character, cherishes a fond belief in the *vis medicatrix naturae.* When confronted with the disorders caused by the Machine in political life, this optimism simply says, "It will right itself," or, again, " With Americaris the thing rights itself." It is not even shaken by the spectacle of the material ravages inflicted by the plundering politicians, but replies, "We can stand it; you cannot ruin *this* country. " This is exactly, both in form and in spirit, the reasoning of the English duke quoted by Mr. Gladstone in a speech in the House: as the duke's son was leading a fast life and spending money right and left, his Grace's steward felt bound to inform him of it. "Indeed," replied the duke with dignity, " there is a great deal to spend." So far as the material effects are concerned, the situation therefore is not supposed to present any gravity. As for the misdeeds of the Machine, considered in themselves, judged from the moral standpoint, there is no need either to make a fuss; they are part and parcel of the infirmities of human nature; men are not angels; "it is human nature." With reference to the "human nature " argument, so frequently and so complacently used by the representatives of the better element, it is, perhaps, permissible to quote a joke from the comic column of an American paOr, better still, a good many citizens, who are only too well informed, deliberately shut their eyes and stop their ears, —'they deny the facts. One would think that, weary of the ever-present spectacle of bosses, they had made up their minds, on waking one fine morning, to cease believing in the reality of it, and to say to themselves that it is nothing but a delusion which takes in sour-minded individuals or credulous foreigners. I myself was charitably told to beware of this pitfall; and, in order to impress upon me the danger which I was running, the example of an illustrious predecessor was pointed out to me, who, on the strength of impressions derived from the particular people he consorted with, had, in his book, attributed to the bosses and to the Machine a greater importance than they really possess. Lastly, when these citizens who assume that they know better are closely pressed and obliged to admit that the bosses are not altogether mythical beings, they declare that bossism is the inevitable outcome of all government, that without the boss there would be chaos.

Here we have the clinching argument, which expresses the real view of the members of the better element; the boss governs in their place, he relieves them of the tedious duty of governing themselves, enables them to attend to their own affairs. And here again is the true explanation of the success of the Machine: it is a government. It possesses most of the attributes of a government in a high degree, except legitimacy of origin and honesty of motive; its staff, the "leaders" and the "workers," are recruited by natural selection and not by a formal process; they are representative of the great mass of the electors; they are united to it and, above all, united among themselves by the closest ties of social cohesion, by feelings of mutual attachment and feudal loyalty toward the chiefs; per. *Tommy.* "Paw, what is human nature?" *Mr.*

Figg. "Human nature, my son, is the excuse generally offered by a man who has been acting like a hog!" The remark on foreign investigators being misled by the bad company they kept during their visit to the United States is of old standing. Tocqueville did not escape it either. Benton says of him: "Tocqueville is evidently not intentionally unjust. But he is the victim of the company he kept while among us; and his book must pay the penalty of the impositions practised upon him." *(Thirty Years' View:* I, 114.) individual responsibility and personal merit are the only principles which govern their relations; firmness, energy, and audacity characterize all their acts. These virtues are exactly those which are wanting to society at large, disintegrated, split up into sets, inert and cowardly. These vital principles of government — absence of formalism, individual responsibility, and personal merit — are exactly the contrary of those which society submits to from the Machine itself, like an exoteric doctrine which, in the old days, made the vulgar an easy prey of the astute holders of the esoteric doctrine. Hence the extreme difficulty of fighting the Machine. The better element must "become mad" with anger in order to rise and recover, by an extraordinary effort, the moral force which should be opposed to the Machine. And, again, the epileptic fit of public spirit is not enough of itself, it cannot fill the moral gulf which divides the better element from the masses, and which has been dug by the selfish indifference of the former and widened by the process of social differentiation. The energetic appeals addressed to the masses by the good citizens who march against the Machine are not altogether a *vox clamantis in deserto.* But to make more sure of reaching the masses and to sweep them into its movement of revolt, the better element must have recourse to the men of the Machine itself, must "fight the devil with fire," by allying itself with the rival Machine or even with a section of the Machine of the predominant party which it is sought to overthrow. Living only for spoil, each Machine stimulates and excites appetites and desires until there comes a moment when it is no longer capable of satisfying them all. Therein resides its organic weakness; sooner or later boss rule produces malcontents, mutineers, who, after having, for a long time perhaps, struggled without success, help to upset it when it is attacked from outside. There must always be a concurrence of circumstances and of forces, a "tidal wave," to use the regular expression, to get the better of the boss. Generally, nothing short of a change in the fortunes of the parties is required to bring about his fall, a change which often is due only to the conjunctures of national politics, that is to say, conjunctures which have nothing to do with the local situation laid to the door of the boss. Thanks to the party system, it is almost always necessary to dislodge the party from power in order to dislodge its boss. But when this has been done, the Organization of the opposite party is always fated to take its place; the tidal wave which has carried away the boss will only have served, after all, to bring in the rival Machine, often under the very flag of the better element which had made alliance with it; the muddy channel of public life which had just been swept clean is defiled once more.

But is there, then, no radical cleansing process? A number of good citizens, during the last quarter of this century, have not despaired, and still do not despair, of finding one and of ensuring its adoption. In fact, this quarter of the century, which has been marked in the highest degree by political corruption, has also witnessed manifold attempts, differing widely in scope, which sought to lift the American democracy out of the condition to which Machine rule had reduced it. To conclude our enquiry, we will now review those attempts and recall for a moment the struggles, often dramatic and always full of instruction, to which they gave rise.

EIGHTH CHAPTER THE STRUGGLES FOB EMANCIPATION

I

The attempts at shaking off the yoke of the party Organization began soon after the Civil War. They were brought about by the corruption of the party in power, of the Republicans, whose mercenary elements supported by party discipline shamelessly exploited the public interest, and under whose auspices monopolies were established for the benefit of large industrial and financial concerns. The movement of revolt, therefore, assumed a double aspect — an economic and a political one. The economic agitation broke out both in the primitive regions of the West, among the farmers who thought themselves injured by the arbitrary tariffs of the railroads, and in the East, where it was directed against the excesses of the industrial protectionism which dated from the Civil War. The farmers' movement created a hotbed of social discontent in the West, which became a permanent menace to the political stability embodied in the traditional parties. The anti-protectionist movement took the form mainly of a propaganda of free trade ideas, and became in its turn a hotbed of free political thought, which attracted prominent men and independent minds from both parties, and constituted a training-school for the greater part of the staff that was to lead, during the next quarter of the century, all the campaigns for reform and liberty. The first great uprising, however, occurred in the political field on the occasion of the presidential election of 1872. The President in office, General Grant, who, in spite of himself, became the embodiment of the regime of party despotism and party corruption, built up on the artificially perpetuated antagonism between the North and the "rebel" South, was a candidate for re-election. The prospect of seeing this regime obtain a new lease of power roused the indignation of several eminent members of the Republican party, who were disgusted with "grantism." These disabused Republicans had just fought, in 1871, a successful battle in Missouri, at the State elections, with the regular Organization of the party, having joined the Democrats and declared for a broader and more generous policy toward the reconquered South, which would obliterate the memory of past strife. Their conciliatory attitude earned the Republican secessionists the name, which they accepted, of Liberal Republicans. On the approach of the presidential election, the Liberal Republicans of Missouri started a general revolt in the whole Union, and decided to run an independent candidate against Grant.

At the head of the movement was a naturalized German, Mr. Carl Schurz. When almost a stripling he took a part, and a romantic one, in the revolutionary events of 1848 in Germany. Having escaped from prison, he arrived, after a few halts, in the United States. Bred on the generous diet of the sentiments which inspired the men of 1848, — sentiments in which one still finds a fountain of youth at the close of this century, which is ending in forgetfulness of its best traditions and contempt of its noblest ideals, — Schurz married his exuberant young life with that of the American democracy. He understood its grand and admirable side, and, while keeping the freedom of a mind precociously ripened by exile, he absorbed the American national spirit to a degree which a foreigner can rarely attain. In a comparatively short time he became a figure in the political world, a diplomatist, a general in the army of the North during the Civil War, a Senator, a remarkable speaker, a brilliant writer. Having risen in the Republican party, and with it, he now took up arms against it to serve the cause of the American democracy; and from that time onwards he will be always found in the forefront of the battle in all the emancipation struggles of the Independents.

The dissentient movement of the Liberal Republicans filled the regular Organization of the party with grave apprehension, and appeared to have a good chance of success, especially if it won the support, as was to be expected, of the Democrats. The main point was to choose as independent candidate, against Grant, a man on whom all the opponents of the regime could unite. To make this choice nothing better was hit upon than to summon a national convention, in accordance with the established custom. The convention met at Cincinnati, and had the aspect rather of a mass-meeting with an endless crowd of delegates, several of whom held their mandate from themselves. The professional politicians were there in force, attracted, like birds of prey, by the odour of carrion. Yet the majority of the convention were animated with pure sentiments, and they cheered with genuine enthusiasm the words of the opening address, which declared "that it is the voice of an exceedingly large and influential portion of the American people that they will no longer be dogs to wear the collar of a party." The convention elected Schurz for its president, and adopted a declaration of principles which vehemently condemned Grant's administration and demanded the complete obliteration of the effects of the Civil AVar in the laws and in their application, and a radical reform of the civil service. When the vote for nominating the candidate was taken, the convention found itself a prey of the manoeuvres and intrigue to which national conventions so easily fall a victim. Among the candidates proposed, the man who seemed to specially commend himself was Charles Francis Adams, the grandson of the President Quincy Adams, supported by Schurz and several other eminent men, and by the independent press. The friends of another less favoured candidate, wishing to defeat Adams and Schurz, resolved to run a third candidate, Horace Greeley, the celebrated journalist, who had been one of the foremost combatants in the struggle against slavery. Besides, a considerable section of the members of the convention were not able to throw off the old man entirely; they still clung by too many mental fibres to the Republican party, which they wanted rather to purify than to destroy. Greeley, an uncompromising Republican of old standing, had, in their eyes, the advantage of combining the new aspirations that animated them with the old traditions of the party, down to protectionism, of which he was one of the most determined champions. However, at the first ballots, Adams was well ahead each time; but at the fifth ballot a few delegates suddenly transferred their votes to Greeley, the assembly, like all convention crowds, was seized with a "stampede," and Greeley unexpectedly came out the winner.

This result was a most unfortunate one. The very great popularity which Greeley really enjoyed in the country was not of a kind to qualify him for the ch.ief magistracy of the Republic, especially under the circumstances. A man of remarkable talent, of great moral enthusiasm, of a lofty mind, his judgment was far from unerring, his experience as statesman was nil, and he was too well known for his eccentric conduct to be taken seriously as future chief of the State. An out-and-out protectionist, he had to rely mainly on the support of adherents of free trade. Greeley's candidature was thus not only a tactical error, but a logical absurdity; and with such a standard-bearer the movement of the Independents was undoubtedly doomed to failure. There was no means of reconsidering the choice, without a fresh split, for they had tied their hands, having accepted the procedure of a national convention and the formal sanction which attaches to its decisions. Mr. Schurz and several of his friends thought for a moment of rallying the real Independents, who were freed from all allegiance to the Republican party, and of proposing a candidate for the Presidency without a national convention. But it was too late. Swallowing their profound disappointment, they closed their ranks around Greeley, and fought bravely against Grant and the Republican Organization, but they were not followed by several of those who appeared at the outset to make common cause with them. The national convention of the Democratic party adopted Greeley's candidature on its own account; the latter's position was not improved thereby, and eventually he was beaten, not having succeeded in detaching enough Republicans and in rallying enough Democrats. Grant remained master of the White House, with the result that "grantism" entered on a fresh phase of development.

Thus the movement of the Liberal Republicans failed, and, one may say, failed stupidly. For there are good reasons for agreeing with one of the principal of them, G. W. Julian, the veteran of the anti-slavery struggles, that "Adams would have been elected if nominated, aud that the work of reform would thus have been thoroughly inaugurated, and the whole current of American politics radically changed." And there i *Political Recollections,* 310.

are equally good reasons for adding that Adams' candidature might have been adopted with greater certainty, and proposed to the country with sufficient authority apart from a so-called representative national convention filled with an unruly mob incapable of deliberation, and at the mercy of all kinds of manoeuvres and impulses. The Cincinnati convention showed once more, in this respect, that new wine could not be put into old bottles with impunity. The very heated election campaign which followed the convention was also an object lesson. The rancorous violence with which the Republicans turned against the dissentients only brought out more strongly the political and moral antinomy between the system of stereotyped parties and the actual needs of the day. The Liberal Republicans were " branded as 'apostates' from their anti-slavery faith; but slavery, replied the dissentients, had perished for ever."... "They were called rebels, but the war had been over seven years and a half. "... "It was charged that they changed sides in politics; but the sides themselves had been changed by events, and the substitution of new issues for the old." The alliance of the Liberal Republicans and of the Democrats, concluded under these circumstances, set up against the malignant attitude of the Republicans not only a moral example, but a new method of political action which offered a solution of the antinomy in question. This method lifted reality above convention, and instead of keeping men rooted in the disagreements and the animosities of the past, brought them together or separated them in accordance with the factors of the new situations. "While facing the savage warfare of their former friends, Liberal Republicans were suddenly brought into the most friendly and intimate relations with the men whose recreancy to humanity they had unsparingly denounced for years. They were now working with these men because the subjects on which they had been divided were withdrawn, and the country had entered upon a new dispensation." Co-operation for a political object between men who had been deeply divided on another question, was so novel a thing that the Liberal Republicans were astonished and touched to "discover that the men whom they had been denouncing with such hot indigna tion for so many years were, after all, very much like other people."

Discouraged by the miserable failure of the movement of 1872, the independent Republicans changed their tactics. Their number increased, owing to the scandals of Grant's second administration, but they gave up the plan of forming a "third party," an independent party. They thought it wiser and more effective to play a see-saw game between the two parties, joining forces with that which should bring forward better candidates and better measures than the other. These new tactics were adopted on.the approach of the presidential election of 1876, in a conference of the leading Independents of both parties, summoned by W. C. Bryant, Carl Schurz, and a few others. The conference met at New York (Fifth Avenue Conference) and addressed an appeal to the people, drafted by Schurz, which proclaimed the pressing duty of "re-establishing the moral character of our government and elevating the tone of our political life," by choosing for President not a man possessing virtue of the passive kind, but a champion of radical reforms. The candidates adopted shortly afterwards by the national conventions of the parties, Hayes and Tilden, having both appeared to combine these conditions more or less, the Independents kept in the background.

The candidature of Grant for a third term, launched on the eve of the elections of 1880, brought them back on the scene. This candidature, contrary to the precedent created by Washington, which did not allow the same man to occupy the Presidency for more than two terms, was contrived by a few senatorial bosses. It not only threatened the country with a return of "grantism," of the political corruption which had marked the General's two administrations, but was an audacious attempt by the Machine to lay hands on the national government; the Machine stepped out of the local sphere, which had been till then the theatre of its operations, to extend its power. The Independents accepted the challenge and took the field. In 1879 they had fought an out-post engagement, *Political Recollections,* 346.

at the election of Governor and other high State officials in the State of New York, of which the vote was to be decisive in the impending presidential election. The committee of the Republican Independents, which was formed for the occasion, selected for its target, so to speak, two candidates of the Republican Organization, those for the posts of Governor and State engineer respectively, who embodied the spirit and the methods of the Machine. Adopting all the other candidates of the Republican ticket, the committee of the Independents called on the electors to protest against the Machine, by not voting for the two first candidates, by striking out their names on the printed voting-paper. It was not a revolt against the party that was proposed to them, but a domestic cleansing process, "not to bolt, but to scratch; not to desert the party, but to attempt its purification from within." The plan of scratching adopted by the Independents, which earned them the name of "scratchers," was intended by its authors to supply at once a means of keeping the local Machine in check and giving a solemn warning to the concocters of the "third term." The result of the "scratchers' movement" was not particularly brilliant, but it was not without moral import: twenty thousand or so electors of the State of New York abstained from voting for the two boycotted candidates, thanks to which, one of them was beaten and the other came in last on the ticket. The skirmish of the "scratchers" was followed by a lively agitation led by the Independents, who founded clubs and associations of their followers, circulated political writings, delivered lectures, and, in general, prepared the public mind for resistance. Independents from some other States (Massachusetts, Rhode Island, Pennsylvania) joined the "scratchers" and sent their representatives to Chicago, where the Republican national convention was being held, to put pressure on the delegates and make them reject Grant and every "politician" candidate. To a certain extent, perhaps, owing to their remonstrances, but mainly owing to the rivalries of the politicians, Grant was defeated at the convention, as well as his principal rival among "the politicians," J. G. Blaine, by a "dark horse" — Garfield. The Independents were no longer under the necessity of following up their warlike intentions.

But four years later, in 1884, this necessity presented itself. J. G. Blaine, who had long been lying in wait for the Presidency, appeared to have it in his grasp this time. He was the most conspicuous and the most capable Republican politician; he embodied the "bloody shirt" policy pursued by the party towards the South, and the ultra-American spirit in international relations; he enjoyed throughout the country, especially in the West, an immense popularity, owing to the personal magnetism which he possessed in a high degree. But his political integrity was very questionable; he was repeatedly accused, without being able to clear himself, of having used his official positions for his personal gain. Is a man of this stamp, it was asked, worthy to hold the chief magistracy of the Republic? The Independents decided to oppose his candidature. The Republican national convention paid no heed to this opposition and nominated, by a large majority, Blaine for the Presidency and Logan, a crack senatorial boss, for the Vice-Presidency. The next day the Independents proclaimed themselves in a state of revolt. The investiture conferred on Blaine by the national convention made it the duty of every follower of the party to vote for him unconditionally. Is party obligation superior to the moral obligation of every citizen to keep an unworthy man out of power? Can party morality relieve a citizen from the respect due to elementary honesty? Must the individual conscience surrender to the formal decision of this or that meeting? Such was the sphere into which the Independents lifted the discussion. They appealed to their fellow-citizens to shake off their blind party loyalty; to throw over Blaine without hesitation under the circumstances; they no longer said, "Do not bolt, but scratch," but proclaimed the "divine right of bolting " They declared themselves ready to vote for the Democratic candidate if the person nominated for this purpose was an honourable man. Meeting the views thus expressed by the Independent Republicans half-way, the Democratic national convention adopted the candidature of a new man, whose whole political conduct was a living protest against the methods of professional politicians and party mercenaries or bigots — Mr. Grover Cleveland. The Independent Republicans at once rallied to him with emphasis, not in order to become an appendage of the Democratic party, but solely for the particular occasion, in order to ensure the best choice of the future head of the State, while preserving the liberty of their political conscience.

A good many Independents thought it necessary for the safe-guarding of this liberty to go farther and adopt a candidate of their own "who would fully and specifically represent a conscience vote," while others wanted to found a new party on a permanent basis to take the place of the old corrupt and decrepit parties. "We want not," they said, "an independent party: an independent party is one balancing between the two parties; we want to found a new party in our country, a party of national principles, and which can look forward to a national triumph. " But all idea of a "third party" was soon laid aside. It did not find favour with some because it was a "party," because it was likely to imprison men's minds in a new organization. One of the most eminent representatives of the Independents, Charles Francis Adams, mentioned above, had expressed this idea with much force, during the preceding campaign, of 1880, directed against the "third term," and in which the plan of a "third party " had also been agitated: "We do not want more organization, more discipline, more 'machine '... We want more men of thought and character, who are able to stand up before us in the full dignity of their personality; and we don't want so many organs. Therefore, when men come to me, as they continually do, particularly young men, and are discontented and mutinous, and suggest the possibility of getting up a third party, I have but one reply — 'I don't want a third party.' I don't want any party; there will always, in this country at any rate, be enough of these who will act with parties, but under present conditions I want to stand on my own legs." Most of the leaders of the independent movement looked on a "third party " as ill timed for altogether concrete reasons: the Democrats and the Independents united could defeat Blaine, divided they would ensure his victory.

Report of the National Executive Committee of Republicans and Independents. Presidential campaign of 1884. New York, 1885, p. 16. Quoted by R. L. Bridgman, *The Independents in*

Massachusetts in ISM, Boston, 1885, p. 9.

» *Individuality in Politics.* Lecture on the 21st April, 1880, at New York. VOL. II — 2 o

The Independent Republicans organized themselves definitely, on the basis of an alliance with the Democrats, in a great free conference, which met at New York, on the 22d July, 1884, and was attended by several hundreds of members, representing most of the States of the North. The conference entrusted a national committee, under the presidency of G. W. Curtis, with the management of the campaign. It was a remarkably vigorous one, in spite of the extremely unfavourable conditions under which the Independents had to fight. They had no local organization; they were attacked with violence, reviled, and derided. A contemptuous nickname was fastened on them, that of "Mugwumps." The word, which was taken from the language of the Indians, had a great success, like that other word of the same language — "caucus," but a success of a more elevated kind. In the language of the Algonquin Indians, the word "mugwump" or "mukquomp" meant a chief, a superior man. This nickname was applied to the Independents to ridicule their presumption, the moral superiority which they assumed; but soon the Independents consented to be called by this name, and it passed into political language to denote a citizen who does not make a fetich of the party, for whom the party is not an end, but only a means, who preserves the liberty of his mind and of his conscience in his political conduct. The Mugwumps had to create a fighting organization for themselves; the electors disposed to support the movement were invited, by means of advertisements inserted in the newspapers, to send in their names. On the strength of the answers received, the central committees formed by the Independents selected the persons who displayed the most interest and put themselves in direct communication with them. In a short time there were created a considerable number of local committees, of clubs which often dispensed with all formal organization and recruited adherents by a nonpublic propaganda. It was necessary to deal tenderly with the old strongly-rooted prejudices which made the fact of deserting one's party, of appearing not "regular," looked on with horror. In consequence, the appeal for recruits was drawn up in two forms, one being sent to those who were only willing to abstain from voting for Blaine, and the other to those who were ready to vote with the Democrats for Cleveland. The principal scene of action of the independent movement was Massachusetts. It was a regular revival of the spirit which in the old days had led the great abolitionist fight in that State, it was a blaze of moral enthusiasm which fire'd the old Puritan commonwealth and spread beyond it. The young people, who had grown up after the Civil War, and on that account were less swayed by the passions which fostered Republican loyalty, flung themselves headlong into the fray. They became missionaries, and, going out into the highways to win souls, penetrated as far as the West, sometimes being obliged to steer their course at a venture, like the crusaders of Peter the Hermit. The purely moral plane on which the Mugwumps placed the contest for the Presidency, attracted the members of the clergy. Pulpit orators, with Henry Ward Beecher at their head, preached sermons and delivered lectures. Everywhere an oratorical campaign was carried on, one of the most remarkable features of which was the complete absence of hired "spellbinders"; all the help given was disinterested. Schurz was the great protagonist of this campaign; he was indefatigable, exerting his powerful eloquence in city after city, in State after State. The day of battle arrived, and Cleveland was elected President. This result, obtained with the aid of the Mugwumps, was highly significant and pregnant with consequences; it affirmed that the obligations of morality are as indefeasible in political life as in private life; it proclaimed that the conscience of the elector and private judgment cannot be fettered by the ties of party; it naturalized the Mugwump, gave him citizenship in American political life, with the position of arbiter between the parties; it restored the equilibrium between the parties, which had ceased to balance each other, by putting the government in the hands of the Democrats; and in so doing it offered a practical means of demonstrating the absurdity of the belief according to which the welfare of the country is bound up with the predominance of this or that party, — a belief so naively expressed by the worthy woman who said, on hearing of Cleveland's election, "Well, the poor won't have any work this winter, that's certain,"— and shared by so many people who think themselves more intelligent and more clever.

III

The majority of the popular votes obtained by Cleveland over his Republican rival was only twenty-three thousand, and at the expiration of four years the Republican Organization brought back its candidate, Harrison, into the White House. But the effect of the bolt made by the Mugwumps was by no means lost, it contained a moral seed which is never completely thrown away. This bolt was followed twelve years later by a still more formidable bolt, which took place, on this occasion, at the expense of the Democratic party. The revolt which broke out in that party's ranks, in 1896, was caused by the problem of the free coinage of silver. The idea of the miraculous virtue of the white metal having appeared to make considerable way among the masses, the Democratic Organization hastened to commit the party to this policy, following the habitual tactics of the Machine, which, without caring a jot for principles and convictions, espouses those which seem the most profitable to exploit. The regularity of the party enjoined on every elector who went by the name of Democrat the acceptance of the programme and of the presidential candidature of Mr. Bryan, adopted at the national convention of Chicago. But both of them deeply offended the ideas, and especially the interests, of the more cultivated and wealthier section of the Democratic party; frightened by the prospect of the financial catastrophe which the establishment of a depreciated currency might entail, and by the socialistic revolutionary tendencies of certain elements allied with the silverites, some capitalists, some men of good sense, and some timid middle-class people, who had hitherto voted with the Democratic party, concurred in the intention of deserting the regular Organization on this occasion. Their number was very considerable; never had such a bolt been seen before. While often actuated by personal or class preoccupations, the "gold Democrats," as the secessionists were called, were obliged to invoke the general idea of the independence of the elector's conscience. And never before had this idea been so complacently expounded and so widely accepted, even by those at whose expense the bolt was carried out. It was possible to quote the declaration of Mr. Bryan himself, made only a few months before the crisis: "No convention can rob me of my convictions, nor can any party organization drive me to conspire against the prosperity and liberty of my country.... A man's duty to his country is higher than his duty to his party." A number of Democratic electors, who preferred to remain out-and-out "regulars," went so far, however, as to good-naturedly admit the case of *force majeure* which impelled their dissentient co-religionists to secede.

The person of the candidate who, through a concurrence of circumstances, happened unexpectedly to represent the cause of the gold standard, — Mr. McKinley, the protectionist champion,— inspired the gold Democrats with but little enthusiasm; a good many of them found it difficult to overcome their aversion to give their votes to the Republican candidate. Out of consideration for this category of Democrats it was decided to put forward an independent ticket, for their special use, in order that they might be able to vote for "Democratic" candidates, and not be tempted by the old habit of regularity to re-enter the fold at the last moment. The plan of a third ticket met at first with determined resistance from a good many gold Democrats, who thought that the forces opposed to free coinage should not be divided, and that it was better to rally to the McKinley candidature, which had the best chance of beating the silverites. The promoters of the third ticket, whose views prevailed, on their side, had no wish whatever to embarrass McKinley and were under no illusion as to the defeat which awaited their candidates at the poll; but they were anxious to affirm their principles and to keep the waverers and the weak in a state of revolt. The national convention which they summoned at Indianapolis, to nominate their candidates for the Presidency and the Vice-Presidency, gave a formal sanction to the bolt, adopting the name of "National Democratic party " for the secessionists; it drew up a platform and selected Generals Palmer and Buckner as candidates of the party. This convention offered a very different spectacle to that generally offered by these assemblies: the delegates whom it contained presented a real elite in point of sterling moral and intellectual worth; the whole atmosphere breathed sincerity and disinterestedness from the opening to the close. If there had been any prizes to be won, if the candidates chosen at the convention had had any chance of success, it would probably have ended like all conventions. But it was attended solely for the purpose of making a manifestation of principles. The presidential candidate himself, Palmer, intimated clearly to the dissentient Democrats that they could, if they preferred it for the triumph of the cause, bestow their votes, not on him, but on McKinley. Most of the gold Democrats did so, and McKinley was elected, thanks to their support given in spite of their differences of opinion with him on questions other than that of the currency. He was elected, not because he was McKinley, but although he was McKinley. The Republicans did not triumph as Republicans opposed to the Democrats. The victory was not that of a man nor of a party. For the first time, at least since the controversy on slavery, the contest was fought on a special, clearly defined issue. The bolt of the Mugwumps turned on the person of the candidate and appealed to the moral sense which judges the conduct of men in their private or public relations. This time the dispute was once more placed on a moral footing, in order to carry the popular verdict more easily; but public reprobation was solicited no longer against a dishonest man, but against the "dishonest dollar " for the benefit of " honest money." From the domain of personalities people rose to that of abstract general notions; and to make these intelligible to the public mind the appeal to the moral feeling had to be supplemented by a recourse to logic. The cause of private judgment in politics thus took another and a longer step in advance.

At the same time, the new fact of the contest being no longer between two parties armed with their reminiscences and traditions, with their sympathies and antipathies, but between two solutions of a single problem, called for and inaugurated a new mode of action, in the form of special organizations grouping the combatants on the exclusive basis of the special problem in dispute. To defend the cause of the gold standard a "Sound Money League" was founded, with numerous ramifications in the country, which brought together for common action all the opponents of the free coinage of silver, irrespective of their views on other political questions. This league contributed greatly to the defeat of the silverites by its vigorous oratorical campaign in which veteran Mug wumps like Schurz, orthodox Republicans, lifelong Democrats, fought side by side. Soon afterwards, when, in consequence of the war with Spain, the country was agitated by the problem of "Imperialism," of the policy of territorial conquests in which the Republic was becoming entangled, the opposition to this policy took shape in an " Anti-Imperialist League." This free organization brought together men who the day before had been fighting one another on a different issue, silverites and adherents of gold, Republicans who had never deserted their party, and Independents; they resolved, on this particular occasion, to put the currency question all the more completely on one side, that McKinley's administration, like all party governments, was trading on the confusion of the two questions and demanding approval for its imperialist policy because it represented the good cause of "sound money," which should not be jeopardized.

rv

Party regularity beaten down inside the parties, by the bolts to which political conjunctures gave rise, and by the combinations formed by members of various parties on single issues, was also undermined by the independent parties or the "third parties," which we have already seen on the political stage in the guise of the party of "Liberal Republicans." The other "third parties" were, for the most part, formed in opposition to the existing economic regime, they were the expression of the social discontent which arose after the Civil War, especially in the agricultural West, and which I have briefly referred to at the beginning of this chapter. The pursuit of economic panaceas gave birth, in this way, to a whole series of new parties which, after an ephemeral existence, disappeared to revive shortly under another name and promote more or less analogous or kindred objects. First of all came the "Grangers" or "Patrons of Husbandry," a secret association of farmers whose political activity was displayed in the legislative struggle with the railroad companies, especially in Illinois and Wisconsin; then parties of the "Independents" and of "Working-men" in California and Oregon; the "Labour Reformers" in New England; the "Greenbackers," who demanded an unlimited issue of paper money as a specific against all economic evils; the coalition of the "Greenbackers" and of "Labour Parties" combined into an " Independent party," which later on took the name of "the National party"; the "Farmers' Alliances," which resuscitated the Grangers; and, finally, the last and the most considerable independent party, the " People's party " or " Populists," a semi-socialist party largely recruited from among the old Greenbackers, and existing alongside labour or socialist party organizations of less importance. All these parties had this in common, that they sought to "rescue the country from the clutches of the corporations and the monopolists," and looked on the traditional parties as accomplices of these latter and as an obstacle to reform. They had a more or less distinct notion that this obstacle did not reside only in the special character of the ideas or the economic tendencies of the regular parties, but in their very nature, in the character of their organization, their methods, and their manners. Tims, in the profession of faith of one of the first parties started, in the West, against the "monopolies," the "People's Independent party," which was formed in California in 1874, one already finds this idea expressed with great vigour: the doctrine of "party fealty," the ''tyranny of party discipline," and the system of the primaries are denounced as the great political evils which must be combated. The most powerful of the The resolutions adopted in the constitutive assembly of the party declared this in the following terms: "Secondly, That one of the most serious obstacles in the way of political and governmental reform lien in the doctrine of so-called 'party fealty,' that tyrannical rule that degrades the citizen and sinks him to the servile partisan, rendering him the helpless tool of selfish wire-pullers and caucus manipulators. In view of this long-standing evil, the People's independent party now, in its very inception, once for all lays down its fundamental principle that parties are mere instrumentalities to be employed only in the furtherance of good government; that they should be followed no longer than while they act in the interest of the entire people, of which fact each individual must judge for himself; and that it is the duty of the citizen to abandon instantly any party which swerves from the path of right or passes into the control of unscrupulous leaders; and finally, it utterly spurns and repudiates the doctrine that any citizen owes allegiance to any political organization, or that a pure, upright man in public life can or ought to be under special obligation to any source short of the people for office or position. Thirdly, That one of the great evils which earnestly demands correction is the tyranny of party discipline, which is maintained through the system of primaries and caucuses, and professional politicians aided by governmental "third parties" created and developed during the last decade, the Populist party, also declared its hostility to political corruption and to the methods of the old parties which arrested the free development of political life.

The advent of these independent parties, which appealed to the material interests of the masses and which excited antagonism between classes and between different sections of the country, between the agricultural West and the manufacturing capitalist East, did not fail to throw the ranks of the old parties into confusion by detaching from these latter a good number of their adherents, and by introducing fresh elements of uncertainty into their existence. The cause of the emancipation of the elector's political conscience benefited thereby, in consequence, but in an indirect or negative way and to a limited extent. Most of the new parties had but a local existence; their birth, their success, and their disappearance were only incidents of brief duration in the local contests. The Greenbackers and the Populists alone attained the rank of a national party, descended with their candidates into the lists of the presidential election, and succeeded in winning seats in Congress, nay, even in the Senate of the United States. But these successes were often due to the alliances patronage and moneyed power. ... Thirteenth, That we regard the primary election system as now conducted, especially in the large cities, as being practically a device which deprives the honest citizen of his political Influence and clothes the demagogue with power." — Winfield J. Davis, *History of Political Conventions in California, 1849-18'JS,* Sacramento, 1803, pp. 331, 33:i.

The first declaration of the principles of the Populist party, adopted at the Omaha convention in 1892, ran as follows: "The conditions which surround, us best justify our co-operation. We meet in the midst of a nation brought to the verge of moral, political, and material ruin. Corruption dominates the ballot-box, the legislature, the Congress, and touches even the ermine of the bench.... We have witnessed for more than a quarter of a century the struggles of the two great political parties for power and plunder, while grievous wrongs have been indicted upon the suffering people. We charge that the controlling influences dominating both these parties have permitted the existing dreadful condition to develop without serious effort to prevent or restrain them. Neither do they now promise us any substantial reform. They have agreed together to ignore in the campaign every issue but one. They propose to drown the outcries of a plundered people with the uproar of a sham battle over the tariff, so that capitalists, corporations, national hanks, rings, trusts, watered stock, the demonetization of silver, and the oppressions of the usurers, may all he lost sight of. They propose to sacrifice our homes, lives, and children, on the altar of mammon; to destroy the multitude in order to secure corruption funds from the millionnaires." which they made with the old parties whom they denounced, in one place with the Republican party, in another with the Democratic party, joining forces in each case with the party in a minority against the party in power. This being so, the dissolvent action which the Greenbackers and the Populists were able to exert, as a national party, on the old parties, was largely neutralized. In several States where the movement of the new parties displayed exceptional force, the Democratic State conventions, to take the wind out of their sails, even accepted, or rather "captured" their programmes, but the Democratic Organizations did not change their conduct or their methods on that account. The internal life of the Populist party did not prove better fitted for reforming the parties, its organization was often captured by the politicians just as in the old parties. This result was effected with all the more facility that, if the Populists had shaken off the unreasoning doctrine of "regularity," the bulk of their party was hampered by a no less unreasoning faith in the wondrous properties of the unlimited coinage of silver or of other specifics promising the immediate advent of universal happiness. The Utopian character of the favourite remedies of the new parties, or of certain remedies mixed up in their programmes with other proposals worthy of all consideration, has, in its turn, limited the dissolvent action of these parties. It has even brought discredit on the "third parties" in general, aided by the vulgar fallacy which reasons from the particular to the general, and it has helped to popularize the idea that a "third party" is always Utopian, and that a man of good sense joins one or the other of the regular parties.

This discredit brought on the "third parties" has not been removed by another independent party which developed, on parallel lines, with the parties of economic panaceas and which aimed at the solution of a problem of a specially social character — the suppression of alcoholism. This party took the name of Prohibition party, because it demanded the prohibition, by the law, of the manufacture and sale of spirituous drinks. Several States, especially in New England, had passed, even before the Civil War, laws in this direction; but these laws remained a dead letter and were almost all repealed. The growing harm done by alcoholism and the protection granted to the saloon-keeper by the organizations of the political parties in return for electoral services received from them, led to the formation of an independent political party, with the object of destroying the old parties, who were accomplices of the distillers and the saloon-keepers, and of obtaining power in order to carry the much-needed reform. From 1872 onwards the Prohibitionists ran candidates for the Presidency and the VicePresidency of the Republic, who, at first, polled an absurdly small number of votes (rather more than 5500 in 1872, under 10,000 in 1876, close upon 11,500 in 1880). But in 1884 these figures ran up all at once to more than 150,000, in 1888 they reached 244,000, and in 1892 more than 255,000. The growing adhesions to the Prohibitionist cause were partly due to the concern inspired by the development of alcoholism, but, to a great extent, to the disgust with the old parties which was spreading among honest people. A good many electors, without having the slightest faith in the heroic remedy proposed by the Prohibitionists, voted for them because, unlike the old parties, they constituted a "moral" party. Later on, considerations of a similar nature induced some electors to vote for the Populists. The Prohibitionist party thus served as a refuge for disabused electors. In 1884, when the first rush took place, a great number of Republicans flocked to its standard, not wishing to vote for Blaine, and not having courage enough to turn "mugwumps" and vote for the candidate of the Democratic party, which they had always opposed. But at the presidential election of 1896 the prohibitionist vote fell to 132,000, and it continues to decline, because the possibility of making people sober by an act of the legislature is beginning to appear more and more doubtful.

V

The sphere of local politics, that of the States, was much more frequently the scene of resistance to party discipline and Machine rule; but this resistance had less significance, because more often than not it was confused with the rivalries of the national parties and the local quarrels of the "ins" and the "outs." The movement of revolt sometimes assumed considerable proportions, owing to political or economic conjunctures which profoundly stirred the electorate. Thus, for instance, at the congressional elections of 1882, which swept away the Republican party in several States, the cry, "Down with boss rule," resounded all along the line, but it was but one of the factors which determined the "tidal wave"; the danger of an economic crisis, which was then menacing the country, contributed more to the result. Some independent movements did take place, which were pitched battles between the people and the Machine, between unreasoning "regularity" and the political independence of the elector; great bolts brought into power, into governorships and other positions, good candidates of the opposition. Such, for example, among the early revolts of the independent Republicans, was that of Massachusetts in 1874; later on, that of Pennsylvania in 1882. But all these movements, even when victorious, had no lasting effects. The attempts at local independence quickly died away under the concern for the welfare of the party in the sphere of national politics; that anxiety soon revived party passion and brought the dissentients back into the fold. In municipal life opposition to the rings was, generally speaking, as the reader is already aware, likewise confined to spasmodic risings, which left no trace behind them. Yet in this last sphere the separation between municipal affairs and the interests of national politics was somewhat more easy to establish in the public mind. The contests, therefore, with the Machine in the municipal field, stripped of all extraneous considerations, reduced to the simplest expression of their motives and their objects, could be more easily conducted without regard to party traditions, and influence electoral manners in a similar direction. In this respect, certain revolts which took place against the Machine and the bosses in the large cities marked epochs in American political methods for the same reason as did the national movements which we have just been considering.

The first of these municipal risings was brought about in 1871, at New York, by the misdeeds of the famous Tweed ring, which carried on its operations under the flag of the Democratic party. It was not, however, the party of the opposition that led the attack, its organization was no less demoralized than Tammany Hall, as the reader will remember. Public-spirited men with no formal mandate, without the hallmark of a caucus or of a party convention, volunteered to lead the assault against corruption. They formed themselves, of their own authority, into a committee, which became famous under the name of the "Committee of Seventy," and which included men of different professions and political opinions, — lawyers, bankers, merchants, professors, men of letters, clergymen,—united for the occasion in the desire to rescue New York from the domination of the Ring. The Committee instituted an enquiry into the abuses denounced by the press, proved its case, and brought the members of the Ring to justice. Then it organized the election campaign, at the next election, by making the issue turn solely on the question of honest government, by appealing to the electors of all the parties, and by calling on them to vote for honest candidates irrespective of party labels. The Committee also used its influence with the State legislature to prevent the adoption of measures prejudicial to the good government of the city, and to secure the passing of useful laws. The Ring was dislodged, the abuses were partly corrected, but the attempt to set up a municipal government free from party taint was not successful. The endeavours to reconstitute the government on this basis were viewed in the victorious army itself, by the numerous contingents belonging to the Republican party, to the Machine opposed to Tammany, as a plan for robbing them of the fruits of the victory: so strong was the hold on the public mind of traditional party methods. Soon afterwards, the good citizens having relapsed into political lethargy, the city of New York, as we are already aware, found itself once more under the sway of Tammany Hall.

Nevertheless, the "Committee of Seventy," which soon disappeared, had not lived in vain; it had made its mark, independently even of the temporary relief which it had afforded: even before the struggles with party tyranny had begun in the sphere of national politics, it had, in some measure, laid down the new principles of public action, which were about to make laborious progress, at one time in the field of national struggles, at another in that of local contests. In fact, the organization of this "Committee of Seventy," without any popular mandate, broke the prescription established in favour of the democratic formalism which had converted the evolution of the leadership into a mechanical process; it signified that the moral and intellectual worth which commands adhesion by its intrinsic merit constitutes a sufficient claim to the leadership without any need of an investiture or formal visa conferred, in the name of the people, by more or less representative bodies which, in reality,' are more or less pseudorepresentative. The precedent was created, and from that time onward similar '"self-appointed committees" became tolerably common in the struggles with political corruption. Again, the Committee of Seventy, while accepting an alliance with the Republicans and the Democratic factions hostile to Tammany Hall, outlined a new base of operations, consisting not of the stereotyped organization of an existing party, but of a free combination of men without distinction of party effected for a definite object, which of itself is enough to bring about this combination. The greater freedom of movement and the spontaneous use of his own strength thus ensured to the individual for political action, in the extra-legal sphere, were also secured to him in the legal sphere, thanks to the Committee of Seventy: the latter established the legal right of every tax-paying citizen to prevent, by an appeal to the courts of law, the public officials from wasting public property and funds. New ways were pointed out to the citizens of guiding their individual efforts and combining them in the public interest. The struggles against party corruption and tyranny were to be crowned with success, at least with moral success, in the precise degree in which use was made of these new methods of civic liberty and duty.

The most celebrated municipal Ring next to that of Tammany, the Gas Ring of Philadelphia, was overthrown by the same means as Tweed's clique. The reader will recollect how this Ring had made itself absolute master of the Quaker city by capturing the Organization of the party, and with what audacity it systematically exploited the resources of the city. He will also remember what impregnable positions were held by the Ring, how they were fortified by the implicit devotion of the followers of the Republican party to the party flag, by the protectionist interests of which this party was the champion, by the electoral frauds and corruption, and, finally, by the defective municipal organization. As early as 1871 a group of honest members of the Republican party created a "Citizens' Municipal Reform Association" to remedy the abuses. The Association appealed to public opinion by means of meetings, speeches, and literature; opposed or supported candidates at the elections, according as they deserved it, without distinction of party, or sometimes ran independent candidates in its own name; it prosecuted perpetrators of electoral frauds; it obtained from the State legislature several important modifications in the electoral laws and others. But in a few years' time the members of the Association grew weary of their arduous task; the Association broke up, and the Ring remained undisputed master of the field up to 1880, when the struggle was renewed by a self-appointed "Committee of One Hundred," organized on the pattern of the New York "Committee of Seventy," and composed of men honourably known in the business world, without a single politician.

This committee, however, did not include members of different parties, but only Republicans, who wanted to purify local public life by reforming the Republican party and by making use of Republican elements only. The "Committee of One Hundred" started with a strongly-worded reform "declaration of principles," and decided to give its support, at the impending municipal elections, only to candidates who adhered to this declaration. When the convention of the Republican party nominated as its candidate for the mayoralty the mayor in office, who had not shown himself exactly an opponent of the methods of the Ring, the "Committee of One Hundred" hastened to "endorse" this candidate in the hope that he would subscribe to the reform. But once in possession of the "regular" investiture of the party he threw off the mask and refused, at the instigation of the Ring, to sign the declaration of reform. This incident supplied an admirable demonstration of the efficacy of "reform within party," which had and still has attraction for so many minds convinced that no better political lever can be found than one's own party, and that if the latter is corrupt, the remedy is not to desert it, but to try to convert it to better sentiments, to regenerate it. Yet if the "reformers" made it a rule not to abandon the party under any circumstances, what hold could they have over the degenerate members of the party who sail under its colours, how could they get them to mend their ways? This question presented itself in all its inexorable simplicity to the " Committee of One Hundred"; if it did not want to commit suicide, the only course left to it was to turn its back on the party. This is what it did. It withdrew its approval of the candidature of the out-going mayor, intimated to the Democrats that it would accept their candidate if they chose an honourable man, and, when the Democrats acted accordingly, it adopted their candidate. Having put on the same ticket with him, for the post of tax-collector, an independent candidate of Republican origin, the Committee addressed a formal appeal to the "Democrats and other citizens," soliciting their help to carry the ticket. At the request of the Committee, sermons were preached in the churches of all the religious denominations on the duty of the electors. A current of civic enthusiasm ran through the city. The election ended in a signal victory gained by the candidates of the " Committee of One Hundred" over the " regular" Republican candidates.

A formidable breach had been made in the fortress of the Ring, but it still held several municipal posts. The Committee of One Hundred set to work to dislodge them. Abstaining from all intervention in the State and federal elections, it propagated the idea that national politics had nothing to do with municipal elections, which should be decided irrespective of all considerations of party politics. The Committee asserted itself in every local election by choosing the best of the candidates nominated by the regular parties or proposing its own candidates; it sent to every elector's residence circulars giving detailed reasons why this or that candidate should not be supported; it unmasked the municipal plunderers with an array of facts and figures; it offered rewards for any information likely to lead to the discovery and punishment of the electoral tricksters, and maintained a staff of watchers and detectives for their benefit in the polling-rooms; terrorized by this vigilance, the agents of the Ring who perpetrated electoral frauds disappeared, and the result of the vote was no longer falsified, the will of the electors found free expression. In every ward the Committee of One Hundred formed its adherents into associations, which worked under its direction on the lines indi cated. Thanks to all these efforts of the Committee of One Hundred, in a few years the Ring was dislodged, very great improvements were achieved in the administration of the municipality, its defective organization was reformed to a considerable degree, grave abuses were put down. It had been proved that an honest municipal government was not an impossibility, that the Machine was not invincible if all the good citizens, divided by conventional and meaningless party distinctions, united against the thieves. But the proof was shortlived. People grew weary of upholding or supporting the reform movement, the civic apathy of some and the sordid egoism of others reasserted themselves. "The Committee of One Hundred could not retain the spoils system, and thereby attract the workers. Its candidates, when elected, often betrayed it and went over to the regulars, who, they foresaw, had more staying qualities. Its members became tired of the thankless task of spending time and money in what must be a continuous, unending battle. The people became restive and refused their support to what jarred on their conservative ideas, and what they were pleased to call the dictation of an autocratic, self-constituted body. The cry was raised, 'Who made thee a ruler and a judge over us?' They became tired of hearing Aristides to be called the Just." The " Committee of One Hundred" finished its course, leaving a great example in the history of the independent movements directed against the Machine.

No more appropriate method was discovered for making war on the Machine; and whenever in a city the good citizens, weary of boss rule, organized a rising, recourse was had to a "committee of one hundred " or " of two hundred." New York, which had started this kind of committee in 1871, itself felt the need, more than twenty years later, of calling in a new "Committee of Seventy " to save the city from the corruption of Tammany Hall. Engrossed in its business as usual, New York had no idea of the disgraceful regime it was living under, when a clergyman of ardent and indomitable public spirit, Dr. Parkhurst, laid his finger on the sore and procured the appointment of a legislative committee of enquiry (the Lexow Committee). The revelations of this body roused the good citizens Allinson and Penrose, *City Government in Philadelphia,* p. 63.

VOL. II —2 H

from their torpor, "an appeal to the people of the city of NewYork without distinction of parties" was drawn up at a massmeeting for calling on the citizens "to rise above partisanship to the broad plane of citizenship, and to unite in an earnest demand for the nomination and election of fitting candidates, whatever their national party affiliations, and to form a citizens' movement for the government of the city entirely outside of party politics." The chairman of the meeting was instructed to appoint a committee of seventy persons for the conduct of the campaign. These seventy were chosen so as to give a representation to all the parties and to all classes of the community. The committee came to an understanding with the different political organizations opposed to Tammany; in concert with themit nominated candidates for the posts of mayor and other high officials, taken from among the different parties, and delivered a formidable attack on the whole army of Tammany Hall. Tammany was beaten hollow, but the triumph of non-partisanship in municipal government was not altogether complete. The victory having been won by a coalition, the reforming mayor felt bound to distribute the public offices equitably among the allied parties, instead of paying no heed whatever to parties and looking only at the merit of the claimants. In this way, he was led into filling certain posts by men who were not much better than those of Tammany. Nevertheless, the new municipality gave the city of New York a far better government than that of the fallen regime; it put many things to rights, carrying out improvements in the administration of the city which were in exact proportion to the degree in which the respective municipal departments were free from party influence.

That influence took its tribute on all the movements described by the epithet of independent. It was all very well applying the title of "citizens' movement" to the revolts against the bosses which took place in American cities, and giving the name of "citizens' tickets" to their lists of candidates, as opposed to the Machine slates. These names were but a warcry, a cry which a boss, reduced to opposition and to virtuous courses, adopted himself, in order to dislodge the Organization in power more easily. To succeed, the Independents courted or accepted the alliance of a regular party. These alliances concluded against the ruling Machine, when they were victorious, helped the cause of good government, first of all, by the proof which was afforded that the Machine was not invincible, the spell that protected it was broken. Moreover, a purification, at all events a partial and temporary one, of the government was obtained, reforms were secured which the winning side conceded to celebrate its accession and as a reward for the help given by the Independents. These latter, in their turn, having agreed to "fight the devil with fire," were obliged to make allowance for the fire. The Independents, who, without siding with one of the two parties, "endorsed" the best candidates or put forward their own, were similarly more successful in the first case; but when they confined their action to this see-saw game, they were apt to be outwitted by the Machines, which settled their lists of rival candidates in collusion with each other, and thus always won the toss whether the Independents cried heads or tails.

The "citizens' movements" could not become a real force and produce their full effect in purifying local public life unless they were prosecuted without the necessarily onerous alliances with the political parties. After the city of New York, which had been rescued, in 1894, from the power of Tammany, had experienced a few years of the new regime, the Independents thought that the city was ripe for a genuine emancipation movement as regards the parties and the Machines, and they fought a battle which riveted the attention of the whole Union and, it may be added, of the civilized world. The municipal election about to take place (in 1897) assumed an exceptional importance in itself by reason of two facts: the territorial area of the municipality of New York had just been doubled at one stroke by the amalgamation of the cities of New York, Brooklyn, and several small municipalities into a "Greater New York," which contained a population of 3,200,000 inhabitants. The charter which created this monster municipality at the same time concentrated the power in the hands of a few high officials: the mayor, who was to be elected for a term of four years, became the almost absolute chief of an army of 30,000 employees; the comptroller was to have the management of the finances of the city, the annual budget of which reached a total of $80,000,000. On the other hand, the new constitution of the State of New York, adopted in 1815, had provided that the municipal elections were no longer to be held simultaneously with the State elections and the federal elections, in order to prevent municipal interests from being mixed up with political preoccupations. Taking note of this formal separation proclaimed by the constitution, a certain number of citizens organized a "Citizens' Union," with the duty of seeing that the separation was a real one, and that the municipal government was conducted solely in the interest of the city, "that the city should be governed by the People for the People, not by the Bosses for the Bosses."

The Union started a very active propaganda on these lines. Its platform boldly proclaimed the principle of non-partisanship and put forward an exclusively municipal programme. By means of a systematic personal canvass and a wide distribution of printed matter, these ideas were propagated among the masses months before the elections. This time it was a real "campaign of education." Asserting emphatically that the head of the municipality, to perform his duties properly, ought to be free from all obligations towards parties, the Union declared that to enjoy this independence the mayor "must be primarily the nominee, not of a party organization, but of a combination of citizens acting without respect to party." In consequence, the Union, on the eve of grappling with the perennial enemy of good government in New York,—Tammany, *Tlie City for the People!* Campaign book of the Citizens' Union, New York, 1897, p. 6.

"Honest, efficient, and intelligent city government is the object of the Union. Every voter who believes in that object is asked to join, without regard to his opinion as a Republican, a gold Democrat, a silver Democrat, or as a member of any national party whatever. The Union has no concern with Coinage, Free Trade,or Protection,or with National or State partisan politics in any form. The Union demands an honest and efficient administration, good schools, clean streets, more breathing spaces, better housing in the overcrowded parts of the city, betler rapid transit facilities, strict supervision of the city's franchises, a full return for public privileges granted to corporations, and a just and fair enforcement of local statistics and ordinances.... The Citizens' Union is by no means opposed to the national parties; it asks no citizen to abandon his party. The Union merely demands that our city officers shall no longer be chosen because they are ready and able to promote the aims and ambitions of one or the other of the national parties. In national elections we must have national issues, but in city elections city issues alone should be considered " *The City for the People,* Ibid.).

— refused to enter into negotiations with the Republican Organization and the other party organizations opposed to Tammany Hall, did not wait for them to settle a ticket which might perhaps have been acceptable to the good citizens, but itself selected, in perfect independence, as candidate for the post' of mayor, Mr. Seth Low, president of the University of Columbia, who had a brilliant municipal record as a reforming ex-mayor of Brooklyn. To ascertain the reception which Mr. Low's candidature would meet with among the general body of the electors, the Citizens' Union asked for the signatures of all those who approved of it. In a short time it collected more than one hundred thousand signatures from men of every political party and of every rank in life.

This direct appeal to the people, for the choice of a candidate, over the head of all the regular organizations, and this popular investiture which ignored party distinctions, was a veritable revolution in American political methods. And if it became the practice, the occupation of the Machines would be gone. The prospect of the defeat of Tammany was small consolation to its Republican rival; its own existence was endangered. The Republican Organization would have readily consented to the candidature of Mr. Low, who was a Republican in national politics and a very popular candidate, but on condition that this candidature was adopted by it in the first instance; in that case its prestige as Organization would be left intact. In short, it was the monopoly of nominations assumed by the party Organizations that was inexorably challenged. Rejecting the advances of the Republican committee, the Citizens' Union and Mr. Low were determined to remain free of all connexion with the party Organizations up to the end, leaving them to join the Union, and accepting help from whatever quarter it came. Unwilling to submit or to stand aside, the Republican Organization preferred, in order to make the movement of the independents a failure, to deliver Greater New York into the hands of Tammany. The reader is already aware how the Republican Organization set about this; it put forward a third candidate, an orthodox Republican intended to attract the votes of all the " good " Republicans and prevent them from going over to Mr. Low. The campaign was hotly contested, the Machine conducted it in their usual -fashion, by dragging in the future of the party with its glorious past, the currency system, the anarchy and the socialism with which the silverites, headed by Mr. Bryan, menaced the Republic —everything, in fact, except the question of honest government for the city. Mr. Low and his followers were violently denounced as persons who, out of vanity, infatua'tion and egoism, had wantonly laid their hand on the integrity of the party. The members of the Citizens' Union had no tradition, no orthodoxy to invoke; they could appeal only to the intelligence; they had nothing to promise but good government; they could only attract men and lead them on by enthusiasm for the good cause. Enthusiasm of this kind was not wanting: humble workmen brought their day's wages as a contribution to the funds of the campaign, small anonymous donations flowed in; and, what was not less significant, many men of the "better element," of the business world, descended into the lists to fight the good fight, some openly, others under the veil of anonymity. Thus, a few wealthy corporations sent large anonymous subscriptions to the Union, not from modesty, like several small donors, but from fear of the Machines, which would take revenge on them. The Republican boss, it would appear, also received help in money from the bosses of other States.

Out of close on 500,000, votes recorded at the poll, Mr. Low obtained nearly 150,000, the Republican candidate over 100,000, and the Tammany candidate nearly 230,000. The Tammany "tiger" fastened its claws once more on the metropolis of the New World. The result of this great contest made an immense sensation; it saddened not only the friends of " reform" in the United States, but also in Europe, where it was even thought to sound the death-knell of attempts at municipal regeneration and almost of American democratic government. This view was a mistaken one, because it considered the result of the election in itself only, independently of its antecedents. People forgot that non-partisanship, which, for a quarter of a century, had been striving so laboriously to make its way, had hitherto asserted itself in declarations, in war-cries rather than in actual warfare; that it had been fighting with varying success alongside the regular parties, with their aid; that this was the first time that it delivered battle solely on its own account and with its unaided strength against all the Machines combined. To have received, under such conditions, one hundred and fifty thousand votes, deliberately given to a candidate opposed to the bosses, in a city as little capable of displaying public spirit as the city of New York, was undoubtedly a success. The analysis of the vote made this success still more significant: a very considerable number of the votes obtained by Mr. Low came from wards inhabited by the populace and by the lower middle class. No doubt Tammany triumphed once more this time, but on the dark horizon of American public life a bright gleam had appeared.

The result of the election showed that the struggle undertaken against the Machine was not a desperate one, but it also proved — for the hundredth time, it is true, or for the thousandth — that it was not by sudden attacks culminating in a furious assault that the enemy could be overcome; that to lead the electors away from the Machine it was necessary to make efforts just as persistent as the Machine itself makes to win and to retain them. The politicians of the Machine looked after the electors day after day, they attended to this business morning and evening, for years together, and not only during election time. The "reformers" had never acted but in a spasmodic manner, by fits and starts; when they roused themselves it was always too late, the politicians were always a long way ahead of them in the popular mind. The mode of action of the "reformers" was anything but calculated to fill this gap: excellent persons, exceedingly well-meaning, they were too fond of oratorical arguments, they expended their energies in making big speeches, in voting solemn resolutions, in firing off denunciations which were often too vague, of too general a character to hit the culprits exactly and point them out to the world. The " reformers" did not know how, or but seldom made up their minds, to put their shoulder to the wheel, whereas the Machine did nothing else — it "worked" the electors, one by one, caring nothing for the effects of eloquence. Even the more or less successful "citizens' movements," in which the "reformers " took their turn of "work," as, for instance, the movements which have just been related in the preceding pages, were paralyzed in their effects by the exertions which they entailed: the heroic character of these efforts soon wore out the zeal of the "reformers," and filled them with a conceit which made them complacently celebrate a triumph on the occasion of the slightest success. While the members of the committee of seventy or of one hundred and seventy were feasting, were pouring forth torrents of reciprocal congratulations at their banquets and having their photographs taken, the Machine was collecting its battalions and quietly recovering its positions. To checkmate the Machine, or at all events to cope with it, it was necessary to display a less heroic, but more methodical and more steady, activity, to place the free action inaugurated by the citizens' movements on a permanent basis: such were the conclusions which experience suggested and which attempts have been made of late years to put in practice. These attempts opened a new chapter in the history of the independent movements and of American political methods.

VI

The new departure consisted in non-partisan associations, leagues formed on a permanent basis for systematic warfare against civic indifference and political corruption. They had almost always aimed at municipal government, which they sought to emancipate for good and all from the power of the political parties; and they employed the means of action which had nearly all been already resorted to by the temporary organizations of the committees "of seventy " or "of one hundred." The continuous practice, however, of these methods gave them a new scope and an effect which was all the more intense that they became the object of a certain specialization on the part of several leagues. Some of these assumed the functions of vigilance committees, which kept a daily watch on the people's representatives and the officials, and put constant pressure on them to keep them in the path of duty. They also made it their business to detect infringements of the law and prosecute the offenders. Other leagues were rather committees of investigation iind of initiative in legislation; they studied and followed the actual working of the different branches of municipal administration, pointed out their defects or abuses, prepared schemes of reform, drafted legislative proposals, which they enforced on the attention of the constituted authorities and of the assemblies. Others, again, endeavoured to form, by combining together, centres of moral energy and of civic enthusiasm which would provide a steady supply of motive power in public life; they were anxious to create a seat of action and a base of operations, in the material sense of the word, for the use of publicspirited individuals; they tried to bring the citizens together and to include even the humblest electors in the civic alliance by taking them into a social alliance. Some of these free associations made it a rule not to intervene in the elections, while others openly took part in them by deciding between candidates chosen by the parties or even by nominating candidates on their own account, or, again, they simply volunteered the electors information, on men and things, likely to guide them in their vote, without trying to influence them in other ways. Several leagues combined these various methods of action. More or less aggressive, they all exhibited one marked tendency: they tried to exercise an educational action on the public mind, to awaken the civic conscience and keep it on the alert, and to lay siege to the politicians by a daily vigilance rather than dislodge them by a regular assault.

The permanent "citizens'" associations, outside parties, made their appearance at a comparatively remote period. A "Citizens' Association," formed at New York in 1863, was the first of the series; a similar association arose at Chicago ten years later; organizations of the same kind were created in some other places; their career, although a fairly busy one, was rather modest than otherwise. It was not till the second half of the decade 1880-1890 that the outburst of the civic leagues began, which attained a luxuriant development in the following decade. It will be sufficient to mention a few of them representing the different types of these free organizations. Some are founded on a mixed basis — semi-social and semi-civic — in the form of clubs, inaugurated at New York by the City Club about 1892. Offering the comfort of a large club, the City Club brought together a few hundred or so wealthy citizens, all desirous of seeing the municipal government purified. The club helped to accomplish this result by the work of its permanent committees; one, composed of eminent jurists, examined the bills submitted to the legislature which affected the city, or drafted reform bills itself; another committee inquired into and watched the administration of the various municipal departments; a third committee, in order to create an atmosphere of public spirit, covered the city, down to the lowest wards, with a network of local clubs, intended to be a more or less modest reproduction of the central club, and to serve, like it, as a centre of action and a meetingground for the scattered and isolated citizens. These clubs, which were called " good government clubs," were to fill, in the economy of honest government, the place which the drinkingsaloons filled in that of "practical politics." This they did not achieve so far as the humble electors were concerned; they were not successful in bridging the gulf between the people and the rich; they were only " bourgeois " associations. One may say that it was the same with all the civic leagues, and that often this effect was aimed at deliberately: the leagues tried to bind together the "classes," not exactly against the "masses," as such, but against the "masses" who let themselves be exploited by the plundering politicians, and who by throwing their numbers into the scale allowed serious injury to be inflicted on the propertied classes. As the fault lay with the want of public spirit of these very classes, their attempt to reassert themselves could only benefit the public interest, in spite of the somewhat narrow and selfish character of their motives. In fact, the good government clubs of New York helped to awaken an interest in the public weal among wellto-do people. They likewise exercised an educational influence by popularizing the idea of non-partisanship in municipal affairs, by the very fact of their organi zation as well as by their propaganda, and prepared the ground for the movement of the last committee of "seventy," in 1894, and of the "Citizens' Union," in 1897. They also intervened, in a more direct way, in the election campaigns, by providing "workers," "watchers," who kept an eye on the voting to prevent fraud; they looked out for candidates and tried to run candidates of their own. The zeal and the influence of the clubs, however, declined somewhat quickly. The Citizens' Union, which led the campaign on behalf of Seth Low, adopted a permanent organization after the election and annexed the clubs, so to speak. Yet the system of good government clubs, inaugurated at New York, spread to several other cities and assumed much the same aspect there as in the great metropolis.

The civic leagues, which display their activity principally, if not solely, in the recommendation of candidates, are well represented by two associations, — one in the comparatively small city of Cambridge, Massachusetts, which has 80,000 inhabitants, and the other at Chicago, which has nearly 1,800,000. The Cambridge Association (the Library Hall Association) is open to all the electors, without distinction of opinion, who subscribe to the principle of non-partisanship in municipal government, and whose admission is approved by a special vote of the executive committee with a two-thirds' majority. The Association numbers more than four hundred members. They meet on the eve of the annual municipal election, examine the candidatures proposed by the regular parties or by others, discuss the claims of all the candidates publicly, in presence of reporters, and vote on them in secret ballot. The vote is general when more important elective offices are concerned, whereas in the case of ward councillors, the members of the Association residing in the respective wards alone vote in the first instance, and then submit their decision to the full assembly, which usually approves it. The list of all the candidates adopted is printed and sent to each elector. The recommendations of the Association are in great favour with the electors, for they are known to be disinterested. To prevent the Association from being invaded and got at by politicians, who would exploit its reputation as they exploit the name and style of a party in the Machines, the founders of the Library Hall Association, who had adopted a system of close co-optation of members, have also laid down the rule that the approval which it gives to a candidature does not commit even its own members to anything, that every one is free to vote as his own conscience and judgment may dictate, so that no candidate can use the recommendation as a formal investiture. This rule is a fundamental principle with all

1 Cf. "Non-partisan Municipal Elections, Library Hall Association, Cambridge, Mass.," by Geo. G.Wright *(Municipal Affairs,* June, 1900) and the annual reports of that Association.

the independent leagues that intervene in the nomination of candidates and which distinguishes them from the Machines. The distinction has been happily expressed by a well-known champion of good government in the following formula: "The Machine is the discipline of unscrupulous tyranny; the Municipal League that of enlightened, organized liberty."

A babel like the city of Chicago did not lend itself so readily to these consultations among neighbours, which the voters of the Cambridge Association really are, and an open Association would have found it difficult to prevent the intrusion of the politicians who swarmed in the capital of the West. The Municipal Voters' League, created at Chicago, in 1896, at once gave up the " usual farce of direct representation of its general membership," and instead of a representative organization, which would have been a door to let in the politicians, it set up an indefinite dictatorship. The adherents of the League have no voice in its management, they have only the duty of giving it their help; all power is in the hands of a small executive committee, one-third of which is reappointed every year by co-optation. The committee itself appoints in each ward a consultative committee of a few persons, who supply it with information, and, if necessary, manage election campaigns under its orders. At the beginning of election time the committee announces, on behalf of the League, its views on the candidates, through the press or by means of circulars sent to each elector. It is a direct appeal to the people. The votes of every outgoing municipal councillor are analyzed and put before the electors with very sober comments and a laconic conclusion, which declares the candidate for re-election worthy or unworthy of a renewal of confidence. In the case of new candidates, the League institutes a careful enquiry and communicates the result to the electors, either condemning the candidates unreservedly, or approving them with or without reservations. The main, almost the only, point which the League considers in each case is the character and the capacity of the candidates; it does not lay much stress on their municipal programmes, holding that a municipal council com

Speech of M. Herbert Welsh at the second " National Conference for pood city government," at Minneapolis, December, 1894 *Proceedings of the Conference,* etc., Phil., 1895, p. 149).

posed of honest and capable persons will always arrive at the best solutions of municipal questions. In addressing its recommendations to the electors the committee does not set up as possessing an authority other than that attaching to the value of its information; its great object is to place the electors in possession of the facts; each elector is free to adopt or reject the conclusions of the League in regard to the candidates; he is warned.

The success of the League was very marked. The electors accepted its recommendations with alacrity, most of the candidates condemned by it were beaten, and most of those whom it supported were elected. Among these latter some betrayed the confidence of the League, but their power for mischief expired with the next election, when the League, which had found out by experience what manner of men they were, denounced them to the electors. The approval of the League has become a regular qualification for a candidate, and it is sought on all sides. Groups of citizens themselves choose a candidate in their ward and ask for the approval of the League. The latter, after making enquiry, gives it, or, if there are several aspirants equally deserving, points out which of them, according to its information, is likely to poll the most votes against the bad candidate. Often the bosses themselves submit to the League beforehand, in confidence, the candidates whom they intend to bring forward, and if the League rejects them and says it will oppose them, the bosses put better candidates before it. The League, in these cases, allows the Machines to reap the moral benefit of having chosen the good candidates, the public not being aware that it is the League that has forced the hand of the bosses. The League, in fact, does not oppose the Machine *qua* Machine, but only prevents it from filling the municipal body with unworthy representatives. Thanks to the activity of the League, the Council, which in 1895 was a regular den of thieves, was gradually purified at each election, so much so that in four years' time an honest majority was installed in it. No doubt this result A very interesting account of the activity of the League will be found in two recent articles by Mr. Edwin Burritt Smith, one of its principal representatives: "The Municipal Voters' League of Chicago" *(Atlantic Monthly,* June, 1U00), and " Council Reform in Chicago " *(Municipal Affairs,* June, 1900). was obtained because the great mass of citizens, aroused from their torpor and vigorously stimulated by the press, had consented, had felt the need of following the League; the moral dictatorship of a few persons, not even particularly well known in the city, did but supply the leadership, an enlightened and disinterested leadership, which was wanted. If several other Leagues have not achieved the same success, this is because in their cities the two conditions of success — an independent leadership and a population which wants it, or accepts it — were not present.

Among the associations which, without interfering with candidates or elections, discharge the analogous duties of monitors and overseers of municipal administration, may be quoted the Citizens' Association of Boston, that of Albany, and others. They study municipal problems, overhaul contracts and tenders, and municipal accounts, and, by threats of appealing to the public, prevent jobbery or extravagant expenditure. Intimidation of the enemies of the public weal, which is one of the principal functions of the leagues, gave rise, in several of them, to a more militant type of activity, which consisted not so much in preventing abuses as in repressing them, in prosecuting the offenders. The Reform League of Baltimore was one of the first of these associations. Its special work was to keep an eye on, and bring to justice, the electoral tricksters, who falsified the register and the voting operations. Having, year after year, secured the imprisonment of not a few acolytes of the Machine, who committed these frauds, it brought home to them the salutary truth that the influence of the Machine was not always able to ensure them impunity. The League summoned public meetings in order to — strange as the expression may appear — intimidate the police which protected the perpetrators of electoral frauds and make it understand that it risked less in doing its duty honestly than in obeying the Machine. The Baltimore League, in addition to this, used its influence with the legislature to obtain more stringent electoral laws, and pilloried the offending candidates, or officials, by publishing their records. Several Leagues, on the other hand, confine themselves to the special work of enforcing the laws and the regulations which are so often defeated by political influence or by negligence. Such are the Law Enforcement Societies, the Law and Order Leagues, which at one time make up for the shortcomings of the authorities hy instituting legal prosecutions through their detectives and their lawyers, and at another time put pressure on the officials to make them do their duty.

The more or less narrow specialization of the various citizens' leagues, or the parallel existence in one city of societies whose energies devoted to local public life met or crossed, suggested the idea of bringing them into a central focus, where their movements would be combined and controlled for the common end. Again, the disease of political corruption and civic indifference seemed too widely spread for a single organization, a municipal reform league even with a comprehensive programme, to get the better of the mischief; it was considered advisable to bring all the living forces of society into the field against the enemy, to gather into a single army all its organized moral forces, whether organized on a philanthropic, or religious, or economic, or social basis. These ideas took shape in the creation of civic federations. Chicago set the example, which was very soon followed in several cities, such as San Francisco, Detroit, St. Louis, Boston, etc. The organization of the model Federation, that of Chicago, is by no means democratic; based on a self-appointed committee, like that "of seventy" in New York, it has created several committees and sub-committees, which have each taken up a special department of public life. The Federation thus consists of a group of committees linked by a central council. The work of inspection and enquiry carried on by the Federation extends to the schools, to conditions of labour in factories, to conflicts between employers and workmen. The Federation has its police, its staff of detectives, its sanitary inspectors; it prosecutes law-breakers; it resorts to agitation, and at the same time gives lessons in good government, as, for instance, by having the principal streets swept for several months at its own expense and at a cost of twelve dollars per mile instead of the twenty-seven paid by the city. In other places the civic federations have tried to combine the various organizations already in existence. Thus the San Francisco Federation includes the following: the Citizens' Defence Association, the Good Government Club, the Law and Order League, the Union of Practical Progress, the Builders' Exchange, the Federated Trades, the Society for the Prevention of Cruelty to Children, the Golden Gate Union of Christian Endeavour, the Woman's Christian Temperance Union, etc., reinforced by the various Protestant churches. It is the application, in a novel form, of the new method of public action which we have already seen resorted to for the solution of great national problems (currency system, imperialism), a method which substitutes for sectarian union, finding expression in a stereotyped organization, a coalition *ad hoc* in which different forces, each pursuing its special object, unite with one another on common ground for a particular end. There it was a case of temporary combinations of individuals; here we have whole organizations also entering into rational unions, which leave them each full liberty outside.

Several civic leagues, with the Chicago Federation at their head, solicit and receive the help of women. The co-operation of the latter in civic movements is becoming more and more important. Holding aloof from party politics, women descend into the arena to combat the corruption engendered by the parties, sometimes joining the men, sometimes hoisting their own flag, organizing municipal leagues and civic clubs composed of women. Some rush into the electoral fray, others endeavour to arouse public spirit in a less militant fashion, in the social or philanthropic field. Several religious associations, such as the Young People's Societies for Christian Endeavour, having heard the cry which rises to heaven against the neglect of civic duty, strive to cultivate that duty in the minds of their members. Special citizens' leagues are founded under the banner of Christianity " to make Christian principles operative in public affairs." Societies for political education, recently founded in various places, work on the same lines by means of lectures, of discussions. But the most powerful help comes from the independent press. Its importance and its influence are growing daily. The rise of the independent press is alike one of the effects and one of the causes of the public awakening which is working against party politics. It is difficult to exaggerate the services which this press renders in the contests with corrupt politicians, up to the sphere of national politics where in the gravest conjunctures it often defies the prejudices of the majority and the caprices of the mob. The independent newspapers assail the old prejudices and accustom their readers to judge men and things by their intrinsic worth. In so doing they not only meet a public want, but a demand from the public; the proof thereof is that "it pays," that they succeed from a pecuniary point of view. The newspapers devoted to the parties, reinforced by "sensational" papers, which poison the public mind, each in their particular way, are still no doubt in a majority; but the cause of independence in politics already commands a strong garrison in the citadel of the press.

On the whole, thanks to all these varied efforts brought to bear on municipal government, the aspect of things has changed perceptibly for the better. The disorders which marked the administration of the American cities have been remedied to a not inconsiderable extent, and interest in the public welfare, at all events within this limited sphere, has been awakened to a greater degree than has ever been the case since the Civil War. Municipal reform is not only before the public, but fashionable. It has become almost the correct thing to dabble in it. The "reformer," considered as a "visionary," a "crank," an "unpractical man," is in a fair way of being rehabilitated, owing to the movement which is carrying public opinion towards municipal reform. Electoral manners are already strongly influenced by it, party "regularity" is no longer observed with the same strictness at the municipal elections, a "straight ticket" is no longer voted with the same devotion, the "citizens' tickets," including candidates of different political complexions, are habitually victorious. In the sphere of national politics, the cause of civic independence is very far from having made the same progress; there regularity is still the supreme law, as was conclusively proved by the number of votes obtained by Mr. Bryan at the last presidential election (of 189(;); in spite of the extravagant character of the silverite programme, the immense majority of the Democrats persisted in voting for the candidate who bore the party label, and would perhaps have brought him in, but for the secession of the "gold Democrats." Yet the independent movements which have taken place in the sphere of the national parties have not remained unfruitful. If non-parti VOL. II—2 I sanship has made such strides in the municipal field, this is owing to their dissolvent action; mugwumpism, too weak to produce great ravages in the national parties, penetrated into the municipal sphere following the line of least resistance; timid minds, which always try to haggle with the facts or with the ideas that make their way into life, agreed to let mugwumpism have its share in the local elections, while clinging to party regularity in the other elections. However, the national political life itself did not wholly escape the new notions about the independence of the elector's conscience, even apart from the tangible successes which mugwumpism obtained in certain great crises, by contributing to the defeat of Blaine and to that of Bryan; these notions pervaded the political atmosphere, exercising a subtle and deleterious influence on the traditional sentiments of party loyalty. It may not be inappropriate to repeat, in this connection, the passage which I have quoted from an English historian describing the progress of radical ideas in English society on the eve of reforms, and stating that these ideas affected society " not with the result that political partisans were converted, but that while retaining their old distinctive names men reasoned after a new fashion."

A no less important result of the movement which we have just been considering was the evolution of new methods of public action, methods which, perhaps, will stamp or even determine the future of democracy, as I shall show in my conclusions. Born into the world by a laborious process, endeavouring, in a whole series of attempts, to fit themselves into the old grooves, to essay "reform within party," to form "third parties," to see-saw between the regular parties, and, finally, adopting the system of free and independent combinations for the promotion of one definite cause and trying this system on the plainest practical issue in public life, that of good municipal government, the new methods are henceforth part of the patrimony of the American democracy. But the best political methods, the best systems cannot do without the motive power supplied by an aggressive public spirit. A change of views without a corresponding change in action will not suffice.

i *Supra,* Vol. I, p. 41.

The struggles with party tyranny and political corruption which we have followed have produced this motive power in a slight degree only. The need of a better government is already admitted, the perception of civic duty has grown stronger, but the active will is still wanting. Apart from the more or less spasmodic risings, the work of civic improvement embodied in the leagues practically devolves on a few excellent citizens who exhibit great self-devotion, but who are not always supported as they should be, not only by personal exertions, but even by pecuniary assistance. There is a sincere desire to see the Machines and the bosses disappear, but people would like this result to be obtained, if possible, in an automatic way, so to speak, which would make up for personal exertion. There is, therefore, a tendency to look to the legislator to arrange the legal machinery in such a fashion as to defeat the enemies of good government. The utility or the necessity of setting up legislative barriers against them was even thought of as soon as the struggles for emancipation began, and the efforts of the "reformers" were also turned in this direction. The liberating movement was thus carried on under a twofold aspect, —a political and a legislative one; while the former endeavoured to put down the abettors of political corruption by pitched battles, the second tried to undermine their position, to suppress the opportunities for corruption. We have now to consider the attempts at liberation made in the legislative sphere.

NINTH CHAPTER THE STRUGGLES FOR EMANCIPATION *(conclusion)*

I

The first attempts at legislative reform which sought to remedy the state of things brought about by the development of the party Organizations were aimed at the degradation of the public service by the spoils system. This system, which had made public office an electoral coin for rewarding services rendered to the parties or simply to the bosses, had alike demoralized political life and deteriorated the government. The service of the State was transformed into a sort of feudal tenure in which every official held his post as a vassal did his fief, with the same obligation of serving his immediate lord, who, in his turn, owed service to his suzerain. Patronage was the motive power of government and the principal source of political influence, while, again, skill in electoral wire-pulling and "work" done for the party constituted the sole claim to office, at the expense of real merit and even of honesty. Owing to the practice of rotation, the government departments were periodically upset with every change of the party in power. The President and the heads of the departments with whom the appointment to offices rested as a matter of right, and the members of Congress who had snatched it from them, were all continually exposed to the solicitations of the office-seekers. Unceasingly beset by the applicants, they wasted with them the time which they should have given to affairs of State, even in the gravest conjunctures. Lincoln said, a month after his accession, that he wanted to attend to the Southern question, but that the office-seekers took up all his time. His successors have not fared any better. "One The newspapers of August, 1897, described the pursuit of President MoKinley by the office-seekers in the following terms: "The scenes of these last three days at the White House were extraordinary. Frantic is the word third of the working hours of the Senators and the Representatives," as Garfield affirmed when Senator, "is hardly sufficient to meet the demands upon them in reference to appointment to offices." The members of Congress were obliged to pay attention to every aspirant to a place, great or small, who came up to Washington from their State. To countersign his request, to write letters in his favour, was the least of the things which a member of Congress had to do for the first-comer; he had to take personal steps as well, to go and see the head of the department, or even the President, to introduce the applicant personally while often knowing him to be undeserving. In this latter case, a Senator who was conscientious in his fashion would take the additional trouble of destroying the effect of his own recommendation: in presenting an aspirant to the Minister he would pass a glowing eulogium on him after having written a private letter to the Minister the day before telling him not to believe a word of what he was going to say to him in the presence of his enforced protege. Every aspirant wanted to "interview " the President, even when the appointment was not in his gift. The greedy throng rolled on at Washington, and if some came back empty-handed, others succeeded in carrying off the places by sheer importunity. The Republic was regu that describes the anxiety that was manifested to reach the President. Months of waiting for recognition culminated in a scramble that was without sense: anterooms and corridors were thronged. Men elbowed each other and forgot good manners in their forlorn hope to obtain the places for which they had been waiting.... If Mr. McKinley did not see everybody who called these last three days, it was because human endurance and time both failed. Hour after hour, during the day and until late at night, the President met that never-ending file. He neglected his exercise and his meals."

The dispensers of State patronage are also victims of the fierce tenacity of the office-seekers, as is shown by the following small picture of political manners in the State of Kansas, which I take from the newspapers of December, 1898: "The closest contest of the last three days has been between C. of. .. and S. of... for the office of Insurance Commissioner. Mr. C. remained in the city over Sunday and was the first man in the Governor's office to-day. S. came in late Saturday night and was accompanied by Senator B. to the Governor's home. The Governor and his family were dining out at the home of a close personal friend. Mr. S. insisted on following the Governor. When he rang the bell and was announced to the Governor, the latter said: 'I cannot see him now. Tell him to call later.' 'I am here to stay till I see the Governor,' S. said, and he stayed. The Governor left the table and the two men went over the situation in rather a warm discussion on the doorstep." larly looted. "If ever," said Lincoln on this subject, "if ever this free people, if this government itself is ever utterly demoralized, it will come from this wriggle and struggle for office." A few days after the capture of Richmond, Lincoln said to a friend, showing him the crowd of office-seekers who thronged his door: "Look at this. Now we have conquered the rebellion; but here you see something that may become more dangerous to this Republic than the rebellion itself."

It was absolutely necessary to withdraw the selection of officials from political favouritism, from party influence, but how? The experience of European countries appeared to offer the means in the form of a system of admission to office by open competition. In the mother-country itself favouritism had long flourished an4 with equally disastrous effects; the patronage of the Crown, which afterwards passed into the hands of members of Parliament, had been but a source of corruption, and at the best made public office an appanage of the privileged few. The competition system introduced into England, from and after 1853, for admission to the lower-grade appointments, had thrown them open to merit. As early as 1864 Charles Sumner, the famous Republican statesman, tabled a proposal in the Senate for setting up a similar system in the United States. But the real promoter of the reform was a modest representative of Rhode Island, Jenckes, who, amid general indifference to the abuse and to the remedy suggested for it, year after year, from 1867 onwards, indefatigably submitted to Congress a series of bills supported by a remarkable array of data. The measure was favourably received by the better part of public opinion and of the press, led on that occasion by a recently started periodical destined to play a very important and wholesome role in the American press — the *Nation,* of New York. However, Jenckes' bill was rejected in Congress, which held that the existing system of appointment to office was "the best in the world," and that a reform which withdrew the bestowal of places from the influence of the representatives of the people tended to nothing less than the destruction of the republican government and the introduction of monarchy. The places, which cost the members of Congress nothing, provided a large fund with which they could buy electoral services, and they had not the slightest wish to deprive themselves of this resource, in spite of all the annoyance caused them by the importunities of the office-seekers. From that time a duel began between the politicians, with the members of Congress at their head, who clung to the spoils system, and public opinion, which was gradually won over to "civil service reform" on the plan of competitive examination. This reform, in the eyes of its champions, contained-the germ of a veritable revolution in American public life. Its effect was not to be confined to ensuring a better selection of public officials, to introducing more stability into the departments, and to freeing the departmental heads from the intolerable "pressure" of the applicants, but it was also destined to improve political manners and to change the whole economy of the fabric of government and of the party system: favouritism would make way for merit; the public weal would no longer be prostituted to private considerations; public office would cease to be an object of traffic, and would once more become a trust bestowed on behalf of the community and exercised in the general interest; the appointment to offices no longer depending on the good pleasure of the executive, the latter would itself be relieved from the pressure of the members of Congress and would recover its independence, while the legislative, for want of occasion for extra-legal pressure, would be restored to its proper function. Last, but not least, the life of the parties would be thoroughly purified: the Machines would no longer be able to subsist; there being no places to give away, there can be no "workers"; the bosses, being unable to support their men, will be deserted, their creatures will be scattered to the winds, and before long the tribe of mercenary politicians will have perished, from inanition; booty no longer being, because it cannot be, the object of the organized parties, the latter will be able to revert to their proper mission, to reform on the footing of ideas and common principles; at the same time respectable men, who have been driven out of politics by the wire-pullers, will reappear on the scene and resume their position within the free and purified parties. In a word, the tone of political life in general would be raised, the whole political atmosphere would be cleared. Some of the champions of the reform, in their ardent hopes, saw it produce all these effects; others, less sanguine, modestly aimed at the first results, which were to substitute merit for political favouritism and stability for rotation in the selection of officials. Both occupying common ground, they started, soon after the Civil War, a struggle with the politicians which is going on to this day.

The following are the principal phases of this struggle. The original plan of the reform of the civil service dealt with three points: the appointment of the lower-grade officials by competition, the repeal of the law of 1820, which limited the term of office to four years, and the establishment of retiring pensions. But in face of the resistance offered to this plan, the two last proposals were abandoned and all the efforts of the reformers were concentrated on the introduction of competitive examinations. After Jenckes' bill, which was brought in for five consecutive years without success, Congress, being repeatedly requested by President Grant to remedy the abuses in the civil service, adopted the principle of the reform in 1871. A rider inserted in the general appropriation bill empowered the President to make regulations for admission into the civil service conducive to its efficiency, to ascertain the fitness of every candidate, and to entrust the conduct of such enquiries to suitable persons. The President at once appointed a commission under the presidency of G. W. Curtis, that eminent man who to choice gifts as a writer and speaker united a lofty character and the keenest and most disinterested public spirit. The commission drew up a plan of competitive examinations for admission to the subordinate offices, and forthwith put the reform into practice. The agitation for "civil service reform," and the favour with which public opinion appeared to regard it, did not fail to impress the politicians. The latter, always uneasy and anxious to have as many strings to their bow as possible, declared for the reform; on the eve of the presidential election of 1872 several State conventions and all the national conventions inserted it in their platforms. But this was only a show manifestation devoid of all sincerity. As soon as the election was over the politicians resumed their attitude of hostility towards the reform. Grant, who had a genuine wish to see it go through, and who during his first presidency had often recommended it in his messages to Congress, returned to the charge, insisting that the tentative reform effected by administrative action, under the law of 1871, would not bind his successors if it did not obtain legislative sanction. Congress turned a deaf ear to all remonstrances, and even found a means of nipping the movement in the bud, of giving it a painless death; it abstained from voting the appropriations for the expenses of the commission appointed under the act of 1871. The commission was reduced to a nominal existence. Curtis retired. Grant allowed his zeal for the reform, to which all those about him were hostile, to cool down, and, after a final recommendation to Congress, he suspended the rules on competitive examinations.

Everything had to be begun over again. The next President, Hayes, took up the cause of the reform energetically, demanding that it should be "thorough, radical, and complete," but he too was checkmated by Congress. He had appointed as Secretary of the Interior one of the principal champions of the reform, Mr. Carl Schurz, who hastened to introduce the competitive system into his department; he had issued the order, with which we are already familiar, forbidding federal office-holders to take part in caucuses and conventions and to pay political assessments, an order which was but little obeyed; he had also applied the competitive system, and with the best results, to two departments in New York which were the stronghold of the mercenary politicians — the customs and the post-office. But these were isolated and personal acts, so to speak, which required to be made a general and compulsory rule. Congress objected to this, and even continued to refuse the supplies for the commission. The latter, however, did not relinquish its task; debarred from administrative action, it strove with perfect disinterestedness to popularize the idea of the reform by its enquiries and its reports. There arose at the same time, in different parts of the Union, special associations of friends of the reform, without distinction of party, who applied themselves to the propaganda of it. Federated soon afterwards (in 1881) into a League under the presidency of Curtis, who devoted the last years of his life to the cause, these associations canvassed public opinion with remarkable perseverance and patience. The task was by no means easy, for the indifference of opinion was great, the problem had but little interest for the public; the latter had got so accustomed to the spoils system that they considered it part of the natural order of things; it was the resubordination of public office to the public interest which appeared strange. When Mr. Grover Cleveland, on accepting the candidature for the post of Governor, declared that "public office is a public trust," he was granted a patent, so to speak, in this formula. It was almost the correct thing to turn the reform into ridicule; in the lobbies of Congress even it became a joke to pronounce the first word in an offensive way (" snivel service reform"); the competitive examinations were called "Chinese examinations," "a'Chinese system." Arguments of a serious kind, or considered as such, abounded: the reform tended to set up an insolent bureaucracy, an aristocracy of office-holders, an official caste which would endanger public liberties; it was un-American; it was an English importation, borrowed from monarchical institutions; it was contrary to the democratic genius of the American people; it was destructive of the independence of the executive and of its constitutional prerogatives; the system of examinations was pedantic and incapable of bringing out the merits of the candidates; the existing system was necessary for maintaining the cohesion of the parties, and without parties a popular government cannot exist, etc. Slowly, like the drops of water which wear away the stone, the apostles of "civil service reform" destroyed the common prejudices against it, they converted people one by one. The politicians paid attention to this movement, in their fashion, by inserting in the party platforms platonic declarations in its favour, without believing a word of them. There turned out to be among them an *enfant terrible* who naively or cynically drew attention to this contradiction: when an amendment in favour of reform of the civil service was submitted to the national Republican convention of 1880, a certain Flanagan, delegate from Texas, cried out: "But do we come here for anything but the places? what are we here for?" A burst Dorman B. Eaton, who up to his last breath was one of the most devoted and most disinterested champions of the reform, used to relate that towards 1880 he came to Chicago to deliver a lecture on the subject, and that, after advertising it extensively in the newspapers and elsewhere, he found an audience of exactly seven persons in the lecture-room.

of merriment greeted this exclamation, which procured its author a brief notoriety, but the amendment was adopted unanimously. The accession to the Presidency of the candidate chosen at the same convention, of Garfield, did not help the reform, although the new President was known to be one of its resolute supporters. Garfield did nothing for it, deterred probably by the hostility of Congress and the indifference of public opinion. But his tragic death powerfully served the cause of the reform. The revolver shot of a disappointed office-seeker which killed Garfield converted a number of people to "civil service reform." The members of Congress, however, were not among the converts; they gave a cool reception to the bill brought forward in 1880 by the Democratic Senator Pendleton, and without absolutely refusing the appropriations for the commission, granted it a bare pittance. Nothing less than the serious defeat suffered by the Republican party at the congressional elections of 1882 and the prospect of the accession to power of the Democrats were required to change the views of the Republican majority in Congress towards the reform. Reinforced by a certain number of Democrats, that majority promptly passed the Pendleton bill, which in reality was the work of the civil service reform League. II

This bill, which became law on the 16th of January, 1883, is the Magna Charta of civil service reform. It set up, no longer in a permissive fashion like the act of 1871, but on a compulsory basis, competitive examinations for admission into all the branches of the executive civil service of the United States which have been "classified" for that purpose. While including in the "classified service" almost all the departments at Washington and post-offices and custom-houses with not less than 50 employees apiece, the law empowered the President to continue the "classification" of public offices, that is to say, to extend the operation of the law to new branches of the executive civil service. Competitive examinations being considered an inadequate test in the case of some offices, and a useless one in the case of some others, certain categories have been exempted from classification, particularly the most important ones, those which are filled up by the President under the Constitution with the confirmation of the Senate, and the posts which come at the other end of the hierarchical ladder, those of simple labourers or workmen. Classification is, in short, applied or applicable to the small employees only, such as clerks, etc. Besides, certain positions within the classified service may be excepted from the requirement of competitive examination by the rules which the President is empowered to make. The unclassified offices and the excepted ones in the classified service, that is to say, the positions left to the discretion of the departmental chiefs, both by the law and by the President, are filled up in the old way, while to the classified offices the chiefs can only appoint one of the three candidates certified to them as having passed the competitive examination. A federal civil service commission of three members, created by the law to see to the execution of the reform and appointed by the President, superintends the examinations throughout the Union; it selects in each State or Territory a board of examiners, before whom all the candidates have to appear, and it keeps the lists of those who have passed. When a vacancy occurs in a classified department, the chief applies to the federal commission, which communicates to him the three names at the head of the list in the order of merit. The places in the departments at Washington are apportioned among the citizens of the several States and Territories and the District of Columbia upon the basis of population, while the local offices are filled by persons who have been examined in the respective districts. The employees are admitted in the first instance on probation; when they have proved their capacity and their zeal, they are confirmed in their office. Once appointed, they cannot bo removed for political reasons; but the chiefs retain a discretionary power to dismiss their subordinates for reasons unconnected with politics. While forbidding the chiefs to put any political pressure on their subordinates, the law also prohibits them, as the reader is already aware, from soliciting or receiving from them contributions to the party funds.

There had been some ground for apprehension that the law would become a dead letter, because there were too many persons interested in its non-enforcement. Such was not the case. True, attempts were made to evade or even to openly break its provisions, both in the departments at Washington and in the local offices, and these attempts were often successful in spite of the vigilance of the federal commission, which battled manfully with the Ministers themselves. There were cases of dismissal for political reasons; appointments were made to the competitive positions irrespective of examinations, in an underhand or open way; the practice of assessments, as I have already pointed out, had not been entirely discontinued either. But, on the whole, the letter of the law has been obeyed. The same thing cannot be said of its spirit. The officials were no doubt appointed by competition, but they were often taken from among the adherents of the party in power. For a long time the departmental chiefs were not so much to blame for this as the aspirants to office themselves. The latter thought that the profession of the party creed was still the principal qualification, and that passing the examinations was only a subsidiary one. The political complexion, therefore, of the candidates who competed varied with each change of the party in power. The federal commission took a vast deal of trouble, especially in the Southern States, to induce the Democrats to come up for examination. Having very often been obliged to appoint only candidates of their own party, for want of others, the heads of departments also adopted this course deliberately, or sometimes even dismissed their subordinates of the opposite party, replacing them by persons who had also passed the examination, but who belonged to their own party. The abuses are disappearing more and more, thanks to the extreme vigilance of the federal commission, which has always been composed of men sincerely devoted to the reform, and of the civil service reform associations with their central League, presided over by Carl Schurz since the death of Curtis. These private organizations, whose propaganda had powerfully contributed to the passing of the law, now mount guard around it.

Cf. Charles Lyman, President of the United States Civil Service Commission, "Ten Years of Civil Service Reform" *(North American Review,* November, 1893), and also Theodore Roosevelt, " An Object Lesson in Civil Service Reform" *(Atlantic Monthly,* February, 1891).

The offices withdrawn from competition, and they include the most important ones, are still distributed as spoils. This had been the case since 1883, under all the Presidents, not excepting Mr. Cleveland, who, especially during his first administration, yielded reluctantly in order not to endanger "the party," kept together by the spoils. The "clean sweep" was carried out as before, while confined to the posts "unprotected" by the law of 1883; and the spectacle might be witnessed of offices "swept clean," all the employees of which, dismissed in a lump, were engaged in a lump by their successors to teach them their duties, of which they had not the faintest notion. The division of the places into "protected" and "unprotected" ones gave rise to fresh anomalies: it had the effect that in a post-office or customhouse, which had 50 employees, and consequently came under the operation of the law of 1883, the appointments were made without reference to political influences, whereas in an office with only 49 employees the places were distributed on the spoils method. Again, the small employees who held the classified places must have given proof of merit, whereas for their superiors it was enough to have proved their servility towards the party and their skill in manipulating primaries and conventions in its interest. Had not the law of 1883, by the mere fact of its enactment, condemned the spoils system in a general way and imposed on the authorities entrusted with the appointment to offices the duty of taking into consideration only the merit of the candidates? By making competition compulsory for only a part of the offices, the legislator had evidently done so in the interest of the best selection of public servants, which did not admit of the universal application of the competitive system, and assuredly he had never intended to sacrifice the non-classified offices, to leave them to the mercy of the political plunderers. If the letter of the law was not broken by the looting of those offices, the spirit of the law was so in an outrageous way; and it was most flagrantly broken by those very persons who, like President Harrison, had given a solemn pledge that "the spirit and the purpose of reform should be observed in all executive appointments. " "But," as was said by a high official who incurred the same reproach, "a man had never yet been hung for breaking the spirit of a law." Besides, promotion in the service, which, according to the letter of the Act of 1883, ought to be determined also by tests of fitness, is practically still free from any regulation. In consequence, the political influence which was formerly exercised to control appointments as well as promotions, is now directed, without restraint, to the control of promotions.

The effect of the bestowal in the old way of the non-competitive places and of promotions within the classified service was attenuated by the steady extension, with regard to appointments, of the classified service, which at the time of the enactment of the law, in 1883, included only 14,000 places. This extension was brought about partly in an automatic manner, in consequence of the development of the service which raised the number of the employees of an office to 50, and partly by presidential authority. Almost all the Presidents who followed each other after 1883, and especially Mr. Cleveland, have more or less enlarged the "classified" service, yielding to the evidence which proved the immense superiority of the new system and to the trend of public opinion, which was declaring itself, with increasing force, in favour of it. Towards the end of his second administration, in 1896, Mr. Cleveland "classified" more than 30,000 offices. Mr. McKinley was the only President under whom the extension of the reform met with a check. The classification by presidential authority being permissive, the President can revoke or modify at his pleasure his orders or those of his predecessors. Mr. McKinley used this power, for the greater advantage of the politicians, and "excepted" a good many offices from competitive examination. The rules also underwent modifications tending to leave somewhat more discretion to the chiefs in appointing to office. In spite of this untoward reaction, the reform may be considered as definitive. Its enemies are still very numerous, the politicians have not yet disarmed, they continue to assail the principle even of the reform, they make a furious attack on it in Congress when the budget is voted, every year, with unfailing regularity, as if the standing orders of the House required it. They try to strike out the appropriations for the federal civil service commission, but they never succeed in getting a majority for their motion; it is rejected from fear of public opinion if not from conviction. Even McKinley's administration, which has whittled down the reform, thought well, on the other hand, to do homage to it by restricting the discretionary power of dismissal belonging to the chiefs. The latter are now obliged, before removing a subordinate, to give him the reasons for it in writing and with due notice, to enable the employee to submit his defence in writing as well. The formal provisions of the law of 1883, completed by the successive extensions of the classified service, had brought into it rather more than 80,000 offices out of over 200,000 which exist in the federal service. There still remain nearly 120,000 non-classified places, of which about 5000 are "presidential" offices, filled with the confirmation of the Senate, and 22,000 "laborers'" situations. The effect of this considerable number of "unprotected places," aggravated by the enforcement of the law of 1820, which limits the tenure of office to four years, is to leave civil service reform in a very incomplete state.

Moreover, the federal offices form but a part of the fund of corruption; the offices in the service of the States and in that of the municipalities, which afford an abundant supply of spoils, have been withdrawn to a slight extent only from the political plunderers. The competitive system started in the federal administration, for a long time had great difficulty in penetrating into the service of the States and of the cities, and still more in being honestly enforced. Two States only had promptly followed the example set by the federal Legislature: the State of New York passed a law similar to the federal one in 1883, and the State of Massachusetts did the same in 1884. In the first of these States the reform had to pass through a checkered struggle to become a reality; its practical effect was often destroyed by the executive officers, or even by the Legislature, in which the politicians are supreme. On the occasion of the last constitutional revision, in 1895, sanction was obtained for the principle of the reform by a formal clause in the Constitution, but this has not prevented the designs of the politicians, who are always seeking, and often finding, means of nullifying, of "beating," the law. The two States which introduced the "merit system " had hardly any imitators. The State of Indiana alone has recently applied this system to charity institutions. In the last few years the reform has made far more progress in the municipal sphere, where remedies for the rule of rings and bosses are such a crying necessity. It was introduced into Chicago, Evanston (Illinois), Milwaukee, New Orleans, San Francisco, Philadelphia, New Haven, Galveston (Texas), and Seattle (Washington). Lastly, in about a dozen cities (of the States of Wisconsin, Colorado, Ohio, and Florida) the merit system has been applied to only one or two special departments, which were the favourite preserve of the politicians — the police and the fire department. The effect of the reform in those States and cities varies a good deal, but generally it is much less thorough than in the federal service. In some places the provisions enacted are a sham and their administration a farce, in Philadelphia for instance. In others, as in Chicago, the rules are excellent, but the administration of them leaves much to be desired. New York city is almost in the same predicament, while at the other end of the State, in the city of Buffalo, and in one or two of the Massachusetts cities, the rules work very well, perhaps better than in the federal service.

On the whole, to the limited extent in which it was applied, the reform yielded very good results. This could not be otherwise; any honest test set up for admission into the public service, no matter in what it consisted, would have been more conducive to the interests of the service and of public morality than a command of the low arts of the caucus and convention "worker," which constitutes the sole qualification under the spoils system. All the more ground was there for the success of such a suitable test as the competitive system, although not an ideal one for the selection of responsible officials. In point of fact it procured more competent, more honest employees, greatly improved the efficiency of the service, and made it less costly by permitting of the abolition of the sinecures, which were no longer needed to fling to the greedy politicians, now kept at a distance by the necessity of passing the examination. Stability became almost the rule in the competitive service, and in any event presented a singular contrast to the sweeping changes carried out in the "unprotected" service, namely, in the "excepted " positions, and still more in VOL. II —2 K the "unclassified" offices. From a general point of view, the political effects of the reform are not as yet very conspicuous, the bosses and the Machines thrive as before, for, if the supply of spoils has diminished, there are still enough left to inspire their henchmen with hopes and to make them "work." Appointment to office apart from all political influence is such a new and strange thing in the eyes of the politicians that a good many of them cannot even now believe in the reality of the reform. The fact, however, remains that more than 80,000 federal offices and a certain number of posts in the services of the States and of the cities have been wrested from them. All these places are now "taken out of politics." This blow to the spoils system, although not mortal, is a formidable one. True, it was predicted that if the fund of corruption supplied by the offices disappeared, it would be simply replaced by money, without any purification of political life. It appears that these previsions were not entirely without foundation, to judge by the growing use made of money in election contests.

But, in any event, there is one effect produced by the movement of civil service reform which is a permanent gain, and that is the moral effect of the propaganda. After the Civil War, when public spirit seemed to be in a state of coma, when the political conscience of the community, engrossed in the mad pursuit of material prosperity, was, as it were, blunted or deadened, this movement against the spoils system rekindled the extinguished flame of the ideal in American public life, it stirred the choicer spirits to an outburst of generous revolt, it enlisted genuine devotion and unselfish ardour in a crusade to regenerate democracy. The civic enthusiasm which animated the noblest and the most eminent of these men, some of whom had a national reputation, like G. W. Curtis, and others only a provincial notoriety, like S. Teackle Wallis in Maryland, — to mention the dead only, — this enthusiasm Such figures as are available for the past dozen years show that the power of removal is used so freely that in some cases from 70 to 80 per cent of the occupants of excepted positions in a given branch are displaced during one administration. In the unclassified service the proportion is still higher: during the first year of the McKinley administration, for instance,!Xi per cent of the salaried consuls were removed. On the other hand, in the whole competitive departmental service within Washington the average of the removals for some time past has been a little less than 2 per cent a year. spread to a number of young men now scattered all over the Union; it will not die out in them nor, in all probability, with them. The extremely concrete and limited character of the legislative reform, which presented it in a tangible and practical aspect likely to attract adhesions, was an admirable conductor of the idealist fluid. But at the same time the apparent modesty of the plan demanded from its promoters all the more self-sacrifice and profound sense of duty. Having entered on a new abolitionist campaign, they had not the halo which encircled the abolitionists demanding the rights of man for the negro, striving to break the chains of the slaves; *they* appeared to the multitude only as supporters of "Chinese examinations." They had to seek and develop in their own consciences the stimulant often supplied from outside in movements which impress the public imagination. The feeling, therefore, which they cultivated was not the fleeting sentiment which the wave of popular impulse brings and carries away, but a conviction rooted in the mind. That conviction formed with many a sort of permanent fund of political righteousness from which they drew their moral supplies in every great crisis, in all the political struggles which filled this quarter of the century. The body of civil service reformers furnished large contingents of the mugwumps, the independents, and the municipal reformers.

III

After the endeavours to starve the Machine by putting the public offices out of its reach, attempts were made to deprive it of another means of subsistence — of the electoral monopoly which it had acquired. The principal source of its influence was thought to lie in the fact that it had obtained possession of the material organization of the elections, which included especially the printing of the voting-papers and the distribution of them. This last required a large staff of agents, which was further swollen to afford a pretext for employing a great many electors and buying their votes in an underhand way. The considerable outlay necessitated by all these operations, added to the varied expenses of the election campaign, raised election expenditure to such a point that it became impossible for a new party, and all the more for an independent candidate, if he was not very rich, to enter the lists. They would have had to create, for their private use, an organization as highly developed as that of the Machine, which was constructed and worked on the principles of large manufacturing concerns. They were therefore obliged, if only for this reason, to accept, or even to seek, the support of the Machine. Again, the expenditure required gave the Machine a pretext for levying assessments on the candidates and an opportunity for obtaining enormous resources, by selling candidatures for cash. Henry George, the author of " Progress and Poverty," summed up the situation in the following formula: "What we call Machine politics springs from the cost of elections." To checkmate the Machine the first thing to be done, therefore, was to reduce election expenditure.

The acts of fraud, of intimidation, and of corruption which characterized the American elections gave rise to an agitation for the introduction of a strict system of secret voting. The Australian system, which appeared to supply the type of one, and which commanded the assent of the public for that reason, also contained provisions imposing on the public authorities the duty of preparing and distributing the votingpapers, at the expense of the State. The American "reformers" thought that these provisions offered a solution of the problem which preoccupied them, and they started a propaganda in favour of the adoption of the Australian system in its entirety. The Australian Ballot forthwith became a most dangerous rival of civil service reform, as a panacea for the evils which afflicted American political life. It would not put an end only to bribery and intimidation of the electors and to frauds in the taking of the vote, but it would undermine the very foundations of the Machine: it would deprive it of a pretext for interfering with elections, for employing "workers," for levying assessments, and would strip its candidatures of their privileged character; the assent of the. Machine would no longer be required for getting on the printed list; the State, which would henceforth make up this ballot, would enter every candidate on it, whether recommended by a party organization or not, would submit them all, without dis " Money in Elections" *(Xorth American Review,* March, 1883).
tinction, to the electors; a poor man would therefore have the same facilities as a rich man, and an independent the same chances as a party hack, of entering public life. The promoters of the reform succeeded in creating a genuine current of opinion in its favour, sermons were preached in the churches for the Australian Ballot, numerous petitions were addressed to the legislatures, and eventually the reformers ended by intimidating the politicians entrenched in those assemblies: against their will the latter introduced the Australian system. In a few years almost all the States of the Union

adopted the Australian Ballot.

I have already explained, in the proper place, the economy of the system so far as it relates to the secrecy of the vote. The second part of the reform, which introduces the official voting-paper, organizes it in the following manner. On the approach of the elections the names of the candidates put forward are communicated, within the prescribed periods, to the public authority. The latter enters them on the list if the candidatures emanate from a more or less considerable group of electors. The law concedes this character in the first instance to the political parties, by admitting the candidates duly nominated by the conventions and certified as such by the committee of the respective party. Every electoral group is considered as a political party for this purpose which has run candidates at the preceding election, and has, according to the legislation of most of the States, polled a certain minimum of votes, varying, with the States, from 10 to 1 per cent of the total number of the voters. The candidates of the less important "parties " or the independent candidates must, to be entered on the official ballot, be presented by a special petition or nomination paper signed by a certain number of electors. All the candidates named either in the certificates of the committees of the recognized parties, or in the special petitions, are arranged by the public authority on one or more lists. The printed copies of these lists are handed on the polling-day to each elector by the election officers to serve as ballots; retiring forthwith into a booth or a compartment screened from observation, he marks on the list the candidates of his choice, and gives it back properly folded to be deposited in the ballot-box. The elector may not use other voting-papers than the official ones; but he is at liberty to vote for candidates not entered on the official ballot, by writing their names on his voting-paper.

The reader already knows the effects of the provisions of the Australian Ballot relating to secret voting, and will remember that in this respect the reform had a certain success, that without doing away with, or perceptibly lessening corruption, it put an end to the open intimidation and the coercion applied to the electors, and ensured order at the elections. Very different was the result of the introduction of official voting-papers, which was to deprive the Machine of its electoral monopoly. This part of the reform proved an almost complete failure, and in reality it even aggravated the situation. It has made the "heelers" and the "workers " of less importance by rendering their intervention on the polling-day useless. Yet election expenditure is almost as high as before. It was no use making the State pay for the preparation and the distribution of the voting-papers; the levy of the assessments went on just the same, for the very simple reason that the candidates did not depend on the organization of the party for the distribution of the voting-papers only, they received from it their actual title of candidates of the party, which it could grant or refuse. Far from curtailing this arbitrary power, the Australian Ballot has unintentionally given it a legal sanction, by admitting candidates flying the colours of a political party only on a certificate of the committee of the Organization. By conceding the status of party to the great parties only, the law has placed them in a privileged position.

The independent candidatures, which the law, according to the intention of its promoters, was to multiply, have now greater difficulty in arising, thanks to this very law, which requires them to be presented through petitions signed by a certain number of electors. The requisite minimum of signatures, however, is often too high, and it is by no means easy to bring into the field every time a group of electors even before Except in the State of Indiana, where the elector is not allowed to write any new name, on pain of making the voting-paper void; he mmy only replace a complete list of candidates of a party by another list equally complete and printed on a piece of paper which he pastes over the space occupied by the first list.
the election. A good many electors would have no objection to vote for an independent candidate, but they have a constitutional aversion to indulging in the public display of heterodoxy which the petition implies, or, again, they refuse to sign it for fear of incurring the enmity of the men of the Machine, which might injure them in their business and in other ways. The period prescribed for presenting the petition, although rather longer, in certain States, than that imposed on the party committees, is also an obstacle to independent candidatures: the independents cannot usefully exercise the power of bringing forward opposition candidates before they know the selections made by the regular parties; but as these latter take care, for that very reason, to make them known at the last moment only, the independents have not sufficient time to get up the petition. The formalities enjoined by the law offer the ingenuity of the politicians opportunities of raising endless quibbles about the petition and of getting it declared null and void. Before the introduction of the Australian Ballot an independent candidature could arise at any moment and appeal for support without any condition; a small party could have its private ticket printed at slight expense, and all the voting-papers presented in the names of its candidates were admitted and counted.

After having thus curtailed the freedom of candidatures, the provisions of the Australian Ballot dealt a no less heavy blow at the independence of the vote and at the equality of the several candidates' chances of catching the eye of the electorate. When the independent candidates, or the candidates of the small parties, have at last overcome every obstacle and have managed to get on the official list, they find themselves relegated to a back place, behind the candidates of the regular parties, owing to the system of classification adopted. The laws of the different States provided two systems of classification of the candidates on the lists: the first arranged, for each office, all the candidates promiscuously, in alphabetical order, without mention of the parties to which they belonged; the second system arranged them by parties, each party having its column on the list with the name of the party at the top, and the division according to offices being repeated in each column, for the special use of the party. The alphabetical system put all the candidates on a footing of equality, whereas in the second system the candidates of the parties, pointed out as such and placed at the head of the list, were brought to the special notice of the electors. The public authority, which put the list before the elector, made itself as it were a broker of the parties to him. The elector was tempted, instead of discriminating between the candidates, instead of judging the men, to look at the label only. This just suited his indolence of mind. He could, however, while marking the names of the candidates obligingly arranged under the title of the party, refuse the mark to those candidates whom he objected to, "scratch the ticket," as the phrase goes, and also mark some names in the adjoining columns, thus voting what is called a "split ticket." But the law undertook to reduce to a minimum the feeble attempts even at discrimination on the part of the elector, by relieving him of the obligation of marking the names one by one, and enabling him to make a general mark, a cross in a small circle printed for this purpose above the title of the party, to show that he voted for the whole list of the party in a lump. The elector made use of this permission all the more readily that the list is a very long one, that a certain material effort even is required to put a cross against each name. The large number of elective offices and of the candidates of different parties for each office, who are generally classified on a single voting-paper, makes the latter a document of extraordinary dimensions, which has got it the nickname of "blanketballot." How can the elector examine such a list properly during the few minutes at his disposal for marking it, in the isolated compartment into which he withdraws with the paper that he has just received from the election board? Perplexed by the jumble of names and columns on the list, the elector is only too glad to get out of the maze as quickly as possible In three States (Connecticut, New Jersey, and Missouri) the candidates of each party are entered ou a separate list; the elector who comes up to record his vote receives a copy of each list, he selects one of them, and hands it in as a voting-paper. Connecticut has not only separate lists for each party, but even for each set of offices — State otlices, municipal offices, seats in the Legislature, magistrates, etc.

I have in my possession a blanket-ballot of the State of Illinois of moderate dimensions, as it. contains four columns only, whereas often there are twice as many; this voting-paper measures about 18 inches by 21, not including the margins, aud contains 148 names. by putting a cross above one of the first columns. He need not even know how to read the title of the party, the law allows it to be designated by an emblem — an eagle, a cock, a star, a plough, a boat, etc.; all he has to do is to put his cross under this little picture Before the introduction of the blanket-ballot, when a separate voting-paper was deposited for each office, the material effort required to depart from the ticket of the Organization was not considerable, the elector could offer his own voting-paper, written by hand and prepared at home. This bit of paper, which he took out of his pocket and which was called the "vest-pocket ballot," could, in a certain degree, defeat the ticket of the Machine. The elector could "scratch," strike out on the ticket of the Machine with a single pencil line the name of a candidate whom he disapproved of, whereas now he can only accomplish this, according to the laws of most States, by leaving this name alone unmarked. Certain States do give the power to strike out individual names or to indicate the names of the rival candidates whom the electors would like to substitute for the respective candidates in the list of their party; but these operations are too complicated to tempt the average elector to resort to them. In one way or another, the elector is invariably driven to vote a straight ticket, to vote the ticket of a party with his eyes shut. The subordination of the personality of the candidate, of the individual to the ticket, thus became greater than ever. True, the system of alphabetical classification, which was adopted in several States, hardly allowed of voting a straight ticket in a mechanical fashion, but the politicians got rid of this system. They replaced it, in most of the States where it was in force, by the system of classification by parties, aggravated by that of single marks and emblems and by some other devices. They thus brought the efficacy of the reform down to the vanishing point. In so doing they afforded a striking example of their habitual tactics, of their mode of capturing the reforms However, the mental indolence which characterizes the great majority of the electors often found a means of circumventing, so to speak, the alphabetical system: the candidates whose names began with the first letters of the alphabet obtained the most votes.

demanded by public opinion, of the way they bow to "the omnipotence of public opinion before which, in the United States, all tremble, all humble themselves in the dust"; they give it, not the thing itself, but the name of the thing, like a toy which is given to children to keep them quiet. Far from having destroyed the electoral monopoly of the Machine, the Australian Ballot has only consolidated it. The ward boss was by no means exaggerating who said to me, with reference to this reform: "If one had deliberately tried to make things easy for the Machine, one could not have hit on anything better."

This singular result was not due only to the perverse ingenuity of the politicians, but also to the simple-mindedness of the reformers. The latter diagnosed the complaint in a somewhat rough-and-ready fashion, by dwelling on the external symptoms. The monopoly of the material organization of the elections which the Machine had assumed was not the cause, but the consequence, the accompaniment, of the moral electoral monopoly which it had acquired, of the power over men's minds which it had usurped under the mask of party orthodoxy. The remedy prescribed for the disease presented a flagrant logical contradiction: to allow full scope to the independent candidatures and to the free expression of the suffrage, they were submitted to a set of restrictive regulations; to stop the usurpation of the political parties legal recognition was obligingly conceded to them. It is perfectly clear that, in order to ensure the official voting-paper its efficacy as a political instrument at the service of every citizen, it was necessary to put the parties quite on one side in all that concerned the working of the Ballot, in all its phases, not only as regards the classification of the candidates on the lists, but also, and above all, as regards the registration of the candidatures. If, in order to fix a reasonable limit for the number of the candidates to be entered on the official list, those only who represented political groups were placed on it, all the political groups should have been put on a footing of equality, all should have been compelled to lodge a petition, to make the effort indicating their wish to support a particular candidate, without the State asking the members of any group what their political ideas were, or what was their political record. By relieving this or that old-established group of this obligation, on the strength of the political label which it has adopted, the State not only puts a premium on political inertia, on unreasoning adhesion to traditional parties at the expense of free opinion, but it deliberately steps out of its province, for it is no business of the State to hall-mark the political ideas or views of the citizens, nor to settle the conditions on which the hall-mark shall be granted. Before the State there are no members of political parties, but members of the community with rights and duties inscribed in the Constitution for the whole body of citizens. It was through disregarding these elementary truths that the American legislator arrived at results diametrically opposed to those which he was aiming at.

The legislation of the Australian Ballot has been completed, in several States, by laws which also aimed at reducing election expenses, but by dealing with illicit expenditure. I have, in a previous chapter, referred to these laws, which imposed severer penalties on corrupt electoral practices and which regulated expenses incurred by candidates or on their account. The reader is already aware that the effect of these laws is almost *nil.* IV

While not having done what was expected of it, the Australian Ballot introduced a great innovation through the legal recognition which it gave to the political parties: being invested with a legal status, they formally became a part of the machinery of the State. For some time past the legislator had been showing a tendency to recognize the existence of the parties and to make room for them. This movement began about 1870, although traces of it are found as early as before the Civil War. It appeared at first in the form of the representation of minorities, not in the sense assigned to this representation in Europe, where its object is to enable the different shades of public opinion to make themselves heard in deliberative assemblies. The American legislator applied the representation of minorities to the election boards which supervise the taking of the vote, and especially to the administrative local offices filled up by election, the effect of which was rather to divide the *places* among the most powerful parties. On the pretext of protecting minorities, the legislator thus admitted, by implication, that public offices belong to the parties as such, that is to say, he recognized the spoils system, but only tried to introduce a little equity into the distribution of the spoils. The "representation of minorities " applied in this way to elective posts, to a somewhat limited extent however, has been followed and almost replaced of late years by the legal distribution among the parties of certain offices filled up by appointment. These offices became more numerous, the elective method having been abolished for certain places in the local administration; they were better adapted for division, as the appointments rested with a single person and not with a body of electors. According to the system in question, the chiefs who appointed the members of the administrative boards had to fill up these posts so that they were not all occupied by the adherents of a single political party, so that the number of the latter did not exceed a certain proportion fixed by the law. Or again, and more often than not, they had to appoint the members of the two largest parties in equal proportions. The administrative boards thus organized and known euphemistically, in official language, by the name of "non-partisan" boards, are styled in ordinary parlance "bi-partisan" boards. It has been justly remarked that it would be still more accurate to call them " double-partisan."

In the first place this system is applied, in a general way throughout the Union, to the election officers whose business it is to conduct the election or to make the preparations for it. They are paid out of public money, but they must be taken from among the members of the two great parties, and even directly chosen or appointed by the committees of the parties. The ostensible object of these provisions was to prevent the frauds and, in general, the abuses which a party in possession of the electoral machinery could commit at the expense of the other parties. By a similar train of reasoning the system was applied to the administration of the police, whose influence, as we are already aware, constitutes one of the most valuable resources of the Machine. In several cities, therefore, where the police is managed by a board of commissioners, the latter were appointed on the bi-partisan system. It had, however, been also applied, in certain cities, to the service of the fire department and to that of public works, where there was assuredly no material for party oppression. It was nothing but a pretext and a means for ensuring the regular division of the spoils. It had always been customary for the rival Machines to agree to relinquish a share of the offices to one another, to make bargains or "deals." The law which introduced the bi-partisan system has simply given these deals the guarantee of the State. The argument based on the expediency or the necessity of protecting the parties which lay hands on the public interest from one another — this argument, even when it seemed plausible, was exactly on a par with a justification of the attitude of a public authority which, in a spirit of higher justice, would superintend the equitable distribution of the booty among thieves who were quarrelling over it and who were not of equal physical strength.

The application of the bi-partisan system to local administration was powerfully stimulated by the legal recognition of the parties effected under the Australian Ballot; most of the bi-partisan boards date mainly from the last decade, which followed the introduction of the Australian system or witnessed the completion of it. But it was in the electoral sphere especially that the legal recognition of the parties was destined to have a sequel. If the State conferred the status of candidate on the persons certified by the committees of the parties as having been duly chosen in the primaries and the conventions, was it not its duty to make sure that they were so chosen, could it assume a kind of responsibility for acts which were done outside it, was it not bound in that case to exercise some control over them; in a word, ought not the State to bring the primaries and the conventions under its strong arm?

V

It had long been tempted to do so, and had already taken several steps in this direction before the introduction of the Cf. an article, supported by copious data, on this legislative movement in the State of New York, by D. F. Wilcox: "Party Government in Cities" *(Political Science Quarterly,* December, 1899).

Australian Ballot. It was the abuses and the scandals prevailing in the primaries and the conventions that had suggested the idea of the intervention of the State in the inner life of the party organizations. Since, people said, the nominations made in the party meetings are as important as, or even more important than, the legal elections of which they predetermine the material result and anticipate the political effect, why should not the State, which surrounds these latter with so many precautions to ensure the free and truthful expression of the will of the electors, grant the same protection to the elector in the preliminary, but not less important, stage of nominations to elective offices? It was only by recognizing the great fact of party organization, by giving the primaries and the conventions a legal existence, that they could be subjected to restraints and responsibilities which would perceptibly abate the evils which they inflict on the country, and, perhaps, render their action normal and useful. Consequently, the frauds committed in the primaries must be made amenable to the penal law just like those which are committed at elections, and so on. Started during the crisis of the Civil War, which gave rise to a sort of political self-examination, the problem of the legalization of the primaries came definitively before the public after the war, when the abuses of the Caucus grew intolerable. It was discussed in the Press, prizes were offered for the best practical solution of it, it was brought before the legislative assemblies. The idea of legalizing the primaries made progress in the public mind; eminent citizens gave a decided opinion in its favour, as for instance, Mr. Cleveland, just as he was entering on his great political career. But Cf. *The Trial of the Constitution,* by Sidney George Fisher, Philadelphia, 1862, pp. 353-386. The Union League Club of Philadelphia organized, in 1868, a competition of this kind, and the successful essays, to the number of four, were published in book form: "*Essays on Legal Organization,* selected among those submitted in competition for the prizes offered by the Union League of Philadelphia." In his letter accepting the candidature for the post of Governor of the State of New York, in 1882, Mr. Cleveland said: "Ourcitizens for the most part attach themselves to one or the other of the great political parties, and under ordinary circumstances they support the nominees of the party to which they profess fealty. It is quite apparent that under such circumstances the primary election or caucus should be surrounded by such safeguards as will secure absolutely free and uncontrolled action. Here the people themselves are supposed to speak; here they put their own hands to the machinery the legislator was at first somewhat slow in complying with the appeals addressed to him. To begin with, the politicians, who were by no means anxious to be placed under supervision, stifled the attempts at legislation. Again, there arose the grave question of principle, whether the State had the right to regulate "the sayings and doings of private individuals, forming free associations and assembling in more or less private meetings to perform acts which have no legal force, however great their political import may be. An affirmative reply to this question appeared by no means so undisputable, and the legislator, therefore, simply offered the protection of the State to the party associations, taking care not to thrust it on them. The first laws on the subject, passed in 1866, in the State of California, and, in 1871, in the State of Ohio, were drafted on these lines. While enacting a whole series of provisions for ensuring regularity and honesty in the proceedings of the primaries or caucuses, and making offenders amenable to the penal code, these laws left it to the party committees to decide, whenever they convened their adherents for the selection of candidates, whether these meetings should be held in accordance with the rules laid down by the law (" may by resolution adopted at the time of making the call, elect to have such elections conducted in accordance with the rules prescribed in sections. ..."). of government, and in this place should be found the manifestation of the popular will. When by fraud, intimidation, or any other questionable practice, the voice of the people is there smothered, a direct blow is aimed at a most precious right, and one which the law should be swift to protect." The rules laid down for that purpose required the notice issued by the committee to be published a certain specified time beforehand, and to mention the place and date of the meeting, its object, the names of the persons who are to act as presiding officers, the hours during which the poll is to remain open, the qualifications necessary for taking part in the vote, besides those fixed by the law; persons not possessing this double qualification could not vote, and each elector who presented himself conld, on the demand of another elector, be challenged to prove that he had all these qualifications; the committee which decided the case could examine and administer an oath to the citizen whose claims as elector or member of the party were thus disputed; refusal to take the oath, voting without possessing the necessary qualifications, tampering with the voting-papers, intimidation or corruption, disturbing the meetings, etc., were made liable to severe penalties, imposed by the penal code. 2 *The Codes and Statutes of the State of California,* by Th. Hittel, 1876, Vol. I, Ch. XIV, Sect. 1357. *Revised Statutes of Ohio,* Columbus, 1870, Sects. 2916-2921.

The example of the States of California and Ohio was followed by several other States, which passed similar laws, but the practical effect was *nil.* The party organizations, having the option of saddling themselves with the restrictions which they entailed, abstained from doing so; the prospect of laying themselves open to a criminal prosecution for the abuses and the frauds which the politicians of the caucuses were in the habit of committing was by no means attractive to them, and they naturally preferred to run the primaries as they liked, to substitute for the procedure proposed by the law that of "go as you please." The failure of this legislation, coupled with the scandals which went on uninterruptedly in political life, drove a section of opinion into demanding more decisive intervention on the part of the State. The ever increasing agitation in this direction has, in the course of the last twenty years, forced the Legislatures of most of the States to adopt measures dealing with the primaries, that were no longer optional, but compulsory. The politicians did all they could to prevent them from becoming law; but public opinion, exasperated by their practices, insisted and had, or, at all events, appeared to have, as in the case of the Australian Ballot, the last word. In complying with the demands of public opinion, the legislator proceeded step by step, conceding to it on each successive occasion more and more rigorous and comprehensive measures, and extending them, in a few States, gradually from the principal cities to larger areas. Among the States, some did not go beyond the first degrees, while others have already reached the farthest end of the scale, striding over the traditional, if not constitutional, ideas about the limits of the intervention of the State. So that at the present moment the legislation on the subject presents a pretty considerable variety in the different States.

If we leave out the States of Florida, Kansas, Ohio, and Wyoming, in which the laws governing the primaries are of optional application, we find that some States (North Dakota and South Dakota) content themselves with repressing as a misdemeanour the act of voting at a caucus without having the legal capacity of local elector. Several other States (such as Connecticut, Indiana, New Jersey, Pennsylvania) go farther: while still leaving the procedure of the caucus to the good will and pleasure of the organizations, they punish the acts of fraud and corruption committed at the primaries, by electors who vote more than once or give in several voting-papers together, or destroy or tamper with them, or who use violence, threats, or bribery to influence the acts of an elector; as well as those committed by the officers who make a fraudulent declaration of the result of the vote, etc. In two of those States (New Jersey and Pennsylvania) we find, in addition, a beginning of regulation of the procedure of the primary, in the form of an oath administered to the officers, who swear to discharge their duties honestly. Most of the other States which have legislated on the subject, about twenty in number (Colorado, Delaware, Georgia, Illinois, Kentucky, Maine, Massachusetts, Michigan, Minnesota, Mississippi, Missouri, Montana, Nebraska, Nevada, Oregon, South Carolina, Virginia, Washington, Wisconsin), grapple with the matter more closely and more extensively. They punish both acts of fraud and of bribery, and lay down more or less strict rules, of a mandatory character, for the procedure of the primaries, prescribing how and at what time the requisition convening the primaries is to be issued so as to ensure its being properly advertised, how the meeting is to be conducted, how the right of individuals to take part in a primary is to be ascertained, how the votes are to be received and counted. But the enactments even of this category of States, based on a common principle, still present a great diversity. Some of them are compulsory only in a few great cities and are optional in the other parts of the State, while in other States the law applies to the entire State. The provisions enacted in some States are scanty and of a general description, while in several others the rules are plentiful and go into great detail; their object is to leave the party organizations, and sometimes even the electors, as little discretion as possible. The Massachusetts l;vw (Code of 1808) settles the composition of the party committees, the mode of their election, prohibits the presiding officers of the caucuses, including the inspectors, being chosen from among public servants or members of the local committees of the party. The Illinois law (of 1898) compels the central committee of the party to choose the judges and the clerks of the primaries from a list previously submitted and approved by VOL. II — 2 L public authority (the county board). In the State of Missouri (laws of 1891 and 1897) the appointment of inspectors and clerks is also subject, although in a much slighter degree, to the approval of the public authority. To prevent persons not belonging to the party from voting in its primaries, the Kentucky law has thought fit to introduce an official registration of the members of the parties: when the register of the legal voters is made up, each of them who wishes to take part in a primary declares which party he is connected with; being entered in a special column of the register, this declaration is made public by that very fact, in open defiance of the secrecy of the ballot. Other States have endeavoured to set up or outline a legal test of party membership; according to the Wisconsin law (of 1895) it consists in the fact of having voted at the last general election for the regular candidates of the party; the Massachusetts and Illinois laws exclude from the primary the electors who have taken part in a primary of the opposite party in the course of the twelve last preceding months, or, according to the Michigan law (of 1895), since the last election. In certain States, the minute regulation of the procedure of voting extends to the voting-papers, prescribing their exact size and the colour of the paper, or even admitting only official ballots, supplied by the public authority (Massachusetts, Missouri, Wisconsin), as in the Australian system: to be entered on them the candidates must have been previously nominated in party meetings preliminary to the primaries, or by petitions signed by a certain number of electors. The expenses caused by the primaries, including the printing of the voting-papers, are borne sometimes by the parties, sometimes (Massachusetts, Illinois — minus the cost of printing the voting-papers, Wisconsin) by the public treasury (of the county, city, etc.).

Several of the provisions which I have just analyzed show us very clearly the State not stopping at the supervision of the primaries, but trying to do duty for the parties in their affairs. This tendency, which received a vigorous impulse under the Australian Ballot movement, has lately reached its climax in the most recent laws on the subject, passed in 1898 by the State of New York, and in 1899 by California. In them the public authority almost completely steps into the shoes of the parties, as regards the conduct of the primaries, and becomes, in a way, a party manager. The New York, law of 1898 sets up " official primaries " by the side of " non-official primaries. " These last are primaries in the old sense; that is to say, private party meetings, placed, however, under certain restrictions, such as the prohibition to hold them in drinking-saloons, the obligation to convene and hold them under fixed conditions of publicity. The appointment of the party committees, the-selection of candidates for local offices, and the choice of delegates to the conventions must take place in the "official primaries," conducted at the cost of the State under the direction of public officers. Only electors officially enrolled for this purpose, are entitled to vote, as in Kentucky, with this difference, that their declarations of membership of a party remain secret until after the day following the general election. A public officer specially entrusted with the affairs of the primaries (custodian of primary records) divides each ward and assembly district into primary districts, one month before the day of the primary, and establishes two pollingplaces in each district: the first of these is assigned to the party which cast the highest number of votes for Governor at the last election, while the second serves for all the other parties. The operations of the primaries are conducted by inspectors, appointed by representatives of the public authority (in the city of New York by the Board of Police Commissioners), and paid out of the public funds. They are chosen among the adherents of the respective parties, either from a list presented by the party commmittees, or outside it. The law of New York lays down these strict rules not only for the primaries, but also makes them applicable to the proceedings of the conventions of all the political areas, following in this the example of Massachusetts.

The California law on the primaries in certain respects goes still farther than the New York law in assimilating the primary elections of the parties to general elections: the primaries of all the parties are held together, their members all vote at Elsewhere we find (in the laws of Connecticut, Michigan, Ohio), on the subject of conventions, only a few provisions here and there punishing acts of bribery of delegates or forbidding the delegates to give a proxy to any person to represent them at those conventions.

the same time and in the same places, to make it impossible to vote in the primaries of both parties; and a single set of officers, unconnected with the par ties, presides over all the operations; the committees of the parties and their inspectors are thus completely ousted from the primaries. The presiding officers are appointed by the public authority from the general list of the electors, and they are obliged to accept the duty like jurymen.

Thus the legislator has, step by step, ended by completely transforming the character of the primaries: the primary, in the sense of a meeting, of a deliberative assembly of the party, is officially obliterated; it is one election the more added to those which existed under the Constitution. The last stage, represented by the laws of 1898 and 1899, is of course beyond the range of criticism for the moment, so far as practical results are concerned. But the experience of the preceding stages has been a disappointing one. It has not fulfilled the hopes which were entertained of these laws. In the first place, the good citizens were expected henceforth to exhibit a greater interest in the primaries now that they were protected by the law, and that each citizen could be sure that his voice would not be drowned in these meetings, that his vote would not be made away with, etc. In reality nothing of the kind occurred; with a few variations the primaries remained, and still are, in the hands of the politicians. Having failed to rouse the indifference of the good citizens, the laws on the primaries have in no way put down the abuses which tainted their procedure. For, however minute the regulations laid down by the law may be, the observance of them always depends on the party committees and the election "judges" or "inspectors," who are appointed or suggested by these committees; being taken from among their immediate associates, they are naturally inclined to wink at the irregularities and the abuses in which the managing Ring is interested. This was the case even in the States which had surrounded the primaries with minute precautions, for instance in that of Missouri, at St. Louis, where the election inspectors are appointed by the public authority from a list submitted by the representatives of the parties and their factions; the persons submitted for this purpose were generally the reverse of respectable, and the public authority, being powerless, was sometimes led into appointing pickpockets and pugilists as inspectors, "and they did their work" *(Conference*

Besides, and this is a crucial point, the rules embodied in the laws quoted provide no solution whatever for the preliminary question on which the character of the primaries, as meetings really representative of the party, depends; namely, who is entitled to vote in the primaries. Almost all the laws referred to have been obliged to leave it, either expressly or by implication, to the party committees to determine the qualifications required; that is to say, to let this great instrument of oppression remain in their hands. The only restrictions on the power of exclusion by the committees are to be found in the Massachusetts law, which prohibits preventing an elector from taking part in the caucus because he has voted for an independent candidate for a political office (§ 85), and in the New York law, which secures the right of being enrolled in a political party to electors who are members of a special organization in view of the municipal elections (§ 2). The definition by the law of the test of party loyalty for admission to the primaries — such as has been attempted, for instance, in Wisconsin — far from guaranteeing the rights of the elector, constitutes an infringement of his political liberty; for it not only asks him to disclose how he has voted at the last election, but prevents him from co-operating with the party of his choice, if he has changed his opinions since that election. The right of the elector to co-operate with his party, and the honesty of the vote in the primaries, are not, it is true, better guaranteed by the legislation of certain States which thought they would show their liberalism by allowing, subject to taking an oath in case of challenge, any one to vote in the primaries of a party who " has the intention of acting with the party at the next election," or who "is in sympathy with the aims and objects of the party" or declares himself "in good faith" a member of the party. The sanction of the oath applied to intentions and feelings, even if it were justi *on Primaries,* p. 144). At Boston, in Massachusetts, which is far from being a stronghold of the Machine, and where the rules laid down for the caucuses are still more strict than at St. Louis, the conduct of the officers gives rise to loud complaints: "We have found the presiding officers at caucuses inclined to assume large powers, and exercise them in an arbitrary and reprehensible manner. They threaten arrest for trivial causes, and show in various ways a partisan spirit. They too often aim to serve their friends or their faction, rather than the whole body of voters" *(Conference on Primaries,* p. 61).

lied in law and in politics, cannot be effective. In practice, the oath is not enforced at all, to avoid irritating the electors who might perhaps be still won over; or, if it is demanded, it is not much of an obstacle to the frequenters of drinkingsaloons and men of their kidney who lay themselves out for voting in the primaries of both parties; having taken the oath, they vote fraudulently with an untroubled conscience. In short, the law has not been able, and never will be able, to prevent with certainty the undue exclusion or admission of citizens into the counsels of the party, for the peremptory reason that party membership does not admit of regulation by an outside authority. This membership is, by its very nature, based solely on the conformity of feelings existing between the member and the party, a conformity which cannot be defined or laid down by third persons. A State which attempted it would be led into arbitrariness or confusion, as has beea shown by the laws of certain States which we have just analyzed. The State is aa powerless against the despotism wielded over the members by the party or its representatives, legitimate or not, as it is against the despotism wielded by the Church over its followers, each despotism being founded on the willing or passive assent of the very persons on whom it presses. The victims of this despotic power can only liberate themselves from it by liberating their conscience. If they are unable to do this, the arm of the State cannot help them.

The legislation protecting the primaries, with all its minute precautions, could not, of course, be more successful in putting an end to the confabulations which necessarily precede every vote, every working-up of a candidature, nor to the intrigues which surround it; the most advanced laws on the subject have thrust the party organizations out of the Caucus, all the doors of which are now guarded by public authority; but they cannot prevent them from retiring into an antecauous and directing their operations

from there. The " slate," which is made up behind the scenes, and which predetermines the Since the oath was introduced in Boston, by the law of 1897, " the trouble has increased rather than diminished. It is beyond question true that more persons belonging to one party have voted in the caucus of the other party than ever before, and more openly" *(Conference on Primaries,* p. 63).
result of the primaries to such a large extent, is inevitably beyond the reach of the legislator: it is protected by the force of the private arrangements got up beforehand by those concerned, as well as by the inertia of the electoral mass, which gravitates in the orbit of "regularity." The law has been able to lay hand only on the outside apparatus of the primaries, and it can only effectively protect the externals, the publicity and the good order of their meetings, the right of those who take part in the primary to make themselves heard, to record their votes without let or hindrance, the taking and honest counting of all the votes without any distinction, and, at the most, it can also protect the honesty of the vote against corruption, so far as that is possible for the law. In short, the law has only been able to apply to the primaries the police supervision, which is the sum total of the State's power over members of organizations, whether of a religious, political, or any other kind. Thanks to the law, it has perhaps been possible, in some localities, to check those practices of the politicians of the primaries which can be reached by the police power. In any event, the results obtained have not been of great importance. Generally, the frauds committed in the primaries remain unpunished, in spite of the law. The representatives of the public authority, whose duty it is to commence or to conduct the prosecutions, are elective officers whose nominations are made in these primaries, and perhaps with the co-operation of the very people who perpetuate frauds. They would have done their duty if they had been supported or encouraged by public opinion, but the misdeeds of the primaries are not such as excite its wrath; in any event, this wrath is never of long duration, — the next day people are indignant, they inveigh loudly against the politicians, and then they go back to their business. That is the secret of the ineffectiveness and, one might almost say, the uselessness of all these laws protecting the primaries. Public opinion, at least a notable section of it, has, in the course of the last few years, so far realized the importance, the imperative necessity, of purifying the primaries, as to demand laws against the offenders; but it has not yet got the will and the energy to make these laws a reality. At the best, it is still in the phase of *Video meliora proboque, deteriora sequor.* At the conference of citizens from different parts of the Union which met at New York, in 1898, to consult over a "practical reform of primary elections," a representative of the State of Missouri, which possesses, as we have been able to satisfy ourselves, an extremely strict legislation on the subject, remarked: "No laws will count if they cannot be enforced. This has been our trouble in Missouri. The fraud out-paced the law. ... There has been fraud in primary elections here, much of it flagrant, for twenty years. I have known men to be arrested, — a few, — but never one prosecuted earnestly and sent to the penitentiary. I would rather see one hirer of primary repeaters sent to the penitentiary than to have the legislature of Missouri say to me,'We will enact into law any plan for a primary election that you may submit.' "
Thus, after all, the legalization of the primaries proved ineffective, while showing, under a new aspect and in the most conclusive manner, the futility of the introduction of the parties into the sphere of the State, of which introduction that legalization was the last and the longest stage.

VI

While attempts were thus being made to purify the springs of political life by legislative reforms, other efforts of the same kind were brought to bear directly on some particular departments of public life which were most contaminated by corruption. The crying abuses in the municipal sphere appeared to call strongly for special legislative remedies. The awakening of public opinion, which has taken place and gathered strength in the course of the last twenty years, centred on the problem of municipal organization, and gave rise to very numerous legislative experiments, dictated by diverse and often contradictory ideas. The first thorough investigation of the question, made in 1877 by a special legislative commission appointed by Tilden, Governor of the State of New York, pointed out as the *Conference on Primarie», pp. 148, 149.*
It is right to mention an earlier scheme of municipal reform, drawn up in 1867 by a committee of the Union Club of New York, under the presidency of Dorman B. Eaton, and embodied in a printed report. causes of the evil: (1) the incompetence and dishonesty of the men who govern the city; (2) the introduction of party politics into municipal affairs, which was the primary source of the preceding cause; and (3) the improper intervention in local affairs of the legislature, which regulated them at haphazard, by special laws, or even prostituted its power of making these laws to the interests of the predominant political party or to financial undertakings which had designs on municipal property. The leading idea of the authors of this report was that a municipality is in no way a political body, but a business organization with the duty of administering the property of the community, like a joint-stock company which runs a private concern. This idea led them to the conclusion that the municipal shareholders, the ratepayers of the city, ought alone to choose its administrators, to the exclusion of those citizens who, not paying any municipal rates, have no right to dispose of them; and, not feeling the effects of extravagant or untrustworthy management, have no interest in electing honest and competent administrators. The commission, therefore, proposed to establish two municipal as-

semblies; the one chosen by universal suffrage, and the other, composed of six to fifteen members and holding the purse-strings, by the limited suffrage of those who pay a fixed minimum of rates. The fundamental conception of the commission was true in part only: in the modern State the powers of a municipal government are not confined to local economic interests, they include also duties of a public kind, delegated by the State, which consequently affect the interests of all the citizens whether municipal shareholders or not. But even if it were legitimate, the limitation of the municipal electorate could not be efficacious: the incapable or dishonest administrators are not elected exclusively by the votes of the non-ratepayers; the latter only make up the total of the parties among which the "better element" is distributed. It is the division of the good citizens against themselves, it is the division into political parties in the sphere of municipal affairs with which poli "Report of the Committee to devise a Plan for the Government of Cities in the State of New York," Albany. March 6,1877 *(State of Xew York Assembly Documents,* Vol. VI, No. 68). This very remarkable report has lately been reprinted, in its essential part, in *Municipal Affairs,* September, 1899, under the title " Report of the Tilden Commission." tics has no concern, that enables the bad candidates to get in under the party flag. If, instead of fighting one another like the Blues and the Greens of the Roman circus, these "good" citizens united to demand only guarantees of capacity and honesty from the municipal candidates, those who have none to give would not be able to get in. In consequence, as long as the elector persisted in looking at nothing but the party colour of the candidates, the exclusion of the poor citizens from the municipal suffrage would only have had the effect of diminishing the absolute number of the voters, but would not have altered the result of the vote. Lastly, even if the proposed limitation of the electorate could be effectual, it was not realizable: to restrict the power of universal suffrage the consent of universal suffrage was necessary. The legislature of the State of New York, on receipt of the report of the committee, did not care to submit to the people the constitutional change recommended by it. The plan of the committee fell through. On the other hand, it appeared impossible that universal suffrage, in the conditions under which it worked, could ever ensure a better class of members for the city councils. Considering the councils, in a way, as given over to incapacity and dishonesty, the reformers tried to obviate the effects of their mischievous activity by preventing them from acting. They set to work to cut down the jurisdiction and the powers of the city councils. The existing municipal organization had been modelled on the political organization, in which the legislative was placed above the executive, and was even entrusted with functions which belonged rather to the province of the executive. Now the position was reversed, the powers of the mayor were enhanced to such an extent as to make him deliberately a "municipal dictator ": he was in no way accountable to the council, he could appoint and dismiss the chief municipal officers at his pleasure, he exercised a right of veto over the decisions of the council in the extremely limited sphere of authority that was left to it. Responsibility, when divided, broken up among the members of the council, the mayor, and numerous committees or officials, which were often independent of one another, had been practically non-existent. When laid on the mayor, who was chosen directly by the people, it would become a reality, argued the reformers; knowing whom to call to account in case of bad government, the people could strike directly at the culprit; in committing supreme power into the hands of one man, the people will be obliged to be careful in the choice of that man, and they can do this more easily than when they have to elect a more or less numerous assembly.

This system of municipal organization, inaugurated about the years 1882-1885 in Brooklyn, Boston, and New York, was soon introduced into several other cities. It was received with marked favour; it was supposed to provide a specific against municipal disorders; it was cracked up as a great innovation in the art of local government which America offered the world along with the town meeting. Among the brilliant champions of this system a few, like Mr. Seth Low, who was mayor of Brooklyn under the new regime, were able to add to their arguments the most eloquent one of all — their own successful experience.. But, as a whole, the "municipal dictator" system was far from yielding the desired results. Sometimes it brought into power superior men, sometimes politicians of the worst stamp, sometimes it started a sort of municipal revival, at other times it perpetuated the old abuses. The city of Brooklyn itself supplied an instance of these variations, — according as the see-saw of the political parties changed the men in power, — and practically demonstrated that the " municipal dictator" system had no intrinsic efficacy. In fact, all its fundamental ideas, however correct in substance, were stretched too far. Responsibility and absolute concentration of powers do not necessarily go hand in hand. The government of cities by municipal councils and their committees is in no way unsound in itself, the example of Europe proves exactly the contrary. If it was otherwise in the United States, this was because the men of whom the councils were composed were unsound. The direct responsibility to the people of a man invested by them with supreme power is a delusion which has been attended over and over again with the most humiliating results for the political communities Cf. *The City Government of Boston,* by Nathan Matthews, Jr., Boston, 1895, p. 173.
The reader will find the defence of the system in question very effectively stated In *Addresses and Papers on Municipal Government,* by Seth Low. which have been led to adopt this system. It is simply an abdication of liber-

ty on the part of the citizens and an encouragement to every form of despotism. A dictator is accountable to rebellion only, whether made with bullets or, in free countries so called, with ballots. To be real and effective, responsibility must be continuous and unceasing; and this is possible only under the regime of representative assemblies, under the system of control which they ensure. The old sophism of personal responsibility to the people appeared in this particular case all the more gross that, as municipal battles were always fought on party questions, the person of the mayor was mixed up with his party — he rose and fell with it. There was, therefore, in reality, no responsibility but party responsibility. But it was this which by eliminating considerations of individual merit had lowered the municipal councils to such an extent as to create a demand for a dictator. The remedy offered by the autocratic mayor system, therefore, only brought back the very evil which it was intended to cure. It even made it worse: by bestowing power on a single individual, it afforded greater facility for prostituting that power to the interests of the party whenever the mayor was inclined that way; by giving each new mayor the right of changing the municipal officers on the pretext of making their responsibility more effective, it legalized the spoils system; far from eliminating the boss, it increased his influence, an individual being more manageable than an assembly, and the extent of his power offering a larger prey to the greed of the boss. The "municipal dictator" system thus tended to countenance or to confirm party despotism all along the line. The defect in the political recruiting of the city councils was usually aggravated by the indifference of the electors, who did not attach sufficient importance to the choice of their ediles. By concentrating authority in the hands of the mayor, and reducing the powers of the city councils to a cipher, the new system made the electors take still less interest in the composition of these assemblies, it put a premium on their want of public spirit, and tended to take away the last vestige of responsibility from the members of the councils, degraded by the law itself. Thus the new system of municipal organization, which was intended to restore responsibility, threatened to do away with it everywhere. The exceptional qualities of the persons who happened to be in charge of the municipal administration could alone mitigate the defects of the system or even turn them to account in the interest of good government, according to the general possibilities, as old as the world itself, of absolutism with its advantages and its dangers. There was nothing new or peculiar to America which could temper or regulate this absolutism but the power of public opinion, stronger in the United States than elsewhere. But these more or less eminent persons, realizing the ideal of the "good tyrant," had no better chance of getting in than before, for the party system held, as before, the keys of all the public positions. The novelty of the " municipal dictator" system, and the stir raised about it, had caused public opinion to wake up with a start in a good many American cities, and had produced fits of public spirit which made it possible to effect a temporary clean-up in the municipal household and to carry out certain more or less durable improvements. The municipal dictator system offered but one permanent result, a very appreciable one in the eyes of so many American citizens: it saved them the trouble of governing themselves, and gave them the illusion of having found an effective mode of government which worked of itself.

The centralization created at the expense of the city councils by the institution of the autocratic mayor did not stop at his office; certain powers withdrawn from the council were transferred to the State legislature or even to the State governor, who had been entrusted, for instance, with the appointment of the commissioners of police. That is to say, municipal powers were transferred to the bodies or to the officials most exposed to party pressure, from which those powers had to be relieved.

The curtailment of the powers of the city councils gradually extended to one branch after another. In several cities the councils were shorn not only of their administrative prerogatives, but they were limited in their so-called legislative ones — in the right of organizing the administration, of making regulations. Lastly, they were almost entirely stripped of their budgetary powers. The right of initiative in expenditure was taken from them; the budget is framed independently of the city council by a small committee of superior municipal officers (board of estimate), who are not all invariably elected by the people; the council can reduce or strike out the appropriations of the budget submitted to it, but cannot increase them or add new ones, or even, as in New York, has no power over the budget. If the council refuses to vote the budget, it comes into force without their approval after a certain fixed period. It would appear that this system works well. Again, the growing restriction of the elective principle in the appointment to certain offices which are henceforth to be filled up, in several cities, by the mayor or by the heads of departments, as well as the tendency to introduce into municipal government a system of administrative control, also yield, or promise to yield, good results. In one very remarkable case a still more radical remedy has been applied: in the city of Washington elective government has been completely abolished. After the excesses of Boss Sheperd's regime, Congress— which exercises direct powers over the administration of the federal capital made into a neutral district — did away with elective government and put in its place three commissioners, to be appointed by itself. The new regime made Washington the best-governed city in the United States; but, evidently, it could not be introduced elsewhere, that is into the States whose citizens govern themselves; there the solution of the municipal problem could only be achieved on the basis of representative government, which cannot be conceived of without councils invested with real powers. In the meanwhile the limitation of the powers of the councils has not helped to raise the standard of these bodies. Attempts have been made to change the mode of their elections by substituting for voting by wards, which is the common practice, the general ticket from the city at large, but without more success.

Almost at the same time that such heavy blows were dealt at the authority of the councils, the municipal reformers rushed in a diametrically opposite direction by trying to free municipal administration from the control which the legislatures See on this point T. R. Commons, " State Supervision for Cities " *(Publications of the American Academy of Political and Social Science,* Philadelphia, 1895); F. W. Holls, "State Boards of Municipal Control " (*Proceedings of the Fourth National Conference for Good City Government,* Philadelphia, 1890). wielded over it. "Home Rule for the cities" became the watchword and the cry of the day. The reader is already aware that in the absence of an organic municipal law in several States, the cities in those States are governed by special "charters," granted to each by the State legislature, which is free to modify them as it thinks fit. Taking advantage of this state of things, the legislatures constantly intervened to modify the charter of this or that city, sometimes in one point and sometimes in another, by creating or abolishing offices, by imposing certain works and expenditure on the city, etc., without consulting the wishes of the municipalities. The undeniable harm done by this intervention was, to a great extent, but one of the aspects of the subordination of local affairs to party rule, which has made the municipality a battlefield for the State and national parties, and a preserve for the leaders of the organizations in quest of spoils and for the capitalist speculators: the parties or the pirates who operated under their flag worked the legislative power from the capital of the State in order to compass their aims of electoral strategy or piracy,—which accounts for a large proportion of the useless or mischievous laws inflicted by the legislatures on the municipalities. The Home Rule proposed as a remedy would have restored freedom to the cities, but would it have liberated them from party rule, to which they were bound not by this or that organization of powers, but by moral ties; and did not the effect of Home Rule depend on the spirit in which it was to be worked, and might it not just as well supply the dominant political party, free from all restraint, with a new weapon for exploiting the resources of the city with more impunity than ever? The plan adopted for realizing Home Rule was to prohibit the legislatures from legislating on municipal matters by special laws — laws of local concern. This heroic remedy was, however, difficult of application, owing to the inelasticity of the existing municipal organization which made special laws unavoidable. In practice the prohibition of special legislation is generally evaded by means of drafting expedients.

Lastly, among the various reforms of electoral legislation, introduced of late years, one dealt specially with municipal Cf. on this last point F. Goodnow, *Municipal Problems,* New York, 1897, pp. 73-78.
elections; it provided that these elections should take place at a different time from State and federal elections. It was hoped that this arrangement would afford a means of eliminating party preoccupations from local elections. As the elector had to vote for none but municipal candidates, he could choose them with perfect freedom, consulting only the interests of the city and with no fear of endangering the interests of the party in Congress or at the presidential election, which would not be at stake just then. A provision to this effect was inserted, as I have already mentioned, in the last constitution of the State of New York. It was also applied in several other States to the large cities. But the reform did not produce the desired effect, the party organizations only fastened more eagerly on the municipal elections thus brought into prominence, and the average party man continued to vote the party ticket; the association of ideas which led him to vote for the municipal candidates selected by the party organization, along with the other candidates, was brought about not so much by the material juxtaposition of the names on the list as by loyalty to party. Yet the measure is not devoid of utility; it will help to implant the distinction between municipal and political elections in the minds of the general body of electors.

To sum up, the various reforms essayed in municipal organization have, undoubtedly, afforded a partial or temporary alleviation of the evil; but, taken as a whole, the municipal problem still remains unsolved. A learned publicist, who has made this problem his own, remarks: "Our journey in the pathway of municipal reform, begun about the beginning of the century, has led us to the point from which we started. Like persons lost in a fog, we have walked in a circle." Has not the rapid survey made in the foregoing pages of the principal directions in which the reformers bent their steps shown us the key of the position which all or nearly all of them constantly wandered round without touching it, and which is the monopolizing of municipal life by the political parties, the enslavement of the municipal electors to the notion of party "regularity"? This aspect of the case did not altogether escape the notice of those who turned their attention to the Ooodnow *op. cit.,* p. 225.
bad government of the cities, but it provided matter for jeremiads rather than became the guiding-point or the pivot of the efforts at reform, except in the case of the material separation of the municipal from the other elections. The reformers expended the best of their energy in recasting or reconstructing the machinery of municipal government; they thought the evil was due mainly to structural imperfections: "For the general inefficiency of their city governments in the past, Amer-

icans need not blame universal suffrage, nor the other special conditions which affect them. The fault has been organic in the structure of city government. The remedy must be sought in a change of that structure." No doubt there were grave defects in the municipal organization; the problems which they raised were important, extremely important, but, after all, of relative importance. The real crux did not lie there, but in the motive power of the machinery and in the methods by which it was set in motion. Believing in the efficacy of machinery, the legislative reformers expected to obtain the maximum of effect by straining it to the utmost, and they indulged in conceptions which were as one-sided in principle as they were summary in execution: the mayor had not sufficient power in municipal government, he was made a dictator; the legislature intervened in an improper way, it was forbidden to legislate; the municipal council managed the property of the city badly, it was bound hand and foot. The public,, again, whose attention was attracted by these legislative experiments, was lulled by the assurance which they conveyed that a remedy had been discovered and the evil averted.

Besides municipal government, legislative reform grappled with the disease of political corruption in another special sphere — in the legislative assemblies of the States. Issuing from the groove of the primaries and the conventions, and being composed in great part of low, venal politicians, these assemblies had sunk to the last depths of public contempt. Improvement of the legislatures being considered hopeless, attempts were made, as in the case of the city councils, and with even more method, to limit their powers, to leave them Seth Low, *The Problem of City Government,* in the volume above quoted, p. 81.

VOL. II — 2 M as few opportunities of legislating as possible. With this object the reformers tried to insert in the constitutions—. which the ordinary legislatures have not the right to touch — as many general provisions as possible, so much so that the most recent constitutions, made very voluminous, contain many clauses which do not fall within the scope of constitutional law, properly so called, at all, but relate to private, to administrative law. To bring legislation into harmony with the changing requirements of life, frequent revisions of the constitution are preferred to trusting the members of the legislatures. Among the decisions which must be left to the latter, several have to be submitted, under the new constitutions, to popular approval, to the electors of the State or of the part of the State concerned. This plan is being adopted, to an increasing extent, in the case of loans, of extensive public works, etc. Again, there is a tendency to generalize, with regard to the legislatures, the prohibition to pass special laws, which we have already noted in connection with municipal administration. Lastly, to diminish still further the opportunities of the State legislatures for mischievous action, attempts have been made to shorten the duration of their labours by the constitutional limitation of the term of the legislative sessions and especially by the introduction, already carried out in most of the States (in all but six), of biennial sessions. VII

The legislative measures which I have just analyzed form but a small part of the schemes which politicians, publicists, and lastly amateurs have put forward for purifying public life contaminated by the Caucus and for destroying the Machine. If the Caucus and the Machine are still standing, the fault is assuredly not due to any lack of ingenuity on the part of the would-be reformers. I can only refer briefly here to the more important of these proposals.

Some deal with the nomination of candidates and try to change the machinery of it. All the mischief is supposed to proceed from the convention system, which has come between the people and its representatives. Under cover of the right which it has assumed of choosing the candidates, this system has installed in power the mercenary politicians and all the corruption that followed in their train. This usurped authority must be withdrawn from the conventions and restored to the people. The people assembled in party meetings should nominate the candidates for all the elective offices; delegates will no longer be sent to conventions, each elector will be his own delegate. This direct nomination is to be made in the primaries, which will be conducted under the rules laid down for the final elections, with all the legal safeguards introduced by the Australian Ballot. According to certain plans each party will hold its primary separately; according to others, the members of all the parties will vote together, that is to say, at the same time and in the same locality, while stating on behalf of which party they choose the candidates. Following the Australian system, most of the primary schemes provide that a list of the candidates of the party is to be drawn up before the vote, on which will be entered 'the persons put forward for that purpose by a certain number of electors, that is to say by means of "petitions " The concentration of the votes on a few names will be thus prepared. There will 1 Cf.D. C. McMillan, *The Elective Franchise in the United States,* New York, 1898; F. F. Hoffmann, " Primary Elections" *(Pennsylvania Monthly,* August, 1881); the *Evening Post* of New York, December, 1897, statement of the plan of M. F. Brooks; the *Milwaukee Sentinel,* February 22,1897, the schemes of R. M. da Follette and of W. T. Lewis, of Wisconsin; *Daily Capital Journal,* Salem, Oregon, February 18, 1897, the plan of E. Hofer, etc.

To attain the same object, that is to say, to enlighten the minds of the electors on the subject of the candidates to be brought forward at the primary, the author of a curious little book *(The Protection of Majorities,* by Josiah Phillips Quincy, Boston, 1870) proposes to publish a newspaper devoted to the candidatures at the expense of the city. This paper, the *Local Nominator,* distributed gratuitously from house to house, will begin to appear six weeks before the election, and will print communications from any electors who may have candidates to propose or an opinion to express on them. The declaration of each elector will have exactly as much weight as the reputation for good sense and integrity which he enjoys among his neighbours. A farmer, a trader, or a respected clergyman, who would never attend a caucus, can, by means of a paragraph of ten lines in the *Local Nominator,* enter into relations with his fellow-citizens and exchange opinions with them on the electoral situation. The proposer of a candidate would be perfectly free to adduce arguments in his favour, which each elector can ponder over at leisure and in the stillness of his own home, under conditions very different to those presented by the tumultuous caucus meeting. After a month of discussion conducted in this way, and a fortnight before the election, the electors will nominate the candidates. be a special primary; or, to save time arid money, it will be held when the annual registration of the electors takes place: each elector who applies to be registered will at the same time mark the names he prefers on the preliminary list of candidates put forward by the petitions.

Direct nomination of the candidates is not unknown to the existing methods; it has been already tried in the form, for instance, of the Crawford County I'hin, which I have described above and which has not been much of a success, at all events in the large cities. In small places, where everybody knows each other, direct nomination is not attended with any difficulties; but in the large cities the electors are so numerous that they do not know the good candidates any more than the bad ones — the latter are even better known. This system, therefore, has in no way curtailed the power of the wirepullers, nor encouraged candidates of a superior stamp to court the suffrages of the primaries. Fraud and corruption flourish in the direct primaries as elsewhere; corruption is even more rife in them, because they have the last word in the choice of the candidates. In South Carolina, where direct nomination is applied even to State offices, it is going out of favour; complaints are made that by doubling the elections it embitters.electoral contests and keeps up agitation. In the new schemes there is nothing novel but the legal procedure applied to the primary elections, the previous selection of candidatures by the plan of " petitions," and, according to certain schemes, the voting of the members of all the parties together.

Other schemes which also aim at eliminating the conventions dispense with the primary elections themselves, and propose that all the candidates should be presented directly by "petitions." Every group of citizens would put forward its candidate irrespective of party, and the candidate would rely only on his The celebrated jurist, David Dudley Field, had proposed, before the Introduction of the Australian Ballot, an analogous plan (" Open Nominations and Free Elections," *North American Review* for April, 18S7), according to which each elector, on the occasion of his registration, himself takes the initiative in proposing candidates, and those among them who obtain a certain minimum of votes are admitted as candidates, and voting-papers with their names are printed and distributed at public expense.

Conference on Prirnaries, pp. 99-102, the communication on the working of the " Crawford County Plan " at Cleveland, Ohio. own merit and on the approval of the citizens who have given him their signatures. The introduction of Mr. Seth Low, as candidate at the election of mayor of New York, in 1897, made in precisely that way, with the *iclat* which the reader will remember, has furnished striking proof that this plan of "free nominations " is not Utopian, and that it is a serious competitor of the existing method of choosing candidates by the Machines.

Other reformers, without sacrificing the system of primaries and conventions, hope to improve it by introducing into the election of delegates the representation of minorities, which would allow the good citizens to assert themselves in these party assemblies; or, again, by subdividing the electoral districts of the caucuses, to enable all the local electors to meet and mingle as neighbours more or less acquainted with one another.

Starting with the same idea of small electoral districts, several publicists devoted all their attention, not to reform in the modes of nominating candidates, but to the improvement of the system of elections. According to them, it was the imperfection of the electoral system which had given rise to the Caucus with all its attendant evils. Without local organization enabling the citizens to deliberate, the vote is only a delusion and a snare, and the citizen, even if he had a hundred votes, will be only a dummy. The Germanic folkmoot, the Saxon hundreds, the town-meeting of New England, provided this organization. We must go back to them, said these reformers, by basing the electoral system on districts of one hundred to three hundred electors, who can come together without difficulty. These small constituencies will choose the members of all the legislative assemblies by means of elections at several degrees. The elective method will be reduced to a minimum; there will be no more periodical elections; the term of office will no longer be limited; the members of the assemblies will remain in office *quoad bene se gexserint;* but each member can always be removed by the assembly of his division: a member of Congress by the assembly of the State, a member of this F. M. Loomis, "The Exclusion f Partisan Politics from Municipal Affairs" *Proceedings of the Louisville Conference for Good City Government,* Philadelphia, 1897); D. B. Eaton, *The Government of Municipalities,* New York, 18»i, Ch. IX.

latter by the county assembly, etc. The head of the executive will be chosen by the popular branch of the legislature, and can be removed by it; the President of the United States by the House of Representatives, and so on. In this way, while the elective method will be diminished, the responsibility of the public representatives will be made continuous and immediate, and, consequently, more effective.

These proposals, which were set forth, in 1868, by Mr. Charles Goepp, were afterwards revived and developed with much vigour by some writers, notably by Mr. Albert Stickney, in a whole series of writings, and by 'Mr. S. E. Moffett. Mr. Stickney's views are supported by a criticism, as penetrating as it is eloquent, of the existing party regime, which fully exposes its defects and abuses. According to Mr. Stickney's plan the heads of the executive at different grades will also and in like manner be elected by the people, that is to say, by assemblies of delegates emanating from the small, local meetings of the citizens. The members of Congress and the President of the United States can be removed by Congress. Popular election will take place only to fill up vacancies, and an end will be made of those " periodical convulsions of the whole national existence which we call elections." All holders of a public mandate will be protected from the tyranny of party and will serve the people only. Personal merit and character will become their sole qualifications. Individual responsibility for individual acts, the absence of which is the crying defect of the present system, will be ensured. Mr. Moffett, while accepting nearly all of Mr. Stickney's plan, reinforces it with the introduction of direct legislation by the people, of the referendum, and of proportional representation. This scheme will bring about the fundamental reform demanded by American political life — the re-establishment of the close contact between the individual citizen and the agents whom he chooses to manage his public affairs. The people in its primaries must be not only the original source, but the per In a paper presented at the competition mentioned above, which the Union League Club of Philadelphia had proposed on the problem of the primaries; this paper is published in the collection quoted. *A True Republic,* New York, 1879; "The People's Problem" *(Scribner's Monthly,* Vol. XXII, 1881); *Democratic Government,* 1885; *The Political Problem,* 1890. "*Suggestions on Government,* 1894. manent depositary of power. It must control and direct the acts of its executive and legislative servants at every degree of the ladder; it must make known its opinion on measures as well as on men. The right of appeal to the people from the legislative assembly will diminish the intensity of party conflicts, will do away with the necessity of party discipline which is practised at the cost of the independence and the honesty of the members, and will stop legislative corruption. The continuous responsibility of each member to his constituents, who can always remove him, combined with the referendum, will keep the representation at a high level. With the introduction of direct legislation and the abolition of periodical elections, the parties will no longer be permanent or inelastic.

The plan of small electoral districts will bring the elections nearer to the people, and the party conventions will be bereft of their occupation. But what is there to prevent the Caucus from creeping into the small local assemblies, from settling their proceedings beforehand, and from usurping power under the new system as it has done under the present one? To obviate this Mr. Charles P. Clark hit upon a device which he thought would nullify all the previous arrangements of the Caucus clique and frauds in general: the electoral assemblies should be formed by drawing lots, like juries. In every place with more than 2000 inhabitants the electors would be divided, by drawing lots, into five, seven, or nine groups of 250 persons at the most. Summoned secretly by personal notices addressed to each member, each group would choose representative electors, who would appoint to local offices and would select representatives to the college of the county or city electors, and so on. In these colleges of electors the vote of each representative would count in proportion to the number of the citizens whom he represents. Every representative, whether elector or office-holder, can be summarily removed by the assembly which has chosen him. The system of drawing lots, strange as it may appear, can nevertheless invoke "the wisdom of old Greece, which employed it in the selection of juries *(dikasteroi).* Moreover, the lot is sanctioned in both of the Testaments. " *The Commonwealth Reconstructed,* New York, 1878, p. 112; "A Logical System of Municipal Elections" *(Proceedings of the Second National Confer*

Some of the reforms included in the general plans which I have just described have been put forward by several men in public life and writers as *the* reform which of itself would work a cure. Such were the proposals relating to the reduction of the number of elective offices, to direct legislation, and to the referendum, and, especially, to the representation of minorities or proportional representation. It is the system of the majority vote which has warped and degraded representative government and has enabled low politicians to monopolize it. The independent elector not being able to make himself heard in the councils of the nation, one of two things inevitably happens: the elector whose vote is practically nullified loses heart, holds aloof; or he accepts, in despair, the candidates of the caucus of his party solely in order not to separate from the majority and not to let the candidates of the opposite party get in. It is this state of things, brought about by the existing electoral system, which the Caucus exploits and on which it lives. The majority has a monopoly of the representation, and the Caucus has a monopoly of the majority. Once adopt proportional representation, and the electors will no longer be forced to choose between the two candidatures, both equally odious. Large bodies of electors will fall away from the two great organizations and will reduce them to simple political groups within the nation. In a word, the Caucus, now the arch-monopolist, would have to submit to the law of competition. The representation of minorities has *ence for Good City Government,* Philadelphia, 1895, pp. 524-53."). In this last paper will be found an account of the painful experiences of the author of the scheme, who had succeeded in getting it accepted by the city of Oswego, where he resided, for the municipal elections. The State legislature voted the required modification of the municipal charter of Oswego, but the State Governor vetoed the bill. The Lieutenant-Governor, President of the Senate, a Tammany Hall man, is said to have alleged as the reason for the opposition to the bill that Mr. Clark's scheme would be the ruin of the politicians, that if the city of Oswego were allowed to adopt it, the other cities would follow suit, and then, added the representative of Tammany, "What would become of us fellows?" *Cf.* J. W. Sullivan, *Direct Legislation,* New York, 1892.

Simon Sterne, *On Representative Government and Personal Representation,* Philadelphia, 1871; articles by the same author: "Representation" (Lalor's *Cyclopaedia of Political Science),* " The Administration of American Cities" *(International Review,* 1877). M. N. Forney, *Political Reform by tlie Representation of Minorities,* New York, 1894. John R. Commons, *Proportional Representation,* New York, 1896. obtained a partial application in the States of Illinois and Pennsylvania, though without producing perceptible changes in political life. The failure is attributed to the defective character of the special form of minority representation adopted in those States, which is on the limited vote system.

The indifference usually displayed by the "good" citizens towards the public interest has suggested the idea of the compulsory vote, which I have already had occasion to mention, and even of the compulsory acceptance of elective office.

Some proposals, while abstaining from dealing with the whole electoral system, seek to change the modes of election to certain positions, to the Presidency of the United States and to federal senatorships by entrusting the election to the people. The election of the Senators by the State legislatures has given rich nonentities exceptional facilities for obtaining seats in the Senate, if not by direct corruption, at all events through the party organization, which they get hold of by their liberal contributions to the party. The electors of a whole State cannot be bought, of course; but if the Organization adopts these millionnaires as regular candidates for the popular election, will not the final result be the same? The direct election of the President by the people has been the object of proposals which date from a very long time back, from the Jacksonian era, and which were accompanied with the still older proposal tending to substitute the district system for the general ticket system. The authors of amendments to the constitution repeatedly brought forward for this purpose during the last sixty or seventy years, by members of one or the other branch of Congress, from Benton, and afterwards Charles Sumner, down to their successors of today — advocated the reform with the special object of getting rid of the intervention of the "intermediate bodies" in the presidential election, of "doing away with the Caucus or the convention." These proposals in their turn raise the question, what change will there be if the presidential candidates nominated by the national conventions are put straight on the ticket instead of the presidential electors who must vote for them? Would it not See F. W. Holls, "Compulsory Voting" *(Publications of the American Academy of Political Science,* No. 25, Philadelphia, 1892), and A. B. Hart, *Practical Essays on American Government,* New York, 1893.

be simply dispensing with the formality of the vote of the electoral college, apart from the different apportionment of the popular votes for the several candidates, if counted *per capita* by districts instead of, as now, by States?— More radical is the plan which proposes to place the election of the President in the hands of the National Legislature.

Others hold that the evil is due, not so much to the electoral system as to the organization of the public powers, to the separation of the legislative and the executive. Under the present regime the first is without guidance and the second without force. The remedy lies in the establishment of closer relations between the two by the admission of the representatives of the executive into the assemblies, — as in the parliamentary regime, minus the responsibility of the Cabinet, — and by increasing the powers of the executive.

Lastly, in the opinion of certain publicists, all these reforms would be utterly ineffective and useless; it is trying to cleanse the stream without having purified the source. The source of the evil is the unlimited right of suffrage. Without restriction of the right of suffrage nothing will ever be accomplished. On the other hand, however, it is thought that if the working of American political life leaves so much to be desired, this is because the right of suffrage is mutilated, is restricted to one sex. Give women a vote, and the aspect of things will change, political life will be purified.

Having set out in quest of remedies for the abuses engendered or fostered by the Caucus, and having, as it were, gone over the whole field of American political life, the reformers appear to have reached the end, if not the object, of their search. After accompanying them to this extreme point, we can at last pause in the already lengthy investigation of the party system which we have patiently pursued throughout the past and the present career of American democracy. A final survey will enable us to collect and fix in the mind the general impressions conveyed by the multiplicity and the variety of the phenomena that have come under our notice.

See for a discussion of this plan by several writers and men in public life, the *North American Review,* February,

1885. See all the writings of Mr. Gamaliel Bradford, in particular his last work, *Tfie Lesson of Popular Government,* New York, 18ifJ. TENTH CHAPTER SUMMARY

I

The American system of party organization, which we have considered in its various aspects, was the outcome and the expression of triumphant democracy. The eclipse of the old ruling class, which became definitive after the first quarter of the last century, appeared to leave the individual, now a member of the sovereign people, in possession of the field. To secure the full enjoyment of his rights over the commonwealth, and to facilitate the discharge of his political duties, which were growing more and more complicated through the extension of the democratic principle to its furthest limits, and more and more burdensome owing to the great economic outburst which-absorbed every energy — the citizen accepted the services of the party Organization formed on the representative method. This extra-constitutional Organization assumed a twofold function in the economy of the new political system: that of upholding the paramount power of the citizen, and' of ensuring the daily working of the governmental machinery in a democratic community whose volume was continually increasing with unprecedented rapidity, and whose composition was becoming more and more heterogeneous.

In the first of these two undertakings the Organization failed miserably, in the second it achieved a relative success. The government rested almost entirely on the elective system, nearly all the office-holders were elected, and the shortness of their terms of office made it necessary to replace them very frequently. How could the citizen, if left to himself, have grappled with this onerous task, which consisted in filling up such a number of places, and which was continually recurring? The system of nominating conventions, established on the basis of parties, provided a way out of the difficulty. By preparing the election business beforehand, by putting it cut and dried before the elector, the party Organization enabled the citizens to discharge their duty in an automatic way, and thus keep the government machine constantly going. Far from being embarrassed by the growing number of the electors, the party Organization made room for them, installed them in the State. In the case of electors of foreign extraction it did more; it was the first to assimilate the immigrants from the four quarters of the globe with the American population; by sweeping them, almost on their arrival, into its net, it forthwith made these aliens sharers in the struggles and the passions which were agitating the country in which they had just landed. It brought together and sorted all the elements of the political community, well or ill, but in the end everything found its place and settled down. And as in the improved machines of our day, which take in the raw material and turn it out transformed, these accumulated elements supplied the driving power of which the governmental machinery stood in need. The refuse even contributed to this purpose; everything was turned to account, the dregs of the population as well as the elite.

But this result, a highly important one, was obtained at the cost of the citizen's power, of the freedom of his political conscience, and of his influence in the State. Instead of giving him a firmer grasp of the government, the Caucus system has seriously weakened his hold thereon, for it diminished the efficacy of the machinery of government, provided by the constitution, as well as that of the living forces which are its real motor.

The executive was the first to give way. The convention movement claimed to infuse fresh vigour into it by withdrawing the Presidency from the intrigues of aristocratic cliques, such as the Congressional Caucus, and by making it emanate directly from the people. The electoral college, which was established by the framers of the constitution, and which had already been practically reduced to a cipher by that caucus, thenceforth took its orders from universal suffrage. But the latter has never been able to exercise its power itself, the new system has left it only a choice between two candidatures, which is often a choice of two evils, — the candidatures being settled beforehand by professional politicians under the influence of a host of calculations and considerations among which it is not always easy to discover a concern for the public interest. The representative character of the President could not therefore be enhanced under the regime of the democratized Caucus; the President was not able to become, through its agency, the tribune of the people, as he is sometimes represented, since it is not to the people that he primarily owed his office, and it is therefore not to the people or to the people alone that he was responsible, but to the party Organization. Having made itself the real bestower of the candidatures and sole contractor for the presidential election, the Organization laid hold of the Presidency for the party. The President ceased to be head of the nation, and became head of a party. And, even then, he was head of the party only in name; he was not at liberty to assert his initiative, to give the party a policy, to form comprehensive designs and far reaching plans on its behalf, for all the interests of the party were reduced to the immediate preoccupations of its Organization,to its appetites, which sought satisfaction in the patronage entrusted to the President by the constitution. The President was left with the role of grand cup-bearer of the party. Having been lowered to this position, he lost the full scope of his authority in the constitutional sphere. Chief of the executive responsible for the enforcement of the laws, he no longer had the choice of his agents. Associated with the legislative power, he could no longer treat on equal terms with that power, which was his co-ordinate under the constitution. He could obtain its cooperation only by currying favour with it, by sacrificing the independence and the dignity of his office. If he refused to make himself a tool of Congress, he doomed himself to impotence, in spite of his constitutional powers, however extensive these may appear to certain people who are fond of magnifying them and comparing them to the powers of an absolute monarch. In the case of political prerogatives, the possession of them does not imply the ability to exercise them, for this ability is a matter not so much of legal right as of moral authority. The rare attempts at resistance offered to Congress by the Presidents, by Cleveland, for instance, perhaps enhanced the reputation of the men, but did not restore the prestige of the office. The apparently authoritative acts of other Presidents who of late years have involved the country in perilous adventures, far from proving the strength of the presidential office have only brought out its weakness more clearly: the office has not been able to supply the deficiency of character in its incumbents, and they proved themselves powerless to resist the clamour of the fanatics of Congress and of the press, in spite of the constitutional protection with which the separation of powers had encompassed them. Thus the shrinkage undergone by the presidential office paralyzed the efforts of its strongest representatives and encouraged the weakness of the others.

However Congress, which usurped the powers of the executive, which gained what the latter lost, has also lapsed from the high place assigned to it by the framers of the constitution. The Caucus was one of the principal, if not the principal agent of this fall. The Senate of the United States no longer has any resemblance to that august assembly which provoked the admiration of the Tocquevilles. It would be no use looking for the foremost men of the nation there; neither statesmen nor orators are to be found in it. In wisdom, in balance, in dignity, the States' chamber is far inferior to the popular branch of Congress. The Senate no longer acts as a conservative element, as a brake for checking popular impulses, for moderating heedless ardour; on the contrary, it is this assembly which often gives the signal for extravagant conduct either in financial matters or in the sphere of foreign politics. The Senate is, for the most part, filled with men of mediocre or no political intelligence, some of whom, extremely wealthy, multi-millionnaires, look on the senatorial dignity as a title for ennobling their well or ill gotten riches; others, crack wire-pullers, State bosses, or representatives of large private industrial or financial concerns, find the Senate a convenient base of operations for their intrigues and their designs on the public interest; others, again, without convictions or without definite or well-matured ideas but sensitive to every breath of public opinion and fond of vulgar popularity, act as the noisy mouthpieces of every movement which flatters the susceptibilities of the crowd. They represent everything save enlightened opinion, to which they do not pay the slightest heed.

And it is through the Caucus that these men, especially those of the first two categories, get into the Senate; the State Legislatures, which elect the Senators of the United States, are composed of creatures of the Machine, and they bestow the senatorial office on the favourites of the party Organization. In the States ruled by the bosses, the boss, if he wants to go into the Senate, has but to hold up his hand, and the most eminent competitor will be sacrificed to him without further ado, were he of the stamp of the Websters or the Clays. The rich men buy a seat in the Senate from the party Organization for cash, with scarcely any disguise; if they do not "make" the Legislature with their own money, on the method of Jay Gould, they subscribe very liberally to the funds of the Organization; and the latter, to discharge its obligation to them, procures them the dignity of Senator — it orders its liegemen in the Legislature to vote for them.

Whilst the Senate was being filled with men of an inferior type, it was assuming powers higher than those conferred on it by the constitution. It has not only encroached on the province of the executive in the matter of appointments to offices and of negotiation of treaties, but even on that of the House of Representatives; it has nullified the initiative in regard to finance, reserved by the constitution for the popular branch of Congress. By its right of amendment, of which it made an improper use, and by systematic obstruction, which consisted in keeping the bills passed by the House hung up in committee, the Senate brought the House to do its will. This usurpation was carried out, once more, with the powerful help of the Caucus. Having established the focus of the party Organization in the Senate, the Caucus gave that assembly a position of vantage over the Representatives and the executive, who are dependent on that very Organization; it placed the Senators in a sort of ambush, from which they can hit everybody without being struck themselves. They can do this with impunity because the Caucus has freed them from all responsibility; they owe nothing to public opinion, as they are indebted for their seats solely to their relations with the party Organization; and there is no fear of their being called to account on behalf of the public interest by the Machine, and still less by the State Legislature, which is supposed to have elected them and which will expire before them. This irresponsibility, ensured on the other hand by the absolute separation of powers which prevents the legislative and the executive from meeting in the light of day, has but stimulated the tendency to encroachment and to extravagant conduct which have marked the career of the Senate during the last quarter of a century.

The havoc wrought in the House of Representatives is less conspicuous, because the contrast between what it was and what it is, is not so flagrant, and the House even conveys the impression of having gained in dignity. But in reality the standard of the Representatives and their political manners have undoubtedly deteriorated. The men who find their way into the assembly are those who have succeeded in "getting the delegates," or in ingratiating themselves with the Machine or the boss. All their habits and all their political methods have, consequently, been formed by the practice of the petty expedients, of the paltry combinations and compromises on individuals and interests, of the "deals," which are the life-breath of the primaries and conventions. The custom which confines the choice of candidates to local residents helps to narrow the political intelligence and to lower the morality of the people's representatives. And these men enter Congress as slaves of the Machine and the boss, of sordid parochial considerations, or of powerful private interests, industrial or financial, which are so often in league with the Machine. One or other of these servitudes of mind and conscience, or even all combined, is what they have to pay for their seat. The House therefore is simply a diet of representatives of private or local interests, and it has been aptly remarked that every interest is represented in it except the public interest. The members make common cause against the latter by lending each other their votes, on condition that the loan is returned, upon the log-rolling system, in order to obtain the special law or the money appropriation in which The Senators being elected for six years never have to seek re-election from the same Legislature, because the term of the State Legislatures scarcely exceeds the period of two years.

they are each interested. The appropriations are their principal objective and, so to speak, their principal victim. Every year, on the occasion of the River and Harbour or Public Buildings Bill, they indulge in a regular " Beutezug (body-raid)," to use the term recently adopted in Switzerland to describe a raid upon the federal chest for the benefit of the cantons and in the ratio of their respective population. Here, however, no one thinks of any proportions, everybody takes what he can grab for his district or for the "interest" which he represents. The financial extravagances of the House being always sure of support in the Senate, or being exceeded even by that assembly, the federal budget has swollen to an inordinate extent. Enormous sums are voted almost without discussion.

These disorderly modes of financial legislation are, no doubt, largely due to the defective organization of the legislative business: the absolute separation of powers, which excludes the Ministers from the chambers, excludes the spokesmen of the general interest from them, leaves the assemblies without guidance, enables each member or group of members to pursue their own ends; the concentration of the real legislative work in the committees and sub-committees screens it from the supervision of the public and consequently from responsibility. But it is primarily the character of the men whom the party Organization instals in Congress which divests them of their responsibility. Congress has ceased to be a deliberative assembly, it no longer lives by discussion. Here, again, the current legislative methods have greatly contributed to this result. In the House of Representatives, in particular, discussion has been rendered superfluous or impossible by the committee system and by the discretionary power of the Speaker, who appoints the members of the committees by his sole authority and curtails at his pleasure the debates in the House by refusing any member the floor. But if this dicta In the ten years extending from 1889 to 1898 the expenditure of the Union has risen from $299,288,978 to $443,868,882.

In 1899, on introducing the River and Harbour Bill, which involved an expenditure of more than $30,000,000, the member in charge of it asked the House to limit the duration of the general debate to half an hour. There happened to be a representative who held that thirty minutes were not enough, and he asked for one hour; another, improving on him, asked for an hour and a half. The House took a liberal view and granted ninety minutes for the debate. VOL. II — 2 N torial organization has been thrust on the House, it is precisely because the latter is so recruited, owing to the Caucus, as to be filled with men incapable of constituting a deliberative assembly worthy of the name, so much so that the celebrated Speaker Mr. Reed "thanked God" that the "House was not a deliberative body." The Senate has no such stringent procedure, the Senators are given their heads, but real parliamentary discussion has fallen into discredit in that chamber as well. True, its members speechify a great deal, but they only demonstrate that a regime of talk is far from being a regime of discussion. The decline of Congress in this respect is evidenced and completed by its legislative sterility; it does not initiate great measures, it does not solve the problems, the solution of which is demanded by the life of the nation; it acts only on impulses coming from outside, by registering more or less faithfully the decisions which are dictated to it either on behalf of the party in power, or by experts who make up for its incompetence. Thus, the most important measure of late years, which at last settled the grave question of the currency, after a fashion, was prepared by a private conference of citizens of different States, meeting for this purpose at Indianapolis, and devoid of all official authority and without any formal mandate. Congress is deficient at every point; it fails to protect the public purse, to administer the finances, to safeguard the credit of the country, and to pass the necessary laws. Its power, whether legitimate, or usurped, as in the case of the Senate, is expended in demonstrations and manoeuvres which aim at the applause of unthinking mobs, and in the service of private interests. Under the regime of the separation of powers, a degenerate Congress might have been held in check by the executive; the latter might have afforded protection against the extravagances of the legislative; but the executive itself has been weakened by the Caucus, being left with no means of action but its constitutional right of veto, and often not feeling sufficiently strong to make use of this weapon. Thus the Caucus, without preventing, as we have seen, the mischievous effects of the separation of powers, has nullified all its advantages. II

The State Legislatures exhibit in a still greater degree the decline, one would be almost entitled to say the collapse, of representative government. The function which the Constitution of the Union has assigned them in the federal sphere, by entrusting them with the election of the Senators of the United States, is prostituted to the bosses and to millionnaires; at the best, the selections are thrust on these assemblies from outside by the party managers, so that in the upshot their constitutional prerogative is never exercised in an independent manner. Nor do they represent the people better in the sphere of their immediate jurisdiction, in that of the local interests of the State. The finances are administered by the Legislatures without the faintest regard to economy; the waste of the public resources is an ever present and growing evil, even in "conservative" States, such as Massachusetts. The laws are made with singular incompetence and carelessness. Their number is excessive, running into volumes each session; but they are mostly laws of local or private interest. The motives which enter into the making of these laws are often of an obviously mercenary nature. In most of the Legislatures there is a "lobby," which buys legislation and wields such a powerful influence in them that it has earned the name of "third house." In the States ruled by the Machine the majority of the members of the Legislature are simply tools of the boss. By means of the boss or the Machine the rich industrial or financial companies make these members their docile instruments and obtain all sorts of concessions, of "franchises," of fiscal privileges. Discussion in the Legislatures is too often a mere farce, the most important laws are "jammed through," as is said in the State of New York; the legislator's just wait for their cue—"what the old man (the boss) wants." "Vote and don't talk," is the rule of procedure. The moral and intellectual standard of the members of the Legislatures has fallen to the lowest level: side by side with respectable but narrow-minded and weak men there are many who do not scruple to make money out of their seat, accepting bribes or Daring the three years from 1895 to 1898 the public debt of the State of Massachusetts has risen from $4,377,066 to $12,462,379.

blackmailing all those whose interests can be promoted or injured by legislation. They do not stick even at petty dishonesty, obtaining payment for carriage hire and other small expenses which they have never incurred, or getting stationery bought for themselves in enormous quantities and at exorbitant prices, or even ordering albums for their photographs which they have had taken at the cost of the State. Each new Legislature makes people almost regret the old one. The groove of the party Organization, vitiated withal by the custom which confines the choice of representatives to local residents, and by rotation in office, appears incapable of turning out men of a different stamp.

The municipal assemblies are often no better off than the Legislatures: filled with "boodle aldermen," they indulge in the same practices, and with the same disastrous results for the public purse. What bribery leaves undone, is done by incompetence and wasteful habits. When the resources of the city are not plundered by a ring, and its primordial interests are not neglected, the expenditure is too often out of all proportion to the return. In one way or another the administration of the cities, which deals with the greater part of the American population, and which affects its most important economic interests, exhibits the most complete failure of elective government in the United States. The effect is proportional to the cause; it is in the municipal sphere, which is within its immediate reach, that the party Organization has established its first base of operations, and it is there that living interests are most completely subordinated to the interests of the party, or even simply to its label, which covers the malpractices of the public plunderers, in the eyes of its adherents.

The judicial power was more spared than the others: from a feeling of self-preservation the political society of America tried to withdraw the law-courts from the regime of the Caucus; yet they did not entirely escape its dissolvent action.

" In Massachusetts, during each successive session for years, I have heard on every hand: 'This is the worst legislature we have ever had ' " (Moorfield Storey, *The American Legislature.* The Annual Address before the American Bar Association, 1814). Or as has been said to me in several States: *"this time* we have a villainous legislature," *"this time* we have an exceptionally bad legislature."

The functions of federal judges and law officers, to which the President appoints, and the State judicial offices, also filled in certain States by the executive, without being distributed on the spoils system in all its rigour, were pretty often bestowed as a reward on men who had earned the gratitude of the party Organization, or who were backed up by it. But it was chiefly the judiciary elected by the people that was hit by the Caucus. The appointment of judges by election is in itself only too apt to make vulgar wire-pullers of the men who should represent the majesty of the law, to rob them of their independence, and to hamper the impartial administration of justice. A distinguished American jurist and ex-judge says on this subject (in a private letter): "War, famine, and an elective judiciary are calamities to any country, but the worst, in my opinion, is the latter." Introduced into the United States through democratic fanaticism, this system was developed under the impulse given by the Caucus; and after having extended it, the Caucus emphasized some of its dangers and intensified some of its evils. The Caucus stimulated the application of the elective method in the appointment of judges, because its moral and material interests demanded that the number of elective offices should be as large as possible. Being subject to election, the judges had to court the favour of political parties, to put themselves openly under the patronage of the Organizations; and to obtain it, to get "slated," they were obliged to ingratiate themselves with the political brokers, with the Machines and the bosses. The natural result was a lowering of the moral and intellectual standard of the bench, although the pressure of public opinion prevented it from being filled with notoriously undeserving men. If the integrity of the judges is, in the main, fairly satisfactory, their independence is not intact in cases where the interests of the party are involved. In the administration of criminal justice that independence scarcely exists at all, particularly among the law officers whose influence can be most profitably exploited by the party Organization, such as the police magistrates in the large cities and, especially, the public prosecutors; elected under the auspices of the Machine, they become its humble servants and arrest the arm of the law in order to shield its protege's.

Thus, from one end of the scale to the other, the constituted authorities are unequal to their duty; they prove incapable of ensuring the protection of the general interest, or even place the power which has been entrusted to them by the community. at the disposal of private interests. The spring of government is weakened or warped everywhere. We have followed the manifold and varied and often desperate attempts at making up for the inadequacy or the irregularity of governmental action. We have seen the protection of the law and protection against the law or justice bought from disreputable gobetweens: the citizens bought from the representatives of the Machine, with their votes, immunity from administrative persecution, as well as impunity for contraventions and offences; corporations bought, for cash, from the bosses protection against the blackmailers of the Legislatures who threatened them with oppressive laws, just as they bought laws' which created privileges for themselves. Citizens' conferences and leagues legislated in the room and stead of the highest legislative assembly of the Union. Private associations, law enforcement societies, law and order leagues, and others, were founded to bring the transgressors of the law to justice; they organized their police, their detectives, for the purpose of exposing them. In the largest cities of the New World private initiative has had to step in to get the streets cleansed and to provide for other duties which devolve on the municipal administration in a well-ordered community. Even in the rural districts the village improvement societies often perform the same task. To obtain more durable and more regular effects than could be achieved by these spasmodic efforts, attempts were made to straighten the relaxed governmental spring by main force: inadequacy of action being mistaken for inadequacy of powers, the latter were concentrated in the hands of a few persons; dictators were created, from the Speaker of the House of Representatives down to the mayors of cities; the attributions of the State were widened. Again, the failure of elective government having shown itself most conspicuously in the legislative assemblies, the public turned wrathfully upon them. When modern society came into possession of liberty a century ago, it had placed its fondest hopes in parliaments; it had looked on them as the palladium of freedom, as the safest refuge for regenerated humanity against the "tyrants," who haunted the imagination even more than the intellect of the eighteenth century. Bitterly disappointed by experience, the political society of America beat the idol and abruptly set up the executive power again, no longer seeing in it the oppressor, but hoping to find in it a tribune of the people: the President of the United States was expected to neutralize the mischievous action of Congress; the Governor was given the right of veto over the Legislature in the few States where (as in Delaware, for instance) the executive did not enjoy this prerogative; the mayors were invested with extraordinary powers at the expense of the municipal assemblies. At the same time, the State tried to strengthen the neglected public weal by a remarkable development of regulation, of the "police power of government." This movement, which alike met the new requirements of a more complex state of society and was a reaction against the general *laisser-aller* from which the public interest suffered, sometimes assumed such excessive forms that it recalled the days of Colbert, and encroached on the domain of individual rights in the narrowest sense of the word.

On the other hand, despairing of its representatives, the people endeavoured to do without them on as many occasions as possible; not being able to trust any one, it took into its own hands duties which are the object of a representative government: many subjects of ordinary legislation were withdrawn from the jurisdiction of the Legislatures and transferred to the category of constitutional laws, on which the people at large decide without appeal; in municipal administration the referendum is being applied more and more in the matter of regulation, and, above all, in the matter of expenditure; in the administration of justice there is a talk of abolishing the office of public prosecutors, which is prostituted to the politicians, and of leaving criminal prosecutions to private initiative, that is to say, of reverting to the old English system and Thus a recent law of the State of Maine provides that if a child's eye or eyes become reddened or inflamed within four weeks after its birth, the nurse or person in charge of the infant must report the matter to a physician under penalty of fine or imprisonment which may extend to six months. (I take this fact from the Presidential Address of the American Bar Association meeting of 1891.) giving up the institution which at one time appeared to constitute an advance on that rudimentary system by supplying the want of public action.

While the spring of government in general was becoming relaxed, the same fate was overtaking that of local self-government, which in Anglo-Saxon communities had, from time immemorial so to speak, set in motion the whole political machinery. It is the Caucus, again, which is, to a very considerable extent, responsible for this result. It has subordinated all the elections, beginning with those of the township, to the presidential election; they all had to be decided by the same considerations; the local contests in the States and the cities were made to turn on differences of opinion caused by the problems of policy of the Union, and not on those which related to local life. By thus centralizing, in spite of their diversity, the aims and objects pursued at the various points of the political circumference, the Caucus regime undermined State and local autonomy, established or guaranteed by the Constitution, and made the electors lose their interest in local public life. It is true that the constitution itself had impelled the elector in this direction, by investing the Legislatures with the choice of the Senators of the United States: in choosing their representative in the State Legislature, the electors, as citizens of the Union, had to make sure that that representative would vote for a Senator who would interpret in Congress their views on the question of slavery, or protection, or the currency. Again, the material conditions of local public life prevented the citizen from taking an effective and lively interest in it: that life had no fixed territorial limits owing to the frequent rearrangements of the electoral divisions, often undertaken with a party object; the increasing heterogeneity of the population, caused by its habits of migration, by the infusion of the foreign element and by social and economic differentiation, deprived local public life of a fixed moral groove; the extraordinary growth of the cities intensified these effects. In the face of these difficulties and these obstacles that had arisen independently of See on this subject a very interesting letter from Mr. John Brooks Leavitt In the *Evening Post* of New York, September, 1900, and an editorial entitled: "The office of district attorney." the Caucus, the latter started up to discourage all attempts to overcome them; it called out to the electors, who were only too ready, in their perplexity, to adopt a rallying-sign visible to all from a distance, that they had but one course to pursue, that is, to join the colours of one of the great national parties, to follow them at all times and in all places, on pain of jeopardizing the paramount interests of the nation. To neglect local interests thereupon appeared meritorious; the Caucus made remissness a virtue in the citizens. To the Caucus this was clear gain; the subordination of local elections to national issues yielded it the federal patronage, to which every party organization looks for the prestige and the resources necessary to secure the fidelity of its liegemen. This subordination became the foundation stone of the spoils system extended throughout the Union.

It might doubtless be pointed out that by making all the electoral issues turn on national problems, the Caucus helped to bring about that redistribution of influence which has taken place, since the close of the civil war, between the Union and the States, to the advantage of the former — a redistribution which proved beneficial from several points of view, as it has strengthened the moral cohesion of the members of the Union, has set before them more elevated and more comprehensive ideals, in the paths of peace and of liberty, and has enabled the government of the Union to grapple with the new problems of national life, the solution of which was beyond the strength of the particular States. But even if it were admitted that the Caucus regime has contributed to this result, along with so many other factors, such as the outcome of the civil war, the economic revolution, the railroad and the telegraph, which have lessened distances and blended the whole population in common interests and common passions — if it were thus admitted that the Caucus has contributed slightly to a wholesome centralization, it would none the less remain a fact that the Caucus has, on the other hand, brought about a harmful centralization, that which by stifling self-regulated local life and by enfeebling men's initiative and volition dries up the sap of a political community and preys upon the very roots of its existence.

m

If the heavy sacrifices made to party interest at every point of the constitutional sphere could be justified by the necessity of securing at all hazards the benefits of "party government," supposed to be alone capable of supplying the framework for a government by public opinion, the sacrifices have been made almost in vain; far from securing these benefits the Caucus has nullified them in the majority of cases. Party organization has, according to some, made it possible to establish in the American government, based on the separation of powers, the necessary co-ordination between them, to bring the isolated organs of government, namely, the executive and the legislative, into a unity of views and of action. To judge how far party organization has really succeeded in bringing about this agreement between the two powers, and in providing the connecting link supplied by the Cabinet in a government of the English type, it is enough to recall a simple fact: from the retirement of Jackson down to the advent to power of McKinley, apart from the period of the civil war and of the Reconstruction, when the South was not represented or not normally represented in Congress, there has not been a single instance of the President and the majority of the two Houses being of the same party throughout the presidential term. In one or the other House, if not in both, the majority has belonged to the party opposed to the President, at least during the second half of each presidential administration, after the biennial renewal of the House of Representatives, which has almost invariably broken up the majority of the President's party. If the

Caucus did contribute towards establishing harmony between the President and Congress, it was only through the prostitution of the presidential patronage to the members of Congress which it had brought about.

The party Organization was all the less capable of ensuring the co-ordination of powers by legitimate and, so to speak, natural means, that it did not bring into Congress, except in times of crises, compact majorities united by identical principles and aspirations, in which the national conscience was reflected. Principles which might serve as a cement for the parties were a dissolvent for the party Organization, based on the spoils system; the grouping of electors in accordance with their views on the great problems raised by the course of political life was, for the Organization, a menace to the permanence of its fabric, to the very foundation of its existence. To preserve the external unity of the party therefore, that is to say, the name and style under which it conducted its operations, the Organization was always trying to make away with the gravest political problems, which had not yet been irrevocably solved, "to agree to disagree," to juggle with principles and programmes, down to assuming different attitudes on the same question in different parts of the country, according to local interests or prejudices; to taking up on its own account, according to the pressure of the moment and the requirements of the game, causes which it had disregarded or was even opposing the day before. Under these circumstances a party, as a rule, represented nothing but a sign which covered divergences of views, sometimes more profound, and struggles of factions, sometimes more bitter, than those which set it at variance with the opposite party. From the first disintegration of parties, which followed the eclipse of the old ruling class and of the traditional leadership, towards the close of the first quarter of the past century, and ever since the democratized Caucus has undertaken to focus public opinion by means of party conventions, the great parties, viewed as a whole, have been throughout their career nothing but agglomerates artificially brought together and kept together — except the original Republican party, the party of Lincoln, called into existence by a single problem, which sharply divided the public mind. Separated by conventional lines of demarcation, they had no personality of their own, and each drew its self-consciousness from the existence of the other. From time to time the unreality of this situation, and the demoralization which it brought about, evoked cries of revolt, movements of protest in the form of "third parties." Incoherent or inspired by good sense, these outbursts were more or less speedily drowned by the perennial coalition of sordid interests and the traditional prejudices of party orthodoxy, of "regularity."

But the effects of the iron discipline enforced by this coalition, which the party Organization promoted and directed, did not extend very far beyond the electoral sphere; they could scarcely cross the threshold of Congress. Claiming to reduce the variety of opinions and interests to a single formula, the Organization of the party in reality ended by making up the House in such a way that, according to the remark quoted above, all interests were represented in it but the general interest. This result, an apparently unexpected one, was the necessary consequence of the mechanical fashion in which the Organization linked the varied contingents of its electoral army, and of the spirit and purpose in which it pursued its undertaking. Always endeavouring to throw a veil over divergences of views and to eliminate principles, it substituted for the process of analysis and synthesis of opinions, which ought to take place in the electorate to create a legislative assembly animated by one mind and one will, a purely artificial analysis and synthesis, obtained by the saving grace of the party label. As soon as the manifold interests jumbled together under this label got admittance into the House, they naturally reverted to their own particular aspirations, like a bent spring which recovers itself. The party Organization no longer had to repress these centrifugal tendencies, for its object was already attained; its sole concern being to manage the elections and win the prize in the form of patronage and other advantages. The American party Organization takes hardly any interest in the sayings and doings of its Representatives in the House, unlike the English caucuses, which follow the conduct of their members, from one sitting to another, so to speak, which scrutinize their votes and put a certain pressure on them to keep them straight. The American Organization, absorbed in the election business, could hardly do likewise, for want of a general criterion to apply to the behaviour of the Representatives. This test cannot be a conformity with the principles, with the doctrines of the party, since the Organization has none; it does not aim at the triumph of a political creed. It cannot even enforce on its representatives the external conformity which consists in falling in behind certain men, behind leaders; the parties have no recognized leaders in Congress, there is no official head of the majority or of the opposition. An Organization may, no doubt, be interested in a certain vote in the House which closely affects its powerful financial supporters, and, in consequence, put pressure on its representatives; but in that case it does but act for or strengthen one of the numerous private interests into which the House is split up. The interest of the party, viewed from the standpoint of its name and style, also counts for something in the House, that is to say that in many cases the representatives have to consider how their vote will affect their party situation before the electors; but as these cases are very far from occurring at each vote, the interest of the party is not strong enough to override all the other interests.

Thus, by a paradoxical but perfectly natural contrast, party discipline, so strict in the electoral sphere, is slack in Congress, being constantly relaxed by the play of the unco-ordinated private interests which not unfrequently makes the parties cross each other. As there are no principles underlying this confused mass of varied interests, the latter agree only by "deals "; they deal among themselves (log-rolling); they deal with the executive; they deal, in their own mind, with what they imagine to be the popular will or whim, with the county of Buncombe. The system of numerous permanent small committees in which the real work of legislation is done has developed this regime of *do ut des* just as it has been developed thereby: the deals are made more easily in the semi-obscurity of hole-and-corner meetings than in the full light of public discussion. The atmosphere of Congress is, as it were, saturated with opportunist habits of compromise, or with fatalistic resignation. Opposition, in the parliamentary sense of the word, systematic opposition does not exist in it; there is no scope for it there: a man will sacrifice himself for his creed, will go to battle for his ideas, will take his stand on a principle; but where there are neither ideas nor principles at stake, differences can only end in compromises or surrenders. Interests always unite more than superficial divergences of opinion separate. In fact, in the highest legislative assembly of the Union, in the Senate of the United States, Senators of either party may be seen combining against the executive, or separating from the bulk of their party in this or that conjuncture, without the independence of the political conscience being vindicated thereby. The office of dispensers of the federal patronage which the spoils system has cast on the Senators has long since established among them a freemasonry, sanctioned by the famous rule of "senatorial courtesy," which pays little regard to party divisions. In proportion as the moral decomposition of the parties advanced in the last quarter of the nineteenth century, the tendency of their members towards cross-voting extended from the sphere of patronage to that of legislation. In the State Legislatures and *a fortiori* in the municipal assemblies, a powerful boss not only controls the members of his own party, but wields a palpable influence over the members of the opposite party. At the elections themselves the Machines of the rival parties, instead of fighting each other, come to terms, make "deals." Lastly, even when the contest is an honest one, the opposition which the parties are supposed to indulge in is none the less fictitious in reality, for their aspirations and methods being identical, the displacement of one party by the other leaves things as they were, one Machine is installed in the place of another.

In a word, given the manner in which the contingents of the parties sent into Congress by the Caucus are formed, they could not constitute homogeneous, closely united wholes, guided by considerations of general interest, and obeying a single impulse proceeding from common principles and aspirations. The parties as such were, consequently, not capable of initiative or of responsibility; they could not put forward measures, display constructive statesmanship, nor, again, serve as a counterpoise one to the other; that is to say, they were unable to discharge the very duties which are the *raison d'etre* and the justification of parties in a free government. Having reduced party divisions to a difference in titles, the Caucus regime has arrested or perverted all along the line the see-saw *by* which the party system is supposed to ensure good government or, at least, supply a temporary remedy for misgovernment. To obtain this remedy the citizens were obliged to make up for the irregularity of the see-saw by violent strokes, by lynch measures. We are familiar with the periodical, but spasmodic, revolts against the Machines, in which it is sought "to punish some one," to strike at random in the hope that the culprits will be among those hit. The abrupt overthrow of the majority in the House of Representatives in the middle of the presidential term, which has become the regular practice, has exactly the same significance, strange and inexplicable as may often appear the behaviour of electors who change their opinions so soon and at such an illtimed moment. The saying "madness and method too" is appropriate here. Congress engrossed in the rivalries of private interests breeds too many malcontents, and, as it has ceased to be a field for discussion and criticism, it does not even offer the dissatisfied the relief afforded by grievances and recriminations put forward and ventilated in broad day. Exasperated, rightly or wrongly, the malcontents combine in a fortuitous way, sometimes under the flag of one party, sometimes of the other, and fall upon the majority in power, submerge it under a "tidal wave," or crush it by a "landslide" — the terms used to denote the great revulsions of the electorate, now become periodical. This is the game to which the Caucus regime has reduced the play of the party system, so ingenious and so efficacious in the eyes of its theorists.

There are, however, men of sound judgment who hold that the confusion of government, and, in particular, that of congressional government, is due rather to the separation of powers which has not allowed the party system to be practised in Congress more fully under conditions such as obtain in the English Parliament with Cabinet rule. But are not these critics of the present congressional regime, who have argued their point, some with ability and vigour, others with more zeal than discretion, too wedded to political forms as apart from forces? Is not the absence in Congress of rigid party organizations holding as in a vice the contingents sent into the House; of a regular opposition, always in battle array, securing the advantages of publicity and criticism for the labours of Congress; and, lastly-, of recognized party leaders directing these labours and imparting to them unity of views and consistency while relying on the compact and disciplined masses of their adherents — are not these deficiencies, which are ascribed to the regime of the separation of powers, rather the effect than the cause of the evil? In any event, do they not rather indicate that a frame-work of party government is wanting, of the type sanctioned by English experience, a very useful framework perhaps, but to which an inside is indispensable? Now, the inside here is inadequate, it would not have substance enough to fit into the frame-work, even if the latter were forthcoming: the Caucus has impoverished and emasculated it.

To sum up, in the predicament in which the Caucus has placed it, party is utterly incapable of serving as an instrument of government; it is reduced to the level of an electoral contrivance.

IV

This state of things will appear still more evident if we enquire more closely what has become of the element which, under representative government combined with the party system, constitutes the most visible tie between Parliament and the country, between the official political sphere and outside public life — the political leadership. Real leadership can be obtained in a political community only on four essential conditions: the men capable of exercising the leadership must have easy access to public life; these men who are allowed political influence must assume the responsibility attaching to it; for this responsibility to be a reality it must be enforced by proper control; to be efficacious the action of the leaders must be sure of continuity. Now, under the Caucus regime, ideas, convictions, character, disqualify a man for public life; they make him, to use the regular expression, "unavailable," whether it is a case of filling the Presidency of the Republic or the office of mayor of a city. The party Organization always gives the preference to colourless, weak, easily managed men. In any event its assent, its visa, is required for entering public life; and to win its favour, the aspirant must lower himself to the persons who direct it and keep it going, that is, the acolytes of the Caucus. As men of eminence who respect themselves decline, or seldom consent, to do this, all those who should occupy the foremost places in public life are, as a rule, *ipso facto* eliminated therefrom. And if they aspired to wield the authority of a leader outside the ranks of officialism, they would again be stopped by the Caucus regime, unless they are satisfied with acting through the press. In fact, should they wish to gain admittance into the councils of the party, into its extra-legal organization, the professional politicians are there before them. Should they seek to carry their fellow-citizens along by their personal influence, they cannot succeed under a widely extended suffrage without the co-operation of many persons, without a crowd of go-betweens, however great their ability and however high their personal position. That co-operation must be bought in the manner sanctioned by the spoils system: the Caucus has implanted this system too deeply in American public life for it to be possible to get " workers" in any other way, at least for a length of time. If, in theory, the first duty of a leader consists in giving his adherents ideas, his first and only duty, in the United States, is to give them places. To be able to bestow these he must have some sort of hold over the party machinery. One is therefore in a vicious circle whichever way one turns

The social conditions of American life aggravate the situation. The steady growth of the large cities and the social and economic differentiation at work in them prevent men capable of leading from making themselves known and from getting accepted over the heads of the politicians. The levelling spirit with which the American appears to be imbued does not, again, create an atmosphere very favourable to the development of leadership. It would, no doubt, be rash to maintain that natural superiority, that which springs from character and intelligence, is disregarded in the United States; it is just as much appreciated there as anywhere else. But the Americans are in no way a "deferential people, politically deferential," after the heart of the Bagehots. Even deference in general — except to women — is much less developed among them than in the communities of the Old World, steeped in hierarchical traditions. They consequently do not feel the need of cultivating it in the political sphere in particular, and, it must be added, they have hardly any opportunity of so doing. For the natural leaders, of whom American society has a potential supply, abstain from assuming the political'leadership; they shirk the service of the commonwealth from selfish motives.

Again, the men who have entered the official sphere of public life shrink from asserting their political individuality there; they have not the courage of their convictions, if they possess any; they avoid taking up a decided line in the clash of opin *VOL.* II—2 o ion; they are always "non-committal," for fear of compromising themselves and from a wish to be "safe." The unreasoning discipline which the Caucus enforces on behalf of the party, and the innumerable concessions and humiliations through which it drags every aspirant to a public post, have enfeebled the will of men in politics, have destroyed their courage and independence of mind, and almost obliterated their dignity as human beings. The sign of the party is their conscience, when there are no powerful private interests that have precedence; the waves of popular feeling are their compass. And one seems to be listening to the echo of a far-off voice, that has long since died away, when one hears a political veteran like Senator Caffery of Louisiana proclaim (in 1896): "I have my own conscience and judgment to answer to above all censors. When my political action is called up before the bar of that conscience and judgment, I must, and do, present to it a record in entire accordance with their requirements.... A Senator of the United States is not a mere piece of political machinery to register the edicts of popular majorities, swayed and ruled by the superheated zeal of partisan politicians." When one hears a young Representative, like Mr. Littlefield of

Maine, in the course of the last session (1900), give his party a piece of his mind, tell it plainly, in open Congress, that it is trampling on law and justice, one turns round, one looks to see whence comes this voice, whose accents sound so unfamiliar because they have not been heard for so long. From one end of the political scale to the other there is only too great a tendency to evade responsibility. However low the standard of the State Legislatures has fallen, however firmly corruption and waste of public money appear to have taken root in them, it is not so much dishonesty which is the principal failing of the great majority of the members as their timidity, their want of civic courage. Along the whole line, therefore, public men evolve leaders who do not lead, who deliberately put in practice the well-known saying: A story, probably invented but characteristic, is related of a Senator of the United States who was told by the leaders of the party organization of his State thatit was time for him, now that he was a Senator, to do the correct thing as regards his family life and get married. The new Senator declared that if the members of the committee agreed upon a lady, he would marry her. "I am their leader, I must follow them. " But as in political life, even more than in ordinary life, those who lose heart soon lose their following, the authority of public men has sunk to a low ebb. On the great national stage there is no longer any public man who can address the whole country and obtain a hearing (except the President, whose utterances in stirring times, like that occasioned by the war with Spain, naturally attract general attention, whether they are the words of wisdom or not); the nation no longer possesses public men who go before it to light it on the way, who lay down the main lines of policy, who frame great measures. The fallen leadership is picked up in one place by the press, in another by willing citizens, who meet in conferences, or form leagues to initiate measures imperiously demanded by the general interest; it is wielded by men not in public life, and in an irregular and spasmodic way. In the lower sphere of the. States and the cities the type of public man has become a still poorer one; with but few exceptions, the best are those who have no history.

The public man loses heart and shirks responsibility all the more readily that there is hardly any one to keep him up to the mark. Unlike the English M.P., who is supervised by the militant members of the caucus of his division, in the United States a Representative who is unfaithful to his trust has nothing to fear from the party committees; no doubt they hold him in check, but by no means in order to keep him in the path of political righteousness; for this last they care not a rap; they look to nothing but the interests of the "organization " and of its financial supporters, and it is in this connection only that they put pressure on the Representatives. In other respects, the Organization is rather inclined to shield them with the party aegis against the best-founded attacks and accusations; the party press does the same. And when the independent press gives the alarm against those who betray the general interest, the public does not pay heed enough, because it is sick of newspaper invective, and, above all, because its interest in the public weal is exhausted with the elections. As the Caucus has given an extraordinary importance to the election business, to the sayings and doings relating to the candidatures, and to the votes which it works up by making a noise, the whole attention of the citizen has been diverted to this phase of public life; the expression "politics" has become a synonym for election affairs, for the concoction of them, and has almost ceased to be associated with ideas of government and administration. Hence, the citizen who has been wrought into a paroxysm of excitement by the elections sinks into apathy immediately afterwards, and takes no interest in the way in which his representatives discharge their trust. Again, the seats are held for a short time, two years or one. If the member has not justified the confidence of the electors, the remedy lies ready to hand: his term will come to an end very shortly; is it worth while to arraign him and to lose through him one's peace of mind and, above all, one's time, of which one never has too much for one's business? It follows that the citizen is not angry enough with the wrongdoers and does not sufficiently appreciate the welldoers. It follows again that if the former easily escape the deserved reprobation, the latter find it difficult to come out of the ruck and to command acceptance as guides and leaders.

In addition to this public men never remain long in office, the most eminent are subject to the general law which does not allow of continuity in the public service. Exceptions apart, prominent public men are sent back into private life when they are still in their prime and in full possession of their powers. A member of Congress who has sat for eight years continuously is considered a veteran. The principle of rotation in office, the impossibility of entering or re-entering public life save by the narrow and single door of the constituency of residence, the necessity and the difficulty of keeping in the good graces of the local organization of the party, and, also, the competition of more lucrative private callings, are all so many reasons which militate against a man holding a public position for long. With his official rank a man loses all political influence, he is invariably "side-tracked," as the saying goes. No one pays any more attention to him, even if he has filled a post as exalted as the Presidency of the Republic; as soon as his successor is "inaugurated" he is forgotten; he "returns to the practice of law," according to the classic formula; he writes for magazines; sometimes in presidential campaigns he takes the stump for the candidate of his party, lost in the crowd of other speakers however; the newspaper interviewer pays him the polite attention of coming and asking him his views on the great question of the day. He has not to keep up the large correspondence of a Jefferson in retirement at Monticello, or even of a Jackson, who were applied to on all sides for political consultations or recommendations for office. The first Presidents, those of the epoch which preceded the establishment of the convention system, were superior men, and they had a force of attraction of their own, which naturally remained their own when they were out of office just as much as when they were in office. But as the convention system lets into the Presidency, except by accident, only inferior men, without high intelligence and without force of character, its holders, once stripped of their official rank, are stripped *ipso facto* of all influence. In the great majority of cases their political opinions would not carry much weight, and their personal recommendations still less; they could not get a village postmaster appointed if they are not on good terms with the local Machine. This is at least as true of the men who have filled less important positions; their authority has been reduced by the Caucus regime in a still more palpable way to the power of providing the loaves and fishes. Now, a political leader *in partibus* is of still less account than a bishop *in partibus.*

Thus, under the action of which the Caucus was the principal instrument, the race of leaders has decayed in the political society of America. There are none forthcoming even for Congress, for the reason which Mr. Woodrow Wilson has admirably stated with regard to the Senators of the United States: "There cannot be a separate breed of public men reared especially for the Senate." And it is not the introduction of Ministers into the House, desirable as it may be in many respects, that will of itself restore the leadership, as some people too fondly imagine; this change can only bring into notice and facilitate the rise of supreme leaders, it cannot create them. They will reappear when there is room for them, when the political market, so to speak, is thrown open to them. In the meanwhile that market is, and remains, monopolized by worthless counterfeits of the leadership intro *Congressional Government,* p. 195.

duced by the Caucus — the wire-pullers and the bosses. This concrete image of the perversion of the leadership epitomizes that of political life in general and the degeneracy of party in particular. The statesman has had to give way to the political machinist, since politics has been lowered to electioneering considerations and the management of the electors has become the first political duty. This duty, consequently, became the sole *raison d'Mre* of the parties, and the leadership in them rightfully devolved not on experts in questions of government, but on experts in the art of organization.

V

Having failed in its purpose of serving as an instrument of government and of providing the latter with its mainspring in the form of leadership, party has not achieved more success in the fundamental duty which is assigned to it, and which consists in organizing public opinion, in giving it expression. Instead of moulding opinion, the Caucus maimed it by forcing it into, and keeping it within, the groove of the stereotyped parties. It crippled the character and the intelligence of the citizen. Having monopolized the nomination to elective offices, it propagated, to get itself accepted, the convention of "regular " candidatures, introduced by the congressional caucus, aud established it more firmly on that other convention of the will of the majority, which it claimed to represent by the mere character of its constitution. Continually invoking this majority and paying it ritual homage by the routine of its proceedings, it made external conformity the sole criterion which dispensed with private judgment and individual responsibility. Henceforth even a "yellow dog" had to be voted for, once he was put on the party ticket. The ticket could not be meddled with on pain of sacrilege, the party had become an object of fetish worship. For the individual conscience, party piety substituted the discipline of the party. To make that discipline binding, the Caucus created an ethics of its own; it created conventional virtues — "party loyalty," "party regularity," and conventional vices — "bolting," "scratching"; the man who severed his connection with the party was a "kicker," a sort of public malefactor, whereas he who followed the party with his eyes shut was a "patriotic citizen." Political formalism permeated the mind of the citizen, and wrought general havoc therein. It discouraged independence of thought, initiative, and self-confidence; it put a premium on the selfishness of the citizen who wanted to shirk concern for the public welfare and devote all his energies to money-making. Why, indeed, should he concern himself? Did not the party Machine provide the elector with his convictions, did it not prescribe to him his conduct, his political sympathies and antipathies, the choice of men — all cut and dried and ready for use? Being thus pressed and accustomed to fall into line, he soon became afraid of leaving the ranks; the fear of not being regular, of appearing heterodox and schismatical, developed in him that deference to the world's opinion which makes a man lose himself in the crowd in a humble and even cowardly fashion; having grown timid and timorous, he was perfectly content to creep behind the majority, and to drift along with the "people" in its ways as unfathomable as those of Providence. Moral and intellectual opportunism appeared as the sovereign dictate of wisdom as well as of the democratic creed. What Mr. Bryce calls the "fatalism of the multitude" — the tendency to acquiescence and submission and the sense of the insignificance of individual effort which would seem to be characteristic of democratic communities — received an almost dogmatic confirmation.

Civic courage shrivelled up in this atmosphere like a body exposed to the cold. No one ventured to raise his voice and protest loud enough. The victims themselves of the pirates Mr. Chapman, the author of the remarkable little volume already quoted, who fondly believes that " misgovernment in the United States is an incident in the history of commerce," says in reference to the timidity of the American citizen: "The main point is that Americans have by business training been growing more alike every day, and have seized upon any and every authority to aid them in disciplining a recusant. We have then a social life in which caution and formalism prevail. ... The attention of every one in the United States is on some one else's opinion, not on truth.... Each is a half-man, each is afraid of his fellows and for the same reason. Each is commercial, keeps his place by conciliatory methods, and will be punished for contumacy by the loss of his job. Neither of them has an independent opinion on any subject." The two points of view, that of Mr. Chapman and mine, might complete one another. On the other hand, a vivid light is thrown on the phenomenon in question in the chapter of Mr. Bryce's book (*The American Commonwealth, H, 3U seq.),* entitled " The Fatalism of the Multitude." of the machine, gagged representatives of the people, companies blackmailed by the bosses, preferred to submit and hold their peace, rather than appeal to the public. The interest which they believed they had in holding aloof, their selfish cowardice, found an excuse in the exigencies of party. Respect for the convention of party, for form, was too strong even for citizens of perfectly independent means and unimpeachable honesty; their party loyalty inspired them with infinite indulgence for these pirates who chose to hoist the party flag. A despicable boss who sows political demoralization broadcast from day to day for years together, who eats like a cancer into the heart of the Republic, is graciously introduced to the public under the charming euphemism of "the presiding genius of the party organization"; chiefs of the State lawfully invested with power by the people fraternize with this public corrupter, they invite him to their table, they affect to consult him as a Solon on affairs of state — all because this usurper has usurped the name of the party and because they want to affirm their orthodoxy, to proclaim it morning, noon, and night. All the more has the capacity for indignation and resistance dwindled in the mind of the average citizen. Acquiescence in abuses, tolerance of political corruption, spread like a noxious vapour.

Political formalism soon led from tolerance of the evil to connivance at it. "Regularity" being the first consideration, and the triumph of the ticket being the supreme object, the means necessary to compass that object were of no consequence, the end justified them; and electoral corruption took root and spread with the connivance and the pecuniary assistance of citizens who in their private life were incapable of the slightest impropriety. Thus, after having stifled independence of thought, the "yellow dog" maxim perverted the moral sense. Political formalism easily beguiled the citizen by making him draw a distinction between the relations of ordinary life and the conditions of public life; it gave a sanction to the convenient theory of the two moralities. By enfeebling the citizen's initiative and his spontaneous solicitude for the public welfare, it had helped to bring about the separation between society and politics. It accentuated that separation by the divorce of politics from morality.

But this political formalism which curbed the individual, has it not, on the other hand, cemented the edifice of the American Republic, and has it not preserved that edifice from the storms and tempests which a democracy, essentially unstable, is supposed to be so prone to let loose? Has it not prevented the overflow of popular passion, caprice, and infatuation by conducting all the currents of political feeling into the bed of organized parties, and by keeping there, through the discipline which it maintained, the various elements borne along with them? When one thinks of this political community of the United States, young, exuberant, composed of incongruous elements, almost without a past, with no traditions, with more will and ardour than ballast, a society representing in truth a world in a state of ebullition, it is impossible to gainsay the regulating function which party discipline must have discharged there and the services which it must have rendered. It is impossible not to admit that this discipline has been one of the factors of the moral force which brought and kept together the populations of the New World with a power even greater than that of the brute force which founded the empires of the Old World.

Yet if party organization served in the American Republic as a brake, it proved also, and above all, a reactionary force. Having repressed the individual too much, it shackled the public mind, and all the more effectively that its free play was already restricted by the mercantile spirit of the nation and by the written instrument of the constitution. A commercial society is, by its nature, more prone to conservatism than is expedient for its proper development. It fosters the growth of that type of inveterate conservatives who, according to Paul Louis Courier's sally, would, on the day of the creation, have besought the Creator to preserve chaos. The American constitution, in its turn, put a premium on immobility in the social and political spheres. Its framers, full of distrust of the people and anxious to keep advanced democracy out of power, had, by the innumerable precautions which they introduced, made all constitutional change extremely difficult. The constitution of the United States was still comparatively very young (it was in 1819) when an American statesman, Senator Dickerson, remarked, in reference to the barriers with which it had been encompassed, "It interposes such obstacles to the spirit of innovation as not only effectually to prevent all unnecessary alteration, but as, I fear, to prevent the most salutary reform." The subsequent course of events has not belied this forecast. Political changes proposed for the remedy of crying evils, such as were disclosed, for instance, by the method in force for the election of the President, for the choice of the presidential electors, have not been able to pass in spite of efforts repeatedly made throughout a whole century. The attempt to get the Ministers admitted to the sittings of Congress has been equally fruitless. It has been impossible even to carry the trifling amendment which altered the date of the opening of a new Congress from the 4th of March to the 30th of April, to prevent the preceding Congress from breaking up just after it had begun its last session, without having done any useful work. The changes which have been effected, thanks to a liberal interpretation of the letter of the constitution, and which are regarded as a proof of its flexibility and its capacity to adapt itself to new requirements, have been almost all in one direction: the powers of the Union have been extended at the expense of the States, and principally under the impulse given by the civil war and the commercial expansion of the country. The Supreme Court, the guardian of the fundamental pact, made these high-handed changes possible by giving them its sanction. But when it was sought to readjust the burden of taxation as between the poor and the rich by means of an income tax, the same Court quashed the reform by declaring it contrary to the letter of the Constitution.

To immobility of political forms, in the State the stereotyped party organization tended to add immobility of mind in this political society, where growing wealth increased the number of persons who are satisfied with things as they are. To preserve its *cadres,* the Organization was always trying to make opinion crystallize within them, to prevent the new currents of public feeling from gathering volume and flowing into fresh channels. It kept opinion a prisoner inside old formulas which often were nothing but pure conventions. It veiled or *Annals of the Congress of the United States,* sitting of the Senate of January 15th, 1819.
conjured away divergences of views which were making progress in the mind or in the conscience of the nation; and to stop their advance, it did not stick even at fraud or corruption. For more than twenty years before the civil war, it prevented the slavery question from being openly raised and honestly examined. After the war, it juggled with the financial question; it kept alive for years together, simply for the requirements of its business, the rancour of old animosities, and the fear of past dangers; or again, enforced the maintenance of an ultra-protectionism, in spite of the secret convictions of many of its members, by means of party discipline and by the purchase of votes with the " fat" provided by the manufacturers. Party formalism thus puts obstacles in the path of progress and creates dangers to the healthy development of political life, the gravity of which increases in proportion as the nation grows older; it is paving the way for a reaction in an anti-conservative direction, of which the politico-social movements in recent years, such as Populism, "Bryanism," are warnings resembling the mutterings of the coming storm.

While keeping opinion, by main force so to speak, within the old grooves, the party Organization at other times drove it as violently into new courses, full of dangers, when it saw any profit therein for its firm. Thus, only a short time back, we have seen the Democratic Organization take up on its own account the cause of the Silverites and deliver the party to them bound hand and foot, and a number of Democrats fall into line solely out of deference to "regularity." The wild schemes of the champions of free coinage thus appeared to be more strongly supported by public opinion than they were in reality; the Organization gave them a factitious moral force. In this way there came to be established a difference between public opinion and the opinion of the parties, which should be but the mirror of the former. The parties were only to organize opinion; they did "organize" it, by means of the Caucus, so thoroughly that opinion, the real, independent kind, has had, from time to time, to organize itself against the "Organization," to rise in revolt. But these revolts, being essentially accidental, can only occur in an intermittent fashion; in the intervals the free course of opinion is confined by the Organization like a river between banks of sand. To break through the embankments of the Organization the anger of opinion must be lashed into a storm. Mad with rage, opinion steps in to wreak vengeance. Yet the power it exerts on that occasion is a power of repression only. It exerts this indeed with unparalleled force, because nowhere else is it backed so widely by numbers. But it does not attain to the preventive power, which is the highest expression, the ideal, if the word is preferred, of free communities, and with which American institutions and habits appear however to have invested it. That power is debarred from asserting itself: the all-engrossing desire to make money aiding and abetting, political formalism lulls the ceaseless vigilance on which rests the preventive power of opinion.

VI

Thus the Caucus regime has not allowed party to discharge any of its legitimate functions, either in the constitutional or in the extra-constitutional sphere. Everywhere it has made it work the wrong way, by warping and slackening the springs which it should have regulated and accelerated. By reducing party to an instrument of organization pure and simple, the Caucus left it no end to serve but itself. At the same time it gave it, under cover of the formalist principle of "regularity," the electoral monopoly. That monopoly put the public interest at the mercy of party, or rather of the Organization which claimed to represent it. And the Organization, composed in great proportion of greedy mercenaries, systematically exploited that interest. Administration and legislation were prostituted to the Machine. Pope's famous definition of party — "The madness of the many for the gain of the few" — received a most humiliating application.

To humiliation was added ignominy, when the party Organization brought in the moneyed men among those " few." It smoothed the path for what is called plutocracy. One might almost say that it was the Organization which gave a definite and substantial meaning to this very vague expression of plutocracy, which, from the beginning of the century, formed one of the staple resources of the political rhetoricians and the demagogues, as well as, it may be added, of many true friends of the people. It was to the cry of "down with the money power" that the Federalists were dislodged, that Jackson was exalted, that all opposition to the autocracy of the old soldier was stifled. It is the same cry that resounds to-day, throughout the Union, repeated by millions of voices; but it is aimed especially at the economic misdeeds of the money power: the citizens of the United States are represented as victims of a frightful economic oppression, practised by the capitalists, by the trusts, and so many other industrial and financial companies. It is beyond dispute that these capitalists enrich themselves, and that they do so at the expense of the people; yet it is not proved that they impoverish the people, that they rob them. The harm done to the citizen as taxpayer and consumer is very slight: the gigantic concentration of industry enables a few men to grow rich by an infinitesimal illicit toll on each member of the community at large. It is quite possible that the future may bring about grave and disastrous changes in this respect. But up to the present the power of plutocracy in the United States, a very tangible and pernicious one, has shown itself rather in the political sphere.

The mere fact of the existence of large fortunes concentrated in a few hands is of itself a source of permanent demoralization in society: it belittles unassuming and honest work; it gives the rein to desires and appetites; it makes the pursuit of wealth the highest aim, the ideal of life, and drives all other aspirations out of the human mind. One knows how rapid and enormous has been the concentration of capital in the United States since the Civil War. But the realization of these colossal fortunes and fabulous incomes was not, and could not be, due solely to the free play of natural forces. More often than not this free play has been perverted for the benefit of the corporations by the complaisance or by the connivance of the public authorities. From the municipal franchises up to the national property and the ultra-protectionist customs tariff, these authorities surrendered to a few what belonged to all. The stronghold of the general interest, the State, was invaded Before the war there were not more than three millionnaires in the whole Union; at the present day there are nearly four thousand.

on all sides by money. The corporations bought legislation, "protection," and favours of every kind, wholesale and retail; rich men bought seats in the highest legislative assembly more or less disguisedly, obtained seats in the Cabinet, ambassadorships. It seemed as if nothing could resist the well-filled purse, that money was king in the Republic to such an extent as to suggest the well-known saying recorded by Sallust about the *urbs venalis.* Jugurtha's remark, although based on experience, was nevertheless an exaggeration, as the Numidian eventually learnt to his cost. Members of a degenerate ruling class, high dignitaries of State, nay, even tribunes of the people might be bought; but how was it possible to buy the people itself, a whole sovereign people? Party Organization in the United States supplied the answer: all the corrupters who try to bend the power of the State to their own selfish ends have but to identify their interests with those of the party Organization which is conscience-keeper to the members of the sovereign demos; they have only to become its financial supporters. It is in this way that the party Organization has served as a lever to all the great private interests in their designs on the public weal, which have assumed so many aspects in the last thirty years; without that intermediary the corporations and the other more or less fraudulent recipients of political favours could not have attained the object of their desires; they could not have got the better not only of the electoral body, the great majority of whom are certainly honest, but even of their representatives, who are very far from being all venal. The reader will remember the remark of the New York legislator: "I want to be honest, and I am honest; but I am the slave of the Organization." It is the party Organization which has made possible this vast political corruption, practised both on the well and on the evilly disposed by the moneyed men, with safety not only from the vengeance of the law, but even from that of public opinion. It is the Organization which has, lastly, enabled a group of manufacturers to install their man in the White House, and to manage him like a puppet, by dictating to him his foreign policy in accordance with their interests and by making him say that his "plain duty " was one thing one day and another the next. The people apprehended the problem of the money power mainly in its economic aspect of accumulation of wealth, which strikes the imagination more easily. They did not sufficiently realize the fact that the economic monopolists were supported and helped up by the political monopolists, by the holders of the electoral monopoly which the people "themselves had handed over to the party Organization. With childlike rage they fastened violently — as we have already seen them do on several occasions, in connection with municipal disorders and others — on the external effect without scrutinizing its cause, which is less obvious, or the particular conditions which develop and encourage it, apart from the purely economic conditions. In a number of States the people have got special laws passed against trusts, which have remained a dead letter, because they were not enforceable or because they were not enforced by the public authorities under the thumb of the plutocrats. Just now it is proposed to insert in the federal Constitution an amendment directed against trusts, the sole purport of which is in reality to hoodwink irritated and unreflecting opinion; for if this amendment were adopted and enforced, it would have the effect of preventing the operation-not only of trusts, but of the most harmless industrial associations. While thus provoking impotent, because ill-directed, wrath in some, the power of plutocracy in the State accentuated in others that civic depression which makes people look resignedly on all the abuses of public life. The money which wrought this havoc in the State appeared as a mysterious and irresistible force of nature, before which there was nothing left but to bow. A fatalistic belief grew up: "they must have their way," what the "moneyed interest" wants "is bound to pass." Confidence in the integrity of the people's representatives was thenceforth shaken; they were given even less credit for honesty than they deserved, there was too great a tendency to confound them all in the same suspicion. People grew so accustomed to this view of things that but little room was left for indignation; they inclined to a sort of philosophic serenity which often bordered on cynicism, and found food for amusement if not admiration in the exploits of the politicians.

While plutocracy, fortified by the party Machine, was thus degrading the commonwealth and lowering the citizen, it developed, in its turn, the power of the Machine. It supplied the Machine with most of its resources and enabled it to take a fresh flight. It gave a most powerful impulse to that oligarchic or autocratic government of the rings and the bosses which party allowed to grow up in its midst. It not only invested that government with a regular function, making it the chief agent of corruption in the State, the licensed broker between the low desires centring on the public interest and the weakness of the latter's defenders, but enabled it also, by ensuring it an independent position, to defy the forces of law and equity and to consolidate its illegal power over party and over the commonwealth. In all the States where the industrial and financial corporations are numerous, the Machine and the boss, fed with their money as with a sap, flourish like a luxuriant plant that overshadows the whole of public life. In these States, where the Machine is supreme, republican institutions are in truth but an idle form, a plaything wherewith to beguile children. It may be that the government of the bosses is not, administratively speaking, more ruinous for the people than plutocracy is oppressive for them from the economic standpoint. But both of them eat out the heart of the commonwealth. It is no longer "a government of the people, by the people, and for the people." VII

Step by step, proceeding from the more obvious to the less perceptible, we have followed the effects of the Caucus regime in the constitutional order, then in the extra-constitutional political order, in the economic sphere, and into the very mind of the citizen. Viewed in the reverse way, these effects will appear exactly the same; they are like a chain whose links hold together, by whatever end you take it. The evolution of American democracy, as represented by this concatenation, ends in two facts of the utmost gravity: popular government has slipped away from the people, and commercialism in its most sordid aspect has laid hands on the government.

How is it that the people have allowed themselves to be despoiled in this fashion? How has it been possible to get the better of this American nation which has presented the admirable spectacle of a creative force, of an indomitable energy, of a tenacious will that has no parallel? The explanation is a simple one: the people have expended all this moral strength in the material building-up of the commonwealth. In that new world which was a mine of untold riches for whoever cared to work it, material preoccupations have engrossed the American's whole being. They have thrust back all other considerations or have subordinated them to their objects. The desperate race for wealth has absorbed the citizen and has not left him time to attend to the public welfare; it even encouraged his want of public spirit, and converted it almost into a virtue. "To make money " appeared to the American as the destiny of man on earth, and the *raiaon d'etre* of a well-ordered commonwealth was thenceforth, in his eyes, to promote the fulfilment of that destiny. The notion of the moral objects of the State grew dim in the public mind, the State was asked only to ensure or assist the production of wealth. In prosperity, the people had no inkling that the government was slipping from them; on the contrary even, they fancied they had but a firmer grasp of it: the economic policy pursued since the Civil War, the system of ultra-protectionism, gave a great part of the nation the illusion that the government was making wages rise, that it was augmenting material comfort, that it was really serving the people, that it was at their beck and call. A change in the economic situation was required to open the eyes of the agricultural portion of the population, in the West, which did not benefit by the protection of manufactures: when times got bad, the farmer, involved in debt, concluded that the government was not on his side, and he started up to lay hold of the government, as if it was a chattel, to insist upon its regulating all the economic functions of life down to procuring him " cheap money," paper, which the government might, if it liked, issue in unlimited quantity, or specie, in the form of depreciated metal. It was these ideas, expressing the materialistic conception of the State with the utmost naivete, that took shape in Populism and the silver movement. Now, however, these movements of revolt are abating and, it would appear, dying out, owing to the extraordinary commercial prosperity which the country has enjoyed of late years, although the political VOL. II—2 P evils which were at the bottom of the revolt still subsist. In the last presidential campaign (of

1900) the rallying-cry on the Republican side was "a full dinner pail," before which the problem of the future of democracy, raised by the new policy of territorial conquests, was to retire into the background. Citizens who were fairly enlightened and able to reason made no secret of the serious apprehensions which this policy, inaugurated by McKinley's administration, caused them, and of the dangers with which it appeared to them to threaten the very heart of the Republic; but in the end they came to the conclusion that they must vote for the re-election of McKinley because "if he was beaten stocks would go down fifty per cent"; and a good many of these conscientious citizens did not even possess any negotiable securities. Material prosperity being, under the sway of these preoccupations, the sole object of the commonwealth, just as under a "good tyrant," there was but one criterion, in every-day life, of the goodness of the government — the cost of it; the harm which a bad government could do was brought down to a money value. The regime of the politicians was appraised by the amount of the depredations which they committed. If the losses resulting therefrom to the citizen were not too serious, he was quite ready to bear them, were it only to save himself the worry and the trouble required to prevent them. The exceptional facility with which "money was made" in the New World developed a tendency to "live and let live," and to apply freely the old formula, *de minimis praetor non curat.* The American, in fact, is a "big" man. He is free from the meanness which so often characterizes the small bourgeois in Europe. But the exaggerated generosity of the American is more dangerous to the commonwealth than the exaggerated economy of the bourgeois of Europe: it puts a premium on public plundering and blunts civic sensibility; it inclines the American to paraphrase in regard to political corruption the well-known saying: *"La France est assez riche pour payer sa gloire";* the reader will remember the *dicta:* "We can stand it," "You cannot ruin this country!"

But, even if they adopt the narrow standpoint of material prosperity, ought not the Americans to foresee that this prosperity must in the long run be affected by the political disorders, that sooner or later the penalty will be paid for them, even in a purely material form? Of all races in an advanced stage of civilization, the American is the least accessible to long views. The New World in which he lives and acts has freed him from two great servitudes which lie heavy on the denizen of the Old World, — space and time. He is not confined within a narrow and hereditary horizon, he is not tied to a locality, he has no deep root anywhere. The theatre of his activity is an immense continent over which he ranges with the facility and, it may be added, with the satisfaction, of a nomad; there are plenty of people who would be quite content to spend their lives in the Pullman cars. The sphere, too easily shifted, of his activity, which deprives the American of local feeling, is not alone in preventing him from viewing things in their durable aspect. His modes of action also tend to make him utterly careless of the morrow. The boundless horizon of the continent and the resources of its virgin territory enable the American to turn the latter to account in a manner resembling that of the nomad, who moves with his flocks and herds from one place to another when all the pasture has been eaten; the richness of the soil inclines the American to a cultivation which is extensive rather than intensive, not to say to a predatory type of exploitation. The eminently speculative mind of the American, due perhaps to the facility afforded by the New World of getting a quick return from everything, impels him into the same path which leads to large immediate results. Always and everywhere in a hurry to get rich, he does not give a thought to remote consequences; he sees only present advantages. He is preeminently the man of short views, views which are often "big" in point of conception or of greed, but necessarily short. Acting on these views, the politicians eagerly make the most of their ephemeral chance, and the "good " citizens meet them with a serene indifference in order not to let their own chance go by.

This epicureanism *sui generis* of the American, which bids him enjoy the present without troubling about the future, is naturally completed by a robust optimism which looks on all difficulties and all evils as transitory. The economic conditions which gave rise to this feeling have, in the course of American history, afforded ample justification for it and made a truth of the favourite remark which I have already quoted: "It will right itself." In fact, the Americans have passed through more than one serious crisis, often caused by their want of forethought and the extravagance of their financial administration, but they have always come out of them unharmed, thanks to the abundant resources of their country and to the extraordinary luck which they met with at the most trying moments. The most ingenious writer of melodrama could not hit upon better "situations " when the hero in extremities is saved as if by a miracle. Thus, for instance, in 1879 a frightful commercial and industrial crisis, aggravated by dangerous financial measures, breaks out in the United States. A catastrophe appears to be imminent, but at this point an unprecedented harvest turns up, while Europe is at the same moment threatened with a famine. In England, in particular, exceptional cold followed by incessant rain affects the crops; the situation becomes so serious that the Archbishop of Canterbury deems fit to intervene and order the use of the prayer for fine weather. But all is in vain, the harvest proves a failure. America forthwith becomes the Egypt of Joseph for Europe, and her commerce, her industry, and her finances go up at a bound. Thus brilliantly justified by events, optimism is not only a general tendency, but almost a national religion. Next to the "unpractical man," there is no one held in such contempt as a "pessimist." He is almost a public malefactor, he defiles the spring at which the community imbibes strength for fresh efforts in the daily battle of life. The objector, the censor of abuses, is therefore always in bad odour, he is pre-eminently a pessimist. "A man with a grievance" is odious; like the whining youth who complains of his schoolfellows, he only shows his weakness of character; is there not room for every one in this favoured land of America? why does he button-hole busy people and seek to interrupt the march of time? what is the good of his recriminations about the past? yesterday has gone by, it is already far off. Wedded to the present, the American possesses a singular power of forgetfulness, the events of the day before are to him ancient history. Confident in the future, he exhibits a remarkable endurance of present evils, a submissive patience which is ready to forego not only the rights of the citizen, but sometimes the rights of man. He does not remember, he does not feel, he lives in a materialist dream.

VIII

It by no means follows, however, that higher aspirations are wanting to the American. It would be a gross mistake to set down Americans as incapable of idealism; they have an ample store of it in their composition, —engrossed as they appear in the pursuit of the dollar, — but up to the present they have made only a special use of it in their public life. A brilliant writer has remarked that the Jews have put all their idealism into religion. Whether this view is quite correct or not, it might be said, with at least as much truth, that the Americans have put all their idealism into the American nationality, into the common country. That country did not represent, as with the nations of the Old World, a community of sentiments that have accumulated for centuries and forming a fund peculiar to itself which reflects the whole character of the people. The "people of the United States," created by the federal Constitution, had no language of its own, nor religion of its own, nor past of its own, nor even political ideas of its own. The Republic was created out of several pieces with infinite pains, it was wrested " by grinding necessities from a reluctant people," and for a long time afterwards each section pulled in a different direction. The national sentiment which had not the opportunity to develop in time developed in space; there the new nation unfolded its genius: it has, as it were, brought a whole continent out of nothingness; and each strip of ground "reclaimed from the wilderness" demonstrated its vitality, made it conscious of its strength. The integrity of the territory became the essential mark of the moral unity of the nation, the proof of its life. American patriots felt that this life depended on the material ties which knit together the pieces and the bits out of which the federation had been made. The Americans, therefore, have put their whole soul into the Union. The remark of one of the greatest of them, of one who embodied the genius of the nation most forcibly Anatole Leroy-Beaulieu, *Israel Chez les nations.* and vividly, Henry Clay, — " If any one desires to know the leading and paramount object of my public life, the preservation of this Union will furnish him the key"—this remark is applicable to the whole nation in its past and in its present. Its greatness and its shortcomings would be unintelligible otherwise. The idea of the Union burned within the breast of its best sons like a sacred fire; it purified the less pure heart of the others. It lifted them all, in one and the same movement, above the accidental toward the eternal and the infinite. It was the sacred legacy which the mighty dead had bequeathed to the survivors. In the American Walhalla the departed. heroes do not appear to be engaged, as in the paradise of Odin, in perpetual combat: having laid aside with their mortal vesture their rivalries and their enmities, all of them hand in hand, Jackson and Clay, Lincoln and Douglas, Grant and Greeley, join in a fervent cry, which descends to earth like a message from above: "The Union! It must be preserved!"

But while throwing a spell over the mind, the idea of the Union, owing to its very origin, assumed a material form therein; the political conscience of the nation took up a position, so to speak, inside the territorial notion of the fatherland and, entrenched behind it, defied the challenges addressed to itself at other points. When President Buchanan publicly declared, in his speech of the 9th of July, 1860, that property in a man was just as sacred as property in coal or iron, the majority of the nation did not budge. But when nine months later the Southern Confederates attacked Fort Sumter, when they fired on the flag of the Union, that majority flew to arms and astonished the world by the extent of its sacrifices and its self-surrender. Putting his civic conscience, as it were, behind that of the American, the citizen felt the stronger for the United States, which made his heart beat quicker and his blood run faster; and he fostered and developed that feeling by altruism as well as by feelings of a contrary description. Thus the dislike of the English, which is so common in the United States, and which offends good sense and shocks the sentiment of justice, cannot assuredly be attributed to a deficiency of good sense or to want of justice in Jackson's celebrated toast.
the Americans. There is no keener intelligence than theirs, and their heart responds to every appeal of justice from whatever quarter it comes. Separating himself from the Englishman in his heart of hearts, the American means to assert his individuality as an American, as if he were afraid that the tie which bound him to the English people, of the same stock as himself, speaking the same language as himself, was still unsevered.

The patriotic sensibility which thus narrows the political conscience of the American absorbs even the feelings awakened in his breast by the natural features of the continent which is coterminous with the Union, and by the aspect which the creative energy of man lends to it. The citizen of the

New World revels in the perpetual battle which he has to fight to gain possession of this world, to subdue the forces of nature to his will; he exults in this activity, he swells with enthusiasm, which is not all hope of material results; his imagination contributes a great deal thereto, through the contemplation of the greatness of the effort; but it refers this greatness to the American even more than to the man, it merges the latter in the former. So with the natural beauties and resources of the continent. The great lakes, the immense rivers, the vast forests, the boundless prairies, the fertile soil, the invigorating climate, have been allotted by a just and far-seeing Providence to the Americans, like Canaan to the chosen people; the majesty of this nature does but express in a material form the majesty of the American people; the Falls of Niagara were created by the Eternal to testify to the American genius in ages to come. "America is written all over the Falls," writes a celebrated journalist, on a visit to Niagara. "Its roar is that of the nation. Its majestic sweep typifies the grand progress of America. The maddening, dashing, seething, buffing, pitching, uneasy flood typifies the intensity of the American mind and the vitality of American action. Here is the fountain of true, young America; here the breast which gives it milk; here the nurture which gives it vitality."

Next to the territory, and to man who had improved it, Quoted from an article written in 1856, by Samuel Bowles (G. Merriam, *The Life uncl Times of Samuet liowces,* I, 102).

there was a third element with which contemporary America had been created — liberty. It is from liberty that man has drawn the strength with which he has conquered matter; it is she who has removed the obstacles in his path; it is she who has opened to all, down to the humblest members of the community, the same prospects in the "pursuit of happiness"; it is liberty which has welded the component parts of the Union; for the first time in the history of the world an amalgam of peoples, of races, of religions, of tongues, had been made otherwise than by the force of arms, and that motley assemblage, rivalling the confusion of the Tower of Babel, has formed a body with a soul, under the life-giving breath of the principles of the Declaration of Independence. In an indictment which an illustrious historian has recently brought against American democracy he quotes, with certain reservations however, the following passage from Ernest Renan: "If it were necessary that Italy, with her past, or America, with her future, should be blotted out of existence, which would leave the greater void in the breast of humanity? What has all America produced that can compare with a ray of that infinite glory that adorns an Italian town of the second or third order, Florence, Pisa, Siena, Perugia? " This view, though inspired by idealism, is due to a narrow conception of the ideal, and bears the stamp of the epicurean and aristocratic intelligence of the admirable writer and of the materialized spiritualism of the former fervent Catholic who entered into communion with the unseen by means of painted Madonnas and sculptured saints. The Most High dwelleth not only in Gothic cathedrals. America has not been able to serve the ideal by "le grand art," with which Renan consoles himself even for the degradation of a society in which it can be enjoyed, but she has served it in another way. The Declaration of American Independence, like the Declaration of the Rights of Man, has not lifted fewer souls heavenward than all the monuments of Pisa and Siena. Like the French Revolution, America, by bringing the good tidings to the world, has solaced humanity W. H. Leeky, *Democracy and Liberty,* Vol. I. *Etudes d'Histoire Reliaietue,* p. 3VH.

"Renan tins explained in the preface, written subsequently, that his views on America had been suggested to him by a concern for the higher culture imperilled by democratic materialism *(ibid.,* IV, V).

for a space and has filled it with immense hopes, however great the disappointments and disillusions which the future had in store. Besides, the moral springs which both have set flowing are still there, and it is enough to be willing and able to drink at them.

It is all very well to say, with every appearance of reason, that the United States have been not so much a democracy as a great company for the exploration and exploitation of a vast territory, offering liberty and a share in political sovereignty as a sort of bounty to the workmen of whom the uncultivated New World stood in need. What difference in the value of the effects produced is made by the hidden motives of the acts which stir the human heart, which thrill it? Even in a theatre where everybody is aware of stage convention, does the spectator before shedding tears over the corpse of Cordelia carried by King Lear ask himself what were the intentions of Shakespeare or those of the theatrical manager who has produced the play? From the Pilgrim Fathers, who crossed the ocean amid storm and tempest within the frail timbers of the *Mayflower,* down to the poor wretches two centuries and a half later, penned up like cattle in the "emigrant steamers," all journeyed in quest of liberty, without always understanding it as we understand it, often without being able to bring a clear definition of it out of their heavy-laden hearts; they went in search of it as towards an "unknown God," and they found that God. It is in vain that good observers,' but who dwell too much on the surface of things, like Michel Chevalier, have declared that "American liberty is not a mystic, undefined liberty; it is a special liberty corresponding to the special genius of the people and their special mission; it is a liberty of work and locomotion of which the American takes advantage to spread over the vast territory... and turn it to profitable account. " It was a mystic, it was an undefined liberty. This, too, is "written over the Falls of Niagara": "And then the rainbows hovering over and about the scene, do they not signify the promise which America Cf. the observations made on this subject by E. Boutmy, in his *Etudes de Droit Constilutionnel,* pp. 200-210, with the acuteness and penetration that characterize this writer.

Lettren sur *VAmirique du Nord,* Paris, 1838, Vol. II, p. 203. gives to mankind, the hope which it implants in weary-laden hearts, the home which it furnishes to the outcast and wanderer from governmental oppression and social villany elsewhere?" Abraham Lincoln, who embodied the best of the American character, did not view the stream of American destiny otherwise than as flowing in this channel of universal human liberty, dug by the authors of the Declaration of Independence: such was "their majestic interpretation of the economy of the universe.... In their enlightened belief nothing stamped with the divine image and likeness was sent into the world to be trodden on and degraded and imbruted by its fellows. They grasped not only the whole race of men then living, but they reached forward and seized upon the farthest posterity. They erected a beacon to guide their children, and their children's children, and the countless myriads who should inhabit the earth in other ages." How is it that the work of the " Fathers " has lasted? "I have often inquired of myself," said Lincoln, "what great principle or idea it was that kept this confederacy so long together. It was not the mere matter of the separation of the colonies from the motherland, but that sentiment of the Declaration of Independence which gave liberty, not alone to the people of this country, but, I hope, to the world for all future time."

But, on the other hand, while granting that liberty — I repeat, a mystic and undefined liberty — is entitled to figure in the American escutcheon, one must admit that it has become materialized by use. Having served not to beautify an old home, but to build up a new one, as it were with bricks and mortar, it has almost lost its spiritual nature in this rough handiwork. That nature was not utterly destroyed, but it was etherealized, it was consigned to the sphere of a national cult rising above the cares of daily life and opening to men's minds, like a temple to the faithful, only at the hour of prayer. Ideal liberty thus contracted and set within the halo with which the intoxication of material successes had surrounded the image of the Union, did but sanctify the national pride that was inspired by these successes; it did but develop that patriotic sensibility which absorbed the political conscience. The inflated national sentiment grew more and more like the nationalist enthusiasm of which, under different circumstances, many a country of the Old World had furnished, or still furnishes, an example, and which makes the worship of country a pagan cult from which the living God is absent. In the United States that cult found its dogmatic formula in the cry: "Our country, right or wrong!"

The American citizen, attracted by the material side of things, could thenceforth give himself up to it with all the less scruple that he had discharged his debt to the ideal by the patriotic sentiment which he carried in his breast. Yet the daily course of public life demanded more than this general tribute, it claimed the performance of regular moral duties towards the commonwealth. The busy citizen thereupon found new resources, by providing himself with a patriotism of the second degree, that of party. He put into it the same fetishism which satisfied his idealist requirements at small expense, and he gave to it the same dogmatic expression as to his worship of country with a slight variation: "My party, right or wrong!" Invested with a more ritual character, the cult of party enabled the citizen to pay off his every-day civic obligations more easily with the outward observances of devotion.

IX

This coarse formalism was not only a more or less unconscious or more or less hypocritical bargain that the citizen made with his conscience, to which he had not the time to pay its due. It also forced itself on him through certain special tendencies of the American character, developed by religious tradition and by the moral position of the individual in society. The spirit of party, like that of fetishists patriotism, is made up of contempt and dislike for those who are on the other side of the frontier line, and of mechanical attachment to those who are on this side of it. The first sentiment came in a direct line from the Puritan mind which had helped to mould the character of New England. The notions of orthodoxy and of heterodoxy, which made people look with holy horror on all those who were outside the pale of the Church, of the sect, passed straight into the life of the political parties as soon as the latter were formed. They set their mark on the contests of the Federalists and the Anti-Federalists, and even on their innermost feelings in the face of death itself; Ebenezer Webster, the father of Daniel Webster, the illustrious statesman, on his death-bed begged not to be left to die in a non-Federalist city. The reciprocal sentiments of the adherents and the opponents of Jackson and Clay, of the Republicans and the Democrats, not only during the Civil War, but long afterwards, bore the same stamp.

The second factor to which I have alluded, and which impelled the American to herd with his fellows in the party fold, is one of the primordial facts of American social existence — the isolation of the individual. True, nowhere is man more unfettered in his movements, nowhere can the individual launch forth more freely, nowhere are political and, to all appearances, social barriers brought so low as in the United States, and yet nowhere else is man reduced to that atomic condition, so to speak, in which he finds himself on the other side of the Atlantic. His deliverance from the bonds of space and time, which has had the effect of narrowing the mind of the American, of making him a man of short views, recoils on him once more and makes him pay a fresh penalty for his liberty. For the yoke of locality and heredity, heavily as it weighs on the denizen of the Old World, offers him at the same time a moral support. The American lives morally in the vagueness of space; he is, as it were, suspended in the air, he has no fixed groove. The levelled society, without traditions, without a past, in which he lives, does not provide him with one. The only traditional social groove which did exist, and which was supplied by the churches, has been almost worn down by the incessant action of material civilization and the advance of knowledge. To construct, or wait for the construction of new, permanent grooves, the American has neither the time nor the inclination. Obeying the national genius he creates mechanical ones, in the form of associations, as numerous and varied as they are superficial, but all revealing the uneasiness of the American mind assailed by a sort of fear of solitude and, again, by the desire felt by the individual to give himself a special status in the midst of the community at large. Such are the "patriotic" societies of Colonial Dames, Daughters of the Revolution, Sons of the American Revolution, Order of the Old Guard, Sons of Veterans, etc., which seek to bring together men or women who have no tie between them but the fact of descending from ancestors closely or remotely connected with historical events. The same spirit that enters into the formation of these societies, which are becoming more and more numerous, has produced what some persons call, in America, the genealogical craze. It is an endemic craze, harmless enough, which for some years past has raged among adults of both sexes possessing a certain amount of culture, and which consists in looking for their ancestors, in trying to discover them among men as celebrated or as distinguished as possible, with the aid of professional genealogists, that is to say charlatans, or by ransacking libraries and archives themselves.

The great mass of citizens of lower birth who cannot connect themselves by name with their ascendants create a small world for themselves in the so-called secret or fraternal societies. These organizations, which are generally reserved for the humbler classes, often discharge the function of mutual benefit societies. But they are not less appreciated for the sentimental gratifications which the members derive from their "lodges," "tents," "commanderies," "chapters," "temples," "conclaves." A workman who belongs to the "Ancient and Illustrious Order of the Knights of Malta" spends half his weekly wages in buying a knight's sword, which will give him the illusion of being really a member of a noble brotherhood whose name goes back so far into the ages. The epithet "ancient" and the historical or mythical appellations which they adopt for their societies enable them to affirm, in imagination, their collective existence even in the remotest past. There is no profession whose members do not assemble in meeting, as much to discuss questions of common interest, if there are any, as with the object of meeting, of being together for a time. The mere fact of having a trade or an occupation or even an external peculiarity in common is taken as a pretext for pleasure parties; such are the barbers' picnics, the tailors' excursions, the dinners of men weighing more than fourteen stone, and other Ancient Order of United Workmen, Ancient Order of Hibernians of America, Improved Order of Red Men, Knights of Pythias, Ancient Arabic Order of the Nobles of the Mystic Shrine.
gatherings of the same kind, which are readily put down to "American eccentricity," but which in the morbid need of friendly contact that they reveal have rather something pathetic about them. In America everything is done in a crowd, by troops. Even in secluded haunts, which invite the soul to commune with nature, the Americans are uncomfortable alone; there, too, they must have company. In a mountain resort, packed by hundreds in the immense hotels, they hardly leave one another for a moment, remaining the whole day in the brilliant suite of apartments, or on the piazzas, seated in rocking-chairs, or hanging about outside in the immediate vicinity. The mania for being introduced to all comers without the introduction leading even to a conversation, the apparent friendliness with which every one is received, the facility with which people who hardly know each other exchange letters of introduction which do not bind the addressees to anything — are so many more manifestations of the need which is felt of procuring at least the illusion of more or less far-reaching moral ties.

The moral blank created by the absence or the indefiniteness of social grooves is further widened, and the necessity of filling it is further accentuated by the fact that all the moral energies of the American are brought to bear on the outside world in order to conquer it, to get an ever larger share of it. The more a man launches out abroad, the more does he suffer from solitude, the more is he forced to fly from himself, being unable to make his mind his kingdom. The incessant activity of the Americans, who go on working even after they have amassed a fortune, and at an advanced age, down to the last gasp, is not, or is not solely, the effect of an insatiable craving for riches; it is also a means of escaping from the moral void produced by the constant and exclusive contemplation of material things; it is, to some extent, a need, that has become chronic, of diverting the mind. The instability of the material existence itself of the American, who, in the ceaseless endeavour to improve his lot, lives perpetually in the provisional, changing his position, his residence, going up and down in the social scale with kaleidoscopic rapidity,—this instability which makes the formation of natural social grooves more difficult renders the absence or the inadequacy of them still more painful.

In this state of things stereotyped party filled a portion of the moral void; it met an emotional need, it offered a groove exclusive enough to permit of the growth of genuine or conventional feelings of hatred and devotion, and comprehensive enough to unite in these feelings men with no other bond between them, and even dispersed in space. Like the ancient Greek who found in the most distant colonies hi" national deities and the fire from the sacred hearth of his *polis,* the American finds in his nomadic existence everywhere, from the Atlantic to the Pacific, from Maine to Florida, a Republican organization or a Democratic organization, which recalls him to himself, gives him a countenance, and makes him repeat with pride the cry of the New York politician: "I am a Democrat," or "I am a Republican."

Thus idealism itself, in its degenerate aspects of patriotic, political, religious, and social formalism, has combined with the materialistic spirit to deaden the civic conscience and let in the enemies of the public weal.

X

Yet the havoc wrought by the invaders being as extensive and profound as we have seen it to be, how is it that the commonwealth continues to prosper in spite of this, and that the Republic subsists, at least with no apparent diminution of strength? The havoc is no doubt very considerable, but up to the present it has had only a relative significance, thanks to the exceptional position enjoyed by the United States. The fact we have ascertained, that the government has slipped from the people, loses not a little of its import when one bears in mind how small is the place which government occupies in the existence of the New World, how limited are its powers and, consequently, its means of abusing them. The inhabitants of the American Republic are hardly "governed"; a citizen may spend his whole life without coming in contact with representatives of the government, unless he breaks the laws, and even if he does break them. The functions of government are not numerous nor very com A member of Congress told me that on one occasion, being sheriff in his county, he had to get up a rather serious criminal case. The accused, who was plicated. Hence, the barbarous method of recruiting the public service, established by the spoils system, has not done all the harm which it would have done in a country of the Old World. The extreme simplicity of government in America justifies, to a certain extent, the belief which is common among the Americans, and which makes them think they can dispense with a more rational system, namely, that every American is fit for any office. Besides, the abuses of the spoils system — as is generally the case with human things, good or bad — were never pushed to their furthest limits. A certain number of experienced officials were retained to keep the administrative machinery going. A good many members of Congress used their usurped power to appoint competent persons. The deterioration of the public services was thus toned down. The waste and plunder of public property in which the representatives of the people indulged were mitigated by the unbounded resources of a virgin country and by its growing wealth.

Lastly, even the usurpation of power by the bosses, the rings, and the machines, substantial as it was, did not and could not entail the political consequences which the illegal seizure of power produces in the countries of the Old World, or even in Latin America; it has not touched, or has scarcely touched liberty. In the United States the latter has never been the objective of the usurpers; besides, it had been made safe from their possible designs on it. The first fact is due primarily to the cardinal phenomenon to which Tocqueville has already called attention, namely, that the passions of the American people are not of a political, but of a commercial, nature. In that world, awaiting cultivation, the love of power aims less at men than at things. The Ccesar called for by the abdication of American society, engrossed in the pursuit of wealth, made his appearance animated with the same instincts and the same greed of gain. To satisfy them, even provisionally left at liberty, was much annoyed because he was not properly watched and because sufficient attention was not paid him. The Secretary of State of one of the largest States of the Union said to me on this subject: "When we (that is to say the whole staff, changed in consequence of the change of the party in power) entered on our duties, three-fourths of us did not know the A B C of what we had to do, bnt in a week's time we were equal to the situation." when there was grafted on them the desire to sway men's wills, it was enough to exploit the forms of liberty without meddling with its essence, to exploit the electoral regime. This was both safer and more advantageous. The reality of liberty was for the American the first condition of success in life, he had to remain undisputed master of his person, of his comings and goings, and of his property, to obtain the greatest possible return for his efforts. He would, therefore, not from public-spirited but from selfish motives, never have allowed himself to be deprived of the kernel of liberty. On the other hand, he was indifferent to the outer forms of it, forgetting that the forms are the bulwark of the substance. Thereupon the usurpers who exploited the public interest fastened on the forms, and made a speciality of them with eagerness, to obtain, in their turn, the maximum of profit.

Protected in this way by the mercantile instincts and ideals of the nation, personal liberty was not less shielded from possible encroachments by the barriers erected by the constitution. The rights of the individual, essential to his free moral and material development, had been formed into a sacred deposit, the custody of which was intrusted to the sovereign authority of the courts placed for this purpose above all the other public powers: no police, no minister, no parliament can touch them. The strongest and cleverest usurper is equally powerless to overthrow these barriers; all he can attempt is to get round them. Hence, we have seen that the political autocrat developed by the party regime, the boss, has not succeeded in attaining the position of the tyrant of the Greek cities or of the Italian republics; he is an autocrat whose power is wielded in a somewhat limited sphere of public life. All the more has this autocracy been unable to increase to the point of taking the lead of the nation. After the Civil War, when corruption invaded the Republic and government was relaxed, anxious minds looked forward with apprehension to the appearance of the " man on horseback." He has not appeared, nor has the oligarchy of the bosses either, which people were afraid of seeing installed at Washington. The centralizing tendencies developed through the war, as well as by the Caucus regime, even seemed to pave the way for them; but they met with an insurmountable obstacle, also set up by the constitution — the federative organi VOL. II — 2 Q zation of the Republic. A Caesar or a Napoleon, who " bestrides a world like a Colossus," and sways an empire from a capital, can only rise and flourish on a levelled political soil which presents a flat and smooth surface; now the American soil was broken up by a number of political units which, in spite of all vicissitudes, had preserved their individuality. There has been a rough outline of a national boss, but the influence of the personages who more or less realized this type was reduced mainly to the role of a grand wire-puller. Such was, for instance, in the early days of the convention system, the position of Thurlow Weed, who is known to the reader. Quite recently, in 1896, a national boss made his appearance in one of the two great parties, but he hardly attained a higher rank than that of a presidential contractor, of a great electoral speculator. The double organization, federal and local, of the public powers and of the governmental attributions, left as little room in the Union for a mayor of the palace as for an oligarchy. The sphere of political influence was wanting to them, unless it was a question of promoting commercial interests. The Union has no foreign or home "policy," in the European sense of the word, at least it had none until Imperialism recently unsettled the destinies of the American Republic; reduced to administration, the role of government even in this field was as much restricted by the rights reserved to the individual as by the limitation of the powers "delegated" to the Union. However favoured they may have been by the centralizing movement developed after the war, the leaders of the Caucus were not able to turn their influence to account in the sphere of the Union otherwise than by trafficking in patronage or by prostituting that influence to private commercial interests. The great crisis of "Reconstruction" was necessary to enable the party Organization to wield its power in a genuine political sense. Moreover, the very creation of a permanent oligarchical centre was not easy in a country cut up into a number of quasi-autonomous parts' and no longer possessing a ruling class. The "senatorial group," which was formed under Grant, was only an accident, favoured by the same crisis of "Reconstruction," which had practically suspended federal autonomy. The failure of the movement in favour of the election of Grant for a third term, started by a few bosses who belonged to that group, proved, among other things, how little opening there was in the Union for permanent political syndicates of that kind. In this respect the American constitution issued triumphant from the ordeal to which the Caucus regime had subjected it. The part of the constitutional apparatus which contained the elective system yielded to the pressure of that regime, and the shock broke down the two big wheels of the machine, —the executive and the legislative. But the reserved rights of the individual, the' federative organization, and the courts of law as political arbiters between the individual and the State and between the States and the Union, that is to say those parts of the constitution which all vindicated personal liberty under various aspects, withstood the shock, and, presenting the most remarkable example of the success of a political machinery created by a-written instrument, have given a subject of satisfaction and pride to the Americans, and a lesson to the world.

The value of these guarantees which the constitution had provided for liberty is in no way impaired by the fact that the latter found natural guarantees besides in the material conditions of the New World, which was vast and thinly populated: the relative isolation in which its inhabitants lived necessarily diminished the dangers which could threaten their liberty, while the boundless territory, open to all comers and possessing endless resources, enabled them to snap their fingers at everything they found oppressive or irksome. Here man was master of the soil, unlike Europe, where the soil was master of man, and had even reduced him, in the old days, to a condition of serfdom.

Thanks to this combination of circumstances, the American citizen has not felt too seriously the consequences of the fact that the government has slipped from the people. It was the same with the second grave result brought about by the Caucus regime, the subjection of the State to private commercial interests. With them privilege really did invade the State, but it did not pursue political ends. The plutocrats cared even less than the bosses about confiscating the liberties of the people; they thought of one thing only, morning, noon, and night — to enrich themselves as much as possible. Now, as long as it was a question of making money, the American was afraid of-nobody, all he asked for, up to quite recently, was, "Give me elbow-room, and I will take care of the rest"; and in point of fact he got what he wanted. The change in the conditions of this free race, which is being brought about, under our eyes, by the inevitable exhaustion of natural resources and the formidable concentration of capital threatening to restrict freedom of production, was necessary to make individual interests begin to take the alarm.

Of course the moral harm done by the Caucus regime and the dangers to which it exposes the future of the Republic could not be mitigated by constitutional guarantees, nor by the abundant resources of the country, nor by the special nature of the aims of the bosses and the plutocrats. This harm found a partial corrective in the mind of the citizen, who believes that he is still king in the State, and that he can put things to rights there when he chooses. The words of the stump orator, "When the American people will rise in their might and majesty," are by no means a mere formula to his audience. Each one of them believes in this mysterious force which is called "the American people," and which nothing can withstand; he has a mystic faith in the power of opinion, he speaks of it with a sort of religious ecstasy. This faith in opinion makes up for the inadequate strength put forth by it. The citizen does not lift a linger to combat abuses, but his conviction that his mere volition is sufficient to put an end to them keeps up the love of right and the hatred of wrong within him, like a fire which barely emits a spark, but which is not extinguished and may at any moment burst into a generous flame, giving light and warmth.

XI

Yet the degree in which the dissolvent action of the Caucus regime could be neutralized is in danger of considerable diminution, because the United. States are more and more losing the benefit of those exceptional conditions which we have seen check the mischief. Their vast natural resources are beginning to be exhausted, especially the free lands. Of the national lands which were sold at a nominal price, next to none or but few remain. Even in the West fertile land at a moderate price has not been available for the last twenty years or so. Thus, the great safety-valve provided by the abundance of land is being closed. Again, in proportion as the continent is cleared, is covered with large cities containing a dense population, and as industrial civilization advances, social existence assumes a complexity which is no longer compatible with the primitive simplicity of government. The functions of the latter become more numerous, more complicated, and more delicate. The question by whom and under what conditions they are to be exercised assumes a gravity which it did not hitherto present outside agglomerations as important, for instance, as New York or Chicago, where the Caucus regime has appeared in all its repulsiveness, owing precisely to the greater complexity of their social existence. Individual liberty will not be able to serve as an antidote to the same extent as formerly, for the amount of liberty available will naturally grow less. The more complex civilization becomes, the greater becomes the necessity for regulation. The rapid development of the "police power of government," which we are witnessing in the United States, is the outward sign of this need. Naturally encroaching and incapable of precise definition, the exercise of this power will inevitably contract the circle of individual rights, and it may even supply fresh weapons to the Caucus. The example of New York, where the social conditions had necessitated more extensive regulation than in othe'r places, and where the Machines of the city and of the State exploit it with a coolness of which fresh proof is daily forthcoming, is of evil omen in this respect. In any event, it may be said that the *vis medicatrix* of liberty being destined to decrease, society will bear with less fortitude the evils for which it was the remedy.

External liberty is not alone in process of diminution. The moral autonomy of the individual, the consciousness which he had of his liberty, and which, to a certain extent repaired, "The power is indefinite in extent and incapable of definition, though a definition has often been attempted," says F. Stimson in his excellent *Handbook to the Labor Law in the United States,* p. 22. Another jurist, of the highest eminence, expresses himself on the same subject (in a private letter) in the following terms: "The trouble with the Police Power is that nobody can define it, and people are afraid to attempt a definition lest it should become a limitation." as it were in a worn-out frame, the strength wasted through the fault of the Caucus, is also on the decline. This consciousness of his liberty was imparted to the individual mainly by his economic independence. Now, the latter is giving way under the action of the new factors. On one side a formidable industrial concentration is leaving less and less opening for individual enterprise and tending to transform the small producers and traders into wage-receivers. In the country districts the scarcity of land and the competition, daily growing more formidable, of foreign corn, which is contending with the home product for the markets of the world, have in their turn helped to change the conditions of existence to the detriment of individual independence; the small trades which used to make an easy living, are languishing; in the agricultural sphere the small landowner, who is still very numerous, is beginning to give way to the tenant; the number of holdings taken on lease is increasing in the East as well as in the central West; in certain parts of the country, for instance in New England, farmers cannot be found for the farms. This agricultural depression is a motive or a pretext for the emigration to the cities, which is steadily going on. Finding themselves in a pecuniary position that is less advantageous or below what they consider their due, those even who up till lately were in the front rank of the rural population are giving way to a certain moral depression; pinched in their expenditure, they are coiling up, their social spirit'is evaporating, as well as their assurance and their confidence in themselves. They are beginning to turn their eyes towards the State and to look for its helping hand. The example of the ultra protection granted to manufactures is contagious, and it certainly does not encourage, either in those who benefit by it or in others, the spirit of independence and of personal initiative.

The decline of religious feeling, which is incontestable in the country districts as well as in the cities, in spite of the comforting statistics compiled by the representatives of the churches, is tending likewise towards the shrinkage of the individual: apart from the moral influence which religion is held to exercise, and which I have not to inquire into here, there are signs that the growing religious scepticism is severing the ties which the Church formed among its members, and destroying the sphere of common interest and co-operation which it established for them and in which the individual felt he had his being. Until this gap is filled — if it can be filled — the equilibrium of the individual character remains disturbed at yet another point.,

Lastly, the same effect is being produced by the political scepticism which the corruption of the Caucus regime does not fail to develop: confidence in the representatives of the people is diminishing, their integrity is too readily suspected, the view is gaining ground that it is all much of a muchness, and there is even creeping in a doubt as to the efficacy of republican institutions. The serene confidence of the citizen in his power is no longer intact.

The material as well as the moral reserve represented by the territory, by the individual, and by the economy of the constitution being thus diminished, the passive resistance offered by these latent forces to the destructive action of the Caucus regime will be less effective than of yore. The favourite saying of the Americans, "It will right itself," is becoming every day more untrue. Only an active resistance, a vigorous offensive will be able to check the mischief, and maybe even eradicate it.

XII

The task is a gigantic one: the citizen must be re-invested with his power over the commonwealth, and the commonwealth must revert to its proper objects; the separation between society and politics must be put an end to, and the divorce between politics and morality annulled; civic indifference must give place to an alert and vigilant public spirit; the conscience of the citizen must be set free from the formalism which has enslaved it; electors and supreme depositaries of power must be guided in their political conduct by the reason inherent in things, and not by the conventional meaning attached to words; superiority of character and of intelligence, that is to say the real leadership, dethroned by political machinism, must be reinstated in its right to direct the government of the Republic; authority as well as liberty, now usurped by the men who traffic in the public weal under the party flag and in the name of democracy, must be rehabilitated in the body politic.

The immensity of the void to be filled and the obvious difficulty of the undertaking, the complete realization of which seems to partake almost of a Utopia, would appear to carry inevitable failure with them, and-to proclaim the condemnation of American democracy in its present and in its future. The passing of this sentence of condemnation, which would fill some with sadness and others with joy, is, however, deferred by the undeniable fact that a beginning has been made in the performance of the task, that a portion of what has to be done, small as it is, is already accomplished. The last few years, as we have seen, have been marked by an awakening of the civic conscience. The business community displays a much keener interest in local public affairs than formerly. The cultivated set and, in particular, the rising generation, descend into the political arena with an ardour which was unknown a quarter of a century ago. Public morality has advanced: its behests are at least acknowledged, if not obeyed; the homage of platonic respect at any rate is paid to them; society has become more alive to right and wrong. Public opinion is beginning to extricate itself from the narrow and deadly groove of parties. The fetish-like cult of party has fewer fervent worshippers. Party ties are being relaxed in all the organizations, owing to the progress of enlightenment as well as to the feeling of uneasiness which has been working for some time past in American society, of social discontent, whether justified or not, which makes people turn over like sick persons from one side to the other. In the " Solid South" itself economic changes are tending to unsettle parties. Habits of independence, if not freedom of mind, are certainly gainers thereby. Intellectual progress however is incontestable throughout the community, and people unquestionably vote with more discrimination. The personal qualities of the candidate, his moral worth, are becoming more and more appreciated. The expert is gaining ground in public estimation; slowly and laboriously he is undermining the prejudice which is so widely entertained that the public interest can be intrusted to the first comer, to "a plain man like all the rest of us."

These results are not to be despised, but, in truth, they constitute only a small instalment of the whole debt. The further raising of the standard of American political society, the development of the tendencies toward amelioration, which we have just noted, will evidently depend upon the action of the two factors which determine the existence of every political community, that is to say, its p.uturflJvthrgn moral, and its political methods. The future of American democracy liesTn"the improvement of its general culture and OBJ of its political methods. These two factors, as I have already indicated, have not been foreign to the progress already made, during the last twenty or five-and-twenty years. Education, lavishly provided in the American Republic, I mean primary education, has no doubt powerfully contributed to raise the intellectual standard, although, as I have also pointed out, the mechanical character of the methods of instruction is not calculated to develop the judgment of the future citizens and hardly admits of the cultivation of moral emotions. The Universities, which have made a great start of late, have had a most happy effect on the formation of the public mind, and their benefieent activity will not fail to increase in this respect when it is clearly understood that the higher culture is not obtained by an excessive special-

ization of studies, recalling the remark of Mephistopheles in *Faust,* "Dann hat er die Theile in seiner Hand, fehlt, leider! nur das geistige Band; " nor by the cultivation of a vain scholastic erudition; nor even by the transplanting of German University seminaries. The influence of the Universities on the body politic will extend in proportion as the conviction takes shape that in a democracy more than anywhere else the first duty of Universities is not so much to reproduce their own species, as to make men and citizens. The new tendencies which are coming to the front in the most important American Universities warrant great hopes in this connection. The pulpit has perhaps contributed also to the reform of the public mind, but in any event its politico-social role was slight. That of letters and art and of "society " was *nil.* Far more important was the part taken in the liberal Cf. in this order of ideas the statements of the new President of the University of Yale, Mr. A. Hadley, in his inaugural address and in his lecture on "University Ideals," delivered at New York, in February, 1900.
education of the public mind by Mugwumpism, by the political action of the Independents, which they brought to bear from 1871 onward, in a whole series of contests, either in the field of the Union, or in that of the States and the cities. It was a highly practical lesson which bore fruit, although the majority forgot what it had learned very quickly, and the work had to be done over again each time. Atptrwumpism, represented by the independent press and the combatants in the arena, battered down political formalism, party "regularity," and inclined people to judge men and things apart from all conventions.
The attempts at reform in political methods, while contributing to the awakening of public opinion by the agitation and propaganda which they set on foot, were too often characterized by an inadequate appreciation of the moral motive power which is the first condition of the proper working of all political systems. They fastened mostly not so much on the causes as on the apparent effects, and exhibited a constant tendency to resort to external remedies and mechanical expedients. The naive belief in the efficacy of machinery and of the hallmark of the State paralyzed in the citizen the volition and initiative which so imperiously needed to be stimulated. The success of the various experiments in reform, which took shape either in militant action or in legislative measures, was in the direct ratio of the broad-mindedness which the reformers showed with regard to party. Some adopted as basis and instrument the old groove of stereotyped party, and they failed in their undertaking; others placed themselves outside party, and they achieved a success that was more or less durable and more or less promising for the future. "Reform within party," which sought to purify party by persuasion, proved a fiasco; the measures which tended to regenerate it by force borrowed from the State fared no better; the placing of party under the supervision of the public authorities or even its transformation into a wheel of the State machinery, by the legal recognition of parties, by the institution of official nominations of candidates, and by the legalization of the primaries, ended in discomfiture. Being unattended by a clear perception of the nature of the evil which they sought to remedy, of the political formalism and machinism which had caught the American community in their toils, these attempts only made it sink deeper into them. They tended to consolidate the monopoly of the party flag, increased the supply of political machinery, and only succeeded in giving the "good" citizens a fresh pretext for dispensing with personal efforts on behalf of the public weal, while enabling them to display a hypocritical public spirit.

On the other hand, "civil service reform," which put parties entirely on one side and tried to rid the public service of them, was attended with some measure of success. The leagues which set up free and independent associations, irrespective of all party convention and sectarian creed, and for the promotion of a special cause, which appealed to all co-operation and all honest convictions from whatever quarter they came, and united them in an alliance for the service of that cause only — these leagues succeeded many and many a time in saving the Union from humiliations or grave mistakes, in expelling the public malefactors, or at least in blockading them by continually narrowing their field of action, and in purifying the political atmosphere, if only for a moment. Free nominations of candidates, outside parties, were also tried with encouraging results. Do these movements really point out the path in which the improvement of methods demanded by the political life of the United States must be sought? Or does our enquiry suggest other methods again for the best attainment of the ends of democratic government? Ought the new methods of political action to be completed by changes in the legal organization to produce their full effect?

These questions, brought before us by the political evolution of America, which has just been reviewed, lead us back to the conclusions furnished by our study of England. The essence of the problem awaiting solution turns out to be exactly the same. The study of America has but enabled us to see a little more clearly and a little farther. In fact, the longer experience of American democracy has only given extraordinary distinctness to the political phenomena and tendencies which we have seen looming in the young democracy of England. What appeared to us in England as a germ, blossoms in the United States, thanks to conditions which are unfortunately too favourable, into a luxuriant plant. The present intensity of the mischief differs in the two countries, it may be said, almost as day differs from night. But the source and the nature of the evil are the same, and its dangers as well, in the one still somewhat remote, in the other coming to close quarters with deadly effect. They are political formalism and machinism. WiU it be possible to escape from this evil? If not, how will it affect the future of democracy?

SIXTH PART CONCLUSION

I

When we take a comprehensive glance at the phenomena which have been successively brought under our notice and try to find our bearings among them, nothing is visible, at first, but confusion. Going back to the starting point, we see the State in the hands of a class, and society, embodied in that ruling class, dominating the individual and overwhelming him with the whole weight of social, religious, and political convention. But this threefold tyranny gives way and collapses under the pressure of manifold forces of a moral and material kind. The enthusiasm of selfrevealed religious faith, the criticism of reason triumphantly asserting itself, the new appliances of industry, all combine to free the individual from his bonds. In vain do dethroned authority and relaxed social discipline call to their aid the religious tradition, social tradition, the emotions of the heart, the distress inspired by the future, in order to stop the progress of the individual. Everything conspires in his favour, obstacles vanish before him. The autonomous individual is finally proclaimed sovereign in the State. Left to himself in the political sphere by the emancipating process of individualism, and powerless in his atomistic isolation, he fastens on the old party groove and makes it his base of operations. Jealous of his new power, he is not content with being invested with it; to prevent a fresh attack from the old influences, which appear to him more odious than ever, the individual, weary of the moral action of man on his fellow-men, which has kept him for centuries in a state of dependence and submission, strives to regulate even this action, to make its effect subject to formal conditions. He tries to refer directly to himself, as to their source, all the relations in public life, within and without the legal sphere. On the other side of the Atlantic, where he became his own master sooner, he presses forward in this direction with exceptional energy.

But—strange phenomenon—the more he advances the nearer he appears to draw to the starting-point. In fact, after he has gone on for a time it is seen that the role of the individual in the State dwindles to a small affair; he wields only a shadow of the sovereignty which is laid at his feet as pompously as it is hypocritically; he has, in reality, no power over the choice of the men who govern in his name and by his authority; the nation and its rulers are separated; government is a monopoly; it is in the hands of a class which, without forming a caste, constitutes a distinct group in society; it is even often wielded by a single man, who relies on that class and enjoys the powers of an autocrat in spite of the republican forms of the State; the bulk of the community endure this yoke, with indifference or passivity, as in the old times when concern for the public welfare was forbidden them on pain of being treated as rebels; government is at the beck and call of private interests in their designs on the general interest; legislation and administration are bought and sold; public office itself is virtually put up to auction.

It would, in truth, be difficult to find in the history of human societies a more pathetic drama than this ruin of so many generous aspirations, of so many noble efforts, of such high promise and expectations. But the tragic gravity of this spectacle, extorting cries of distress or of joy at the failure of democracy, cannot detain the scientific observer. What he has just seen simply suggests to him the very elementary reflection that, if society, which set forth to realize a new ideal, finds itself after a time near its starting-point, it has evidently moved in a circle or entered on a side-path which has brought it straight back to the starting-point. The inference, then, is that the paths which have been taken to reach the goal were not the right ones. As for the goal itself, it is neither condemned nor justified by experience: the seekers turned their backs on it. Consequently, to arrive at a practical solution, the alL-important point is to single out the paths which have misled society in its pursuit of the new ideal, and then to note those which appear more certain to lead to the goal. Our lengthy investigation has but accumulated the data which will enable us to distinguish, as from a vantage-ground, the one set from the other.

Society entered on its new existence under the auspices of the idea which presided over its birth, which viewed the object of democracy — the greatest happiness of the greatest number — in a narrowly individualist way, by placing it wholly in the abstract and self-sufficing individual. This incomplete and, consequently, erroneous conception, without doing irreparable injury to the intrinsic efficacy of democracy and its final success, was anything but calculated to provide it with a clue for guidance through the difficulties which awaited it. Wedded to this idea, society is seen at first to enter on the path of the elective regime into which the old tradition of the struggles against absolute power impelled it. Representative institutions were, for the subjects, the means of ensuring the security of their persons and property; and each step forward in this direction marked a new conquest in the domain of popular liberties, until, established for good and all, an elective regime became a synonym for that of liberty. Under cover of this political evolution, a prejudice grew up which attributed a sort of mystic virtue to the elective principle in itself, and made it an axiom that the more widely the elective method is applied in public organization, the more liberty there is. When, to accomplish liberty, society started in pursuit of equality, it sought to realize it by the same means: by giving fresh developments to the elective principle. It subjected to universal suffrage the greatest possible number of public functions, and even the extra-legal relations of political influence, in order to assert emphatically the power of the autonomous individual, who was the embodiment of the State. But, thereupon, the electoral business proved so complicated that political society was almost entirely taken up with it. The democracy appeared to live only for electioneering; the task of government was identified with electoral operations; and from a means election became an end. The hypertrophy of the electoral system — which made a Chicago elector, for instance, vote, as at the elections of 1896, a ticket of 370 candidates — necessarily had the effect that society could not properly discharge the duty with which it was overwhelmed; it could neither make its choice with adequate knowledge nor supervise VOL. II — 2 R its representatives; its authority over them became purely nominal. To get out of the difficulty, society demanded or accepted the services of election agencies, of electoral contractors, and, to make sure of their trustworthiness, it subjected them, in their turn, to election. The gravity of the situation, far from being attenuated, only became more obvious. The interposition of third persons between the people and its numerous representatives, the selection of whom it did but ratify, reduced to a minimum the responsibility of the latter to their pretended constituents, and placed the real power in the hands of the election agencies and their managers, who, on pretence of helping bewildered public opinion, thus became its masters.

It follows therefore that, contrary to the current prejudice, the elective principle in government is a spring of limited power; that once the limit is exceeded it becomes, like a strained mechanical spring, incapable of supplying the required impulse, and throws the movement out of order. It follows, again, that the political omnipotence of the people by no means consists in the power of giving an impulse to all the organs of government directly with its own hands, since "its own hands" are set in motion in these cases only from outside, like those of a puppet. A highly developed electoral system is therefore only a purely formal homage to democracy, and produces, in reality, a diminution of its strength. By parcelling out, so to speak, public functions of every kind on the elective method, the people fritter away their authority instead of increasing it; the direct responsibility to themselves, which they try to establish all along the line, is scattered, and, while supposed to be everywhere, is really nowhere. To make it a reality, it is therefore necessary that direct responsibility to the people should be concentrated; that it should apply only to certain well-defined attributions of the public authority, to those which, by their nature, dominate all the others, that is to say, in the modern State, in the first instance, to the legislative functions, and, in the second degree, to those of local selfgovernment. Every extension of the elective regime beyond these limits, to administrative posts and to judicial office, can be admitted only as the lesser of two evils, to wit, in countries which are still at a lower or intermediate stage of political progress, such as Russia, for instance, or even Germany. There an elective administration and judiciary can give public opinion an opportunity of making itself heard; can enable it to exercise a modicum of control over public affairs, of which it is deprived by the political organization; can serve it as a means of civic education; can awaken and stimulate its interest in the public weal, which is still feebly developed; or, again, hold in check a corrupt bureaucracy or withstand a bureaucracy which is honest and capable, but arrogant and dictatorial, and whose representatives fondly imagine that they are made of a different clay from other people. That is to say that the progress of a political community is appraised not by the extension of the elective method in its organization, but by the degree in which it can venture to restrict it and to entrust fearlessly its administration and its courts of law to permanent officials. When a political community has reached true liberty, when public opinion, become supreme, has in hand the legislative power, — the source of all powers, — and commands liberty of the press, of association, and of meeting, the elective method applied to administration ceases to render it the services which it may have rendered to it during its years of growth and struggle, and, serving no useful purpose, recoils even against the political community: it makes the latter exhaust itself in electoral efforts, which are henceforth superfluous and which simply divide and weary its attention, blunt its moral energy, and, in the long run, withdraw public opinion from its real duty, which is that of supervising and controlling the organs of government.

To make the performance of this duty easy for public opinion, and to prevent the elective principle from exceeding the limit of its efficaciousness in the very sphere where its application is justified, in legislation and local self-government, it is material to reduce the employment of the electoral method in that sphere to a minimum. The proposals for abolishing periodical elections, and for allowing the elected to retain their places *quoad bene se gesserint,* offer a solution which is obviously too radical: the periodicity of elections is one of the means which are as indispensable for developing civic education and fostering public spirit as for keeping the representatives in touch with the views and aspirations of their constituents, not to mention the sanction with which periodical elections invest the responsibility of the mandate-holders. But it may be well to inquire if there is not an intermediate solution which would make the sterile agitation of the elections less frequent, while fulfilling the objects of representative government. I shall have an opportunity of reverting to this problem. selves, who examined the dangers and the difficulties of democratic government so closely, had not, it would appear, bestowed a moment's thought on the question as to how the electors should be set in motion and made of one mind, in order to produce the final act investing the elected persons with their mandate. It is probable that the limited horizon of the small republics, with an insignificant population, in which the trainers of the American Constitution lived, as well as the social hierarchy which was still supreme in public life, hid this problem from their eyes. There was no thought even of deciding how qualified and unqualified persons should be distinguished at the elections; there was no attempt, in the United States as well as in England in the old days, to establish any system of electoral lists'. The reader will remember how in England, the State having omitted, even after the Reform Bill, to take in hand electoral registration, private persons stepped into its shoes and exploited this public function in their own interest, to the detriment of the true expression of the popular suffrage.

II

The prejudice which attributed an intrinsic efficacy to the elective system was complicated by another mistake, which it perhaps brought in its train — the no less grave mistake of supposing that the application of this system could be left to itself. This view came direct from the eighteenth century, which had a fond belief in the, so to speak, automatic and universal action of moral ideas, and did not allow for free will and for the weaknesses and resistance of individual volition. It was proclaimed as axioms that mankind had been unhappy because they were ignorant of their rights; that, to be free, it was enough to know and to love liberty, etc. By enacting the elective system, had not enough been done to realize liberty? There seemed to be no inkling that a popular election demands the agreement of a considerable number of persons, an agreement of minds and wills which needs to be established beforehand. Besides, the conception of the abstract individual, which the philosophy of the eighteenth century had made the foundation of political life, encouraged this attitude and justified it. Political society was considered as composed of autonomous individuals who were of equal value; the sum total of their minds expressed the general will; to ascertain this, all that had to be done was to add up the figures — it was useless to analyze them. Universal suffrage, therefore, found its way into democratic communities with the character which still subsists and which constitutes one of its greatest, if not its greatest failing, — that of a synthesis without a previous analysis. The mistake was all the less noticed that representative democracy was an entirely new phenomenon, experience of which had yet to be gained. The republics of antiquity, which haunted the minds of thinkers as well as of statesmen, threw no light on this subject. The founders of the American Republic them

Th the same way private organizations laid hand, in the United States and, later, in England, on the whole procedure which prepares and determines the elections. To control the action of the citizens during this preliminary electoral phase, a very complicated machinery was created, which formed a pendant to the constitutional mechanism. It was accepted all the more readily that it met a real public want. But the more fully it appeared to satisfy that want, the more its action extended in public life, and the more it degraded it. It was like a parasite, which feeds on the vital parts of the body and weakens all its members. In vain did the State, alarmed in the long run, endeavour to protect the general interest, to regulate the play of the extra-legal apparatus introduced into the political organization. It "legalized" the primaries and the party conventions by associating the public authority with them as manager or superintendent. But the evil was by no means averted: as the State omitted to eliminate the representatives of the parties and accepted their organization as a basis for its action, they remained masters of the situation. There was, in truth, no need of this demonstration to prove that it is as idle as it is absurd to entrust, even in part, the custody of the general interest to private interests. If it is necessary to take preservative measures for safeguarding the general interest, it is for the State, its sole representative, to take them and to apply them in all the plenitude of its one and indivisible power. There is no possible *condominium* in the public sphere. When, as we have seen, experience revealed the absence in the political machinery of an apparatus corresponding to the preliminary phase of the electoral operations, it was the duty of the State to create that supplementary apparatus and not allow private initiative to undertake it with a selfish object. The nature of the electoral franchise which is involved in the case, far from being opposed to such an intervention of the State, fully justifies it. No doubt the citizen is free to use his electoral right as he pleases; but to enable him to exercise this liberty it should, like all liberties, be guaranteed by the State, and, if need be, organized by it. Now, the act of voting being complicated, in practice, by a series of preliminary acts, the genuineness of which is of no less moment to the efficacy of representative government than that of the final vote, is it not in the general interest that the guarantees and the legal organization established for this last act should be extended to those which precede and pave the way for it; that is to say, that the State should itself organize, irrespective of political opinions, the preliminary proceedings in which the electors express their views on the candidates to be brought forward at the definitive election?

Yet, however great may be the value of these proceedings, which the State can and ought to take under its safeguard, they are still far from constituting the analysis that should precede the synthesis which is the final act of the election. The registration of candidatures and the previous vote-takings are only an external and purely formal analysis, so to speak. There still remains a deeper and more inward analysis: the study of the electors' opinions on the problems of the day and on the men capable of ensuring the solution of them, and, in general, of representing their fellow-citizens in the councils of the nation. As regards this last analysis, the State can do nothing, it rests entirely with the conscience of the electors. Now their conscience is not completely free under the present regime in spite of the democratic form which it assumes. Yet if the State cannot prevent this state of things, it is partly responsible for it. As it neglected to provide for the preliminary election procedure which constitutes the external analysis, and allowed private organizations to undertake it, the latter availed themselves of this to get in as through a gap, and took possession of the inner analysis on behalf of the electors. The conceptions which these organizations obeyed, and the methods which they employed to discharge the task they assumed, were in direct opposition to freedom of the civic conscience, and they ended in making the elective regime and representative government miscarry.

Ill

The extra-legal organizations which regularly undertook to ensure the coordination of the opinions of the citizens, with a view to the legal manifestation of the general will, adopted a framework of political action created before the advent of democracy — " party," which arranged opinions in fixed and rigid grooves. This old method thrust on a new society was contrary alike to the logic of facts and of reason. It was founded on theological and ecclesiastical conceptions; the grouping of the members of a party exactly resembled that of the adherents of a Church; the principles or the programme of the party constituted a creed invested, like the creed of a Church, with the sanction of orthodoxy and heterodoxy. The adhesion had to be undivided, one could not differ from the party on any article of its faith any more than one can choose between the dogmas of a religion. Like the Church, which takes charge of all the spiritual needs of man, party demanded the whole citizen. Conformity with the party creed was the sole rule of political conduct; it conferred, like religious faith, justifying grace on all the members, present and to come, who enjoyed.it without further effort on their part. No act of the party, no wrong committed by it, could destroy or impair its efficacy or communicate it to the heterodox party: they were governed by the theological principle of hereditary merit and demerit. Two organizations, the two earliest in point of date, did just recognize each other's right to existence, but subject to the duty of every citizen to profess the creed of the one or the other, according to his origin, just as under the regime established by the Agreement of Augsburg, which, after sanguinary struggles, recognized the reformed confession side by side with the Catholic religion, by classifying all the subjects on the principle *cujw regio ejus religio.* A place was vouchsafed to "His Majesty's Opposition"; but all other opposition was "illegitimate." Those who were outside the recognized parties were looked on with the hatred and disgust which the churches, making common cause for once in a way, reserve for those who are outside the recognized cults. The "free-thinkers," the political " infidels," were proclaimed "*hostes humani generis,* who are entitled to no favour or mercy from any honest man," "a pestiferous and demoralizing brood."

The party system which rested on these conceptions, so contrary to the modern spirit, had not, since the advent of democracy, a more rational justification in the facts. Its historic foundation had collapsed. The old divergences, which divided society into two hostile camps, had fallen into the background after the definitive conquest of the fundamental liberties which placed everybody on an equal footing in the State, and ensured to each man the untrammelled development of his moral and material personality. The new problems were no longer of a nature to divide men's minds for generations, and could no longer give rise on each side to ties as lasting as the old ones. At the same time the problems became infinitely more numerous and varied; the emancipation of the individual and the growing diversity of the social conditions of a more complex civilization had substituted everywhere, — in men's ideas, interests, aspirations, — variety for unity and a sort of perpetual flux for the comparative stagnation of the old days. The more numerous problems naturally produced more numerous divisions, which could not be marshalled into two opposing On the approach of a general election in England, I asked a distinguished member of the majority of the House of Commons whether he would have to fight for his seat. He replied that that depended on whether he would have to deal with the *legitimate* opposition only or meet two opponents at the same time. Thus, the candidate who, belonging neither to the Tory nor to the Liberal party, would have stood for Parliament, would have intervened in an " illegitimate " manner.

-See above, Vol. II, p. 93.

I lines as formerly, but which mingled and crossed each other in men's minds, and all the more easily that the ties formed by the old combinations were relaxed.

This contradiction could not be solved by the theory of the natural dualism of the human mind which the champions of the system were fond of advancing — a theory according to which the human race is divided into those who wish to keep things as they are and those who desire to change them, from which it would follow that there must, and always will be, two permanent parties. No doubt each problem may be viewed under two different aspects, some upholding the *pro* and others the *con.* But is it natural that the same persons should always, in all things, take, the one set the negative, the other the affirmative side? Is it reasonable to admit that a man who desires to preserve the Established Church should necessarily wish to keep the dirt in the streets and public thoroughfares, as Mr. Chamberlain asserted in the days when he belonged to the Radical party? It is in theology, again, that one would have to look for the justification of this theory, which is put forward as a datum of political anthropology or psychology. The proof of this pretended fact can only be found in the Calvinist dogma of predestination, according to which the Creator took care to divide mankind beforehand into the elect and the damned — unless one prefers the more profane explanation of the dramatic author, who supposes that, by an operation of nature, all human beings come into the world Liberals or Conservatives. In any event, were the division between conservatives and progressives really ever so hard and fast, this immobility can only be that of the spirit which each side represents, and not that of the means by which they try to make it predominant in public life, since means must always adapt themselves to varying circumstances. In practice, therefore, this supposed foreordained division is but an idle form or even an illusion, as we have so often seen in the

'See above, Vol. I, p. 485.

" I often think it's comical,
How Nature always does contrive
That every boy and every gal
That's born into the world alive,
Is either a little Liberal
Or else a little Conservative." — W. S. Gilrrrt. course of our enquiry. We have found that "conservatism" itself cannot'rest on negation pure and simple, and cannot, in consequence, be crystallized for all time in a rigid organization. It is all very well for it to adopt or at least proclaim as its duty, the " maintenance of institutions," it cannot always sit with its hands 'folded. In fact, "How are institutions maintained," we have been led to ask, "By never laying hand on them? But in that case is there not a great risk of their being allowed to fall into ruin under the ravages of time? If, on the other hand, in order to preserve the edifice the injured or decaying parts must be renewed and constantly changed, it is only in particular cases that the question can be put, whether the change proposed is conservative or destructive; and it would be impossible before the cases giving rise to these questions had occurred to give an anticipatory and general answer to them and adopt it as an unvarying rule of conduct."

Thus the system of stereotyped parties, on which it was sought to found democratic government, was, in its principle, as artificial as irrational and out of date. The methods by which it was carried out could not help being of the same nature. The problems preoccupying public opinion being numerous and varied, it was necessary, instead of grouping the men in accordance with the issues, to adapt the issues to fixed groups of men. With this object confusion of the questions of the day was erected into a system; they were huddled together into "omnibus" programmes; they were put one on the top of another; they were shuffled like a pack of cards, some being played at one time and some at another; at a pinch those which caused irreconcilable divergencies were made away with. That is to say, that to obtain the analysis of the opinions of the electors, — the task which the Organization of the parties undertook to facilitate and which was its principal *raison d'Hre,*—nothing better was hit upon than to mix up systematically the opinions that had to be analyzed. Consequently, what was pompously called the national verdict was, as a rule, tainted with ambiguity and uncertainty; a group of electors gave or refused its approval to the party or to its champions in consideration of this or that point of the composite programme which they put forward, another group

See above, Vol. II, p. 537.

did the same on the ground of some other point. And after "the voice of the country had spoken," people did not know exactly what it had said, and very often were entitled to wrangle over the meaning of the vote; for, however paramount a particular question may have been in the public mind, considerations foreign to it constantly entered into the "popular verdict." As it was difficult to establish unanimity on the basis of the various problems which the party took up, the electors were made to rally round the firm of the party, round its sign and its ancient renown. To gain their adhesion more easily, an appeal was addressed rather to their feelings, not to say to their senses. The maxim of the Primrose League — " Do not argue, but take them in socially " — became the rule in a somewhat more comprehensive form, —" Do not argue, but take them in sentimentally." Thus, to ensure the working of a regime supposed to be that of reason, the minimum of action was brought to bear on the intelligence. More or less consciously, but systematically, the parties discarded the analysis of the general will, on which the new regime rested, and tried to obtain the political synthesis through tradition and feelings, just as under the regime which democracy had replaced, but with this difference, that the synthesis of the old political society acted spontaneously. By reviving this method deliberately after the fall of the old regime, the system of stereotyped parties simply carried on the work of the counter-revolution, which, in the form of the Oxford Movement, of the Young England Movement, etc., tried to stem the current which emancipated the individual. The champions of the counter-revolution preached return to tradition, to discipline, appealed to the imagination, to popular emotion, and not to the reason of man. The party system put these precepts in practice and, unwittingly, undertook as it were to carry out the designs of the sworn enemies of democratic government, that government which it was its mission to perpetuate.

While applying the old method to democratic government, the party system introduced into it two modern practices — popular election and free association. But the employment of these practices, far from mitigating the defects of the method, only aggravated them. In the first place, it disguised its reactionary tendencies from the very persons who carried out the method. The champions of the counter-revolution, who inveighed against " the reason of man," fought without a mask; and they had only to enter the lists for people to know what to make of them, whereas the party system, clothed with the forms of popular election and association, appeared in all the glamour of democratic principles. In the second place, the extension of the election and association basis to extra-legal political relations imposed fresh efforts on the citizens, which did but increase the very difficulties which party organization was to obviate. Over and above the numerous elections prescribed by the law, which were quite enough to bewilder the citizen, there were elections for choosing the representatives of the party. Besides the acts of the constitutional representatives of the people, the electors had also to follow and weigh those of the several series of representatives of the parties. The citizens were not equal to this task, and the over-strained spring of elective government became further relaxed, proving once more, and still more decisively, that the efficacy of the elective principle is limited.

The practice of free association has in no way been able to remedy this defect, because the association principle also has its limits, which cannot be exceeded with impunity. The association which was made the basis of the party system had no fixed limits; it represented a sort of *integral* association, like that by means of which certain social reformers have endeavoured, and still endeavour, to organize economic life, with a view to abolishing pauperism. Whether the universal association which the individual enters with his whole economic personality, to attain all the objects of his material existence, is possible or not — I have not to discuss the point here; but in political life, founded on liberty, an analogous association, into which the citizen brings his whole political personality, to achieve his aims in the State, can never ensure its members this result. An association for political action, which is a combination of efforts aiming at a moral object, always implies the voluntary and conscious co-operation of its members. By joining the association they subordinate their freedom of initiative to the unity of management which constitutes the strength of the union, but they cannot part with the spontaneity of their action, and of their energy, which alone makes the effort fruitful and gives the result obtained its value, if not its efficacy. However insignificant may be the personal share of a member in the work of the association, however nearly it approaches to a simple adhesion, this adhesion must be a continuous adhesion, which is unceasingly renewed in his mind, which is always present to it like the faith of the believer, and not a capital sunk in the association. It is therefore necessary that, while accepting the direction imparted to the whole, the member of the association should always be in a position to keep its object in view, and to discern the limits of the obligations which it lays upon him. Now, the intellectual vision and the power of attention of the average man are very limited, it is hardly possible for him to apply them to a large area or to a highly diversified prospect; he can only follow action confined to a restricted sphere, like that of the parish, or extending beyond it, but with a single object clearly visible to all and entailing only a temporary duty. Once these limits are exceeded, his sight becomes dazed, his attention is divided and wearied, and if he continues to follow the course prescribed, he does it in a passive manner. The members of a political association pursuing a variety of objects are, therefore, units simply placed side by side; and this form of association leads back to that social atomism for which the association principle was to be the grand remedy. Their spontaneous energy and their individual impulse being, as it were, smothered under the multiplicity of the aims proposed, they are obliged to trust to a few persons, to the first comers who take them in tow, that is to say, to submit to a moral monopoly which it was the very object of free co-operation to abolish. Reduced to a passive co-operation, they derive their strength not from the spirit of association, which elevates men's minds by making them one, but from *esprit de corps,* that base form of fellowship which unites by excluding, whose binding force is not so much mutual affection as contempt for, and hatred of, outsiders, or at least the pharisaic satisfaction of not resembling them, which develops not so much a collective conscience as a collective pride or self-love, acting as sole inspirer of conduct, and taking precedence of all other considerations, including even those of truth and justice. Through out the whole of our enquiry the party system has but supplied us, in a concrete form, with a continuous demonstration of all these effects of universal association applied to political action.

rv

The democratization of the party system was thus nothing but a change of form and could not cure the original defect, either of its principle, or of the methods by which it was carried out. Thenceforth the system could only produce effects which were the negation of democracy. Incapable of realizing its essence, the system reduced political relations to an external conformity, which warped their moral spring and ended by enslaving the mind of the citizens and opening the door to corruption. In calling each individual to the dignity of citizen, democracy had laid upon him the duty, if he wished to enjoy his rights, of exercising his judgment and keeping his conscience on the alert. The system of stereotyped parties diverted him from the fulfilment of this duty. It offered him a criterion of political good and evil, the purely formal character of which made its application automatic and dispensed with the necessity of personal effort. The indolence natural to man, indolence of mind and indolence of conscience, makes him only too ready to abstain from displaying personal energy, whenever he finds plausible pretexts for so doing. In proportion as these pretexts are taken from him, or, on the contrary, are liberally supplied to him, by education, by the habits of his particular environment, or by special circumstances, the conduct of man, whether in private or in public life, will incline towards the independence or towards the subjection of his personality, will be guided by or screened from individual responsibility; in a word, will enhance human dignity or obscure it. The convention of party, embodied in stereotyped organizations, put before the citizen not only pretexts, but a sort of categorical imperative; "regularity" made personal remissness a virtue, and adhesion to the party a fetish-like worship, which reduced the duties of the citizen to ritual performances.

Stricken by political formalism in the independence of their thought, in the energy of their will, and in the autonomy of the individual conscience, the citizens, too weak to counteract the failings inherent in democratic government and to bring out its innate strength, allowed the former to increase and the latter to diminish.

The first postulate of democratic government is the active participation of the great mass of the citizens. Now this great mass is naturally passive. The maxim of Montesquieu, who attributed virtue to democracy as a "principle" or a "spring," has no foundation in reality. In all democracies, small or great, virtue is only an ideal, the notion of which is more or less distinctly kept in view but which does not predominate anywhere in practice; and there is little sign that its reign is near at hand or even probable. Established, apparently, on a mechanical association of ideas, — republic, antiquity, Plutarch, virtue, — Montesquieu's maxim is not more true in the corrected definition which he gave of it when bringing it down from the heights of "moral virtue and Christian virtue" to "political virtue,"or, as we should say in the language of to-day, public spirit. "Political virtue " is supposed to consist, according to Montesquieu's revised definition, in the "love of country, that is to say, the love of equality." Even if it attains a high degree of intensity, "love of country" cannot of itself "set going republican government." The vilest citizen can indulge in the luxury of professing love of country. Dr. Johnson had no need to live as late as the second half of the nineteenth century, when "patriotism" had become, according to Herr Nordau's expression, one of the "conventional lies of civilization," to define it as "the last refuge of a scoundrel." "The love of equality" is not sufficient either to furnish a substance to public spirit on which a democracy can live. A democracy cannot be saved, as in certain religions, by faith alone; works are what is all essential to it. Public spirit ought to be strenuous, nay, even militant; the citizen ought to be ever in the breach, his gaze fixed on the public weal, and ready to give it, with disinterestedness, his time and his energies. Now this public spirit is wanting to all the de Montesquieu almost admits this when he indirectly defines virtue: "The love of country, the desire for true glory, self-renunciation, the sacrifice of one's dearest interests, and all those heroic virtues which we find in the ancients and of which we have only heard by report." *(Esprit des Lois,* Part. Ill, chap. V.) mocracies with which we are acquainted, and it would appear even that they are radically incapable of displaying it continuously, whether they are democratic communities of AngloSaxon or of Latin race. Their public spirit is exhibited only in an intermittent and spasmodic way; it consists of outbreaks of civic virtue, sudden, and often violent, like volcanic eruptions, which at one moment are all fire and flame, but which leave behind them nothing but lava, but mud that has cooled down.

It may even be said that of all non-despotic regimes that of democracy is the least capable of public spirit, in the conditions of modern civilization. The advent of democracy coincided with, and, to some extent, was caused by, a social evolution, which has made life more and more complex, has multiplied and intensified private interests — cares as well as pleasures — both of a moral and of a material kind. Thus it came about that, from the time the public weal has demanded the greatest attention from each citizen, the great majority have found themselves less than ever in a position to respond to this appeal; the citizen, who is human, is naturally inclined by a selfish instinct to place concern for his livelihood, and the other personal preoccupations which absorb him, before the interests of the commonwealth, which appear to him more remote and less urgent, if they do not leave him completely indifferent. The greater the number, in modern society, of persons admitted to citizenship, the less the interest taken in the public welfare is sustained; platonie interest alone becomes more widely spread. The citizen is barely able, or willing, to give the public weal his odd moments. On the other hand, a regime of enlightened despotism, supported by a trained and honest bureaucracy, or a parliamentary aristocracy like that which ruled England for so long, is far more favourably situated for displaying public spirit. The law of division of labour, which turns against public spirit in democracies, benefits it under non-democratic regimes. It enables those who wield power in them, by various titles, to devote themselves freely to the public, welfare and to identify their interests, their ambitions, and their moral aspirations with the best fulfilment of their public task. They need not even be inspired by pure duty; whether they take to public affairs, believing in the mission of an upper class, as a point of honour, or out of dilettantism, or from a disinterested love of sporting excitement, the public interest, more or less broadly understood, will not be neglected.

To the economic and social conditions which divert the attention of the citizen from public affairs and lull his vigilance, is also added, in democratic communities, the extreme confidence inspired by the, possession of unlimited power. Member of the sovereign demos, each citizen refers to himself, consciously or unconsciously, the irresistible strength of the people, which relieves him from all uneasiness on the score of the public interest. He readily fancies that he will always be able to intervene soon enough to set things to rights, if need be. Like the Roman *imperator*, he thinks that he has but to stamp on the ground and legions will start from it, or he repeats the more modern phrase of the stump orator with which we are already acquainted: "When the American people will rise in their might and majesty." In the case of a sovereign or of a ruling class, whether reasonable or timorous, the infatuation inspired by power may be moderated by the fear that some day or other the people, injured in its interests or its rights, will kick against the pricks. But in a democratic State master and people are one and the same.

However distressing may be the reflections suggested by this want of active public spirit in democracies, the fact must be frankly admitted, and allowance must be made for it in political organization, in order to make good the deficiency as far as possible, by encouraging everything that favours the laborious growth of public spirit and by avoiding everything that checks it. The first problem, therefore, which arises in democratic practice is the following: how to so organize political action as to develop spontaneous and regular impulse, to stimulate individual energies and not let them fall asleep. The party system offered its solution: Let the citizens choose a party, let them enlist in it for good and all, let them give it full powers, and it will undertake to supply the required impetus. Put forward with every semblance of political piety, this solution found favour with the citizens, and enabled them to sink, with an untroubled conscience, into their habitual apathy. Their selfishness, which the industrial civilization of our day fosters only too much, was, so to speak, rehabiliVol. 11 — 2 s tated in their own eyes; it was able to wear the cloak of the general interest. Giving way, more or less consciously, to this feeling, the citizens spread around them an atmosphere of political cant, in which genuine devotion to the public welfare withers and wastes away. This was the case especially with that class of society which is the hotbed of all forms of cant, the bourgeoisie, or the "better element," as it is called in the United States. They raised political indifferentism to the level of a virtue, and this aloofness has combined with the ignorance of the masses to repress public spirit. But the moral torpor brought on by party convention did not fail to paralyze the parties themselves. Obliged by the representative system to obtain a periodical renewal of their mandate, the parties themselves encountered the passivity of the electors, and were forced on each occasion to exert extraordinary efforts to overcome it for a moment. They had recourse to heroic means, and, acting mostly on the emotions, threw the electors into a state of paroxysm, which, by a natural reaction, was invariably followed by complete prostration.

V

While it lulled to sleep the public spirit which ought to watch over the commonwealth, party convention fastened on the power of social intimidation with which democracy, by reason of its institutions, is armed in a high degree. This power, which consists in keeping everybody in the path of duty, by the operation of the laws as well as by that of public opinion, is the regulating force of all government. To exercise power is simply to intimidate, to exert a moral constraint in order to obtain obedience, to compel men's wills by the idea of the consequences which disobedience will entail. A despot cannot, any more than a republican minister, make a material and full use of the power which is supposed to reside in him; it would not go beyond his muscular strength. The power to intimidate which governs political society is complete when it reaches all the members, rulers as well as ruled. It acts through the very idea of the force which it possesses, material or moral force, without any need, however, for a real display; in the great majority of cases it is enough that the idea of the force available should be present in men's minds, for their wills to be impelled in the direction whither the force exerted in a tangible form would drive them. The effectiveness with which the power of intimidation acts depends, consequently, in the first place, on the amount of the force which it commands or which it represents..But this amount cannot be purely material, even when it is a questiou of brute force. The number of arms relied on is an essential element of it, but by no means the only one, for these arms themselves obey consciences and minds, and the consciences and minds must co-operate in the work of intimidation. Of all regimes democratic government best combines these conditions, so far at least as political forms are concerned. As all the citizens are allowed a share in the government of the commonwealth, and as power emanates directly from the whole nation, the democratic regime has on its side the maximum of brute force and of moral force. Every law is supposed to be made with the assent of the humblest of the citizens, and the citizen who obeys the laws and the custodians of them appears to obey only himself. If he wished to swerve from the path of duty, the citizen, either as ruler or ruled, would come into collision with the whole united power of numbers armed with the weapons which he himself will have helped to forge. The fiction of spontaneous assent is thus added to the reality of the most formidable external constraint which can be exerted, constituting, in society, a power of intimidation from which no one escapes, and to which every one can fly for refuge.

Now, this power which ensures democratic government an incontestable superiority over other regimes, the political formalism introduced by the party system has undermined at various points, and has prevented from asserting itself in all its fulness. In a general way it may be said that party convention has wrested from the citizens the weapon of moral constraint, and has turned it against them. It is all very well for the, members of the sovereign people to have numbers and right on their side, they are reduced to impotence, their minds and their consciences capitulate to what is put before them as the interest of the party. Those who claim to represent it have but to dangle before them the exigencies of the party to gain possession of their wills, as by a mesmeric pass. The people give their adhesion, as soon as the party is in question, to acts which they would otherwise have condemned. They vote meekly for a "yellow dog," because it wears the collar of the party. They witness the disorders of public life unmoved, because these disorders are covered by the flag of their party. The pirates who bring them about and profit thereby are bold, because they know that the votaries of the party, constrained by the principle of regularity, "will wheel into line." Instead of being intimidated, it is they who intimidate, by holding up the bugbear of political heterodoxy. A handful of bandits, or to put it at the best, of vulgar selfseekers, thus keep in check a whole people armed from head to foot. No doubt the people may, at any moment, wake from their hypnotic slumber, and recovering, by the mere play of democratic institutions, their power of intimidation, may make it felt in an irresistible way. But is not continuity the first condition of the exercise of power? If the power is asserted at intervals only, it evidently loses a great deal. The character even of its action undergoes a profound change: it takes effect only when the mischief is done, that is to say, that the power represses more than it intimidates. We have been able to verify this, in the United States in particular, when examining the conditions in which public opinion acts there. I have therefore been led to draw a distinction between the repressive and the preventive power of opinion, and to point out how the latter, which alone realizes the ideal of democracy — while realizing in the highest degree the power of social intimidation — is too often debarred from asserting itself.

But it is not only a quantitative diminution that party convention has inflicted on the power of social intimidation. It has also lowered it in quality, by profoundly affecting the nature of the fear which it inspires. It is this nature which distinguishes the various political regimes from one another. Contrary to the theory of Montesquieu, who reserves fear as a "spring" or "principle" for despotic government, it is really the regulating principle of all government, since every government is founded on constraint. Under a despotic government swayed by caprice, the fear inspired by power is necessarily the coarse fear of material pains and privations; whereas in governments controlled by the law it is capable of becoming gradually ennobled to the point of being transformed, in the best type of citizens, into the fear of forfeiting one's moral dignity in case of neglect of the public interest. The evolution in this direction of the feeling of fear in the relations of rulers and ruled stamps and sums up the progress of political society and of civilization in general. The structure of democratic government presents the most favourable conditions for this evolution: in non-popular regimes where there always remains a ruling class or individual beyond the reach of the power of social intimidation, who can do much, and against whom little can be done, the citizens stand in fear of irreparable acts of highhandedness on their part; whereas, under a popular government, where no one escapes the power of intimidation wielded by the whole community, it is no longer men, but equal laws for all, that inspire apprehension; fear loses, so to speak, its material nature and assumes a moral aspect. Yet the democratic form of the government can impart a moral character to the external constraint only, to that of the authorities and of the laws. But man is also subjected, in the social state, to another constraint, that of public opinion, which eludes the best organized government. This inward constraint can be ennobled only by the raising of the intellectual standard of the community, it can be improved only by the development of the moral autonomy of its members. If these influences are wanting, or are prevented from making themselves felt, may not the fear of public opinion become all the more oppressive that the democratic regime concedes to opinions a power in the State, that is to say, that it increases their capacity of intimidation without being able to assign limits to it? In that case, is not each individual, in a democratic community, in danger of living in fear of everybody? While enjoying, owing to the universality of the power of intimidation, the maximum of material liberty, is not the citizen menaced in his moral liberty? And as external constraint in the State rests, after all, on public opinion, is not the material liberty of the citizen itself indirectly menaced? Here we have the latent weakness in the power of social intimidation, which democratic government brings out with the same intensity as it brings out its strength. The democratic communities most advanced in point of culture axe still very far from having reached a moral and intellectual standard high enough to overcome this weakness. Consequently, we see the brute pressure of opinion display itself without disguise in them, and weigh heavily on every one. A man who has the courage of his opinions is very rare under a democratic regime, he must be almost a hero to face the multitude: it is so numerous, so all-pervading; where is he to take refuge? from whom is he to seek aid and protection against it, since each individual is an item of it? So long as it was a question of external constraint, which threatened the citizen in his person and property, every one was on his side, drawn towards him by the obvious identity of their interests. But as soon as the constraint of opinion comes into play, this identity disappears in the eyes of the great majority, and the individual has to confront them alone. Consequently, no one walks with head erect in public life, everybody skulks along. There is no one in a democratic State who can address the sovereign people in the language of the Cortes of Aragon, which saluted each new king with these words: "We who are as good as you..." Every man vies with his neighbour in professing himself the humble, the most humble, servant of the multitude. In truth, the moral oppression of numbers has been exercised at all times and in all places since men have lived in the social state. Outside the constituted authorities was set up the authority of opinion, with powers as unlimited as they were intangible, and extending its jurisdiction not only over the acts, but even over the manifestations of the thought of the individual. The brute force of numbers which it represented was formidable enough to procure for it alike submission and general respect. People were not content with bowing before its power; they admired its virtues, they invested it with a moral and intellectual superiority, they credited it not only with the robust qualities of the mind, such as good sense, "*le gros bon sens,*" but even with the delicate qualities, such as *"esprit";* the age which most valued *"esprit"* did not hesitate to admit that Monsieur Everybody had more of it than Monsieur de Voltaire. This was democracy by way of anticipation, brute democracy, the "theory of equality applied to minds," according to an expression of Tocqueville. When democracy was installed in the State, the practical supremacy which Mr. Everybody enjoyed obtained a legal confirmation, and asserted itself in public life with all the greater force that it became weak in social life, where the breaking up of the old ties had abated the tyranny of the environment. Each environment and each order of social, economic, and religious relations represented so many strongholds garrisoned by opinion. When the progress of private liberty forced it to evacuate these fortresses, wholly or in part, and to make them over to the jurisdiction of the individual conscience, opinion moved with the main body of its army into the more circumscribed field of public life. Being thus led to concentrate itself, it appeared all the more formidable in that particular field that it could enforce its will not only by moral coercion, but also by the power of legal coercion, with which the democratic regime had just invested it. Thus, for instance, while religious worship, formerly the basis and the bond of union of the commonwealth, was more and more left to personal preferences, the worship of country, and all the feelings and doings connected with it, found themselves placed under the jealous and implacable sway of opinion, which inspires a fear as indefinite as are the numbers and the political power of the multitude.

Again, with opinion becoming more intimidating, the individual found himself weakened, impoverished. He had now to face, not a special environment, but the whole body of opinion, with ever-receding limits, which were beyond the grasp of his imagination itself. Besides, in the days when he lived under the pressure of the circumscribed environment he took shelter behind it, as behind a fortress, against all pressure from outside; when these forts were dismantled he had to meet opinion in public life alone and in the open field. The natural tendency, therefore, of the individual to retire before the majority was accentuated. Whether this tendency assumes the fatalistic aspect of a blind submission to an irresistible force, of which Mr. Bryce has given such an admirable analysis in his chapter already quoted, "The Fatalism of the Multitude," or whether it takes other forms, such as the simple fear of appearing peculiar, of being alone in one's opinion, of incurring disapproval, or even the wish to fawn upon power, in the upshot the citizen under a democratic regime, however enterprising and bold he may be in private life, is, in public life, without initiative, timorous, and, to be plain-spokeu, cowardly. Cowardice coexists perfectly well in his breast with the civic infatuation which we have observed in him. This double current of feeling corresponds to the distinction which Rousseau drew when he said that the members of the body politic are alike "*citizens,* as sharers in sovereign power, and *subjects,* as amenable to the laws of the State." The *subject* is timorous, the *citizen* is infatuated and presumptuous; the cowardice of the one hides behind the infatuation of the other, and these two feelings combine to keep individual will passive and inert and to discourage personal effort.

Of all the citizens in a democratic State, those who hold office are the most timorous: they are dependent on the first comer; the Man in the Street has their fate in his hands; in every passer-by they see a master whose favour must be conciliated. They try to please him by lowering themselves to him; but as they have little knowledge of his views, they appraise them, for fear of miscalculation, as low as possible, and adjust themselves thereto. Every one invested, or seeking to be invested, with a portion of public authority is *ipso facto* shorn of his dignity as a man. Human dignity is conceived only as a homage to be laid at the feet of the sovereign multitude. "These are my convictions," concluded a stump orator in the United States emphatically, "and if you do not like them... I will change them." To the low types which the human race has produced, from Cain down to Tartuffe, the age of democracy has added a new one — the politician. And it is not the least despicable. There is a sombre grandeur in the crime of Cain and its expiation; this is not entirely wanting even in Harpagon, chained body and mind to one all-absorbing passion, like Prometheus to his rock. Nothing of the kind is to be found in the motley soul of the politician; it is made up of innumerable pettinesses, with but one trait to give them unity — cowardice.

The timorous attitude of the governed does not spring exactly from the same motives as that of the representatives of public authority, it is not guided by the coarse personal interest which inspires the latter, and does not present the same odious aspect; but both are of the same nature, both meet in their effects and combine to form a sort of blind circle in which democratic government revolves; the cowardice of the ruled encourages the rulers, and the cowardice of the latter demoralizes the former. The very character of its generality tempers, it is true the effects of the cowardice on government; as nobody has enough pluck, little pluck is exhibited either for good or for ill. We have seen how, in the United States, the most corrupt politicians are kept within certain limits by fear of the elector; they are too pusillanimous to proceed to extremities. The electors, knowing that after all the politicians will not do a great deal of harm, quietly allow them to go a good part of the way; they are too faint-hearted to stop them at the start. It is a sort of mutual insurance through cowardice that governs the relations between the rulers and the ruled.

Herein lies one of the greatest defects of democratic government, to which the so numerous critics of democracy have hitherto hardly paid attention. They have fastened rather on its apparent failings, they have considered mostly its external working, they have vied with one another in pointing out the want of stability of the democratic regime or its fragility, as Sir H. Sumner Maine says, its incapacity for the conduct of affairs, its weakness in action, the general mediocrity of its leaders, the influence which demagogues easily gain over it, the oppression of minorities by majorities, the extravagance and corruption in the disposal of public money. Those even among the critics of democracy who have probed its sores more deeply, who have closely investigated the way in which democratic government affects the human mind and the motives of the individual's conduct in society, have hardly got beyond the motives which spring, so to speak, from the very definition of democracy, from its equalizing nature, which arouses the passions of jealousy and envy, which tends to the levelling of men and things, which seeks to degrade superiority of mind and character, and to establish an equality in the distribution of wealth. It is true that Tocqueville, in dwelling with much vigour on the dangers with which the omnipotence of the majority threatens democracy, has brought out the moral oppression wielded by numbers; he has described it in passages that can never be forgotten; but he has not distinguished it clearly enough from the legal coercion which the majority wields and which it is capable of abusing, nor has he deduced the consequences which it may entail for the working of the political order. Almost every time that he seems on the point of grappling with the subject, he diverges from it to return to the problem of the legal omnipotence of the majority, and finally to point out the necessity of averting the danger by an improved organization of the public powers. The problem is in no way a legislative one; the best organization of the public powers in a democratic government cannot affect the moral sway of numbers and its action on the rulers and the ruled. Tocqueville insists, and with more emphasis than was required, on the tyrannical power wielded by the majority in America over thought in general; he denounces more correctly the " courtier-like spirit" in the United States, but comes to the conclusion that these "effects of the tyranny of the majority have hitherto exercised more influence on the manners than on the conduct of society." Whatever may have been the case in Tocqueville's time, at the present day the dissolvent action of the moral pressure of the multitude presents more gravity from the political than from the social point of view. The atmosphere of general cowardice which surrounds democratic government is pre-eminently a political problem. To it may be applied what Tocqueville says, with less reason, of the omnipotence of the majority: "I have spoken before of the defects which are natural to government by democracy; there is not one of them which does not increase along with the power of the majority."

The chief of these defects, such as the general mediocrity, the influence of demagogues, the want of public spirit, the weakening of the action of the laws, either arise from the fundamental cowardice of the rulers and the ruled, or are but aspects of it. This cowardice relegates to the second or third rank most of the other indictments, more or less justified, and often even little justified, which are brought against democracy. For instance, the classic charge of democratic inconstancy, which recalls the argument of variations with which Bossuet combats the Reformation: if the reformers are obliged to reform themselves every day, so that they cannot say when the innovations will come to an end, and can never *Be la dimocratic en Amirique,* 13th ed., in two volumes, I, 310.

Ibid., 300.

please themselves, it is evident that they are not in possession of the truth. The agitations incident to democratic government are often only surface agitations, which do not affect the real life of the country. In so far as they are substantial and pregnant with consequences, they are the inevitable and often beneficent effect of the growing complexity of social relations which is at work in all modern societies and which tends to bring about an ever greater amount of justice in those relations, "so that one cannot say when the innovations will come to an end." The monarchical and anti-democratic form of certain empires in northern and central Europe, for instance, does not appear in the least to guarantee them from abrupt and constant changes of their whole policy, from variations in the "Kurs," etc. Democratic government is not, after all, less stable than other forms of government, only it slowly, but steadily, undermines the moral basis of the commonwealth. It is all very well for it to enhance the dignity of the humble citizen by bestowing political equality on him; the feeling of general dependence which it diffuses demoralizes every public man, produces, in the long run, a moral decline, and tends to make cowardice a principle of government. How is this tendency to be checked? That is one of the cardinal problems of democracy.

Party convention does but foster and develop the tendency. The ritual cult with which it surrounds the "majority," the "party," gives a quasi-concrete form to the undefined authority of numbers which strikes the imagination of the individual and casts a spell over his will; it makes this authority still more urgent, more irresistible. Party " regularity" sets up an external standard for political conduct, which thrusts back the unseen guide, conscience, which puts a sort of barrier between it and the citizen; he cannot cross this barrier without the risk of being caught in the very act of "irregularity" by the first passer-by; all eyes are upon him to see if he follows the route indicated by the visible sign; how can he help falling into line? The life of the party is, consequently, only one long school of servile submission. All the lessons the citizen receives in it are lessons in cowardice; the first of them, which teaches that there is no salvation for a citizen outside a permanent party, prepares him for every kind of surrender and withdrawal. Those who have no political aims follow these lessons and assimilate them passively, while those who want public office study them as a science or as an art; and at the end of their apprenticeship their mind is schooled, like the body of an acrobat, to every sort of contortion.

The power of intimidation, therefore, wielded over them by numbers, arouses in them only a vulgar fear, which is devoid of all concern for what the individual owes to himself and which looks only to.the external consequences of conduct. Now, in all relations involving dependence those who are a prey to a vulgar fear always try to circumvent those who inspire it: servility invariably has deceit for its corollary. We have seen how, in the United States, the politicians dupe the "people" while quailing before them. To the conditions which ensure the maximum of efficiency of the power of social intimidation, must therefore be added yet another: the character of the incentives at its disposal; it will become more real in proportion as the nature of the fear, or, to use the more legal or more metaphysical term given to it, of the responsibility which it inspires, becomes loftier. Party convention tends systematically to lower this, by keeping it at the level of an unreasoning conformism resting on the general inertness which that convention itself develops. The responsibility which governs the relations of the rulers and the ruled is already deficient in elevation, owing to the state of the popular mind and conscience, still somewhat unenlightened. Party convention prevents it from gaining elevation. It keeps the force of public opinion in the condition of brute force.

VI

No doubt there is a counterpoise to this force in opinion itself; "opinion " is not an entity, it is made up of manifold and divers opinions which can hold one another in check and evolve a moral force capable of quelling or intimidating brute force. One man's opinion backed by reason and justice can impress many, the force of numbers will bow before it. But for this result to be achieved, it is necessary that all opinions should be free to assert themselves, and not only for counting heads, but for action. If opinions are merely allowed to muster in order to bestow a legal or other authority on the majority, there is only a change in the form of the exercise of power; the arbitrariness of force is no more excluded from it than before. This arbitrariness can be tempered, if not curbed, only by the free play of opinion allowing individual opinions to influence one another, to counterbalance one another by fighting in open combat and with equal weapons. That is the cardinal political function of opinion which brings out in a new aspect the power of social intimidation protecting every member of the community from the abuses of force, whatever shape they may assume. This function of opinion thus gives democracy its special character and distinguishes it from other regimes. The mere power of opinion is not a sufficient criterion, for every government rests, after all, on public opinion; a government pure and simple of opinion is only a despotism pure and simple. The difference between a government that goes by the name of free and those which are not so is that of the motive power of opinion; in the latter kind, opinion is determined mainly by prejudice and sentiment, crystallized in tradition, whereas, under a democratic regime,— if it is a genuine one,— it is determined mainly by reason asserting itself in discussion. But here the convention of party intervenes again; it does not allow discussion. Not that it stifles the material liberty of discussion, but it affects it injuriously by attacking moral liberty. It is all very well for a citizen to possess the right of speaking and writing, his mouth is stopped by the argument that his opinion is an insult to the honour of the party, to its glorious flag, an affront to "regularity." Minorities are deprived of the only weapon with which they can overawe majorities, intimidate them. They are disabled. If there is a fight, it is never fair and above-board; the majority is always screened by convention, which prevents the loyal grapple of opinions..And it is not even always on the real majority that party convention thus bestows the monopoly. By putting obstacles in the way of the free assertion of individual opinions, it does not allow them to be honestly counted, so that it is difficult to know on which side the majority really is. It thus lets a minority easily usurp the title of a majority. True, the majority, genuine or spurious, can be shifted. But party convention impedes the formation of new political associations by crystallizing opinion. It is a permanent obstacle to the evolution of new ideas and to the fulfilment of that evolution's twofold mission, which is to prepare a better future and to mitigate the abuses of the present. Unfettered, the evolution of ideas is a sort of *memento mori* addressed to the great ones of the hour, individuals, constituted majorities, ideas, prejudices, and saying to them: "You are but the present, the future belongs to the future!"

Thus, by hampering or warping the free play of opinion, political formalism not only undermines the regime of discussion which tempers the despotism of government by opinion, not only lends a sanction to the absolutism of majorities, but ends by affecting the ideal itself. This source, from which every free community derives its vital strength, is, so to speak, the special and natural property of democracy: democratic government springs therefrom, it holds its title-deeds from the ideal, and can only justify the enjoyment of them by always going back to it. Thus the ideal is, in a way, officially the patron saint of the commonwealth under democracy. Every one invokes it, everybody pays it homage, at least with the lips, it has its place of honour in all the solemn manifestations of public life; whereas, under non-popular regimes, its seat is empty, and the rulers too often see only the ghost of Banquo there. Not that before democracy the ideal was unknown in the life of communities, and that it has not shaped their destinies. It was born almost with man. But from its birth it was lost in the heavenliness of religion and turned towards a supra-terrestrial world. The democratic movement secularized the ideal, and humanized it by establishing the seat of it in what used to be called the vale of tears, to illumine and cheer the life of the terrestrial city, and to elevate the lot of its humblest members, all bidden to enjoy the rights of human dignity in the State and in society. The human ideal, repressed before the advent of democracy, succeeded by its own strength in opening itself a path and in asserting itself triumphantly under various forms, whether the Renaissance, or the Reformation, or the French Revolution. But these were nearly always violent explosions, the flame of which more than once died out and was rekindled only by dint of great efforts and hard struggles, often stained by bloodshed. Democracy gave the ideal a permanent home. More than that, it enabled this home to be established in broad daylight. True, the ideal lived in the catacombs, but it could only prepare men for martyrdom there. To generate life, it must have the light and the warmth of day. Democracy ensured it them. This exceptional faculty of fostering and developing the ideal, which is inherent in democracy, constitutes its great force along with its power of social intimidation. It completes the influence of that power; it may even be described as the highest and noblest manifestation in which the action of social intimidation culminates, like a heavenly body at its zenith — that action which, step by step, by elevating and ennobling itself, develops the primordial principles of life in political society, and realizes the latter's material as well as moral objects in an indissoluble association. Material liberty, security against arbitrariness, which the fear of equal laws for all ensures to every citizen, finds its supreme guarantee in absolute liberty of opinion, in its moral liberty, which is never genuine if it cannot put the ideal between it and the jailers of the mind behind whom stand the jailers of the body.

But, on the other hand, the very fact that in democracy the seat of the ideal is established in the market-place and is the object of a regular cult, exposes it to the danger of this cult degenerating into a purely ritual one, from which belief has departed. The sacramental formulas may be in every mouth, they may be engraved on the walls of every public edifice, but they will be as empty as a dried-up river whose bed is all sand and pebbles. To prevent the ideal running dry in this way, it must be fed continually from those invisible sources in which it rises — the individual conscience and mind. External conformism tends to choke those sources in politics as well as elsewhere, by preventing them from flowing freely. It is all very well for it to propose an ideal itself or to thrust itself on the community in the name of the ideal, it can only put forward a counterfeit of the ideal, because it assigns a limit to the aspirations of reason and of individual conscience; In a few pages in a separate place (Appendix I) the considerations developed above, relating to the power of social intimidation as a principle of political life, will be defined in regard to some important points which could not be dealt with in the body of the book without interrupting the continuity of the argument.
owing to that very fact, this ideal ends by being destructive of its own objects. The eclipse of the ideal, therefore, is not brought about solely by materialism pure and simple, but also by giving currency to a conventional ideal, just as religious faith does not decay solely because people believe no longer in God, but also, and mainly, because they have ceased to feel the living God within them. In both cases worship is reduced sooner or later to those cults in regard to which one wonders how the ministers themselves can look at one another without laughing. Hence the profound and universal significance of the commandment: "Thou shalt not make to thyself any graven image nor the likeness of anything that is in heaven above." In democracy, party convention is, along with spurious patriotism, the most apt to constitute an idol for the use of the community, because it appeals to the people at large and unites them in the same fetishism, that is to say, it is the most apt to lower the ideal of the whole community. VII
The citizens, thus morally disarmed by political formalism, cannot expect any effectual help outside themselves; they will search in vain elsewhere for guides and advisers, whom they need more than ever in the impotence and isolation to which they are reduced: this formalism has destroyed also the moral ascendency of man over man, the ascendency which man exercises over his fellows through his superiority. The individuals capable of exerting this influence constitute an element indispensable to good government in any community, but they are even more necessary to democracy than to other regimes. Equality of rights cannot make up for the natural inequality of brains and character. Again, the authority of leaders cannot be wielded unconditionally over men called to political equality. To keep in the right path a democracy then has need of guides; but they can only compel ad-

hesion and discharge their function if they constitute a natural elite in the levelled ranks of society. How to encourage the rise of this elite in public life is one of the fundamental problems of democracy. Almost from the advent of democracy a few great minds, bent on the renewal of society, caught sight of the problem. Thus, St. Simon and the St. Simonians saw that the French Revolution had dissolved the old spiritual power; that in the society sprung from the Revolution the government of the mind had been left vacant; and that the spiritual power must be reconstituted on new foundations. They realized that the new spiritual power must have its source in the perfectly voluntary adhesion of the governed, and that it must be based on merit; that the ablest was the man to wield it. Developing the doctrine of tne master, the St. Simonians assigned to the spiritual power not only a place of honour in the government of society, but conceded it even the exclusive right of exercising this government in the temporal, as well as in the spiritual sphere, with an absolute authority which was equivalent to that claimed by the Catholic Church, and which, in truth, was only a transposition of it. Mixed up with the temporal power, the spiritual power lost its character, and this confusion nullified the whole movement of the emancipation of the individual and the citizen. Auguste Comte, who was also preoccupied with the organization of the spiritual power, unlike the St. Simonians, maintained the separation between the two powers, — the purely moral power and the purely political power. But the founder of Positivism, in his turn, managed to organize the spiritual power on the same basis as the Roman Church, the authority of which was not even absolute enough in his eyes. Social renovators, the St. Simonians and Auguste Comte sought inspiration in the past; they tried to organize by means of authority a world called to liberty; the select few, the "intellectual superiors," as Comte called them, entrusted with the direction of men's minds, were to form only a hierarchy of despots.

Democratic practice, founded on the convention of parties, offered no better solution of the problem. Out of hatred of the aristocratic leadership, or considered by it as such, which it found in possession, it endeavoured to regulate even the exercise of influence in political society, and succeeded only in driving personal ascendency out of public life, that is to say, solved the problem the wrong way. The formalism introduced by it subordinated the exercise of the action of man on man to external criteria, which disqualified character and knowledge. Seconded by democratic prejudice, which requires VOL. Ii—2t as rulers "plain men like all the rest of us," it put forward mediocrity and incapacity, when it did not enforce the rule of notorious robbers, for the simple reason that they represented the "party," and that the "cause" was paramount. Thus repressed, the natural demand for leaders of men asserted itself notwithstanding, and sought satisfaction by indirect channels. Under the auspices of democratic formalism itself, the representative party organization which it built up gave birth to an illegitimate personal government — the bosses. Their leadership, untrammelled by mere forms, but also by moral responsibility, proves a mischievous one, and "mugwumps," without a mandate, rise against them. "Self-appointed committees" are formed, civic leagues are organized. Once more it is a personal power, the negation of democratic formalism, that these volunteers bring forward against the public malefactors sheltered behind party convention. And the people, who at first accepted the bosses, follow the mugwumps in moments of distress. It is the old cry, as Carlyle says: "Guide me, govern me; I am mad and miserable, I cannot guide myself!" But it is not despots, after the heart of the Carlyles and the Auguste Comtes, that the people want; it is not for this that they overthrew the old regime; they want men.

Now, men cannot be found, or cannot be found in sufficient numbers, where the feeling of personal responsibility is weakened, where individual will and initiative are enfeebled, where the moral liberty of opinion is impaired, where the ideal is only a sounding brass and a tinkling cymbal. The spring of human personality once relaxed, it can be replaced only by a mechanical motor; and people try to make up for moral effort by machinery. Centralization, however harmful to local autonomy, is thereupon welcomed; the State is relied on, its regulation is accepted or applied for; new laws are constantly demanded because, in order to comply with the old ones, a moral effort would be required, whereas to obtain new laws it is enough to turn the handle of the legislative machine. A fetichistic property is fondly attributed to it; the State has but to lay its hands on this or that sore of the body politic, and it will heal of itself. "Legalize" — that is the panacea which for some time past has been cried up, in and out of season, in the greatest democracy of the world. Legalize the voting-paper, and corruption will disappear, and the political pirates will hide their heads; legalize the primaries, and civic indifference will give place to public spirit. The confusion produced in men's minds by this faith in legal machinery has even just reached the point of demanding quite seriously that the State should take in the political parties in order to render them harmless, that it should make them component parts of its own mechanism. Where the sphere of the machinery of the State comes to an end, it is made up for by extralegal automatism, established by convention: a blind obedience is yielded to conventions which are taken for realities; duty is held to lie in external conformism; certain men are followed, not in consequence of their intrinsic worth, moral and intellectual, but because they are the embodiment of conventional conformity. Government thus tends to become *mechanical* instead of *personal.*

It is into one or the other of these two categories, in fact, that all political systems are resolvable. The classic division of forms of government, which has been in vogue since Aristotle's day, with more or less important variations, has had its scholastic, and even its political utility, but it no longer corresponds, if it has ever corresponded, to the reality of things. This or that monarchical government is in no way distinguishable from a republican government, save as regards the title and the mode of appointment of the nominal head of the State. Again, a government that goes by the name of democratic may walk in the paths of an absolute government. The forms of governments do not betoken their special nature any more than costume indicates the rank of those that wear it, as it did in the old days when the dress distinguished the nobleman from the commoner, the-bourgeois from the peasant. The same progress of brummagem civilization which has levelled costume.has popularized the apparently most advanced forms of government, while making them often an imposture. The traditional classifications are, in reality, all based on external signs, especially on the distribution of the sovereignty or on that of the powers. No doubt, Kant contributed a very important correction by establishing a difference between the "form of the sovereignty" and the "form of the government," *die Form der Beherrschung* (forma imperii) and *die Regierungsart* (forma regiminis). The first classifies governments according to the number of the persons who hold the sovereignty (autocracy, aristocracy, and democracy), while the second classifies them by the manner in which the State makes use of its power: they are republican or despotic according as the executive power is separated from the legislative or mixed up with it. This distinction, a more profound one, which was drawn by the author of *Zum eivigen Frieden,* and which aims at the mode in which power is exercised, does not, however, go beyond the organization of government; it reaches the latter's internal structure, but it is still forms of government that are in question, and not its essence, however close may be the correlation between them. What really distinguishes the different regimes is the way in which they work; and this depends not only on the governmental machinery, but also, and above all, on the motive power and the manner in which it is applied. This motive power, represented by the individual, manifests itself in two aspects, according as human personality is conscious of itself, of its rights, and of its duties, or according as the human being is reduced to a chattel, to an instrument. In the first case government is *personal* and responsible; in the second, it is *mechanical* and devoid of responsibility.

These are the two extreme types between which the government of human societies oscillates, approximating now to the one, now to the other, according as the one or the other is the predominant trait of its necessarily composite character. For the so-called *simple* forms of government, as opposed to *mixed* governments, is yet another of those scholastic conceptions which constitute almost the whole stock-in-trade of the traditional political philosophy. It does not correspond to the reality of things, even from the standpoint of the Architectonic classification of governments according to the organization of the supreme power, as has been already remarked in the eighteenth century, by Rousseau and by Paley. The character of governments is composite, because that of the individuals who conduct them, and of the communities in which "Properly speaking there is no such thing as a simple government" *(Conirat Social,* Book III, eh. 7).

Moral and Political Philosophy, Part VI, ch. fi. they are carried on, is composite. All possess a personal element and a mechanical element, and they are distinguishable only by the distribution of these elements. The more individuality is developed and asserts itself in a political community, and the greater the number of those in whom it is capable of asserting itself, the nearer does this community approximate to the first type of government, because the members of it, and in particular the rulers, are in that case more inclined to respect the rights and the wants of their fellowcitizens, in other words, are more effectively held to responsibility. On the other hand, wherever the great mass of citizens are unable to assert their personality, the rulers manage them as they please, like puppets, or consider them as an instrument for their own use; while in their own case responsibility disappears, or dwindles, and their personality, morally deteriorated, is reduced to its elementary, its crude nature. Their relations with the ruled, incapable of being determined by the action of man on man, of mind on mind, are determined only by mechanical impulses. The power wielded by them, therefore, in these conditions, is a gross personal power, of the kind that every-day language describes by the simple words "personal power," which have, consequently, received an invidious acceptation as being synonymous with absolutism. To remedy the evils of irresponsible, or insufficiently responsible personal power, the representative regime was introduced or extended, not because it possessed an intrinsic efficacy, — it has none, — but because it enabled the citizens to take cognizance of themselves, to assert their individuality, and, in consequence, to establish or strengthen the responsibility of the rulers. Now, it is these results that party convention attacks, and *mechanical* government driven out at one door, to make way for responsible government, is re-entering by another.

With it are necessarily returning the old abuses as well, in somewhat new forms, more in keeping with contemporary civilization. They consist not so much in direct attacks on the person and property, as in indirect exploitation of the public weal for the benefit of selfish passions and private interests. They easily get a footing because, just as in the old days, the attention of the citizens, reduced to inert instruments, is lulled to rest. They creep in unobserved all the more readily that they are screened by the political parties whose flag covers them and conceals them from the bulk of the adherents of the party. The protectionist greed of the manufacturers, who try to mulct the consumer throughout the country for their own gain, shelters itself behind the party as quietly and as successfully as the appetites of a Ring in a municipality. At the same time that it protects their schemes, party conformism ensures them the co-operation or the connivance of the depositaries of public authority. Character and personal merit generally having been disqualified by the application of the external criterion of conformity to the selection of men, the public service lies open to persons who are ready — some through weakness, others from interest — to betray the public weal, and even to make themselves the agents or the prime movers of the most shameless corruption, of the kind described by a New York paper in the terms already quoted above: "The government of the city, in fact, became a huge market; the officers might as well have sat at little tables and sold their wares openly." VIII

In helping to instal or reinstal corruption in public life, party formalism has reached the extreme limits of its action, which has been one long degradation of democratic government. It has added to all the difficulties of that regime; it has aggravated them, as it were, deliberately. It found itself face to face with a series of problems which confronted democratic government: how to counteract the want of public spirit peculiar to democracies; how to check the general cowardice which characterizes them; how to transform fear into a sense of the moral responsibility which would bring the power of social intimidation to its maximum of elevation and, consequently, of efficiency; how to temper the despotism of public opinion, to protect minorities against majorities, and, in general, to strengthen the individual as against the sovereign multitude; how to promote the rise in democracy of an elite to guide it; how to prevent the ideal, which is its life-blood, from wasting

See above, Vol. II, p. 167.

away; how, in a word, to maintain and develop its living forces and not to allow the democratic regime to sink into an automatic contrivance without a soul and without a conscience, which would only fall an easier prey to selfish appetites and ambitions. All these problems party formalism has solved the wrong way, or it has increased the gradient of the incline down which these difficulties were pushing democracy. It has repressed the individual and lowered the standard of political society; it has deadened individual responsibility, put a premium on cowardice in public life, obstructed the free course of opinion, while leaving the individual defenceless against it, debased the ideal, degraded public morality, and reduced the citizen to a helpless instrument, which all those who exploit the public interest may manipulate as they please.

No doubt these results, which are the culminating point of the formalism instituted by party convention and kept up by a permanent organization, have not all manifested themselves in their complete logical fulness. Even in America the havoc wrought by the Caucus regime has not reached its furthest limits. If Tammany Hall is in the United States, it is not the United States. Besides, the American Republic had found itself placed in exceptional conditions, which absorbed the moral energy of the nation and made it acquiesce blindly in political formalism and endure all its consequences, including even political corruption, without murmuring. But these, so to speak, unique conditions have but encouraged the evil, which would have arisen without them, and which was due to more general and less fortuitous causes. Party regularity, systematically injected into a democratic society with an instrument as highly perfected and of such approved democratic make as the Caucus, constitutes of itself a virus strong enough to poison the blood of a community; the rapidity and intensity alone with which its effects will be manifested may vary according to the special environment and the more or less propitious conjunctures. The experience furnished by England, however short and however different in kind, confirms more than it contradicts this conclusion: when one returns to it after the study of America, one recognizes in the form of symptoms, of more or less remote, but still distinct indications, a number of pathological phenomena of the American practice, unfolding themselves with a remarkable logical sequence. This result was foreseen to a certain extent, although the cause was perhaps not very clearly realized. When the Caucus took up its abode in England, an American, on a visit to that country, said: "You are afraid of the cattle plague coming among you" (it was in 1878 when the rinderpest was threatening the country). "That is nothing. But if you find any one importing into England the organization of the 'caucus,' slaughter him at the very first outport. Bury him deep in quicklime in the biggest pit you can dig; for if the disease he brings once gets a foothold in your political life, it will make it rotten through and through, until it becomes an abomination unto all men." Commenting on these remarks, the *Times* recognized the justice of them, and added: "There is no magic in the English nature to keep us free from the evils to which politics in the United States has succumbed." The sponsors of the English Caucus, with Mr. Chamberlain at their head, thought they had successfully met these apprehensions when they pointed out that the class of professional politicians did not exist in England, and that the change of office-holders following on the change of the party in power was not the custom there as in America. They appear to have had no inkling that these phenomena of American public life were not so much the cause of the evil, as its effects or its contributories; that political corruption does not consist solely of material corruption; that one can pervert the mind of a nation and lead it to degradation without making money thereby. It is not even necessary to be a self-seeker and a busy-body, to achieve this; one may even be animated with the purest intentions. In this connection it is enough to recall the episode, related in its proper place, of the struggle between the Liberal Association of Newcastle-on-Tyne and Joseph Cowen. It furnished a singularly eloquent demonstration of the way in which party conformism acts on men's minds, eloquent not only from Cowen's personality, but still more from that of his opponents, who were led by an excellent citizen, whose ardour was equalled only by his disinterestedness. That, however, did not prevent this excellent citizen and his lieutenants from helping, in spite of themselves, but to the best of their ability, to push the young i *Times* of 31st July, 1873.

democracy of England down the incline which leads to the surrender of the conscience and the mind of the citizen; for, once more, "there is no magic in the English nature," no more than in any other.

It is the general characteristic of conformism to lead to the enslavement of the mind, and political formalism has not been alone in producing this result. Social convention and religious convention have also always tended in this direction, and, in degrees which differ according to the special environments, are still influencing societies. But it is political formalism that is the protagonist in public life at the present day. The democratic movement has, in a way, left it in possession of the field, by driving social and religious conformism from public life into the seclusion of private life; and it has rejuvenated, or modernized political formalism, by providing it with a new stock of conventions, in the front rank of which is party convention. Installed in the very heart of the democratic system, formalism by its action completely justifies the saying that there is nothing new under the sun. It is the never-ending war on the liberty of the human mind and on the dignity of the human being that it wages. It is only a new aspect which it presents of the old tyranny that fastens on humanity and that does but vary its forms, but reappear in different shapes, — tyranny of priests, tyranny of rulers, tyranny of nobles, tyranny of caste, of nationality, of race, etc. In vain is it supposed at certain moments to have been overthrown, the heads of the hydra are ever ready to spring up again. And there is no possibility, it would appear, of cutting off all of them at once: the general idea of liberty has infinite difficulty in gaining acceptance; it is of no avail to bring home to the universal conscience that there is but one justice, one equity, one humanity; as soon as a new application of the principle presents itself, the lesson is forgotten, and the demonstration has to be begun over again. It may be that this will be so for all time, and that, on pain of moral suicide, the time-honoured struggle for the defence of the liberty of the mind and the dignity of man will have to be unceasingly renewed.

This struggle, which is becoming more easy, from a certain point of view, owing to the spread of enlightenment, is, on the other hand, more difficult to carry on than formerly: the enemy of liberty has donned its armour, and its champions often find it hard to recognize him and to recognize one another, whereas in the old days, when he proclaimed as his sole motto *credo quia absurdum,* no confusion was possible, and all those who took their stand on reason and liberty ranged themselves against him to a man. Besides, the economy of the forces of the combatants has changed, as in real war, since the introduction of large masses of men on the battlefield. Formerly, when the public mind was embodied in a caste or a privileged class, one could set up against its corruption the virgin social strata, which constituted an untilled moral soil capable of yielding a more generous crop. The "people," denied access to social and political influence, were, to some extent, looked on as the Germans of Tacitus, rude, but full of native vigour, in contrast to the refined and effeminate Romans. This popular reserve is no longer intact; it is contaminated as well, owing to the democratic regime, which has taken it into the political machinery, and to the progress of that surface civilization which gives a wide currency to all conventions, from those of the toilette down to those of the moral sphere. True, the masses are not less accessible to reason than the so-called upper classes; but, pending their submission to it, they increase the active force of ignorance and of prejudice which liberty has to combat, and provide those who control that force with positions of all the greater strength that the popular adhesion appears to be conscious and almost deliberate.

Political formalism, which relies more than any other, in the modern State, on liberty and on the power of the masses, is, consequently, the most difficult to combat, and the most pregnant with dangers for democracy. Party formalism brings these difficulties and these dangers to their highest pitch because to the moral constraint wielded by party convention, under the mask of liberty, it adds the strength of organization. Organization gives substance to convention, brings out its latent power, intensifies it, and makes it produce the maximum of its effect. It introduces discipline, which thrusts back conscience and private judgment, stifles the spirit of criticism, independence of thought, and the citizen's spontaneity of action. Its fixed *cadre?* confine opinion as within a prison. The play of its machinery, which is necessarily uniform and rigid, reduces opinion to a dead level. It starts opinion in a factitious way, and perverts its movements or, what comes to the same thing, represents them in a false light. Blended with the party, the permanent organization from a means becomes an end. The integrity of its *cadres,* the apparent unity of the party, becomes the supreme preoccupation to which everything is, in the long run, subordinated, — principles, personal convictions, dictates of public morality, and even those of private morality. The upkeep of the complicated machinery of the organization, which demands daily care, compels the acceptance of the more or less interested services of the professionals; and as the success of the party depends on their "work," they acquire an important or even predominant position in it, which, sooner or later, delivers the party into their hands and enables them to exploit it in one way or another, and, under cover of it, to lay hand even on the public interest. The more perfect the organization at the disposal of party convention is, the better it accomplishes these results, that is to say, the more it demoralizes' the party and lowers public life. But, on the other hand, to maintain themselves, the parties have more and more need of a strong organization, which alone can make up for the nullity of the convention on which they rest. The upshot, then, is a vicious circle. What is the issue from it? Is nothing left, then, but to give up forming parties? By no means.

IX

The growing complexity of social life has rendered more necessary than ever the union of individual efforts. The development of political life, by calling on every citizen to share in the government, obliges him to come to an understanding with his fellow-citizens in order to discharge his civic duty. In a word, the realization by each man of his objects in society and in the State implies co-operation, and this is not possible without organization. But because organization is necessary to attain an object by means of common efforts, it does not follow that it justifies the moral servitude of man and the degradation of public life. *Der Oott der Eisen toaclisen liess der wollte keine Knechte.* Organization must serve, not to lower the individual, but to enhance his strength, not to absorb his personality, but to enable him to assert himself more effectively. The combinations of citizens for a political end, which are called "parties," are indispensable wherever the citizen has the right and the duty to speak his mind and to act; but party must cease to be an instrument of tyranny and corruption, and must be restored to its proper function.

According to Burke's well-known formula, a party is "a body of men united for promoting, by their joint endeavours, the national interest upon some particular principle in which they are all agreed." However elastic may be this definition given by the great champion of the party system, it assigns to party very precise limits: party is a special combination, its basis is agreement on a particular principle, and its end is the realization of ah object or objects of public interest. These iimits have been exceeded in practice. The struggles which had to be carried on in England for liberty before representative government became a reality, as well as the rivalries of the great families, gave rise to the formation of parties, and led them to make the possession of power their objective. The exercise of power by the victorious party was not intended only to gratify ambition and greed, but was necessary as the sole means of ensuring the triumph in practical life of the conception of public policy represented by that party. The antagonism which existed between the conceptions embodied by the parties affected the very foundations of political society, it was so profound, and the passions of the parties were, consequently, so violent and so irreconcilable, that even after the victory, in time of peace so to speak, the conquest had to be defended as in time of war; one or other of the two parties had to hold the citadel of the State in order to overawe the opponent and secure the untrammelled application of the fundamental principles of the public policy which it supported. But soon these principles were recognized by every one; they no longer were in danger from any party, for they had sunk into the national conscience and were protected by a new power which had arisen in the meantime and which all parties thenceforth humbly invoked — the power of opinion. While guaran The God who created iron dU not mean men to be slaves. — Arntjt. teeing to every citizen the enjoyment of liberty, the new constitutional order placed at his disposal the means of pursuing political aims and of attaining them without having to seize on power for this purpose: it was enough to appeal to public opinion and to win it over to his cause.

However, the parties which had tasted power had little notion of giving it up, and by a tacit agreement they wielded it alternately, according to the changing fortunes of their contests. The confusion, at first unavoidable, between party conceived as a combination of free citizens pursuing a political object, and party as a troop storming the heights of power in order to divide the spoils, was perpetuated. "Party government" became a regular institution. Its legitimacy and its necessity were accepted as a political dogma owing to the very human tendency to cloak selfish aspirations under considerations of the general interest, and to that common philosophy which always professed, even before Hegel, that everything which is real is rational. On the Continent, where English institutions and the real springs of the regime of liberty enjoyed by the English have never been clearly understood, people hastened, on the introduction of the representative system, to borrow from England the mould in which an accident had cast liberty, and it was adopted as the very essence of free institutions. The mistake was all the more natural that in almost every continental country the struggles for liberty were far from being at an end, and that things were still in that transitional phase when the old regime had fallen without the new one having taken firm root, and when a fresh attack from the conquered reactionary forces was still to be apprehended. But in countries such as England or the United States, where the democratic regime is established beyond dispute, and liberty occupies an unassailable position, the tenure of power by a party which entrenches itself in it as in a fortress has become an anachronism, and the pretended necessity of this domination of the party, in order to make the political principles of the majority prevail in the government, is no longer aught but a pure convention, not to say an imposition. That there are still countries in which democratic institutions are as yet imperfectly consolidated, are even only a make-believe, and where, consequently, the seizure of power is the condition of liberty, is undeniable. But it is not on these countries, which have still to serve their apprenticeship in democracy, that the methods of democratic government should be modelled; the transitional must not be taken as a pattern for the definitive. In a country which has already achieved liberty the formula attributed to Gambetta, "One can only govern with one's own party," is as meaningless as would be the formula, "One can only go to law before one's own judges." Moreover, did not Gambetta himself, after the definitive triumph of the Republic, and once he had come into power, think it right and expedient to depart from this rule and to bestow the most important posts in the foreign office and war office on political opponents? His party, bred in the narrow school of the formula, could not forgive him the broadmindedness with which he tried to emancipate himself therefrom; they punished him for it by driving him from power.

How, in fact, will it be possible henceforth to justify the maxim which lays down that "one can only govern with one's party?" The task of government comprises two functions — to make laws and to execute them. The enforcement of the laws lies, by its very nature, outside all divergence of political principles; there cannot be several conceptions or several ways of executing the laws under a regime which is not one of mere arbitrariness. Wherever liberty reigns, the advent of a party to power, whatever it may be, cannot add to or subtract from the liberties of the citizens or the security of their persons and their property. In England, for instance, when the Tories are at the helm, are liberty of the press, freedom of conscience, the right of meeting and of association, in any degree less than under a Liberal Ministry? Does the Habeas Corpus Act cease to be respected? A Liberal government which takes the place of a Tory government has neither chains to break nor bonds to loose. In the United States, a citizen is as much his own master under a Republican as under a Democratic administration. Even in the only province where the executive is at liberty to impart a special direction to its activity, in that of foreign policy, governments, to whatever party they belong, find themselves obliged, by the force of things, to follow the same line of conduct. Thus in England, Tory and Liberal Ministries scarcely differ in their foreign policy. Even in France, under the third Republic, in which Ministries succeed each other with kaleidoscopic rapidity, foreign policy does not vary. There does not appear, therefore, to be any reason why the exercise of the executive power should belong to one party more than to another. It demands only honest and capable administrators. To keep them in the path of duty there is henceforth an authority far more powerful than that of a dominant party — opinion, armed with the irresistible weapon of publicity, in the press, on the platform, in parliament. And if there is at the present day anything which screens the representatives of the executive from the responsibility to which the fierce light of publicity exposes them, it is too often the dominant party, of which these representatives are, under the existing system, the liegemen rather than servants of the whole nation.

If, however, the executive function of government cannot be a source of dissension to the citizens, it is not so with the discharge of its legislative function. The divergences which tend to split the community into different camps are natural, necessary, and beneficial here. The more the regime of liberty is firmly established in a country, the more do these divergences arise spontaneously, and the more it is necessary, in order to give them a solution, that the citizens should form combinations and groups, and do battle with all the weapons which liberty places at their disposal. But why should the stake of these contests be power? Power can only be obtained by getting a majority; but if one has the majority on one's side, it is sufficient to carry the desired reform or to prevent that which is dreaded. Thanks to the regime of popular sovereignty, it is easy to bring about the most sweeping changes in the legal sphere without any need for anxiety about the attitude of the executive power: whether it will or no, it is bound to submit; whereas in non-popular regimes one must step over the bodies of the holders of power and take their place in order to obtain a change in the established order. If, for instance, in a country which lives under the economic regime of free trade, the protectionists wish to put an end to it, they have but to start an active propaganda in the country for the formation of a protectionist party, and as soon as they have obtained a majority in tne parliament, the latter will pass as high a customs tariff as it likes. The representatives of the executive, even if they are all free-traders to a man, will evidently not refuse to order the collection of or to collect the new customs duties. And if the protectionist party was bent, nevertheless, on seizing power, this would evidently be for an object other than the triumph of protectionist ideas, that triumph being already assured. It would be seeking power for the sake of power itself only. Once in possession of it, its main preoccupation would be to keep itself there; and it could succeed in this only by bringing in its train all the evils engendered, as we have seen, by the present party system.

That these evils necessarily spring from the exercise of power proposed as the end and aim of party, is capable of mathematical proof, so to speak. To win or hold power, the party is obliged to provide itself with a permanent organization. This cannot be formed and kept up without the help of professionals. As the latter have to be rewarded in some mode or other, the party is induced to lay hand for this purpose on public offices, of which it makes an electoral coin, and to traffic in the influence procured by power in yet other ways, from the apparently harmless bestowal of honorary titles down to the concession of public works, of contracts, of "franchises "; and extending even to the stay of criminal proceedings, to the remission of fines and penalties, to the passing of laws for the benefit of private interests. To prevent the great mass of adherents on whom rests the power of the party from escaping it, their minds and their wills must be inveigled by every kind of device. As the parties are no longer cemented by principles and ideas, once the question or questions which had divided them are settled, they have recourse to mechanical cohesion: they unite their contingents in a superstitious respect for pure forms, in a fetish-like worship of the "party," inculcate a loyalty to its name and style, and thus establish a moral mortmain over men's minds. The right of private judgment and the independence of the conscience are a perpetual menace to their ascendency, just as under the regime of a despot, and the parties try to stifle them as a despot would — they only adopt other means. They stereotype opinion in creeds which enforce on it a rigid discipline, they conceal the divergences of views that arise by composite programmes in which the most varied problems are jumbled together, which promise everything to everybody, which reconcile contradiction by rhetorical artifices, masterpieces of shuffling and humbug. Those electors who are in agreement with the party on a single point of its programme only are obliged, in order to get that point carried, to vote for all the rest, in spite of their convictions. The national verdict is perverted, the aim of representative government is missed; but the party cannot capture its positions or keep them otherwise. To the moral tyranny of political prejudice, to subterfuge, to deception, it is also obliged too often, not to say always, to add the weapon of corruption. Success is obtainable on no other terms. And as it is the supreme end, it justifies everything, even in the eyes of honest people. In order not to jeopardize the party, they consent to throw over received morality, agree to all kinds of discreditable transactions, and accept co-operators and associates of every description. Under the pressure of the pretended interests of the party, the maxim *omnia serviliter pro dominatione* obtains an application and an extension which would have disconcerted Tacitus himself. The moral and material corruption which the party leaves behind it in its pursuit of power penetrates into the furthest recesses of public life: as the domination of the party is never complete so long as it does not occupy all the strongholds of the electoral sphere, it introduces politics everywhere with the latter's criterion of "regularity " that takes precedence of all other qualifications, moral and intellectual; it invades local public life, strips it of its character, infects it with its own evil ways. Even the solution of the vital problems of the nation is subordinated by the parties to the possession of power; they play heads and tails with these problems, they put forward some and thrust back others according as they seem likely to conciliate or estrange the majority of the day. While assuming various forms and aspects according to the different environments and conjunctures, this demoralizing action is the inevitable penalty for the exercise of power by a party and for the permanent existence of the party — these two concomitant and almost convertible causes. As soon as a party, were it created for the noblest object, perpetuates itself, it tends inevitably towards power, and as soon as it makes that VOL. ii—2u its end, its master passion is to maintain itself against all opposition, with no scruple as to the means. It is enough to recall the career of the Republican party which was founded by the Lincolns to combat slaveholding, and which, from having perpetuated itself after it had solved the problem of slavery, became a hotbed of corruption. The demoralizing action of a permanent party is spread and accentuated in proportion as it becomes destitute of principles, and as the line of demarcation which separates it from the rival parties grows fainter. And the higher the penalty that has to be paid, the more useless does it become if we admit, as I have just shown, that party government is not, or is no longer, necessary to realize the objects of a free government.

X

This being so, is not the solution demanded by the problem of parties an obvious one? Does it not consist in discarding the use of permanent parties with power as their end, and in restoring and reserving to party its essential character of a combination of citizens formed specially for a particular political issue? This solution would strip party of its object, which had only a temporary and accidental political value, and would reinstate it in the function which is its perpetual *raison d'etre.* Party as a general contractor for the numerous and varied problems present and to come, awaiting solution, would give place to special organizations, limited to particular objects. It would cease to be a medley of groups and individuals united by a fictitious agreement, and would constitute an association, the homogeneity of which would be ensured by its single aim. Party holding its members, once they have joined it, in a vice-like grasp would give place to combinations forming and re-forming spontaneously, according to the changing problems of life and the play of opinion brought about thereby. Citizens who part company on one question would join forces on another.

The change in methods of political action which would be effected on this basis would entirely remodel the working of democratic government. It would more or less profoundly affect the solution of most of the problems which we have seen raised by the collapse of the old regime and by the experience that has been gained of democracy, and it would open new horizons to political speculation itself.

The new method will begin by striking at the first conditions of the corruption and the tyranny engendered by the present party regime. It will inevitably shake their material foundation, which is the permanence of organization, and their moral foundation, which is the conformism of the adherents. The temporary and special character of the parties created on the new method will not permit of the enrolment and maintenance of those standing armies with whose help power was won and exploited. On the other hand, as the new parties will be only organizations limited to a particular issue and to the period of time necessary to settle it, party "regularity" will no longer have an object: a permanent homage cannot be paid to what is transitory. Organized *ad hoc,* party will no longer be able to produce by way of title a sort of apostolic succession or to hang out an old sign which has the power of attracting customers. No longer able to rely on a sentimental devotion to its name and style, it will have, in spite of itself, so to speak, to rest on the adhesion of minds and consciences to something well defined, to a clearly specified cause, the triumph of which is sought in political life and of which it will constitute itself the champion. Thus enlisted in the exclusive service of that cause, party organization will revert to its function of means and will cease to be an end; formerly a tyrannical master, it will have to become a docile servant.

By giving the citizen this new basis of action, the new method will allow, and will even compel him to take a less passive part in the government, to discharge his civic duties in a more conscious way. Instead of giving a wholesale and anticipatory adhesion to a single organization and to the direction which it will impart to all the political problems that may arise, the citizen will be enabled and obliged to make up his mind on each of the great questions that will divide public opinion. By joining one of the parties which will be formed on this occasion, he will know exactly what he wants, what is the issue, to what he gives his adhesion, where he is going, and how far he will go. The aim of the association being circumscribed, he will be able to follow the efforts made to realize it; his attention, no longer distracted by the multiplicity of objects with which a party burdens itself under the present system, will be concentrated, and will not weary so quickly. Again, the limited task of this association will not allow the citizen to go to sleep, so to speak, on the adhesion which he has given it. New problems will appeal to him, new parties will be formed to solve them, and he will have to decide what attitude he should take up with regard to them. He will be forced to examine his conscience oftener than he does now. He has associated himself, for instance, with a party which aims at the separation of Church and State; but thereupon a new problem rises on the political horizon, the protection by customs duties of agriculture or of the national industries, or, again, the regulation of labour, in the form of the "eight hours' question" or in some other shape. The elector will no longer be able, in this new conjuncture, to "follow his party" automatically; the party formed for the separation of Church and State, even if it is not yet dissolved, would be unable to give him a lead, for its members, united on the question of a State Church, hold opposite views on the "eight hours' question." The elector will therefore be obliged to form an opinion, or a tentative opinion, in order to know what party he shall join this time, that which is opposed to all regulation of labour or that which supports it. The appeal addressed to the elector by the respective organizations on behalf of the cause which they represent will be heard far more effectively than under the present regime: confronted with a single well-defined question, the elector will be able to understand what is said to him, whereas now he is not. Those who have conducted election campaigns among the masses are unanimous on this point, they all agree that it is impossible to make the electors understand more than one question at a time, but that, on the other hand, if one deals with a single problem and takes trouble — one must take a great deal — to explain it well, one can drive it into the popular mind; the slums of New York and of Chicago themselves have furnished decisive experiences in this respect. Thus the citizen who nowadays is encouraged, and often even compelled, to surrender his judgment, will, on the contrary, be stimulated to exercise it; the energy of his will and the activity of his mind, instead of being lulled to rest, will be kept awake. Indolence of mind being shaken off, that of conscience will be so too, for the one is connected with the other; the man who seldom exerts his mind loses the habit of consulting his conscience. A more alert intelligence and conscience will yield a stronger sense of individual responsibility.

This sense will be all the more stimulated that the new method will enhance the moral liberty of the citizen to an unrivalled extent, while strengthening the discipline without which no common action demanding the co-operation of the many is possible. The adhesion of the citizen to a single issue organization will naturally be undivided and unreserved; limited to a particular cause, it will be more intense; his gaze fixed on the one object in view, the adherent will follow the leader without looking to the right or to the left. The subordination of the *ego,* which is the end of discipline and the basis of all association, will be fully exhibited here, and yet it will be for the citizen a sacrifice as easy as it will be little degrading. The absolute subordination of the *ego* is attainable only by an angel or an animal, to borrow the celebrated antithesis of Pascal. The new political method will enable the citizen to subordinate his *ego* as a man. It will never insist on the total deposit of his personality in the common stock, it will require of him partial contributions only, sometimes on one occasion, sometimes on another, leaving him always his own master for all that does not concern the conjuncture in question. Sacrifice demanded by small instalments, so to speak, will appear trifling to the citizen, and he will submit to it with devotion as well as discernment. Discipline will be as little irksome as degrading to him; strictly limited in its application to a particular occasion, it will no longer be able to enslave the individual conscience and judgment.

On the contrary, the limited nature of the pledges given by the citizen will keep alive his independence of mind like a fire which it will not let die out. With whatever combination he connects himself, he will always be able to differ from his associates on all points other than those which have brought them together. However extensive the common ground on which they have taken their stand, there will remain for each man a still vaster area over which his mind can range with all the more freedom that this area will never have fixed limits. The limits will recede continually in proportion as the problems and the persons change: connected in regard to one problem with certain persons, the citizen will shake off this connection as soon as another problem is involved; and this other problem will give him fresh associates, who, in their turn, will lose all hold over him as soon as they have another object in view, and so on *ad infinitum.* In this way there will be provided for the liberty of the individual mind innumerable outlets, which will afford it inviolable refuges where it may reflect, may regain possession of itself, before choosing the route which it will take. In a word, as he will never wholly surrender himself, the citizen in devoting himself will always feel his own master, and will always be able to realize his liberty as a free man. Under the system of permanent parties he can do so only as a rebellious slave, and even then he recovers his liberty just for a moment; if he shakes off the servitude of one party, it is to accept the yoke of another, for in the latter as well as in the former he falls immediately, as soon as he enters it, into the bondage of "regularity." The new method puts an end to this state of moral mortmain, it liberates the mind and the conscience.

Protected from the moral constraint wielded over him by the tradition of "party," freed from the nightmare of "regularity" which oppressed his imagination, the citizen whom we have seen cringing to numbers, timorous and cowardly, will be able to hold up his head and regain confidence in himself. He will not cease to fear the multitude; a sociable being, he will be always haunted by this fear, but the multitude will appear less terrifying to him when its forces, instead of being concentrated in the universal and perpetual groove of permanent party, will be divided among several special and temporary organizations. The definite nature of these will be self-evident to the citizen, and he will find in this demonstration continually presented to his mind a protection against his own weakness of character. Respect for the world's opinion will have less hold over him, when he knows that he will not always have to co-operate with the same persons, that in a new conjuncture he may very well be out of sight and reach of many of them. The "majority" will no longer inspire him with a mystic fear when, ceasing to be embodied in a permanent organization and to represent the abiding force of unlimited numbers, it will appear in its adventitious character, when it will be seen to change with the problems, when elements which constitute the nucleus of the majority in one case will be seen to be in a minority in another. In short, the individual will be less inclined to bow before the multitude with a fatalistic resignation, to surrender his will and his dignity, and will be more stimulated to take cognizance of himself and to walk in public life with a firmer step.

XI

The intimidatory power of opinion which democracy has let loose will thus find limits marked out for it by the new method of political action which the principle of democracy could not assign to it. This method will ensure the citizen a greater moral autonomy, and by that means will contribute to the solution of one of the fundamental problems of democratic government — the decentralization of the power of opinion. The problem of decentralization has hitherto been considered only in relation to the State, from the standpoint of the legal power. A favourite theme of political discussion, brought into vogue by the Liberal school, decentralization has become in the long run a subject for academical disquisitions. While lances were being broken in its honour, the legal power was enveloped, as it were, by a new power, that of opinion, and the exercise of the former was subordinated to the latter. Henceforth it was the power of opinion which imparted the direction, which gave the legal forms their substance, and, consequently, its structure was of no less moment than the organization of the constituted powers. Now, the power of opinion on making its appearance provided itself with highly centralized organs — the press and the permanent parties. The dangers which were observed in the centralization of the State reappeared in another form, in cases even where they were supposed to have been averted by the establishment of a local self-government or of a federative organization into the bargain. The development of the provincial press was a great step towards liberation from the tyranny wielded from the centre; but it could only effect decentralization to a slight extent, because the permanent parties continued to exist and to give the cue to the provincial press as well as to that of the capital. In the United States even, where the clearing of a vast continent has brought about, with the aid of the telegraph, the creation of a powerful local press unparalleled in the world, the decentralization of the press is purely nominal, so far as the political tendency is concerned. The great majority of the newspapers, from Maine to Florida, from the Atlantic to the Pacific, are under the sway of one or other of the two great permanent parties, whose word of command is transmitted all along the line. The reader will remember how the headquarters of the American parties manage, by means of the "patent inside" practice, to secure the publication of the articles they want, even in the prints of the most out-ofthe-way spots. The new method of political action which I advocate will realize the desired decentralization. It will break up the centralizing mould of organized opinion, and will ensure the latter, in the form of single issue associations, manifold centres from which opinion will be projected in its various aspects. And in doing this, it will not only have struck at the centralizing forms, but it will have brought decentralization even into the political preoccupations that fill the life of a community by giving each its autonomy and letting it pursue its ends with its own means. While it will prevent the congestion of opinion, the new method will allow it to reap the full benefit of the useful side of centralized action, namely, the unity of control which makes the efforts converge towards the common object.

The new method, by establishing the principle of autonomy in the government of opinion, will not only have the effect of tempering the despotism of opinion, of decentralizing its power, but it will also enable opinions to come forward with more freedom and to assert themselves with more sincerity. Instead of being jumbled together in an ill-assorted compound and kept mechanically in the fixed grooves of permanent parties, they will be able to combine and recombine at will, according to their natural affinities, in homogeneous categories. A freetrader opposed to the unlimited coinage of silver will no longer be forced to join the protectionist party because the latter has thought fit to declare against free coinage. An adherent of local veto for the drink traffic will no longer find himself obliged to vote for Irish Home Rule, because the party which supports Home Rule has agreed to take up local veto as well. The questions on which the electors will have to express their opinion being no longer mixed up, everybody will be able to express his opinion frankly and unambiguously. Adherents and opponents of the specified causes on which the electoral battles will be fought will be able to muster separately and without confusion; the taking of the popular vote will no longer be a conjuring trick; the will of the majority will be elicited in a clear and unmistakable manner; it will no longer be necessary to decipher the electoral verdict as if it were a charade or a riddle, its purport will be exactly known. It will no longer be possible, after having raised a McKinley to the presidency in order to stop the Silverites, to take advantage of his championship of protectionism to assert that the country has given a fresh sanction to this policy by recording its votes for this personage, and to enact a still more prohibitive tariff, a Dingley tariff. The result of the national deliberations will be all the more sincere that the questions at issue will not only be raised in a distinct manner, but may always be examined for their own sake and not from the standpoint of the interests of the "party," of the consequences that this or that solution may have for its welfare, for the prestige of its firm, for its future, and I know not what besides.

Stripped of extraneous considerations and restored to their intrinsic importance, political problems will be submitted to and developed before public opinion in a more natural, more spontaneous way, so to speak, than under the present regime, in which they are taken up or dropped by a party according as they can help or impede it in its race for power. Henceforth they will engross opinion to the extent that men's minds, well or ill informed, will be engrossed by them, neither more nor less. It will no longer be possible to hustle public opinion as xinder the system of permanent parties, where we see the party organizers modify their policy as the manager of a theatre changes his playbill, introduce at a moment's notice new items into their programmes, and thrust them on their followers by the force of party discipline, without giving them time to grasp the first elements of the problem thus suddenly raised. Deprived of the factitious support of the title of a permanent party, and coming before public opinion in its own name, every problem will necessarily have to appeal to it, to canvass it at more or less length, and therefore to advantage, whether the solution be a positive or a negative one. This means that the methods of political propaganda will change. There will be less inducement to resort to those sensational practices which aim at the emotions and the senses, because they will be of less use. Confronted by a particular question, which has to be explained to the multitude, and which in no way involves the fate of a party, politicians will have more need to convert men's minds than to take them by storm in the hurly-burly of the "Chinese business," which "is styled in polite language political education," to use the expression of a dignitary of the American Caucus. The political education of the masses in the true sense of the word will become possible. At present it is a material impossibility, both in point of time and of space. When, from considerations of party tactics, a question is sprung upon the public in view of the next election, there is no time left to convince the electors, even if one wished to do so; all that can be done is to act on their imagination, to impress it by noisy proceedings, in order to carry votes. When the question does not arise unexpectedly, when it is not the want of time that is prohibitive, then the crowded state of the composite programme of which it forms part is an obstacle. A permanent party which has set up as general contractor for the political problems awaiting solution is always obliged to deal with several of them at the same time. Now, as John Bright said in a phrase that has passed into a proverb, "You cannot get twenty wagons at once through Temple Bar. " We have seen the very party which professes, and with sincerity, the greatest zeal for political See above, Vol. II,

p. 366.
This is what was said to me in so many words, at the beginning of the presidential campaign of 18% in the United States, by a member of the National Republican Committee, who was directing the contest in one of the largest States of the Union, classed among the "doubtful " ones: "The silver question will be put on a sentimental basis; the maintenance of the gold standard will be advocated in the name of the national honour; an appeal will be made to popular feeling; there is no time to conduct an educational campaign to persuade people that free coinage is a fallacy." education, the English Liberal party, grappling with this difficulty. We have seen that it is as impossible for it to enlighten the masses on all questions at once as to select one of them for this purpose and sacrifice all the rest to it. Being unable to make a serious impression on the minds of those whom it wishes to carry along with it, the Liberal Organization is reduced to the resource of "raising enthusiasm."
With the system of temporary single issue organizations all these difficulties disappear. A party will be able, and bound, to devote itself wholly to making converts to the cause which it is promoting; there will be nothing left for it but to turn propagandist; every inch of ground won by it will be so only through the efforts made to win men's minds. If there are several causes contending for the favour of public opinion, the political education will be carried on with all the more fulness and energy; each of the rival organizations which will represent the various causes will be obliged to make a direct appeal to every intelligence. Political society will be transformed into a vast school, and democratic government will become really a government of discussion. This teaching and this discussion, however numerous the rival organizations conducting them may be, will be free from all confusion; for no organization will ever teach more than one thing at a time, and the subjects taught will be quite optional, once the organization of parties is freed from that method of "cramming" which characterizes the organization of studies in so many educational systems. Appealed to by various causes, the elector will bestow his attention on that which appears to him, rightly or wrongly, as the most important or the most urgent, and will give his vote to the standard-bearer of that cause. The cause which musters the most combatants for and against it, will naturally be first in the electoral steeple-chase. The movements which obtain but few adherents will be last, with liberty to start afresh at the next race in greater strength, if they succeed in making converts. No opinion will be able to thrust itself on the community if it has not conquered the majority of the electorate; but no opinion, no movement, will find itself excluded at the outset, as in the present day, because it does not fit in with the views or the calculations of the existing parties, or because it appears to be premature. Every political movement, left free, by the new method, to expand like a plant in the sun, will be able to ripen if it has vital force. On the other hand, if it does not arrive at maturity, it will have far more difficulty in asserting itself under the new method, which subjects all opinions to a natural probation unknown to the present system.

The restitution of their autonomy to political problems, while thus contributing to liberate opinion, will not fail to improve those who are supposed to represent it in the State, the politicians, and to bring about generally a marked change in the relations of the electors with their representatives, of the rulers and the ruled. Under the present system of permanent parties burdened with omnibus programmes, a candidate or a member is, in the very great majority of cases, necessarily a humbug. It is to him that John Bright's sally in the debate on the "minorities clause" applies, he it is "who produces like a conjurer port, champagne, milk, and water out of the same bottle." Not only has he to be, in political matters, a sort of doctor *de omni re scibili et quibuadam aliis,* to possess a ready-made solution for all possible problems, but he has to pledge himself to solve these problems, however varied and numerous they may be, at the earliest date. He has to make promises right and left, and as it is impossible for him to keep them, he becomes a professional liar, although at bottom he is perhaps not more dishonest than other men. "Necessity which has no law" impels him, in spite of himself, to disregard truth, sincerity, uprightness. This will be always the case as long as the object is to muster under a common standard and for all time the greatest possible number of electors, without taking into consideration their divergences on many questions; under this system the candidate will always be obliged to hedge continually, to discourage nobody, and to carry on a regular flirtation with every one, with whoever is likely to join the "party. " But once the new method will have introduced the grouping of the electors according to the problems of the day, the candidate or the member, instead of playing the part of Moliere's Don Juan, will be able and obliged to choose and honourably espouse the cause which he feels capable of defending. He will, of course, be able to i
See above, Vol. I, p. 111.
give his adhesion to more than one political movement, to offer himself as champion to several organizations, and to ask for the votes of their adherents. But he will have an obvious interest in not overloading himself with causes to defend, for the more he takes a special line, the more marked will be the confidence with which he will inspire the electors concerned and the greater will be their readiness to vote for him. As a rule, he will be likely to lose more votes than he will gain by dividing himself among several causes, if they are not more or less akin. He will do better to make his choice. If he is a man of convictions, he will hoist the standard of the cause which he has most at heart; if he aims only at success, he will have to exert his powers of perception, to discern the winning

cause, and plump for it. Thus he will be always led to take up a distinct and straightforward attitude, even if he is actuated by interested motives.

Elected as champion of a cause or of certain specified causes, the member will find himself in closer relations with his constituents and under a far more effective responsibility toward them. The electors, who, thanks to the new method, will be able to assert their individuality better and will be less easily duped, will inspire the politicians with a more wholesome fear. As the mandate will be more limited than at present, it will be easier for the electors to watch the way in which it is discharged. The member will no longer be able to hide behind the name and style of the party; when he is called to account, he will no longer be able to invite his fellow-citizens to ascend the Capitol in order to render thanks to the gods for victories formerly won by the party. It is by his own merits and shortcomings alone that he will be judged.

When the criterion of personal merit will thus have been restored to the front rank in place of the conventional criterion of party, men of sterling worth will have a better chance of success; they will no longer be necessarily ousted by the politicians who appeal to party orthodoxy. Besides, the multiplicity of the political organizations and their special character will favour the rise of this elite. The more the sphere of action is restricted or the end in view circumscribed, the closer becomes the contact of the men who are co-operating for it and the easier is it for them to know and appreciate one another; superior men thus come to the front and command a following with more facility. This facility will increase with the number of the special parties, which will be so many centres where the leaders will be formed and whence they will shed their influence over the community. The variety of these organizations will bring about in the general body of leaders produced by them a variety of temperaments and a freedom of mind far greater than can be turned out by the single mould of permanent party. In short, a great step will be taken toward the solution of that grave problem of the leadership which arises in democracy.

This does not mean that the professional politician will be eliminated and that the occupation of the wirepuller will be gone, but they will never play in the temporary parties the same role that they play in the permanent parties. Every organization stands in need of a machinery, and consequently of machinists; this applies especially to organizations used for setting in motion large masses of men, as is the case under democratic government. It will not be possible then to dispense with the services of "organizers" of various degrees. But these auxiliaries will never be able to become the masters, for they will no longer be the depositaries of the creed of the party, the high priests of its cult: no more fetish-worship, no more priests. Will the single issue parties be composed exclusively of convinced adherents, bent solely on the triumph of the cause? Certainly not; there is no public combination without its parasites. There will therefore be plenty of people who will make the parties a simple stepping-stone for their political career, or who will exploit them in another way, but their manoeuvres will be much less dangerous, because they will be unable to wear the cloak of party piety, and will no longer have that convenient base of operations at present afforded by the permanent groove of party. They will always have to contend with the state of affairs created by the solution of continuity of the single issue parties. The great private interests, the mercantile interests, may also be able to exploit a special party, they will even be in a position to facilitate the organization of them on the method of Jay Gould, who "made" legislatures with his own money; but success will be far less certain, and for the same reason: they will not be able to use the title of a permanent party as a mark. Manufacturers may found a protectionist party, but they will no longer be able to invoke the *manes* of Abraham Lincoln and the glory of the Republican party to get a prohibitive tariff passed for themselves; they will have to fight under their own colours.

The new method will thus let in more light everywhere and will enforce more straightforwardness, more sincerity; it will deprive some of the pretext for disregarding these qualities, from others it will raise the mask which conceals their passions or their greed, whether it be the mask of liberty worn by the moral coercion of "regularity," the mask of right with which party tyranny disguises itself, or the mask of the general interest used by the mercenaries and the exploiters of the name and style of parties. Honest citizens will no longer have to play into the hands of these men out of political piety; anxiety about the maintenance of the party once eliminated, one will no longer have to make the sacrifices which were made for it and to consent to acts which would be looked on as reprehensible in private life. The conventional morality of politics will lose one of its essential aliments. In short, the new method will help to raise the moral standard of the electors as well as of the people's representatives, of the ruled as well as of the rulers, by removing from each the opportunity for temptation; while, on the other hand, it will contribute to this result by stimulating their sense of responsibility; that is to say, it will apply the two best means that exist for the improvement of mankind.

XII

The method of temporary parties for a single issue thus offers a beginning of a solution, or one of the means for the solution, of most of the political problems which we have seen arise in democracy. This virtue of the new method lies in a simple but great fact: the method is founded on the vital principle of the order of things sprung from the democratic revolution, on the principle of *union instead of unity.* The old order one and indivisible has passed away with the society which served it as a basis. And it is as impossible to re-establish the former as to revive the latter. We have witnessed, especially in England, the failure of all the attempts made to reconstitute the unity of society: they were pursuing a chimera. Neither in the religious sphere, nor in social relations, nor in the State, is unity any longer possible since the advent of the era of liberty, in which ideas and interests are bent on asserting themselves in all their variety. The problem raised by the democratic counter-revolution — " How are the elements of the nation to be again blended together " — is meaningless, for it is only homogeneous bodies that can be blended together. Divergent social elements can be kept in unity by tyranny only, whether it be the tyranny armed with the sword, or the moral tyranny which began with theocracy and has continued in the form of social conventions. As soon as the absolute authority of the sword or of tradition declines, the harmony of the elements which constitute society can be restored only by the agreement of wills — by union. But as in emancipated society the conflicting aspirations and interests are of an infinite complexity and multiplicity, this harmony cannot be a sort of universal and pre-existing harmony founded on an immutable basis. If even such a harmony were possible, how could the wills assent to it without destroying themselves; how can self-conscious wills at a given moment determine to forego volition? An agreement of wills, therefore, cannot be effected once for all and about everything, but it must be continually differentiated and renewed according to the changing relations of facts and ideas. Just as the organic world is kept in equilibrium and constantly renewed by the ceaseless transmutation of matter, so the harmony of the elements and the forces of which society is composed is to be ensured by the union of wills displaying itself in varied and successive combinations.

The new social synthesis required by emancipated society lies there, in this free union of wills. If it has not been found, the reason is that its seekers looked towards the past, haunted by the idea of unity conceived in a fashion that recalls Caligula. And, after all, the dream of the imperial madman was a less extravagant one: he wanted humanity to have a single head in order to make it die more easily; whereas the modern advocates of unity feel the same wish in order to See above, Vol. I, p. 63.

make it live more easily. The unity which it is sought to reconstruct will never be aught but a mechanical one; vital cohesion will always be wanting to it. That cohesion cannot be supplied by sentiment nor replaced by organization. There is henceforth no possibility of a "political creed" which "can be a permanent source of inspiration," whether it be stamped with the hallmark of reactionary tradition or proceed from a revolutionary mysticism. The most highly centralized organization, whether it be cast in the Caesarean or in the Jacobin mould, will furnish but a vain shadow of unity. In the new society, which is no longer cemented by sentiment and habit, social cohesion, to be effective, must spring mainly from a consciousness of the common interests that are evolved from the variety of social aspirations, and from a consciousness of the rights and of the duties towards the commonwealth accruing therefrom to each of its members. This twofold consciousness produces the union of wills and develops it, and thus provides the new social synthesis with its motor. The conditions favourable to its working are ensured it by that very democratic regime which had created the want of a new synthesis. For democracy has come into this world both to destroy and to fulfil. In breaking up the old structure, it pulled down the barriers which divided the citizens into classes and closed groups; it demolished the strongholds from which a ruling class lorded it over the common herd that grovelled below; the henceforth levelled ground was *ipso facto* to become ground on which the members of the community could meet and draw near one another. As they all found themselves placed on a footing of equality there, they were able — which was impossible for them before — to get into touch, to learn to know one another, and to come to an understanding on what united them in the midst of what separated them. Thus democracy, far from reducing society to atoms, from "setting class against class," as the champions of the counter-revolution maintained, inclined divergent social interests to come to an understanding, and at the same time pointed out to them, in a way, the most appropriate mode of action for this purpose: by doing away with the fixed limits of classes, by razing the Capitol as well as the Aventine, it made those struggles obsolete which, like civil 1 See above, Vol. I, p. 63.

Vol. II — 2 x wars, divided society into two camps; it invited antagonists, instead of clinging to the inflexibility of a complete political or social system, to lessen the divergences, by splitting them up, so to speak, and adjusting them to the practical needs and possibilities of the moment. Recourse to brute force being once eliminated, this was the only feasible plan for the solution of the problems of society, and especially of those which present the gravest and most complex aspect, for it is as impossible for a social order to be preserved without change as to be radically transformed at a single stroke; the life of societies is nothing but a series of partial and provisional compromises.

The theoretical principles of modern government have precisely the same basis. The doctrines of the sovereignty of the people, of the social contract, of the general will, these much criticised and decried theories supply the modern State with an impregnable foundation if it is cemented by the principle of union substituted for unity. Once divine right, once the right of an individual or of a class to exercise sovereign power, is no longer admitted, that power cannot reside elsewhere than in the nation at large, and cannot be wielded by any will other than the general will. The assent of the citizens being consequently necessary to give the laws their force, the relations of the State with the citizens, and of the members of the State among one another, are found to rest on a basis identical with that which in law goes by the name of contract. Has not one of the severest critics of democracy, Sir Henry Sumner Maine, himself admitted that contract is the culmination of modern civilization in social relations? The men of the eighteenth century were therefore perfectly justified in proclaiming their principles, they only made the mistake of conceiving the realization of them in political life under the metaphysical form of unity; they had conceived the individual in his abstract isolation (as I have shown in the first chapters of this book), and they viewed society in the same way. This mistake was their undoing: it vitiated all the conclusions which they drew from their principles.

Rousseau's "general will," in which resides the sovereignty of the people, is the constant will of a "moral being," with an existence of its own outside and above the particular wills, and invested with an absolute power, one and indivisible. Now, how can it be constant, single, always identical with itself, when it is — as Rousseau himself points out rather clumsily, in confused mathematical phraseology — but a resultant of the particular wills, wills essentially liable to vary? One thing or the other: either it is not a resultant of these wills, or it is not necessarily identical with itself; but in either case it ceases to be "general," and then the sovereignty of the people is left in the air. That is to say, that the unity of the "general will" comes to nothing even in pure logic. In practice, the result is just the same. For the "general will" to be able to constitute itself, for it to live, the particular wills must be immolated to it; since if a single one of them subsists, and asserts itself for a single moment, the general will is no longer intact, that is to say, it is nonexistent. In the association formed under the social contract, therefore, each member is obliged, by the very fact of the constitution of the association, to make a total surrender to the community of all his rights, so that the association obtains an unlimited power over him, — the State is absolute master of all the property of its members, of their opinions, and of their lives even.

Whether it be owing to the influence of the political ideas of antiquity which Rousseau had come under, or whether it proceed from another source, the mistake in reasoning which led him to this monstrous result arises solely from the fact that he viewed the general will as an entity, whereas in reality it is not, as the philosophers would say, a being, but a phenomenon; it is the expression of relations between beings, the manifestation of particular wills tending to a common aim, or, to revert to the terms already employed, the resultant of the particular wills which are manifested on an object of common interest. That is to say, that far from being personified in a logical phantom and being crystallized there for all time, the general will assumes, in a living society, expressions as " Subtract from the particular wills the pluses and the minuses which cancel one another; the total remaining from the differences is the general will" *(Contrat Social,* Part II, Chap. V).
Rousseau himself says: 'The sovereign acts bylaws.... What is a law? It is a public and solemn declaration of the general will on an object of common interest" *(Lettres icritcs de la montagne,* Letter VI, Part I). manifold and diverse as are the movements of the particular wills brought about by the objects of common interest. This amended notion of the general will once substituted for that which served as a starting-point for Rousseau's arguments, everything in the doctrines of the sovereignty of the people, of the general will, and of the social contract, holds together with a logic as rigorous as Rousseau's logic appears to be. The inconsistencies which he piled up disappear, and the criticism of these doctrines falls to the ground.
The general will, as I have just defined it, no longer wields an absolute power, which crushes the "subjects "; it carries its limitation within itself, since it is nothing but a manifestation of wills aiming at particular objects and exhausting itself with those objects, and since this effect can even be annulled by a fresh combination of particular wills, like a judgment of a lower by a higher court. "The total surrender of each member, with all his rights," is henceforth objectless. The apparently more restricted surrender of rights to which Rousseau consents, and which is reduced to the "part whose use is of importance to the community," the sovereign, by the way, being the sole "judge of this importance," has no *raison d'etre* either: there is nothing to be "judged" and nobody to "act as judge"; the office of that mystic personage who is referred to under the title of "sovereign," and who is to deal at his discretion with the rights of the citizens, is done away with. In the State there is nothing but citizens, who always remain erect and retain the custody of all their rights, which are only limited, whenever the common interest appears to enjoin new obligations, by a new manifestation of the general will, by a new understanding among the citizens, concluded either by themselves or by their representatives in their room and stead.

Representation, which Rousseau has shown to be incompatible with the sovereignty of the people, ceases to be so or to appear so directly the general will is no longer considered as an absolute entity. "Sovereignty consists essentially in the general will, and will cannot be represented," says Rousseau; "it is the same or it is different; there is no middle form." Consequently, the general will represented is no *Contrat Social,* Part III. Chap. XV.
longer general, it is destroyed; and wherever the people are too numerous to act in person, they cannot exercise their sovereign rights, in other words, cannot be free "if the *polis* is not very small." All this dialectical fabric collapses under the simple remark that the general will is not the constant will of a "moral being," but simply expresses the attitude of the particular wills

which meet on an object of common interest. The representatives, then, do but represent this attitude, and in no way the wills themselves, which remain exactly what they were before: free to manifest themselves in new common modes, that is to say, to manifest the general will in new conjunctures, indefinitely. If the agreement between the general will and its representatives implied a perpetual agreement, one would be justified in remarking with Rousseau that "the sovereign can of course say, at present I want what so-and-so wants, or at least what he says he wants; but he cannot say, what this man will want tomorrow I shall still want, since it is absurd that the general will should fetter itself for the future." The characteristic of the general will, according to its amended notion, consists precisely in that it will never be able to say, "What this man will want to-morrow I shall still want," since "to-morrow" presupposes a new agreement of wills. It is therefore not true that " will fetters itself for fie future" by giving itself representatives. No doubt the representatives may exceed the limits within which they should keep, but that is a simple question of precautions to be taken, which concerns the political art, and which in no way affects the actual principle of representation.

The doctrinaire opponents of democracy, like Guizot, — who in reality have themselves only plagiarized Rousseau, by substituting for the sovereignty of the "general will" that of "reason," placed outside individuals, promoted, in its turn, into an entity formed by the same process of logical abstraction, and likewise invested with omnipotence, —have drawn from Rousseau's argument on the incompatibility of representation with the general will the conclusion that the sovereignty of the people is an absurdity. But once it is established that *Contrat Social,* Part II, Chap. I.

Cf. *Histoire des origines du qouvernement repr4sentatif en Europe,* by Guizot, I, 90-115; II, 129-153. this incompatibility is imaginary, it is their conclusion that turns out absurd. The corrected notion of the general will also disposes of the other objections which these critics made to the sovereignty of the people and which they thought irrefutable. Unless the right is conceded to the minority "not to obey what may have been decided against its opinion," that is to say, "unless society is kept in a permanent state of dissolution," the sovereignty of the people, according to Guizot, "dwindles into the sovereignty of the majority. 'This argument is radically unsound, because there is no majority and minority, but majorities and minorities, and as everybody helps at one moment or another to form the majorities, the sovereignty really resides in the nation at large, and not in a part of it. A majority, considered in itself, has no absolute right, nor even existence of its own; it manifests only the power of the general body, the power of the people, founded on right; it marks the passing of that power into action. Whenever it is set in motion, the aggregate of forces which make up the people can evidently move only in the direction of the majority; but the direction of a movement is not the movement itself nor the centripetal and centrifugal forces which compose it. As for the minority, that is to say, the elements of the people whose tendency did not prevail in the general movement, it cannot be said that that movement was accomplished against their will, since they took part in it; the result only disappointed them, but in no way did violence to their will. In the same way is refuted the objection of those critics who, thinking that they have demonstrated that "on the principle of the sovereignty of the people absolute right resides in the majority," extract from it the conclusion that "from this flows, almost necessarily, the oppression of the minority." It does indeed "flow" from it, if the majority and the minority are conceived as entities. But if we admit that the expression of the general will, viewed in accordance with the real state of things, presupposes majoriti.« and minorit/es, whose constituent elements change continually with circumstances, what becomes of the source of this alleged necessary oppression? Would not the possibility for the "oppressors" of to-day to find themselves among the "oppressed" of to-morrow act as a curb on the tyrannical propen sities of the majority — which are not deniable — if majority and minority were not crystallized in a permanent form?

The principle of union substituted for unity thus nullifies the absurd and disastrous consequences to which the doctrine of the sovereignty of the people leads in Rousseau, as well as the absurd consequences which its opponents have sought to impute to this doctrine. At the same time, it enables us to obtain from it the desirable results which Rousseau vainly endeavoured to establish. His principal task was to "find a form of association which would defend and protect the person and the property of each member with the whole strength of the community, and by which each combining with all would nevertheless obey himself only, and remain as free as before." The *Control Social,* whatever its author may say, has not "given the solution of this fundamental problem," since, when all is said and done, the member obeys a will which is outside him, a being superior to him, which is all-powerful over him. On the other hand, the principle which I uphold brings us nearer to the solution sought for. Rousseau's assertion that the citizen obeys himself only in obeying the general will ceases to be the obvious sophism that it is in his argument, if the general will is understood in the sense which I give it; for in that case the general will is no longer outside the member, and the latter really helps to influence its decision on each occasion; at all events, he sketches out the main lines which his spokesmen and his representatives define and develop. Even when it is the opinion contrary to his own that prevails, his will is simply held in abeyance on that particular point, and there is nothing' to prevent it asserting itself in other directions with perfect freedom. He is therefore far more likely to "remain as free as before" than the member according to Rousseau, who pledges himself once for all to obey the "general will," without even knowing or being able to foresee what the tenor of its decisions will be. As he recovers in each new conjuncture his capacity of free contracting party, and can thus always feel "his own master," it is he, and not the member according to Rousseau, who obtains that "moral liberty" (Part I, Chap. VIII) which the social contract is to ensure. It is in regard to him, then, that the "moral equality" established by the fundamental pact becomes a reality, and it is of his fellows that one may say that "men who can be unequal in point of strength and genius all become equal by agreement and by right" (Part I, Chap. IX); whereas the members according to Rousseau " become by agreement all equal" in bondage to the "general will." Rousseau's *dictum* therefore — "it is if you like an aggregation, but not an association" (Part I, Chap. V) — may be turned against him. There can be no question of association for a collective body in which the adhesion of the parts is not, or is no longer, spontaneous; their free union continually renewable can alone make it a veritable association.

Without this condition, the contract itself is only a fiction, and the contractual character of the association is exhausted in the act which constitutes it. Thus in Rousseau, this act once performed, there are no longer contracting parties, but only a "sovereign" and "subjects." If, on the contrary, the association is founded on my principle, Rousseau's whole fabric rises anew; the contractual character of the association is no longer an illusion; it is, so to speak, its living and immortal soul, for the peremptory reason that this principle — to express the whole in a single sentence, which sums up the foregoing — implies not a social contract, but social contracts, which follow each other in an indefinite succession. And if we "must always go back to a first convention," it may be said that this convention, this original social contract, consists of a single clause, providing that there shall be social contracts. That is to say, it stipulates that the members of society, all equal in point of right, shall not use force in their relations, but that they shall negotiate an understanding whenever social life has raised a problem of common interest; and that the understanding thus concluded shall be law. This is the "single clause " to which the "fundamental pact" of modern society is reduced, instead of the "single clause" of Rousseau's contract, namely, "the total surrender of each member with all his rights." According to this pact, it is liberty, it is the autonomy of the individual, that is the rule; and it is only through ulterior agreements on the part of those concerned that it can be departed from. And to make the foundations of this liberty safe from the caprices of future majorities, the hypothesis of the contract, developed still further, enables the contracting parties to reserve, by an addition to the social pact, the primordial liberties of the citizen, on which society will be set as upon a rock amidst the fluctuations of life that will continually necessitate new agreements. Thus the fundamental pact, with the clause of social contracts, far from fettering the contracting parties or keeping society in a permanent state of dissolution, will give a double guarantee to liberty, and will ensure stability as well as unbounded progress; under its safeguard the citizens will not cease for a single instant to be free, while being subject to the rule which they have adopted themselves; and society, founded on this impregnable basis of individual liberties, will be all the better able to renew its life continually and to work out a destiny growing daily more worthy of mankind.

XIII

The new method of political action thus appears to be recommended by the data of experience, as well as by the reasoning of speculative thought. By a coincidence that is somewhat rare in practice, experience and reason combine to give a sort of warranty that this method is capable of solving the great problem of political society, which is to ensure the co-operation necessary to accomplish its objects, while safeguarding individual liberty. It appears alike better suited to the conditions of a complex society with a multiplicity of interests; more supple, more elastic in its application to the new social relations; more in keeping with the temperament of modern democracies, which are refractory to sustained political action and weak in public spirit; able to meet these deficiencies, to help in awakening public spirit, in re-establishing individual responsibility, and in raising public morality, by the mere play of the forces which it sets in motion. To the extent that the present system of stereotyped parties has appeared to us artificial, irrational, obsolete, and disappointing in its results, the new method presents itself as in harmony with the nature of things, with reason, with the modern spirit, and with the object which it has to realize.

There will, of course, be no lack of objections; but they can hardly be of a decisive nature. For the most part, they have been anticipated in the foregoing pages. Already, at the solemn inauguration of the English Caucus, in 1877, its promoters exclaimed, in order to prove the superiority of this institution: "But if a special agitation were set on foot for each political question, what an enormous waste of energy, of time, and abilities would be entailed. Instead of having an Educational League to promote national education, a Reform Union to secure parliamentary reform, a Liberation Society to obtain religious equality, instead of all these organizations, would it not be better to form once and for all a federation which, by focussing the opinion of the majority of the population in great centres of political activity, would be able to speak on any question that might arise, with all the authority of the voice of the nation?" These observations, made at Birmingham, are inspired by conceptions suited to industrial life, in which goods are turned out more cheaply by the saving of labour effected in their manufacture, thanks to the use of machinery and to the curtailment of working expenses rendered possible by the concentration of production. But the individuals who compose a free society are not machines, and political activity has nothing in common with industrial output; its strength is derived from individual consciences, and its productivity increases in the ratio, not of the energy economized, but of the energy expended. The more opportunities are multiplied for the citizen to display initiative and volition, the more will political life be intense and fruitful. The curtailment of "working expenses" in political action is simply a curtailment of the citizen's expenditure of thought; it is realized in the highest degree under absolute regimes, where a single individual thinks, or is supposed to think, for everybody; there, indeed, we find no "waste of energy, of time, of abilities."

But will not the existence of several organizations for dif ferent objects be a source of confusion of every kind? Will not these organizations cross and clash with one another in contending for adherents, and will not the latter be led to fight in one organization those who are their associates in another? Such complications are quite imaginary; they could occur only if the various organizations were founded on a

See above, Vol. I, p. 175.

creed or formed otherwise than by the conscious union of wills. The liberty which will be the basis of these organizations carries with it the principle that brings order out of confusion, by differentiating interests and ideas, and separating them from the personality of those who represent them. In communities where individual liberty is not yet achieved, interests and ideas are not sufficiently differentiated, and men feel the need of sharing pains and pleasures, aversions and attachments, of not parting from one another for fear of losing their way in life. Wherever liberty has not yet become an institution, people find it difficult to separate the man from his ideas, or to make a distinction between them; the opposition shown to any one's opinions is considered as an insult or a personal attack, and the agreement arrived at with him on certain points does not admit of divergencies on others. But in societies in an advanced stage of civilization, where clannish habits and ecclesiastical notions of a universal creed have been shaken off, men easily conceive of one another under various aspects and in changing combinations, without any unsettlement of their personal relations. One constantly sees nowadays persons who belong to rival religious sects make common cause outside the Churches; people agree in politics and differ in scientific, literary, or other controversies; they oppose one another in a profession, at the bar, on the stock exchange, or elsewhere, and resume amicable relations as soon as they have quitted the particular field of contention. These comings and goings in different directions denote an order all the more perfect that they assert the moral liberty of human personality. Why should the same attitude, applied in a methodical manner to political problems, which have in their turn been differentiated, be productive of confusion?

But will not the confusion occur in spite of this, and to a greater degree, in the consideration of political questions by public opinion? Who is to settle the order in which they will be submitted to the national deliberations? How will the electors, tossed from one special organization to another, be able, in electing their member, to give distinct replies to the questions raised, if there are several of them? How will it be known on what question the electoral verdict turns, unless plebiscitary pollings are frankly taken on the problems of the day independently of the elections of the representatives; and in this latter case, on what basis will these elections be held? I' have already replied in anticipation to these objections by pointing out that the candidates who are the standard-bearers of the most important or the most urgent causes, in the eyes of the electors, will come in first in the electoral steeple-chase; the classification of the questions will, therefore, in a way, take place automatically, and the electors will be able to express their views unmistakably on them, when choosing their representatives, without there being any need to submit them one by one to a particular vote. The opinion of the electors, on the things as well as on the men, will only be more clearly elicited.

On the hypothesis that the distribution of the political problems among several special parties can be effected without confusion, will not the national thought and will undergo a sort of frittering away, destructive of those general views which secure consistency in purpose and order in political action, which assign to each problem its time and place, according to the predominant needs and aspirations of the nation? This frittering process will be purely apparent, both in comparison with the present system and as regards the new one. Under the former, the questions which are brought together in the programme of a party form an amalgam and not a body; they are joined and disjoined according to opportunist calculations and preoccupations. Far from aggravating this state ot things, — which would not be very easy, — the new method will rather favour the main currents of political thought and will check the unimportant ones. Now that the two parties operate like two rival syndicates, by picking up votes from every quarter, each vote counts, thanks to the accession of strength which it may bring to either syndicate; its value is reckoned, not by what it is, but by what it adds. The parties therefore are often obliged to conciliate even the representatives of the fanciful movements, of the fads and the crotchets. But when the causes now brought together under a common flag will be separated, and left to their own resources, — because alliances between different and more or less ephemeral organizations will be neither easy nor useful, —there will take place a sort of readjustment in the value of the electoral votes; the votes of the adherents of the secondary causes, being no longer so readily available as reinforcements, will be depreciated in the electoral market. As a rule, they will be dispersed in the great mass of universal suffrage and will neutralize one another, leaving the field open to the adherents and the opponents of the more important causes, that is to say, of those which will have already won over notable sections of opinion.

If the breaking-up of the problems entailed by the new method presents no drawbacks whatever for the working of political life, will this hold good for the elector? Instead of sifting the problems one by one, will he not prefer to accept in a lump the omnibus programmes guaranteed by the old brand of the parties? This is quite possible. But what does it mean, except that the elector does not want liberty, and would rather remain a slave? True, we cannot apply to him the Mosaic law, which enjoined that a slave who preferred slavery to freedom should have his ear bored through; but we have another duty towards him: we must strike off his fetters and throw open the doors of his dungeon. He must be enabled to become free, and once in possession of liberty, he will learn to be a man.

But, will it really be a matter for congratulation if the elector prefers spontaneously to embrace a single cause rather than enlist in a party with a general programme? Shall we not have to fear him as one fears the classic *homo unius libri,* to dread his exclusive devotion to a single cause, his fanaticism and his intolerance, which may hinder the compromises on which politics and communities live? By no means; the new method obviates this danger, which, moreover, is far greater for the permanent parties, whose divergences are as irreconcilable as those of the Churches, because they are organized on the same basis. These divergences set at variance two creeds, two traditions, two firms, two collective *amourspropres,* parted as by a gulf. Under the new system, the member of a special party will find on his side opponents of yesterday, and on the other side allies of yesterday, and he will be naturally led to distinguish the men from the momentary divergences that separate them, and to make allowance for ideas and feelings that differ from his own. The temporary single issue parties will thus supply, by the very force of their constitution and their object, a sort of inoculation against party rabies and sectarian fanaticism; they will become schools of tolerance and broad-mindedness.

But, as against this, will not the relations of the electors with their representatives become more rigid? Once the member is no longer elected because his political feelings correspond with those of his constituents, but on account of the strict agreement of their views on a specified question, will not the representative become a. mere delegate, and the elections simple plebiscites? In reality the bases of representative government will not be changed. The representative will not be chosen solely to interpret the will of his electors on this or that problem, but also to watch the government. As the performance of this last duty does not admit of an imperative mandate, the member will be chosen for his knowledge and his character, and not only for the concordance of his views with those of his constituents on the problem of the day. The elections will have only so much of the plebiscite as may be useful for ensuring more straightforwardness in the national verdict,—which already, under the present system, is often transformed into a plebiscite, but in an underhand and misleading manner,—and will have nothing of it which may affect the nature of representative government.

All this being admitted, does there not remain, it will be said, one insurmountable objection: how will it be possible to recruit political parties, and to train men to lead them, without the allurement of power? Human nature being what it is, are not "the spoils " in one form or another the incentive from which there is no escape, and which it is better to regulate than to ignore or struggle against? In the eighteenth century there were eminent thinkers who held that corruption, then practised by the Crown, was essential to the perfection of the British parliamentary regime. Hume said so; Alexander Hamilton repeated his words before the Constitutional Convention of 1787. To-day, after the lapse of more than a century, every schoolboy knows that if the old English parliamentary regime lived on corruption, it also died of it. Must a similar experience be recommended, in the face of this, to democracy? Before assenting to such a proposition, it is perhaps permissible to propose another method, without being taxed as a visionary.

But why spend time in foreseeing the objections which may be urged against the new method of political action? To all these objections there is a reply of a very summary kind, and of an irresistible eloquence, which is supplied by the facts: the existing system is collapsing, and from the ruin and disorder accumulated by it the new method is already emerging, as a human being comes into the world amid the throes of childbirth. The old parties are breaking up with daily increasing rapidity, they can no longer contain the incongruous elements brought together under the common flag; it is all very well for them to go on bearing the old names, to wrap themselves in the ancient traditions; these names and these traditions do not succeed even in disguising the absence of common ideas and aspirations, which is too obvious to admit of concealment. Compact and stable majorities are only a historical reminiscence. The crumbling of parties is the rule; intestine strife, schisms, artifices, and manoeuvres intended to conceal them are the very essence of their existence. Some, like the parties that go by the name of Liberal, live, not to say vegetate, Ob the credit of their past, which is becoming visibly exhausted; others carry on their business by appealing to the vulgar instincts of the multitude, by exploiting their ignorance and their credulity, by flattering their passions and their prejudices; others, again, live from hand to mouth by means of expedients, of hagglings, of unprincipled coalitions which are formed for sharing power, as rogues combine to commit a robbery. The gravity of this state of affairs varies in different countries with the political manners and the more or less deep roots of the parties; but no country is free from the evil; England itself is already attacked. Everywhere, although in different degrees, parties formed on the traditional basis have lost the power of discharging the double function which was the object of their existence: to unify the various shades of opinion, to make them a body with a soul, and by counterbalancing one another to ensure the regular play of the political forces. Instead of achieving these results, the system produces only disorder and paralysis of the political forces, when it is not corruption pure and simple. The politicians and the defenders of things as they are none the less continue to justify the maintenance of this system by the necessity of "party government" in a representative regime, reasoning like Ugolino, who devoured his children to preserve them a father. But with many less ingenious people, the unreality and the corruption of the parties provoke disgust, and they would be only too glad to find a substitute for this system. They welcome the idea of a "national party," which they imagine to be essentially pure and honest; simple folk allow themselves to be taken in tow by political sharpers who choose to exploit the title of "national party," as has been seen in the Boulangist adventure in France. The same disgust inspired by the old parties has of late years helped the formation, in different countries, of Socialist, Populist, and other parties, as the reader will recollect. And what is not less significant, is that among those who apply the present system themselves, belief in it is no longer intact. Some, who remain indifferent to the moral havoc wrought by the system, but who feel its practical difficulties, would like to restrict the action of the parties, in a manner, it is true, which would in reality end in their complete destruction.3 Others view this eventuality without any displeasure, and naively dream of substituting for the present parties parties of "right" against parties of "wrong," being evidently unaware that every one can "The idea of a ' national party' has been in the air for many years, and we have good reason to think that the idea has already taken root in many minds throughout the country. The experiences of the last five years have disgusted intelligent Englishmen with the system of party government" (Home Affairs: "A National Party," *Fortnightly Review*, Vol. XLII, 1887); cf. in the same volume R. B. Haldane, " Is a National Party possible?"; " The National Party" *(Nineteenth Century*, Nov. 188!)).

During the fight in the United States, in 180fi, with the Silverites, who had been taken in by the Democratic party, a member of the Republican national committee confided to me his opinion that several questions ought to be entirely withdrawn from party politics — the customs tariff, the currency, and the public service — and be dealt with on their own merits. But once withdraw these questions from the American parties, and what *pabulum* would be left to them *1* In an interview which I had with the chairman of a Liberal Association in the cast of England, the conversation fell on the crumbling of parties. "I," he remarked, " take a hopeful view of it." — " Yet you and your Association do all you can to check this movement and to maintain party unity." — "Yes, but that is to ensure stability of government." — "Yet you think that the present parties are doomed?" — " Undoubtedly." — " What will there adopt the label of "national party," or "party of justice and uprightness "; and that if these parties are to have, like those of the present day, the exercise of power for their aim and end, that is to say, are to be organized on the same basis as these, they may be exploited in the same way by selfish interests and passions. Amid the confusion of their thought, darkened by traditional forms, they are groping about for a more genuine and more "moral" basis of political action than the conventional groove of the existing parties.

This basis we have seen laid in the struggles for emancipation throughout the United States, in the form of "committees of seventy" or of "one hundred," of the "citizens' movements," of the "mugwumps," of the "leagues," or "civic federations," all of which represented free associations of men brought together for a particular cause, and completely setting aside, for the nonce, their views on other political questions. In these movements the new method received its baptism of fire and showed what it could do. By its means it has been possible to combine all the living forces of American society for the struggle against political corruption, and to win victories which enable us not to despair of American democracy and of the government of the people by the people. In the sphere of the great national questions, as well as in municipal life, everywhere the "leagues" have been the instigators of the civic awakening; all the great reforms which have been passed to purify political life, beginning with that of the civil service, are due to their initiative or to their efforts; they have broken the prescription set up in favour of party tyranny and corruption, by opposing to the traditional conventions and the rigid forms that congeal and stifle everything that falls into their grasp, liberty of movement for the citizen in public life and the full light of free consideration.

The same method, inspired by the same leading ideas, is passing more and more into the legal forms of political action: the growing restriction of the powers of the State legislatures, legislation by means of constitutional amendments, submitted on each occasion to popular ratification, or by frequent revisions of the constitution, effected by constituent assemblies elected be to take their place?" — " Henceforth there will he only two parties, the party of right and the party of wrong." VOL. II — 2 Y *ad hoc,* the development of the referendum in matters of current legislation, are so many devices aimed at the arbitrariness and the corruption of the parties, which are entrenched behind the legislatures, so many measures for holding in check the permanent and crystallized forces, in which selfish designs of every kind so easily take refuge. These designs are combated by temporary combinations, which interpret more faithfully the aspirations of current opinion, the real and not the factitious opinion, and prevent the formal and the conventional from taking root in public life.

If this method is coming into more and more regular use in the United States, it is not unknown in England either. The three great reforms which renewed England during the second quarter of the nineteenth century, which have given religious freedom, parliamentary reform, and economic liberty, to what are they due but to the efforts of the special organizations which acted outside the permanent parties or even against them, — the Catholic Association, the Political Unions, and the league of leagues, the AntiCorn-Law League? Do they not correspond with the conception of the old Liberalism and of the old English Radicalism, popular organizations of this kind formed for the realization of a precise and well-defined object rallying the combatants round an idea which appeals to the individual mind and conscience? Again, the first extra-constitutional organizations which the second half of the eighteenth century witnessed in England, were they not also formed on the same basis of free associations of a temporary nature, and not working for the parties, but aimed at the coteries which had monopolized Parliament; and did not the parliamentary parties subsequently seize on the weapon of extra-constitutional organization in order to get control of the electorate? The remark of Madame de Stael may be repeated in this connection: "It is liberty that is ancient and despotism that is modern."

This, in fact, is the antithesis which sums up the opposition of the two modes of political action, one of which is embodied in "party," and the other in "league." "Down with 'party,'" and "Up with 'league,'" that is the cry of the political evo 1 Cf. above, Vol. I, pp. 132-135, 218-221.
Considerations sur la Revolution franc;aise, Chap. II. lution which is beginning to take shape. The struggle between these two political methods has begun; the first is continually retreating, the second is advancing in spite of obstacles, because it is the logic of things, the mirror of life, the earnest of the future. And it is not, it is no longer, an idle dream, a mystic longing, to apply to this impending change the words of the poet: —

"Ring out a slowly dying cause, And ancient forms of party strife;
Ring in the nobler modes of life,
With sweeter manners, purer laws."

XIV

The advantages of the new method of political action once secured, the great electoral problem stated above, the problem of the organization of universal suffrage in the preliminary electoral phase, is more than half solved. The working of democracy, based on the electoral system, has revealed a grave difficulty: how this system is to be put in practice, how to obtain in a vast electorate that previous agreement of wills and intellects without which the election is but a game of chance or a series of confused and disorderly proceedings. The principle of the elective system is inadequate to solve the problem; it is powerless to fill the gap by itself. As the State had ignored the matter, private organizations thrust their services as election contractors on the community; but the price which they charged for them turned out ruinous for democracy. In order that their interested services may be dispensed with, the State, I have said, must take the place of these extra-legal organizations in such of their operations as concern the general interest. In establishing the necessity and the legitimacy of this liberating intervention of the State, I have, however, pointed out how inadequate it would be; for even if the State undertook to introduce the candidates to the electors and superintended the preliminary pollings for selecting them, the choice, the classification of the candidates according to their opinions and their merits, would have to be made by the electors themselves, in their minds and in their See above, Vol. II, pp. 611, 612.
consciences. Now, the extra-legal organizations have succeeded in monopolizing iind in exploiting electoral action, not solely owing to the carelessness of the State, which neglected to take the necessary measures, but also owing to certain habits of mind which they have developed in the citizens, to modes of action which they forced on the latter, and which have enabled them to obtain a sort of lien over the intellects and the consciences of the electors. As long as no means have been discovered of removing this moral lien, the intervention of the State in the preliminary electoral operations, however beneficial it unquestionably may be, will not be enough to destroy the monopoly of party, so disastrous for democracy.

The means of removing this lien has been found. It is the new method of political action that provides it, by substituting for stereotyped parties temporary organizations with limited objects. It is this method which, by the moral liberty it ensures, will give their full value and their full force to the preliminary official polls, intended to supply the instrument of analysis and synthesis of electoral opinion which is wanting at present to universal suffrage. The economy of the combination, that is to say, of the legal regulation of candidatures with the new method of extra-legal public action, is as simple as it is farreaching and fruitful in its consequences. The electors will all be invited, without distinction of party, to express their opinion, in an official poll, on the candidatures put

forward, to pick and choose between them. Those which have polled the largest number of votes will be submitted to the definitive vote of the same electors, after a due interval of time for the discussion of the claims of the selected candidates. To be entered on the preliminary list of candidates, drawn up by the public authority, the aspirants to a seat should be put before that authority by a more or less considerable number of electors, as is required by the " Australian system " in the United States for the independent candidatures which do not emanate from organized parties. But here the law will completely ignore party distinctions and will put all the candidates on a footing of equality, by providing that each shall be introduced by a group of electors. This will serve alike to preclude the exaggerated multiplicity of candidatures and to elicit a first deliberate manifestation of the political views of the different groups of electors. For this last purpose the number of the signatures required in support of the declarations of candidatures will have to be high enough to prevent the recommendation of the wire-pullers alone from being sufficient, and not so high as to complicate the procedure of the introduction of candidates. The public authority, in its turn, will introduce all the candidates, without any distinctive mark, to the general body of the electors summoned to the preliminary poll. This poll will yield a complete census of all the shades of electoral opinion; they will be reviewed like troops before the battle; it will be possible to reconnoitre the electoral ground, which, under the existing system, is more often than not hidden from the view of the electors. At present they wander about on it as in a fog, and are obliged, in order not to lose their way, to accept the password of a party, to follow the flag. Henceforth they will be able to find their bearings before taking the decisive step; fully enlightened by the result of the preliminary poll, they will be able, at the definitive vote, to make up their minds without constraint and with ample knowledge of what they are about. They will be able to rid themselves of the importunities of the mercenary guides and of the necessity of accepting their offers of help. The traffic in political labels and the monopoly of the candidatures, enjoyed by committees and caucuses, will be done away with. Under the present system, in which the respective strength of the various political opinions often remains a puzzle even after the election, and by which the act of the election is performed in a single stage, without any possibility of reconsidering it, the tyrannical authority of the wire-pullers and the blind discipline of the electors are a necessity: as the candidate who polls the most votes at the first ballot, which is also the last, will be returned, care must be taken not to scatter one's votes; they must all be given to the only candidate, whether he is a good selection or not. Even thoughtful and independent-minded electors are obliged to submit to this, for fear of bringing in a candidate who is still less congenial to them; they choose, if it can be called a choice, the lesser of two evils; they vote not so much for their candidate as against the rival candidate.
In English-speaking countries there is, with hut very few exceptions, no second ballot.
The plan of preliminary polls will put an end to this state of things: it will no longer be possible to intimidate the electors by the risk of letting the rival candidate get in at the outset; passive discipline will henceforth be objectless.

Yet the beneficial results which the preliminary polls will not fail to produce would be difficult of realization if the change were confined to this legal reform: the electors would no doubt have secured the possibility of getting rid of the interested go-betweens and of making a free and deliberate choice; but they would not yet have the power of doing so, for the very simple reason that a previous agreement on their part would be almost as necessary for the preliminary poll as it is at present for the single election. The introductions of candidates made by groups of electors will give the electorate at large a few hints, but very imperfect ones. That being so, will not the present party system regain a very considerable portion of the ground which it had lost? It is more than probable that the elector in his bewilderment will let himself once more be taken in tow by the parties, who will obligingly tell him for whom to vote at the preliminary poll. No doubt, the fact that this poll will not be definitive and that the elector will have the option of changing his vote at the final election will greatly curtail the tyrannical power of the parties and the machines. But if one is obliged, as is probable, to accept the guidance of the parties in the preliminary poll, they will inevitably predetermine the result of the definitive election; the electors will be able to choose only between the candidates introduced by the parties at the poll; that is to say, they will have, as in the present day, a choice between two evils only. These difficulties will be completely met by the system of "leagues ": the previous agreement of the electors in view of the poll will be effected by the leagues; each league will come forward with its electoral contingents arrayed in compact masses and united heart and soul by the particular political object which has given rise to its formation; it will arrive at the general rendez-vous of the poll with colours flying, proclaiming far and wide the name of its cause, as well as the names of its champions whom it wishes to see returned to Parliament. The poll will be only a numerical abstract of the forces represented by the ideas and opinions which are contending for political supremacy; the purely external analysis — to use the terms which I have already employed — which it will have produced, and which I have shown to be inadequate in itself, will but express the inward analysis that has already taken place in the minds of the members of the different leagues.
In short, thanks to the leagues, the previous agreement between the members of the different groups of electors and

the record of this agreement, which are the *raison d'etre* of the preliminary poll, will be something real and genuine. It is the method of leagues that will give life to the system of preliminary polls, which otherwise would be likely to remain a dead letter. And, on the other hand, it is the legal organization of these polls that will furnish a substance and an expression to this method of analysis and classification of electoral opinion, and each provision of the law, framed on the plan which I have sketched out, will help to realize it the better in political life. The preliminary poll, followed by the discussion of the claims of the candidates who are at the head of it, will lead up to the final election as to a synthesis, — a synthesis worthy of the name, for it will have been really founded on an analysis. Carried out on these bases, the preliminary electoral organization solves, from a certain point of view, the whole problem of the organization of universal suffrage, the greatest present weakness of which consists, as we have seen, in the fact that its working resembles a synthesis without a previous analysis.

XV

Other solutions of the electoral problem have, it is true, been proposed in the course of the last few decades. They consisted in reforms of the system of representation. Two plans have especially occupied public opinion. One of them, by a singular association of ideas, not to say of words, linked reform of the organization of universal suffrage with the *organic* conception of the State and Society, with that theory which sets up a complete parallelism between the life of a community and Some supplementary details will be found in Appendix II, where I have entered in a general summary the changes to be introduced in the organization of the public powers with regard to all the points which I am considering in this Conclusion.

that of a human being. This parallelism, which is referred to in many a political writer or orator by way of metaphor or apologue, from antiquity downwards, was developed and raised to the level of a system in the course of the nineteenth century. After having been barely outlined in the speculations of Fichte and Schelling, the organic theory of the State bloomed in Germany like a luxuriant plant. The creator of sociology, Auguste Comte, gave a limited but conspicuous place in his theories to the organic conception of society. In England Mr. Herbert Spencer, in his turn, extended to it his powerful patronage. But in proportion as it spread, this idea shared the fate that sometimes befalls conceptions of the intellect, which, in one aspect or another, border on the tangible reality, and which, in consequence, are apt to strike every imagination — they become turbid, like torrents which, starting from mountain heights, flow over vast plains and lose themselves in the mud. The analogy between society and the human body was pushed to the point of discovering in the structure and in the working of society molecules, cells, tissues, organs, apparatus of orgaus, etc. Its exponents ended by translating social science into natural science, as poetry is set to music, and, taking anatomical and physiological terms for political realities, drew conclusions from them for the organization of society. Persons of very different mental breadth and culture, while often disavowing the profession of the organic theory in all its rigour, concurred in the idea that the disease of existing political society is due to the fact that it does not rest on an " organic" basis; dispersed like atoms, the social elements need an "organic grouping"; universal suffrage works in a deplorable manner because it is "inorganic," etc. And yet "society has an organic frame"; it is "divided into collective organisms." These "organisms" supply the political order with a readymade structure. What are they? They are the "collectivities of interests," the "social interests." Representative government, therefore, to become a reality and a source of life, to substitute order for anarchy, should be founded on the " representation of social interests," each group of interests or each Tho excellent little work of A. T. van Krieken, *Ueber dle sogenannte organische Staatstheorie,* Leipzig, 1873, may be consulted with advantage. I borrow most of these terms and formulas from the most eloquent chain professional category forming an electoral college, which would send representatives to Parliament. That is the mode of grouping of the electors which is required; that is the "organic grouping" because it corresponds to the living reality. On these "organic" notions is grafted in some persons a certain mediaeval romanticism, which looks back, with a pleasing emotion, to the corporate life in the "free" communes of the olden time; in others a vague socialistic feeling; in others, again, irreconcilable opponents of the order of things sprung from the Revolution, or soured reactionaries, are added the wish and the hope to stem the current of the Revolution by means of a sort of " corporate representation," to curb the brute force of num-bers; in a word, to muzzle the "many-headed beast." Thanks to these various sentiments, resting on the organic theory of society, the "representation of interests" has been proposed as the grand electoral remedy, and brought into the forefront of political discussion.

I, for my part, hold that this mode of representation would be as mischievous in its consequences as it is erroneous in its conception. It is absolutely false that there is any analogy between social phenomena, in which free will plays such an important part, and biological phenomena. The relationship between social studies, or, to use the fashionable word, "sociology," and biology is imaginary. The terms "organic," "inorganic," "organism" are meaningless when applied to the regulation of political relations. They may be employed in every-day language to express an idea more easily, — and I have perhaps myself happened to use them in this way, —but it is inadmissible to erect a political edifice on metaphors, at the risk of building it in the air. The "social organisms," the

"collective organisms," which are offered as a political framework, are in reality nothing but a pure abstraction in existing society: let a single group of social interests be pointed out to us which resembles an organism, that is to say, an organized body with a separate life, a group which serves its members as a complete sphere pion of the "representation of interests," M. Ad. Prins *(La dimocratie et le rtgime parlementaire,* Briix. 1884, *V Organisation de la liberii et Ie. devoir social,* Brux. 1895), some of whose ideas I do not share, but the loftiness of whose inspiration I readily admit.
of existence. A combination of individuals, either economic or professional, or pursuing a moral aim, represents only certain interests of these individuals; it represents the latter united under a certain aspect, and it is enough to view them under another aspect for the combination to disappear. It is an illusion to believe, in present conditions, that by substituting the group for the individual as a basis of political life, we "cease to consider society in its metaphysical unity," and "take as a pivot realities, that is to say, collectivities sprung, so to speak, spontaneously from the very heart of a country." An abstract entity can be made out of a group as well as out of an individual. the concrete origin of the subject of the abstraction makes no difference; an individual springs just as well from the very heart of the nation. If the individual has become a logical phantom in the French philosophers of the eighteenth century, and, as I have pointed out, even in Bentham, this is because they viewed the relative in him under the aspect of the absolute, and transformed him into a being complete in himself. Now the champions of the representation of "collective organisms" proceed in precisely the same way with the economic or professional categories, each of which they transform into a permanent and complete sphere of political life in all its manifestations. It is therefore through the same prism of "metaphysical unity" that they view the groupings of "social interests." To clothe them with a substantial form they are obliged to reduce them to groupings of interests in the narrow, utilitarian sense of the word.
But if political representation is organized on the basis of these groupings, it will be merely organizing the selfish interests in the State; if this mode of classification is adopted for universal suffrage, it will be simply increasing confusion and aggravating the evil of the existing representative regime. "Interests" are already only too much represented in political assemblies. The reader will remember the remark applied to the American House of Representatives, that every interest is represented in it except the general interest. Everywhere people are only too much guided by preoccupations of groups, of trade-unions, of localities, even when Prins, *La dimocratie,* 196.
it is not avowed with the candour of the representative of an Alpine constituency in Switzerland who voted against the phylloxera law because there were no vines in his canton. There cannot be too many efforts made to induce the electors, and consequently their representatives, to step out of the narrow groove of the particular and to take their stand on the general, on the national. It would be a grievous mistake and a sad misfortune if, after centuries of struggle for emancipation, the antagonisms of interests and the selfishness of classes were invested with a legal form conferring on them political individuality. No doubt, a community lives on interests, as man lives on bread, but in a society whose life is not a mere greedy scramble, interests ought to be made dependent on ideas, which, divested of the personal, that is to say, of the narrow and paltry element, are alone able to establish the harmony of justice among the diverging tendencies. Far from facilitating the manifestation and the classification of political opinions, the separate groups of interests would hamper them systematically, placed as they always will be, by the law itself, in the contracted sphere of their special preoccupations. Every political problem unconnected with these preoccupations will throw the members of the " social combination" into confusion. The question will be put to the citizens, but the electors will always have to reply, whatever the subject may be, as traders, as agriculturalists, or as manufacturers, etc. The group may be as " organic" as you please, its members will be like " dispersed atoms " when confronted with all the variety of national questions; they will often exhibit more divergence and more incoherence in their opinions than many a citizen belonging to different groups of interests. Even supposing that professional freemasonry produces a community of views strong enough *idem sentire de republica,* this community of views will still have to be brought out at the elections. How will this be done, especially in a large combination numbering thousands of members? The problem of establishing a previous agreement of the electors remains therefore untouched, and the system of "organic representation," of "representation of interests," leaves everything as it was! If there is anything worth noticing in the ideas on Quoted by Numa Droz (ex-President of the Swiss Confederation), *Etudes el portraits politiques,* 1895, p. 95. which it is founded, it is that the only combination which can supply a sphere for electoral action is the "grouping of similar interests"; but as this similitude can only assert itself really within the limits of a particular problem, "the only combination which is truly organic (I, who am ignorant of biology, will substitute for the word 'organic' the word 'rational') and truly free," is a combination according to the problems. In other words, the system of representation of the interests identified with social groups condemns itself in a way, and brings us back to the method which I advocate, as the only one that can solve the great electoral problem.
On the other hand, if there is any ground for the complaint that the authorized representatives of the "interests" find it difficult to get into the legislatures, which are monopolized by

lawyers and unqualified politicians, this evil might be remedied without abandoning the whole national representation to the "interests." The authentic representatives of economic and other interests might be provided with a particular means of entering the chambers and giving the latter the benefit of their special knowledge. A place might be found for them in the upper house, in the senate, by bestowing a proportion of the seats on the great social organizations and the constituted bodies — chambers of commerce, agricultural societies, trades' unions and masters' associations, learned societies, universities, churches, great public bodies (such as, in France, the *Cour de Cassation,* the *Conseil d'Etat,* and the *Cour des Comptes).* Their sole mission being, from their special competence, to advise the representatives, direct and indirect, of universal suffrage, these spokesmen of the "interests" would play the part of experts, of technical assessors, in the assemblies. To prevent them losing this character, and to preclude the creation of a new category of politicians, or, at all events, of a class of political mandarins, it would be well to limit the duration of their mandate to the discussion of a single budget. This measure will besides facilitate the rotation which it would be necessary to establish between the different sections of the country, which would appoint special representatives by turns, as the number of seats that might be reserved for them in the senate would not allow, for instance, trades-unions of every industry and of every district to be all represented at the same time.

XVI

A second method of classifying the opinions of the electors which has been proposed of late years, and which has attracted far more attention than the representation of interests, is that of proportional representation, which would admit into national assemblies not only the predominant opinions, but all opinions in the exact ratio of their numerical strength. In the earlier part of this book we have witnessed the introduction of this problem into politics by T. Hare and J. S. Mill. The reader will remember the exceptional importance which the illustrious philosopher attached to the idea of " personal representation" for the future of democracy, and the qualifications which I have been led to make on this subject, while recognizing the grandeur of Hare's conception and the clear-sightedness with which he had discerned the new conditions in which political society had to work. Since the days of Hare and J. S. Mill, the idea has made considerable progress in the world, it has found ardent champions in all latitudes, and it is proposed as the great, the best means of organizing universal suffrage and regenerating political life at the same time. The opposition which the idea encountered from writers and legislative assemblies has not been less determined, although it was not inspired by the generous feelings that animated its champions who engaged in a crusade against the majority system, that iniquitous and brutal system which confers all power on the half plus one of the persons voting, crushes minorities by reducing them to a sort of political slavery, warps the foundations of representative government, and inevitably spreads demoralization and corruption in public life. Various forms of proportional representation were contrived, which were to ensure a more and more correct reproduction of all opinions. The objections which were made, and which are still being made, to these schemes are by no means all conclusive. Some, which condemn proportional representation, because it would lead to a crumbling away of parties and stifle the "organic" spirit of the nation, to use a term with which we are already acquainted, or because the electoral procedure entailed by it would be extremely complicated, are unwarranted or exaggerated. Other objections do not deserve discussion; they only prove the tenacity of the prejudices and the inveterate habits which are blindly opposed to all innovation. But it is also unquestionable that proportionalism would be attended with serious drawbacks. And it would be surprising if this were otherwise. The material of a political regime is limited like that of a single garment in which repairs can be made only with pieces cut out of the fabric itself. Every political reform intended to fill a gap in the regime makes a hole in it at some other place, which can be perceived at once, or will only be revealed later on by experience. The practical proposals which I have just made myself, and which I am about to supplement in the following pages, will probably not escape this fate either. The sole point is to make a correct estimate of what will be gained and what lost by the change. That is the whole secret of the political art. Equally free from the religious enthusiasm which animates the champions of proportional representation and from the lofty disdain professed for it by its opponents, I, for my part, hold that, all things considered, this reform would show a balance of advantages for representative government, because it is able to ensure a more equitable distribution of political influence and, at any rate, to convey the idea of it to the electors, to give minorities a standing, to increase, in certain respects, the independence of the elector, and to make the monopoly of the dominant parties less exclusive.

But while admitting that these important results may be obtained, I cannot help seeing that this reform of representation would not of itself solve the problem of the organization of universal suffrage. It deals with one part of this problem only, with that which constitutes the last act of the electoral drama; of the preceding acts the plans of proportional representation take no account, as if they were accomplished automatically, as if they were something that goes of itself. The system proposed by the eminent initiator of the reform, Thomas Hare, is the first to reveal this omission, and in the most flagrant manner. I will recall the main lines of this system here: each elector has but one vote, can return but one member, whatever the number of the

1 See above, Vol. I, pp. 104-112.

seats to be filled up; but he is free to put down on his voting-paper the names of several candidates in the order of his preferences, firstly the one whom he wishes as his first choice, and then the one whom he wants next, and so on. When the yotes are counted, the first step is to divide tha-tolal number of the voting-papers bylihafc-of the seats to be filledjip; the quotient determines the number of suffrages necessaryf or a candidate to be elected. The electoral quotient once fixed, the votes of the candidates who head the lists are first counted. As soon as a candidate has reached the figure of the electoral quotient, he is declared to be elected, and the voting-papers which contained his name are eliminated. If his name is still found on the remaining voting-papers, it is disregarded, and its place is taken by the candidate who comes second on the voting-paper and who now moves up, for the counting of the votes, into the first line, being followed by the candidates mentioned after him on the voting-papers, who thus all go up one line. The counting of the votes is continued on the same plan until the number of seats to be filled up is exhausted. When instead of a surplus of votes the candidates of the first choice have a deficit, this can be made up, in a similar way, by the subsidiary votes, of the second or third line, bestowed by other electors, on condition that their vote is no longer of use to their first or their second choice. The candidates of the first choice who cannot obtain the electoral quotient are eliminated, and their votes are transferred, on the above plan, to the candidates who come after them on the voting-paper. Whenever, in spite of the transfers effected, there still remain seats for which no one has obtained the quotient, the one who gets nearest to it is declared elected. Thanks to this plan, which demands from the elector no effort but that of writing on the voting-paper his favourite candidates in the order of his preferences, each group of electors whose number is equal to the quotient is sure to obtain one representative, and not more than one. No vote or suffrage of eventual preference, given to a candidate able to attain the quotient, will be lost; that is to say, that each elector will have his representative, his member, expressly chosen by him, and the members will be the really free and deliberate choice of the electors and the genuine representatives of public opinion in all its varied shades.

Yet a closer scrutiny of this plan shows that the admirable results which it holds out can be obtained only on condition of a previous agreement as to the names of the candidates to be put down, or even as to their number, and as to the order in which the preferences will be given in view of the transfer of votes. If an understanding is not arrived at beforehand on each of these points, the votes may easily be scattered and be distributed in a way that does not correspond to the effective strength of the different opinions (for instance, the adherents of an opinion who organized themselves thoroughly will get the better of the representatives of another opinion who are twice as numerous, but not organized); or, again, it will happen that no candidate reaches the quotient, or that the latter may be assigned, by means of the transfer of suffrages, to candidates who are the last choices at the expense of those who have been put in the first line (but in too great numbers to obtain the electoral quotient). To obviate these untoward results, nothing short of a very elaborate organization would be required. The grouping implied by Hare's plan may be one of absolute liberty and remarkable elasticity; it must, however, be made. On what basis and in what way will it be made? To this there is no reply in Hare. He sees only two personages on the electoral stage, the candidate and the elector, and appears to be unaware of the presence of third persons, the fellow-citizens of this elector, without whom the latter is powerless. He claims for his system the title of "systemjjf indivjdiiarkuidependejice,'' but is it not the independence of a man who is suspended in the air?

This uncertainty as to the way in which the electors would combine to ensure the quotient to a candidate of their preference, and the risk of scattering the electoral votes to no purpose, has had something to do with the favour which was shown to another system of proportional representation, described briefly by the name of "system of lists." The fundamental principle of this system, somewhat varied forms of It is possible that the estimate of probabilities might considerably weaken the force of these objections, but they would none the less subsist. *The Election of Representatives,* Lond. , 4th ed., 1873, p. 130.
which have been devised and which has been adopted in Switzerland and, quite recently, in Belgium, is that the electors vote for candidates classified by parties, each party having its list. When the votes are counted, the seats are distributed among the parties in proportion to the votes obtained by the respective lists; and once this distribution is made, the seats falling to each party are assigned to the candidates on its list who have received the most support. The number of lists not being limited, every combination of electors may bring forward its own concurrently with the existing parties, and if it reaches the party quotient, it will have its share of parliamentary representation. This system, which is meant to ensure to all opinions a place corresponding to their numerical strength, and in a safer and easier way than Hare's plan, in reality does not ensure anything more than the correct representation of parties. Now, the distributive justice to be realized in representation is due first and foremost to the electors and not to the parties, which are too often artificial and conventional entities, and are the first to pervert the representation, by forcing the hand of the electors through the moral coercion which they wield over them; the tyranny of the majority plan is but a complement of the tyranny of the parties over their members. Will that oppression be put an end to by the system of lists? This seems to be doubtful. The

success of the list being set up by the law itself as the supreme object, little heed will be paid to the individuality of the candidates, the label will be voted for more than ever, the notion of "regularity" will survive, and with it the organization of stereotyped permanent parties. The free competition of the parties, secured by the system of competition of the lists, will curtail the power of the regular parties; it will make a breach in their rampart, but will not demolish it, for it is not the dualism of parties only that is the source of their electoral monopoly and their oppressive power, but still more their permanent character, which confers on them, to repeat an expression already employed, a sort of moral mortmain over the electors. And the permanent parties will retain their privileged position so long as the electors, for want of another method of electoral combination, are obliged to accept their promptings, in order not to scatter and squander their votes. VOL. II—2 Z

The free competition of lists will provide an outlet for independent minds, for an elite. But the citizens at large would not be able to benefit by this liberating enactment unless it has a basis of electoral combination independent of the regular parties. Proportionalism does not supply this, it does not fill the gap; the justice which it offers remains in the air; it is the apex of an edifice which has neither walls nor foundation.

These walls and this foundation are provided by the method which I advocate. Superadded to this method, proportional representation is a happy completion of it; it bestows a legal sanction on the practical autonomy ensured by my method to the various opinions, it instals those opinions in the political assemblies, it marks the place there which belongs to them. Brought together, by the operation of this method, on the basis of particular problems, classified and combined according to their rational affinities, opinions *proportionalize themselves* by the natural play of things, without any mathematical or other contrivance; at the preliminary poll each opinion, embodied in a league, will give forth all its votes, and nothing but its votes. If a proportionalist system is added thereto in the counting of the votes at the definitive election, the equitable distribution of votes effected by the preliminary poll will be able to pass, so to speak, straight into the precincts of Parliament, or, to use another metaphor, these votes will be coined into parliamentary mandates representing their exact value. That is the service which legal proportionalism will render, and it can never do more; it cannot create the value, the precious metal must be brought to it after having been laboriously extracted from the political soil. The method which I recommend will offer the means of extracting the metal and will enable it to be supplied properly cut and of exact weight, all ready for the hall-mark. The difficulties and drawbacks which appeared to attend the application of the proportional system vanish, once it is combined with this method. The "system of lists" will no longer threaten to realize a spurious justice, a purely arithmetical justice, in representation, because the parties will no longer be artificial and conventional entities, but conscious unions of wills, brought about by a particular problem; the notion of "regularity" being eliminated, none of the "competing lists " will be a mere label or a sign; the respective strength of the various parties being known beforehand, thanks to the preliminary poll, there will be less temptation to vote blindly for the names put on the list in order to make its success more certain.

Hare's system, theoretically more perfect, will be still better rehabilitated: it left unsolved the question how the electors, able to procure for a candidate the electoral quotient by their united votes, are to bring about this union; the system of leagues and of the preliminary poll will do it. The scattering of votes, which seemed likely to rob the system of its advantages, is obviated by the double concentration effected through the leagues and the preliminary polls. The uncertainty as to the strength of the various opinions and the popularity of different candidates, which would have led to haphazard decisions in regard to the number of candidates to be brought forward and the order of preference to be given them, is dispelled by the results of the preliminary poll and replaced by exact calculations. The complication in the counting of the votes, due to the transfer of preferential suffrages, will be greatly reduced, thanks to the diminution of the number of the candidates, some of whom will be eliminated by the preliminary poll, and to the greater concentration of the votes on the names of those who have obtained most support in that poll. Thus, by leaning on the method which I recommend, Hare's system recovers its stability, can be easily and usefully applied, and the theoretical superiority which it possesses over the other systems of proportional representation—in securing the electors a more equitable distribution of the seats with the greatest amount of individual 1 mean, of course, not the original plan, —expounded by Mill, which supposed that the whole country would form a single electoral college and that isolated electors belonging even to different districts could combine to procure the quotient for a candidate of their choice, and form ideal constituencies, — but Hare's system applied to constituencies with geographical boundaries and a limited number of seats, as it is worked in Denmark (on the plan of Andrae, Hare's emulator), and as it has just been introduced in the colony of Tasmania, where it yields, it would appear, good results.

I allude especially to the different varieties of the system of lists and *a fortiori* to the two other types of representation of minorities — the limited vote and the cumulative vote, with which the reader is acquainted (see Vol. I, pp. Ill, 1(i2, lfri), and the inadequacy of which is admitted. The reader will remember that it was the system of the limited vote, introduced by the English Reform Bill of 1867. that gave rise to the formation of the Birmingham Caucus and succumbed to its efforts. independence in the choice of the candidates — becomes by this method a living reality.

If even the proportionalist principle were rejected — which would be a pity — Hare's plan might still be of use; it contains an idea independent of the proportional system, but almost as fruitful as that of personal representation — the preferential vote. Being adaptable at once to all the electoral modes in force, — general ticket, district system, direct elections, elections by two stages, — it would supply a valuable instrument for the classification of opinions, and would also serve as a lever for elevating political manners. It would lead even the most party-ridden elector to compare, to judge, to marshal the various shades of opinion and the merits of the men. As the second or the third choices of the elector, to be effective, will have to fall on candidates of more or less different complexion to his own, the system of preferences will widen his horizon and will counteract blind sectarian intolerance and narrow cliquish exclusiveness. The candidates, in their turn, having to conciliate the electors of the adjoining shades of opinion in order to get their subsidiary votes, will conduct their campaigns with more moderation and decency; they will have more to lose than gain by those rancorous attacks and slandering matches indulged in by candidates of different fractions of the party and their friends who have fallen out even more than by candidates of diametrically opposite opinions, and which are a disgrace to representative government and a source of profound demoralization to the masses. The moderation which they will have to display will have nothing in common with the opportunism and the fenceriding practised nowadays by so many candidates who try to please everybody: to succeed, a candidate will always have to be put in the first line by a considerable number of electors; and he cannot become their choice unless he inspires them with implicit confidence, which he will be unable to win by equivocal declarations and ambiguous attitudes. The votes in the top line will come first of all from the militant members of the party, who will have to be spoken to plainly; on the other hand, to obtain the subsidiary votes of other groups of electors, the candidate will be equally obliged to state frankly how far the agreement between him and tbem extends, and his greatest skill will consist in honesty to everybody. Combined with the method of leagues and of preliminary pollings, the preferential vote will enhance their power of true classification and effective combination of opinions, and, consequently, the genuineness of representation, even independently of the application of the proportional system. The preferential vote might be applied at the preliminary poll, minus the operation of the transfer of votes, however, which will not be needed in this electoral phase, since it is not yet a question of the definitive election. The preferential vote at the preliminary poll will be confined to a simple indication of preferences on the voting-papers, which, however, will be of great assistance as a guide to the electors for the definitive election and will facilitate their final understanding; while at the definitive election the preferential vote, followed by the transfer of votes, will help to bring about the concentration of the votes, all the elements of which will have been already prepared in a-manner as rational as it is effective.

I will not dwell upon the mode of election by two stages, which certain politicians and writers consider a very suitable means for the organization of universal suffrage. All that there is to be said on the value of this mode has been said by J. S. Mill; his verdict cannot be reversed. I will only point out that the method advocated by me possesses all the advantages attributed to election by two stages, and is free from its undeniable defects. The office of filter of public opinion, wrongly assigned to it, is discharged by my method with a fulness and a genuineness to which no other can lay claim. It is this method which brings "the light in the election and the honesty in the law" that Taine expects from the two stages system.; It comes to the rescue of universal suffrage, inadequately informed about men and questions, to enlighten the conscience and the intellect of the electors on both, and not to ask them to abdicate in favour of some intermediate power and pay no heed to the sequel which is beyond their influence. On the contrary, it keeps the elector's mind constantly on the alert, from the moment of the inception of the *Consiileratiom on Representative Government,* Chap. IX, " Should there be two stages of election?" *Du xufTraye universel et de la mani 'erc de voter,* 1872, p. 44.

candidatures, and even before it, down to the time of the final vote; it works for his political education; it rouses and stimulates his civic energy; it does not allow him to shift his responsibility to other shoulders, it develops it in him as well as in those who solicit his vote. Universal suffrage is not shorn of its power nor maimed in its influence by a more or less surreptitious device; it remains the *fans et origo* of every political act throughout all the phases of electoral life.

The preliminary pollings will even impose additioual duties and efforts on the citizens, which, from a certain point of view, appears to involve a grave drawback: a double election campaign will not fail to heighten the electoral fever and to rouse men's passions more. In a general way, it may be said on this point that political agitation, even of the most intense kind, is not necessarily an evil; it is unwholesome when it is artificial, when it turns on a subject of pure convention, when it beats the air; but it is not sterile when it is enlisted in the service of a genuine cause, when it awakens the conscience of the citizen, and intensifies the sense of his rights and of his duties to the public weal. To make sure of obtaining the results of wholesome agitation, it is no doubt important to avoid electoral *surmenage.* But this consists not so much in the multiplicity of the electoral operations as in the frequency of elections. It would therefore be desirable, in adapting the rule *uon multa sed multum* to the occasion, to intensify the action of the electors, to demand from them the maximum of their efforts at a given moment, but also to make the interval between the manifestations of this action as long as possible. The preliminary pollings, applied to general elections held at longer intervals, would but enhance the value of the national verdict, which would be given with more reflection and with a sense of responsibility increased in proportion to the greater duration of the mandate. To keep the nation and its representatives in touch with one another, in spite of the longer intervals between the elections, it will be enough to adopt the system of renewal of assemblies by instalments, which will enable the new aspirations of public opinion to penetrate regularly into the House with the minimum of disturbance for the country. I would accept for assemblies chosen by universal suffrage, if not the periodicity of elections established, for instance, for the French Senate, a third of which is renewed every three years, at any rate that which is fixed for the American Senate, which is renewed to the extent of one-third every two years.

But would not the long duration of the parliamentary mandate, extending to six years and more, make the mandate-holder too independent towards his constituents? would it not weaken his sense of responsibility? The latter is not unimpaired even in the present day, under the regime of more frequent elections. It does happen that in important conjunctures a member behaves in a way which a great number of his constituents, perhaps the majority of them, entirely disapprove. But when he seeks re-election, the political situation has radically changed, the grievances of the past are thrust into the background by the preoccupations of the present, and, under cover of these, the member gets off scot-free and can begin his old game over again. In any event, the punishment does not follow the offence; justice in electoral matters walks with a halting step, as it does elsewhere. What would happen if the term of the mandate were prolonged? The reader will remember that among the various cures for the political disease proposed in the United States, there was one for ensuring the continuous responsibility of the representative by giving his constituents the right of unseating him at any moment, as Bentham had already suggested. Heroic as this remedy, which clashes with our habits, may appear, I hold that it deserves serious consideration. To keep the representative up to the mark, and get the electors to have an eye always on him, is not a result to be despised if it can be obtained by this plan. It woidd be a better means of keeping the member in the right path than the imperative mandate, for this makes the mandate-holder a machine and destroys real responsibility, whereas dismissal coming after the event would leave him his liberty, that is his responsibility, but would render it genuine, would give it a sanction by making removal follow on misbehaviour. No doubt if the principle of dismissal were adopted, its application would have to be subjected to precautions against the improper use that might be made of it: thus dismissal would have to be pronounced by a number of electors Cf. on this point Henry Sidgwick, *The Elements of Politics,* Lond. 1897, p. 555 *et seq.* equal to not less than half of the voters at the last election; if the member no longer possesses the confidence of half the electors of his constituency, it is only right that he should lose his seat. This system, of course, could not be applied to proportional representation, under which the particular electors of each member cannot be distinguished. On this point Mr. Moffet, the American publicist already quoted, devoted as he is to proportionalism, abandons it in favour of the dismissal of representatives, because he considers that their continuous responsibility is of more importance for the proper working of representative government. — I have shown that the elective method of appointment to public office ought to be limited to legislatures and to assemblies of local self-government. The judges in particular ought not to be subject to popular election; but to prevent them from shirking their responsibility to the people and hiding behind an inadequate hierarchical supervision, or even behind the *esprit de corps* of an irremovable judiciary, the citizens might be given the right, not of removing the judges, but of impeaching them in the supreme court, which would decide the case after a public trial. The law will fix the number of electors whose intervention would be necessary for the impeachment of the offending judge; there will be no need to make it as high as that for the dismissal of a member of Parliament; but it will have to be substantial enough to prevent such a grave controversy being raised without sufficient foundation.

XVII

On the hypothesis that the method which I advocate, completed by the changes proposed in the electoral system, yields all the desired results in the electoral phase of political life, how will the next phase be adapted to it, that which begins with the entrance of the elected representatives into the precincts of the legislative assembly? If there are no longer permanent parties in the country, there will no longer be a permanent majority in the chamber; and then arises the old question of the Duke of Wellington, frightened by the prospect of tho abolition of the rotten boroughs: "How will the King's *Suggestions on Government,* p. 175. government be carried on? " — how will parliamentary government work? In reality, the catastrophe would not be more terrible than that which so alarmed the hero of Waterloo; now as then, it would be nothing more than the destruction of something rotten. The orthodox doctrine of parliamentary government, which presupposes "two great parties" in the chamber, and, under the English system, a ministry naturally homogeneous and united and jointly responsible to the chamber, has had its day. The "two great parties" have ceased to exist; in almost all parliamentary countries the assembly is now composed of more or less numerous shifting groups, which do not admit of any permanent classification. In consequence the majority, at least the constant majority, is a fiction, the homogeneity of ministries a farce, their solidarity a blind, and their responsibility a delusion. Warped in its foundations, the regime inevitably produces all those evils which have become the very essence of parliamentary life: the chamber being divided, it can only give birth to a weak government, which is continually fighting for its life; to keep in power, the ministry is obliged to make concessions right and left, to manoeuvre and to abandon all idea of a firm and consistent policy; needing the votes of the members, it is forced to obtain them by endless civilities, which enable the representatives to reward the devotion of their electors; the interference of members and favouritism become the rule in administration; the power of the ministers, which is coined so extensively into electoral favours, excites jealousies and ambitions, and their precarious position, which makes them an easy prey, encourages the intrigues and the coalitions directed against them; the overthrow or the maintenance of the ministry being the real objective of parliamentary debate, questions are not considered for their own sake, but are gambled with according to the needs of the moment; the same practices being available to all alike, coalitions are broken almost as soon as formed and lead to ministerial crises at frequent intervals; the ministries, being the outcome of coalitions, are combinations of heterogeneous elements just placed side by side, of conflicting interests and aspirations which *ipso facto* neutralize one another; the solidarity of the ministers is reduced to a desire to remain together in power as long as possible. And no change seems to be of any avail; with no way out of it, apparently, this state of affairs ends only in discrediting parliamentary government and in keeping the country in a state of constant uneasiness.

The perfect logic with which the critics of parliamentary ways establish this rigorous connection of cause and effect leads most of them to the following conclusion: a genuine majority must be constituted! we must revert to the reality of parliamentary government! And they do not notice the conclusion which stares them in the face, so to speak, to wit, that if parliamentary majorities are constantly breaking up, the reason is that these majorities are artificial; that if they are artificial, the reason is that there are no more natural ones, that they cannot be obtained any longer, and that new foundations must be sought for the tottering edifice in the place of those which have collapsed. The inexorable realities of life proclaim this only too eloquently, it is all of no avail; electors and members are still exhorted to constitute the "two great parties "; to excite their emulation, the example is quoted to them of that highly practical English people, which is careful to divide itself regularly into Whigs and Tories, and there seems to be no inkling that the great parties are like the proverbial Eolaud's mare, which possessed every good quality, but had the misfortune to be dead. Instead of clinging to obsolete forms, would it not be better to try to extract the essence of parliamentary government, and, while frankly admitting its new predicament, to adapt it to that predicament? To secure this result, it would only be necessary to extend to parliamentary life the principle which governs the new social relations, and which is that of union substituted for unity. Parliamentary relations cannot be aught but a reproduction of those that exist outside the precincts of Parliament; and it is a perversion of language, not to say worse, to apply the epithets "normal and rational" to the working of parliamentarism on the basis of a one and indivisible majority which is henceforth contrary to nature. Conformably to the new principle of political life, the chamber can be only a rendezvous of the representatives of the various national aspirations, met to come to understandings which will adjust the divergent interests in the way that is most equitable for all. The work of Parliament will be a continual series of compromises, settled by majorities whose composition may vary from one question to another, but which will in each case present a genuine reflection of the views and feelings of the true, of the only majority that can have been constituted on the basis of the particular question. The laws will no longer be the imperious decisions of a dominant majority, delivered against the will of a minority always reduced, if not to silence, at all events to impotence, but medium solutions arrived at with the real co-operation of the whole body of national representatives, who on each occasion combine freely to say yes or no according to their convictions and the wishes of their constituents. What can be more rational and more equitable?

But if the composition of the majorities varies from one question to another, how will they be able to give birth to and keep alive a government? Will not the existence of a homogeneous ministry and its collective responsibility to the chamber be made impossible, especially under regimes of the English type? Undoubtedly; but far from being a misfortune, this eventuality will be the salvation of parliamentary government, and will ensure the success of the new parliamentary method, which otherwise would be but an idle dream of the millennium. The homogeneity and the solidarity of the ministry are, like party government, of which they are the expression, better founded in history than in reason; created in England on the occasion and in view of the struggle of Parliament against the Crown, they no longer correspond to political necessities and are no longer of use for preserving a government of opinion; on the contrary even. To curb the royal prerogative, Parliament thrust on the Crown ministers taken from its midst, belonging to the party in a majority; being all identified with that party, they only championed its claims the better; all united among themselves against the Crown, forming a sort of chain, they prevented the Crown from getting the better of them singly. On the other hand, the creation of homogeneous Cabinets on rigid party lines had marked an advance on the practice of motley coalitions of the great families, which combined under the leadership of a distinguished chief, the head of a group, to exploit power, without paying heed to public opinion, whose influence was as yet *nil;* the rigid party lines symbolized principles and convictions (hence Burke's enthusiasm for parties). In the plan of the Cabinet representing the dominant party, which was directed against the Crown, the latter, defeated and resigned, soon found its advantage: the ministry shielded it, ensured it the immunity of its new "irresponsible" position, and served as a buffer between it and Parliament, as well as between Parliament and the nation. But when public opinion had become supreme and every power bowed before it, all these precautions and all these advantages became objectless. The ministry had been the garrison of Parliament in the fortress of the Crown; this fortress was dismantled. Its function of buffer itself could henceforth be dispensed with; there was no longer any collision possible between the Crown and Parliament, nor between the House and the nation, the Crown being reduced to complete impotence, and the House submissively registering the will of the nation, ever since it has ceased to represent the privileges of a ruling class. In the present day, when public opinion invested with the political suffrage has but to make a sign for all the holders of power to do humble obeisance, these weapons intended for the defence of popular liberties — the solidarity of party, the homogeneous ministry, and the collective responsibility of ministers — are as out-ofdate as the moats, the drawbridges, and the towers of mediaeval castles in the age of gunpowder and dynamite; they do but impede the free circulation of the forces of opinion.

The responsibility which is supposed to govern parliamentary relations comes to nothing but general irresponsibility: the members, obliged to follow their party, on pain of depriving it of power, are dispensed from following the voice of their conscience, their responsibility disappears in that of the party; it is the party that comes up for judgment before the electors, and whether it is convicted or acquitted, all its members are censured or commended without distinction, the good as well as the bad; it is not so much they and their merit or demerit that are involved, as the government which they support or oppose. The ministers, in their turn, easily hide behind the collective title: however incompetent or culpable they may be, it is impossible to punish one of them without punishing all; when one is called to account, the whole Cabinet demands a "vote of confidence," and in nine cases out of ten makes its own adherents Swallow their resentment. It is almost always an accident that causes the fall of the ministry; and so long as this accident does not occur, the followers of the ministry defend it servilely with their persons, like the janissaries who faithfully mounted guard around a sultan up to the moment when they chose to assassinate him. In England, where these accidents are uncommon, because, especially since the extension of the suffrage, the members pledge themselves before the electors to support a particular party leader, who is head of the Cabinet or may become so, the irresponsibility of the ministry to Parliament is still greater; whatever may be the private views of those who form the majority, the ministry is sure to last out the term of the legislature, if its majority is not too small; it is accountable, in reality, only to the electors from whom it practically holds office, that is to say, it will have to come before them again and ask them for a bill of indemnity for itself and its docile supporters. In the meanwhile, it can do very much what it likes; granted that it takes care not to run counter to the opinion of the country and wantonly compromise the welfare of the party, still it escapes the effective control of the representatives of the nation, which might protect it against its impulses or its failings, prevent it from committing blunders, perhaps irreparable and disastrous for the country. This control — it is idle to blink the fact — is almost non-existent; the role of a "private member" is reduced to a cipher; the greater part of his parliamentary activity consists in walking up and down the division lobbies; he is simply a voting machine. Thus the solidarity of the ministers and that of the members of the majority, which place both of them in a position of reciprocal dependence, do but paralyze at one time governmental activity, wherever there are no longer stable majorities, at another parliamentary control, if not both together, as in continental countries. But as this dependence is the basis of the power of the parties, parliamentarism, founded on party government, is landed in the deadlock of *nec tecum vivere possum nec sine te.*

This Gordian knot would be cut by the abolition of the collective responsibility of the ministers: the life of ministries would no longer depend on tho good pleasure of party majorities; the latter would no longer be able to create and sustain Cabinets, and they would no longer have any interest in constituting themselves, once power is put out of their reach. But while doing away with the abuses and difficulties entailed by the hold which the dominant parties possessed over the government, the change of parliamentary methods proposed by me would not abolish the legitimate dependence of the government on the representatives of the nation; this dependence will be fully secured by the individual responsibility of the ministers. In proposing to protect them from the discretionary power of the members of the legislatures, I have no intention whatever of borrowing the doctrinaire solution of the separation of the legislative and the executive, which for some time past has been urged as a remedy for the evils of parliamentarism, the example of the United States being quoted, but inaptly, in support of it. We are acquainted with the serious inconveniences produced by the separation of powers, established by the framers of the American constitution and accentuated in practice; we have seen how it has completely miscarried, and, instead of ensuring the independence of the executive, has helped to put it under the thumb of the legislative. The exclusion of the ministers from Congress has not enabled them to dispense with the assistance of the legislative to govern successfully, and the executive has had to pay for this assistance in the form of favours to the dominant party with all the more promptness that its head owed his election to that party. If it is party that creates or sustains the executive, the latter will find it demauding its wages everywhere, within the precincts of Parliament as well as outside them — that is the lesson taught by experience. The legal separation of the powers will always remain a vain precaution so long as power is wielded by parties. To safeguard the reciprocal independence and the responsibility of the legislative and of the executive, it is, on the contrary, highly desirable to place them face to face, under the eye of that all-powerful arbiter, public opinion.

The mainspring of representative government is not its machinery, however perfected; it is the light that it sheds on the acts of the rulers; it is the publicity which attaches to all See above, Vol. II, pp. 130-132.
their sayings and doings. If this light is insufficient, the most ingenious governmental mechanism gets out of order, and the best men who have to work it deteriorate; if there is plenty of light, it makes up for the defects of the institutions and raises the character of the men by increasing their responsibility; it dispels selfishness and ambition, it silences greed and vanity, individual as well as collective; it regulates the movements of the divergent social and political forces, it provides them with checks and balances, it establishes an equilibrium between them better than any machinery. Consequently, the first criterion of political institutions, as well as of political methods, is the greater or lesser degree of light and openness, of publicity and responsibility, which they admit of in the relations of the rulers with the ruled and among them. I have shown how the practice of collective ministerial responsibility has ended in decreasing the light inside parliament; at one time it is the solidarity of the Cabinet that intercepts it, at another the solidarity of the majority, of the party. Great care must therefore be taken not to allow these already flickering rays to be still further obstructed by a constitutional partition between the legislative and. the executive. The prime function of a parliament, that which is its *raison d'etre,* is the control of the executive; how can it exercise this control if the ministers are hidden from it? The sphere of the national interests entrusted to the legislative and the executive being one and indivisible, the co-operation of these two powers is a matter of necessity; how will they be able to co-operate if they are kept at a distance from each other? Yet, if the presence of the ministers in the assemblies and their direct collaboration with the representatives of the nation is the *conditio sine qua non* of the good working of representative government, the ministers must not be the plaything of parties, of their shifting majorities; the assembly must not encroach on the province of the executive, just as it must not itself be dragged at the heel of ministers controlling legislation as well as administration. "For the powers to be always distinct, it is not necessary that they should be entirely separated," said Mounier, the celebrated member of the *Constituante* of 1789. I agree with this proposition, and I complete it by another, which is its counterpart: "For the powers to be united, it is not necessary that they should be blended." The continuance of the ministers in the assemblies and the substitution for their collective responsibility of individual responsibility would quite meet the double preoccupation expressed by these propositions, and would bring everything into right focus both in the legal organization and in the practical methods of parliamentary life.

This plan, without modifying in any way the essence of the rights and the reciprocal duties of the national representation and of the executive, will rectify their mutual relations and their functions which are so perverted at the present day. It will begin by establishing stability in the government and the effective responsibility of those who govern. It will no longer be possible to raise those parliamentary storms which carry off all the ministers with a single gust, because one of them has lost the confidence of the chamber or has brought forward a bill of which it disapproves, or, again, because their opponents want to step into their shoes. The ministers will be removable only one by one, by attacking each singly and bringing definite charges against him. Under these circumstances they will have nothing to fear from the manoeuvres of the parties: as they will no longer form a body, there can no longer be a ministerial party and an anti-ministerial party, for the same member may be the supporter of one minister and the opponent of another; still less is it possible, without being landed in absurdities, to admit the hypothesis of a ministerial party and an anti-ministerial party organized and kept up for the sake of each minister separately. A minister therefore will be able to live and act outside or above parties. No doubt it will be always possible to get up an attack on him; but if the onslaught is not sufficiently justified by the public interest to attract a majority spontaneously, it would have little chance of success: when the minister is overthrown, there will be only one office available for the whole victorious army; how is it to be divided? The game will not be worth the candle. Besides, to get rid of a minister, it will no longer be possible to employ the easy tactics in vogue at the present day: the indictment which is brought against a jointly responsible ministry is often made up of constructive charges, it is its "policy" that is arraigned, or is supposed to be arraigned; but when the conduct of a particular minister has to be reviewed, the discussion must be *ad hominem* and *ad rem.* As a rule, the favourite plan is to upset a Cabinet even without any direct indictment, on an incident or on a quibble, by lying in wait behind a measure or even a question of procedure, a question of the order of business." It will be impossible to play this game with a minister individually responsible, whose shortcomings will have to be demonstrated in an explicit debate. If the minister is not openly censured for clearly specified faults, if the vote of the chamber bears only on the measure brought in or supported by him, he will not have to resign, unless he considers that it is impossible for him to carry out the directions of the chamber. But, on the other hand, if he is not free from reproach, he will not be able to hide behind the Cabinet. The member, in his turn, will not be obliged to wink at a reprehensible act of a minister, or even to vote for a ministerial measure of which he disapproves, for fear of plunging the country into a ministerial crisis; he will recover his liberty, as well as his responsibility.

The new position thus assigned to ministers in assemblies will change the character of the men who hold office, and the way in which they discharge their duties. A minister will be selected for his special competence and not for his merits as a political gladiator or his talents as a tactician skilled in piloting the ministerial bark through the shoals of Parliament. There will be no need to belong to a political syndicate to attain to or to keep in power; a great financier, a skilful diplomatist, an eminent administrator will no longer be excluded because they do not belong to the dominant political persuasion. But while being specialists, they are not to be purely specialists; to defend their views before a national assembly, to make an impression on it, they will have to be recruited from among broad-minded and far-seeing men, they must have the making of statesmen. As he will not have to be always in the breach fighting for his ministerial life, a minister will be able to devote himself to the study and the despatch of the business of his department, without leaving the real management of it to the permanent officials. Being no longer condemned to the precarious existence of a member of a Cabinet, he will be better able to resist the solicitations of the members who VOL. II—3 a demand favours for their constituents. Similarly, when addressing the chamber, he will be able to speak the truth, without having to ask himself whether the Cabinet will suffer for it or not; he will be able to give a piece of his mind to any one who may require it; he will be the representative of the general interest as opposed to particular interests; he may become a sort of tribune of the people confronting the plutocratic or other oligarchies which install themselves in democratic assemblies as easily as under the regime of privilege.

Taking part in political discussions whenever they think fit, and sharing with the chambers the right of legislative initiative, the ministers will continue to discharge the office of connecting link between the two powers, which, to the champions of the cabinet system, with Bagehot at their head, appears to constitute its *raiso7i d'etre* and its special merit. Their collaboration will not be less valuable than it is now, nor less efficacious; on the contrary. As the ministers will no longer be politicians of the lobby or the platform, but expert specialists, they will be better able to "aid the Chamber with the knowledge that experience, practice of affairs and familiarity with difficulties of execution continually impart to the executive power," to use the words of Mirabeau. Their authority will be less formal, because they will no longer be heads of disciplined parties nor dispensers of "spoils to the victors," but it will be more flexible and more insinuating, because it will be founded on their personal qualities as superior men, as statesmen able to serve as guides, as torch-bearers to earnest men who are seeking their way. The leadership of the ministers will gain in moral strength what it will lose, apparently, in material strength; they will be leaders of men without being managers of men or captains conducting troops to the assault. This change in the position of the ministers will inevitably be accompanied by a marked curtailment of their formal attributions; being no longer the representatives and the heads of a parliamentary majority, they will no longer have the necessary authority for the control of the chamber, nor the responsibility attaching thereto; they will no longer be able to act as general contractors for the work of the assembly and gather into their own hands all the threads of parliamentary activity. There will necessarily take place a division. a sort of decentralization, in the discharge of their present duties, which would be a welcome change; for the responsible Cabinet, in order to meet its obligations and consolidate its authority, has been led to take so many duties upon itself that it can no longer bear the burden of them, and its failing powers of control do but contribute to the parliamentary paralysis. To manage the business of the assembly the ministers will have to divide their duties or even make them over to the chair, who might be assisted for this purpose by a semiofficial committee of representatives of the various groups, on the model, for instance, of the *Senioren-Convent* in the German Reichstag.

As regards the preparation of legislative measures, the abolition of the cabinet system will necessitate a development of the system of standing committees, which might yield excellent results on these two conditions, that they are not hole-and-corner committees as in the American Congress, and not composed on a party basis, as in the French Chamber, for instance, where the main preoccupation, when important committees are appointed, is not so much to choose competent members as to eliminate the minority

or reduce it as much as possible. The duty of the committees is not to take decisions, but to prepare the materials for them by a thorough discussion of every aspect of the question. It would therefore be proper to appoint champions of every different view, irrespective of party distinctions and of the numerical strength of parties in the chamber. The committees will present their report, and the chamber will afterwards decide in the plenitude of its independence and its power. The neutral composition of the standing committees will prevent that usurpation of power which is apprehended by some persons from the example of the committees of the National Convention in the French Revolution; once they cease to represent the dominant party, their decisions will only have the significance of deliberations of experts who have carefully studied the question. The publicity of their procedure will remove any lingering danger and will ensure their labours A confirmation of this view Trill be found in an instructive article in the *Quarterly Review,* of October, 1901, entitled "The Paralysis of Parliament," which reviews the work of the session of V.KH, or rather the waste of that session of the House of Commons.
the maximum of efficacy: the ministers will always be at liberty to attend the sittings of the committees and to speak in them, and not allowed only, as in the French Parliament, to submit their observations and withdraw immediately afterwards. The same option of attending the sittings of the committees, but without the right of speaking in them, might be extended to all the members, who, in this way, would get a better notion of things. There would be only the committee on foreign affairs and perhaps that on military affairs in which the presence of members who are not committee-men could not be allowed.

The function of connecting-link between the legislative and the executive discharged by the ministers, associated so closely with the work of the chamber and of its committees, will be in no way impaired by the fact that they will no longer be united themselves by a collective responsibility. Independence does not necessarily entail isolation. *If* a question arises which concerns more than one department, nothing would prevent the respective ministers from coming to an understanding. Neighbours have no need to be formed into a Cabinet to talk over a matter of common interest. If the ministers cannot agree, the chamber will decide between them, and all the more equitably that there will no longer be a majority to defend a minister at all hazards nor an organized opposition to attack him. The cases in which all the ministers must act in concert are not common, but, once more, nothing will prevent them, in such cases, from holding councils. Instead of the "Council of ministers," there will be councils of ministers, who will meet whenever the need or expediency of meeting makes itself felt. In ordinary circumstances it is the settlement of the budget that will require these consultations. Foreign or home complications may also make them necessary. The colleagues of the minister concerned will give him the benefit of their knowledge and experience, which will lighten his moral responsibility, but leave him alone answerable to the chamber. The councils of ministers could be presided over by the head of the State, who would play the part of moderator, of arbiter, and would find in this function, as well as in the selection of ministers, a means of escape from the position of *"pore ft Vengrais,"* which did not suit Napoleon as First Consul.

The duties of ministers and their relations with the legislative once settled on the basis which has just been stated, the life of the chamber, considered in itself, will be completely renewed. As the ministers' places and the fate of parties will no longer be at stake, every measure may be examined for itself, honestly and straightforwardly; the chamber will become a real deliberating assembly, instead of an arena of the parties, a theatre of civil war. There will always be contests of opinions and interests in it, but the combatants will be obliged to fight without a mask and to confine their strife to the sphere of those opinions and those interests. Ambitions, intrigues, and electioneering preoccupations will assuredly not be banished from the chamber, but they will no longer be able to enjoy such free scope, to hide behind the general interests as easily as they do now. The fear that the chamber may sink into impotence and anarchy in consequence of the disappearance of a " government majority " and a systematic opposition, is unfounded. The functions of both will only be better discharged under the new conditions. The criticism of the acts of the government will be more effective, because it will be more free; when the ministry and the majority are no longer hand and glove, a reprehensible act of a minister will raise against him the upright and the sound-thinking men in every quarter of the chamber; the offending minister may be brought to book without any fear of playing into the hands of the "other side" and weakening one's own, and without arousing the scepticism of public opinion, which nowadays has no illusions about the sincerity of the Opposition. Nor will the legislative business suffer from the multiplicity of the groups in the chamber or from the disappearance of the omnibus programmes. Every great question that is stirring the country will have, shanks to the league system, its spokesmen in the chamber, who will try to make the latter take it up, will collect all the legislative material, will draft bills, will conduct the discussion of them, will pilot the assembly through the difficulties and details of the question which they will have mastered better than any one else. If they are not numerous enough, and have not succeeded in obtaining sufficient adhesions in the other groups, the conclusion will be that the country is not yet ripe for the solution of the problem. The parliament would then legislate on other less contentious matters, and, in general, would legislate less and devote itself more to supervising the government and public expenditure, which ought to be its first duty. The same thing will take place when the champions of a certain reform have carried their point and accomplished their mission. Maybe when a great question has been settled, it will not be possible, under the system of leagues for limited objects, to take up another important measure before the renewal of the chamber, which will have brought a new question into the foreground. But do we see chambers in the present day solve several great problems during the life of one parliament? It is a matter of congratulation when a single important reform has been carried by the end of it. Without delaying the measures really demanded by public opinion, the useful reforms, the new system, which will take the place of the factotum majority, will simply ripen them, and at the same time provide a natural cheek on the extravagant use of the members' legislative initiative, which is now vainly combated by artificial and often arbitrary means.

All these results, crowned by the free unions of the members of different groups according to their opinions on the particular questions, will be brought about by the abolition of the collective responsibility of the ministers, because it will have made the exercise of power by the parties an impossibility. So long as power remains within the reach of parties, the formation of spontaneous and genuine majorities, determined by the problems of the day and carried out with the sole object of solving them, will remain a pious wish; so long as there are "spoils" in prospect, the most monstrous coalitions, the most artificial majorities, will be the most natural ones. It is when vice does not pay that virtue is most easily cultivated. The "spoils" are the natural consequence of the hold which the parties possess over the executive; and they possess it because they create and sustain the executive. In governments of the English type, it is the ministry which they create and sustain; in regimes of the American type, it is the President, who is a sort of prime minister, but appointed for a term. Under regimes of the first kind, the party creates the executive, thanks to the system of the collective responsibility of the ministers; and in governments on the American pattern, it creates the head of the executive, thanks to the system of popular election, which also ends in an election by the parties. Consequently, if the abolition of the collective responsibility of the ministers can stop the exploitation of power by the parties under regimes of the English type, this result would be fully attained in the United States only by the abolition of the popular election of the President. His election would have to be entrusted to the national legislature, which will be able to perform this duty most satisfactorily when it is no longer organized on the basis of party majorities. No doubt democratic formalism would stoutly oppose such a reform. It is the same feeling that leads advanced political circles in Switzerland to demand the appointment of the federal executive by the people; this innovation would undoubtedly be one of the greatest political misfortunes that could befall the gallant little Alpine Republic, if the experience of America proves anything. According to this experience one must insist on the withdrawal of the. presidential election from the people; the risk that one runs of being treated by the latter as Gil Bias was treated by the Archbishop of Grenada in no way affects the exigencies of the logical situation.

Once deprived, by one means or another, of their hold over the executive, the permanent parties will be decapitated, and with them the political formalism which dominates and oppresses the life of contemporary democracies. The finishing blow will be given to it by the introduction of the new methods into parliaments, which will re-establish therein the control of the representatives of the nation and the responsibility of the rulers, which will enable and oblige both to walk according to the reason of things, and not according to conventions, which will replace representative government, now struggling with shams, in the sphere of realities. This last and final victory over formalism will have been systematically prepared by the new method of political action, which in all its stages, from the formation of the smallest branch of a league onwards, will have been guided by the same idea — free union and individual responsibility.

XVIII

Of course this victory over political formalism, if it is to be genuine, must be won first of all in the mind of the elector. The reforms which have just been examined, the alterations proposed in the working of parliamentary government, the modifications in the electoral system, the new modes of combination of the electors, all imply a profound change in the role of parties and in political manners, changes which are beyond the reach of the legislator. There is no legal authority which can issue and enforce the following decree: (1) Permanent parties are and shall be dissolved; (2) the pursuit of power is expressly forbidden to parties; (3) the electors shall henceforth display public spirit. To make such an enactment enforceable, it is necessary to change the mental attitude of the electors, to eradicate those conventional notions, those prejudices which have taken possession of their minds, and which make them believe that the citizen who follows his party blindly is a "patriot," and that the prostitution of power to a party is a pious action. These *idols,* as Bacon would say, must be destroyed. Men must be taught to use their judgment, and to act independently. It is on the accomplishment of this work of liberation that the whole future of democracy depends. Hitherto the victorious struggle which democracy has carried on in the world has been mainly, and necessarily, a struggle for material liberty; moral liberty, which consists in thinking and acting as free reason dictates, has yet to be achieved by it. It has carried the *habeas corpus* by force, but the decisive battle of democracy will be fought on the *habeas animum.*

The greatness and the poverty of contemporary democracy turn on this distinction between the two formulas. Through the mere fact of having realized material liberty, democracy has given more happiness to the nations than the other regimes had ever afforded them; "the greatest happiness of the greatest number" has never been less distant from its realization than in the present day. The critics and the detractors of democracy forget this fact as well as the condition in which mankind lived under the former regimes, and they fasten on democracy as if these regimes belonged to the golden age of the history of humanity. The disorders of which democratic government has presented or continues to present the spectacle in certain countries are paralleled or equalled, to say the least of it, by the experience of the anterior regimes; but the latter had no political liberty to compensate them and to cure their ills, and they have passed away. Democracy has brought with it liberty, and it has renewed the life of societies. This liberty has been realized in its highest degree, other circumstances contributing thereto, in the United States, and never has the earth resounded with so mighty a song of triumph as that endless psean chanted by American life with a joyousness and a fervour which inanimate objects themselves seem to share. But nowhere also has it appeared more clearly than in the United States that political freedom, which can build up external liberty only, is not complete without the citizen's independence of mind, and without the spontaneous and vigilant energy of his will. In the absence of this independence and this vigilance, demagogism and corruption have entered the house in broad day as a thief enters in the night. Democracy thenceforth received a check, and not through excess of liberty, as so many of its critics imagine, but from a deficiency of it, from a want of moral liberty in this government of free reason.

To retrieve this check and prevent complete ruin, the remedy is obvious: reason and liberty, and a double dose of reason and liberty! It is not by cultivating the emotions, which we have seen play such a preponderant part in existing political methods, it is not by working up sentiment, even with the best intentions, that the mind of the citizen can be reformed. Not that in civic life the action of sentiment is to be despised; nothing can be founded without sentiment; but nothing durable can be founded with sentiment alone; to build on it is to build on a quicksand; to build on reason is to build on a rock. Of course this reason is not knowledge only; reduced to the external cultivation of the intellect, to the simple furnishing of the mind, it cannot form the man nor the citizen. To the reason of knowledge must be allied that of duty. The judgment as well as the will, to be exercised freely and spontaneously, that is to say effectively, must have their motor in the moral force that is within us. It is therefore just as necessary to enlighten the conscience of the elector as his mind. The individual conscience contains.the furnace which feeds public virtue, and it is on individual responsibility that the commonwealth ultimately rests. This responsibility sustains the life of the commonwealth like that central tire which, according to Buffon, sustains the life of the earth, and the gradual extinction of which will entail the death of our globe.

But the awakened intellects and consciences and the sense of individual responsibility developed in the citizen would not of themselves be enough to ensure the free and spontaneous action without which democracy will remain all on the surface. It is obvious that inward liberty cannot assert itself in public life without outward liberty, that, as the one without the other cannot keep the commonwealth alive, the latter has an equal need of free institutions and of manners in keeping with the institutions. This equation, which Tacitus has already referred to in his famous apostrophe *Quid leges sine moribus,* is however not yet complete, for besides the institutions and the manners, besides the legal means for realizing the object of political society, and of the spirit which animates it, there is a third factor, the co-operation of which is not less necessary, and which has not been sufficiently appreciated: the methods for making the means serve the end, the political methods. They too must be in harmony with the institutions and the manners; if not, they will warp the former, as ill-regulated machinery is warped, and will paralyze or hamper the will and the best intentions of those who work them. It is on the efficacy of the political methods of a regime that the success of the regime itself consequently depends in the end, and in this sense it may be said that everything in governments resolves itself into a question of methods. Democracy, being a regime of free reason, can succeed only if it employs methods imbued with the same spirit. Now hitherto it has only employed contrary methods, imbued with the spirit of the old regime, in which men and things were not rated at their intrinsic worth, but according to conventional notions and external and arbitrary classifications. That democracy has not always been free to shake off the old methods, that more often than not a combination of traditions and circumstances has kept it chained to them, explains the fact, but does not get rid of it. Consequently, to the reason for the comparative failure of democracy which I have given, by attributing it to a deficiency of moral liberty, must be added — what, after all, is but a complementary aspect of it — the unsuitable methods which democracy has adopted. The moral remedy, therefore, cannot be complete unless it affects the methods, or in other words, the *habeas animum* will not be realized unless the political methods change in the same direction. All the modifications in the legal and extra-legal organization, which have been suggested here, have been so only with a view to this result; they have no intrinsic self-sufficing efficacy, they are but means for developing the liberty of the civic mind and conscience, and for making them pass from power into action. The system of leagues for specified objects and limited periods of time is but a device for awakening and combining the civic intellects and consciences; the sole object of the preliminary polls is to bring out their free agreement and to stimulate it by giving it a legal sanction; the preferential vote also tends to quicken and encourage the private judgment of the elector for the best discharge of his public duty; the abolition of the collective responsibility of ministers to parliament has the same psychological object in view, that is, to get the intellects and consciences to become their own masters in order to guide their wills freely, in public life, according to the general interest, in a word, to restore to each and all the responsibility which is non-existent or perverted by a conventional standard of conduct and by unsuitable methods.

Intellectual culture, moral culture, renewal of political methods, all having the individual conscience and individual responsibility for their objective, naturally aim at society over the individual. Controversy alone has been able to set up, for its needs, an antagonism between the two, to separate what is inseparable. Individualism, which makes the individual, free, cognizant of himself, of his rights and of his duties, the corner-stone of democracy, cannot be affected by the discredit which has been cast on it; it is not enough to distort the meaning of words and degrade them, to degrade the ideas and the things which they represent. True individualism, which is in no way synonymous with selfishness and disregard of social justice, is fully alive to the social aspect of the phenomena which are reflected in groups or classes of society and assume a greater luminous intensity there. All the factors of the political renovation, which have just been reviewed, present themselves also under a more or less accentuated social aspect. Intellectual culture, on the one hand, is specially necessary for the masses, who have been recently invested with the suffrage, and as yet have too little leisure, if not inclination, to learn. After having vainly resisted the extension of the parliamentary franchise to the working-men of the English cities, Robert Lowe avenged himself for his defeat by the sarcastic sally: "Now we shall have to educate our masters." The remark is almost as true at the present day as in 1867. But it requires another as its complement: "Now we shall have to educate ourselves," for the class above the labourers and artisans is still remarkably ignorant. Its members no doubt can read and write very well, and cast accounts still better, but in matters relating to the commonwealth they often display an ignorance which is sometimes really incredible. The problem of the cultivation of the civic conscience assumes a still greater acuteness in the case of this class. Everywhere they exhibit complete indifference to the public weal; everywhere, and from the outset, as soon as they have come into power, they have held aloof, either devoting themselves The reader will remember the violent and well-founded reproaches addressed on this subject by Disraeli, in the Young England period, to the English middle class, which had been just admitted to the parliamentary franchise (Vol. I, p. 5o). In France the bourgeoisie has shown even more readiness to throw down the burdens of the political power which it had demanded with such ardour. Cf. in this connexion and as to the way in which the bourgeoisie, by its apathy or its anxiety for its own position, caused France to lose liberty more than once in the course of the century which followed the Revolution, an article by M. George Villain entitled " Les classes dirigeantes et le pouvoir politique" *(Revue politique et purlementaire,* January, 1901). This writer quotes a curious appeal, for stimulating the ardour of the electors, addressed by a commissioner of the executive Directory attached to a municipal department of Paris to one of the members of a charitable committee, in Messidor, year IV: "As you are in touch with the people, you are requested to represent to them how important it is for the public welfare that they should go to the communal assemblies. Point out to them the irreparable harm done by the carelessness of virtuous men who omit to attend the primary assemblies and leave the field open to scoundrels who, under cover of the revolutionary government, could rob and murder us with impunity. Enlighten the people on the choice of their officers. On that choice depends the enforcement of the laws and the strengthening of the Republic. " These lines might just as well have been written at New York in 1901. The classic exhortation in the United States — "attend the primaries" — is even to be found exclusively to the accumulation and enjoyment of wealth, or from indolence and apathy. This attitude of the bourgeoisie singularly complicates the problem of democracy and of universal suifrage; it is not only a question of the masses, of the "vile multitude," as the representatives of the bourgeoisie used to say, but also and above all of that select class itself; to the ignorance of the masses is added the ferocious selfishness of the "better element."

For this reason and for others besides, the question of political methods presents itself as a social question as well. The free unions which form the basis of the new method of political action will not be able to achieve complete success so long as the separation of classes which characterizes existing social relations subsists, the separation between the rich and the poor, between the educated and the uneducated. It is this separation which, other circumstances contributing, has given a check to democratic government in large agglomerations such as New York, for instance, as the reader is aware. What can the best methods do in such surroundings? Union in the political sphere will not be fruitful and solid unless it is cemented by the confidence which springs from the contact of men in non-political relations. It needs the *social spirit* wrongly attributed to the old society, which could not realize it because it was founded on privilege. Democratic society was called to realize it, but was prevented from doing so by the social differentiation due to the rise of industry as well as to the progress of knowledge, and by the selfishness of the class which has benefited most from the industrial transformation. The action of man on man is a spring of government as necessary in democracy as under other regimes; the incentives alone to this action and the spirit in which it is exercised must change, and be guided by sentiments of a more disinterested nature and more respectful of human dignity than those of which the old regimes have left the reminiscence. Democratic society cannot do without leadership, which in a naive pride it thought itself bound and able to shake off; the experience of the representative Caucus, by means of which it there in so many words. Barely one expression need be changed: for "virtuous men " substitute " the better element." Cf. the first part of this work.

fancied that it had exorcised the leadership, and which forced one on it in most humiliating circumstances, has supplied a demonstration of this which would be decisive, in the absence of others. Social spirit, the action of man on man, and the leadership, which are so many steps of a ladder, must be reestablished; but this cannot be effected in modern society by class ascendency, nor by tradition or custom, which have had their day, nor, and still less, by a coercive organization, which will never have its day, even if it inscribes the word " solidarity" in gigantic red letters on its banner. They will be able to develop only in an atmosphere of free influences, established spontaneously by the adhesion of the reason and the conscience of those over whom they are wielded to the reason and the conscience of those who wield them. Even class selfishness, to what jurisdiction can it be made amenable? What tribunal can sentence it to mend its ways and enforce the decision, but that of reason and of individual conscience? Social renovation cannot be accomplished otherwise, and without social renovation the renovation of democratic government cannot produce its full effect. Thus the social aspect itself of the problem of democracy makes it depend on the individual. Democracy turns, like the earth on its axis, on the individual conceived as a conscience, moral conscience and intellectual conscience; at least this must be so if it is to fulfil its destiny.

Supposing, it will be said, that all these conditions on which the formalism that oppresses democratic government can be overcome are clearly discerned, will they be easy to fulfil? Is it not a dream of the millennium to expect the victory from them? That depends on what is understood by victory in the sphere of political and social transformations. If we mean the complete realization of the end proposed, if we fancy that the enemy ean be dislodged and made to surrender at discretion by vigorous assaults or skilful stratagems, we are under an illusion. It is not thus that social or political revolutions are accomplished. The evolution of societies resembles the movements of the beam of what is known in mechanics as an *unstable balance,* in which the two forces applied on each side of the beam, *power* and *resistance,* are never in equilibrium. Represented in social life by opposite principles, they are in constant strife, each being in regard to the other at one time power and at another resistance. Able to gain one from the other a more or less considerable space on the indefinite line of the beam of the social balance, they can only shift it or bend it farther in the one or the other direction. If one of the contending forces succeeds in changing the inclination of the lever to its own advantage, it has won. That is to say that the victories which bring about the political or social transformations consist of changes in the trend of society towards the one or the other of the opposing principles. However far they may go, these changes never entail the absolute triumph of a principle, they never get to the end of the beam, — the force of resistance, that of men and of things, being never destroyed, — but they turn or move society in the direction leading to that ideal point to which it can draw nearer by means of fresh efforts, without ever reaching it. To gain a few points on the indefinite series of degrees — that is the task which confronts each generation and which should satisfy its ambition and its ardour, and also its pride when the task is performed. The immensity of the efforts necessary to obtain an apparently so slender result constitutes their grandeur, which gives life its *raison cVMre* and makes it worth living. Moreover, two degrees, two degrees and no more, may turn the scale; one degree in advance and one degree to the rear of the fulcrum of the beam, and the trend, as regards the forces which are contending for supremacy in society, is towards good, towards truth, towards happiness, or the position is reversed, and the trend is towards evil, towards error, towards ruin. The main thing for a society which does not let itself drift is to discern the right point to make for and always work towards it, and so diminish as much as possible the distance which must separate them.

In the particular problem under our consideration the object is in reality just the same. In the war which has to be waged against formalism, there can be no question of banishing it forever from the realm, of installing the citizen's independence of thought and autonomy of conscience as absolute sovereigns, of flooding the commonwealth with public spirit, of making the politicians virtuous, of putting an end to political corruption, of eliminating party spirit, etc. Formalism will never lose its rights; it is inevitable in every body of men, the great majority of whom are naturally incapable of discriminating and judging, and necessarily accept an external rule for their conduct, follow a conventional token, look to the sign or the label. This is especially the case in the life of a democracy, owing to the great number of citizens; purely formal criterions will always act like a magnet on their minds. It is not a question of doing away with formalism, but of diminishing its influence, and increasing that of judgment, of which the world will never have enough. Sentiment will always act on the majority of mortals with more force than reason, but it is desirable to lessen the power of blind impulses and to let rational motives have a greater share in the conduct of the citizens. Once more, in pitting reason and the individual conscience against formalism, the point is by no means to transform each elector into a cartesian philosopher and into a moralist always bent on "knowing himself." The average elector will always fall into line, but it is material that he should do so in a less passive, less servile way, that he should look as often as possible where he is going, that those whom he follows should not be so sure of his automatic adhesion as to lead him as they please. The *mechanical* element will never be eliminated from government, but a larger share of influence should be given in it to the *personal* and responsible element, which enables individuality to develop and assert itself in political life. Political greed, designs on the public weal, will disappear only with mankind, but as many obstacles as possible should be put in their path. It is the same thing with party spirit; whether it is a survival of ancient barbarism, as Sir H. Sumner Maine believed, or whether it is a product of civilization, it will always creep in among men who come together for common action; but it should not be allowed to obtrude itself and bear sway under the guise of loftier motives, it should be thrust back as much as possible and exposed more and more to the searching light It is related that Edmund Burke, when dining with Pitt, in September, 1791, insisted strongly on the dangers with which the contagion of French revolutionary principles threatened the country. Pitt, who was not so pessimistic, remarked: "Never fear, Mr. Burke, depend on it we shall go on as we are till the Day of Judgment." — "Very likely, sir," replied Burke, "His the day of *no judgment* that I am afraid of." of day. But to obtain these effects, even in a slight degree, to diminish the evil, the idea of good must be present to men's minds, must be put before them; then they will be able to steer their course by it.

The new departure which seems to us indispensable for democratic society, how will it come about, and will it come about at all? Its realization will be subject to the general conditions of social formations and transformations, which are effected by the association of ideas and of material facts, and by their dissociation. The change of political conceptions in the direction of the individual conceived as a conscience, and of free unions, which are to become the principles of democratic organization, is linked with the moral crisis that contemporary society is passing through. This crisis, one of the gravest that humanity has experienced since the advent of Christianity, affects all the forms assumed by the notion of good and evil, of right and wrong — religion, social morality, political morality. Everywhere it is endeavouring to substitute the rational basis for the theological and the conventional basis. The one is tottering and collapsing, the other is not yet established. People are living in a state of uncertainty, are passing through what is commonly called the period of transition, which is a time of hope, but also of mortal anguish for those even who are only too willing to hope.

The crisis of democracy is, in the first place, a long-standing crisis of political morality, a crisis which seemed to be ended with the establishment of democratic forms, but which is still very far from being so. It will approach its solution, if it can receive one, alike more easily and with more difficulty than the great crisis of which it is a special aspect: it does not appear, in the eyes of the immense majority, to affect the conventional foundations of morality, political life being viewed by that majority as an external domain; consequently, the desired transformation will not encounter the same dogged resistance that would be offered by the traditional ecclesiastical and social notions which sway private life. But on the other hand, for that very reason, it will not appeal to the conscience with the same peremptoriness as the problem of personal conduct, it will not be able to bring into play, to use a theological term, the "salvation of the soul"; the impulse, instead VOL. II—3 R of coming from inside, will have to come from outside, from the pressure of material facts, of interests. Now interests, which are by their nature eminently conservative, yield only to the *ultima ratio* of grinding necessity. The resistance of interests, including intellectual habits, which are a form of human selfishness rather than a tendency of the mind, will be all the more formidable that it will not be inspired solely by sordid preoccupations, it will not rely exclusively on mercenary politicians and the crowd of unthinking electors, but also on men of loftier thought and purer heart. As the problem is in fact a moral one, it will suggest to these men whether they would not do better to uphold a system, bad in itself, in order to render its effect less mischievous, whether they would not be making a mistake in refusing this system the countenance of their honesty and their knowledge, at the risk of aggravating the harm which it does to society. It is a grave question for the conscience, which is raised in a general way by moral notions which are doomed, but not replaced, and on which society still lives. This conscientious scruple, how will it be met by well-meaning men, able to serve the commonwealth, and confronted with the existing party system, which is still the accepted groove of political activity? Even if they are devoid of ambition, will they hold aloof, because it is proved that the system of permanent parties, and the exercise of power by parties, are an evil and a mortal danger for democracy? Will they stand with arms folded until this antiquated system collapses for good and all? That is not very likely, as a rule they will say: "The king's government must be carried on." It is one of the tragic features of " periods of transition," this forced support of obsolete and artificial systems by upright and honest men, a support which, without being able to save what is doomed, increases moral confusion by keeping up the uncertainty as to right and wrong in the public mind, and defers the hour of reform. The new departure which has to be taken by democratic government will certainly encounter a serious obstacle from this quarter. It may also happen that reform will be precipitated, that the duration of the transition period will be curtailed, owing to the warmer reception that may be accorded to the new ideas by more enlightened minds, but above all to the dissolvent action of the abuses and ravages of an overstrained system, seconded by that powerful auxiliary known as the chapter of accidents.

" But, on the other hand, is it possible that the new departure may not be able to take place at all, and that democracy may succumb to the crisis in which it is struggling? Undoubtedly, unless the blissful theory of necessary progress is admitted, a theory not warranted by experience, in which the march of societies appears to resemble the movements of an unstable balance. There is no proof that democracy will come off victorious, but there is no proof either of the contrary. The spectacle which it presents, to us from day to day is not a very encouraging one; the tidings of the crushing defeats sustained by the democratic ideal now in one country and now in another reach us too frequently, and often extort the cry, *Redde mihi legiones,* by suggesting painful reflections on the dreams of youth and the hopes of mature age. But this experience has as yet nothing final about it, democratic government has not yet given the measure of its capacity; democratic institutions, left too often to their intrinsic force, have not always had the necessary accompaniment of corresponding manners, and have never had that of corresponding political methods; the "new wine has been put into old bottles." It is therefore premature to speak, as people do, of the failure of democracy; it is still far from having said its last word, and no one can foretell what that last word may be. There is only one thing that may be asserted: if democracy does not succeed in filling its forms with a moral substance and in adapting its modes of action thereto, it will run the risk of meeting the fate of previous political civilizations, which perished through inability to realize liberty. The example of the most brilliant of those civilizations, the Graco-Roman civilization, is a standing proof that the sacred flame of the commonwealth, if it is not kindled in the independent conscience, dies out, however bright the light which it may shed; that the formalism which becomes the cement of the body politic disintegrates it. In vain did the *poll's* of antiquity, in a desperate movement of self-preservation, put Socrates to death; it only signed its own death warrant. It is the same problem of formalism which, after centuries full of vicissitudes, rises before modern society, as threatening as ever, although the possibility of a catastrophe, to put it at the worst, is very remote. Our civilization possesses a force of resistance far superior to that of the society of antiquity, where the individual was completely absorbed in the *polis,* and all the manifestations of life, private as well as public, were confined within a single groove. When the decay of the old religious beliefs shattered this groove, society crumbled into dust. Thanks to the emancipation of the individual, which the Stoics inaugurated, and of which the Reformation, the French Revolution, and the advent of industrialism have ensured the triumph, our civilization is provided with a good many strongholds; the differentiation Qf thought and of modern life has created several centres of resistance in it: religion separated from the State, free science, art, independent letters, liberated economic activity, untrammelled social activity; the living springs of society can no longer be all corrupted. In vain does the formalism which in divers ways seeks to lead society back to uniformity diminish its force of resistance, the means of defence which individualism has stored up ensure the new society for a long time to come an advantage such as none of the previous societies have possessed. At the same time the democratic regime may count upon that general condition of which all regimes without exception get the benefit, and to which the great Swedish chancellor, Oxenstierna, referred when he said: *"Nescis, miJUi, qnantilla prudentia homines regantur;"* "How little wisdom is required for the government of mankind."

Whether the crisis of democracy takes this or that course, whether it is solved in one way or another — all the considerations involved in this question are a mere mental exercise from the standpoint of the practical problem which must be grappled with by democracy and which consists in achieving the *habeas animum.* Even if it were demonstrated that all the efforts made for this object are doomed to failure, that there is nothing left but to sound the knell of democracy with all the hopes that humanity has placed upon it, we should have to act precisely as if the final triumph of democratic government were a mathematical certainty. The reason for this is simple: to die fighting is better than a living death. But in the meanwhile, it is the political and social forms anterior to democracy which are dead. Therefore, leaving the dead to bury their dead, as the saying is, we must devote ourselves to the work of life, and at the voice of conscience which calls to duty, "ach contribute his personal efforts as bricks and mortar for building the walls of the free democratic city, the supreme refuge of human dignity: APPENDIXES APPENDIX I THE POWER OF SOCIAL INTIMIDATION AS A PRINCIPLE OF POLITICAL LIFE

The regulating principle of all government is the fear or the responsibility which tends to keep every member of the community in the path of duty, which influences their wills through the prospect of the consequences that would be entailed by neglect of duty. In propounding this idea I remarked that it would be erroneous, for this reason, to reserve fear as a "spring" or "principle" for despotic government, as Montesquieu does. That government, it may be added here, has another "spring," — *terror,*—because the exercise of power under despotic rule baffles all calculation; a despot or his ministers can have subjects beheaded, flung into prison, or transported to the other end of the kingdom without any reason being assigned therefor. On the other hand, under regimes in which the relations of the rulers and the ruled are governed by laws, whether written or not written, the injunctions of which, either express or implied, indicate what transgressors are liable to, there is no place for terror, but only for the fear of incurring the consequences attached beforehand to the evil deeds in the mind and the conscience of the agent. The object of the fear, or the *sanction,* —to use Bent ham's term, — to which one is exposed in public life is of four kinds: the legal sanction, the political sanction, the sanction of public opinion, and the inward sanction. In the first case the sanction is established by the express provisions of the law, and consists of penalties inflicted on the wrong-doers; in the second case the sanction comes from the working of the institutions: thus, under representative government, a minister or a member of Parliament, without incurring any punishment See above, Vol. II, p. 626 *et seq.* from the law, runs the risk of losing his position if he acts in a way considered as contrary to his duty by those entitled to decide; in the third case no harm is to be apprehended save the disapprobation of public opinion; in the fourth case it is only the censure of one's own conscience that has to be dreaded. The fact that among the motives which determ ine the conduct of a citizen may be found the noblest and the most spontaneous, so to speak, in no way invalidates the correctness of the formula which embraces them all under the single heading of fear as the supreme regulator of governments. Fear is the general incentive, although it differs according to the nature of those on whom it acts; in some persons it appeals to the coarse emotions implied by the term in its vulgar sense, while in others it strikes finer chords of the mind. One can be intimidated even by the action of the gentlest moral virtues; by their sole manifestation they make men bow humbly and submissively before their majesty. Certain languages therefore have but one expression for rendering feelings of veneration and of intense fear; and the idea of reverential dread is associated with the notion of goodness itself, as in the words of Milton: "How awful goodness is." It is not absolutely necessary either for the social result of intimidation that it should proceed directly from outside. The inward sanction and the moral freedom of conscience in no way exclude social intimidation. In the decisions of conscience on the duties of man towards himself a distinction must be drawn between the duties of the individual taken singly and those of the individual as a member of society. Only a man living the life of a hermit depends morally on himself without any qualification; the duties which his human dignity enjoins on him, even in the desert where he lives, are determined by his conscience without the slightest intervention from outside. But this is no longer the case when he forms part of society; the duties enjoined on him by his human dignity are widened by those which he has towards society. Through the mere fact of surrounding him, society confronts him with his duties, says to him: "You have obligations towards your fellow-men, consider them, examine your conscience, you shall be your own judge, and if the verdict is guilty, you shall be Abash'rt the devil stood,

And felt how awful goodness is. — *Paradise Lost.*

your own executioner." He is left to himself, he goes his own way, and he decides without appeal. Society, then, has nothing to do with the matter, it will be said. Yes, but who has indicted him, who has set up the gibbet to which he will eventually be dragged by himself, but society? Of what forces but those of society at large does this punitory power of the individual conscience form part?

The four sanctions which constitute the resources of the power of social intimidation overlie and complete one another. None of the lower sanctions is strong enough by itself; each, in a way, calls for the next which possesses a higher force, until they culminate in the supreme sanction, which is the inward sanction. The injunctions of the laws, even if sanctioned by the severest penalties and supported by the most formidable brute force, cannot obtain full acceptance if they are not accepted by men's minds and consciences. *A fortiori* must the dictates of duty commend themselves by their moral force in social relations, which are beyond the reach of the law. And they will commend themselves all the more completely in proportion as this moral force gains in fulness, in proportion as those who inspire fear and those in whom they inspire it are swayed by purer and more enlightened motives. Whatever be the social sanction, if it exacts obedience through interest only, it cannot intimidate sufficiently. If I obey the law solely from interest, if I bow to public opinion for the same reason, I shall not do so whenever I have an interest in not doing so; I shall therefore, in that case, escape the power of the law, I shall pay no heed to public opinion, I shall defy them. If I am never to escape their power, I must be held to it, not only by interest, but by duty. It is then only that each sanction, that of the laws, or of the working of the institutions, or of public opinion, will, each in its sphere, produce its full intimidatory effect. But for them to determine my duty, they must be of such a nature as to commend themselves to my conscience. If the law is unjust, I shall, on the contrary, make a point of disobeying it as soon as I can; if public opinion is tyrannical or ill informed, I shall resist it from a sense of duty; in any event, I shall try to elude their action. All their material power will not be strong enough to make me consider as right and wise what my conscience and my reason condemn, and force the free adhesion of my will. In short, their power of intimidation, in this case also, will not be complete. Besides, it may very well not be so even if it appeals to duty; that will depend on the nature of the duty, according as it is a true expression of the moral obligation or a factitious, conventional one. In this latter case enlightened consciences will not respond to its appeal; they will defy it. Under a despotic government, for instance, blind obedience to the sovereign's caprices, even if they are iniquitous, is honestly considered as a duty; but the moral conscience thus warped rights itself some day or other, and defeats the tyrannical power of the ruler. In republics, it is held to be a civic duty to vote for "yellow dogs " if they are regular candidates, and the act of "bolting" is looked on as a moral misdemeanour; but "mugwumps" arise, set at defiance public opinion, which professes this duty and tries to enforce it, and win the day. It follows, thus, that to be complete and absolute, the power of social intimidation, however great may be the material force of numbers by which it is backed, is obliged to moralize itself more and more to the point of taking up its abode in the conscience, free and enlightened, of the members of the community. By simply obeying, in a way, its own logic, *fear* is led to make force the handmaid of justice, and to press, in its own interest so to speak, in order to attain the maximum of its action, towards the continuous elevation of the idea of justice and of the notion of duty, and of the criteria by which they are recognized in practice. Under these circumstances, the power of social intimidation is not only an irresistible weapon in the hands of the multitude, but also becomes a means of defence and of action for the individual confronted with numbers. Henceforth he can meet the despotism of public opinion with a moral force capable of overawing it: as soon as free reason supported by the conscience can assert itself, there is no longer any place for the absolute sway of the majority, one may defy the majority by criticizing its opinions, by attacking its prejudices; a man may hold his own against numbers, may overawe the multitude by moral authority, although he be one against a thousand.

The property of the power of social intimidation as a principle of political life and the conditions on which it attains the maximum of its efficiency once recognized, the best political regime will turn out to be that which is the most favourable to their realization. I have pointed out the superiority possessed in this respect by democratic government over the other regimes. We can now sum up all the elements of this superiority in the general remark that it is the only regime under which the four sanctions of the power of social intimidation can be realized. The fulness of the legal sanction, which results from equal laws for all, is ensured in it through the fact that they are made by the representatives of all. Under a nonpopular regime equal laws for all may doubtless also be passed; but what guarantee is there that they will command the respect of everybody, that they will be observed by all and for all, when they emanate from a government founded on privilege? The political sanction would be wanting to these laws or would be confined to a part of the nation. It would, on the contrary, be complete in democracy, where all share in the government. The sanction of public opinion cannot be real either, under a non-democratic regime, because public opinion cannot manifest itself there with perfect liberty. The inward sanction itself, apparently quite independent of the political organization of societies, cannot produce its full effect as regards the citizen except under a free government. How could the citizen feel and develop within him a sense of his social obligations in a community of slaves? How could such a community appeal to his conscience, remind him of his civic duty when it acknowledges none, cowering as it is in subjection? Like a plant which fades away, however deep its roots, if it cannot open its buds in the sun, the civic conscience shrivels and withers wherever the citizen is denied free growth and expansion. The individual conscience, by falling back on itself, can no doubt ensure itself liberty at all times and in all places, but it will not live for the commonwealth, and the commonwealth will not be able to live by it nor without it. Epictetus though a slave was the freest man on earth; but all the Stoics put together, however fruitful the germs which they sowed were destined to be for future ages, could not prevent the *polis* of antiquity from dying, they could only act as chief mourners to it with an admirable dignity.

The democratic regime and the regime in which the power of social intimidation can best assert itself are thus convertible terms. What people are agreed to consider as democratic principles are, in reality, only the expression and the amplification, in the organization of public life, of the principle of social intimidation; it is this principle which is their foundation and their practical *raison d'etre.* The participation of all the citizens in the government has no substantial basis save the necessity of affording each member of the community the protection of his personality. If there is a category of citizens excluded from the government, how will they be able to make themselves respected by those who enjoy the right of ruling the commonwealth and who may turn it against them? This consideration justifies, in principle, the bestowal of. the political franchise on every citizen. It is useless to look for his title in the law of nature or in some mystic right of the "people. " Borrowing the phrase of Laplace, I say: "I do not need this hypothesis." When we have to pass to the application of the principle of universal suffrage to a given community, I only ask if the persons in question would be capable of intimidating the rulers. If they are children or adults who are still in political infancy, the answer is obvious: it is no use investing them with the suffrage; they will be made fools of with absolute impunity. When the question is on what basis the regime of universal suffrage shall be founded, on the parliamentary basis or on the plebiscitary or Caesarean basis, the point is decided by the same consideration. And when a philosopher observes that "a democracy which makes use of the franchise to give itself a master, a democracy which exchanges the free election of its representatives for the plebiscite, a Caesarean democracy, in a word, is a veritable monstrosity; it has really destroyed its *raison d'etre,"* I applaud this noble language; but for my part I content myself with the simple remark that if the citizens of a democracy give themselves a Caesar, he will snap his fingers at them afterwards — they will not be able to intimidate him. When it is said that the people are incapable of governing themselves, and that universal suffrage and parliamentarism are, consequently, an absurdity, if ever there was one, I agree on the first point, but I hold that the conclusion drawn therefrom is altogether erroneous: the political function of the masses in a democracy is not to goveru it,— they probably will never be able to do so in spite of all the rights of popular initiative, of direct legislation bestowed on them, — but to intimidate the rulers. The real question, here again, is whether they are capable of intimidating, and to what extent they are so; what is the nature of the responsibility which they enforce. That the masses already possess, in most democracies of the present day, the capacity of seriously intimidating the rulers, is beyond a doubt. It is through this that solid progress has been achieved in society; whether they will or no, the rulers are obliged to pay heed to popular needs and aspirations. Too often they cheat, as a dishonest tradesman cheats an unwary purchaser in the quality or the weight of his wares; but no more than he can they avoid, as they formerly could, supplying their customers with the goods. The great difficulty of the existing political situation is that the masses, as yet ill-informed and not clear-sighted enough, do not sufficiently intimidate the politicians, that they appeal to the lower sanctions, to their vulgar motives. The intimidation which they wield over them appears to say to them: You owe us your obedience, your servility, even if it involves trickery and falsehood, instead of saying to them: You owe us your conscience, your honesty, even if it offends our feelings and our prejudices. The spread of education among the masses, their increased power of exercising their judgment, are therefore not so much of value, in political life, for the direct use which they will make of them, —except, of course, the more enlightened choice of their representatives, — as for the better intimidation of those who govern in the name of the people and trade upon its want of perspicacity. These rulers will behave differently when they have to deal with better-informed electors; the latter will intimidate them more, will inspire them with a loftier kind of fear. This is why it is doubly important in a democracy to raise the moral and intellectual standard of the masses; with it will rise automatically the moral standard of those who are supposed to be superior to them.

What has just been said on the subject of universal suffrage is quite as true of the other principles of modern public policy. All the political liberties on which universal suffrage rests, and which are considered as guarantees of freedom, are but forms or instruments of the power of social intimidation, protecting the members of the body politic from the abuses of force: liberty of the press, of meeting, of association, guarantees of individual liberty. It is the same with the fundamental principles of the organization of the public powers: elective mode of appointing to the leading positions in the State, separation of powers, publicity given to the acts of the public authority, from Parliament down to the lowest tribunal, etc. But all these principles of contemporary public life, elaborated by political speculation and consecrated by the institutions of the peoples that go by the name of free, by no means exhaust the resources of the power of social intimidation; it has another at its command: to turn these principles to account in practice as fully as possible, it strengthens them with a higher principle, that of liberty of mind. This liberty, generally ranked as a philosophic liberty, is enrolled by it in the direct service of the commonwealth; it makes it the guardian of the liberties which have been called "necessary liberties," and, in so doing, places it at their head as the liberty most necessary to a community, — a liberty without which all the others are likely to decay. I have given a so to speak experimental demonstration of this, by showing how, when the reason, the will, and the conscience are captured by conventional notions, when moral responsibility is impaired, when the free play of opinion is impeded, when the ideal is stifled, the inevitable result is corruption in the State. After having thus deduced from the as it were tangible facts the laws of public life, which ideological philosophy can put forward only as postulates, 1 establish in the same manner the controlling principle of these laws, and, as I find it in the moral domain, I realize in practice the unity of politics and morality.

This final result, arrived at by a method which disclaims all connection with metaphysics, and still more my starting-point, which is the psychological phenomenon of fear controlling, under various aspects, the conduct of the citizen, may suggest the doctrine of the English Utilitarians. The resemblances are superficial and illusory. Between the doctrine of Bentham, and even between that of J. S. Mill, and my view a gulf is fixed. I must insist somewhat on this point in order to complete my demonstration. The Utilitarians base the identity of morals and politics on the identification of private interest with public interest. Now, these two interests are in reality in perpetual conflict, and there is no possibility of ever getting rid of it. The point is, in public life, not to mix up private interest with the interest of all, to reconcile the irreconcilable, but to subordinate the former to the latter, to enlist it in its service, or, at all events, to restrain it whenever the object of society, which is justice, so requires. To achieve this I rely on the various sanctions which appeal to the various aspects of human nature. Egoism becoming altruism in all men by the association of their interests remains for me a mystery and an idyl, which do not grow more real through the improved theory of J. S. Mill, according to which the harmony between individual happiness and the general happiness is created by the association of ideas in the human mind. As a practical moralist, I know no human mind in the abstract, I know only human minds, some base, others mediocre, others noble. While taking things as they are and considering humanity under the aspect of the relative, I differentiate moral action by means of the scale of the social sanctions. To make all the members of society walk in the path of social duty, I endeavour to establish the responsibility of each to all by founding it on obligations of a varied nature, but with the constant preoccupation of placing an ever greater number of citizens under the authority of the higher and, consequently, more effective sanction. Each sanction therefore remains what it is, it does not change its nature, black does not become white by some indefinable process of association of interests or ideas; there are only individuals who pass, so to speak, from one moral class to another with the progress of institutions and of manners. I consequently escape the verbal quibbles and the confusion in which Bentham, for instance, is landed, who unconsciously plays, not to say juggles, with his principle of interest, by using this term sometimes in the popular sense, sometimes in the sense of wellunderstood interest, which converts itself into altruism. I have no need of this sleight of hand. But it is not only from the logical standpoint that my position is the better one; my prospects as a practical moralist are so as well. The obstinate identification of private interest with public interest, in spite of the reality, imprisons the Utilitarians in a sort of circle, VOL. II — 3 c whereas I can move freely along the never-ending path of the moral improvement of humanity. To pass from selfishness to disinterestedness the J. S. Mills themselves are obliged to make dialectical, not to say sophistical, jumps, whereas I proceed straight from one stage to another, slowly but surely. In a word, to logical phantoms I oppose the reality; instead of the absolute principle of interest which claims to establish social equilibrium, I assign as moving spring to public life the relative principle of individual responsibility capable of development, and not in order to realize the millenary dream of perfect equilibrium, but to improve society as much as possible; I do not say, like the Utilitarians: organize interest, but, organize the moral authority of social intimidation, organize individual responsibility for liberty and through liberty.

APPENDIX II ORGANIZATION OF THE PUBLIC POWERS

Part I

1. The head of the State, except when he succeeds by dynastic right, is elected by the members of the national legislature, on an absolute majority of votes, for seven years. He is not re-eligible. 2. The ministers are appointed by the head of the State. They represent the government in the Chambers, and sit in them *ex officio* with right of debate, as well as in their committees. The ministers are removed by the head of the State on a resolution of either Chamber, passed in the case of each minister after a public debate in which the minister concerned is heard in his defence.

Part II 1. The national legislature is composed of two assemblies: the Senate and the Chamber of Deputies.

This draft scheme of organization of the public powers, which sums up and completes the proposals on the subject developed in the Conclusion, contains, in addition to the fundamental provisions, some clauses embodying the details of the electoral system sketched out. These clauses are printed in small type.

I have not space to annotate this draft on the points which have not been examined in the body of the work; but the principles and the considerations which have suggested the above provisions are self-evident, so to speak, and it is only in two or three cases that I have deemed it expedient to give some explanations in the form of notes at the bottom of the page.

2. The senators are elected through indirect universal suffrage, by electors of the second degree; their number is fixed, and apportioned among the several provinces according to their respective population, or, under federative constitutions, among each state or canton equally. They are appointed for nine years, and are renewable to the extent of one-third, every three years.

An additional number of seats, equal to one-quarter of the number of senators elected on the above plan, is assigned to associate senators, appointed by the constituted bodies, social, economic, and other groups which are specified for that purpose in the law. The associate senators enjoy the same rights and immunities as the other members of the Senate, in the exercise of their functions.

3. The members of the Chamber of Deputies are elected by direct universal suffrage for six years, and are renewable to the extent of one-third, every two years.

The candidates for the Chamber of Deputies are nominated by universal suffrage, in a preliminary poll, from among the persons who shall have made, within the period fixed by law, a declaration of their candidature, countersigned by a number of electors not less than that prescribed by the law.

These declarations, accompanied by a statement of the opinions of the declarants, from which all mention of party is rigorously excluded, are made known to the electors by means of electoral circulars, distributed from

This clause, the object of which is to get a certain intellectual effort out of the elector and to prevent him from voting for a candidate simply on the strength of his label, would be a useless precaution where there are only two or three rival candidates at the election, in England, for instance, and where it is easy to give the dullest electors their cue. But the case would be different in countries where, as In the United States, the number of candidates between whom an elector has to decide at an election is very considerable. The reader will remember how the ignorance of the American elector and his intellectual indolence are assisted by the delivery to him of official voting-papers with the names of the candidates grouped by parties, the title of which is indicated at the top of the column, or even, for the benefit of the illiterate voters, by a preconcerted small picture (an eagle, a ship, a plough, etc).; the elector has only to make a mark under the picture, and he has voted the whole party ticket.

house to house by the public authority, within the three days following the closure of the lists of the candidates.

The preliminary poll for the nomination of the candidates takes place fifteen days after the distribution of their declarations, in the forms and according to the procedure in force for the elections.

The declarants, who have obtained the most votes at the preliminary poll, are proclaimed candidates to the number of three times that of the seats to be filled up.

Their names, accompanied by their electoral programmes or manifestoes, which reproduce their first declarations as well as their new declarations, are made known to the electors by the means provided for the declarations of the candidatures.

The definitive election takes place fifteen days after the preliminary poll. Only electors who have voted at the preliminary poll can take part in it.

The electors vote for all the admitted candidates whom they approve, without restriction of number, by order of preference, that is to say, by indicating, besides the persons whom they select as their first choice, other persons subsidiarily. The subsidiary votes are assigned to the candidates in accordance with the provisions of the electoral law.

The voting-papers, which are drawn up, prepared, and distributed by the public authority, contain the names of all the candidates in alphabetical order, and without any indication of their political opinions. The electors signify their choice by marking the names with figures, 1, 2, 3, etc., in the order of preference.

The candidates who have obtained the required number of votes, with or without the addition of the subsidiary ones, are proclaimed elected.

In constituencies with several seats, the latter may be distributed among the candidates who have received the most support at the poll according to the proportional method fixed by the law.

The seat of a deputy becomes vacant before the expiration of the term of his mandate, in addition to vacancy through The object of this provision is not only to enable the electors to become acquainted with the opinions of the rival candidates and compare them at leisure in the stillness of their homes, but also to check the growth of billsticking, which has of late assumed alarming proportions, has singularly enhanced election expenditure in countries where, as in France, it was very moderate a short time back, and which exercises an untoward influence on electoral manners in other respects as well.

The law will provide for this according to the electoral system in force: single-member ticket or general ticket, majority vote or proportional vote. death, resignation, or legal incapacity, if a petition for his removal is addressed to the president of the Chamber, signed by a number of electors of his constituency, being not less than half of the number of electors on the register at the last election.

Pakt III 1. The members of the judiciary are appointed for life by the head of the State.

2. The judges are removed by the head of the State, on the proposal of the Supreme Court, set in motion by the government, or by the judges of the courts and tribunals of the respective jurisdiction, or by the citizens amenable to the jurisdiction, represented for this purpose by a number of persons fixed by the law. The decision of the Supreme Court is delivered after a public hearing of both sides. 3. The public prosecutors are removed by the head of the State, on the proposal of their hierarchical chiefs. INDEX

CPSIA information can be obtained at www.ICGtesting.com
Printed in the USA
BVOW07s1714280414

351936BV00012B/762/P

9 781230 226125